Class 4575, 2-6-2 tank No. 4593 comes to a halt in Pensford Station with the 10.50 am Frome to Bristol train on the 10th October 1959.
(Hugh Ballantyne)

THROUGH COUNTRYSIDE
Standard Class 3 2-6-2T No. 82040 passes Whitchurch Halt in its beautiful North Somerset setting, with the 10.50am Frome to Bristol train on 31st October 1959.

Hugh Ballantyne

Mike Vincent

Oxford Publishing Co.

THE RURAL RAILWAYMAN
Porter George Denning (and bike!) pose for posterity at Midsomer Norton & Welton station in the mid-1930s.

Philip Chapman

Title page: PENSFORD: THE VIADUCT & VILLAGE
This rather evocative view shows the village and the viaduct at Pensford. It was probably taken in Edwardian times and the water lying in the area below the viaduct itself shows quite clearly why the contractors on this stretch had problems constructing this particular piece of Victorian engineering.

John Kingman

A FOULIS-OPC Railway Book

British Library Cataloguing in Publication Data
Vincent, Mike
Through countryside and coalfield: the GWR's Bristol and North Somerset Railway.
1. North Somerset. Railway Services. Great Western Railway, history
I. Title
385'.09423'8

ISBN 0-86093-428-4

Library of Congress catalog card number
89-81505

Published by:
Haynes Publishing Group
Sparkford, Near Yeovil, Somerset. BA22 7JJ

Haynes Publications Inc.
861 Lawrence Drive, Newbury Park, California 91320, USA.

Printed by: J. H. Haynes & Co. Ltd

Dedication

To my daughter, Anna – for fun!

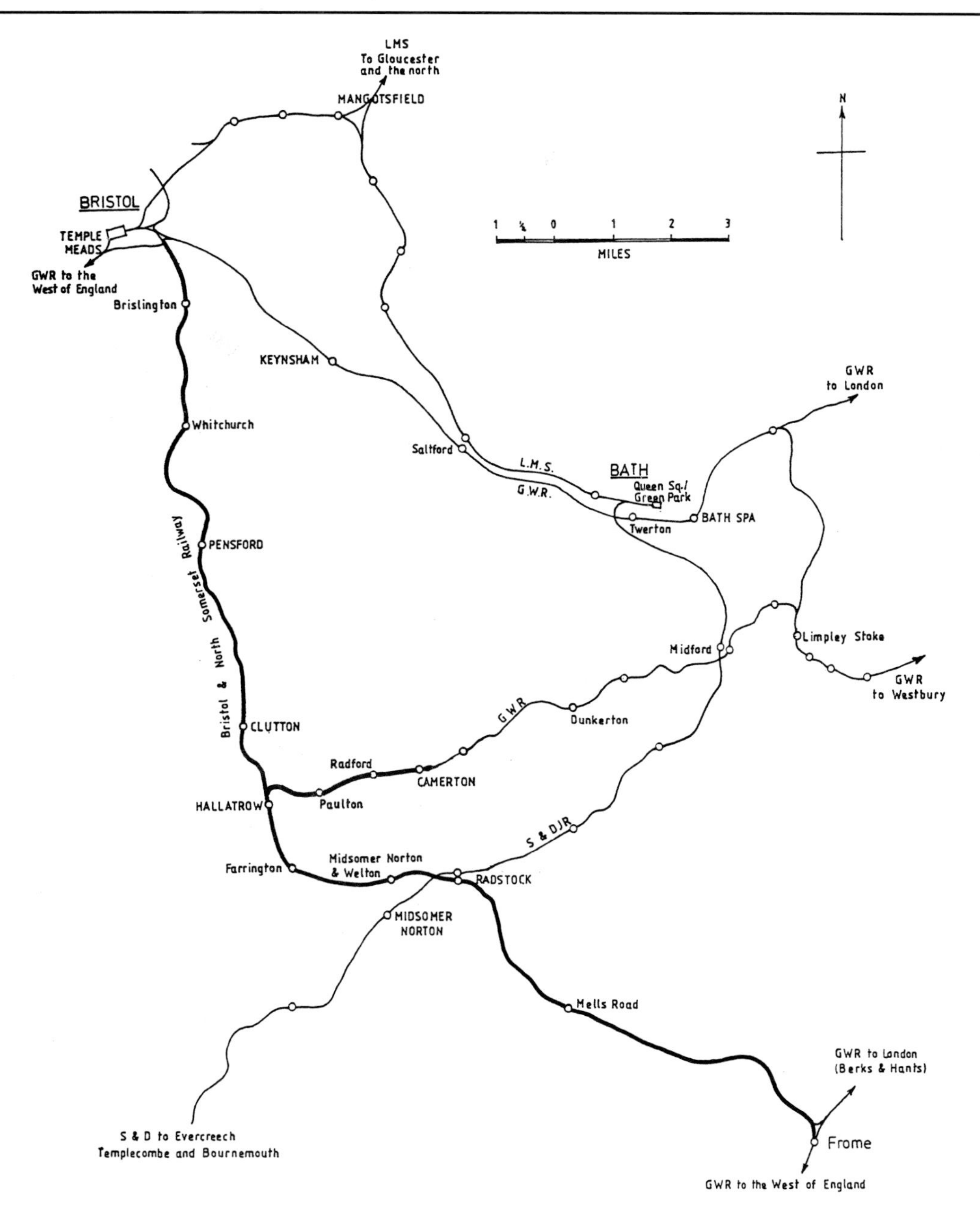

THE BRISTOL & NORTH SOMERSET RAILWAY AND ITS NEIGHBOURING RAILWAYS AND CONNECTIONS.

Contents

Preface

It seems fair to say that certain childhood images stay with you all of your adult life. This book's development started because of some long-standing childhood images.

When I was about nine years of age I lived in Glastonbury, Somerset and, because of prolonged illness, I travelled regularly by road to hospital in Bristol. One feature strongly-looked for on the journey was the colliery and railway viaduct at Pensford. Why, I asked myself, was there a coal mine in this beautiful and rural part of Somerset? Where did the trains come from and where did they go? How was that magnificent railway viaduct built and who built it? Was the railway that it carried really so important that it justified such a massive and beautiful piece of Victorian engineering?

The questions lay dormant for many years, rising to the surface only when I passed through the village of Pensford itself. Then, some good few years later and two railway histories on, I came back to Pensford and the Bristol & North Somerset Railway as I now knew it to be. Friends encouraged me to write a history of the line in spite of my initial (rather weak) protestations! The journey into another era and another railway had begun.

Come back to North Somerset with me and discover some of the answers and some of the questions thrown up by the life story of the Bristol & North Somerset Railway between Bristol (Temple Meads) and Radstock (West) and its Great Western connection onwards to Frome.

Acknowledgements

Strange as it may seem, the Bristol & North Somerset railway, even though it was an important cross-country line, was actually quite difficult to research, although a good deal of information was already in existence on the coalfield. However, as my network of contacts spread across North Somerset it became very clear that there was a ready source of railwaymen, industrialists and interested individuals who were waiting and willing to help. I am extremely grateful to absolutely everyone who gave me assistance with this book but I am particularly appreciative of the following for the time and hospitality they so freely gave me during the research:
Robin Atthill, Roy Ball, Ray Bishop, David Carter, Geoff Carter and family, Mr Cook, Philip Chapman, Dennis Chedgy, John Childs, Mr Ching, Amos Church, Gerald Dagger, M. E. J. Deane, Brian Denton, Mr Doel, John Durnford, Ken Evans, Derek Fear, Derek Fleming, Mr Gait, Ron Gardner, D. J. Gill, G. F. Gillham, Ernest Goulding, R. Hacker, Mr & Mrs Hawkins, Mr Keen, John Kingman, John Keeping, Mr Ladd, John Leach, A. Lecouteur, the late H. Loader, E. Lyons, J. W. Mann for all his help with plans, Michael McGarvie, Steve McNicol, the Ministry of Defence, the late E. Mountford, George Nailor, Terry Paget, Mr & Mrs Perry of Temple Cloud, David Pollard, Gerald Plummer, C. Smith, Frank Smith, Martin Smith, Derek Stoyel, Mr Tarling, Ken Tiley, R. E. Toop, Mike Tozer, Tim Venton, Kevin Weston, E. White, B. Williamson, H. J. Wyatt, and Mike Wyatt.

Amongst those who deserve a special mention are Reverend Brian Armen, for help with the motive power appendix; Alan and Joan Gregory for much help and support; Ian Ford for information on and enthusiasm for the Somerset Coalfield, Chris Handley for being an excellent critic, draughtsman and motivator and without whom this book would have been very much the poorer; Bill Harbor for consistently doing the impossible with photographs; Roger Hateley for assistance with the appendix on industrial locomotives; Dick Kelham for an enormous amount of work at the Public Record Office and for information so freely given; Terry Lyons for getting me started in the first place (!). John Morris, Chris Osment, Alan Price – all three helping tremendously with the signalling appendix and Gerald Quartley for photographs, friendship and good conversation. I would also like to thank Mr David Warnock and Mr Bob Parsons for all the information they gave to get me started and to keep me going! Finally, an especial round of thanks goes to Mr Wilfred White for his research and photographs on Marcroft Wagon Works at Radstock.

I am further indebted to the following for the photographs and plans that appear in this book:
Reverend Brian Armen, Hugh Ballantyne, British Rail (Western), Kim Bultitude, R. C. Bunyar, Geoff Carter, H. C. Casserley, Philip Chapman, A. Church, John Cornwell, Ken Evans' collection, Dave Fisher, the late Peter A. Fry, G. F. Gillham, Roger Hateley, Chris Howell, G. Hounsell, F. Jones, John Kingman, Tony Lecouteur, Lens of Sutton, John Loaring, Colin G. Maggs, Mike Miller (and his absolutely superb photographic collection!), Marcroft Wagon Works, A. H. Parsons, Bob Parsons, Ivo Peters, John Pritchard, Gerald Quartley, Dennis Rendell, R. C. Riley, Mrs G. Shearn, Tony Wadley, Mrs T. Weaver, Mark B. Warburton, P. J. Williams, and Barbara Zadarnowski

In addition to all those individuals mentioned above, I have made use of a number of organisations and I am most pleased to be able to thank them here:
ARC, Avon County Reference Library, Bath Reference Library, Bristol Archives Office, Bristol Evening Post, British Library, British Rail offices at Bristol and Paddington, County Records Office (Taunton), Frome Library, Gloucester Reference Library, Industrial Railway Society, the Public Record Office at Kew, Signalling Record Society, the SLS, Somerset Guardian and Tarmac.

I would also like to thank my publishers for taking on this title so quickly and so enthusiastically, and in particular, to Peter Nicholson for his thorough and committed help.

Last but by no means least, I would want to finish by offering my grateful thanks to Eileen and Anna who probably know more about the unsociability of writing books and articles than anyone else I know.

The Bristol and North Somerset Railway

Bristol – Hallatrow – Radstock (West) – Frome

THE BRISTOL & NORTH SOMERSET RAILWAY
Here beginneth the Bristol & North Somerset Railway: the Great Western station at Radstock (West). *Lens of Sutton*

Location: Bristol (North Somerset Junction) to Radstock, and Branch to Camerton

Act of Incorporation: Bristol & North Somerset Railway Act, 21st July 1863.

Other Particulars Concerning Line: The Act of Incorporation authorised the line from Bristol to Radstock. The line was worked by the Great Western Railway under Agreements dated 25th May 1866 and 25th June 1867.
The Camerton Branch was authorised by the Bristol & North Somerset Railway Act of 21st July 1873 section 4.
The Hallatrow Loop was authorised by the Great Western Railway Act of 15th August 1904 section 5.

Amalgamated with GWR: As from 1st July 1884 by Great Western Railway (No. 1) Act of 7th August 1884 section 54.

Dates of Opening: Bristol (North Somerset Junction) to Radstock 3rd September 1873
Camerton Branch 1st March 1882
Hallatrow Loop 9th May 1910

1
The Bristol/Radstock (West) – Frome Branch

An Introduction and Overview

The former cross-country railway between Bristol, Hallatrow, Radstock and Frome was a significant, if somewhat unnoticed line, that used to swing and sway, uphill and down vale, through the North Somerset countryside and coalfield. Although worked as an entity from the 1880s onwards, the railway was actually constructed by two separate companies: the Wilts, Somerset & Weymouth Railway building the section between Frome and Radstock, whilst the Bristol & North Somerset Railway slowly and painfully constructed the difficult section between Bristol and Radstock. Nonetheless, once built, the Bristol, Radstock and Frome line played an important role in handling the products of the local coal mines and stone quarries, across the Mendip hills. This was an area in which, before the coming of the railways, the then-existing roads and canals had become increasingly inadequate and quite unable to move these products efficiently.

Although the Somerset Coalfield had developed initially on the southern slopes of the Mendip hills, by 1800 it was centred on the town of Radstock. From here collieries were to be found dotted throughout "hills and valleys in every direction". Up until this time coal had been moved by packhorse and by cart but, in 1805, the Somersetshire Coal Canal had opened for some ten miles along the valley of the River Cam. Feeding into the Kennet & Avon Canal on the outskirts of Bath at the Dundas Aqueduct in the River Avon's beautiful valley near Limpley Stoke, the new waterway terminated at a basin between Timsbury and Paulton on the coalfield itself, the coal was delivered from surrounding collieries by a number of tramways. Another branch of this canal had been planned to run to Radstock, but this was not a success however, and saw little use. Instead, a tramway was built along the unused towing path. Serving a number of other collieries, this particular iron road opened in 1815.

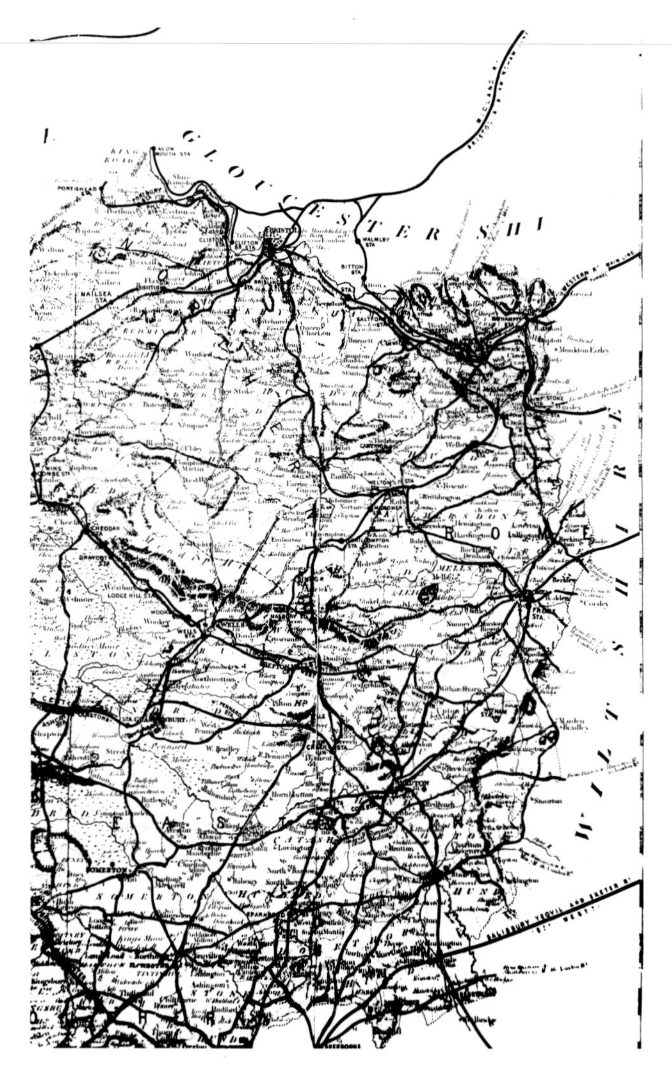

THE RAILWAYS OF NORTH AND EAST SOMERSET TAKEN FROM CRUTCHLEY'S COUNTY MAP OF SOMERSET (1877-1883)
Original plan: Bath Reference Library

BRISLINGTON STATION
Distance from Bristol (Temple Meads) 2m 7ch.
The delightful station at Brislington opened for business on 3rd September 1873. It closed its doors to passengers on 2nd November 1959. Freight traffic lingered on, however, until 7th October 1963. *Lens of Sutton*

BRISLINGTON: THE STATION GARDEN
This photograph shows the beautiful station garden at Brislington c1900. The stationmaster has every reason to be proud. Indeed, creative and delightful garden arrangements seem to have been a lasting feature of this railway, running as it did, through a once-important and bustling coalfield.

Author's collection

BRIDGE UNDER REPAIR AT BRISLINGTON
This interesting and somewhat unusual photograph shows bridge reconstruction work taking place in the Brislington area of Bristol. Believed to be Bloomfield Road bridge, the event has obviously gathered quite a collection of onlookers and, as always, the engineers and builders seem quite happy to stop work to face the camera.

C. Thorne/Mike Miller

During the 1840s and 1850s broad gauge railways came into the area when, in 1844 and after several false starts, a plan was put together to build a railway from Frome to Radstock. This short branch was part of a much larger scheme to build a broad gauge Wiltshire & Somerset Railway between Corsham and Salisbury. The intended railway was to throw off a multitude of branches to serve various Wiltshire and Somerset towns such as Devizes, Bradford-on-Avon and Frome, there being another offshoot from the latter town to Radstock to tap the black riches of the Somerset Coalfield. In the fading months of 1844 the scope of the scheme was broadened and its title lengthened. It was now the Wilts, Somerset and Weymouth Railway.

All did not go smoothly for railway construction in the late 1840s and, in 1850, the whole project was taken over by the Great Western Railway. However, even at this stage the scheme had become a real financial liability in that it had already cost half a million pounds. Nonetheless, the GWR's directors were anxious to get the section between Frome and Radstock completed because of the wealth of coal traffic that awaited the broad gauge there. Even the $\frac{1}{4}$ mile branch to the coal mining town was not easy to build, land acquisition proved difficult and it was not until 14th November 1854 that the single-line, freight-only branch actually opened for traffic.

Over the next 20 years a large number of might-have-been schemes for further railway developments were proposed for North Somerset and the Bristol area. Many, indeed most, of them fell by the trackside. Nevertheless, in 1863 the Bristol & North Somerset Railway Company was given the go-ahead by an Act dated 21st July of that year. The main spine of the railway was the Mendip section between Bristol and Radstock, although important connecting lines were to be built to serve the harbour, the GWR and the Midland Railway in the Bristol area, and the then-building Somerset & Dorset Railway south of Radstock. The rails were on their way!

In 1863 the railway's construction began at two points. On the 7th October the first sod of the Bristol/Radstock section was turned at Clutton. It poured with rain and, as our story will show, the outlook for the railway was very grey and stormy during the 1860s in particular. On 8th October the first rail of the tramway that was designed to link the Bristol & North Somerset with the City Docks in Bristol was "laid".

Throughout the Company's early history, the lack of finance was a grinding and persistent problem and, although adventurous in outlook, the B&NSR could not even afford to build

Left: WHITCHURCH HALT
Distance from Bristol 4m 15ch. This typical GWR halt was opened to passengers on 1st January 1925. After an uneventful career it closed some 35 years later on 2nd November 1959.

Author's collection

Right: WHITCHURCH HALT
Class 4575 2-6-2T No. 5542 lets the smoke go while working a Radstock and Frome train in the last year of passenger working (1959).

Collection M. B. Warburton

WHITCHURCH HALT

Original plan: British Rail (Western)

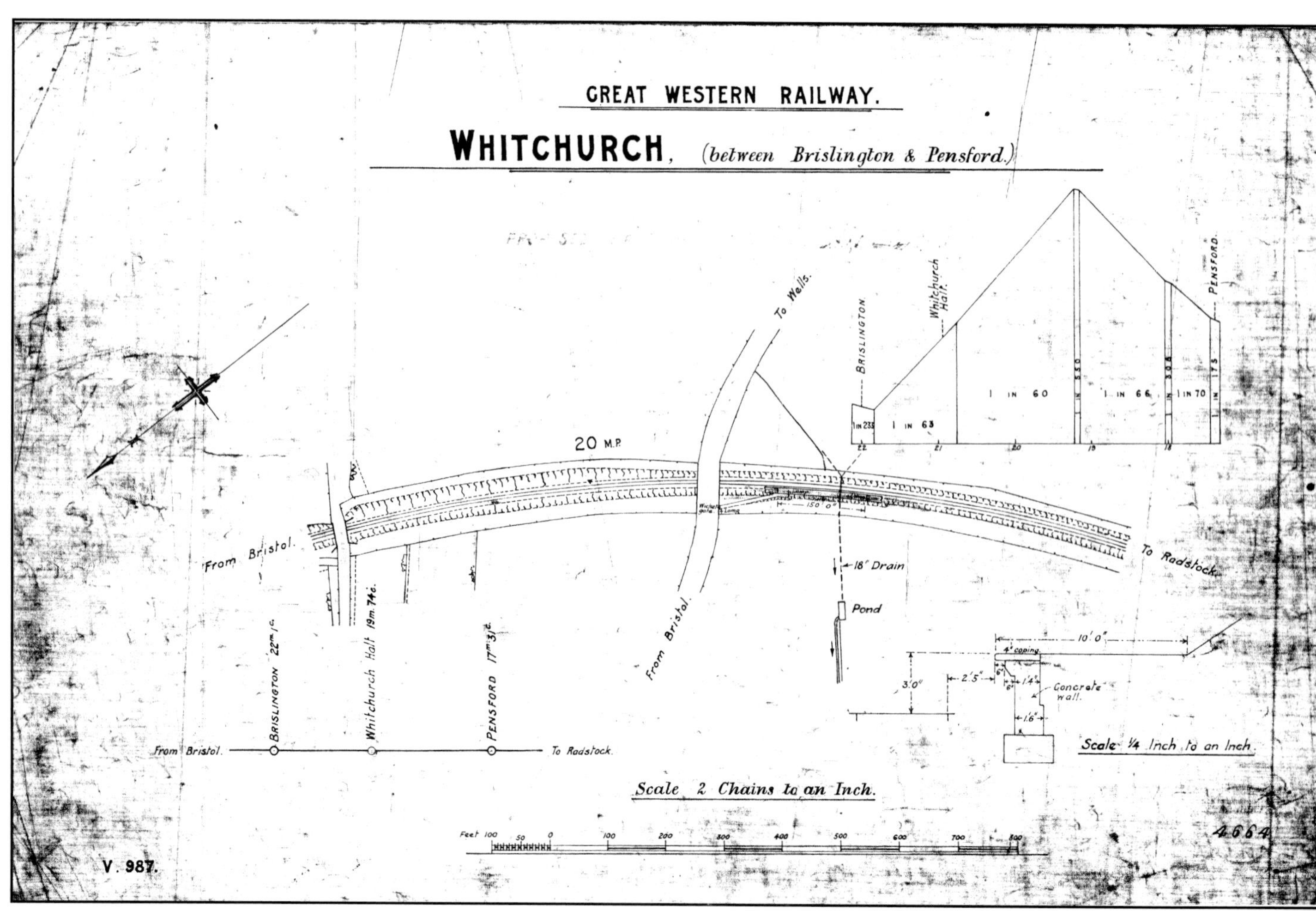

Above: PENSFORD STATION
Distance from Bristol 6m 58ch.
The station at Pensford opened on 3rd September 1873, closing to passengers on 2nd November 1959 when the line's passenger service was withdrawn. The crossing loop shown here was taken out of use in March 1960, its removal taking place in September of that year. The signal box closed on 14th June 1964 with the goods sidings being taken out of use on 6th March 1966.

This view, looking towards Bristol, shows the station and signal box in the early years of the present century. Someone's spuds seem to be drying nicely!

Mr D. White (Pensford)

Left: PENSFORD & BROMLEY COLLIERIES' SIDINGS SIGNAL BOX
A general view showing the box and sidings at Pensford & Bromley Collieries' Sidings on 13th September 1959.

Hugh Ballantyne

the lines sanctioned by its 1863 Act, let alone new extensions to serve the additional parts of Bristol and North Somerset that it would have liked to have served. Indeed, so bad were the North Somerset's financial problems during the 1867-1870 period that a new company had eventually to be set up and this took over in 1870. However, this three-year period in the late 1860s stands out as a sorry and shameful example of Victorian white-collar crime and incompetence leading to total liabilities for the B&NSR of around £300,000!

At long last, and in spite of difficulties both financial and constructional, the North Somerset Railway opened to passenger and freight traffic on 3rd September 1873. It had stations at Brislington, Pensford, Clutton, Hallatrow, Welton and Radstock. Laid to standard gauge, through running to Frome was not possible until the Radstock/Frome section had itself been converted to standard gauge, this change taking place in June 1874. On 5th July 1875 a through passenger service began running between Bristol and Frome via Radstock.

As the Company moved through the late 1870s and into the early 1880s, its financial problems loomed large yet again. Matters reached a head when, in January 1882, the courts instructed the North Somerset to pay the £113,000 it owed the Earl of Warwick. Unfortunately, there was no cash to hand and it was left to the Court of Chancery to take care of the Company's affairs. Would the Great Western Railway provide a way out?

In the past the larger company had not found the terms offered to it for the North Somerset's takeover to be attractive enough. However, in 1882, the deadlock was broken when a proposal to build a railway connecting the London & South Western Railway near Andover with Radstock was put forward. Remarkably enough, this project, with its threat of LSWR infiltration into the Somerset Coalfield, seemed to be just the nudge the GWR needed to take over the Bristol/Radstock line and, on 1st July 1884, the local company was absorbed!

As part of its original 1863 Act, the Bristol & North Somerset had put forward a scheme to build a branch from its main line at Hallatrow to Camerton in the valley of the beautiful River Cam. However, because of the Company's financial problems, it was not until 1882 that this section actually opened for passenger and goods traffic. An even longer period of time was to elapse before this short, but important,

CLUTTON STATION
Distance from Bristol 9m 74ch.
Clutton station is seen here looking towards Hallatrow and showing the signal box and the maze of crossings at the south end of the station. Opened on 3rd September 1873, the station closed to passengers on 2nd November 1959. The bulk of the sidings and the signal box were taken out of use on 14th June 1964.
Author's collection

CLUTTON SIGNAL BOX DURING THE 1920s
This picture of the signal box at Clutton is believed to have been taken at some time during the 1920s. The man inside the box was one of the regular signalmen at that time, Mr Albert Gibbs. By all accounts, Mr Gibbs was a keen gardener growing cacti, chrysanthemums and other flowers in the box which was kept in spotless condition. On Saturday mornings he always had a big polish throughout the box and anyone visiting would find brown paper down on the floor to protect it! This would stay in place until Sunday morning, by which time the polish would have dried.
Mrs Weaver

Left:
FARRINGTON GURNEY HALT
Distance from Bristol 12m 49ch.
Pannier tank No. 8741 arrives at Farrington Gurney Halt on a train to Radstock and Frome on 12th September 1959. The platform here was 150 feet long and was unstaffed. Tickets for this halt were issued by the landlord/lady at the nearby Miners' Arms public house. As this photograph shows, the halt would just take a two-car train.

The halt opened for passenger and parcels traffic on 11th July 1927 in response to the threat thrown up by growing bus competition. It closed completely on 2nd November 1959.

Peter A. Fry

Right: MIDSOMER NORTON & WELTON STATION
Distance from Bristol 14m 41ch.
This view shows the attractive scene of the station at Midsomer Norton & Welton which was opened to passengers on 3rd September 1873. It closed for passengers on 2nd November 1959, the sidings and single line to Radstock (West) being taken out of use some nine years later on 31st December 1968.

Author's collection

THE B&NSR BETWEEN RADSTOCK & MIDSOMER NORTON

This plan shows the Bristol & North Somerset Railway between Radstock and Midsomer Norton & Welton. It was taken from a survey of 1880.

Original plan: British Rail (Western)

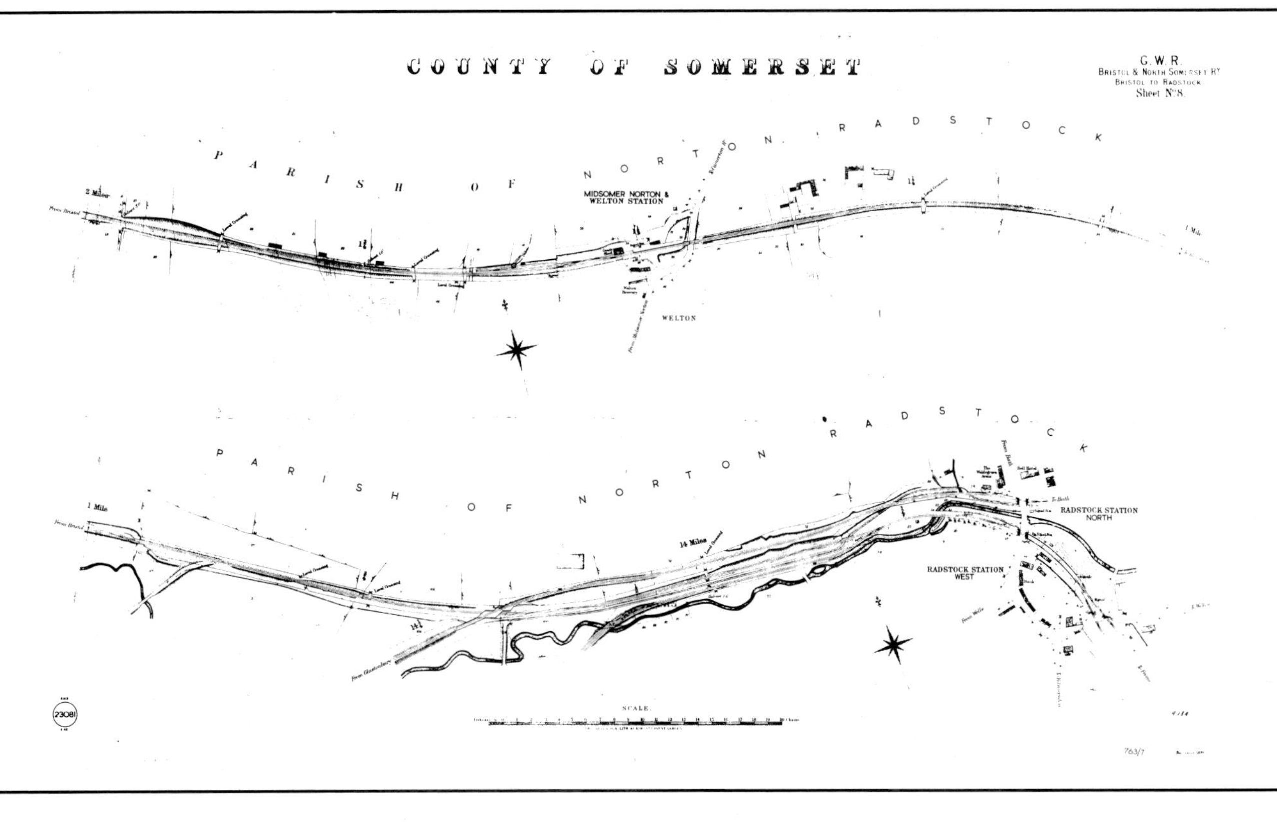

Left: HALLATROW STATION (JUNCTION FOR THE CAMERTON BRANCH)
Distance from Bristol 11m 31ch. A view of Hallatrow looking north towards Free's Quarry and Clutton. Hallatrow opened on 3rd September 1873. It became a junction when the line to Camerton opened in 1882. In 1910 the Hallatrow-Camerton section was extend through to Limpley Stoke on the Bath-Trowbridge line. It lost that junction status very quickly however, when the Camerton-Hallatrow section itself closed in 1932. Hallatrow station closed to passenger traffic on 2nd November 1959, the sidings and signal box here being taken out of use on 14th June 1964.

Gerald Quartley

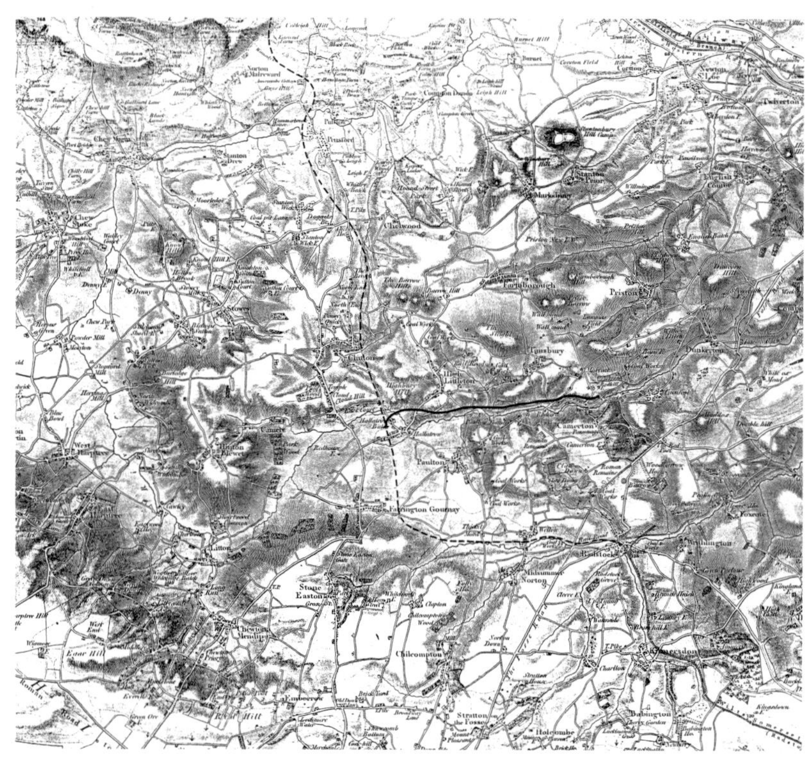

THE CENTRAL SECTION OF THE BRISTOL & NORTH SOMERSET RAILWAY 1873

The proposed railway to Camerton is clearly shown.

Original plan Somerset Record Office

Below: CAMERTON STATION
Distance from Hallatrow 3m 34ch.

Opened:	(passengers)	1st April 1882.
	(goods)	1st March 1882.
Closed:	(passengers)	
	Hallatrow-Camerton	21st September 1925.
	(goods)	
	Camerton-Limpley Stoke	15th February 1951.

This period postcard photograph shows the station at Camerton before the extension to Dunkerton and Limpley Stoke was opened.

Courtesy Bob Parsons

RADSTOCK (WEST) STATION
The Bristol & North Somerset Railway's southern terminus, Radstock (West) was situated at 15m 72ch from Bristol.
This station was opened for passengers on 3rd September 1873. The photograph shows the station returning to some peace and quiet with the departure of a Bristol-bound goods. Closed for passenger traffic on 2nd November 1959, the station buildings were demolished during 1963.

Author's collection

stub was linked with the Bath-Trowbridge-Westbury route at Limpley Stoke. This latter development took place in two stages: the first of these (between Camerton and Dunkerton Colliery), opening to freight traffic in 1907. The remainder of the route between Dunkerton Colliery and Limpley Stoke opened to passenger traffic on 9th May 1910.

Some five years later and with wartime pressure on, the line's railmotor services were withdrawn on 22nd March 1915. They were reinstated on 9th July 1923 but, with bus competition, they succumbed for good in 1925. The section of track between Hallatrow and Camerton became disused and was lifted during the 1930s while the last commercial freight on the Camerton/Limpley Stoke section ran on 14th February 1951, a year after the closure of the colliery at Camerton. This section was finally lifted by 1958.

Back on the main Bristol/Radstock route, the early years of the 20th century brought many changes to the North Somerset. Station improvement and rebuilding schemes at Brislington, Hallatrow and Mells Road stations, the last two of major importance, all helped to shape the face of an increasingly important cross-country route between Bristol, Radstock and Frome. Of course, the line was extremely busy during the First World War.

After the war, the railway settled down to carry a wide variety of goods as well as its regular passenger and excursion traffic. In the 1920s, new halts were opened at Whitchurch (Som.) and at Farrington Gurney to combat increasing road competition. The golden days of the Edwardian period would never again return to the North Somerset, although during the Second World War the line was predictably busy. The coalfield was hard at work and this meant good business. In addition, the line served as a useful diversionary route from Bristol to the South Coast, although its sharp gradients proved to be something of a barrier to the fullest exploitation of this role.

MELLS ROAD (HALT)
Distance from Bristol 18m 70ch.
This station opened for passenger traffic on 4th March 1887. It became an unstaffed halt in September 1956, closing for passenger business on 2nd November 1959. This particular photograph shows its last days as a halt and was taken in October 1959.

Collection M. B. Warburton

FROME STATION: CHANGE HERE FOR THE NORTH SOMERSET
Distance from Bristol via Radstock (West) 24m 16ch.
Prairie tank No. 5570 simmers and steams gently on a grey and miserable day in 1934. On 21st April of that year an attentive footplate crew get ready to move off with what appears to be a Bristol-bound train. "All aboard please the North Somerset and its stations await!".

H. C. Casserley

Kelly's Directory for 1897 shows the stationmasters at the stations on the North Somerset & Camerton railways:

Brislington	Mr John Royle Williams
Pensford	Mr William Henry Brook
Clutton	Mr William Herbert Collins
Hallatrow	Mr Henry Jefferies
Camerton	Mr Frederick Price
Welton	Mr Goldsworth Beer
Radstock	Mr Walter Thomas Davis
Mells Road	Mr William Williams
Frome*	Mr George Peach

*Kelly's Directory also reminds us that "An omnibus from the George Hotel, Market Place, meets every train". This was surely rail/road integration at its very best!

Once the war came to an end, the railway returned to a working routine not unlike the one that had existed pre-war. Nevertheless, major changes were on the way. The increasing use of road transport, particularly the spread of the motor car, some very poorly-sited stations in relation to modern-day needs and a complacent and unenterprising railway management after nationalisation had taken place in 1948, all coalesced to ensure that the writing was on the wall for the North Somerset at some stage in the not-too-distant future.

In 1959, and in spite of substantial amounts of coal, parcels and GPO traffic remaining with the branch, British Railways (Western Region) proposed the removal of the passenger service between Bristol, Radstock (GW) and Frome. The WR put forward a particularly poorly framed and fought case to the South Western Transport Users' Consultative Committee, but the end was all-too-clear and, on 2nd November 1959, the branch lost its regular passenger service.

Although the passenger trains had been removed, the rails of the Bristol, Radstock (GW) and Frome line were still kept well-burnished by substantial amounts of freight traffic, including coal, stone and general goods. On 15th August 1966, however, the Radstock/Mells Road section closed to all traffic, although fortuitously, the permanent way was left in place. Two years later, on 10th July 1968, the Bristol & North Somerset Railway between Bristol and Radstock was also closed, all freight traffic going out from Radstock over the hastily reinstated rails through Mells Road and Frome.

Not all was gloom and despondency, however, for the death of the former Bristol & North Somerset was soon followed by the gradual, but firm and exciting, rebirth of stone traffic on part of the Wilts, Somerset & Weymouth Railway between Radstock and Frome. Coal was no longer king, the last colliery in Somerset having closed in 1973, but stone traffic was strong and growing from ARC's Whatley Quarry near Frome. In the autumn of 1988, when this section of the book was written the Frome/Whatley Quarry section was still busy with trains, although the occasional trip workings of wagons for repair at Marcroft's works at Radstock had ceased with the closure of that firm's facility at the end of June 1988.

MELLS ROAD STATION

This plan of Mells Road station shows the changes that were to take place in the station's reduction in status to a halt in 1956.

Original plan: British Rail (Western)

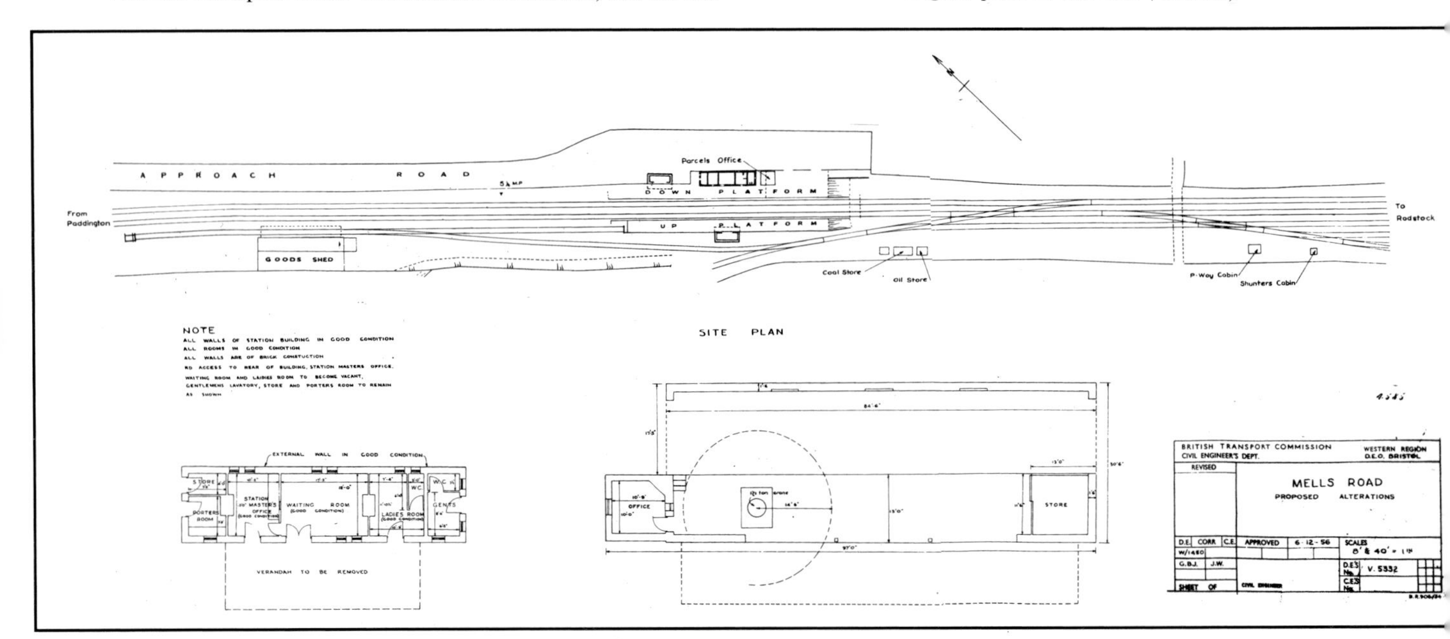

HALCYON DAYS AND HEAT AT HAPSFORD
On a lovely summer's day, a Frome-bound 4575 class 2-6-2T No. 5508 and train head past Hapsford. All's well with the railway world it would seem! However, some four months after this photograph was taken this location would see only freight trains. This particular sunny day was 4th July 1959.
Peter A. Fry

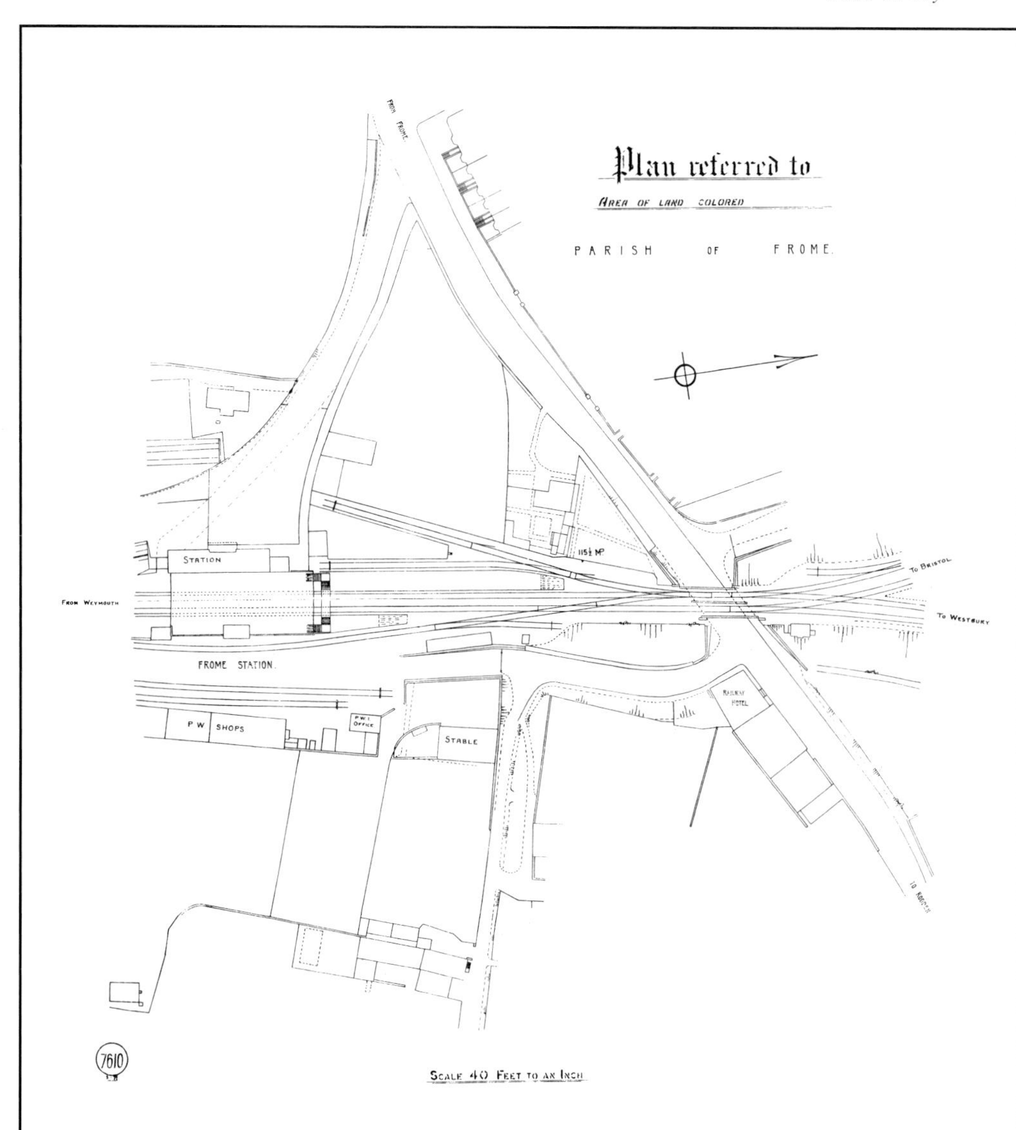

FROME STATION

This plan of Frome station shows the Bristol/Westbury end of the station. The North Somerset line's bay platform can be seen clearly alongside mile post 115½. The Bristol line veers round to the signal box at West Junction, the double track becoming single from there.

Original plan: Gerald Quartley

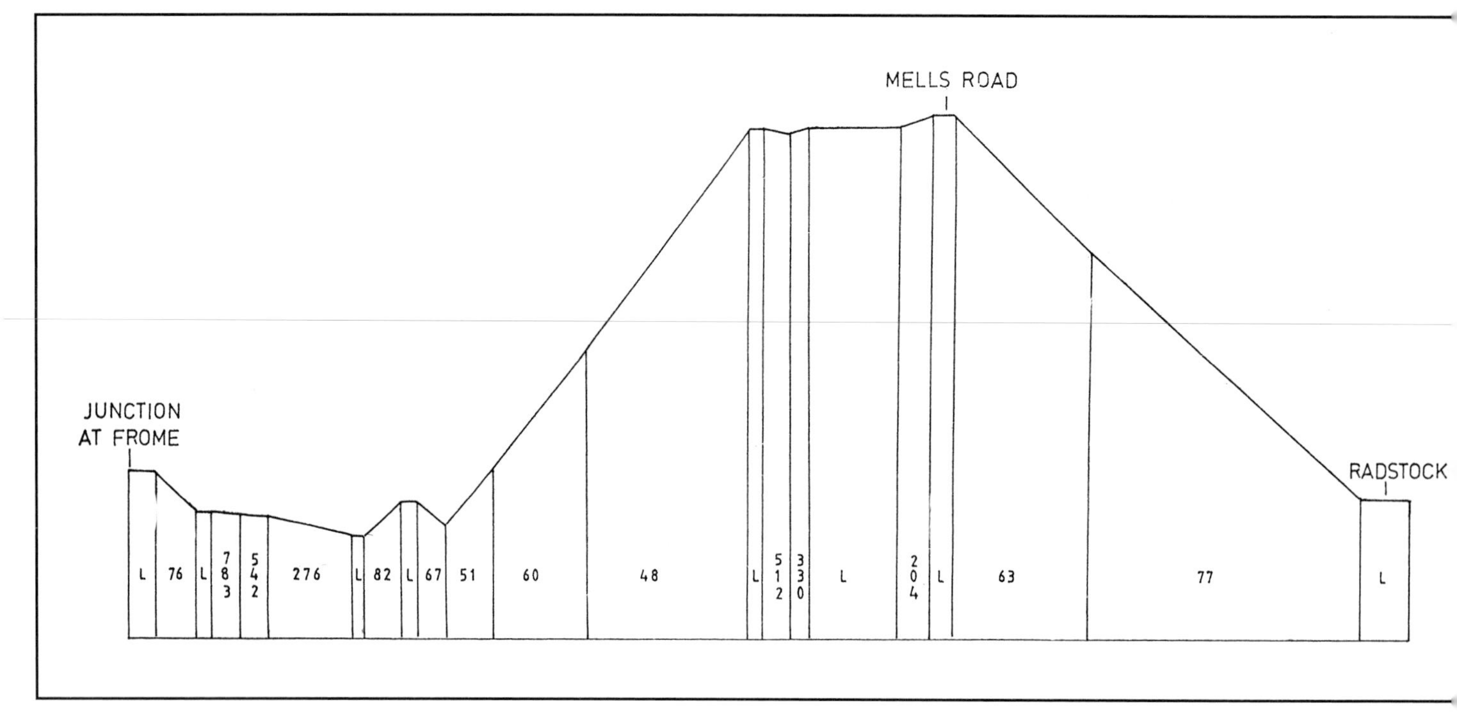

GRADIENT PROFILE, FROME-RADSTOCK SECTION

Original document: John Morris

The North Somerset may have gone but the memories remain vivid and I hope that this book will help to re-kindle fond images and pictures for those who knew the line and that it will give interesting and exciting insights for those for whom this book is a first glimpse into the history of the former Bristol & North Somerset Railway.

RADSTOCK: "CAPITAL" OF THE SOMERSET COALFIELD
With the Waldegrave Arms on the right, this photograph looks down towards the two level crossings in the centre of Radstock. The nearest crossing and signal box belong to the Somerset & Dorset Railway, while behind the S&D's gates can be seen the North Somerset signal box.

Although the earliest mining in the coalfield had centred on the Nettlebridge Valley, it was the Radstock district, with its green and several valleys, that saw tremendous growth in its coal production during the 18th and 19th centuries.

John Kingman

A Coalfield Cameo: The Somerset Coalfield

"The usual lightning sketch of Somerset is cheese and cider, soft hills, cottages and cream. It is not a county that many associate with the roar and dirty work of coal mining, although Somerset's coalfields once made an important contribution to the country's energy supply."

The Romans were believed to have dug outcropping coal in

COLLIERIES AT CLUTTON

Burchells Colliery in 1913. *Bob Parsons/Ken Tiley*

RADSTOCK 1917

This thorough diagram of Radstock taken from the Midland Railway's Distance Diagram of 1917 clearly shows the complex of railways around Radstock in the busy years of the First World War. *Original diagram: SDRT/Chris Handley*

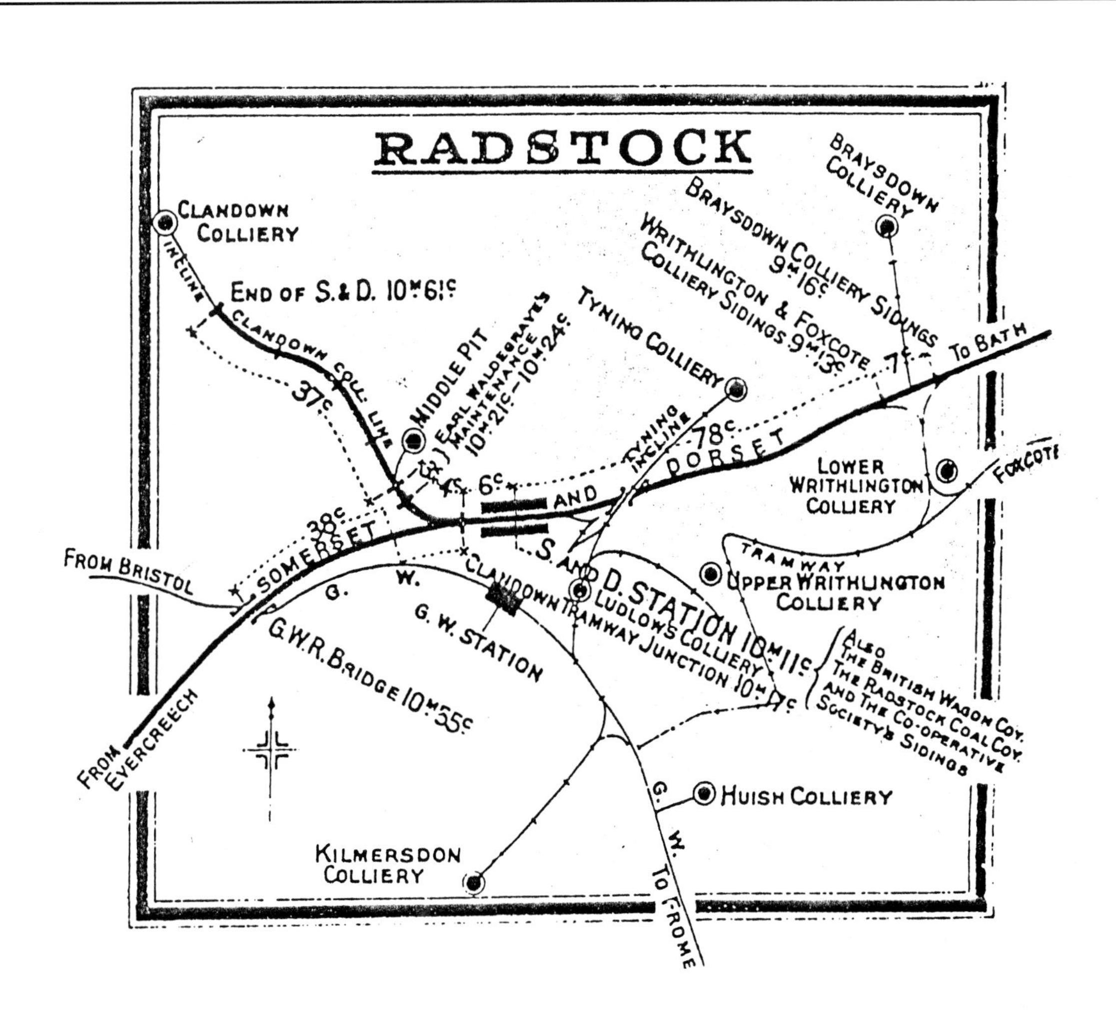

the Mendip hills. This was used to smelt lead ore and to fuel temple fires in the Roman spa of Bath. However, it was in the 15th century when timber was becoming scarcer as a source of fuel that coal was in demand by smithies and lime kilns. It was then that mining started on a commercial scale. In the years after 1750 some 80 pits were sunk in the Somerset Coalfields while, in the early years of the 1800s, the Somersetshire Coal Canal was opened giving coal owners access to wider markets by way of the Kennet & Avon Canal. In the days of the coalfield's production peak around the early years of the 20th century, the coalfield employed some 10,000 men and more than a million tons of coal a year were raised. At nationalisation in 1947, 13 collieries were still at work. Tonnage was then about 600,000 a year. In 1973 the last pit in the area, Kilmersdon Colliery at Radstock, wound its last ton of coal.

In the 18th and 19th centuries, Somerset miners had figured occasionally in food riots. From out of these grew the miners' societies that formed the basis of the later trade unions. The most bitter struggle in the coalfield occurred during 1909 at Dunkerton Colliery where angry miners stoned the home of the manager and the manager's son retaliated by firing his shotgun into the crowd, wounding several of the men. For the Somerset Coalfield, however, this was very much a "one-off" incident. The kind of militancy to be found in the Welsh and Yorkshire pits was never truly to be seen in the rolling hills of rural Somerset.

In addition, the coal of the county was never up to the quality of, say, the Welsh coal and this fact, combined with the savagely difficult working conditions and the later decline in the market for coal, led to the total rundown of the industry.

But what an individual coalfield it was! There were twisted and distorted coal veins with such names as Blew Pott, Dungy Drift and Stinking Vein while the pits themselves often had a real "earthy" feel to them with such fascinating names as Atkin's Gout, Fry's Bottom, Ruth's Arse, Woody Heighgrove and Vobster. These were the names and the pits that formed the basis and central focus of many a North Somerset community and of the men and women living in those communities.

A manuscript by James Twyford in the Ammerdown Collection – *Observations on Coal Works* – gives an extremely detailed account of conditions at the close of the 17th century. Twyford sets his face against the earlier system of granting leases to individual colliers and asserts that "the Coal-works should never be let, but wrought for the person in possession of the inheritance". He advised any owners of coal-bearing land to adventure for coal on their own account and to get a skilled collier as manager.

The mines of those days appear to have been sloping adits, or lanes, cut into the coal bearing rocks.

> "They usually or always sink one pit first; when the air is bad they sink another pit about six yards distant on the same course as near as can, and cut a lane of communication from one pit to another to give air, or else, when one pit is sinking, they put down trunks, and make a trunk-hole to let the air to the nose of the shides or pipes, and so carry the air into the lane. About midsummer the air is usually bad when the hedges are full of leaves, then they sink an iron grate about ten yards into the pit with burning coals, which draws the stenched or stagnated air from the bottom and lane."

The "breakers" of coal, as the coal-face workers were called, worked by turns or tasks. They cut into the seams with a mattock and broke very large pieces of coal away with a wedge. This coal was loaded into carts, which were pulled by carters – usually boys. The carters kept a tally of the loads hewn by each of the breakers, who were paid according to their output.

In the Mendip mines the workers were provided with "the coal they burn, and working coats and waistcoats, that is drawers or breeches, and also shirts whilst they are working, but not otherwise, but at Paulton the men find all". (For full details of the coalfield, please see Chapter 6.)

Class 6100,2-6-2T No.6148 climbing away from Clutton with the 5.00 pm coal train from Radstock. *Ivo Peters*

2
Plans, Proposals and Possibilities

From the 1840s until the early years of the 20th century two major railway companies were in contention for the passenger and freight traffic of the South West of England. These two warring companies were the Great Western Railway and the London & South Western Railway. Their territorial battles lie at the heart of the problems encountered by the small, initially privately financed railway whose history we are concerned with in this book: namely the Bristol & North Somerset Railway Company.

Once the GWR's London-Bristol axis was laid in and the LSWR had its artery from London to Southampton in place, it was logical that Wessex, that swathe of land encompassing Berkshire, Hampshire, Gloucestershire, Wiltshire, the modern county of Avon, Dorset and most of Somerset, would become the arena of dispute and tussle that it in fact, did develop into during the early years of those two railway companies' stories. It is against this background that we need to place the unfolding of the railway plans for the region south of Bristol, stretching deep into Somerset and serving that county's once extensive and well established coalfield under the Mendip hills.

The historical position was well outlined by Mr Phinn QC when opening the case for the promoters of the Bristol & North Somerset Railway's Act of 1863 when he said,

> ". . . The district (North Somerset) being situated between two great companies, had frequently been made by them the scene of their disagreements and instead of the local wants of the district being catered for, elements of antagonism had been imported into the question, and the consequence was that the district still remained (in 1863) without any railway accommodation at all."

Although this comment was made well ahead in time of some of the developments we will be concerned with in this chapter, the key issue of inter-railway company competition, and the delays that this competition threw up, is something we need to bear in mind both here, and in the following chapters, for this fierce and, at times, very unpleasant competition would continue for many years to come. Indeed, it would last even into the early years of the 20th century.

By the 1840s coal had been mined for hundreds of years in North Somerset. Nevertheless, the removal of that coal from the ground and its subsequent transportation once above ground had always been a major problem. A significant breakthrough apparently occurred on the transport side when the Somersetshire Coal Canal was opened in 1805 to Paulton. In addition, an offshoot of the canal ran from Midford to Radstock. However, since this canal did not directly link in with any of the collieries in Radstock, an important town in the coalfield and surrounding areas, a series of short tramways had to be built to connect neighbouring tramways with this canal. It would seem that these tramways were all opened around about the same time. In spite of all these attempts to improve the local communications, the branch of the canal from Midford to Radstock was a failure and, by 1825, it had been replaced by a tramroad. With the main arm of the canal and its connected tramways in operation the SCC was, for quite some time, the most prosperous canal in the South of England and its shareholders were at the receiving end of some very comfortable dividends. Indeed, by 1840, Somerset coal was

WELTON IN THE OLD DAYS

This 1822 map of Midsomer Norton and Welton shows the collieries at Old and New Welton the mill leat with its extension to Old Welton Colliery and the Stone Cross. *Chris Handley*

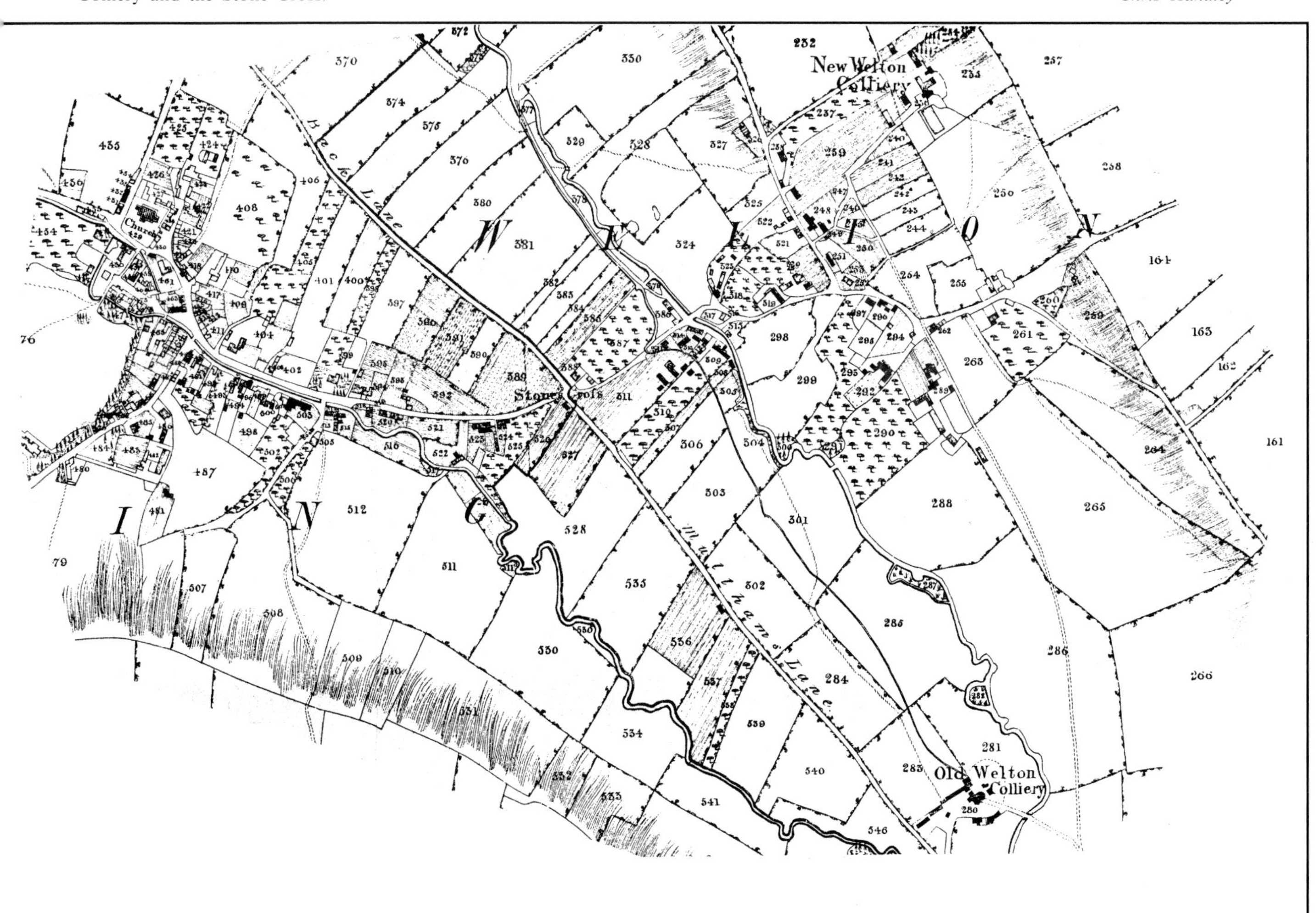

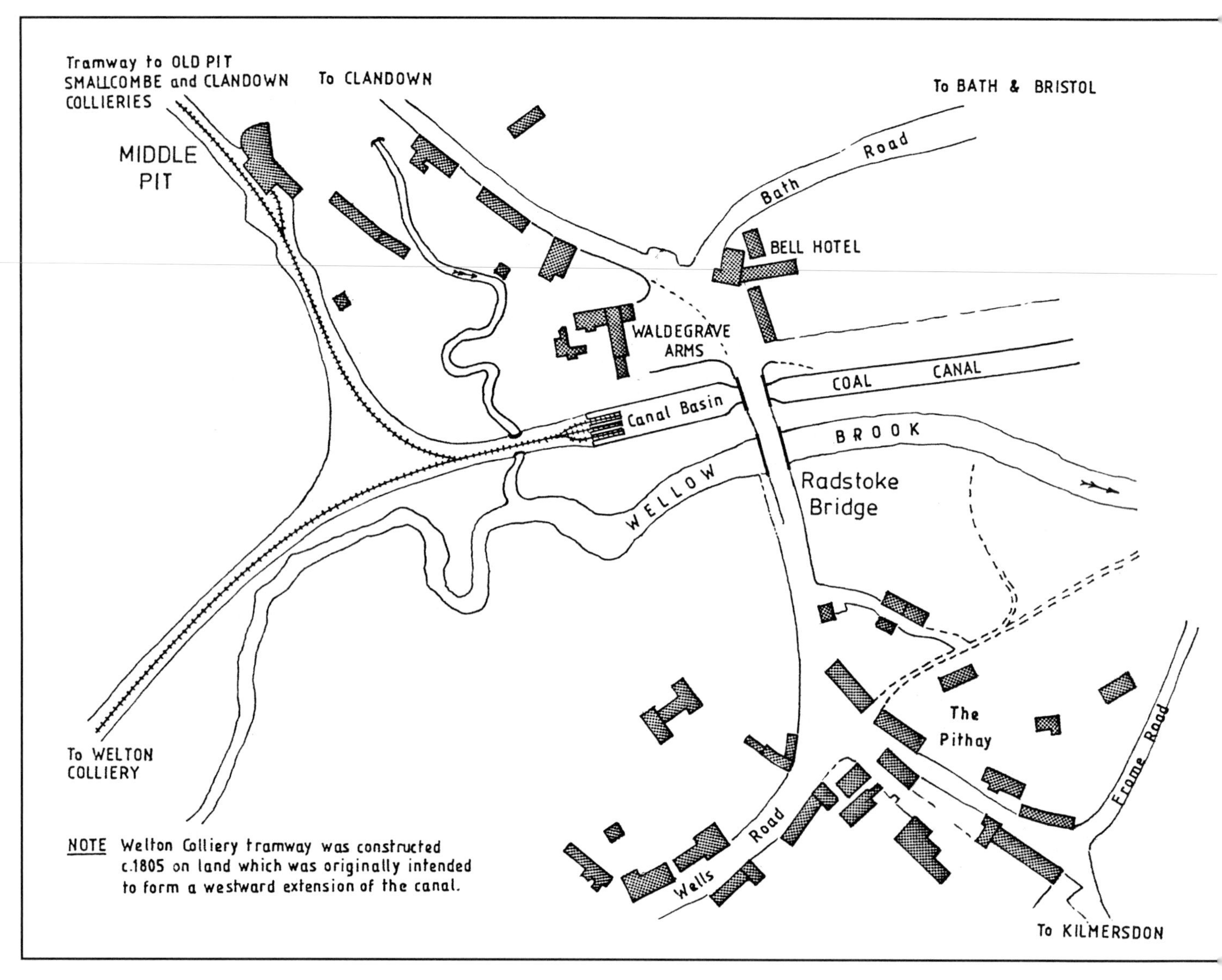

The Somersetshire Coal Canal's Basin at Radstock *Original plan: Chris Handley*

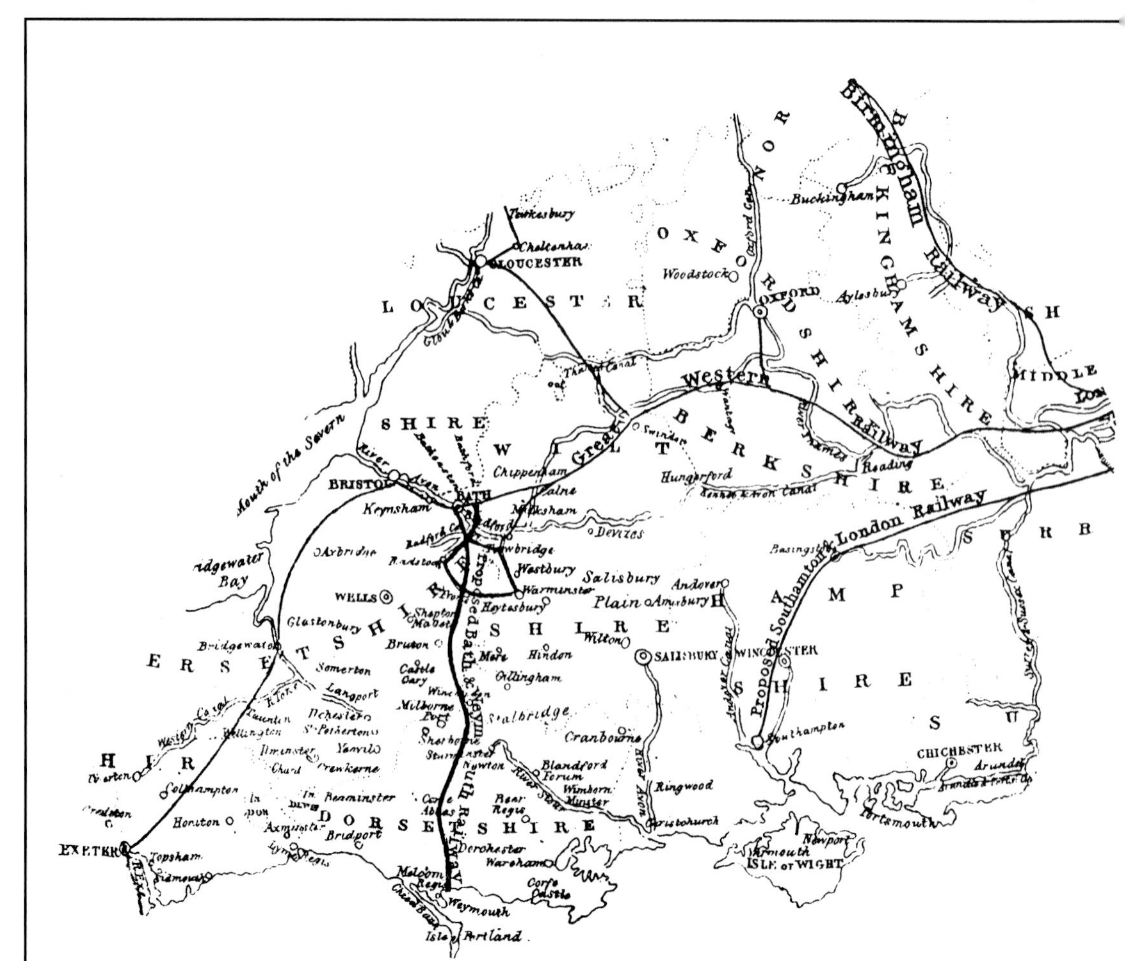

The Bath and Weymouth Great Western Union Railway 1836

This map, taken from the company's prospectus, shows the route of the proposed railway.

Original plan: Bath Reference Library

being taken out of the county by the SCC and its associated canals, the Kennet & Avon and the Wilts & Berks, to such places in the Thames Valley as Abingdon and Pangbourne.

Kenneth Clew, in his excellent book on the SCC sums the position up admirably when he says:

> "These years (the 1830s) were the golden years of the canal age as far as the three canals – Kennet & Avon, Wilts & Berks and Somerset Coal – were concerned. The period of prosperity for the W&B and K&A was to be short-lived as the Great Western Railway line (Bristol-London) was under construction and, when completed (1841), would form a challenge to the future trade."

During the mid-1830s, the railway challenge was being thrown at the Somersetshire Coal Canal from several directions. There was, of course, the GWR line to Paddington, but in addition, the grand-sounding "Bath & Weymouth: Great Western Union Railway" was proposed.

This line was to have run from Bath to Weymouth, via Frome, Wincanton, Stalbridge and Dorchester. It would also have had connecting branches from the Somerset Coalfield at Radstock; from Bradford-on-Avon and from Warminster and Frome. Its capital was to have been £1,000,000 in 10,000 shares of £100 each. The engineers were Messrs Hopkins & Sons. It was reckoned that the key lines from the collieries could be completed within twelve months of the Act of Incorporation being granted. The Warminster and Frome sections would have been brought into operation some 18 months after the line's act had been passed. The main line to Weymouth was to be ready in some three to four years. These periods of time seem to reflect a remarkable sense of optimism and unreality! In fact, none of the lines were ever built.

However, the scheme had helped to generate local railway interest for, just as the national network of rails was growing, so the pressure was now on to develop the iron lines locally. The seeds had already been planted. With the railway between Bristol & London in use and a railway between the Bristol and English Channels running through and serving the prosperous Somerset Coalfield in prospect at least, the railway roots had been well and truly dug in. So, it was not surprising that, within the coalfield itself, a strong pressure group was built up to get a railway line into the area. In the mid-1840s the challenge was taken up by a local company which was, at least in name, private. Strongly backed by the GWR as one of its attempts to stop the LSWR gaining more ground in the West Country, the new enterprise was to be known as the Wilts & Somerset Railway.

The new railway was to have started near Chippenham on the Great Western's main line from Paddington to Bristol. From here it was to run to Salisbury. There were to be branches to Devizes, Bradford-on-Avon and Frome. From Frome there would have been a short, but key mineral-only line to Radstock. This would tap the coalfield. During the autumn of 1844 the aspirations of the Wilts & Somerset widened. With growing local hopes, the scope of the company was increased. It was decided to extend the line beyond Frome to Weymouth and to change the company's name to the Wilts, Somerset & Weymouth Railway. There was also pressure to extend the mineral-only line beyond Radstock through the coalfield at Timsbury. From here it would have run to Twerton, a small station just west of Bath on the GWR's Bristol-Bath-London line, but this latter extension was never built.

In 1845 an Act was passed authorising the Wilts, Somerset & Weymouth Railway's construction. Essentially, the railway's backbone was made up of two north/south lines. One of these core routes would join the Bristol-Bath-London line at Thingley Junction near Chippenham and would run down to Frome. From here the lines would split into two: one branch running through Yeovil to Weymouth, the other running down through Warminster to Salisbury. As in the company's previous plan, a short stub was to be built from Frome, through the Mells area to Radstock to tap the as yet under-tapped

ANNO OCTAVO & NONO

VICTORIÆ REGINÆ.

****

Cap. liii.

An Act for making a Railway from the *Great Western* Railway to the City of *Salisbury* and Town of *Weymouth*, with other Railways in connexion therewith, to be called "The *Wilts, Somerset, and Weymouth* Railway."

[30th *June* 1845.]

WHEREAS the making of a Railway from and out of the *Great Western* Railway at or near *Thingley* in the Parish of *Corsham* in the County of *Wilts* to the City of *Salisbury*, and of another Railway from and out of such first-mentioned intended Railway in the Parish of *Upton Scudamore* in the said County of *Wilts* to *Yeovil* in the County of *Somerset*, and to the Boroughs of *Dorchester* and *Melcombe Regis* in the County of *Dorset*, and of another Railway from and out of such first-mentioned intended Railway in the Parish of *Melksham* in the said County of *Wilts* to the Borough of *Devizes*, and of another Railway from and out of the same first-mentioned intended Railway at or near to *Staverton* in the Parish of *Trowbridge* in the said County of *Wilts*, to or near to the Town of *Bradford* in the same County, and of another Railway or Railways from and out of the said secondly-mentioned

[*Local.*] 12 *M*

mentioned intended Railway in the Parish of *Frome Selwood* in the said County of *Somerset* to certain Collieries and Coal Works in the Parish of *Radstoke* in the said County of *Somerset*, and of another Railway from and out of the said secondly-mentioned intended Railway in the Parish of *Bradford Abbas* in the County of *Dorset* to the Town of *Sherborne* in the same County, and of another Railway from and out of the said secondly-mentioned intended Railway near the Town of *Maiden Newton* in the said County of *Dorset* to or near to the Town and Harbour of *Bridport* in the same County, would be of great public Advantage, by opening an additional, certain, and expeditious Means of Communication between the said Places, and also by facilitating Communication between more distant Towns and Places: And whereas an Act has been passed during the present Session of Parliament, intituled *An Act for consolidating in One Act certain Provisions usually inserted in Acts with respect to the Constitution of Companies incorporated for carrying on Undertakings of a public Nature*, called "The Companies Clauses Consolidation Act, 1845:" And whereas another Act has been passed during the present Session of Parliament, intituled *An Act for consolidating in One Act certain Provisions usually inserted in Acts authorizing the taking of Lands for Undertakings of a public Nature*, called "The Lands Clauses Consolidation Act, 1845:" And whereas another Act has been passed during the present Session of Parliament, intituled *An Act for consolidating in One Act certain Provisions usually inserted in Acts authorizing the making of Railways*, called "The Railways Clauses Consolidation Act, 1845:" And whereas the Persons hereafter named are willing at their own Expence to carry such Undertaking into execution; but the same cannot be effected without the Authority of Parliament: May it therefore please Your Majesty that it may be enacted; and be it enacted by the Queen's most Excellent Majesty, by and with the Advice and Consent of the Lords Spiritual and Temporal, and Commons, in this present Parliament assembled, and by the Authority of the same, That the Provisions of the said Companies Clauses Consolidation Act, 1845, the Lands Clauses Consolidation Act, 1845, and the Railway Clauses Consolidation Act, 1845, shall be incorporated with and form Part of this Act, save as to such Parts thereof as may be modified by or be inconsistent with the Provisions of this Act.

(Margin notes: 8 & 9 Vict. c. 16. — 8 & 9 Vict. c. 18. — 8 & 9 Vict. c. 20. — Incorporation of recited Acts with this Act.)

Short Title. II. And be it enacted, That in citing this Act in other Acts of Parliament, and in legal Instruments, it shall be sufficient to use the Expression "The *Wilts, Somerset, and Weymouth* Railway Act, 1845."

Subscribers incorporated. III. And be it enacted, That Sir *John Wither Awdry*, *Thomas O. Bennett* Esquire, *Henry Butcher* junior, Esquire, *John Clark* Esquire, *Thomas Clark* Esquire, *Edward Cooper* Esquire, *Ezekiel Edmonds* Esquire, *Michael John Festing* Esquire, the Reverend *Canon Fisher*, *Robert Frederic Gower* Esquire, Major *Thomas H. Grubbe*, *Jesse Gouldsmith* Esquire, the Reverend *J. D. Hastings*, *William Goodenough Hayter* Esquire, M.P., the Reverend *Thomas T. Heathcote*, Sir *Hugh Hoare* Baronet, Sir *Ralph Lopez* Baronet, M.P., Reverend *C. Lucas*, *Henry Gaisford Gibbs Ludlow* Esquire, *John*

resources of the coalfields.

Built by the contractors Tredwells, J. Pritchard and possibly Roland Brotherhood, the first section of the Wilts, Somerset & Weymouth to open to traffic was the 14 mile link from Thingley Junction to Westbury in Wiltshire. Opened in 1848, little progress was made after that time for the serious after effects of the "Railway Mania" of 1846/47 had set in and finance was very difficult to come by. Since land had already been bought for most of the project, it must have appeared strange to see a half-built railway with unfinished earthworks, incomplete bridges and unlaid permanent way. However, help was in sight for the GWR took over the local company in a way we shall see repeated later in our story with the Bristol & North Somerset Railway. The Wilts, Somerset & Weymouth was absorbed by the larger company on the 14th March 1850. After the GWR took over, things got moving again and Frome was reached in the autumn of 1850.

A very useful source of information that throws some interesting insights onto the construction of the station at Frome and into the Frome-Radstock mineral-only branch, whose construction was to follow over the 1850-54 period, has been provided by a Frome man, Mr Thomas Green. Green maintained a diary which noted, on 5th August 1850, that he went into the "new railway station in course of erection" while, one month later, on 5th September, he "met Mr Barnes the contractor of the railway station". Some three days after this Thomas "walked to the railway at Clink where they were putting down the rails". By the 25th of the same month the railway station at Frome was very nearly complete.

October 7th 1850 should have been a great day for Frome for it was on that particular day that the railway line from Westbury to Frome opened. Thomas Green writes of the weather that it was "fine but blowing. Frome railway station opened this morning at 7 o'clock by special train to Oxford and four regular trains to Chippenham. Walked to station at ten and saw the half past ten go out and horse buses and coaches to meet it came in and a new coach from Yeovil through Bruton and (Castle) Cary".

Though rather scathing, a contemporary account of the opening of the railway to Frome from The Times throws more light on the occasion:

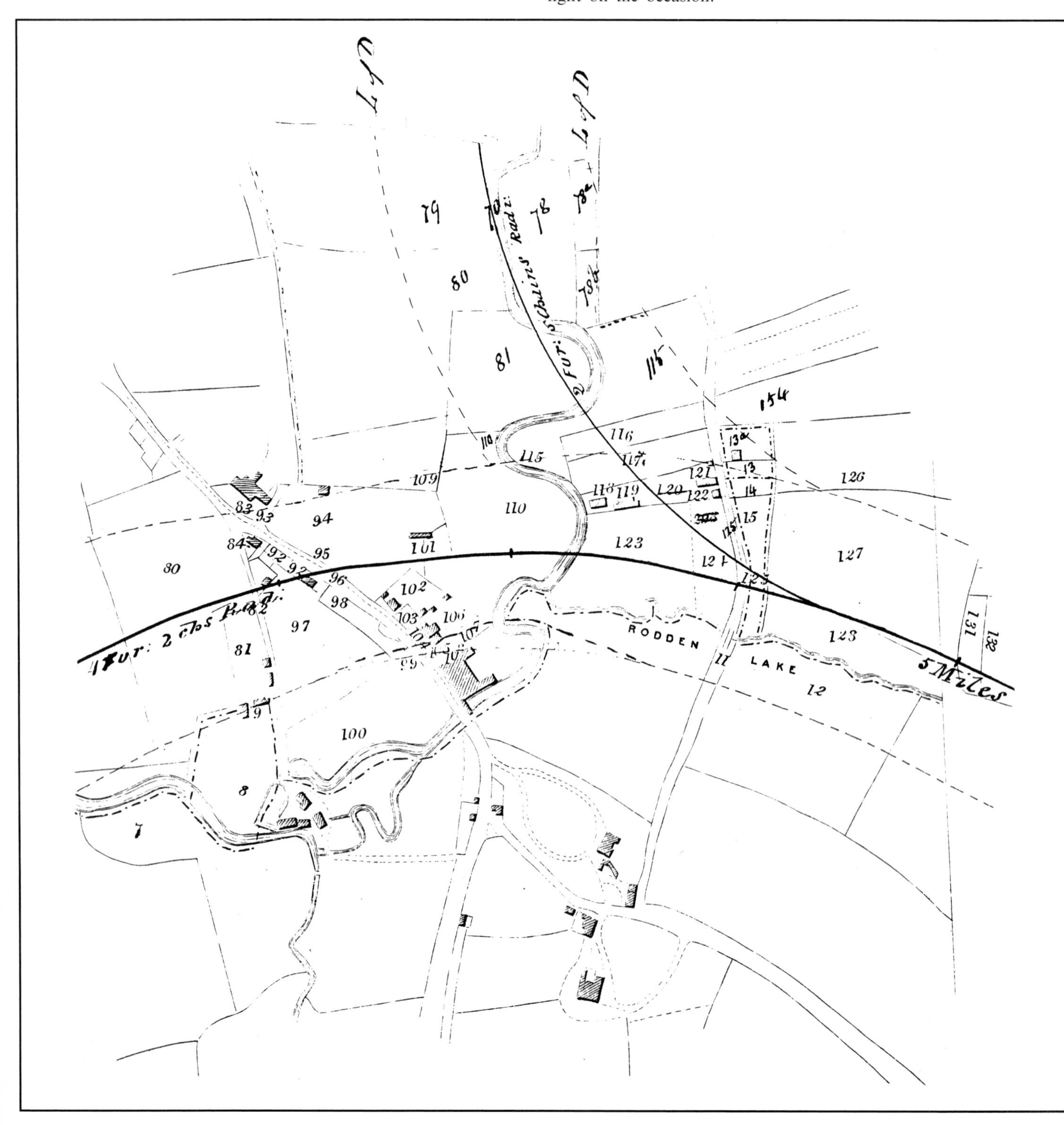

The Wilts, Somerset & Weymouth's
Frome Deviation 1845

Original plan: Somerset Record Office

FROME STATION
Opened in 1850, the station at Frome was designed by J. R. Hannaford, one of Brunel's many assistants. The station's goods shed was also designed by Hannaford. However, there can be no doubt that Frome is a characteristically Brunellian station on what is very much a Brunellian line.

Now restored, the station shows how well historically important buildings can be adapted to modern day use, a process at which British Rail can be especially good when it wishes to or, as in this case, when it has been goaded into so doing! With a pannier tank and brake van at the starting signals, this photograph shows the station during the late 1950s.

Author's collection

> "Our reporter was dispatched to Frome to chronicle the usual rejoicings and public demonstrations which occur when a line first connects a town with railway communication. But our reporter returns with a blank notebook. Frome is an exception to his experience of similar occasions. There was no enthusiasm in the place to be recorded."

However, the newspaper did note that celebrations were encountered at Westbury. The people in this Wiltshire town were obviously much happier about the coming of the railway! The Times continued:

> "But at Frome no officials welcomed the commencement of a mode of communication undoubtedly calculated to exercise considerable influence on the trade and commerce of the town. The bells of the parish church were silent, no flags were hoisted, no cannon discharged, the workpeople of the town, who had been granted a holiday, had no other occupation than wandering to and from the station to watch the arrival and departure of the trains. The whole population, by their listlessness and apathy seemed to exemplify the truth of the saying, "A want of occupation is not rest, the mind that's vacant is a mind distressed."

The paper's reporter could not even pass comment on the celebration dinner that took place at the Crown Hotel for the last train left Frome at 5.10pm! This particular dinner was chaired by Henry Miller and it seems that not all the 50 tickets available were used. The special excursion to Oxford, mentioned by Thomas Green in his diary, cost 3s 6d (17½p). According to The Times reporter less than 100 people travelled on it.

Once the WS&WR had reached Frome its construction continued on southwards towards Salisbury Plain and, in September 1851, the single line reached Warminster. By this time the enormous sum of £1,433,000 had been spent on the new southward-stretching railway, of which some three quarters of a million was tied up on the section beyond Frome towards Yeovil and beyond Warminster towards Salisbury. It was not until 1854 that the GWR eventually decided to restart work on the two main lines out of Frome. At last, on 30th June 1856, the line to Salisbury was opened to passenger traffic, while, on 1st September, the Frome-Yeovil section also opened for passenger business. Both lines were single and on the broad gauge. The line from Yeovil onwards to Weymouth opened on 20th January 1857.

It would seem opportune at this point to slip back a little in time and see what had happened with regard to the planned mineral-only line to Radstock. Eight contractors competed for the short branch and they, and their tenders, were as follows:

C. E. Lansdell	£19,680
Messrs Roach & Pilditch	£21,380
Messrs Fowler	£21,334
William Fitzpatrick	£22,491
William Few	£23,700
Joseph Diggle	£27,500
William Baker	£34,000

The contract put forward by Messrs Roach and Pilditch was the one accepted. I. K. Brunel was the line's chief engineer while the post of resident engineer was filled by Mr R. J. Ward. The firm of Barnes and Taylor were responsible for laying the branch's permanent way. The cost of the line worked out at around £11,000 per mile.

On 31st May 1851, the year in which special excursions were run from Frome to the Great Exhibition at the Crystal Palace in London, Thomas Green wrote in his diary, "walked to Pilly Vale to see progress of (the) Radstock Railway". Pilly Vale is now called Willow Vale and the Frome-Radstock line cuts through the end building of the row of cottages which is now the present No. 17 Willow Vale. In 1851, the railway company purchased the premises from James Anthony Wickham of

FROME SHED

(1) With the maltings dominating the Frome shed scene, pannier tanks simmer quietly one evening in November 1961. This small loco shed was located to the south of Frome station and was built entirely of timber apart from its slate roof. As can be clearly seen, the adjoining office was brick built. *John Keeping*

(2) With locomotives Nos 7727, 4553 and 5530 to the fore, Frome shed is just five years away from official closure, this coming in September 1963. The photograph was taken in the North Somerset's twilight year of 1958. *Peter A. Fry*

Mr Brunel who was present at the Meeting, requested to know the views of the Directors relative to a Contract for laying the Permanent way on the Oxford & Birmingham Line and he was instructed to ascertain from Messrs Peto & Betts the Terms upon which they will engage to Construct it.—

Mr Brunel reported that Messrs Roach & Pilditch had agreed to Construct the Works of the Radstock Branch of the Wilts & Somerset Line receiving in payment the Company's 4½ Pcent fixed Stock which they undertake to hold in their own names for one year after the completion of the Works. This arrangement was approved_ and the Engineer was instructed to confer with the Solicitors for drawing up the necessary Contract for the Works_ according to his Specification and Conditions.—

An Interesting GWR Board Minute
6th February 1851
Original document: Public Record Office, Kew

Norton Hill House and soon set to work demolishing part of the building. Indeed, the blocked-off windows and doorway still remain, scars to the work carried out on the railway side of the building.

Even with this short stretch of track there were problems in that some of the land required for the route was difficult to obtain. Nonetheless, by November 1854 the broad gauge from Frome terminated close to the centre of Radstock just beyond Ludlows Pit. On 15th November 1854 Thomas Green noted "Radstock railway opened this day" while the Bristol Mercury for 18th November commented on the opening in the following caustic way:

> "The portion of this line between Frome and Radstock which from various causes has been so long in construction, was opened for the conveyance of minerals on Tuesday."

As one would expect the line had previously been inspected by a Board of Trade inspector who, in this instance, was Colonel Yolland, a name we shall find continually cropping up in our narrative.

Yolland made his inspection and report on 23rd October 1854 which stated that:

> "The whole of the permanent way on this line of about 8½ miles in length, is laid with a single line of rails, and the works appear to be in good order throughout; but no arrangements have yet been made for working the line for passenger traffic at Radstock as no accommodation or platform has yet been provided and the station is not as yet entirely inclosed . . . Some slight portions of fencing also require to be completed and some Policemen's Boxes have yet to be placed at the Public Crossings, but I am informed that the fencing and the placing (of) the Policemen's Boxes will be attended to without delay.
>
> I learn also that there is no present intention to commence working the line for Passenger Traffic.
>
> I am therefore of (the) opinion that taking into consideration the incompleteness of the works that this line cannot be opened for Traffic, without danger to the public using the same."

However, some three weeks later, all the faults had been ironed out to the satisfaction of the Board of Trade for, as we have seen, the line opened for freight traffic only.

At the Radstock end, under an agreement of 17th February 1853, a short siding was constructed from the GWR linking the nearby pit at Ludlows into the broad gauge network. Other collieries in the area however, found access to the GWR's mineral-only line to be somewhat more difficult and costly in that in order to get to the broad gauge their coal had to cross land owned by one of the best known, and most powerful of the Somerset coal owners, the Waldegraves. (For further details of Radstock's coal owners, see accompanying table.)

For the benefit of crossing Waldegrave land, the other coal owners had to pay both rent and royalties to Lady Waldegrave who, upon the death of her husband, the seventh Earl in 1846, had taken over sole responsibility for the Waldegrave Estates in North Somerset. In return, she provided a short tramway in the vicinity of Ludlows Pit which connected the Somersetshire Coal Canal's tramway to a new coal tipping dock adjacent to the broad gauge tracks. The consequence of this arrangement was that most of the local colliery proprietors were forced to pay for the privilege of using not one but two tramways, thus significantly raising the cost of their coal production over that of the Waldegraves.

Not surprisingly, this way of doing things was not universally popular with the coal owners and, on 28th November 1855, a group of them met at Radstock to discuss a proposal to build a broad gauge line linking the GWR at Radstock with both the East Somerset Railway (at that time being proposed between Witham and Shepton Mallet) and with collieries at Clandown, Wellsway, Norton Hill, Old Welton and Upper and Lower Writhlington, all of these pits being fairly close to Radstock itself. The Rector of Radstock, Mr H. N. Ward, and Mr J. Rees-Mogg, a local landowner, were both involved, although it would seem that Mr Ward was the key agent for change.

THE RADSTOCK BRANCH

The Wilts, Somerset & Weymouth Railway's route near Mells in advance of the construction of the Radstock Branch.

Original plan: Lord Oxford

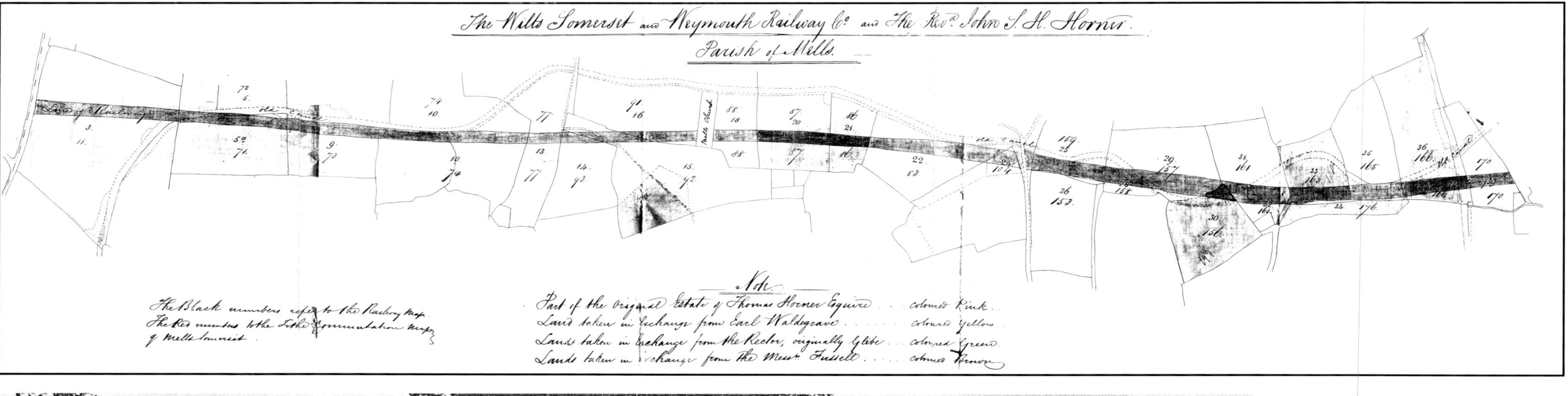

WELL LADEN THROUGH WILLOW VALE, FROME
Class 33 diesel-electric locomotives Nos 33045 and 33054 head a heavy train of loaded stone hoppers through Willow Vale, Frome bound for their destination at Totton, near Southampton. The cottages mentioned in the text can just be seen to the left of the photograph. This ARC action took place on 11th August 1982.

Mike Miller

Colliery Ownership in the Radstock Area in 1850

Very conveniently up to the year 1850, collieries around the Radstock area could be divided into three ownership groups, namely The Duchy of Cornwall Mines, The Earl Waldegrave Collieries and The Writhlington Collieries.

The Duchy Of Cornwall Collieries

This group consisted of three large collieries worked on land in the area owned by the Duchy of Cornwall. In each case, the work was carried out by private companies under lease arrangements.

Old Welton Colliery*	Opened c1783
Clandown Colliery	Opened c1811
Welton Hill Colliery*	Opened c1815

The Earl Waldegrave's Radstock Collieries

Although relatively late into the North Somerset mining business, this became one of the best known colliery groups during the 19th century. The family, Lords of the Manor of Radstock, leased their land, at first, to private mining companies but later went on to form their own company, managing their own affairs.

Old Pit	Opened c1763
Smallcombe Colliery	Opened c1798
Middle Pit	Opened c1779
Ludlows Colliery*	Opened c1784
Wellsway Colliery*	Opened c1833
Tyning Colliery*	Opened c1837

The Writhlington Collieries

Trading under the general title of The Writhlington Collieries Ltd, this group became a powerful and long-lasting organisation in the Radstock community.

Upper Writhlington Colliery	Opened c1805
Huish Colliery*	Opened c1824
Shoscombe Colliery	Opened c1828
Lower Writhlington Colliery	Opened c1829
Braysdown Colliery	Opened c1845

*Collieries of direct concern to the history of the Bristol & North Somerset Railway. (Source: Chris Handley.)

At the meeting the plan received a good deal of support. However, it was felt that:

" . . . in consequence of the great expense of the works (over £42,000) contemplated by Mr Ward it is desirable that at present a broad gauge horse railway only with self-acting inclines to connect them with the GWR terminus at Radstock should be made: . . . and that a tunnel for a single line of railway . . . (should be built) . . . "

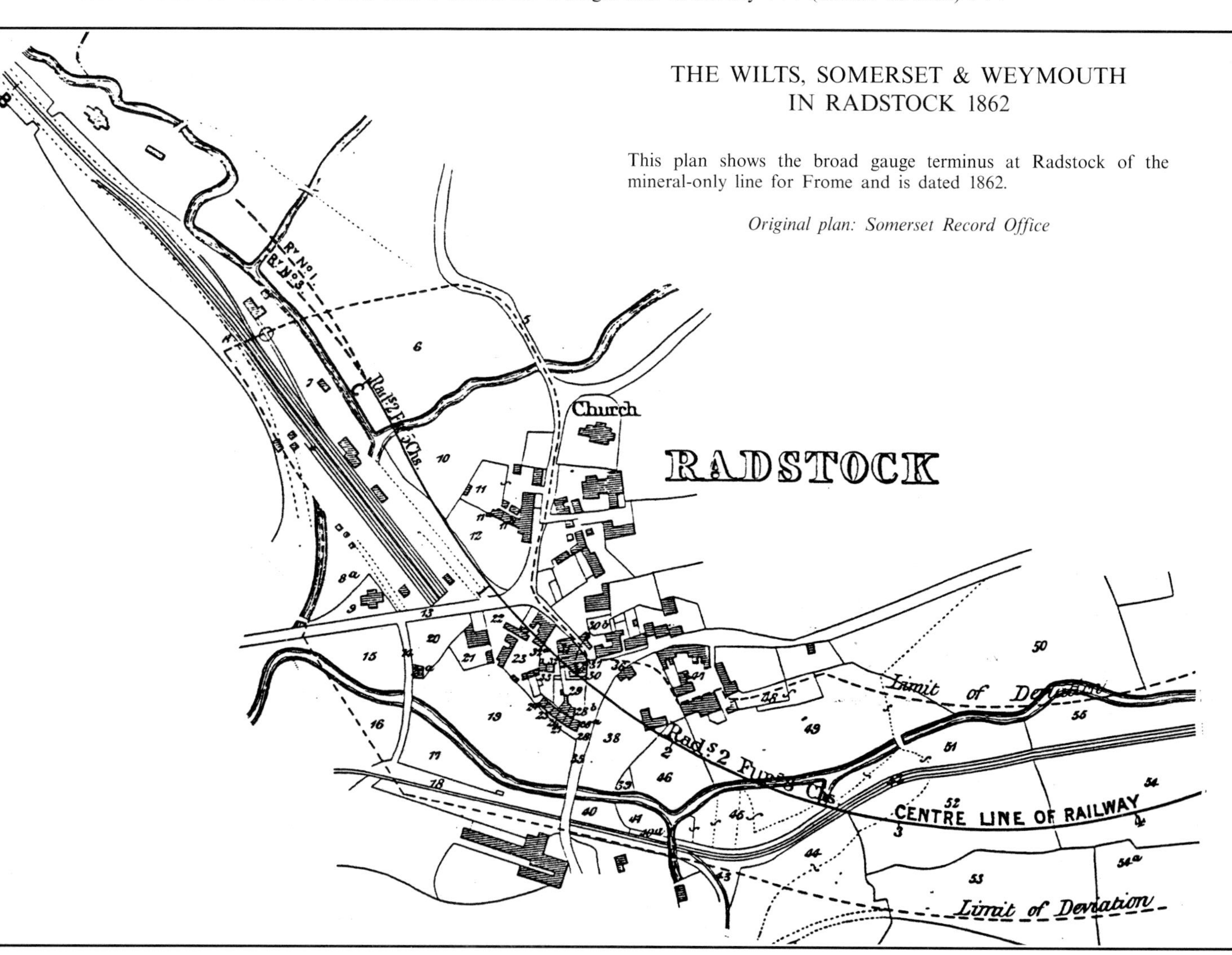

THE WILTS, SOMERSET & WEYMOUTH IN RADSTOCK 1862

This plan shows the broad gauge terminus at Radstock of the mineral-only line for Frome and is dated 1862.

Original plan: Somerset Record Office

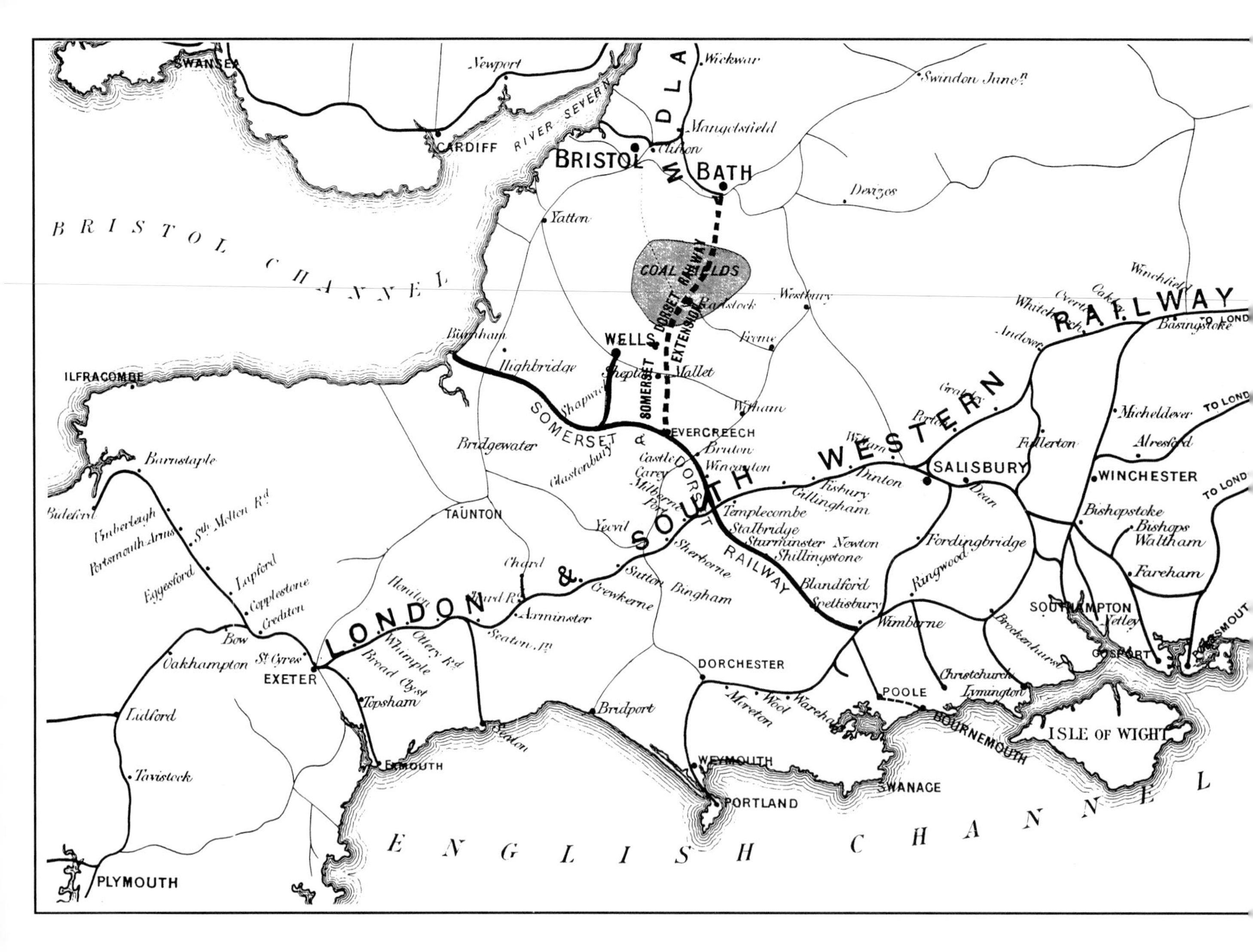

The latter was presumably needed to link the Writhlington pits by a railway under Frome Hill at Radstock with the GWR's broad gauge empire? The motion was carried as, indeed, was another which gave Mr Ward the go-ahead to cost the scheme out once more. This he did and, in December 1855, he produced a revised estimate of nearly £21,500. This was still too much for the colliery owners to bear and the line was never built.

As we shall see, this was one of very many railway schemes that never saw the light of day in the Somerset Coalfield and it might well be a good time to have a closer look at some of the fascinating ideas that were never turned into concrete reality. For example, in the 1846/47 "Railway Mania" period, the GWR had received parliamentary permission to build a broad gauge railway from Twerton, just outside Bath, to Radstock and Midsomer Norton. However, because times were financially very hard for the GWR, and all other railway companies, for that matter this plan was never carried out. In the parliamentary discussion of the 1863 Bristol & North Somerset Railway Act the promoters made the following comments about this 1847 scheme when they said,

> ". . . The fact remained that the GWR undertook to supply a railway which should develop the resources of the mineral fields. The company had been charged with criminal neglect in not making that line! Every member of the (House of Commons) committee knew what took place in 1848 when there was a panic as regarded railways such as this country had never seen before or since, under the influence of which all railway schemes, good, bad and indifferent, perished together from sheer want of funds."

Another scheme that fell by the wayside in North Somerset was put forward in 1852 when it was proposed to link, by rail, the Bristol Channel with the English Channel near Poole. This line was to be of standard gauge. Again, nothing became of this particular plan.

THE SOMERSET & DORSET JOINT RAILWAY SWEEPS INTO NORTH SOMERSET: EVERCREECH JUNCTION-BATH 1874

The Somerset & Dorset Joint Railway was formed in 1862 by the amalgamation of the Somerset Central and Dorset Central Railways to form a through route between Burnham-on-Sea and Wimborne. The Somerset Central opened in 1854 between Highbridge and Glastonbury, being extended to Burnham-on-Sea in 1858 and Wells in 1859. The Dorset Central opened between Wimborne and Blandford in 1860. In 1862 the two companies combined whilst the section of line between Glastonbury and Templecombe was also opened. In 1863 Blandford to Templecombe opened for business. The through route between the Bristol and English Channels was complete.

In 1874 an extension was opened from Evercreech Junction to Bath and this linked the standard gauge Midland and London & South Western Railways smack through the heart of the GWR's territory. However, with its finances drained, the S&D could not cope with the extra traffic generated and so, in 1875 and much to the GWR's annoyance, the company was leased jointly by the MR and the LSWR. In 1885, the opening of the cut-off line avoiding reversal at Wimborne, and of the Bridgwater branch in 1890 meant that the system was now complete and it was not long before the Bath-Bournemouth spine became the main traffic artery.

Original plan: (dated 1870) Somerset Record Office

With J. F. Tone as its chief engineer and H. Copperthwaite as its resident engineer, the next likely looking scheme to succeed was the North Somerset Railway project of 1860. To be of standard gauge, the NSR was to have run from a connection with the Somerset Central Railway at Wells northwards to Bristol. Leaving Wells, the line's route would have been up past the "County Lunatic Asylum" to the hamlet of East Horrington. From here it would have forged up over the Mendips passing close to the village of Binegar. From there the route would have taken the tracks on past Ston Easton to Farrington Gurney where, if all the proposed connections had been built, there would have been a triangular junction.

The first part of the three arms of this junction would, quite naturally, have been the Wells to Bristol main line. Secondly, there would have been a junction from the Bristol direction towards Radstock, the line running down through Welton. Eventually, if traffic had materialised in abundance, the third arm of the junction would have linked the Wells line directly into the Radstock branch. From Farrington north the line would have continued towards Bristol along virtually the same route as that later taken by the Bristol & North Somerset Railway as built under that company's 1863 Act. In other words, it would have headed towards and through Clutton, Pensford, Brislington and thence into Bristol. In Bristol itself the North Somerset Railway would have run up and over the GWR's main Bristol-London line, hitching into the Midland near the junction of the company's lines from Gloucester and the North, with those of the GWR from Bath and the East.

The North Somerset scheme of 1860 would also have led to the construction of a branch to serve collieries in the Cam Valley. This short, but vitally important spur, would have left the main South-North/Wells-Bristol route near the village of Clutton and would have run, via an eastward-swinging curve, to a terminus at Radford Mill, near Camerton. The junction for this branch would have joined the main line with a connection facing towards Bristol. This, in itself, is quite an interesting feature in that many of the other, later-proposed lines to Camerton joined the Radstock-Bristol section with a junction facing towards Radstock. Indeed, when it was finally opened in 1882, the branch line from the Cam Valley allowed through running towards Radstock and not towards Bristol.

A significant and important proposal, in that it set the routes for many of the later North Somerset schemes, the North Somerset of 1860 showed some steep gradients. For example, much of the first six miles out of Wells were to be at 1 in 47. The Radstock branch to Farrington Gurney was also rather see-saw in nature. However, the Camerton line was reasonably level, having much milder gradients. In spite of all the interest, the new railway was never built. It may have been mainly due to the fact that it was standard gauge and this implied that the promoters' ultimate object was to get a 4ft 8½in gauge link between the Midlands and the South, hence the scheme's lack of support amongst broad gauge interests.

In 1861, however, the GWR reacted to the pressure for a north-south standard gauge railway in the Wessex area, by putting forward proposals to build a broad gauge route to the LSWR's territory at Southampton. The LSWR retaliated by proposing a standard gauge line to Bristol. This latter railway, the Bristol & South Western Railway, for which a bill was deposited in 1862, would have left the Salisbury & Exeter Railway (opened 1860) near Templecombe, in Somerset. It would have thrust northwards into broad gauge territory through Wincanton and Bruton to Radstock, weaving these three towns together along much the same route as that actually taken by

The Radstock & Keynsham Railway 1862

Original plan: Somerset Record Office

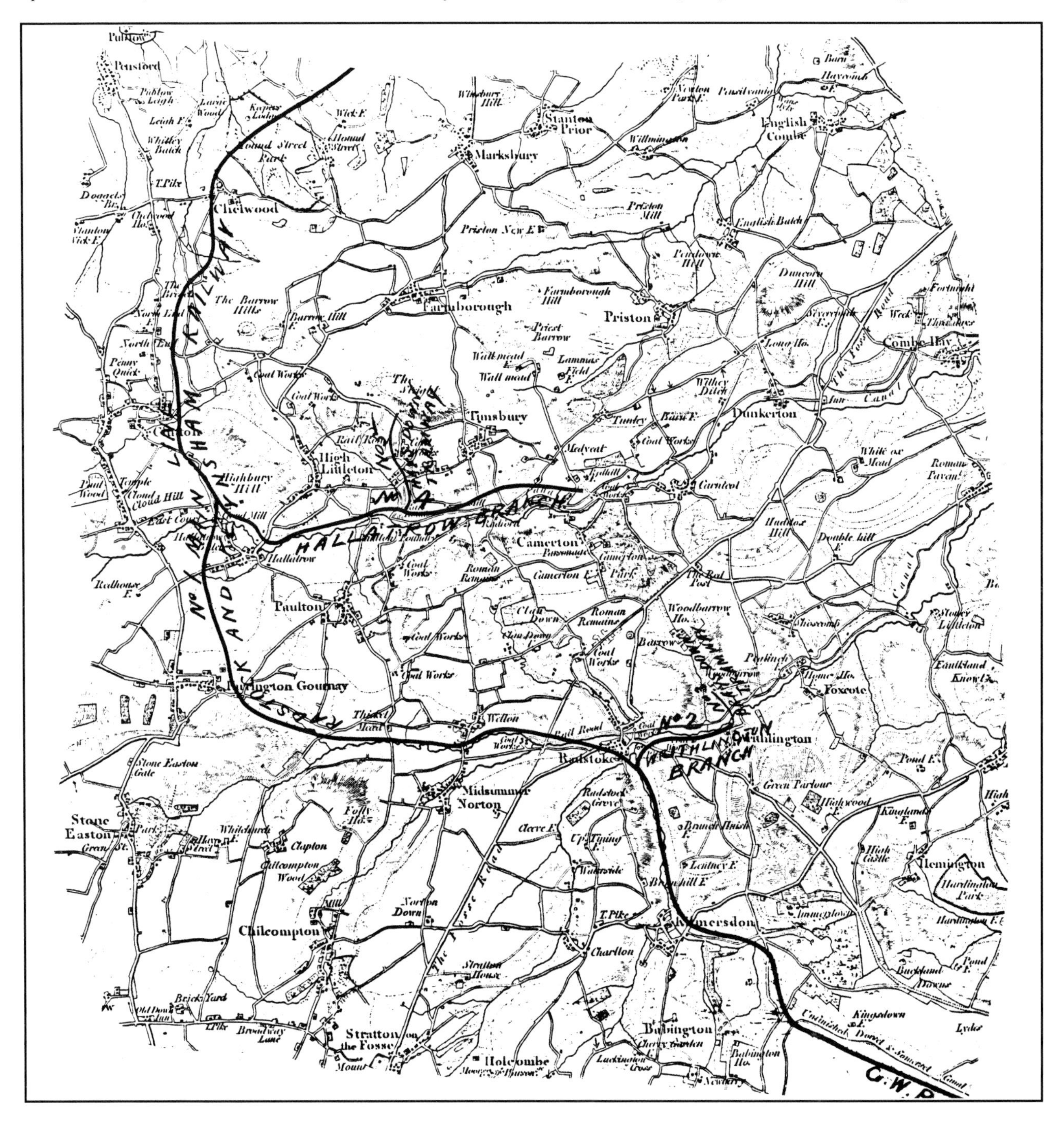

the Somerset & Dorset's Evercreech-Bath line when that railway opened in 1874. The section north of Radstock was substantially the same as that taken by the Bristol & North Somerset Railway when that eventually opened in 1873. In Bristol the terminus was to be close to the GWR's station at Temple Meads. A branch from Hallatrow to Camerton to get at Cam Valley coal was also included in these proposals.

It would have been a tough line to work with some 1 in 50 gradients. Single track at first it would later have been doubled if traffic demanded this. In addition, it would have put the Somerset Coalfield in direct contact with the 1,000 miles of track then being operated by the LSWR. Mr A. Scott, the LSWR'S Traffic Manager stated in parliamentary evidence that he would propose having two engines for the coal trains, each train consisting of 21 wagons containing six tons each. It would take three trains a day to work 100,000 tons of coal a year. The bill was, however, thrown out, as was the Great Western's bill for a broad gauge line to Southampton. Nevertheless, the two companies had been badly shaken by the whole business so, on 23rd October 1862, they made a 'peace treaty' by which the GWR retained its monopolistic hold on the Bristol-London traffic. Strangely enough, considerable improvements took place in the GWR's Bristol-Paddington services while the B&SWR bill was undergoing the parliamentary process!

Two other proposed railways put forward in 1862 were the Radstock & Keynsham Railway and the Somerset Coal Railway. The Radstock & Keynsham was another line that got caught up in the territorial squabbles of the GWR and the LSWR. This particular scheme went before the same parliamentary committee that was discussing the GWR's scheme to get to Southampton and the LSWR's counter-proposals to get towards Bristol. It came as no surprise, therefore, when the Radstock & Keynsham was thrown out! It could have been quite a useful railway with branches to serve the pits at Timsbury, Camerton and Writhlington.

The other scheme of the time, the Somerset Coal Railway, found especial favour with the coal owners. On the standard gauge, this line would have run from the S & D at Wincanton through to Radstock and would have terminated at Timsbury.

This was yet another line which, to the frustration of the coal owners, was never built! The years were rolling by. Would the railways ever be built that would help to encourage the development of the coalfield? As one coal owner rather succinctly put it in 1861, " . . . the great bulk of this coalfield is dormant . . . for the want of railway accommodation".

At long last, in September 1862, local private enterprise got together and, at a meeting held in Midsomer Norton, put

THE SOMERSET COAL RAILWAY 1862

This plan shows the northern section of the railway with its terminus at Timsbury. The broad gauge extension from the Great Western Railway and Ludlows Pit at Radstock to Tyning Colliery, opened in 1857, can be seen clearly.

Original plan: Somerset Record Office

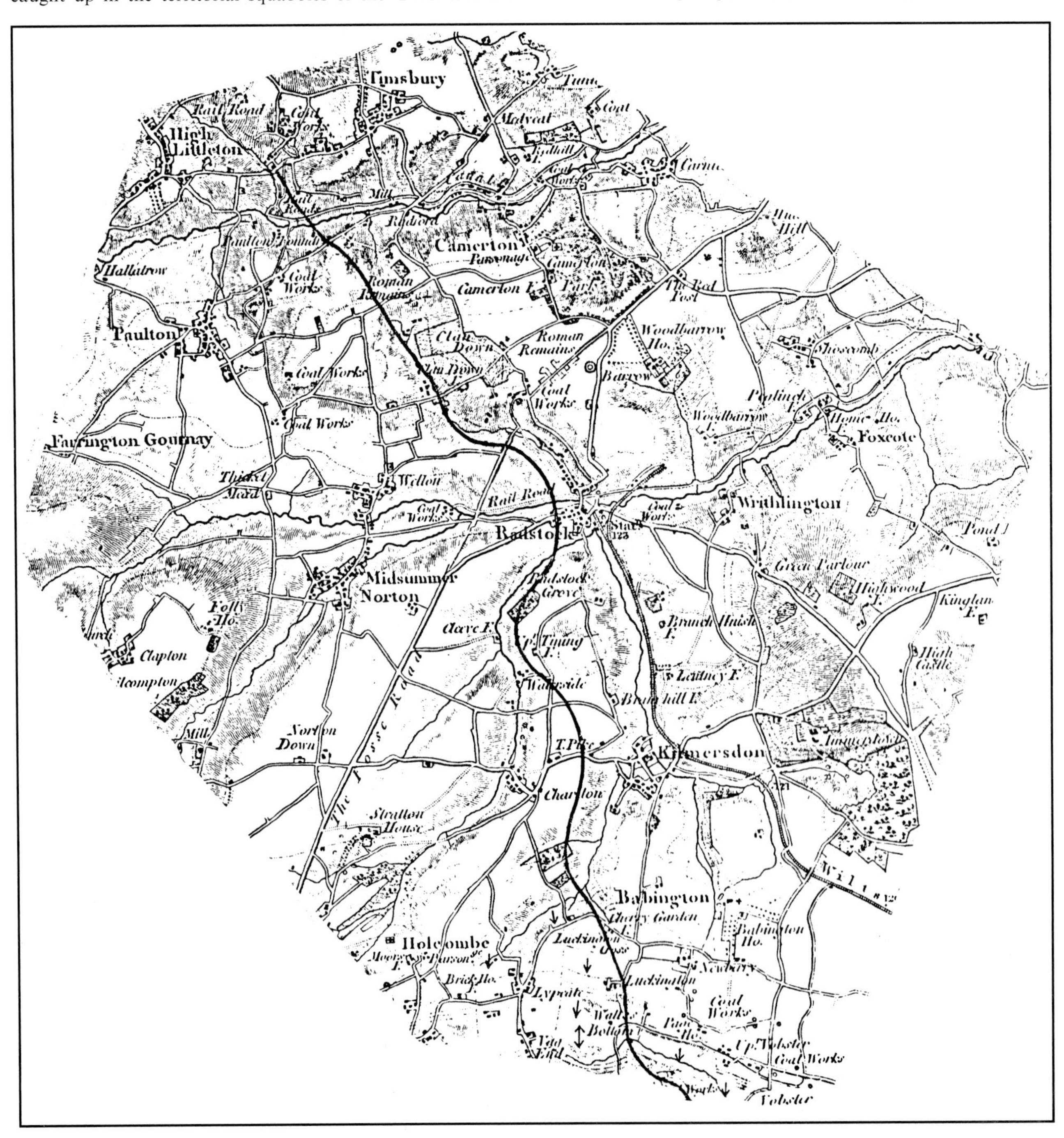

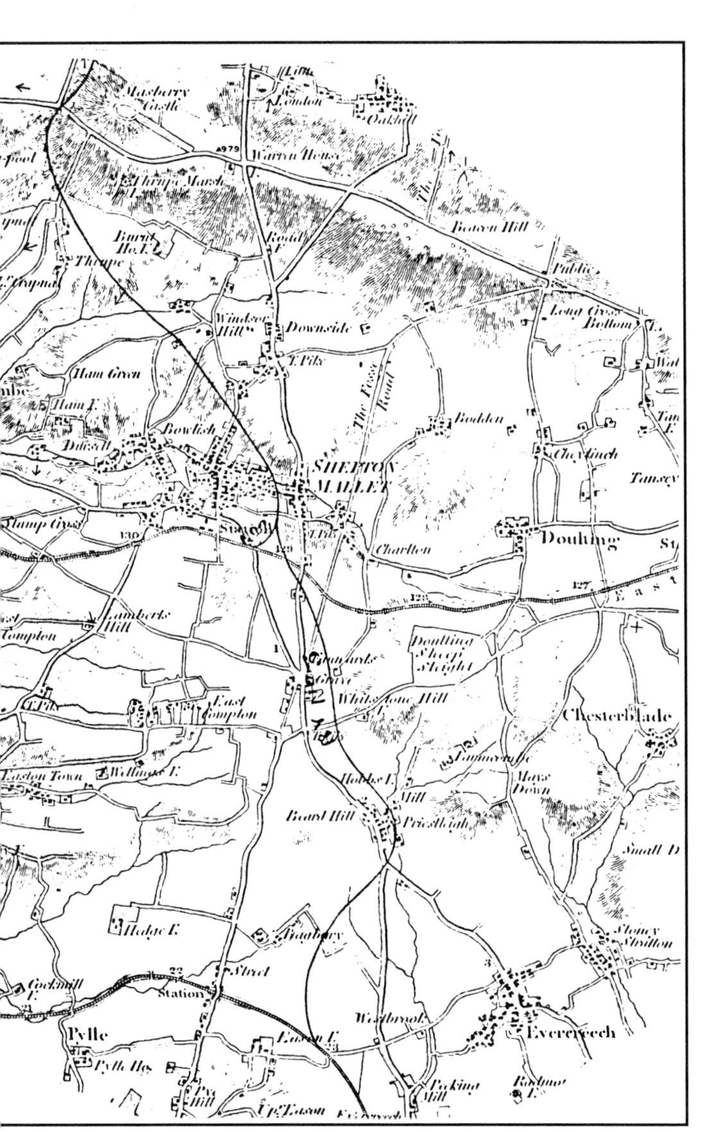

Left: THE BRISTOL & NORTH SOMERSET RAILWAY (SOUTHERN EXTENSION) 1864

This plan shows the proposed junction of the railway with the Somerset & Dorset near Evercreech. In addition, it shows the proposed connection with the East Somerset Railway at Shepton Mallet. North of Shepton the line would have continued on through Binegar and Chilcompton to Farrington where it would have joined the intended line from Radstock to Bristol.

Original plan: Somerset Record Office

forward a project that would, one day, link Bristol with the collieries at Radstock. It would then continue south to join up with the Somerset & Dorset line near Bruton. At the Bristol end there would be junctions with both broad and standard gauge lines and there would be a tramway to the then important and busy City Docks at the Floating Harbour. South of Bristol the railway would pass through Pensford, Clutton and Welton. There would be a branch to Camerton with a junction, facing towards Radstock, near the tiny hamlet of Hallatrow. At the end of November 1862 the *Bristol & North Somerset Railway* bill was deposited.

In the next chapter we will look at the bothered beginnings and troubled times of the Bristol & North Somerset in much more detail but, for the time being at least, it will be easier and clearer if we keep the picture as broad as possible. Once into 1863, notwithstanding a rather serious internal disagreement regarding what gauge the railway was to be built, the B&NSR bill came before the House of Commons' Committee.

Below: THE RADSTOCK & BATH RAILWAY 1865 SESSION

This plan shows the tunnel under Radstock that was to be built for this particular railway. The "railway station" in the centre of the plan is the terminus of the mineral-only line from Frome.

Original plan: Somerset Record Office.

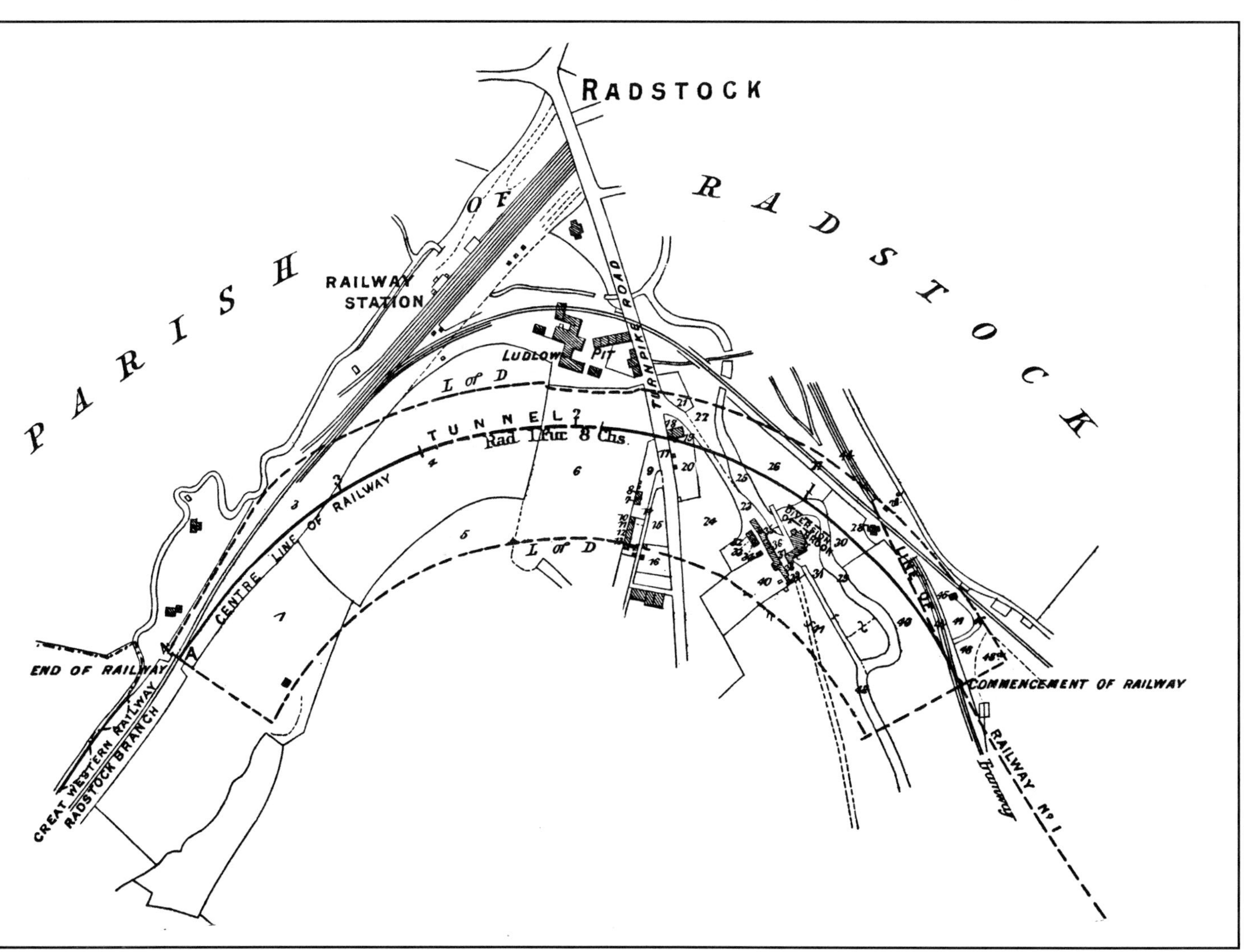

It was successful and, in late June 1863, it moved to the House of Lords. It succeeded there too and the Bristol &North Somerset Railway bill became law on 21st July 1863. This allowed the raising of £275,000 in £20 shares. Loans could, with conditions, be raised to the tune of £91,000.

During October 1863, the secretary of the Bristol & North Somerset, Mr John Bingham, met Mr Robert Read, the secretary of the Somerset & Dorset Railway and they agreed that both companies would put forward bills, in the next parliamentary session, for new railways to Shepton Mallet. However, here was yet another flight of fancy, for nothing came out of these proposals. In the meantime, the Bristol & North Somerset had made the first of what was to be many attempts to get the GWR to work their new line, once it was built, in return for a proportion of the receipts. It also wanted the GWR's Frome-Radstock mineral-only line to be opened for passengers once the Bristol-Radstock section was completed. The GWR simply turned down flat the idea of an operating agreement between the two companies.

Work on the railway was agonisingly slow and incredibly unsure but, in October 1864, negotiations began again with the Somerset & Dorset, following which the B&NSR and the S&D reached an agreement by which they would both promote bills to construct lines to Shepton Mallet in the 1865 parliamentary session. Were the two companies going to develop a closer relationship – even amalgamate perhaps?

During 1865 the Somersetshire Coal Canal showed some fight back against the railways when it said that it was going to put forward a bill for a broad gauge railway, the Radstock & Bath Railway, which would join Radstock to the Wilts, Somerset & Weymouth's route at Monkton Combe on the section between Bath and Bradford-on-Avon. As part of this plan this new railway would replace the Coal Canal's tramroad between Radstock and Midford. On a tit-for-tat basis, the Bristol & North Somerset then put forward a plan to build a new line from Camerton direct to Bath. This railway, the B&NSR (Bristol-Bath Lines) Act would have had connections to both the GWR near Twerton, and to the proposed Midland line from Mangotsfield into Bath (Queen Square). In response to this threat, the SCC decided to abandon its broad gauge bill, while the North Somerset's own bill also subsequently failed due to the opposition of some influential landowners in the area!

During October 1865 the North Somerset and the S&D resumed their discussions about amalgamation. Following agreement on 1st November of that year the two companies deposited a joint bill for their amalgamation, or for the S&D to buy or lease the North Somerset. In the 1866 parliamentary session the North Somerset deposited bills for a line to Shepton Mallet (the B&NSR Southern Extension) and for a deviation of its proposed 1863 line at Radstock (the B&NSR Deviation) Act. A third bill was also introduced authorising new routes in the Nettlebridge Valley (the B&NSR/GWR: New Lines) Act.

However, crisis and chaos were on the way for, in May 1866, the apparently amicable relationship between the B&NSR and the S&D came to an abrupt end when the beleaguered North Somerset heard of an agreement made by the S&D that compelled the railway, then in existence only between Burnham-on-Sea and Blandford, to send much of its traffic via the Bristol & Exeter Company's Taunton-Bristol line. The North Somerset's secretary, Mr Bingham, was therefore told to withdraw the bill for amalgamation and the one allowing new construction to take place down to Shepton Mallet.

As 1866 went grinding on, the North Somerset had to accept that they were nowhere near completing their Bristol-Radstock main line. The national financial crisis of that year came crashing down upon the Company and, as we shall see in Chapter 4, it was not until 1870 that the company started to raise its head weakly above water again. However, the events of 1866 had a profound effect not only upon the North Somerset Company but also upon its larger and all-pervading neighbour, the Great Western. Indeed, it is very important to remember that, in relation to the North Somerset's development during the 1860s, '70s and '80s, the GWR was having a pretty hard time of it financially as well.

Booker in his work *The GWR: A New History* reminds us that:

> "In the summer of 1864 Gooch resigned (and) he left a railway which was now deep in trouble. The cost of nearly twenty years of expansion had cut remorselessly into dividends . . . A renewed outburst of railway speculation in 1863 threatened the system at a dozen or more points."

In 1865, Gooch returned to the GWR and set in motion massive internal economies but:

> "The 'Black Friday' collapse in May 1866 of the bankers Overend & Gurney along with other firms who had been over-speculating hit (the company) hard. The collapse came when nearly £14 million of renewable debentures was in circulation and more than £1 million outstanding in temporary loans. Appeals to the Bank of England fell on deaf ears. Shares began to tumble (and) insolvency was only narrowly averted.
>
> From now on a policy of rigid economy stamped Gooch's conservative image on the company for nearly twenty years . . . Brunel's railway, ended the sixties and seventies lapped in deep lethargy – too poor to be enterprising, too mean to be smart. Even in the 1880s Foxwell was still noting that its porters handled passengers' luggage with heartfelt inertia . . . "

To the author, it seems very important to bear in mind this broader view during the whole of the early part of this story because, to a certain extent at least, these more general factors clearly help to explain the GWR's actions (or lack of action, as the case may be!) in relation to the Bristol & North Somerset's slow evolution over the next twenty years.

It is also crucial to remember that:

> "Gooch's drastic medicine worked. Other railways had been badly hit in the 1866 collapse; few weathered the storm as the Great Western. Dividends were again being paid by 1868."

On the other hand, if the 1866 crash had been difficult for the GWR, it had been absolutely disastrous for the Bristol & North Somerset Company. Its business affairs were already under close inspection by a committee of investigation. There was widespread mismanagement, resignations and prosecutions. It was going to take quite some sorting out and, until this had been cleared up, all construction work was at a standstill. Some three years were to pass before things started to move again for the North Somerset. By 1870 the Company had got its cash problems reasonably sorted out and, in 1870, was in the process of getting an act (the B&NSR Deviation at Radstock Act) to change the course of the route planned under its original 1863 Act.

In 1868 the Somerset & Dorset had fallen into receivership although, by 1870, it too had pulled itself enough out of the mire to allow the receivers to be discharged. In spite of its problems, the Company was on the move again, this time towards Bath, since it was clear that the way to Bristol was blocked by their former partners, the North Somerset Company. In November 1870, the S&D proposed to build a 26 mile long line from its existing railway at Evercreech hard up over the Mendip hills. From the junction at Evercreech it would wind its tortuous and uphill way to Bath via Shepton Mallet, Midsomer Norton, Radstock and Wellow. Like the B&NSR the coalfield traffic was a central goal for the S&D. At its northern stronghold of Bath, the newly-built S&D Extension would link into the Midland Railway's line between Mangotsfield and Bath. This section of track opened in 1869 and gave through connections into the Midlands.

The S&D's proposals came as a great shock to the Somersetshire Coal Canal since the new railway would offer certain and very threatening competition to its own tramway to Radstock. The canal company made the best of a very bad job and, in February 1871, it sold its Radstock tramway to the S&D. Construction of the Bath Extension moved with amazing speed. It was the hare of the race. The tortoise, however, in the shape of the North Somerset did at last, in September 1873, open throughout from Bristol to Radstock. Less than a

Left: THE GWR'S STATION AT SHEPTON MALLET
The Somerset town of Shepton Mallet featured in many might-have-been railway schemes of the 1860s. However, the GWR, whose station is shown here, actually reached the town from Witham in November 1858. An extension through to Wells followed in March 1861. The town was also later served by the Somerset & Dorset Railway. This company arrived on the Shepton scene in July 1874 when their metals were extended through from Evercreech Junction to Bath.

Today, Shepton Mallet has no British Rail service at all! *Lens of Sutton*

year later, in July 1874, the Somerset & Dorset opened its new railway, thus linking, by standard gauge, Bath with the South Coast.

The construction of the S&D's line to Bath brought four trains each way a day to S&D metals. Two of these carried through coaches from Bournemouth to Birmingham for, from the start, the local company had built up a good relationship with the Midland Railway. This relationship again highlights the inter-company rivalry present in this area and brings this chapter full circle for, when the S&D again (!) became bankrupt, it went, first of all, to the GWR for help. In turn, the GWR consulted the LSWR who, after all, had strong connections with the S&D at its southern end. The next move, however, put Paddington's nose very much out of joint in that the LSWR informed the Midland Railway. These two companies then made an offer to the S&D which was accepted. An agreement and a bill ratifying the agreement followed later.

Quite naturally, the GWR was incensed about the whole affair. Indeed, it may well have soured the GWR's view of the Radstock /North Somerset areas for some years to come, who knows? It certainly soured the relationship between the Bristol & North Somerset and the Somerset & Dorset. The sourness lasted for a good few years. However, let us move on from sourness and examine slowness; let us investigate more deeply the setting-up and the setting-out of the Bristol & North Somerset Railway in the 1862/3 period.

Below: FROME STATION 1900
"Taxi, Sir?" A hansom cab, its driver and passenger are seen here about to leave Frome station in 1900. This is one of those photographs that show "ordinary", everyday scenes that (railway) historians are always glad to see captured on film. *Michael McGarvie*

RELAYING AT RADSTOCK
This excellent photograph, although slightly marked in its upper part, shows a large number of permanent way men replacing bridge rail on the GWR's connection from its Radstock-Frome Branch into Ludlows Colliery. Apart from the actual relaying work itself, there are some other fascinating items that deserve closer attention. On the left can be seen the station's turntable, while on the adjacent platform can be seen a grounded passenger brake, possibly deriving from the 1850s period. The photograph was probably taken just before the First World War. *P. J. Williams*

3
The North Somerset Makes Tracks

In 1861, after the failure of the various proposals to connect the Somerset Coalfield with Bristol, there was a great deal of local pressure to get a line built over the Mendips from Radstock to Bristol. This pressure was particularly strong after the rejection of the LSWR's proposals of that year, namely the Bristol & South Western Railway. Indeed, one of that scheme's strongest supporters, the Rector of Paulton, Mr Henry Milward, called an initial meeting of some of the neighbourhood's most influential individuals to get their own line to Bristol. After this a public meeting at Midsomer Norton was then called on 23rd September 1862 in order to raise public interest in the idea. The scheme put forward at this meeting was for a railway from Bristol running south to join the then existing Somerset & Dorset line near Bruton. This proposal met with general approval.

The meeting set up a provisional committee whose job it was to get the scheme off the ground. Not surprisingly, this committee was made up of most of the local coal and landowners. In addition, the meeting was responsible for promoting an independent bill for the 1863 parliamentary session. At the beginning of October 1862 the agent for the unsuccessful LSWR bill, Mr John Bingham, was appointed agent for the Bristol & North Somerset Railway's bill. This was deposited on 20th November 1862.

Under the bill the following railways were to be built. One line was to run from a junction with the Somerset & Dorset near Bruton, passing through Shepton Mallet and climbing over Mendip to Radstock. A second railway took the North Somerset north from Radstock to Bristol. On this section the line was to pass through Welton (for Midsomer Norton), Clutton and Pensford running into Bristol through Whitchurch, Brislington and St Philip's Marsh. A third railway to be built would have been a branch from Radstock to serve the pits at Writhlington while another branch, this time from near Hallatrow with a junction facing towards Radstock, would have run to Camerton. Finally, railways in Bristol would have linked the North Somerset with the GWR, the Midland Railway, and Horton Street. A tramway was also to be laid to the Floating Harbour.

However, it was at about this time that the GWR and the LSWR published an agreement limiting their territorial battles. This meant that the London & South Western's support for the B&NSR's bill evaporated. The secretary of the North Somerset therefore suggested that the proposed section from Evercreech to Radstock should be abandoned for the time being. This was an important move in that when this section was eventually built it was actually part of the S&D's main route! Further ripples were also caused within the provisional committee when Bingham suggested that the route between Radstock and Bristol should be built to the broad gauge!

The Bristol & North Somerset Railway Bill came before the House of Commons Committee on 5th March 1863. During the parliamentary discussions on the project some very interesting facts emerged about various aspects of the proposed North Somerset Railway. For example, details of construction were provided by Mr James Frazer who was, along with Messrs Piercy, joint engineer for the North Somerset. He said that the projected line would be 15 miles 34 chains in length. There was also to be a spur at Bristol some 57 chains in length linking it to the GWR, while a tramway was to run off the North Somerset to connect the Docks with the ever-growing railway system. This was to be 1 mile 36 chains in length. The ruling

THE GWR'S ENGINE SHED AT RADSTOCK (EXTERIOR VIEW)
The GWR's engine shed at Radstock was opened in 1866. It measured 74ft by 20ft and was of stone construction. Its roof was slated. The shed's facilities were as follows an office, a water tank, a sand house, a store and, after 1873, a pumphouse. In 1874, along with the rest of the Radstock-Frome branch the broad gauge shed was "narrowed". In 1894 a coal stage was added while, in the same year, a 41ft 6in diameter turntable was added. At some later date the position of this was altered slightly.

On 1st January 1901 the shed's allocation was Class 517 No. 1459. The shed was officially closed at some time in 1920.

J. W. Mann

THE GWR'S ENGINE SHED AT RADSTOCK (INTERIOR VIEW)
This excellent photograph shows the interior of the former loco shed which is today the only building remaining intact from the whole of the GWR's installations at Radstock. Until the firm's departure in 1988, this shed was used by Marcroft as a shot-blasting shop. Part of the pit once used for the maintenance of locomotives can be seen at the far end of the shed.

Marcroft, Radstock

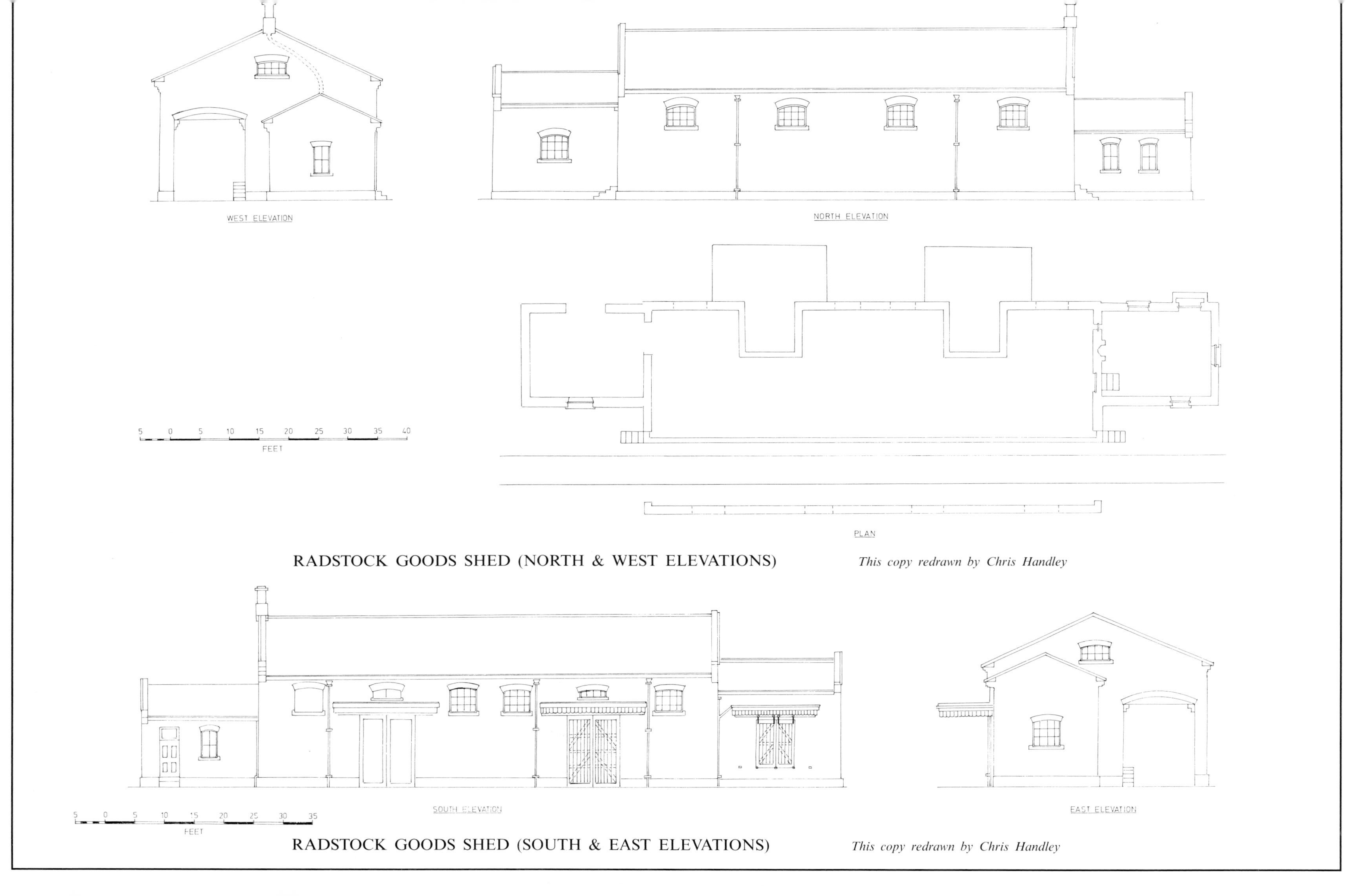

RADSTOCK GOODS SHED (NORTH & WEST ELEVATIONS)

This copy redrawn by Chris Handley

RADSTOCK GOODS SHED (SOUTH & EAST ELEVATIONS)

This copy redrawn by Chris Handley

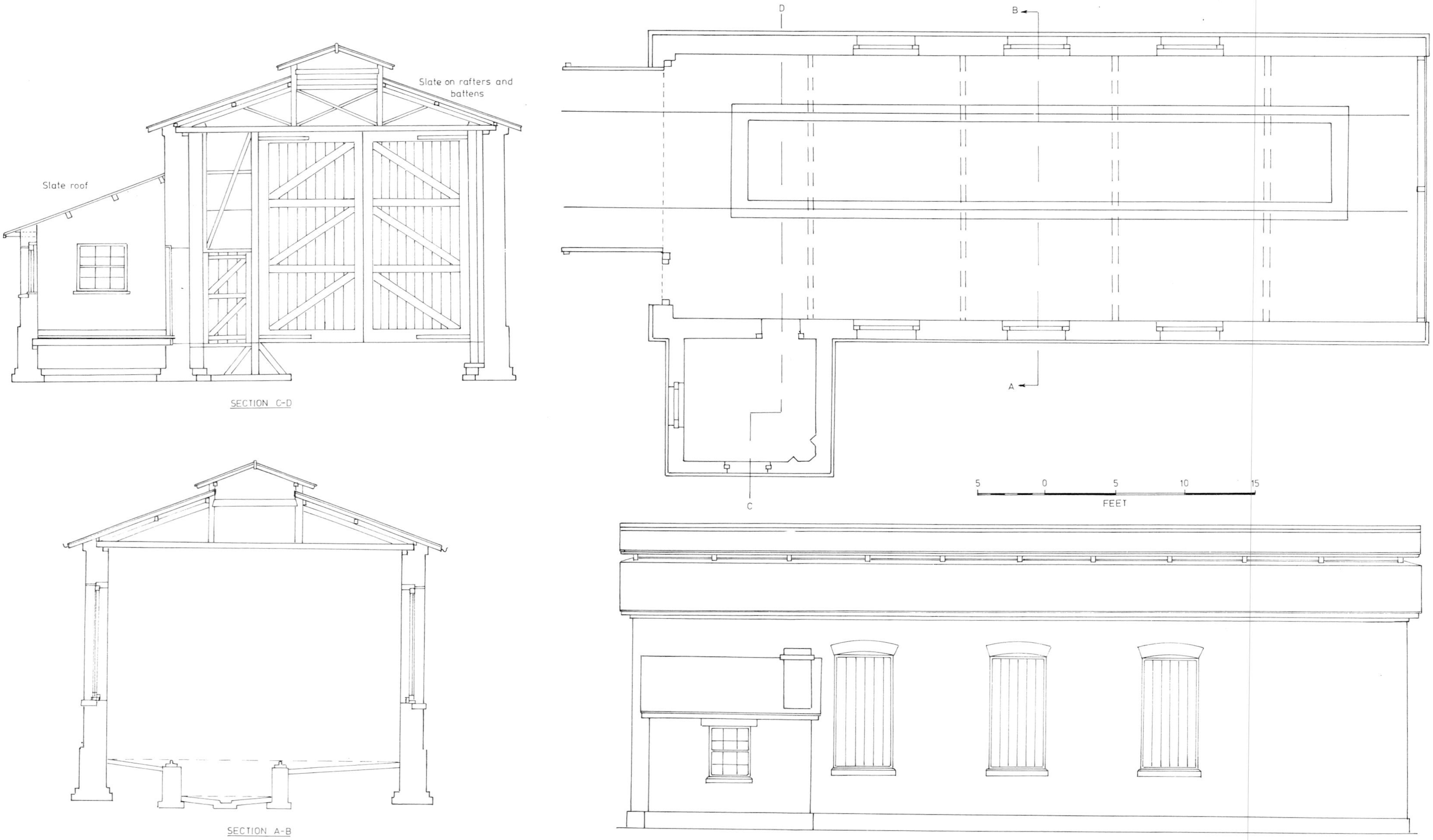

RADSTOCK ENGINE SHED

Original drawing dated 2nd February 1861 *This copy redrawn by Chris Handley*

Above: THE GWR'S GOODS SHED AT RADSTOCK
This turn-of-the-century photograph across Radstock shows, to the extreme right, the GWR's goods yard and shed. This shed, the second to be built to serve Radstock goods yard, was constructed in 1874 and contained one through siding and loading dock within it. The original goods shed was smaller in size and was probably built around 1856.

Chris Howell

Above: THE GWR's RADSTOCK GOODS SHED c1969

R. T. S. Dagger

Right: THE GOODS SHED AND SIDINGS AT RADSTOCK c1969

R. T. S. Dagger

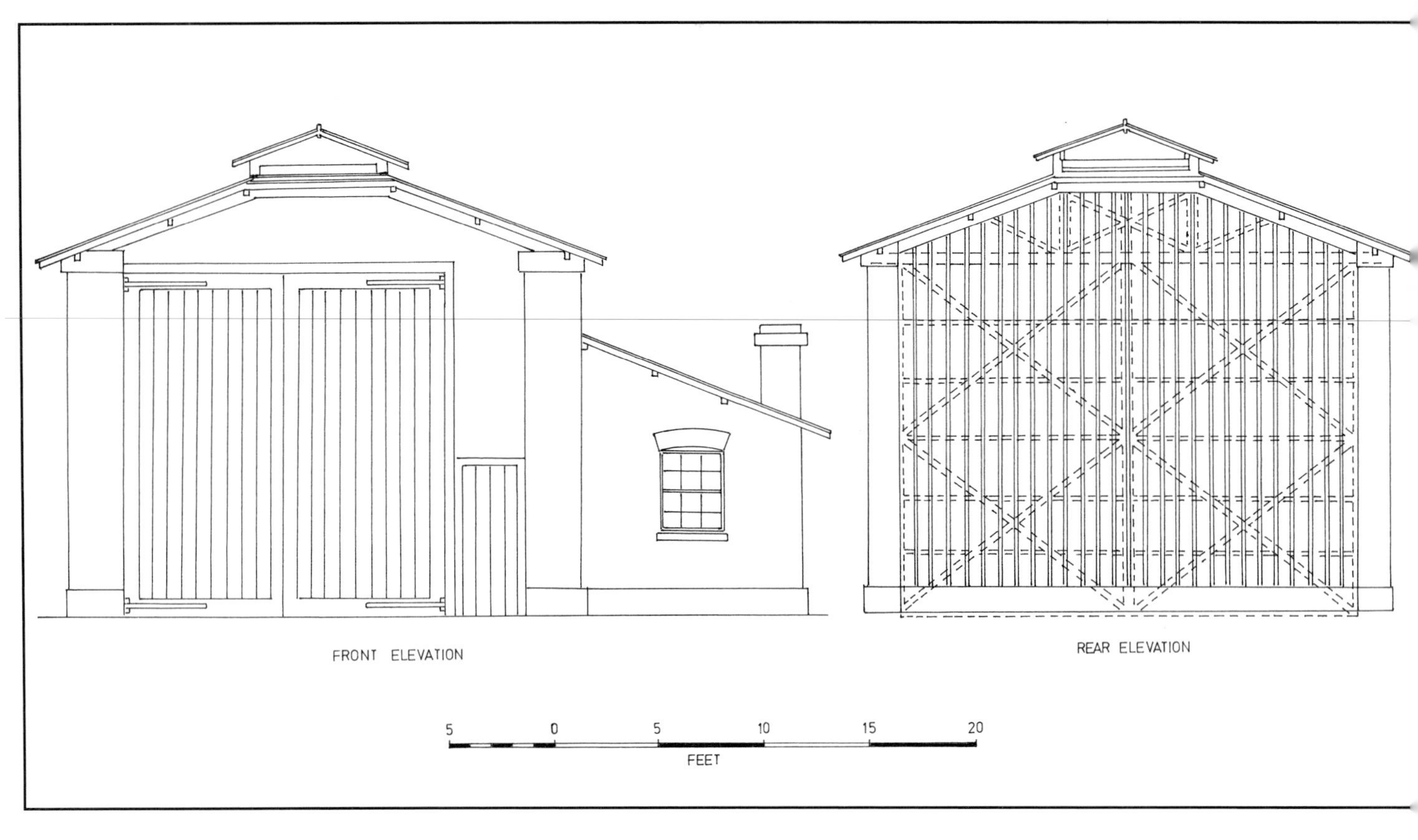

RADSTOCK ENGINE SHED

Original drawing: dated 2nd February 1861 *This copy redrawn by Chris Handley*

THE BRISTOL & NORTH SOMERSET RAILWAY

This plan shows the absurd junction at St Philip's, in Bristol, as referred to in the text.

Original plan: Somerset Record Office

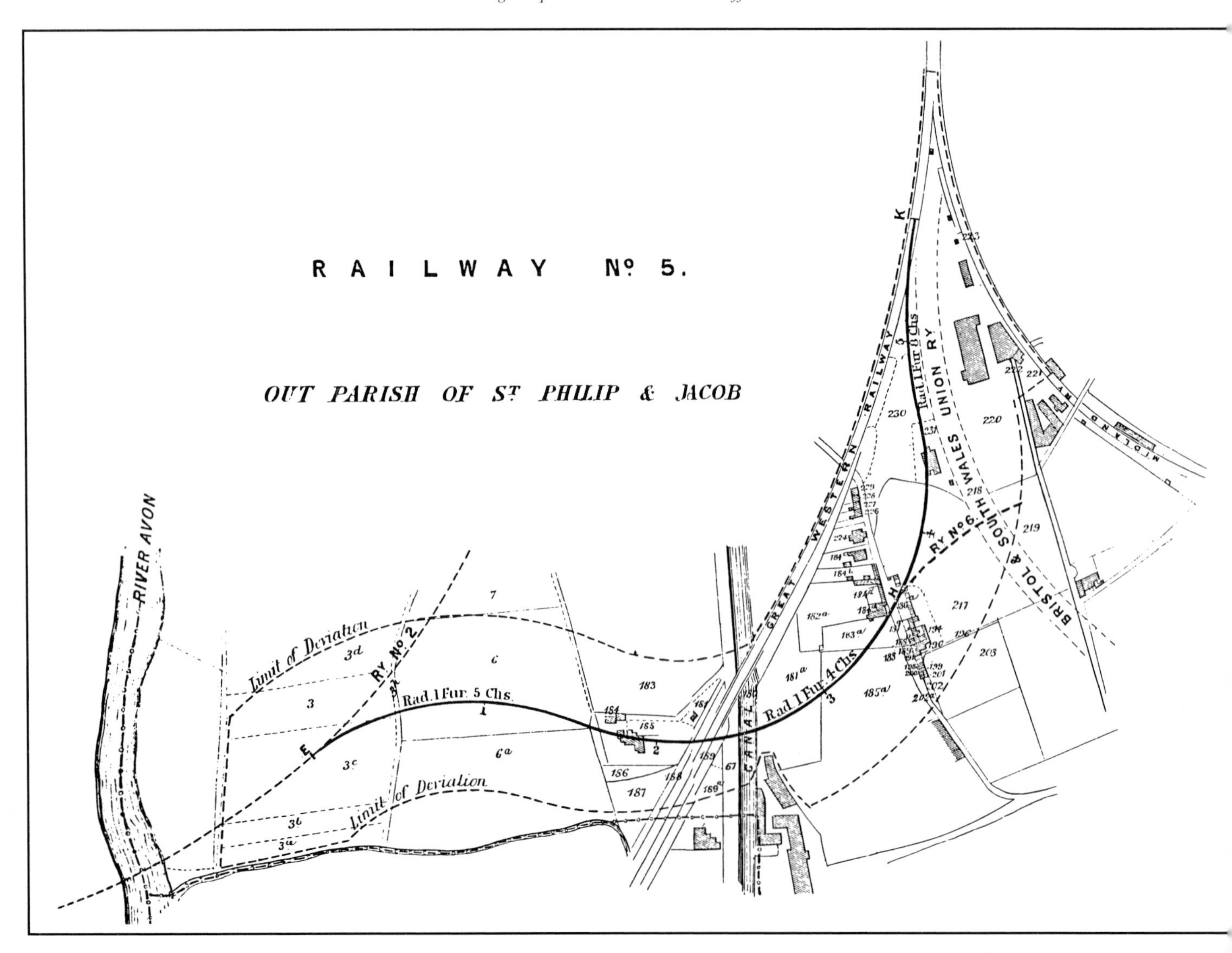

gradient was to be 1 in 60 while the worst curve, which was to be at the junction with the GWR at Radstock, was one of 20 chains.

In view of the events to follow, Frazer's comments that there were "no engineering difficulties to encounter" seems wildly optimistic as was his further statement that the line "was so laid out as to accommodate the coal pits in the district". It might have been planned that way but, in actuality, the North Somerset had enormous trouble getting sidings built to take the coal traffic out from the line's adjacent pits!

The estimated cost of the main line between Radstock and Bristol, including land and works, was £216,000 while the tramway in Bristol was to cost £6,500. The outlay on the Camerton branch was estimated at £28,640. With characteristic brashness, Mr Frazer had absolutely no doubt that the work could be done within these estimates! The House of Commons' Committee was obviously also well impressed – the North Somerset's bill was allowed to go forward to the House of Lords.

The hearing in the upper chamber began on 30th June 1863. The promoters made a strong case by saying that the proposal under discussion had a great deal of support in and around Bristol and across a wide swathe of North Somerset. The scheme's opponents forcefully made the point that the line was heavily under-subscribed and that the Company would need more cash – how right events would prove them to be!

In its opposition to the bill, the Great Western, through its Chief Civil Engineer, Mr Fowler stated that "the company needed rest and (it) would not subscribe to or lease any new line". He advised the GWR to oppose this particular scheme on the basis that it was not "laid out conveniently for working with the existing system". By this he was referring to the connection at Bristol where the North Somerset was to have passed under the GWR's Bristol-Bath line at St Philips so that it could make a junction with the Midland. Unfortunately, that junction had since been abandoned and the North Somerset was left in the absurd position of going under the GWR and then coming back up again to form a junction with it!

However, in spite of the serious misgivings expressed by various opponents of the bill, the House of Lords' Committee decided that the bill could go ahead and so, on 21st July 1863, it became law. The act named seven interim directors. These would take the reins of the company until a fresh group of directors could be elected; at the first half-yearly meeting.

Once their act had been passed the provisional committee organised a celebration dinner. This was held on Tuesday 21st July at Midsomer Norton. It was at this dinner that John Bingham was offered, and accepted, the post of company secretary. For the Company, the seeds of its own destruction were already being sown! With the line's construction now not far off, one of the influential proponents of the line, the Reverend Ommaney of Chew Magna, expressed his concern that the men who would be needed to build the line would "cause disorder in several parishes". It was therefore suggested that a committee should be formed in Bristol, with sub-committees at Chew Magna, Paulton, Midsomer Norton and Radstock, "to watch over the religious interests of the people brought into the neighbourhood for constructing the railway".

On 3rd September 1863 the first half-yearly meeting of the Bristol & North Somerset Railway Company was held at Midsomer Norton. As the Act had stated new directors were to be elected; this election was carried out at the meeting. The eight individuals elected to the Board of Directors were: Mr John Colthurst of Clifton, Bristol (Chairman), Mr Thomas Harris Smith of Midsomer Norton (Vice Chairman), Mr Henry Box of Chewton Mendip, Mr Joseph Langford of Timsbury, Mr James Perrin of Temple Cloud, Mr James Thatcher of Midsomer Norton and Messrs Cary and Jameson, both of whom came from London.

By this time contracts had been let, the Company's initial contractors being Messrs Bethell & Walton. It seemed that after many proposals and even more plans, the Company was on the move. With its Act of Incorporation behind it, the future looked rosy for the Bristol & North Somerset. Indeed, on the constructional side, a two pronged campaign of attack was planned with special opening ceremonies at Clutton, on the Radstock-Bristol main line, and at the Floating Harbour, in Bristol. For the first ceremony at Clutton, the directors agreed, in September 1863, to ask Lord Warwick, Lady Waldegrave and Mrs Milward to see if one of them would like to turn the first sod. However, the directors received no response from the first two and were probably very relieved when Mrs Milward agreed to do the job!

At the ceremony at the Floating Harbour it was only fitting that the then Mayoress of Bristol, Mrs Sholto Vere Hare, should be requested to 'lay' the first rail of the proposed tramway linking the North Somerset's new cross-country route with the City Docks. Railway historians are, indeed, fortunate that both ceremonies were very well covered by the Illustrated London News for 17th October 1863 and it is from that source that the following extracts are taken.

Of the cutting of the first sod at Clutton we are told,

Left: THE BRISTOL & NORTH SOMERSET RAILWAY CUTTING THE FIRST SOD AT CLUTTON, 7th October 1863.
"At various times within the last 40 years efforts have been made to provide railway accommodation for the district, but the contentions of rival promoters, financial difficulties, and non-success before Parliamentary Committees prevented the success of various schemes which were set afoot, until at length a bill, promoted by some of the most influential residents in the district, passed through Parliament in 1863, and amidst manifestations of general satisfaction, the first sod of the present line was turned at Clutton, on 7th October in that year, by Mrs Milward, wife of the present vicar of Paulton, who was one of the most active promoters of the scheme.

A beginning was thus made but the end was destined to be far distant." (Bath Chronicle, 4th September 1873)

Author's collection

"The event took place in a field in the occupation of Mr Gibbon, and belonging to the Earl of Warwick, situated a little in the rear of Clutton. Thither repaired the thousands of colliers and school children who were to be honoured with a commemorative entertainment, and a large number of spectators who came from a distance. Just at 1 o'clock, when the authorities were about to commence the proceedings, the rain descended and continued almost without intermission, so that almost all the business, even the dining, had to be accomplished under umbrellas.

After some delay a short break in the rainfall was taken advantage of, and the proceedings . . . were commenced by Mr Bingham, the secretary, reading an address to Mrs Milward, which treated very ably of the proceedings which had transpired in connection with the undertaking, and congratulated the Rev. Prebendary Milward on the success which had attended his persistent efforts to serve this neighbourhood. Mrs Milward replied in a suitable address, after which the Old Hundredth Psalm was sung by the children, colliers and visitors. The united voices of the multitude joined harmoniously, and the singing was very effective. The Rev. Prebendary Ommaney, of Chew Magna, and the Rural Dean . . . then read a form of prayer that had been prepared for the occasion. The fine March of the Israelites, from the oratorio of "Eli" was next played by a band of musicians, under Mr J.O. Brook . . .

"Mrs Milward then proceeded to turn the first sod. For this purpose she was presented by the contractors with a handsome mahogany wheelbarrow, ornamented with silver, and a silver spade, with a prettily-turned mahogany handle and silver ornamentations. By the assistance of two navvies, rendered with an address and a carefulness that might not have been anticipated, the lady discharged the duty she undertook most satisfactorily, lifting several sods with her handsome spade into her pretty barrow, which she then wheeled across the platform, emptied, and returned with her little vehicle amid the hearty plaudits of the company.

Three cheers having been given for Mrs Milward, three for the Sheriff, three for the directors, and three for Mr Milward, the National Anthem was sung by the great gathering, and, the prayers having been concluded, the 3,000 colliers were marched off to their tents, where each man was supplied with a pound of bread, a pound of beef, and a quart of beer. The school children were also bountifully regaled. The "dejeuner" given by the directors of the line to the visitors took place in a spacious tent put up in the field."

The extract continues with this description of the events that took place at Bristol's Floating Harbour the following day, 8th October.

"The first rail of the tramway connecting the North Somerset Railway with the Floating Harbour at Bristol was laid by the Mayoress Mrs Sholto Vere Hare. The ceremony took place on a piece of ground on the towing path behind St Raphael's Church, where a platform had been erected for the accommodation of invited guests. The shipping was also well filled with spectators, and from Mr Terrell's rope-walk to the edge of the water. With the exception of a small space reserved by the police, there was one dense mass of human beings. Rows of flags from various buildings, the rigging of vessels in the floating harbour, and, in fact, every salient point, imparted animation to the scene. The company was welcomed to the spot by the cheery strains of the artillery band and the merry peals of the bells of glorious old St Mary Redcliffe.

The work allotted to the Mayoress – which consisted of the filling of a highly ornamental barrow with earth, lifted with a silver spade, and wheeling it along a plank and overturning it – was efficiently performed, and was completed amid the applause of the large assemblage which the event had brought together. A large party afterwards adjourned to Mr Hyde's sail loft, which had been decorated for the occasion, and where an elegant dejeuner was served, and several speeches were delivered.

The silver ornamentations on the wheelbarrow and handle of the spade presented to Mrs Milward . . . (at Clutton the previous day) . . . and on the barrow and spade of the Mayoress of Bristol, which are exactly alike, were the work of Messrs Mapin Bros, of London Bridge. Upon Mrs Milward's spade is engraved the arms of the Milward family . . . Mrs Hare's spade bears the crest of the Hare family, and underneath "Presented to Mrs Elizabeth Hare, Mayoress of Bristol, October 8th, 1863." To which is to be added, "In commemoration of laying the first rail of the tramway of the Bristol and North Somerset Railway."

Although we will continue our look at the way the railway was actually built in the next chapter, let us, for the moment at least, concentrate very closely on those precise areas of the region in which the North Somerset Company wanted to blossom and grow. On 30th November 1863, the Company deposited a bill for an extension of its proposed Camerton branch to Bath. Like so many other schemes it was never built and the North Somerset (now Avon!) villages of High Littleton, Timsbury and Englishcombe were all permanently denied the benefits of rail transport.

In the same year, 1863, the Company also deposited its Bristol & North Somerset Railway (Extension) Act. Made up of a large number of railways, the key one was drawn to leave the main North Somerset line at Farrington Gurney, heading southwards to Shepton Mallet where there would have been

Left: BRISTOL HARBOUR TRAMWAY, 8th October 1863 Mrs Hare, the then Mayoress of Bristol, lays the first rail of the Bristol Harbour Tramway in connection with the construction of the Bristol & North Somerset Railway.

Author's collection

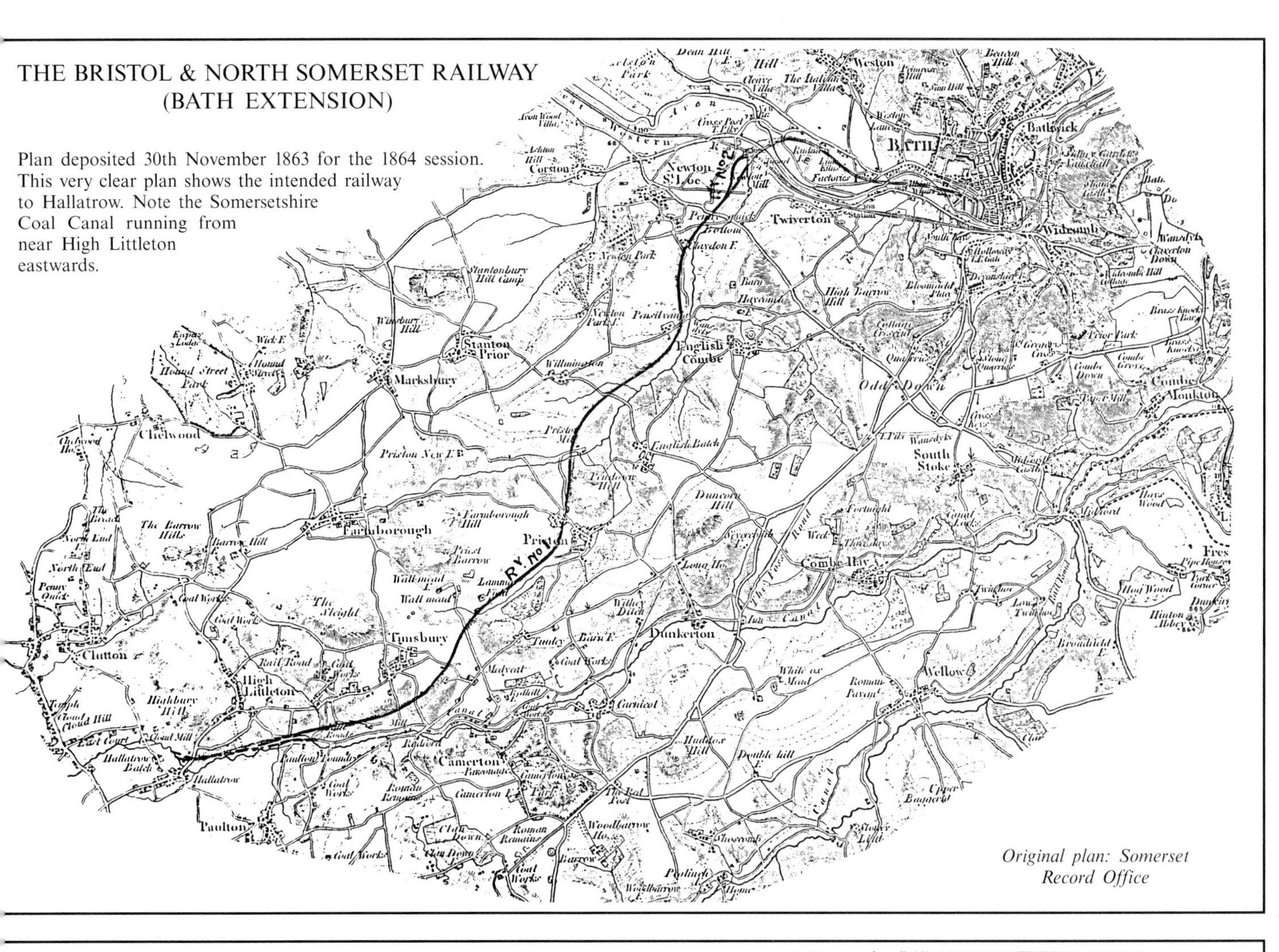

THE BRISTOL & NORTH SOMERSET RAILWAY (BATH EXTENSION)

Plan deposited 30th November 1863 for the 1864 session. This very clear plan shows the intended railway to Hallatrow. Note the Somersetshire Coal Canal running from near High Littleton eastwards.

Original plan: Somerset Record Office

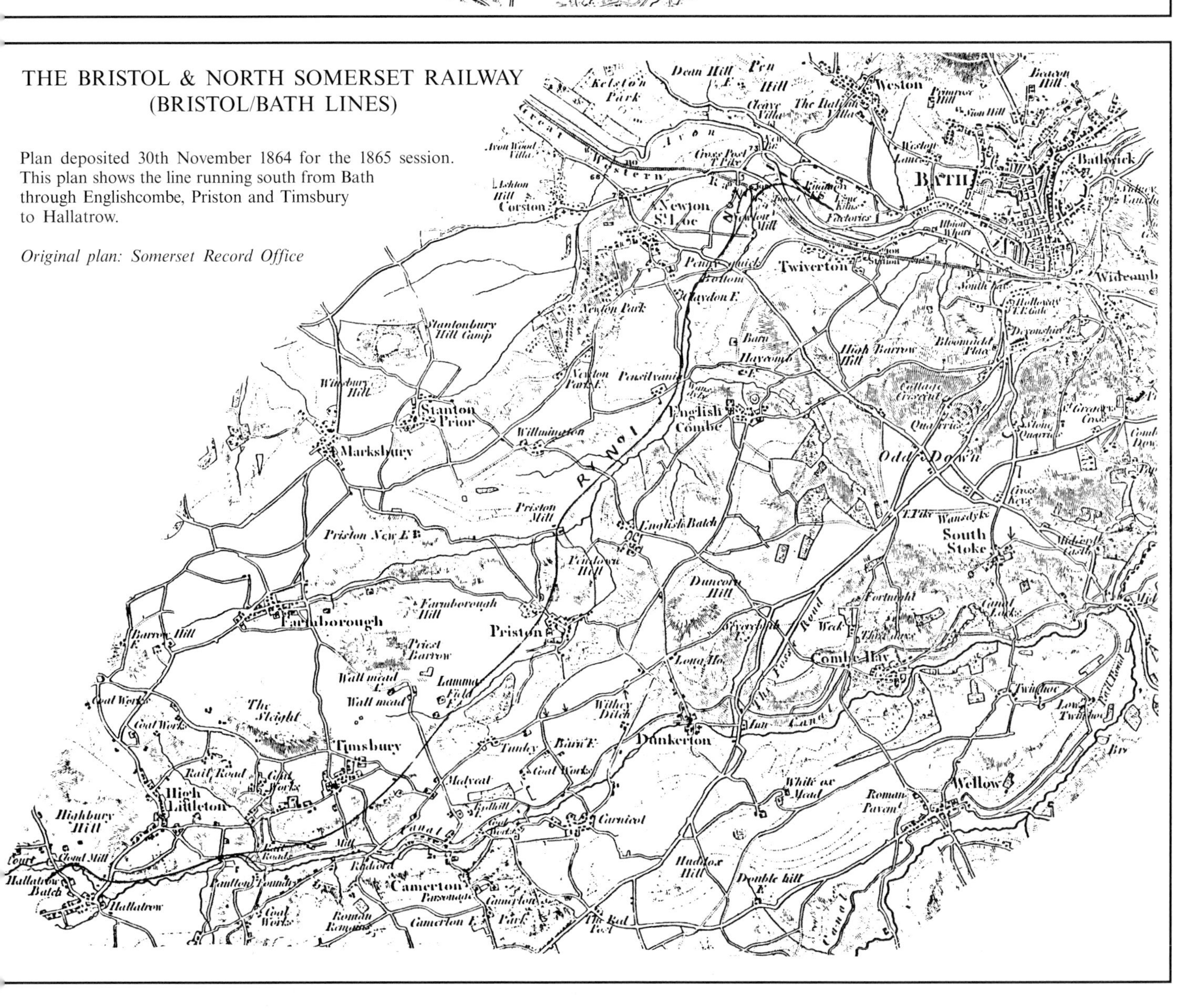

THE BRISTOL & NORTH SOMERSET RAILWAY (BRISTOL/BATH LINES)

Plan deposited 30th November 1864 for the 1865 session. This plan shows the line running south from Bath through Englishcombe, Priston and Timsbury to Hallatrow.

Original plan: Somerset Record Office

a connection into the East Somerset Railway. Another line was to have been constructed up the Nettlebridge Valley, while the bill would also have allowed the construction of various branches in the Bristol area, with lines to the Midland, the GWR and tramways to the docks.

The 30th of November 1864 produced three new bills for the following parliamentary session. One of these called for a railway serving the pits at Writhlington. It would then have run up through Wellow and Midford to join the Bath-Bradford-on-Avon-Trowbridge line at Monkton Combe. This scheme was yet another plan that was never given the all-clear. The other two acts of that year were somewhat more involved. The Bristol & North Somerset Railway (Southern Extension) Act was proposing to build a railway running from Farrington Gurney to Shepton Mallet with the associated branch to the East Somerset Railway at Shepton. From here there would have been a southward stretching of the line with a section being built between Shepton Mallet and the Somerset & Dorset at Evercreech. Another railway would have served the Nettlebridge Valley while a further two lines involved deviations to the original plans for the railway at Radstock.

The final bill of the trio for the 1865 session was the B&NSR (Bristol & Bath Lines) Act. The route outlined in this bill was in many respects identical to the Bath Extension Act deposited for the 1864 session, leaving the proposed Cam Valley stub near Hallatrow from where it would have run to the Midland Railway making a junction with the latter between Newton St Loe and Twerton just to the west of Bath. Like its predecessor the bill also included a short branch which would have fed into the GWR close to the latter village. Four other railways listed under this act were concerned with new works in the Bristol Docks' area and with connections to the Midland, GWR and quays in the City Docks' district.

Mention of Bristol gently leads us on to reflect that just as the early 1860s threw up a great number of interesting, if unbuilt, proposals for railways across North Somerset so that very same period also generated a number of quite fascinating ideas and schemes for railways across the Bristol region. The cross-Bristol schemes had, in many cases, at least one element in common – namely that of linking central Bristol with the fashionable area of Clifton.

In 1861 the Bristol & Clifton Railway scheme was put forward in an attempt to link Temple Meads station with Clifton. Although unsuccessful, this particular project encouraged the submission of an 1862/3 scheme to build a central railway station in the heart of Bristol itself. A railway would have been built connecting that central station with the GWR, MR, and the Bristol & North Somerset who wanted a central terminus to link its proposed Radstock-Bristol railway with the city centre. It was therefore quite natural that the North Somerset gave this new scheme strong support.

In the original 1862 scheme the intention was to build a central station over the Floating Harbour between two of the major bridges in the city's central area, namely the Stonebridge and the Drawbridge. From this central location lines would have run to the Midland Railway at that company's station at St Philip's and to the GWR at the London end of Temple Meads, thus giving access to Paddington. There would also have been a link connecting the North Somerset with the central station while there would have been access for the Bristol & Exeter's trains as well. In this form the line would have been essentially a branch pulling in these various railways to a terminus in the heart of Bristol. Ironically enough, it would not have given a real service between Bristol & Clifton!

However, when the above plan went to parliament in the 1864 session it had been modified so that the central terminus had become a through station, the line now driving southwards towards and under the Floating Harbour and the New Cut to emerge and weave in with the Bristol & Exeter beyond Bedminster. In many ways it is interesting to compare this scheme with that of the planned Bristol Metro system put forward in the late 1970s! The 1864 line's cost was estimated at around £300,000 which was to be the subscribed capital for the new line. The Bristol & North Somerset was to subscribe £50,000 but, for various reasons, the scheme was eventually thrown out and supporters of a new railway between Bristol and Clifton put forward proposals which later led to the construction of the Clifton Extension Railway of 1874.

Throughout our story we shall see that financial problems badly afflicted the life of the Bristol & North Somerset Railway until it was taken over by the GWR in 1884. It never had enough cash to build lines that would have provided it with lucrative traffic quickly. One of the areas of the Somerset Coalfield that often figured in potential routes was the Nettlebridge Valley, south of Radstock. This southern area of the coalfield ran eastwards in a slightly sweeping arc, from the Binegar/Chilcompton area, taking in collieries around Stratton on the Fosse, Benter, Nettlebridge itself, Holcombe, Coleford, Vobster and Mells. In this district there had been many small workings and, although few lasted beyond 1800, many of the sites ran back at least 600 years. Indeed, the earliest workings of the Somerset Coalfield were in the Nettlebridge Valley where, as Robin Atthill notes, ". . . the proprietors of these coal works were either groups of working colliers, or (were) local business men investing small amounts of capital,

Below: MELLS ROAD – A RED BRICK WAYSIDE STATION
"After 1870 it seems that a new feeling overcame the Chief Engineer's drawing office and red brick wayside stations were constructed in a quite standardised and uncompromising manner. By "uncompromising" I mean that they were not disguised as lodge gate houses, or mediaeval monasteries, but were merely railway stations and were not afraid to appear as such. Marlow and Mells Road stations, although separated by scores of miles and in a totally different geographical area, were identical." (A. Vaughan)

Lens of Sutton

or landowners who . . . drew their royalty from the coal mined on their estates".

This area of the coalfield was generally a rich source of inspiration for railway schemes during the 1860s and early 1870s. However, relatively early in the development of railways within the coalfield, the eastern end of the arc was served by a broad gauge line. This was the Newbury Railway which ran into the mineral-only branch between Frome and Radstock on the site of what later became Mells Road station. The Newbury Railway ran to Vobster Quarry and Newbury Colliery and was promoted by the Westbury Iron Company to serve its Newbury Colliery.

This branch off a branch was built without a formal agreement with the GWR so it is very difficult to pin down the exact date of its construction. However, it is believed that it was open in 1857, it was certainly in place by 1864, and the contractor may have been Rowland Brotherhood, bearing in mind that he was also an original shareholder in the Westbury Iron Company. At the Vobster end of the branch railway a narrow gauge tramway was laid in to serve the collieries there. The new railway had such a positive impact on the coal owners that three new pits, at Mells, Vobster Breach and Mackintosh, were sunk not long after the Newbury Railway's opening. However, we will have a much closer look at this district's development in Chapter 11.

Further west along the Nettlebridge Valley, away from the Newbury Railway, the Bristol & North Somerset Railway was involved with various projected schemes during the 1860s and '70s to serve this part of the coalfield. Indeed, the Company had made provision under its Extension Act to build a railway down the Nettlebridge Valley as part of its ambitions to get a railway from Farrington Gurney to Shepton Mallet. This particular proposal had strong support from coal owners in the Valley. The North Somerset's Board therefore agreed to build a branch to serve the area provided that:

The coal owners opposed any other companies' attempts to build similar lines.
The coal owners would help to finance the line.
The deputation of coal owners at the Board meeting could show that the new branch would be profitable.

All these things the coal owners obviously did, for the bill went forward to parliament, only to be rejected, however, by the House of Commons!

Another attempt to get at the mineral wealth of the Nettlebridge Valley was made in a proposal of 1863 for an act in the 1864 parliamentary session. Again, however, this was unsuccessful. A more hopeful attempt developed with the promotion of the B&NSR (Southern Extension) Act which was deposited on 30th November 1864. Railway number four of this authorised a branch down the Nettlebridge Valley. As we have seen, this bill was also rejected!

Another similarly titled bill was the B&NSR (Southern Extension/Amended) Act put forward in the 1866 parliamentary session which also included the Nettlebridge Valley in its provision. For part of its length the railway envisaged in this plan would have followed the course of the abandoned Dorset & Somerset Canal past Coleford to join the Radstock-Frome Branch near Mells Road Goods. Yes, you have guessed, this one was never built either!

Incidentally, one of the reasons for the 1866 Southern Extension Act was the East Somerset Railway's plan for an extension. This broad gauge project consisted of a seven mile line from the East Somerset itself near Shepton Mallet. It would have run through Coleford and Vobster to a triangular junction near the GWR's Goods Shed at Mells Road. From Coleford a five mile long branch through the Nettlebridge Valley would have ended up in a terminus near Old Down. A non-starter, the end of the story is predictable with the scheme being thrown out by parliament. In 1868 the project was dragged out for a second airing, this time under the guise of the Mendip Mineral Railway, but the bill was withdrawn in 1869.

The GWR and B&NSR deposited a joint act in 1866, their New Lines' Act, which proposed another Nettlebridge branch

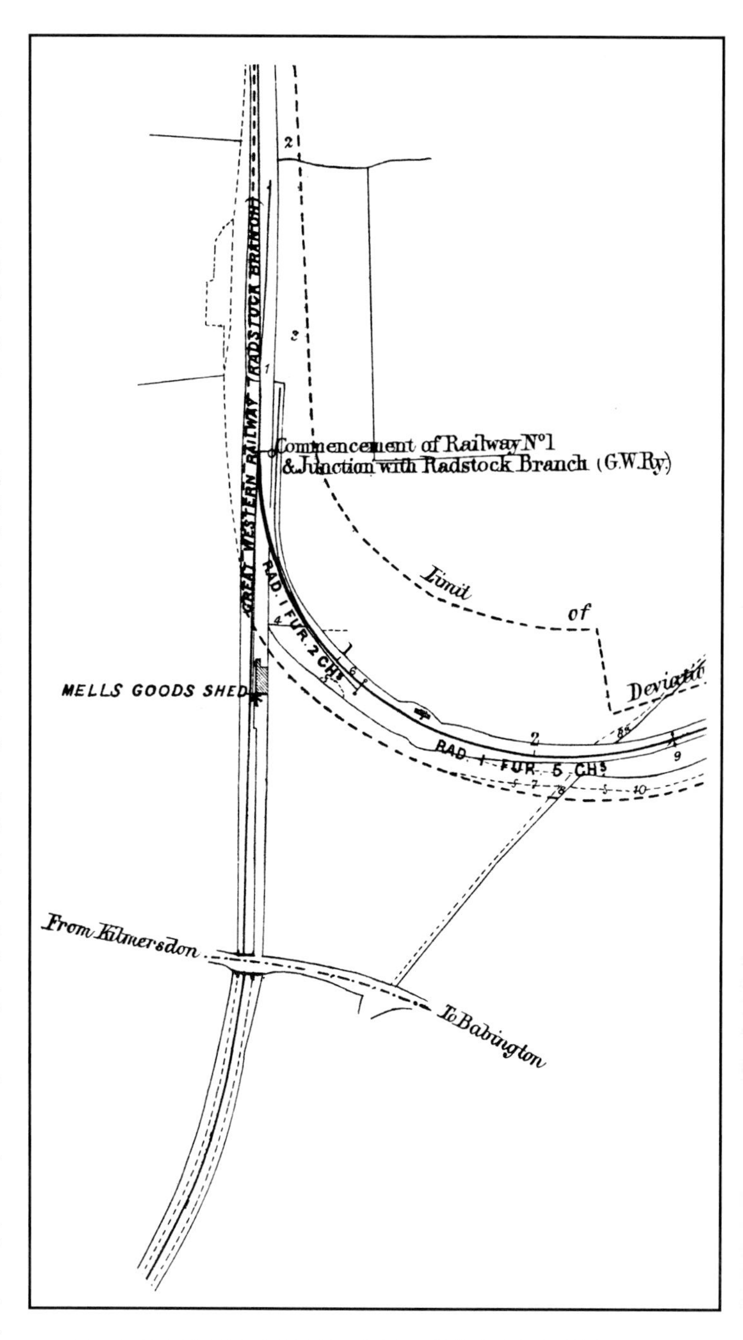

THE NETTLEBRIDGE VALLEY RAILWAY
1874 SESSION

Collection: Lord Oxford

running from Mells Goods through Nettlebridge to a terminus at Moorewood between Chilcompton and Binegar. This scheme, along with a similar one in 1874, never saw the light of day. The 1874 scheme was to make use of the private railway of the Westbury Iron Company Limited, the Newbury Railway in other words, and was to have run from this railway to the Somerset & Dorset Railway, at that point in time virtually complete, between Binegar and Chilcompton. This line's proposed route is more clearly shown by the plan above and those in Chapter 11 As you have come to expect by now this was another scheme that gathered dust on the shelf and it too was never built. After this time it would seem that railway promoters lost interest in Nettlebridge for the area was never served by a standard gauge railway in the shape or form of the many schemes detailed in this chapter.

One final, but very important financial act of 1866, the Bristol & North Somerset (Additional Capital) Act, allowed the Company to raise £100,000 by the issue of new shares. It was also given the go-ahead to borrow another £33,500. In 1868 yet a further act gave the Company permission to change the junction arrangements of its Radstock-Bristol section where it met the GWR in Bristol. The connection here had always been difficult, perhaps even downright daft, but under the 1868 proposals the Company was to build a new line, just over three

Left: MELLS COLLIERY IN WORKING CONDITION
This view of Mells Colliery shows it during its second lease of life. Originally opened about 1863, the colliery had been closed as unprofitable by 1881. Reopened just before the First World War Mells, along with Newbury Colliery, went into receivership around 1930. This busy view was taken around 1920.

John Kingman

Below: MELLS STATION IN A MESS
Taken in 1985, this rather depressing photograph shows the former station site at Mells Road. With the goods-only line arching its way down over Mells bank in the background, the sleeper storage depot stands guard over what used to be an attractive and tidy wayside station.

Barbara Zadarnowski

furlongs in length, from its Avon Bridge to the GWR main line to Paddington, to the west of Temple Meads station. This later became the site of North Somerset Junction as we know it today. The Act also confirmed that all the railways and tramways of the Company were to be on the standard gauge.

In 1866, a bill had passed through parliament allowing the Bristol & Exeter and the GWR, in partnership with Bristol Corporation, to build the Bristol Harbour Railway and Wharf Depot at Wapping, since the North Somerset was having such trouble completing its harbour tramway. In addition, the joint scheme was put forward to ease heavy road traffic through what were, even in those days, overcrowded city streets. Goods that were being transferred by road from the harbour, then still not rail-connected, to the main line companies' tracks at Bristol, would be able to move directly from ship to rail, and vice versa, at the dockside. The cost of the scheme was estimated at £165,000. It was to be equally divided between the Bristol & Exeter, the GWR and the Corporation and, considering the line was only three-quarters of a mile in length, it takes very little to see just how expensive it was.

The route was engineered by Charles Richardson and work began in August 1868, by which time the North Somerset was in very deep trouble. The Harbour Railway forced the demolition of the old vicarage at the well-known and well-loved, beautiful old Bristol church of St Mary Redcliffe. At the same time, nearly all of one side of Guinea Street was overthrown to let the railway through. Its construction meant the boring of a 282 yard tunnel under the churchyard at Redcliffe and for this the Church received £2,500 in compensation. Incidentally, with the money received, some land was purchased at Arno's Vale in Brislington and many of the bodies formerly buried at Redcliffe were reburied there.

In 1869 the railway companies decided to increase the size of the wharfage provided for in the scheme. They applied for further parliamentary powers while the Corporation agreed to a 400 feet extension of the wharf west of Princes Street bridge.

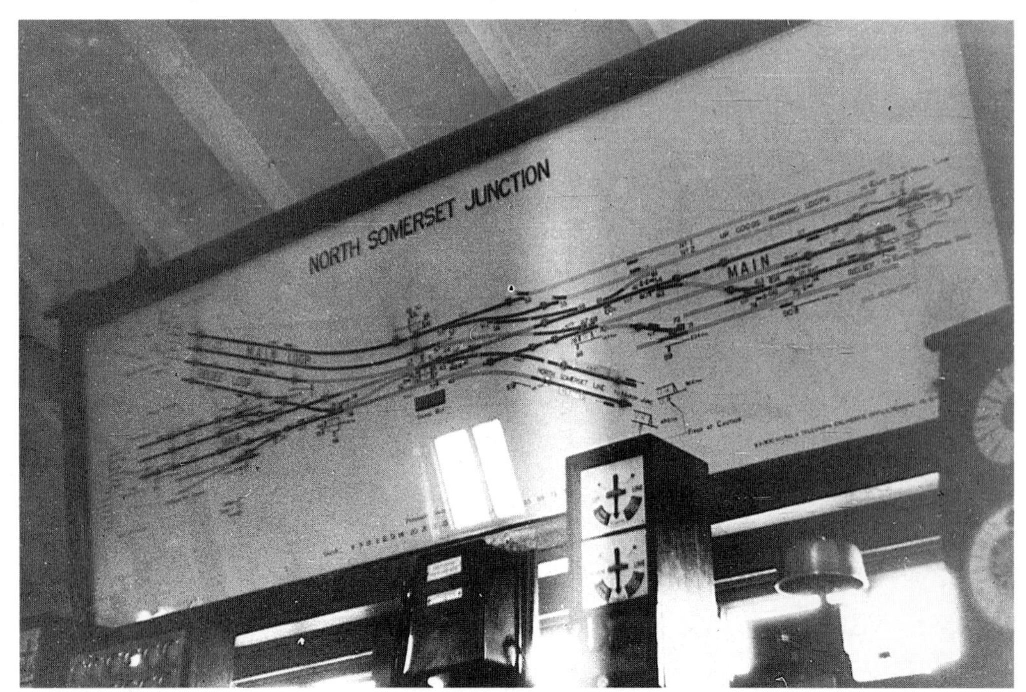

Left: NORTH SOMERSET JUNCTION SIGNAL BOX
This interior view of the second signal box built at North Somerset Junction shows the track diagram. From this it can be seen that the box was responsible for controlling an important series of junctions on the Paddington line to the east of the station at Bristol (Temple Meads).

Mr White (Keynsham)

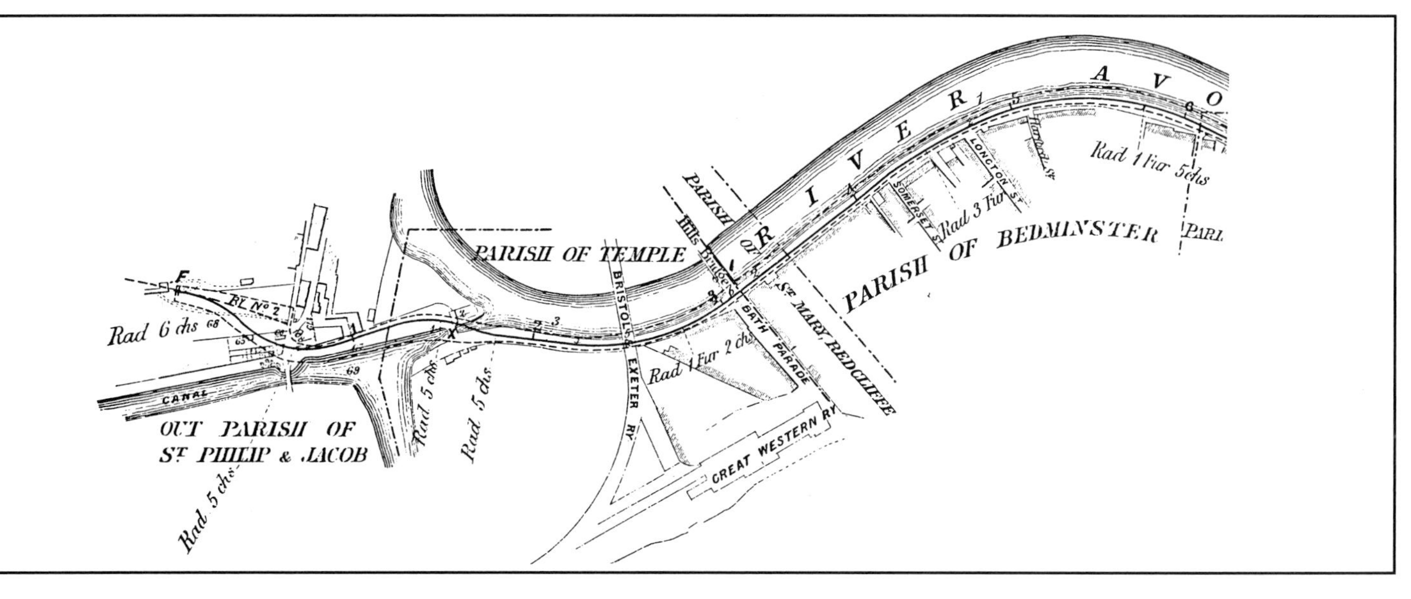

THE NORTH SOMERSET'S PROPOSED TRAMWAY TO THE FLOATING HARBOUR

This plan shows the section from near Temple Meads to St Mary Redcliffe.

Original plan: Somerset Record Office

In the same year the North Somerset obtained a new act in order to finish its harbour tramway but, this was not to be, and in 1871, the proposed line, which even then was still unfinished, was abandoned. However, the Bristol Harbour Railway was moving ahead and, after an inspection by Colonel Yolland on 26th February 1872, it opened for freight traffic on 11th March 1872. Running from Temple Meads, under Redcliffe, across the Bathurst Basin by a celebrated bascule bridge, through to the City Docks at Wapping, it was an immediate success.

In all this the irony was that although the North Somerset had been first on the docklands' scene in Bristol, its financial and other related problems meant that yet again it had lost out in its fight for traffic. Of all the routes it had proposed in its original 1863 act, only one, the Bristol-Radstock main line, was ever actually completed by the North Somerset company itself. All the others fell by the wayside, condemned to disintegration and decay.

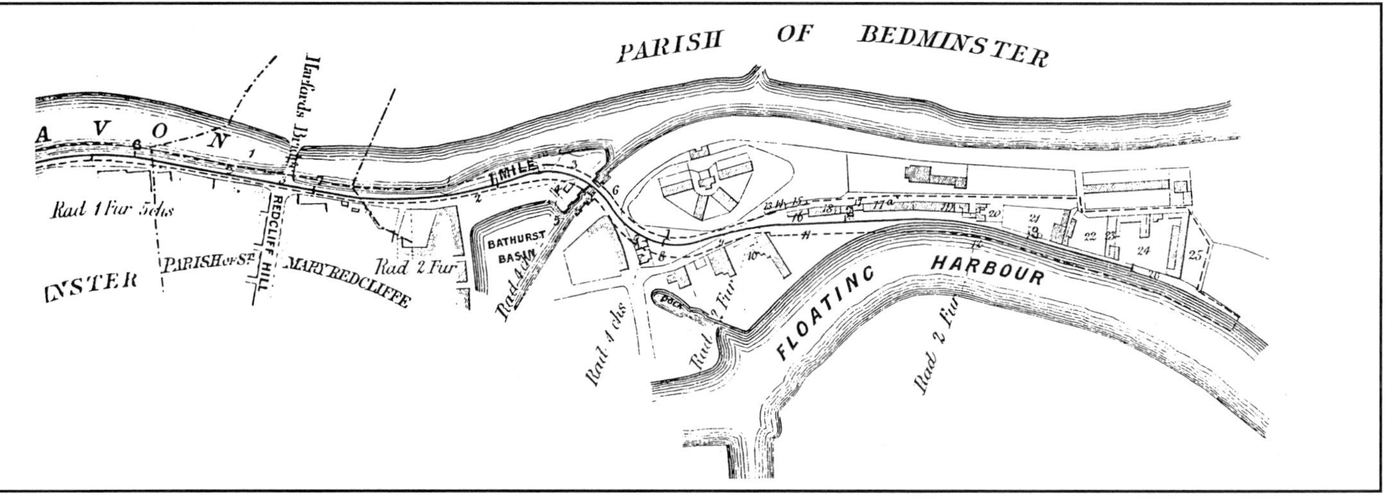

THE NORTH SOMERSET'S PROPOSED TRAMWAY TO THE FLOATING HARBOUR

This plan shows the section from St Mary Redcliffe to Wapping.

Original plan: Somerset Record Office

Left: BRISTOL HARBOUR RAILWAY – THE BATHURST BASIN BASCULE BRIDGE
This picture, taken on the 4th January 1964, shows the last 'Modified Hall' worked train down from Temple Meads to Wapping. Hauled by No. 6988 *Swithland Hall* and driven by Driver Holden, the train is seen thumping its way across the bascule bridge at Bathurst Basin.

D. J. Pollard

4
Contractors, Construction and Catastrophe

NO BUSTLE AT BRISLINGTON
On 17th March 1955, Prairie tank No. 5508 comes quietly to a stand at Brislington station on its journey from Bristol to Frome. The tidy station buildings and yard are in marked contrast to the present use of part of the site as a scrapyard. Quietness, and a small cluster of passengers, reflect a typical day in the station's history.

M. B. Warburton

With the ceremonies and celebrations completed, the engineers, Mr James Frazer and Messrs Piercy, along with the contractors, Bethell & Walton, started to turn the North Somerset's paper plans into concrete reality. However, the contractors had financial problems almost as soon as they started work. In December 1863 a letter was received from them, by the Board of Directors, asking for an advance of £1,000 in cash and another £1,000 in shares. The Board agreed to give them the shares. By February 1864 the contractors had been given bonds worth a further £2,500 but wanted a further £1,000 in cash and £7,500 in bonds. Eventually the Company agreed to give them £500 in cash and the bonds they wanted. However, by March 1864, the Company's secretary reported that the contract for the works had still not been carried out by Bethell & Walton and so the Board gave them formal notice that they required the work to be done immediately.

On 9th April 1864 the secretary, Mr Bingham, and Mr Cooke (working on behalf of the Company's solicitors) met the contractors in London. Bethell & Walton had declined to complete the contract. The Board said they would get no more cash until the work was finished, in reply to which the contractors left the meeting saying that they *would* now stop work! The directors then authorised notices to be served on the contractors forbidding them to remove any engineering plant or equipment being used by the contractors.

Because of these problems, on 12th April 1864, there were discussions held with the contracting firm of Lawrence & Fry. Meanwhile, by mid-April, Mr Bingham had still been unable to come to an amicable agreement with Mr Bethell, who produced an account for £17,000, or with Mr Walton who, in turn, demanded a settlement of £25,000! Therefore, under a firmly agreed set of conditions, Lawrence & Fry agreed to take the North Somerset's contract on. Indeed, by the morning of 5th May 1864 they had taken possession of the works and work was already under way. In the meantime, the directors had decided that the shares held by their former contractors, Bethell & Walton, should all be declared forfeit for non-payment of calls. They really were adding salt to the wound!

By early June it was all too apparent that the Company was again in a difficult position. It was unable to complete its land purchases and there were still outstanding claims on the Company. It desperately needed further cash straight away. Worse was to come for, on 27th June 1864, there was an announcement in The Times that Lawrence & Fry had been declared bankrupt.

In mid-July Mr Bingham was writing to possible future contractors. By the end of the month the contract with Lawrence & Fry had finally been cancelled and the Company decided it simply had to stop work! In early August the very well known contractor, Thomas Brassey, offered to complete the work. This offer was immediately accepted. However, he wanted cash and, since a large part of the North Somerset's capital was still unsubscribed and since the Company had no power to compulsorily purchase the land, Thomas Brassey was unwilling to go ahead with the deal. Nevertheless, he did say that, provided the directors could complete their share capital, he was prepared to meet the Board and discuss arrangements for payment in a mix of cash, debenture stock and paid up shares.

It was also decided at this time that the work at Pensford should continue. Indeed, by early September, the state of the line's works was such that five piers of Pensford Viaduct had been begun, as had work on the foundations of the Avon Bridge near Brislington. Several small arches and culverts on the line had also been completed while, in Bristol itself, the wall beside the River Avon, for the Harbour Tramway, had been built for a length of about half a mile.

In late September, a new initiative was put forward. This came from Mr Lawrence who, working on his own presumably now, proposed that he should complete the job. Payment

PENSFORD PASTORAL
With the viaduct dominating the village, as it still does, Pensford seems hardly threatened by the advance of progress when this photograph was taken. In those days it seems roads were for having your photograph taken in – sensible people travelling by train, of course!
A. Church

TO THE CHANNEL ISLANDS VIA PENSFORD AND THE B&NSR
A heavily retouched postcard shows the seemingly timeless scene at Pensford station. The many posters on the station's end wall advertise a variety of products and services but one advertisement must catch the eye; namely the one that extols the beauty of the Channel Islands.

It seems strange to think of there being a direct link between Pensford and Jersey and Guernsey but, it must be remembered that, post World War Two, the 5.55pm perhaps in the shape of a pannier tank and a "B" set, connected with the Weymouth-Paddington Channel Islands boat train at Frome. This "fast" train over the branch, stopping only at Radstock and Pensford, boasted express passenger headlights and added special interest to the day-to-day working of the North Somerset.
A. Church

would come one third in cash, one third in debenture stock and one third in shares. At a meeting on 11th October, Lawrence repeated this offer, which was very fortunate since Thomas Brassey had now decided that he was unwilling to proceed because the share capital had not been raised. Gratefully, the Board accepted Lawrence's offer. By late October 1864 the contract with Lawrence was sealed.

At this time, discussions were taking place concerning the visit to Radstock of Mr Bingham and the Company's engineer regarding a possible diversion of the B&NSR's line in that area. Mr Fraser, the engineer, had sent new plans to the directors and these showed a new route following the line of the Somersetshire Coal Canal's Tramroad. At a meeting held on 22nd October, the directors agreed this new route. On 2nd November, Mr Bingham and Mr Rees-Mogg met representatives of the SCC in Bath regarding the possible use of part of the tramroad. Mr Cook, representing the SCC, told the North Somerset's representatives that he, and others, were proposing a new railway from Dundas Aqueduct, on the Kennet & Avon Canal near Bath, to Radstock but they had no objection to the North Somerset's proposed change of route. At a directors' meeting held on 10th November, Mr Bingham was told to write to Mr Cook suggesting that he postpone his new railway scheme, for the North Somerset directors were willing to put off their planned line from Radstock to Bath if the promoters of the canal-into-railway scheme would do the same. This they agreed to do.

By 1865 progress had slowed yet again and by March, there were more financial disagreements between the Company and the contractor, Lawrence. The latter had been offered a cash payment but in order to get this he had to agree to an eight per cent reduction in all his prices. Obviously the quality of the work and the relationship with the directors was bound to go downhill. On reflection, it would seem that March 1865 was to prove to be a very difficult month for the North Somerset company in that Mr Fraser, the engineer, had come across errors in plans and sections which he claimed were not his fault. On the other hand, the directors held the view that since he had not checked these amended plans and sections, he was responsible for these mistakes and should go! From 6th April Mr Piercy was to be the sole engineer in charge but, unexpectedly for the directors, Mr Piercy and Mr Fraser began an action against the Company. The Board then decided that Mr Piercy had abandoned his post by this action and that he too should go! The directors agreed to appoint Mr J.F. Tone as engineer and, in August 1865, he was officially given the post. His first job was to recommend that the line from Farrington Gurney be re-surveyed. This the Board agreed to do.

Mr Tone was also a key person in other matters when, in October 1865, Mr Bingham reported that Mr Tone had been retained to survey an important new line to Andover from Bristol, namely the Andover, Radstock & Bristol Railway. The directors thought that it would be a good idea for the North Somerset to find money for the deposit on this bill. Lawrence was consulted and it was agreed that if he got the contract for the line, he would contribute two thirds of the cost for the bill. It was further agreed that either the North Somerset's directors would deposit the Andover Bill or that a new company should be formed with B&NSR representatives on the board.

Incidentally, just before we leave 1865, one small, but rather interesting issue to arise was that, in spite of all of the financial problems that had come up in the spring of the year, that good-hearted fellow, Mr Bingham, called attention to the fact that the navvies engaged on the work on the line were living in very difficult conditions. He gave, as an example, the state of the lodging houses at Pensford. Here, he said, there was an instance of ten men living in one room of a cottage. He called for immediate assistance with this problem, asking that more houses be made available and that teaching be given to the navvies' children. The directors agreed to appoint a chaplain and a scripture reader with another to follow later. It was reassuring to know that whatever the Company's financial needs were, the North Somerset's navvies spiritual needs were being attended to!

Joking apart, however, the situation considerably worsened as the Bristol & North Somerset Company entered the financial crisis year of 1866. Nationally, the economic situation was very bad; locally on the North Somerset, things were heading for disaster. By late August 1866, the contractor had asked for an immediate lump sum payment of £9,900. The directors were unprepared to make such a payment and they were also unprepared to pay Lawrence another sum, due in four weeks time.

RAILWAYS AT RADSTOCK
This excellent panorama of Radstock shows both the Somerset & Dorset station (on the left with the train passing through towards Bath) and the GWR station (on the right). The line swinging away to the left in the foreground is the standard gauge Clandown branch while the white, clearly marked path in the "Y" of the S&D and the branch to Clandown is the route of the former tramway to Clandown and pits in the Welton area. The photograph was probably taken in 1909.

Lens of Sutton/Chris Howell

Instead it was decided that he should get bonds worth nearly £30,000.

An engineer's report, made in August 1866, showed that because of the Company's financial problems little progress had been made on the constructional side. Nevertheless, Mr Tone, the engineer, had reached agreement with his GWR counterpart about improvements to the junctions at both Bristol and Radstock. These improvements were going to save the North Somerset money at a time when such savings were desperately needed!

Things continued to go from bad to worse on the money side. At a meeting held on 11th October 1866 Mr Bingham reported that he had met Mr Lawrence and had told him that he could not, in fact, sell plant and equipment since it was owned by the Company. Lawrence was called into the meeting and he agreed *not* to sell machinery etc but he persisted in his wish to sell materials. Indeed, he was just about to put the following advertisement in *The Builder:*

Bristol & North Somerset Railway

W.H. Williams & Co. for W.F. Lawrence to auction at contractor's works, Avon Bridge, Brislington 16-10-1866, Whitchurch 17-10-1866 and Viaduct Works, Pensford 18-10-1866; all materials purchased for construction of above railway (timber, rails, bricks, etc).

(No mention is made of any locomotives.)

In fact, it would appear that none of these particular sales took place. Lawrence decided to cancel them instead. Mr Tone recommended, nevertheless, that a new contractor should be called in. If this happened, Mr Lawrence would get some cash and stock as recompense. What actually happened is that matters were sorted out it seems, at a meeting held at Paddington, on 12th October, when the North Somerset and Mr Lawrence agreed to continue to work together.

Nevertheless, things were still going extraordinarily poorly for the Company, so much so that a committee had been especially set up and, during March and April 1867, was delving deeply into the Company's disturbed financial problems. On 16th March Mr Tone agreed compensation with Mr Lawrence totalling £33,193. This sum had been given by the Company as a result of events that had taken place in the 1866 financial collapse. As we have already seen, payments were due to the contractor. These were not forthcoming, the contractors stopped work and the contract was terminated by mutual consent. Lawrence therefore decided to lay a claim against the North Somerset company and this compensation was the result of that claim. Incidentally, at the time Mr Tone awarded the compensation, he said that he thought it would cost somewhere between £100,000 and £110,000 to finish the line excluding the price of the land! Perhaps, if work began at once the line could be opened by late Autumn 1867. Again, this was another case of misplaced optimism!

Out in the field, the heavy work still to be done was on the Pensford-Bristol section. Mr Tone stated that he could more easily finish the section from Radstock to Pensford. If the land was made available quickly the Company might well be able to lay a connection with the GWR at Radstock by the end of Summer 1867. This would allow the Company to handle the highly profitable coal traffic very quickly. He, therefore, recommended that this part of the work be completed first and the directors agreed. However, other far more pressing and important events were about to sweep all other considerations aside.

The bombshell came at the annual half-yearly meeting of the Company held on 4th May 1867. At this meeting the Board disclosed that they were totally in the hands of the creditors who were, as the directors themselves put it, ". . . suing (the Company) from one end of the line to the other!" Judgements against the North Somerset were coming from north and south, left, right and centre. The problems with Mr Lawrence's contract had certainly not helped things, while on top of all this, the company secretary, the elusive John Bingham, had not been available to give an account as to what had been happening to the Company's finances.

The report of the committee of investigation was not complete in that many people had still not put in all their claims. Nevertheless, the picture that was emerging was showing all too clearly the disastrous state of the Company's finances. It would seem that out of the 13,750 shares the Company was authorised to issue by the 1863 Act, only 804 were applied for and distributed. In addition to these, there were 355 shares issued in payment for land and for professional services. Another 2,026 shares had been issued to contractors for work done. On top of this, it was clear that loans had been taken out by some of the directors of the Company to the tune of £180,000, these directors giving their own promissory notes as security. White-collar crime was clearly alive and thriving in the North Somerset company!

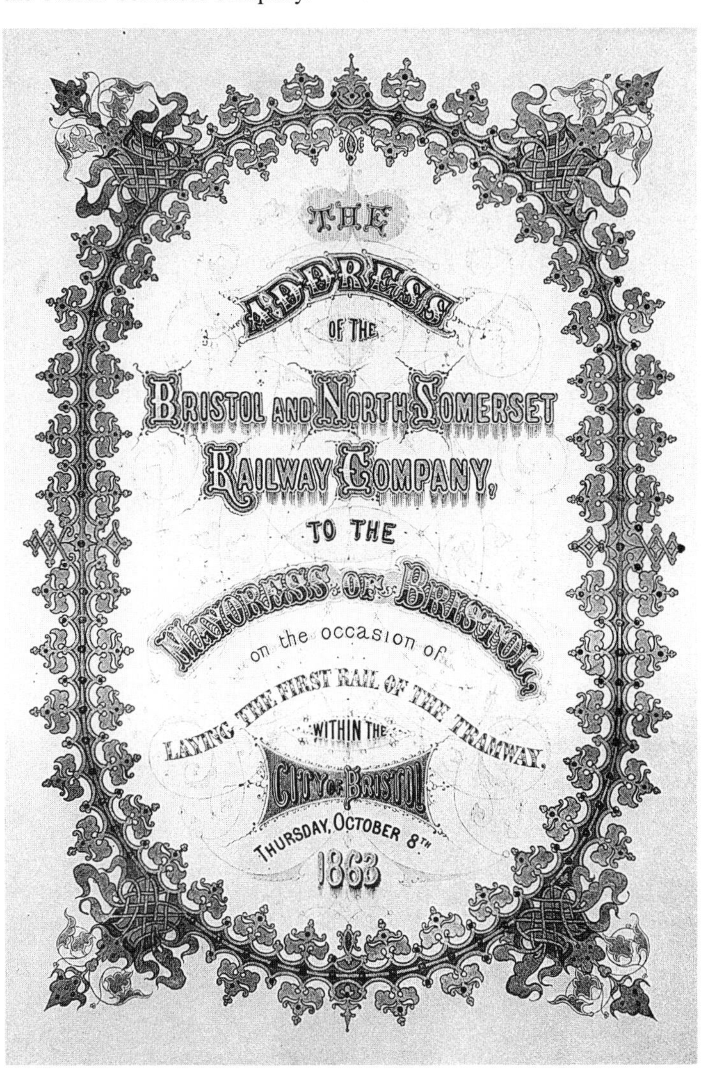

BRISTOL HARBOUR RAILWAY
THE ADDRESS – 8th October 1863
This photograph shows the cover page of the address of the B&NSR Company's rail laying ceremony for the Harbour Tramway. What optimism lay behind this page in the address given to the crowds gathered on the quayside near St Raphael's Church! Little did anyone know the problems that lay ahead of the Company in connecting Bristol Docks with Radstock coal.

Avon County Reference Library, Bristol

In all, the B&NSR's total receipts stood at £220,000 but the amount which seems to have been spent on the line's construction stood at no more than £124,000! This latter sum did *not* include payment for land nor did it include compensation claims which, at the time of the inquiry, amounted to nearly £32,000. There were also legal and parliamentary charges of over £28,500. Overall, the liabilities of the Company came to very nearly £300,000, an enormous sum for the mid-1860s.

Not surprisingly, there were ". . . great irregularities in keeping the books of the Company and transactions involving large

T. HARRIS SMITH & THE B&NSR
T.Harris Smith was an important and influential individual in the promotion and eventual construction of the Bristol & North Somerset Railway.
Collection David Warnock/Midsomer Norton Library

amounts seem to have been entered into by some of the directors and by the secretary of the company." One of the more honest directors on the Board, Mr T.H. Smith, hoped that the picture was now complete but he feared that they would never get the full story from their former secretary, John Bingham.

Bingham maintained that the North Somerset actually owed him £11,000 but his account was never put to the Company. Perhaps he had too much to hide? It was also quite clear that many of the sums owing to creditors hung on what Mr Bingham would have to say. The report of enquiry summed things up rather well when it said ". . . £100,000 or £50,000 had been spent; they knew it was gone somewhere, but they did not know where."!

Late in May, Mr Bingham replied to the directors through a letter sent to the local Bristol newspapers. He stated that, due to ill health, he had been unable to attend the meeting held on 4th May. He also said that he had made an appointment to meet the committee (of inquiry) with his accounts but, due to his eldest son's illness, he could not keep that appointment. Nevertheless, he was now ready to see the directors and show them his entire accounts. He went on to add, "Since that adjourned meeting I have been applied to by the so-called board of directors to furnish all my accounts, including my Parliamentary agent's bill and they are being prepared as rapidly as possible".

The matter dragged its way into early June, when on the evening of Thursday the 6th, the report of the committee of investigation was finally published. It said much as had been said at the May meeting. However, it did add one or two interesting points. One of these concerned the settlement that Mr Tone, the engineer, had made with Lawrence, the contractor. The committee felt that the Company had not been properly represented in this matter and that if it had been, the outcome would have been much more favourable to the Company. The published report states that " . . . the arbitrator allowed Messrs Lawrence & Company credit for £70,500, which was an error, but he was induced to do so by . . . Mr Lawrence and . . . (this was) . . . confirmed by the late secretary".

The total list of the Company's liabilities, as far as could be judged, amounted to over £275,000. In addition, "additional bills of an unclear nature" still had to be added. The report concludes that, ". . . one of the accounts (still) not given is that of the late secretary whose repeated promises to furnish it . . . remain unfulfilled". In all, it was a very sorry story in which some extremely dirty linen was washed in an extremely public way.

As for everyone's scapegoat of the piece, John Bingham, he received what, on reflection, seems to be his just deserts for, some three years later on 7th June 1870 at Bristol's Central Criminal Court, he pleaded guilty to a charge accusing him of having forged and altered an endorsement for £536 17s 6d (£536.87½) with intent to defraud. He was sentenced to twelve months hard labour. At long last the law had caught up with him but there can be no doubt that he (and others!) had experienced a very good run with their own (and other people's) money.

After the financial crises and collapses of 1866 and 1867 and, after the formation of a new company in 1870, changes in both contractor and engineer were forthcoming. By the summer of 1870 the engineer in charge had become Mr William Clarke, a former Assistant Chief Engineer with the London & North Western Railway. It was he who took the project through to its completion in 1873.

Once the Bristol & North Somerset Railway Act of 31st July 1868 had been obtained, the directors had told William Clarke to survey the line to see exactly what the position was. He was also asked to give some kind of estimate as to the cost of completion. It would seem that he carried out his survey in the summer of 1869, reporting in the autumn of the same year. As part of this report, further changes were to take place in the Radstock area and because of the scope of these changes, it became necessary to obtain a further Act, the B&NSR (Deviation at Radstock) Act of 30th November 1869. This diversion provided for far less demolition of property in the area, was less expensive and provided a better junction with the GWR. The Somersetshire Coal Canal opposed the Bristol & North Somerset's Radstock bill in both houses of Parliament but, in spite of this opposition, the bill became law on 14th July 1870.

In July 1870, the directors sought estimates for the railway's completion from various new contractors. One of these, Messrs John Perry and Sons, of Stratford, East London, offered to complete the job for £90,000. This was accepted, the directors aiming to open the line between Bristol and Pensford in the spring of 1871. It was hoped that the rest of the branch would be ready by the autumn of the same year. In order to get things moving it was suggested that work between Radstock and Bristol should be undertaken in two sections, these being as follows:

Contract No. 1 which would cover the Radstock to Cloud Hill section, Cloud Hill being just to the north of Hallatrow station as built and,

Contract No. 2 which would deal with the Cloud Hill to Bristol part of the route.

By the end of October 1870 the contract with Perry had been confirmed. However the planned-for rate of progress was not to be achieved for, at a directors' meeting held in early April 1871, it was reported that little gain had been made on the line during the 1870/1 winter. This was again due to the fact that few funds were forthcoming. It is, therefore, to see in the minutes those well-used and well-chosen words: ". . . little progress of works . . ."!

During the spring of 1871 the Board received letters from people living in the Whitchurch and Farrington Gurney areas. They wanted the company to provide them with stations. The North Somerset board agreed to meet these people with the

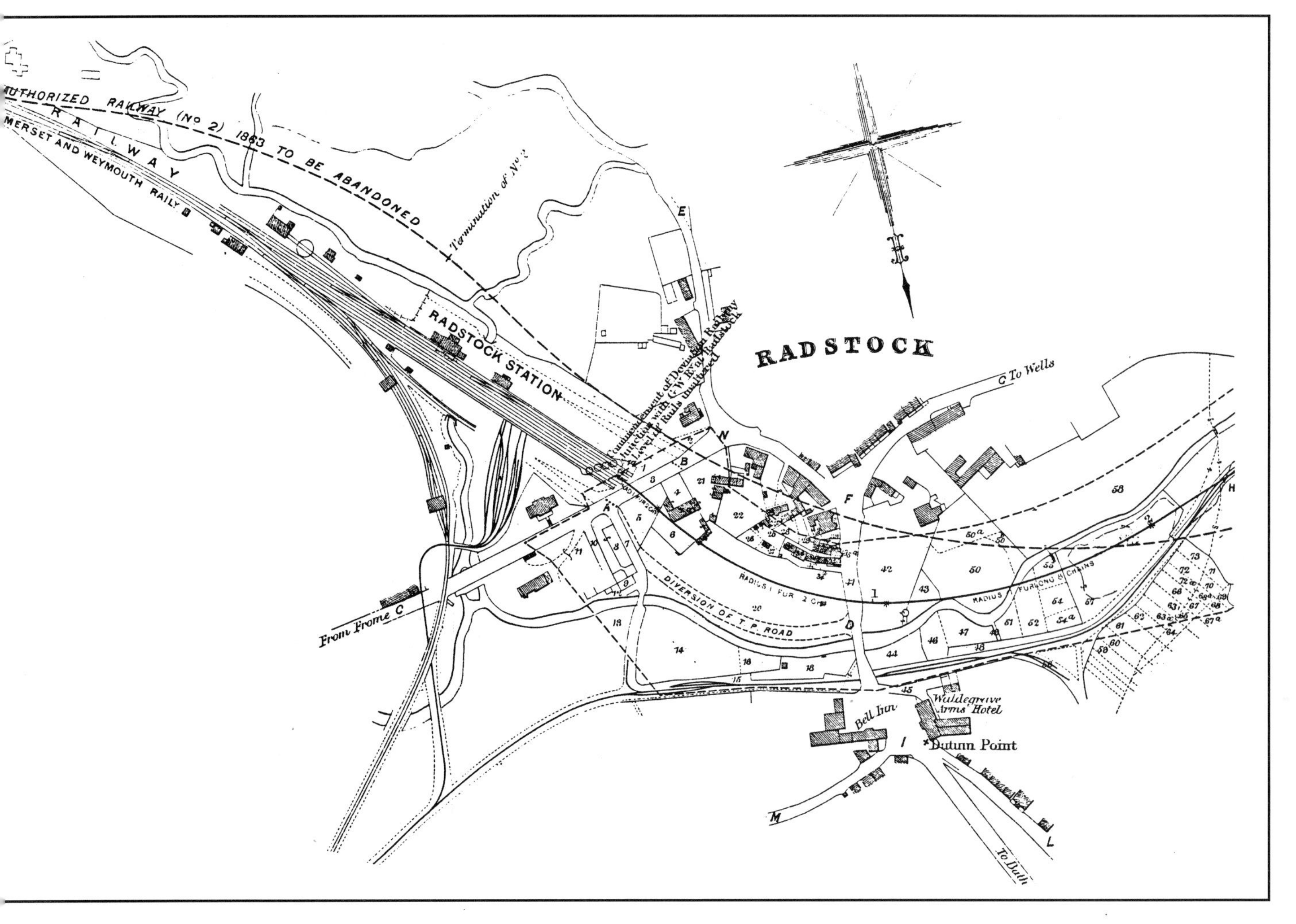

THE BRISTOL & NORTH SOMERSET RAILWAY (DEVIATION AT RADSTOCK) ACT: 1870 SESSION

Original plan: Somerset Record Office

intention of getting the residents themselves to subscribe to some of the costs of providing those stations. The residents must have been unsuccessful in their attempts for the halts at Whitchurch and Farrington were not actually built until 1925 and 1927 respectively!

At the end of August 1871 it was announced that Pensford Viaduct needed further alterations and strengthening. The viaduct itself and a nearby embankment were also discussed again at a meeting in November. There was obviously real concern here on the part of the directors, as well there might be, for such an important structure on the line. At a late January meeting the problems at Pensford came up yet again. Clearly, because of the various problems at Pensford and because of the unexpectedly high cost of providing siding accommodation along the line, more cash would be needed for these essential works. However, the GWR had said that it would be prepared to construct more sidings at Bristol and these would ease the North Somerset's burden. In addition, the GWR were about to relay the Radstock terminus of the Frome-Radstock line, partially as a sweetener to the local coal owners who were getting annoyed at the length of delay there had been in converting the line to Salisbury to standard gauge. At the same

THE NORTH SOMERSET RAILWAY COMES TO RADSTOCK
This very useful photograph shows the coming of the North Somerset Railway to Radstock itself. In the left background can be seen the Waldegrave Arms, a pub still in use at the present time. In the same area of the picture, but this time nearer the camera, can be seen piles of earth, signs of the railway's march into the town.

Some demolition has clearly taken place although if the B&NSR's original 1862 route had gone ahead much of the centre of Radstock would have had to have been removed to make way for the line! The route taken under an 1870 Act required far less removal of property. However, it did require diverting the Frome turnpike from which this photo was taken.
(The view was likely captured by the photographer c1871/2.)

Radstock Library

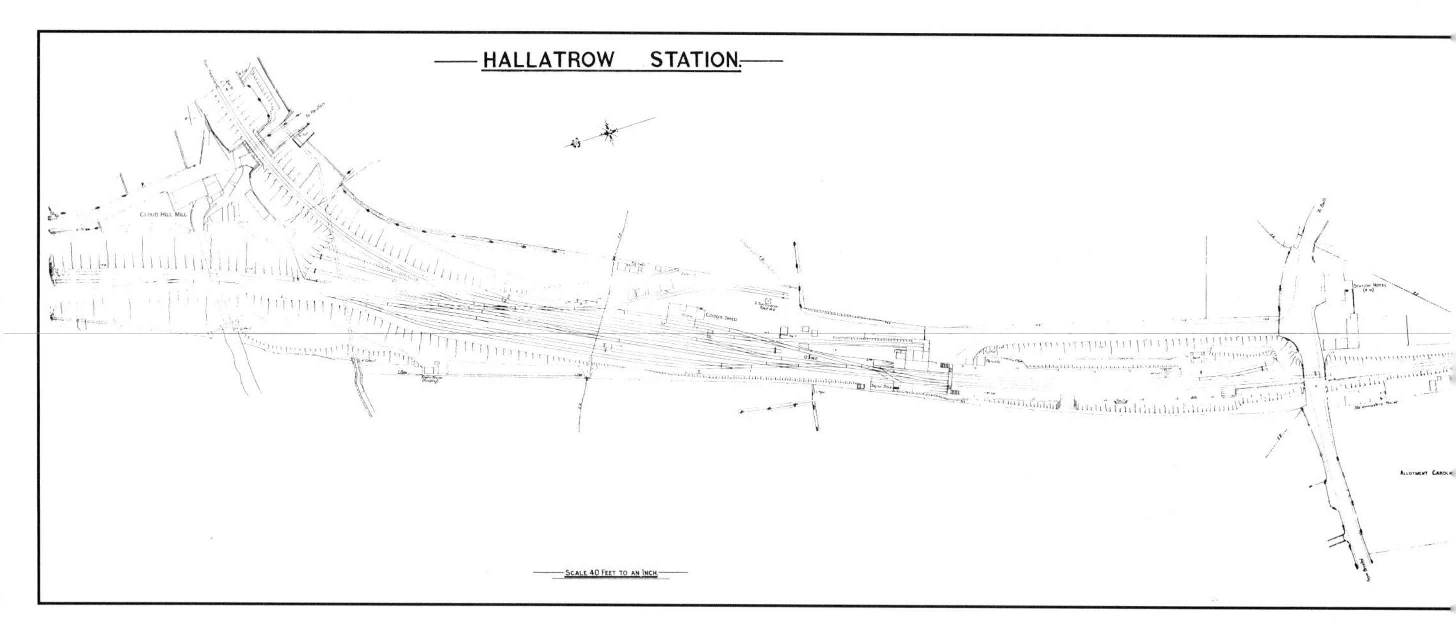

HALLATROW STATION: JUNCTION FOR THE CAMERTON BRANCH *Original plan: British Rail (Western)*

Below: EDWARDIAN HALLATROW

With movement and action evident in the goods yard, Hallatrow station bathes in the sunshine in the early years of the 20th century. Here we have a pleasant country junction just before some very major changes took place.

The area to the left of the picture became the site of the new passing loop and platform, these being installed in 1909. At the same time, the signal box in the left distance was replaced by a new and larger box of 55 working and 12 spare levers. Milk churns indicate that this particular source of income was well established by this time. *Collection Dave Fisher*

meeting Mr Clarke submitted plans for the stations while a memo from Mr Perry estimated that, "barring accidents" (!), the railway should be completed by 2nd July 1872.

In March 1872, the directors ordered advertisements to be placed for tenders for the line's stations and these were, in fact, 'captured' and built (on a 'standard' model) by William Clarke, the Company's engineer. All was not running smoothly, however, for, at a directors' meeting held on 6th February 1873, it was disclosed that negotiations had been entered into with Mr John Mackay of Shrewsbury for the completion of the line. Nominally this was to be under Mr Perry's number two contract, that is, between Cloud Hill and Bristol, but it did not include work on Pensford Viaduct itself. Mr Perry had agreed to complete contract number one *and* the viaduct by 1st May 1873 and it certainly seems as if he was really hard-pressed to do this. Mr Mackay was thus taken on with the understanding that he would complete the contract by the end of May 1873, for £9,000.

This involvement of Mr Mackay seems to have come about due to the production of an independent report by a Mr Thomas E. Harrison. Mr Harrison was an engineer employed at the insistence of the Earl of Warwick to check exactly what the state of affairs was on the route. Harrison had thoroughly inspected the railway on the 16th and 17th January 1873 and his close scrutiny was also extended to the viaduct and the two landslips at Pensford. He noted that the original design of the viaduct had been altered and, as a result, there had been some slight signs of settlement in the face work of some of

Above: THE YEARS PASS FOR PENSFORD
With a single line through the now deserted station, Pensford awaits its ultimate fate. This picture, taken in the early 1960s, shows that in spite of the removal of the North Somerset's passenger service in November 1959, the track was kept in pretty good condition for the freight traffic still remaining. *Lens of Sutton*

the bases of the piers. There had been a very heavy slip in one of the cuttings and this, he felt, should be taken out and used to infill a slip in the embankment to the north of the station. This embankment was on very treacherous ground and so large, stone drains had been put in to improve matters.

Throughout the length of the line Harrison had seen many heavy slips both in cuttings and embankments, more so than he had ever seen on any other railway of similar length. He did add that, although there were instances with some of the smaller slips where greater care and more drainage would have helped, in general terms, the blame was not with the contractor. He did, nevertheless, go on to say that there was a poor finish on most of the work and that the line's general appearance was very untidy. He could make no prediction as to when the works would be completed with the number of men and the amount of machinery currently employed, but he did believe that with much greater effort all round the line *could* be ready in three months.

Below: JUST AN ORDINARY DAY!
Pannier tank No. 3735 comes smartly downhill on the 10.17am (SO) Bristol to Frome train and is about to go under the S&D's main line near Radstock. The scene was captured on 10th October 1959. *Hugh Ballantyne*

Right: REPOINTING AT PENSFORD
This enlargement of a more general view of Pensford Viaduct shows repointing taking place. It is believed that this work was being carried out just before the First World War. The photograph gives an excellent idea of the forest of wooden scaffolding needed.

The man in the bottom left hand corner is a Mr Light from nearby Woollard. *Mrs Ethel Tucker/Bob Parsons*

Following on from this report, it is quite clear that the directors' meeting held on 6th February 1873 was a key one in that several crucial constructional issues were resolved.

First, it was decided to end the contract of 19th October 1870 between the B&NSR and John Perry for the construction of section two from Cloud Hill to Bristol, with the exception of the work on Pensford Viaduct, which he was now left free to complete.

Second, that building work on the North Somerset be suspended on the evening of 31st January 1873. The following day two representatives from the Company and two from the contractor would inspect the line to see what work had been done. Within 28 days, Perry, the contractor, was to deliver a full account of all work done on contract number two, including that carried out on the viaduct at Pensford.

Third, that the Company was at liberty to appoint another contractor if they felt it was necessary. It is at this point that John Mackay comes into our story.

From this time on, progress becomes much more apparent, so much so that, by the end of March 1873, the line was almost completed, the various slips and works all having been virtually attended to. By early July, the line is clearly well nigh finished for an advertisement placed in *The Builder* at that time read as follows:

Bristol & North Somerset Line

T. Melhuish for J. Perry & Co. of Tredegar Works, Bow*: to auction on 22/23rd July 1873 at Hallatrow Depot, remainder of plant used in the construction of the above line, including two 6-wheel saddle tank locomotives.

*Perry had moved from Stratford to Bow in 1872.

Finally, at a board meeting held on 5th August 1873 Mr Clarke reported on the state of the works. He said that arrangements had already been made for the Board of Trade's inspector to visit the line and that its opening should follow in September. On 3rd September 1873 the opening took place and it is to this that we now turn our attention.

5
Completion and Takeover by the GWR

WET RAILS AT RADSTOCK
With dampness in the air and on the sleepers and rails, pannier tank No. 9762 leaves Radstock and heads in the Mells Road direction with a solitary brake van in tow. The date is 11th January 1961.

P. J. Williams

On 2nd September 1873 Colonel Rich completed his inspection and report on the Bristol & North Somerset line between Bristol (North Somerset Junction) and Radstock. In it he stated that the new addition to the railway network was single although land had been acquired and fenced off so that a second track could be added when finances allowed and traffic levels demanded this.

Stations were constructed at Brislington, Pensford, Clutton, Hallatrow, Welton and Radstock. Interestingly enough, Rich actually got the order of the stations wrong in his report in that, working south from Bristol, he puts Hallatrow before Clutton. He noted, with some concern, that all of the stations, with the exception of Radstock itself, were on gradients varying from 1 in 70 to 1 in 200 but as he himself says "... (since) they are placed in the hollows near the bottoms of the inclines and ... (since) ... it would be difficult to alter them, I recommend that they be permitted to remain as they are ...(!)" The line was well ballasted throughout.

At the time of inspection, there were 20 overbridges, 26 underbridges and five viaducts in use on the branch. Of the viaducts the one over the River Avon near North Somerset Junction had stone piers and wrought iron girderwork. The masterpiece, however, and the one that had caused all the trouble during building was the one at Pensford. This magnificent edifice consisted of 16 semi-circular brick arches on stone piers, 14 of these arches having spans varying between 51ft and 55ft 11in with two spans of 28ft.

Colonel Rich noted that several things needed to be done. He was concerned that several bridges had showed signs of slight settlement. He suggested that the cracks should be pointed and that they should be carefully watched for some time to come. He also required that one of the three sets of facing points at Pensford station should be taken out of use while the rails on the Avon Viaduct in Bristol and on the overbridge at Pensford station should be much more firmly fixed to their respective bridges.

He mentioned the level crossing at Radstock which was worked from the adjacent signal box ("Radstock No. 1" or as its later replacement became known "Radstock North"), the gates here being interlocked with the signals controlled from this box. In some of the line's other signal boxes clocks were needed. Rich noticed that the shelves holding telegraph equipment interfered with the signalmen's view of the signals that they were working and with the actual working of the levers themselves. He therefore ordered that this equipment should be placed to the sides of the signal cabins concerned.

In addition, line and signal diagrams were required in the boxes. At Radstock, the signal and point locking, arranged at this time for working the 'up' and 'down' lines separately, was to be changed so that the station could be worked on a single line basis – this way of working being in force until such time as the railway was opened all the way to Frome on the standard gauge. Once this had become reality then the station would become a passing place.

All the points and signals on the North Somerset were worked from boxes and were interlocked. At the time of Rich's

RADSTOCK NORTH SIGNAL BOX DIAGRAM *Signalling Record Society*

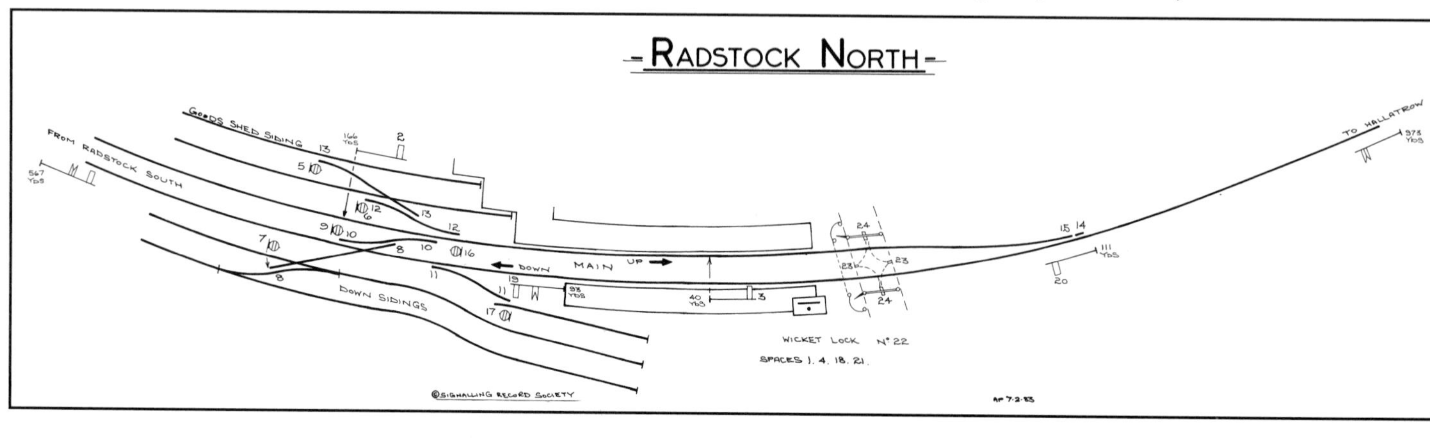

inspection the arrangements for working the branch on the block telegraph system were nearly completed. One rather nice, minor touch was that Rich noted that ". . . there are turntables at Radstock and at Birmingham which are the terminal stations . . ."! He concludes his report with the pointed comment that " . . . the Great Western station at Bristol (Temple Meads) is in process of reconstruction. This very necessary work appears to progress very slowly indeed".

Nevertheless, in spite of all these comments about the unfinished nature of the works, Rich pronounced the line fit for passenger traffic. The local press had the following things to say about its opening:

"It was with something like surprise that the public learnt at the end of last week that the line of railway which will connect Bristol with the Somerset coalfields would be opened for traffic tomorrow*. Not that the time which had been occupied in bringing the undertaking to a termination has been short, for few railway ventures of its size have been so long in completion.

The Great Western Railway Company have undertaken to work the line, and at present it is intended to run four trains a day each way, with the exception of Sunday which, it is believed will be a dies non (a non-day) upon the branch. The first train will leave Radstock at 7.15 tomorrow morning* arriving in Bristol about an hour later, while the first train in the other direction will start from the Bristol terminus at 7.40 on Tuesday morning*. There are stations at Brislington, Pensford, Clutton, Hallatrow, Welton and Radstock with sidings at each."

(Source: Western Daily Press 1st September 1873.* Note that the paper actually got the date of the line's opening wrong!)

The Bath Chronicle of 4th September added that:

"Besides opening up communication with the extensive collieries of Lord Warwick and the Countess Waldegrave at Radstock and other mineral properties in the neighbourhood, . . . (the line) . . . will open up a district rich in agricultural products, and there are several extensive breweries to the proprietors of which it must be a great convenience."

Once the excitement over the opening had died down, the everyday events and meetings came to the fore again. At a meeting held on 19th February 1874, with the railway now complete and in use through to Bristol, the North Somerset's directors discussed the claim for payment made by one of the route's contractors, Mr Mackay. He wanted £6,500 for settlement in full. The directors agreed to this figure, no doubt being only too pleased to have the line finished at long last!

By early July 1874 an agreement had been prepared regarding the GWR's financing of the North Somerset's goods sidings and sheds, the security for this work being based on the ailing company's preference stock. The meeting also heard that the Company's other contractor, Mr Perry & Son, had recently agreed to accepting £2,500 in cash plus £14,500 in deferred debenture stock for the work they had done in constructing the line. It would seem that some of the debts, at least, were being paid and the problems were on the way to solution.

At an autumn meeting held in November 1874 another important issue was raised when the North Somerset directors were reminded of the fact that, under an agreement dated 25th May 1866, the GWR were obliged, by 1st May 1867, to open the Radstock-Frome section of line to passenger traffic, irrespective of what gauge problems there might be. This particular item is worthy of further discussion in that as far back as November 1864 the GWR's Board of Directors had agreed to lay standard gauge trackage from Bristol to Salisbury. In 1866 the Company had entered into the May agreement

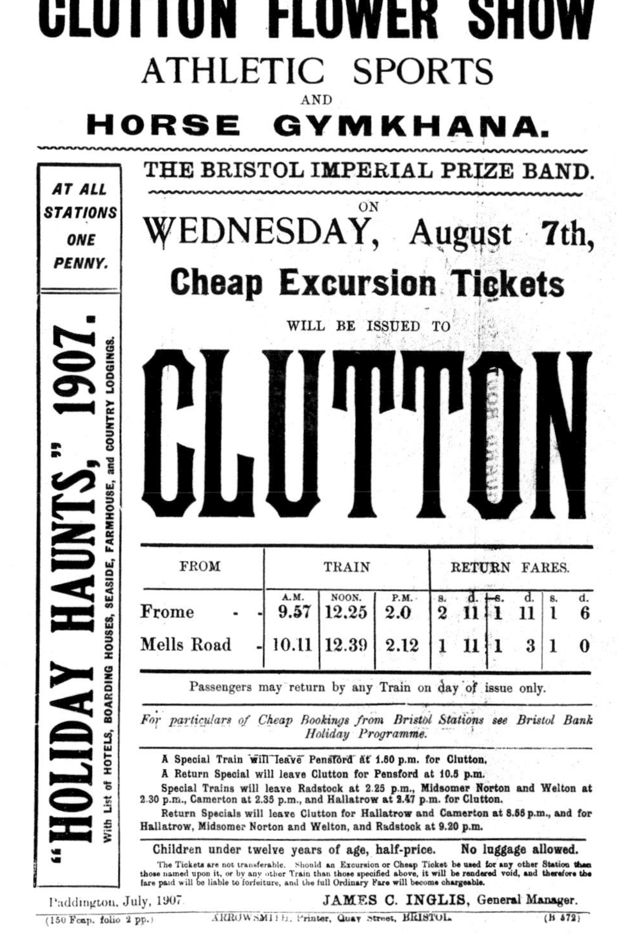

GREAT WESTERN RAILWAY.

CLUTTON FLOWER SHOW

ATHLETIC SPORTS

AND

HORSE GYMKHANA.

THE BRISTOL IMPERIAL PRIZE BAND.

ON

WEDNESDAY, August 7th,

Cheap Excursion Tickets

WILL BE ISSUED TO

CLUTTON

FROM	TRAIN			RETURN FARES.					
	A.M.	NOON.	P.M.	s.	d.	s.	d.	s.	d.
Frome	9.57	12.25	2.0	2	11	1	11	1	6
Mells Road	10.11	12.39	2.12	1	11	1	3	1	0

Passengers may return by any Train on day of issue only.

For particulars of Cheap Bookings from Bristol Stations see Bristol Bank Holiday Programme.

A Special Train will leave Pensford at 1.50 p.m. for Clutton.

A Return Special will leave Clutton for Pensford at 10.5 p.m.

Special Trains will leave Radstock at 2.25 p.m., Midsomer Norton and Welton at 2.30 p.m., Camerton at 2.35 p.m., and Hallatrow at 2.47 p.m. for Clutton.

Return Specials will leave Clutton for Hallatrow and Camerton at 8.55 p.m., and for Hallatrow, Midsomer Norton and Welton, and Radstock at 9.20 p.m.

Children under twelve years of age, half-price. No luggage allowed.

The Tickets are not transferable. Should an Excursion or Cheap Ticket be used for any other Station than those named upon it, or by any other Train than those specified above, it will be rendered void, and therefore the fare paid will be liable to forfeiture, and the full Ordinary Fare will become chargeable.

AT ALL STATIONS ONE PENNY.

"HOLIDAY HAUNTS," 1907.

With List of HOTELS, BOARDING HOUSES, SEASIDE, FARMHOUSE, and COUNTRY LODGINGS.

Paddington, July, 1907. JAMES C. INGLIS, General Manager.

(150 Fcap. folio 2 pp.) ARROWSMITH, Printer, Quay Street, BRISTOL. (B 572)

DAYS OUT ON THE LINE 1907:
Clutton Show in the summer.

GREAT WESTERN RAILWAY.

WESTERN LEAGUE MATCH, DIVISION 2.

WEYMOUTH TOWN v. RADSTOCK TOWN.

KICK-OFF 3.30 p.m.

On SATURDAY, Sept. 28th,

A HALF-DAY EXCURSION

WILL RUN TO

WEYMOUTH

LEAVING	AT	Return Fares, Third Class.
	A.M.	
BRISTOL – CLIFTON DOWN	11 37	3/-
BRISTOL – REDLAND	11 39	3/-
BRISTOL – MONTPELIER	11 41	3/-
BRISTOL – STAPLETON ROAD	11 46	3/-
BRISTOL – LAWRENCE HILL	11 53	3/-
BRISTOL – TEMPLE MEADS	11 41	3/-
	P.M.	
BRISLINGTON	12 5	3/-
PENSFORD	12 18	3/-
CLUTTON	12 28	2/6
HALLATROW	12 32	2/6
MIDSOMER NORTON & WELTON	12 42	2/6
RADSTOCK	12 48	2/6
MELLS ROAD	1 0	2/6
FROME	1 15	2/6

The Return Train will leave Weymouth at 8.45 p.m. the same day.

BRISTOL.—Tickets for all G.W. Excursions from Clifton Down, Redland, Montpelier, Ashley Hill, Stapleton Road, Lawrence Hill, Temple Meads, or Bedminster Stations, can be obtained in advance at the G.W.R. Office, 3 High Street, City, and 17 Pritchard Street, Portland Square; also (unless otherwise stated) at Messrs. Cook & Son's Agency, 49 Corn Street, City; at Mr. H. W. Gapper's Office, 2 Cromwell Road, Montpelier (Zetland Road Junction); and at "Pickford's" Office, Star Life Buildings, St. Augustine's Parade.

Tickets for all G. W. Excursions from Stapleton Road or Lawrence Hill stations can be obtained in advance at the G.W.R. Office, Regent Street, Kingswood.

Tickets for all G.W. Excursions from Clifton Down and Temple Meads Stations can be obtained in advance at the G.W.R. Office, 11 The Mall, Clifton.

Excursion programmes and bills can be obtained at above offices, also at the following G.W.R. Receiving Offices:—48 East Street, Bedminster; Assembly Rooms, Prince Street; 6 Bridge Street, City; Byron Place, Triangle, Clifton; 115 Redcliffe Street; Mr. Hiles, 78 Gloucester Road, Bishopston; Mr. Bowkett, 224 Hotwells Road; Messrs. Sloper & Co., Tobacconists, 3 West Street, St. Philip's; Miss Burgess, Stationer, Broad Street, Staple Hill; Mr. Daniel, 3 Cheapside, Fishponds Road; The Domestic Supply and Bazaar Company, 22 Sandy Park Road, New Brislington; Mr. Dunn, Tobacconist, 6 Stokes Croft; Mr. J. H. Baynham, 156 St. Michael's Hill, Kingsdown; & G.W.R. Office, Gloucester Road, Avonmouth Docks, and at the Polytechnic Touring Association Office, 6 Bridge Street, City.

Children under Twelve years of Age, Half-price. No Luggage allowed.

The Tickets are not transferable. Should an Excursion or Cheap Ticket be used for any other Station than those named upon it, or by any other Train than those specified, it will be rendered void, and therefore the fare paid will be liable to forfeiture, and the full Ordinary Fare will become chargeable.

For information respecting Tourist, Pleasure Party arrangements, and Excursion and Special Trips on the Great Western Railway, application should be made to Mr. C. Kislingbury, Divisional Superintendent, Temple Meads Station, Bristol, or at any of the Stations.

FREQUENT RAIL MOTORS

In addition to Ordinary Train Service on many parts of the System.

THROUGH CARRIAGES on principal Express Trains BETWEEN LONDON and PROVINCIAL TOWNS.

CORRIDOR COACHES

First, Second and Third Class Lavatory Compartments.

Reserved Compartments for Ladies.

Paddington, Sept., 1907. JAMES C. INGLIS, General Manager.

(Bristol—13,000 R. 8vo, 2 pp.) Arrowsmith, Printer, Quay Street, Bristol. (B 794)

Away games in the autumn. *Original handbills: M. Wyatt*

mentioned above but, due to the collapse of the North Somerset company, nothing further was done.

In 1870 a new agreement was drawn up and signed. This confirmed that the GWR *would* provide standard gauge facilities between Radstock and Salisbury. In 1871 the GWR's directors put forward a somewhat strange proposal in which the GWR would lay an additional standard gauge line alongside the then existing broad gauge track from Frome westwards to the London & South Western Railway beyond Yeovil. The whole project was to have cost some £54,000.

However, this proposal was not turned into reality and nothing more was done about the 1870 agreement until February 1874 when the GWR directors gave the following report about their intentions:

"By the terms of an Agreement with the Bristol & North Somerset Company and the principal colliery proprietors of the Radstock District, this Company is under engagement to lay the 'narrow gauge' between Radstock and Salisbury on or before the 3rd September next.

In view of this obligation, the Directors have had to consider the best mode of dealing with the question of Gauge on the Wilts, Somerset & Weymouth, and the Berks & Hants Railways, and they are of the opinion that the convenience of the public will be best met, and the interests of the Proprietors best secured, by the alteration from broad to 'narrow gauge' of all the lines in the district which these railways accommodate.

This alteration will necessitate an extension of the Mixed Gauge over a portion of the Main Line between Swindon and Bristol, and the Directors recommend that at the same time a second line of rails should be laid on the Wilts, Somerset & Weymouth Railway between Frome and Witham and between Westbury and Warminster, where earthworks and bridges have already been constructed for a double line. In connection with the conversion of the gauge the station accommodation will be enlarged and improved to meet the requirements of the increasing traffic.

The cost of carrying out the alterations and additions to the permanent way, stations and works involved in this arrangement is estimated at £290,000."

Work began almost at once, laying in the third additional rail on the GWR's main line between Swindon and Thingley Junction (near Chippenham) and between Bristol and Bathampton. For the conversion work on the Wilts, Somerset & Weymouth Railway, however, the company decided to carry out the narrowing operation during the long, light summer days of June 1874. The event was well reported in the local press, the Bath Chronicle for 25th June having the following item covering the story:

Left: GANGERS & PLATELAYERS (1)
Ganger Poole on the Four Foot
Ganger Bill Poole stands on the North Somerset main line, to the north of Clutton station. By all accounts, Bill Poole set very high standards in his work on the permanent way, so much so that he eventually went on to become a Permanent Way Inspector. Incidentally, the trucks to the right of Ganger Poole are standing on the long connection that ran from Clutton goods yard to the colliery at Fry's Bottom.

Mrs Weaver

Below: GANGERS & PLATELAYERS (2)
Laying into Ludlows
This beautiful photograph shows a motley crew of permanent way men working on the track at Ludlows Colliery, Radstock. It would seem likely that this photograph was taken in 1874 when the gauge was narrowed on the Radstock-Frome section of the GWR; a marvellous collection of men, expressions and hats and some baulked road track all help to make this a photograph worthy of much closer study.
A. Church

Above: GANGERS & PLATELAYERS (3)
A Gaggle of Gangers at Clutton
It is believed that this group photograph shows two of the North Somerset's permanent way gangs at Clutton. One gang is obviously that based at Clutton; the other was presumably the one stationed either at Pensford, to the north, or Hallatrow, to the south.
Identifiable members of the group are back row, extreme right – Mr Albert Gibbs (signalman at Clutton); bottom row, fourth from left – Mr Dan Perry (ganger); ganger on extreme right, Mr Silas Bailey. Mr Parfitt is the man with the pole, front row, extreme left.

Mrs Weaver

"Hundreds of labourers have been busily engaged for some days in the service of the Great Western Railway Company, carrying out the works connected with the change from broad to 'narrow gauge' on the various branches of the line between Reading and Devizes, Holt Junction, Bath, Salisbury, Chippenham, Weymouth, Radstock, Wells and Frome and the short lines in conjunction therewith.

The work of conversion commenced on (the previous) Friday morning, the line being closed on that and the following two

Below: GANGERS & PLATELAYERS (4)
A Greater Gaggle of Gangers at Clutton
This picture probably shows not only the regular Clutton p.w. gang but also another "foreign" gang from Bristol. It could have been the case that some major relaying work was going on in the district! Mr A. Gibbs can be seen again in the back row, extreme right while Mr Parfitt dominates the centre of the picture. Both this and the above view are believed to have been taken in the 1920s, perhaps a little earlier.
Note the profusion of pocket watches!

Mrs Weaver

days, but passenger traffic was resumed on the Monday morning subject to special timetables which had been issued some time previously. On the 1st of July new timetables will be issued and the service on the branches will, we are told, be greatly improved. The following account shows the magnitude of the task and the precautions that had to be taken.

For some days previous to the commencement of the work the broad gauge stock was gradually worked off the line, and on Thursday evening (18th June) each stationmaster had to give a certificate that his station and district was clear of broad gauge rolling stock, the last trains of which arrived at the Chippenham end of the line about midnight, and was sent to appointed depots. Immediately afterwards the line was handed over to the engineers, who were entrusted with the supervision of the work between Chippenham and Weymouth, Bathampton and Weymouth and various branches in connection, the largest of which was that from Wells to Witham. About 2,000 men were engaged in the work, the company having concentrated a number of men on various sections of the work. Each man received 1s 3d (6p) per day for rations, and the company found oatmeal and good water for making a wholesome and strengthening beverage. Sheds were also erected where sleeping accommodation was scanty, and the men worked 17 or 18 out of each 24 hours, their energy and steadiness being remarkable."

Once the network of lines had been changed to standard gauge the Frome-Radstock Branch was inspected in June 1875 for the Board of Trade by Colonel Yolland. Perhaps, we should use the word 're-inspected' for, as we saw in Chapter 2, it was Colonel Yolland who had originally inspected the mineral branch on its opening some 21 years before! Incidentally, it would seem that the GWR had intended to open the Frome-Radstock section for passengers as well but notice to do this was subsequently withdrawn and, since that time back in 1854, it had simply carried freight traffic.

Yolland's later report, dated 25th June 1875 made the following points and comments. One of the first statements he made highlighted the inaccuracy of the information the GWR had given him. Apparently the details he had received from the company had described the line as being single between Radstock and Frome. In fact, as part of the route's upgrading it had been doubled between Radstock and Mells Road. Yolland suggested that " . . . the GWR Company should be requested to supply correct details of the present line as requested . . ."!

It would seem that the mineral line had been fairly extensively relaid in 1861. However, at the time of Yolland's visit the GWR was in the process of taking out and replacing many of the worn rails. Along the length inspected there were eleven over underbridges in addition to five viaducts. Yolland wrote that for the production of his report, he had not had access to any plans or drawings of the bridges or viaducts concerned but he did go on to say that ". . . although they have been constructed for upwards of twenty years they are standing well, with the exception that in some, the stone has suffered from the action of the weather, and repairs have been required and in some places, are still in hand – and with respect to the underbridges and viaducts where timber is used for supporting the permanent way, they did not present any unusual deflection under a rolling load. The viaducts (however) will require to be carefully looked after, as they are mostly of wood, and after such an interval of time, decayed portions will continually require from time to time to be taken out."

Pressure and a Petition from the Mells Area: 1874

On 31st July 1874 a petition was sent to the directors of the GWR from the inhabitants of the area around Buckland Dinham. Since the GWR was in the process of preparing the mineral only line from Radstock to Frome for passenger traffic the local people obviously felt that now was a good time to have a go at getting "a local station, or stopping place, of a simple kind" built in the neighbourhood. The petitioners made a strong case, including the point that both Radstock & Frome stations were inconveniently sited for Buckland Dinham and Great Elm parishes adding that, "It is worthy of observation that Limestone Quarries, and Iron Works already exist in the locality, in addition to which a Coal Mine is in course of being sunk*. Considerations of an engineering character must no doubt arise in determining the position of a station, but subject to these, we would indicate a point near the Great Elm railway arch as suited to the wants of both Parishes, or as an alternative, a point near the railway bridge at Chantry, in the Parish of Buckland Dinham". The petition was, unfortunately, unsuccessful, and it was not until 1887 that a station was eventually opened at Mells Road, some three miles from the village of the same name!

*The coal mine mentioned here was at Buckland Dinham. Full details of its sinking were given in the Western Gazette for 15th March 1874. We are told that "the preliminary borings for coal at Buckland Dinham carried on by the Diamond Boring Company for Mr J. Oxley of Frome have been sufficiently successful to justify the sinking of a shaft. The site is on the south side of Buckland Down in the valley between Barrow Hill and the road leading from Buckland Down to Mells, and consequently in an advantageous situation with regard to Radstock Railway". However, in spite of this initial optimism, the venture was unsuccessful.

This photograph shows some of those who signed the 1874 petition to the GWR: a close examination of the names reveals some very influential members of the community.

Original document: Public Record Office

Above: WILLOW VALE BRIDGE, FROME
BEFORE REBUILDING – 1902
This view shows the old wooden railway bridge in Willow Vale, near Frome, just before it was rebuilt in the early years of the 20th century.

British Rail (Western)

Below: WILLOW VALE BRIDGE FROME
AFTER REBUILDING – 1903
The same location is shown here just one year later. This substantial bridge remains in use and in this form at the present time.

British Rail (Western)

In 1875, it would appear that there were three level crossings between Radstock and Frome but that in that parliamentary session the GWR were putting through legislation to do away with these. All of the crossings then in use had their own protecting signals. On the signalling side, all preparations had been made for working the double line on the Absolute Block System while the single section was to be worked by Train Staff. These methods of working had not, however, been confirmed at the time of Yolland's inspection. He also mentioned that the GWR were going to establish " . . . an Electric Communication . . ." between No. 1 and No. 2 signal boxes at Radstock, the "Gates" and the "Yard" respectively.

Huish's Colliery Sidings and Incline also drew his attention. He was concerned that the self-acting incline, down which coal tubs were bringing their valuable cargo from the pithead at Huish to sidings on the Radstock-Frome branch, might break away and hurtle across the GWR's passenger lines. In order to make sure that this did not happen, a strong and solid stone wall was to be built between the colliery siding and the passenger lines.

One additional point made by Yolland that, I feel, is worthy of note concerns a misunderstanding made by the man from the Board of Trade. He had obviously misinterpreted the warm local dialect for, in his report, he mentions that ". . . there is a steep incline from a colliery on a hill near Radstock (Whittinson and Hewitts) . . . ". This clearly refers to Huish and the phrase should, of course have read "Writhlington and Huish"! It is apparent that the inspector did not get the right message on this particular occasion.

At the Frome end of the branch, the single catch point situated at the junction of the coal siding with the Radstock branch near Frome West box was to be changed into a double junction with a dead-end spur. However, the short connecting third side link of the triangular junction arrangement at Frome, connecting Frome North and West boxes was incomplete at the time of Yolland's inspection. He could not give it the go-ahead and suggested that it would have to be re-examined at some later date. This was, in fact, precisely what happened and the chord, now an important part of the route of the stone traffic out of Whatley Quarry, was re-inspected in early September 1875. It was passed fit for traffic by Captain Tyler who was, at that time, inspecting the siding at Frome Market.

In concluding his report, Yolland recommended that the whole of the Radstock-Frome section should be very carefully gone over and all worn and damaged rails should be taken out and replaced by new ones without delay. However, he was unwilling to postpone, yet again, the opening of the line

Above: FROME MARKET SIDING
'Hymek' No. D7007 approaches Frome and is about to pass under the A361 main road near the town centre with a train from North Somerset Quarry Sidings. On the left is the loop line which served Frome Market. The old cattle pens can still be seen alongside this loop. The photograph was taken on 29th December 1967.

In September 1875, Frome Market Siding was inspected by Captain Tyler of the Board of Trade whose report on it read as follows "A loop siding has been added to the single line of the Radstock branch, and a signal cabin has been provided together with a locking frame, and the levers for working the points are interlocked with levers working signals in both directions. It is, however, proposed to keep a signalman on one day only in every week, and to lock it up on other days. The siding is only to be used by trains in possession of the train staff, which serves for securing safety on the single line. The signals in the two directions being interlocked with each other, it is at present impossible to lower them all at the same time. A special provision will therefore be required, to avoid compelling engine drivers, on days when the cabin is unoccupied, to run past signals at danger. For this purpose it will be necessary either to take the locks off the signal levers, so that they may be interlocked with the point levers only, or to adopt some means of causing all the signal arms to be kept down during the six days when the signals are not at work.

In any case, it is necessary to provide for the certainty of the apparatus being in proper working order on the one day in the week on which it will be worked, and for the employment at the cabin of a thoroughly responsible man on that day."

With this full report, and subject to the carrying out of his observations, Captain Tyler agreed to Market Siding being brought into use.

Hugh Ballantyne

and Frome were connected by through passenger trains which ran *via Radstock!*

"The opening of this branch of the GWR (Radstock-Frome) took place yesterday, the first train leaving Frome at 7.20am, in charge of Messrs Graham (District Superintendent), and Morrison, Liddiard and Robson (inspectors). The engine employed was driven by Mr Dennis Haycroft, and was profusely ornamented with flowers, evergreens and small coloured flags. The boon conferred upon the travelling public by the opening of this small branch is considerable. Improved communication is opened between Bristol and the Weymouth branch, in which Frome will especially benefit. Hitherto the journey to Bristol from Frome has occupied two hours; via Radstock it can be accomplished in an hour and a quarter, without change of carriage. There is now a double line of rails between Radstock and Mells, and it is intended to continue the second line to Frome*. The difference in the distance between the old and new routes to Bristol from Frome is nine miles only; the saving in time between the two is due to the train running direct between the two places. . . ."

Below: SERVICE TIMETABLE: 1877

Original: M. Wyatt

GREAT WESTERN RAILWAY.

BRISTOL TO RADSTOCK AND FROME.

Distance.	STATIONS.	UP TRAINS.—WEEK DAYS. 1 Coal.	2 Passenger.	3 Coal.	4 Coal.	5 Goods and Coal. A	6 Coal.	7 Passenger.	8 Coal.	9 Coal.	10 Passenger.	11 Coal.	12 Passenger.	13 Coal.	14 Coal.	15 Goods & Coal.	16 Passenger.	17	18	SUNDAY 1 Passenger.	2 Passenger.
		A.M.	A.M.	A.M.	A.M.	A.M.	A.M.	A.M.	A.M.	A.M.	P.M.	P.M.	P.M.	P.M.	P.M.	P.M.	P.M.			A.M.	P.M.
	Bristol dep.	.	**6 50**	.	.	7 20	.	**9 15**	.	.	**12 30**	.	**2 35**	.	.	3 30	**6 50**	.	.	**8 10**	5
2¼	Brislington ,,	..	6 57	..	..	7 35	..	9 22	..	..	—	..	2 42	..	..	4 0	6 57	..	..	8 17	5
6¾	Pensford arr.	...	—	...	...	7 55	...	—	...	...	—	...	—	...	...	4 20	—	...	...	—	—
	Pensford dep.	.	7 10	.	.	× 8 20	.	9 35	.	.	× 12 45	.	2 55	.	.	× 4 55	7 10	.	.	8 30	6
10	Clutton ,,	..	7 20	..	..	8 40	..	9 45	..	..	12 55	..	3 5	..	..	5 15	7 20	..	..	8 40	6
1¼	Hallatrow ,,	...	7 25	...	...	9 0	...	9 50	...	...	1 0	...	3 10	...	...	5 30	7 25	...	...	8 45	6
13½	Old Mills Siding ,,	.	—	.	.	CR	.	—	.	.	—	.	—	.	.	5 50	—	.	.	—	
14½	Welton ,,	..	7 35	..	..	9 20	..	10 0	..	..	1 10	..	3 20	..	..	6 15	7 35	..	..	8 55	6
	Wells Way ,,	...	—	...	..	—	...	—	...	...	—	...	—	...	...	—	—	...	...	—	
16	**Radstock** arr.	.	**7 40**	.		9 25	.	**10 5**	.	.	**1 15** ✗	.	**3 25**	.	.	6 25	**7 40** ✗	.	.	**9 0**	**6**
	Radstock dep.	6 0	**7 42**	8 5	..	..	9 30	**10 7**	11 0	..	**1 17**	1 30	**3 27**	..	3 45	...	**7 42**	..	..	**9 2**	**6**
19	Mells arr.	6 20	—	8 25	...	...	9 50	—	11 20	...	—	1 50	—	...	4 5	...	—	...	...	—	—
	Mells dep.	.	✗ 7 50	..	9 15	.	.	10 15	.	11 55	1 25	.	3 35	2 30	.	5 0	7 50	.	.	9 10	6
24¾	**Frome** arr.	..	**8 5**	..	9 40	..	..	**10 30**	..	12 20	**1 40**	..	**3 50**	2 55	..	5 25	8 5	..	..	**9 25**	**7**

✗ This mark indicates where Trains cross each other.

RADSTOCK AND FROME TO BRISTOL—*continued.*

Distance.	STATIONS.	DOWN TRAINS—WEEK DAYS. 1 Coal.	2 Passenger.	3 Coal.	4 Coal.	5 Coal.	6 Passenger.	7 Coal.	8 Coal.	9 Passenger.	10 Coal.	11 Coal.	12 Passenger.	13 Coal.	14 Coal.	15 Goods & Coal.	16 Passenger.	17	18	SUNDAYS 1 Passenger.	2 Passenger.
		A.M.	A.M.	A.M.	A.M.	A.M.	A.M.	A.M.	A.M.	P.M.	P.M.	P.M.	P.M.	P.M.	P.M.	P.M.	P.M.			A.M.	P.M.
	Frome dep.	.	**7 20**	8 30	.	.	**10 50**	.	11 15	**12 55**	.	1 50	**4 0**	.	4 15	.	**7 10**	.	.	**9 45**	**7**
5¾	Mells arr.	..	—	8 55	..	..	—	..	11 40	—	..	2 15	—	..	4 40	..	—	..	..	—	—
	Mells dep.	6 30	✗ 7 35	.	8 35	10 0	11 5	11 30	Goods	1 10	2 10	.	4 15	4 20	.	.	7 25	.	.	10 0	7
8¾	**Radstock** arr.	6 45	**7 43**	..	8 50	10 15	**11 13**	11 45	& Coal	**1 18** ✗	2 25	..	**4 23**	4 35	..	..	**7 33** ✗	..	..	**10 8**	**8**
	Radstock dep.	...	**7 45**	...	...	...	**11 15**	...	11 30	**1 20**	...	...	**4 25**	...	...	8 0	**7 40**	...	...	**10 10**	**8**
...	Wells Way	.	—	.	.	.	—	.	—	—	.	.	—	.	.	—	—	.	.	—	—
0¼	Welton	..	7 50	..	.	..	11 20	..	11 50	1 25	..	..	4 30	..	..	8 15	7 45	..	..	10 15	8
11¼	Old Mills Siding	...	—	...	...	...	—	...	—	—	...	...	—	...	...	CR	—	...	...	—	—
13½	Hallatrow	.	8 0	.	.	.	11 30	.	12 10	1 35	.	.	4 40	.	.	8 35	7 55	.	.	10 25	8
14¾	Clutton	..	8 5	..	..	..	11 35	..	CR	1 40	..	..	4 45	..	..	8 55	8 0	..	..	10 30	8
18	Pensford arr.	...	—	...	...	...	—	...	12 40	—	...	...	—	...	...	9 10	—	...	...	—	—
	Pensford dep.	.	× 8 15	.	.	.	11 45	.	× 12 45	1 50	.	.	× 4 55	.	.	9 30	8 10	.	.	10 40	8
22¼	Brislington ,,	..	8 27	..	..	..	11 57	..	1 5	2 2	..	..	5 7	..	..	9 50	8 22	..	..	10 52	8
24¾	**Bristol** arr.	...	**8 35**	...	...	...	**12 5**	...	1 15	**2 10**	...	...	**5 15**	...	...	10 0	**8 30**	...	...	**11 0**	**9**

A This Train will make a trip to Wells Way and back (between the arrival of the 9.15 a.m. from Bristol, and the departure of the 11,15 a.m. from Radstock), when required. The Guard to receive his instructions from Mr. Rowley.

CROSSING INSTRUCTIONS.

The 7.20 a.m. Bristol Goods and the 7.20 a.m. Frome Passenger Trains cross at Pensford.
The 12.30 p.m. ,, Passenger ,, 11.30 a.m. Radstock Goods ,, ,, ,, ,,
The 3.30 p.m. ,, Goods ,, 4. 0 p.m. Frome Passenger ,, ,, ,, ,,
The 6.50 a.m. ,, Passenger ,, 7.20 a.m. Frome Passenger ,, ,, ,, Mells
The 12.30 p.m. ,, ,, ,, 12.55 p.m. ,, ,, ,, ,, ,, Radstock.
The 6.50 p.m. ,, ,, ,, 7.10 p.m. ,, ,, ,, ,, ,, ,,

The Line from Bristol to Radstock is single (Pensford is the intermediate Crossing Station), from Radstock to Mells, double, and from Mells to Frome Junction, single. The single portions are worked by Train Staff and Auxiliary Disc Telegraph. The following are the particulars of the Staffs and Tickets.

SECTION.	Form of Staff and Tickets.	Colour of Ticket.
Bristol and Pensford.	Square.	Red.
Pensford and Radstock.	Triangular	Blue.
Mells and Frome Junction	Round.	White.

whether it be for this reason or because the points and signals had not, in all cases, been connected up to their respective levers in the signal boxes! Instead he stated that " . . . provided these few requirements were attended to – and provided also that a satisfactory undertaking as to the mode of working be received from the company . . ." the line could open for through traffic.

On 5th July 1875 all was clearly well, for at long last, Bristol

*This was never, in fact, laid in.
(Source: Western Daily Press Tuesday 6th July 1875)

WEYMOUTH WANDERINGS
With a full head of steam, ex-GWR Mogul No. 7316 of the 4300 class bashes up towards Mells Road Halt with a Weymouth excursion on 5th August 1959. Weymouth had always been a popular destination for specials off the North Somerset branch.

George Tucker (1822-1910), a colliery blacksmith at Radstock, provided evidence of these railway trips way back in the 1870s. In his diary he mentions that in July 1875 the Wesleyans went to Weymouth over the GWR as did the enginemen, bailiffs and mechanics from Writhlington pits.

P. J. Williams

Although the Bristol & North Somerset Railway was now open for passenger and freight traffic, it was still not financially successful. Theoretically open for both kinds of traffic, it was essentially only handling passengers since its most important potential traffic, namely coal, could not be handled because, at this point in time at least, there was a shortage of sidings at pits served by the new line. On top of all these problems the opening of the Somerset & Dorset's Bath Extension in 1874 meant that cheap coal was now actually coming *into* the area from the Midlands!

However, there were some bright signs in that the Directors' Report for 1874/75 stated that arrangements for completing the sidings had been made and that advertisements had been issued for tenders for their immediate construction. The report also gave the line's gross receipts over the period from 1st July 1874 to 30th June 1875 as being some £11,967. Nevertheless, the gloomy outlook continued and a year later there was still considerable worry and discussion about the unsatisfactory state of traffic leading out of the GWR's way of working the branch.

Indeed, so much concern was felt that at a board meeting held in July 1877 the working of the North Somerset came under very close scrutiny. The directors were hopeful that steps could be taken to put things right in order that the Company's debt to the Earl of Warwick could be cleared and a dividend might be paid! The key problem, however, was that the GWR was still not giving the local company any through traffic. On top of all these other problems the shareholders showed little interest in the line; the value of the company's shares had dropped while in 1876 the Company had lost over £5,600!

In August 1877 the Board had told the shareholders that certain proposals were being made to the GWR for the improvement of traffic on the line. In addition, they had secured the services of Mr Cawkwell, a former General Manager of the London & North Western Railway, and the GWR had agreed to meet him to discuss complaints raised by the North Somerset company. Of course, the key issue was still the one of there being no through goods traffic with the GWR. On top of all this, an order had been taken out by the Board of Trade concerning the level crossings at Radstock. The Board of Trade wanted these replaced. In reality, both the North Somerset and the Somerset & Dorset ignored this order and the level crossings in the centre of the town remained a notable part of the local Radstock scene until well into the 1970s!

At yet another meeting, this time held on 23rd October 1877, the Board discussed the state of play in its negotiations with the GWR. On the Great Western's side, Mr Grierson was prepared to alter the train arrangements and, he said that if the North Somerset board wished to discuss any questions regarding the purchase of the B&NSR by his company, it would be possible for fresh proposals to be put to the GWR's board of directors. After careful consideration, this was, in fact, what happened, but agreement was still not reached between the two companies. Because of this failure to agree, the North Somerset decided to prepare a bill for the 1878 parliamentary session to put an end to the then existing arrangements with the GWR. The bill would allow the North Somerset to work the line and would, in addition, allow the Company to continue using the level crossing at Radstock.

In the new year, 1878, little progress was made with the North Somerset's negotiations with the GWR. Indeed, concern with the lack of progress was highlighted in the way that the North Somerset cancelled its half-yearly meeting to allow the discussions to continue. In April, the debate concerning the Company's liabilities, including the North Somerset's problems with land owned by Lady Waldegrave and with the level crossing at Radstock, continued. By the end of April more bad news

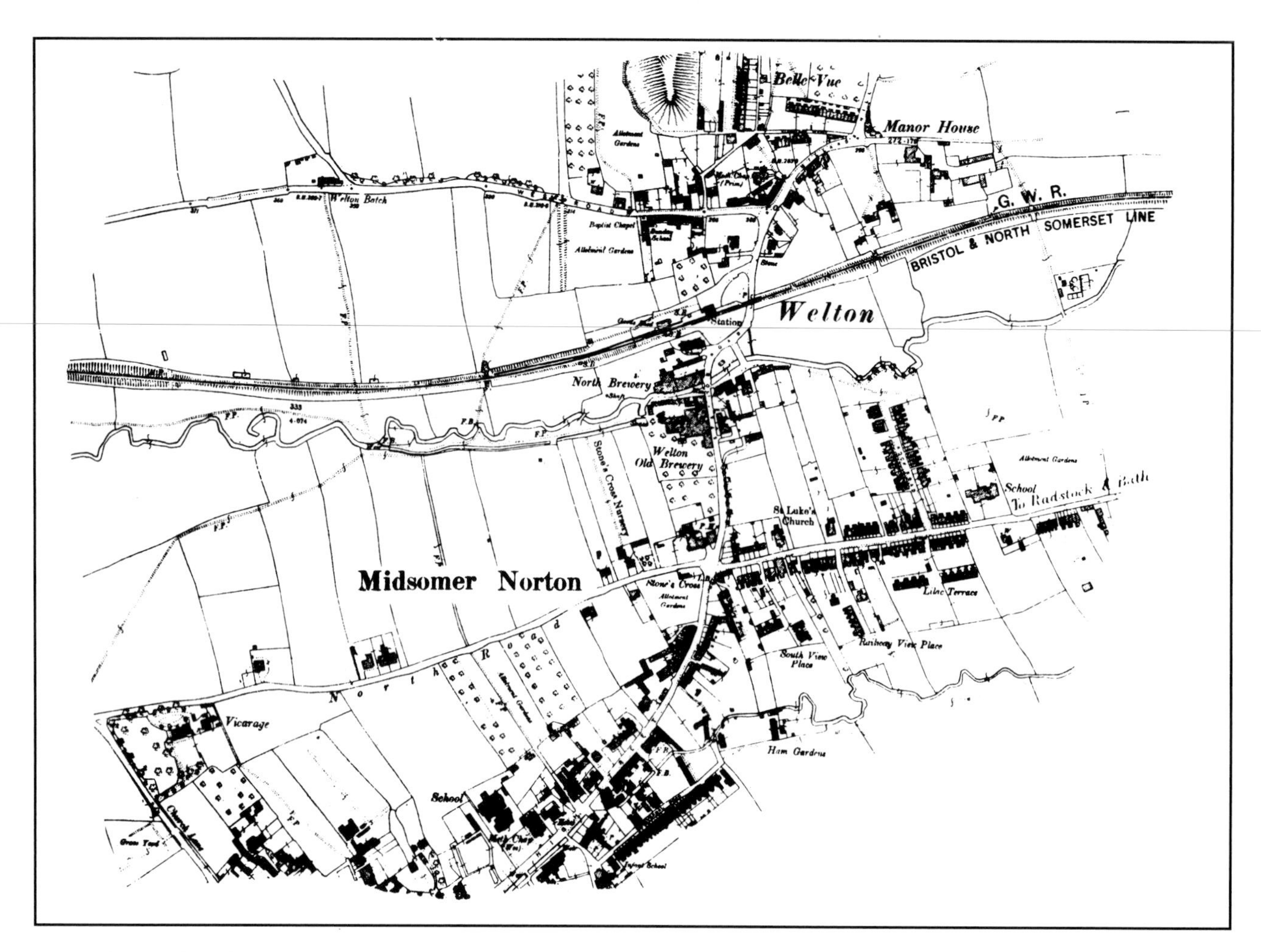

WELTON STATION & VILLAGE 1888

Original plan: A. Church

was showered on the Company in that the GWR had refused to entertain the North Somerset's new proposals. By September 1878, the conversations at Paddington were at an end. In addition, arrangements were being made to give up surplus land at Radstock with a view to getting the account with Lady Waldegrave settled. Arbitration with the GWR on the matter of sidings and other works along the line were also given the go-ahead.

The Coming of the Bristol & North Somerset Railway and its Impact upon the Rural Way of Life

Mr Amos Church of Welton tells the following story that gives some personal insight into the impact that the coming of the Bristol & North Somerset Railway had upon the rural way of life.

Mr Church's grandfather told of the time he was living with his parents at Millards Hill Farm and when the old Somerset & Dorset tramroad was still serving the pit at Welton Hill. At that time, however, around 1879/80 the North Somerset was still the area's big attraction since the line's regular passenger service offered delights previously unimagined by the inhabitants of Welton.

Mr Church's great grandmother was determined to see the sights of London and she travelled up on the first excursion from Welton station to the metropolis. She had saved the fare of £3, which must have seemed quite a lot of money in the late 1870s.

The return train from London arrived back at Welton station at around 1.30am the following morning. When she knocked on her own front door, her husband, Mr Church's great grandfather, Uriah, shouted out from the bedroom window, "Who's there?" She replied, "It's your wife!" "Oh no, you're not!" he retorted, "She's gone to London!".

Since he refused to open the door until daybreak, she had to sleep in the barn!

With thanks to A. Church.

People at Pensford During the 1870s and 1880s

The station book at Pensford for January 1879 has the following entries:

> "Elly, Joseph, Signalman, on duty in time to give line clear for 6.50am passenger train. Dinner time 1.00pm to 2.00pm. Off duty after receiving line clear for last passenger train 9.00pm. Meal times subject to trains.
>
> Price, Thomas Henry, General Porter, on duty at 7.00am. Breakfast 8.40am to 9.10am. Dinner and tea time one hour the former, and half hour the latter, to be taken without interfering with trains, to speak to signalman upon leaving so that he may look to safety of station and answer enquiries during the time. Off duty after last train. No duty paper supplied.
>
> On Sundays the duties are performed by Elly and Price separately and then together. Waiting rooms and offices to receive the same attention as on other days."

(Original document courtesy Mr H. Wyatt)

The following are details of what are believed to be the duties of the stationmaster at Pensford. They are outlined in a notice dated the 12th August 1885:

> To personally receive and deliver Train Staff and Train Ticket.
>
> To see that all signal and platform lamps are kept clean and lighted at the proper time also that the Booking Office, Waiting Rooms, Signal Box and all offices are kept clean and tidy.
>
> To visit signal box often and see that the duties are properly performed and that the necessary entries are properly made in the Line Clear Book and to sign same daily.
>
> To test the signal and points often.
>
> To see that all tickets are cancelled immediately after being collected and sent to Audit Office daily, responsible for the collection of all monies and accounts; to strictly comply with all rules in Book

of General Instructions and Special Instructions for the safe working of the line (see rules 103 to 143) and to see that the same are acted up to, not to be absent from duty during duty hours except by Authority and proper arrangements made for the performance of your duties.
To transact all businesses in a manner most conducive to the interest of the Company.
To be relieved by the signalman from duty every third Sunday, also daily for the first trains, the signalman then being responsible for the working of the Train Staff or Ticket as per Mr Walton's notice dated 12th August 1885.
To go to meals when convenient . . . (and) not to miss any trains.

On duty at 7.30am, off duty at passing the last train.

The stationmaster at this time was thought to be a Mr J.R. Langdon.
(Original document courtesy Mr H. Wyatt)

By 1880 things were no better and discussions were still continuing on further terms put forward by the GWR for the North Somerset's amalgamation with the Great Western. Early in 1881 new terms were put forward by the GWR but these were turned down by the North Somerset's shareholders, of all people! Indeed, a large number of them made it clear to both sets of directors that they did not want to sell the line. At a meeting in May 1881, the Chairman of the North Somerset's board admitted that he knew that what the GWR was proposing to pay did not give the ordinary shareholder very much. Nevertheless, he had reminded them that these negotiations had been going on for quite a long time now!

He went on to say that they were now working the railway by agreement with the GWR that, and as far as the shareholders were concerned, it was not being worked successfully as far as their interests went. The Company was paying £8,500 per year as part of that agreement and this sum would continue to rise until, in 1888, it would reach £11,550. The Board had looked very carefully into the figures. It felt that the Company was paying the absolute maximum it could afford. There had been a continuous battle over and about the line and the directors thought that it would be to the benefit of everyone involved to bring things to a settlement in the way they had put forward. The GWR were certainly not going to give any more than they currently had on offer because the figures that had been mentioned actually represented more, in fact, than the North Somerset earned!

However, they also realised that if the matter was not agreed to by at least three quarters of the shareholders who voted, the matter would fall through yet again. As we have seen, that is precisely what happened.

"A Frightful Accident Occurred on the GWR at Radstock"

"A frightful accident occurred on the GWR at Radstock on Thursday morning. About 10.00am a porter named James Higgs was engaged with others, shunting some trucks loaded with coal, and he had just attached a chain to the trucks, the order being given to the driver of the engine to proceed when, by some means, he was caught by the chain and thrown down. Four of the trucks passed over his thighs mangling them in a most frightful manner. He was conveyed to the waiting room of the station and attended to by Dr Worger of Radstock who rendered every assistance and recommended his immediate removal to the Bristol General Hospital. Mr Rowley, stationmaster, at once despatched a special engine and carriage to Bristol but when the injured man arrived at the hospital, life was extinct. The poor fellow, who had been many years in the company's service, leaves a wife and children."
(Source: Western Daily Press 23rd January 1881)

Following the rejection of the Board of Directors' advice to take the GWR's offer, changes took place in the membership of the Board, adding even more uncertainty to an already uncertain phase in the line's history. By the summer of 1881 things had got so serious that the Earl of Warwick, who was still owed some £113,000 by the Company, decided to set legal proceedings in motion. In January 1882, the courts found in favour of the Earl but, unfortunately for the North Somerset, the directors had no cash to meet the judgement. The Court of Chancery took charge of the Company's affairs and appointed three of the line's directors to be receivers and managers of the Company. However, yet another shock was on the way for both the North Somerset and the GWR. This would be enough to help to break the deadlock that had existed

RADSTOCK LOOKING TOWARDS THE GWR STATION FROME ABOVE LUDLOWS COLLIERY c1900
This rather pleasing view across Radstock shows Ludlows Colliery in the right foreground and the GWR station with its early wooden signal box in the middle distance. The GWR goods yard can be seen on the left, while the S&D station (with train) can be seen on the right. The photograph was very likely taken in the early years of the 20th century.
Gerald Quartley

between the two companies for so many years. This shock was thrown up by another proposed railway in the area, a line with the grand title of the Bristol & South Western Junction Railway.

This particular project created an enormous amount of interest when the bill allowing its construction was deposited in the autumn of 1882. The bill's intention was the construction of a railway connecting the LSWR near Andover with the town of Radstock. It would have run via Amesbury and Westbury across the Wiltshire Downs. At Radstock the new route would have divided into two, one branch swinging over onto the North Somerset line, the other hitching into the Somerset & Dorset's main line near Wellow, south of Bath. Trains could therefore get into Bristol by both routes. The most direct was by the North Somerset's metals. The longer, slightly more circuitous option, was via the Somerset & Dorset and Midland main lines via Bath.

Mr ROWLEY OF RADSTOCK (GWR)
Mr Rowley came to Radstock when its sole railway connection with the outside world was the mineral-only line to Frome. It would seem that he started work on the GWR at Radstock in 1857, retiring some forty years later on 26th March 1897. By 1861 he was a commercial agent on the railway and, at some time between then and 1881, he became station master, possibly in September 1873 when the station opened its doors for passenger businesss.

On his retirement in 1897 the staff at Radstock station gave him a gold mounted walking stick which was engraved "Presented to Mr C. A. Rowley by the staff at Radstock Station March 1897".

Tony Lecouteur

The bill made provision for the doubling of the North Somerset between Radstock and Bristol and gave the LSWR compulsory running powers over the GWR's North Somerset branch. Indeed, the promoters of the new route regarded the North Somerset as an essential element in their overall scheme in that it gave them the principal access into Bristol.

In the city itself a short link was to be made with a new central station. This spur line would have branched off the North Somerset's route between North Somerset Junction and its crossing of the River Avon. It would have run through a mass of working class properties in the areas situated between St Philip's Marsh and the city centre. At that time, the River Frome, in the area around today's centre, was open to the skies and, as part of the scheme, it was intended that the line's passenger terminus would have been built on a section of the Floating Harbour (into which the River Frome emptied), the latter being especially covered over for the purpose! A goods station was also to have been constructed and this would have been built at Lewins Mead, on a site just to the north of today's modern city centre. The distance from the B&SWJR's passenger terminus to Waterloo would have been roughly 130 miles, some twelve miles longer than the GWR's direct route to London via Bath.

John Latimer, the noted Bristol historian and writer, had the following comments to make about the public's response to the project:

Mr CARTER OF RADSTOCK (GWR)
This charming photograph shows a Mr Carter who was a porter/signalman at Radstock (GWR) station from the early 1920s through to 1938. As signalman he worked first at the "Gates" (North signal box) and then at the "Yard" (South signal box)

Mrs G. Shearn

> "The scheme met with an amount of approval rarely accorded to local plans of improvement, the provisional committee formed for promoting the Bill comprising the majority of the Council and of the leading mercantile firms, while the Merchants' Society made a liberal grant towards the expenses; the Chamber of Commerce forwarded petitions in favour of the scheme, and meetings in its support were held in every ward. In fact, as was observed at the time, Bristolians presented the rare spectacle of being unanimous."

Problems did arise, however, and not everyone agreed that it was a good scheme, notably the GWR itself who opposed the railway before Parliament. The company said that it did not believe that the Bristol & South Western Junction Railway would take away any of its express passenger traffic, although it had to concede that it would, in all probability, lose some of its third class business.

In addition, the Midland Railway opposed the scheme, particularly those parts of the bill relating to the use of the North Somerset. It also objected to the building of the central station. Early in April 1883, just before the bill came before the Committee of the House of Commons, the promoters agreed to drop those parts objected to by the Midland and a modified plan was put forward. This proposed a line from Andover to join the Somerset & Dorset at Wellow. From there to Bath the track was to have been doubled, trains from Bath to Bristol being taken on their way by the Midland. Making these alterations would cut the cost from its original (and massive) £1,866,000 to a mere (!) £790,000. Indeed, scrapping the central terminus would in itself have saved around £600,000! As a might-have-been the plan was magnificent and the thought of catching a train to London from the very heart of Bristol is, in a way perhaps, even more thought-provoking today than it was in 1883.

After a very hard struggle with the GWR before the House of Commons' Committee, it was decided that the bill's preamble had not been proved. It was thrown out. Nonetheless, the GWR had been badly frightened. It was, therefore, not surprising that the scheme had some important side effects, one of which was that, shortly afterwards, the GWR and the LSWR boards entered into a peace agreement by which they both agreed not to involve themselves in aggressive moves, one towards the other, over the next ten years.

In addition, in July 1883, new fast trains to London from Bristol were put into service on the GWR. These left Temple Meads at 9.35am, arriving at Paddington at 12.25pm, a total journey time of 2 hours 50 minutes. In the evening, the return working left the London terminus at 6.20pm, arriving back at Bristol at 9.15pm, a run of some 2 hours 55 minutes. Both trains carried third class passengers for whom poor provision had been a regular complaint in Bristol.

Finally, and most importantly for the North Somerset company, it would seem that the Bristol & South Western Junction's plan was just the push that the GWR needed to take over the small, impecunious line struggling through the North Somerset Coalfield. And so, at a half-yearly meeting of the GWR held at Paddington on 14th February 1884, approval was given to the bill for vesting in the GWR, the Bristol & North Somerset Railway Company.

The small, local company was absorbed on 1st July 1884, the actual assimilation process continuing on through the summer of the same year. It would seem that the threat of the Bristol & South Western Junction scheme had given the GWR's directors quite a nasty fright and, very quickly, they went ahead and purchased this struggling little line: a stretch of railway with which they had toyed and by which they had been bothered for some twenty odd years!

Another interesting and also unbuilt scheme of the 1880s was the Radstock, Wrington & Congresbury Junction Railway, an impressive title for a small country railway intended to wander through the Yeo Valley from the Bristol & Exeter Railway at Congresbury (on the Wells to Yatton branch) to Farrington Gurney on the Bristol & North Somerset Railway. The provisional prospectus for the proposed line showed a capital of £180,000 in £10 shares. Borrowing powers of £60,000 were also covered.

The new line was to be about 14½ miles long, while its cost was put at around £141,000. The engineer, Mr R. Price Williams of 38 Parliament Street, Westminster, London, said that the intended cost per mile of the new line would be about £9,500 which compared very favourably with the average cost of £25,000 per mile for the North Somerset Railway. The project had been well received by the local landowners and had the Great Western's full support. Indeed, an agreement was signed with the GWR on 11th May 1882 for that company to operate the intended route for 50% of the gross receipts. The future looked good.

Furthermore, the provisional prospectus looked very much on the bright side when it came to the proposed line's traffic potential:

> "A considerable passenger traffic may thus be looked for, but an important feature in the undertaking is the traffic in minerals. The intended railway will skirt the northern base of the Mendip hills, known to be rich in iron, lead, and other mineral deposits, hitherto unavailable from the absence of the means of the cheap transport. At and near Farrington Gurney and Radstock numerous collieries are already in operation, the produce of which will find the shortest and cheapest route to the West of England by means of the intended railway. It is believed that coal pits are about to be sunk at Blue Bowl and Ubley, upon the route of the new line. There is no doubt of the existence of beds of coal; and iron ore is now extensively worked in the neighbourhood of Winford, to the northward of the line, where there is at present no railway accommodation. From surveys made, a railway connexion with these appears to be feasible, and may form a future extension and valuable traffic."

THE ROUTE OF THE PROPOSED RADSTOCK, WRINGTON & CONGRESBURY JUNCTION RAILWAY: 1882

Original plan: Somerset Record Office

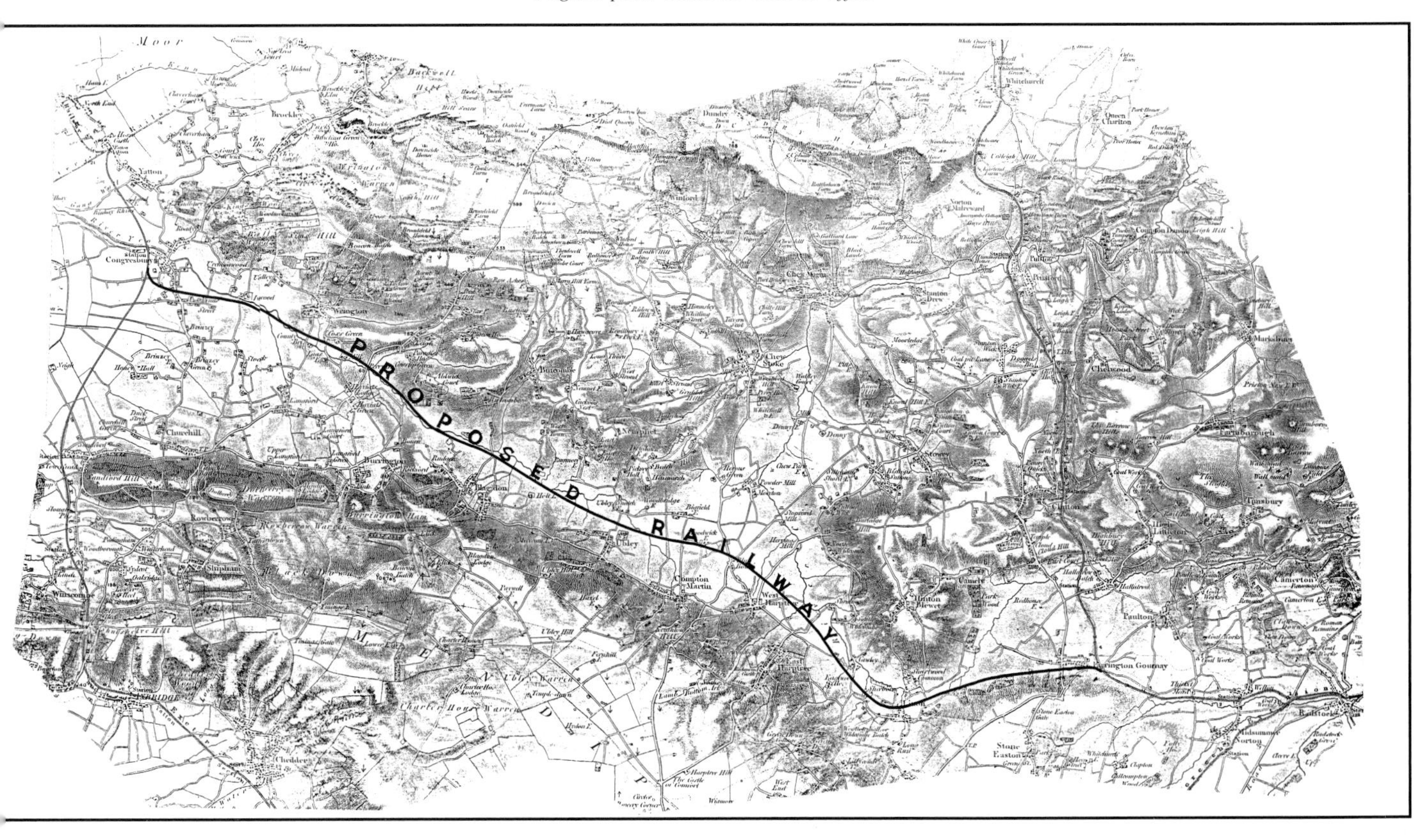

A report in the Bath Chronicle for 27th April 1882 gave further details of the new line. It was opposed by the North Somerset since they felt it would take traffic away from them. However, a strong lobby of landowners, ably supported by McMurtrie in Radstock, were very much in favour. They were probably sick of the B&NSR by now and wanted an alternative to the service provided by that company.

In the House of Commons, and after consulting in private, the committee investigating the proposed line decided that the bill's preamble had been proved and so, on 18th August 1882, the Radstock, Wrington & Congresbury Junction Railway received the Royal Assent. However, in spite of the enthusiasm and optimism of the promoters, sufficient capital could not be raised and the project had to be abandoned. The company was finally dissolved by an act dated 4th June 1886.

Greater success did, however, come to the long-suffering villagers of Mells and its surrounding countryside for, in 1887, a station was built and opened on a site adjacent to Mells Road good shed. The Somerset Standard for 26th February reported that on the following Friday, 4th March 1887, the station at Mells Road would officially open for passenger and parcels traffic. All trains from Frome and Bristol would call there – and that is all the newspaper had to say on the matter. The Somerset & Wilts Journal did not even report that much! It only very briefly commented on the almost-hidden, extra name in the GWR timetable for March. On reflection, it seems a strange sense of news value the editors of the time must have had, to hardly mention the opening of a railway station, but to give some twelve column inches to a breathless account of the local hunt's last meet! Certainly the railways were no longer as newsworthy as they once had been.

Interestingly enough, it would appear from the Inspecting Officer's report on the 1887 works at Mells that only new

AT MELLS AND HEADING FOR MARCROFT'S WAGON WORKS
On 14th April 1978 a Thos Hill 4-wheel diesel hydraulic locomotive, belonging to the quarry firm of ARC, is seen at Mells Road, heading for repairs at Marcroft's Wagon Works at Radstock.

Mike Miller

Right: MELLS ROAD 1985
This view shows the former station site at Mells Road in April 1985. It was taken looking towards Radstock and follows the now single line as it humps its way down Mells bank. The grey skies reflect an unhappy scene of decay and desolation. Evidence of the sleeper depot can be seen to the left of the picture.

Barbara Zadarnowski

Below: THE GOODS SHED AT MELLS (GWR) *Collection: Lord Oxford*

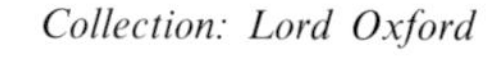

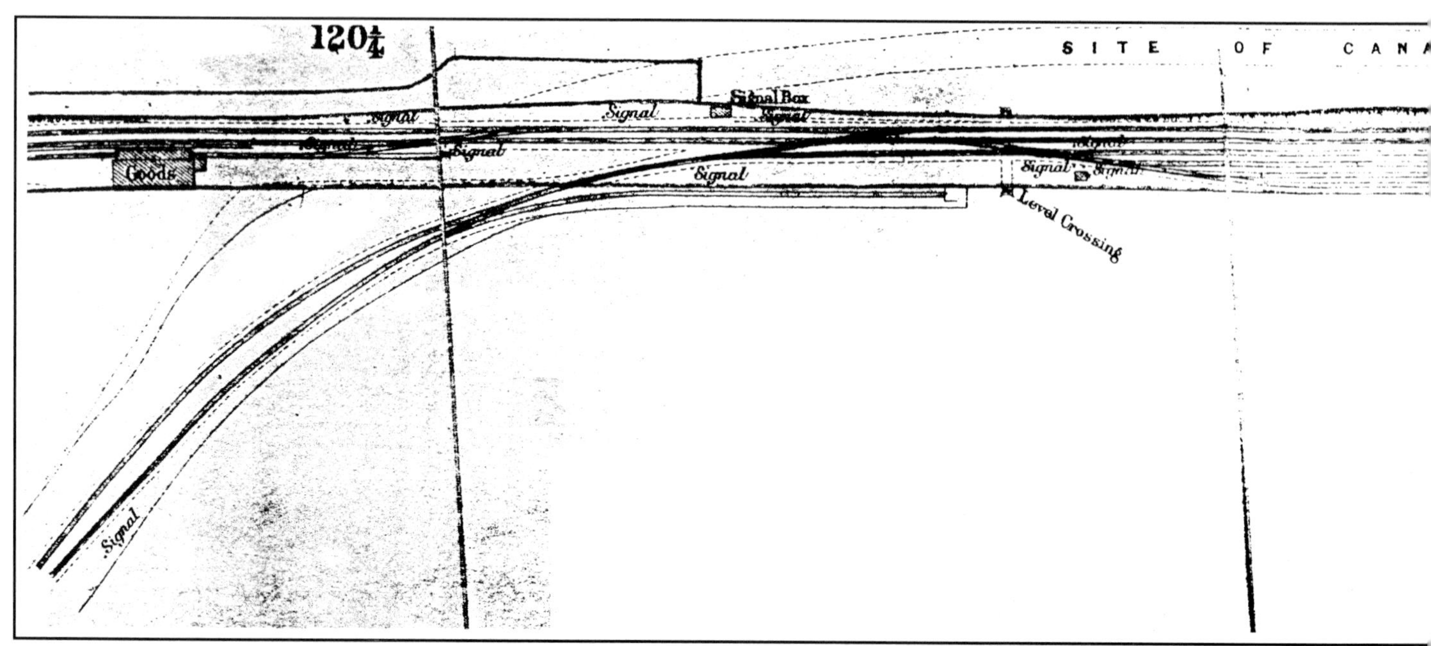

THE CONSTRUCTION OF EAST DEPOT: UP AND DOWN SIDINGS, ST ANNE'S, BRISTOL
This view, taken c1889, shows the construction of Bristol, East Depot, 'Up and Down' sidings. These two groups of sidings were opened c1890. Around this time, the North Somerset branch, which can be seen in the left background of this picture, ran southbound towards Brislington on a slightly straighter alignment. However, in 1892, a triangular junction was brought into use from the down sidings, seen here to the left, and this forced the North Somerset branch to swing around a tighter curve into the Bristol-Paddington main line at North Somerset Junction.

(Note the GWR's original London line heading towards Bath still on the mixed gauge.)

R. Winstone

items constructed at that time were the platforms themselves. Further alterations were carried out in 1910/1911 when, among other things, the platforms were lengthened. Possibly the station buildings had been brought into use by then? The work at Mells was a concrete example of the fact that the GWR was now in charge of the North Somerset. At long, long last through and local traffic, both passenger and freight, were being encouraged.

Another instance of this overall development of the branch from Bristol right through to Frome occurred in 1890 at Clutton station. In May of that year the GWR informed the Board of Trade that they were about to provide an additional platform on the eastern side of the station. There was also to be an increase in the number of sidings provided. However, in order to make a start on this work, some major re-organisation of the pointwork at the Radstock end had to be brought about and new facing points would have to be installed so that the station's freight traffic could be worked. On 7th May 1890 the Board of Trade gave provisional clearance for the work to be carried out, official approval following on the 9th.

On 21st June the GWR informed the Board of Trade that the work at Clutton would be finished and ready for examination by 1st July. However, the actual inspection by Colonel Rich did not take place until 1st September when Rich reported that he had gone over the new arrangements. The points and signals were interlocked and were worked from a new signal cabin which contained 26 working and 3 spare levers. Rich was satisfied with the quality of the new arrangements and recommended that they be brought into immediate use.

However, it seems that we have moved rather a long way forward in time in our discussions about the development of what are essentially the passenger services and facilities provided by the North Somerset branch. Let us now move back a little chronologically and examine, in more depth, the working of the line's main reason for being, namely its freight traffic and, in particular, its coal trade.

EAST DEPOT, UP AND DOWN SIDINGS ST ANNE'S, BRISTOL
With an 'up' HST accelerating hard towards the Georgian city of Bath, this photograph is taken from the same location as the view above except that some 96 years have elapsed in the meantime! Many changes have taken place not least of which is the fact that both sets of sidings were officially closed in August 1967. By 1985, when this picture was taken, the Down Sidings had been taken over by the civil engineering department while the Up Loop and Sidings were disused and rusting; quite clearly modern railways are long, thin creations!

Kim Bultitude

6
Collieries, Connections and the North Somerset Railway

THE SOMERSET COALFIELD
Ludlows Colliery, Radstock. *Original: Tony Lecouteur*

In the "Coalfield Cameo – The Somerset Coalfield" a brief introduction was given to the overall development of the Somerset Coalfield. In this, the book's most substantial chapter, we are going to examine much more closely the development of those collieries that were either directly linked into or, at some period, fed some of their output onto the North Somerset Railway between Bristol and the Radstock district. In Chapter 11, "Inclined Planes, Wagon Works and Industrial Lines", we shall continue to look at collieries in North Somerset by concerning ourselves with those formerly found in the Mells and Newbury areas. Pits in the Cam Valley will be examined in the next chapter, "Hallatrow: Change for the Camerton Line" while the sketch map on page 71 gives an overall view of all collieries, in both this and other chapters, in which we have a particular interest.

Clattering over North Somerset Junction and heading south from Bristol, the area around Pensford provides us with the first two pits that we shall look at in more detail. The first of these, at Bromley, was linked to the second at Pensford, by a tramway. In turn, this latter colliery was connected to the Bristol/Radstock line by a self-acting incline, the colliery pithead being some 100ft *above* the railway. By 1912 this incline was in operation and remained so until the colliery itself closed in the late 1950s.

Bromley Colliery

Bromley Colliery appears to have had all the elements of a slight and unimportant colliery in the Somerset Coalfield. With its small sized shaft and twisting underground roadways, its low output and diminutive tramway tubs, it would seem to have been an early example of the "small is beautiful" philosophy! The earliest mention of the pit is in 1893. In 1909 proposals were put forward for the sinking of a neighbouring pit at Pensford and, at that time, ownership of Bromley moved from the Bromley Colliery Company to the Pensford & Bromley Collieries Limited. The business umbilical cord had been developed and soon a more physical connection would grow between the sites of the two pits.

In order to send its coal away, a tramway was built from the pithead at Bromley to the emergent colliery at Pensford. From Pensford Colliery the coal would be transferred to the GWR's North Somerset line. The tramway, which was of 2ft gauge was just about one mile in length and ran in a virtually straight line, and in a south-westerly direction, from Pensford Colliery. At first, propulsion on the tramway was provided by an 0-4-0 side tank locomotive built by the Avonside Engine Company of Bristol (builder's No. 1593) which, not surprisingly in the circumstances, carried the name *Bromley No. 1.* However, its tendency to come off the rails and be unable to pull the loads required of it, made it an unpopular purchase and around January 1913 it was sold to the Old Delabole Slate Company Limited in Cornwall.

Obviously unhappy with locomotives providing the power for the tramway the company installed a main-and-tail rope haulage system. In this form the tramway lasted until the pit's

Left: COLLIERY FEEDERS TO THE GWR'S BRISTOL-RADSTOCK-FROME LINE

Chris Handley

closure in 1957. At first the main-and-tail engine was installed at Bromley Pit but about 1916 it was moved across to Pensford Colliery. Nonetheless, the tramway did add to the cost of the coal obtained at Bromley. Indeed, the cost of digging out and raising coal in the difficult conditions run up against by the miners at Bromley Pit meant that costs were always high. The colliery struggled through what was, in many ways, a precarious existence until nationalisation and once the NCB came on the scene it was clear that Bromley's time would soon be up. And so it was! On 18th May 1957 the colliery stopped shifting Somerset coal and today very little remains of a pastoral pit.

It is perhaps worth adding in here that Bromley Colliery was the last in Somerset to use horses, of which there were four at closure, for hauling coal tubs underground. The four, whose names were Paul, Tiger, Wake and Temple (Ginger), were well looked after by Mr Walter Tovey of Stanton Drew. Paul, the last of the four to finish work, was used to help in the dismantling of the pit, hauling machinery, rails, steel roof supports, etc underground until he too was finally retired. As for the 75 men then employed at Bromley, they were all offered, and with the exception of two, took the offer of transferring to the nearby Pensford Colliery which, ironically enough, was itself closed some eighteen months later.

Pensford Colliery

One of the newer collieries in the Somerset Coalfield, Pensford and its tips were, and in the case of the latter, are still a prominent and well-known sight, or blot, depending on your viewpoint, on the North Somerset countryside. On Christmas Day 1909 the colliery's existence was confirmed when the earliest known lease on the pit was signed. The following year two 14ft diameter shafts were sunk but tremendous difficulties were met with water and by the year of the outbreak of the First World War

Below: BRISTOL-BOUND THROUGH BRISLINGTON
With Somerset coal in tow, 2251 class 0-6-0 No. 3215 shuffles through Brislington heading towards Bristol. It is 1958 and the line's decline is not far away.

M.B. Warburton/R. Griffiths

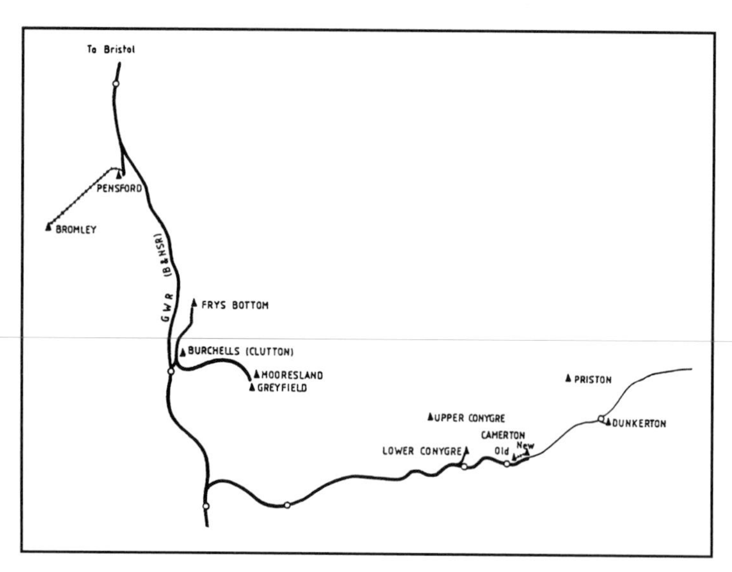

COLLIERY FEEDERS TO THE NORTH SOMERSET LINE (NORTHERN SECTION)

Chris Handley

in 1914, the two shafts were still unfinished. The war then delayed the pit's progress and it was not until 1917 that *regular* winding of coal began.

Because of the difference in height between the pithead of the colliery and the North Somerset (the railway was at a much lower level than the pithead), an incline was needed and was built under an agreement signed on 9th September 1910. However, the initial layout put forward would have made working somewhat awkward and so new plans were proposed on 15th March 1911. These increased the length of the incline but, in consequence, reduced its steepness. With these changes put into action the incline was then built, and it was at work in 1912. More details of its actual working can be found in chapter eleven. At the foot of the incline exchange sidings with the GWR were provided, and wagons were gravity worked into these.

On the railway side the new works brought into use to serve the colliery were inspected by Board of Trade Inspector Yorke and he produced the following report on 2nd March 1912:

"I have inspected the new works near Pensford on the Radstock branch of the GWR. The line is single and worked on the electric train staff system. The new works comprise a loop for goods trains, having connections with the main line at each end. A new signal box has been built which contains 26 levers in use and 6 spaces.

I noticed that the semaphore signals leading from the loop on to the main line are fitted with white lights for danger. These lights should be red, in accordance with Board of Trade regulations.

Owing to the gradient, it is necessary that all trains doing work at the sidings should be placed in the loop before any shunting commences.

Subject to these two conditions being complied with, I can recommend the Board of Trade to sanction the use of these new works."

In spite of all these new arrangements to take away the coal and because of the cost of them, the pit's original owners, the Pensford & Bromley Collieries Limited, ran at a loss after 1918. A new company was formed, this being registered on 5th February 1921. However, the new company's finances were still very uncertain, particularly during the 1930s, and it was not until 1939 that profits started to be commonly made.

Around 1930, Pensford was one of the first pits in Somerset to make regular use of coal cutters. However, one of the disadvantages of using them was that they generated a good deal of rubbish. This dirt and debris was tipped between the incline and the GWR's North Somerset line and it was this tip that slipped late in December 1946, burying the main line. Although the NCB had prepared a modernisation plan for Pensford, full mechanisation could not be implemented due to difficult geological conditions. It therefore came as no real surprise that in November 1958 the decision was taken to bring the pit's life to an end, and on 13th December, the last coal was wound.

The closure took place in two stages during November 1958 and the 328 men affected were offered employment at other collieries in the Somerset & Bristol Group. Pensford's labour force was thus cut in half on 17th November and, about a month later, the number of men working at the colliery was cut again, leaving some 60-70 colliers to withdraw machinery and materials from the now-dying pit.

According to the local press the NCB had said that since nationalisation they had tried various methods to keep coal production up at Pensford but geological disturbances had meant that broken and faulted coal seams had led to conditions which required that working had to be changed almost daily. Planning ahead had been almost impossible and it had eventually proved impracticable to work the pit, even at a "reasonable loss". In addition, production from other Somerset & Bristol Group collieries had very much improved but that at Pensford had lagged behind. In 1948 Pensford had produced some 90,000 tons of coal a year; in 1957 that figure had dropped to 72,000 tons, whilst in the first half of 1958 this was down again to 28,000 tons. The Somerset & Bristol Group as a whole had produced some 624,000 tons in 1957.

Nationally more coal was being dug up than was being burnt at this time and so collieries were having to stockpile it on the surface. In Somerset, they were also stockpiling but, in contrast with the rest of the country where large coal for household use was in short supply and small coal was piling up, Somerset was able to dispose of all its small coal and had just over 6,000 tons of large coal unsold on the surface. Coal was stockpiled in this way at Kilmersdon, Old Mills, New Rock (near Chilcompton) and Harry Stoke (near Filton in Bristol).

PREPARATIONS FOR WORK AT PENSFORD COLLIERY
With difficulties being encountered underground, the pit at Pensford is seen here during sinking operations in the 1910-1914 period. This photograph was probably taken around 1912.

John Kingman

THE BROMLEY COLLIERY TRAMWAY
This view of the luxuriant Somerset countryside shows tubs and a somewhat well-rounded miner, on their way from Bromley Colliery to Pensford Colliery. Through the trees, Bromley Pit can be seen in the background. The photograph was taken on 23rd August 1956.
Colin G. Maggs

PENSFORD COLLIERY IN THE FIFTIES
This aerial shot of Pensford Colliery shows a wealth of mining and railway detail. The North Somerset Railway can be glimpsed briefly in the middle distance, while the route of the tramway to Bromley Colliery followed the line of the hedge seen directly behind the long building in the centre left of the picture, situated to the left of the base of the chimney.
Dennis Rendell

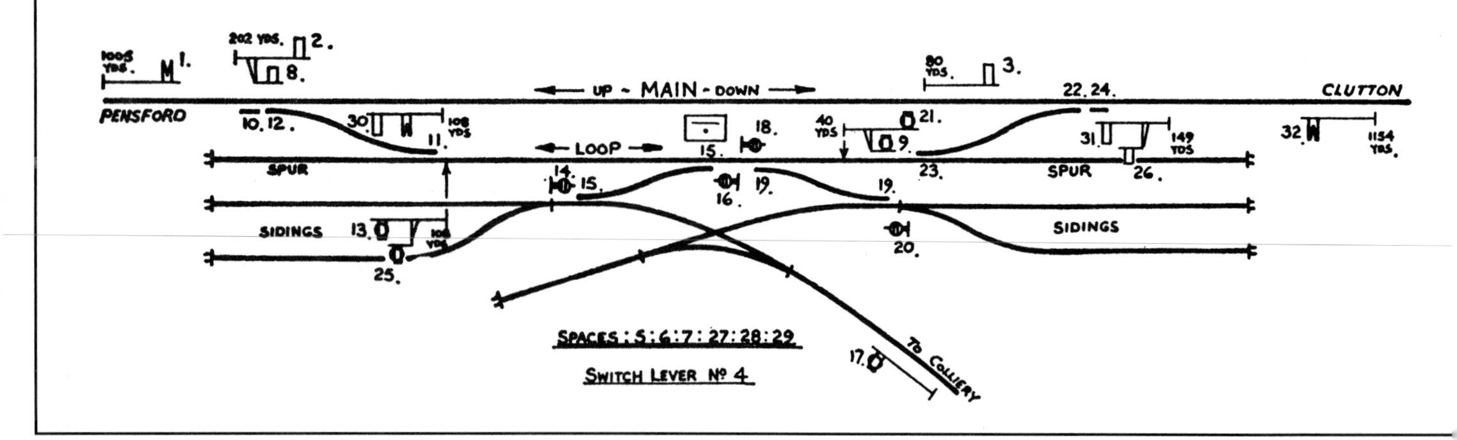

THE SIGNAL BOX DIAGRAM FOR PENSFORD & BROMLEY COLLIERIES SIDINGS SIGNAL BOX

Original diagram: Signalling Record Society *Drawn by G.A. Pryer*

CLUTTON – A GENERAL VIEW
This view of Clutton shows the GWR station in the centre distance, with the line from Radstock to Bristol running from left to right. The railway sweeping around to the left foreground went off to Greyfield Colliery. The original postcard from which this photograph was taken carried a message to one of the local farms asking for four quarts of milk to be delivered the following day!

Mr & Mrs W. Perry

Returning to the history of Pensford Pit, on 9th July 1959 the various siding agreements with the former GWR were brought to a finish by British Railways. The rails were soon removed and the North Somerset branch was robbed of yet another rich source of traffic.

Collieries at Clutton: Fry's Bottom, Greyfield, Burchells and Mooresland

Around Clutton, the next area of concern, there were four collieries, all on land owned by the Earl of Warwick, that fed coal into the Bristol & North Somerset. These four pits were Fry's Bottom, Greyfield, Burchells and Mooresland, the latter pair being much smaller than the former.

The first mention of coal mining in the Clutton area comes from a survey of 1610 which tells us that:

> "There be now three pits near widow Blacker's house, the highest about four fathoms, the middle six fathoms."

It was continued by saying that the underground roadway (the lane) was:

> "A good quoits cast in length with two cross lanes . . . They (the men) now work in two pits at once and have below, two or three men and five boys and also

GREYFIELD COLLIERY
This photograph shows the pithead and the screens at Greyfield Colliery. It would seem that this view was taken from the spoil tips of the colliery, possibly around the turn of the century. The line to Clutton station would have run from the left of this picture passing the site of Greyfield Brickworks on its way down to the GWR.

A.H. Parsons

GREYFIELD COLLIERY
A quiet moment floats by at Greyfield Colliery. Human beings are noticeably absent from the yard although a number of horses enliven this mining scene.
John Kingman

three men to wind up the coals. At the end of every lane a man worketh and there maketh his bench."

The coal was pulled up in buckets by windlass, while the coal was described by Collinson in 1791 as being:

". . . covered with stony stratum, which the miners call wark. It splits like slate and abounds with impressions of fern and other plants. Over this is another stratum called the Thorney Cliff which is intermixed with arborescent marcasites. The coal is often tinged with sulphur . . . it was so strongly impregnated with it, that in all its joints it seemed to be covered with leaf gold. In another wark, nearly 3-cwt of good leadore was found growing to a vein of coal."

Fry's Bottom Colliery

Fry's Bottom Colliery, the first of the Clutton pits in which we have a particular interest, was at work by 1838, but it was not until some 25 years later, on 6th May 1863 that the Bristol & North Somerset Railway came on to the scene. On that date an agreement was made with the Earl of Warwick, as we know already, a very important and key supporter of the B&NSR project, and of the North Somerset company itself, in which the developing railway was given permission to build a siding, three-quarters of a mile long from the intended station at Clutton to the colliery. As part of this arrangement it was agreed that the siding should form only one junction with the main Bristol-Radstock line. It was also agreed that this siding should be finished within one year of the North Somerset Railway's opening.

This last condition leads us to have to make some speculative reflections on the actual opening date of the siding to Fry's Bottom for, although the Bristol-Radstock line came into

Below: THE SECOND SCHEDULE TO THE AGREEMENT OF 11TH AUGUST 1875

Original document: Public Record Office

3.—Estimated Cost of the Grayfield Branch.

Length ... 1 M. 11·69 Chains.

			£	s.	d.
26,000	Cubic yards excavation ...	@ 1s. 2d.	1,516	13	4
	Turnpike road bridge ...		400	0	0
	Stream bridges and drains ...		300	0	0
2,007	Lineal yards permanent way ...	@ 25s. 0d.	2,508	15	0
4,000	„ „ fencing ...	@ 2s. 3d.	450	0	0
	Accommodation works ...		150	0	0
	Junction and sidings ...		480	0	0
	Engineering ...		200	0	0
			6,005	8	4
	Contingencies ...		300	10	10
	Total ...		£6,305	19	2

3.—Estimated Cost of Sundry Works.

Welton.

			£	s.	d.
	Goods shed ...		750	0	0
	Addition to roads ...		300	0	0
601	Cubic yards excavation and carting to tip	@ 1s. 6d.	51	16	6
82	„ masonry ...	„ 18s. 0d.	73	16	0
45	Cubic feet oak coping ...	„ 4s. 0d.	9	0	0
77	„ creosoted memel ...	„ 2s. 3d.	8	13	3
	Carried forward ...		£1,193	5	9

	£	s.	d.
1. Fry's Bottom (as particularised below) ...	3,872	16	9
2. Greyfield ditto ...	6,305	19	2
3. Sundry works ditto ...	2,284	19	10
	£12,463	15	9

1.—Estimated Cost of the Fry's Bottom Branch.

Length ... 0 M. 67 Chains.

			£	s.	d.
20,000	Cubic yards excavation ...	@ 1s. 2d.	1,166	13	0
	Underpinning bridge ...		60	0	0
	Cattle arch ...		160	0	0
	Culverting ...		50	0	0
1,474	Lineal yards permanent way ...	@ 25s. 0d.	1,842	10	0
1,380	Fencing ...	@ 2s. 3d.	155	5	0
	Accommodation works ...		50	0	0
	Engineering ...		200	0	0
			3,684	8	0
	Contingencies ...		188	8	9
	Total ...		£3,872	16	9

operation on 3rd September 1873 it would seem that the connection and associated sidings to both Fry's Bottom and Greyfield Collieries had *not*, at that time at least, been constructed. An agreement dated 11th August 1875 clearly stated that the sidings to both pits were about to be built, the contractors being named as Frederick George Saunders and Thomas Merriman Ward. It was also very clear that both the Earl of Warwick and the GWR, who also signed the agreement with the North Somerset and the contractors, were very keen to get the tracks into these pits into place, although the Earl himself had refused to put any more of his own money into the North Somerset!

The agreement stipulated that all the new work was to be finished by 25th March 1876, so presumably fairly close to that time, these works would have been brought into use, some two and a half years after the Bristol-Radstock portion had been completed. No wonder the railway company was in such dire financial straits and no wonder its potential customers were increasingly frustrated with it! Once in operation it seems likely that the long siding would have been worked, initially at least, by horses. Less than twenty years on, on 31st July 1895, the pit was shut for good, work having been suspended since 1887. Even today, however, much of the siding's trackbed is clear to see.

Greyfield Colliery

Greyfield Pit came into existence through an indenture of 9th March 1833. In this the Earl of Warwick agreed to lease mineral rights to John Savage Cameron. This also gave Cameron the right to sink a pit and although there were two winding shafts, these were sunk at different times. A third shaft was also brought into use for ventilation purposes only and was to be found to the north of the two coaling shafts. In addition, a fourth shaft was provided to clear the workings of water, a major problem encountered in the pit's later years. Greyfield Colliery was producing around 12,000 tons of coal a year in the mid-1840s while, by 1889, this had increased to around 60,000 tons. It was therefore one of the more important collieries in the Somerset Coalfield and a good deal of this output was most likely put onto the North Somerset Railway.

However, access to the colliery was initially a problem in that it had no road access. In the mid-1830s the colliery was served by a double track tramroad incline which was built from the pithead to a coal depot situated on the High Littleton to Bath road. This did not survive for too long and, in 1847, a broad gauge railway was proposed but, like so many other potential lines on offer at this time, this one came to nothing! During the construction of the Bristol & North Somerset Railway it would seem that coal from Greyfield was taken by horse and wagon to the railway at Hallatrow, this section coming into use before the northern section. These wagons put a heavy stress on the local roads and the Turnpike Trust instituted a toll to pay for the damage done, each cartload having to pay this toll.

Under the same agreement as that mentioned in the description of Fry's Bottom (6th May 1863) a siding was to be laid off the Bristol & North Somerset to serve Greyfield. As we have also seen, under an agreement of 11th August 1875, it seems most likely that it was not until around, or some time after, 25th March 1876 that Greyfield Colliery was linked into the B&NSR. As both pits were at a higher level than the North Somerset's station at Clutton, it looks likely that empty wagons for both pits were hauled by horse-power to the pitheads, the loaded trucks then being allowed to run by force of gravity down to the GWR's goods yard. Men rode these trucks to the station so that if for any reason they came to a stand, the men could get them going again. Both sidings were the GWR's responsibility in terms of maintenance as long as the collieries were in work.

The first locomotive used on the Greyfield siding was an 0-4-0 saddle tank, built in 1885, by the firm of R. & W. Hawthorn, of Forth Bank Works, Newcastle upon Tyne (builder's No. 2040). Painted black, it was named *Frances*, although it was known locally as "The Coffee Pot". It was believed scrapped on site around 1895, the year Fry's Bottom Colliery closed. However, a new locomotive had arrived in 1894 when another 0-4-0ST, this time one new from the builders, the Bristol loco-building firm of Peckett's (builder's No. 581) arrived at Clutton. Named *Daisy* after the then Lady Warwick, this locomotive became a familiar sight chuffing backwards and forwards from Greyfield to the GWR station. The locomotive received a new steel boiler in 1904, while another one was fitted in the wartime year of 1916. By this time the locomotive was working at Burchells Pit and around 1922 it moved to Denbighshire, Burchells having closed late the previous year.

In September 1909 Greyfield was very seriously flooded when water from old coal workings swamped the pit. Although no human lives were lost, six pit ponies used in the colliery were drowned. By the end of the month, however, the pit was clear of water and the miners were back at their arduous labours. In May 1911, after a batch of redundancies some two years earlier in December 1909, another 152 men and boys were given the sack and the colliery closed. The reason for the closure was that the owner of the colliery, Lord Warwick, had refused to pay heavy royalties demanded of him for coal to be worked by the pit under a neighbouring estate. Incidentally, some of Greyfield's machinery was sent to the colliery at Burchells and it is to this pit that we now move.

THE EARL OF WARWICK'S COLLIERIES AT CLUTTON: GREYFIELD

A nonchalant crew pose on *Daisy*, one of the locomotives used on the standard gauge branch from Greyfield Colliery to the B&NSR/GWR station at Clutton. *Daisy* was a Peckett 0-4-0ST, (builder's No. 581) built in 1894. It came to Clutton new from the builders and stayed there until around 1922 when it was bought by Wynnstay Collieries Limited in Denbighshire.

John Cornwell

Burchells Colliery

Before Greyfield had suffered from its severe attack of flooding in 1909, it was becoming more and more clear that the writing was on the wall for this particular pit. It was therefore not altogether surprising when, towards the end of 1908, the Clutton Coal Company was formed and began construction work at two places close to the village. One site, an old shaft close to the railway linking the GWR with the colliery at Fry's Bottom and situated roughly half-way along that railway and to its eastern side, was an old shaft which was re-opened. The second site, a new drift was begun to the west of the GWR. This site was right in the heart of the village and turned what had been a lovely farm into an ugly pit. This drift was probably at work in 1910, the men who had been displaced from Greyfield moving across to take up employment at nearby Burchells. It must have been an interesting sight to see the miners wandering off to work with candles or carbide lamps attached to the front of their caps! On the other side of the North Somerset's shining metals the shaft was served by a short siding off the siding that fed the former colliery at Fry's Bottom. Wagons into and out of this siding were shunted by *Daisy*.

However, Burchells was not destined to be working long for, in September 1918, the first rumblings of closure were heard. On 27th April 1920 the pit was partially closed due to a swamping of the workings from the flooded Greyfield Colliery. The end, however, eventually followed in 1921 when, on 25th August of that year, most mining ceased. Although Lady Warwick was keen to see the colliery remain open, it was not to be and by 11th October all underground salvage had finished. *Daisy* had returned to Pecketts for resale. The slag heaps were later planted with trees and the ugly sore that had once been a pit was wiped from the landscape.

Right: BURCHELLS COLLIERY, CLUTTON
This interesting and unusual picture of construction work in progress at the new drift at Burchells, was probably taken at some time around 1909.

John Kingman

Below: BURCHELLS COLLIERY c1910
This striking photograph shows the new drift at Burchells Colliery. It was probably taken around 1910. The miner looks intensely and, somewhat suspiciously perhaps at the photographer, as a long line of narrow gauge tubs stretches between them!

John Kingman

Left: THE COLLIERY AT FARRINGTON (1)

Dennis Rendell

One final point worth noting about Burchells is that behind its tips, a small drift mine was brought into use at some time after 1921. This drift, Knapp Hill, was later abandoned in 1923. However, it is not at all clear whether coal from this drift ever found its way on to the former Fry's Bottom siding and then on to the GWR at Clutton.

Mooresland Colliery

Mooresland Colliery was situated very close to Greyfield, in fact slightly to the north east of it and some one hundred yards from the railway siding linking Clutton station with Greyfield Pit. Mooresland had originally been an independent pit which had been sunk to the Radstock series of seams at some point after 1840. At some later stage Mooresland's coal output was transferred via a narrow gauge tramway and a drift which ran from Greyfield pithead under the GWR line to Clutton onto Mooresland itself. Known as "The Cuckoo" this drift ran to the bottom of Mooresland Colliery's shafts. At some stage these latter shafts were taken out of use for coal winding and the coal was brought, via drift and tramway, to Greyfield. The shafts at Mooresland then remained in use only for ventilation purposes. On 4th June 1904 the Cuckoo Drift and the workings at Mooresland were abandoned. Around 1906 the GWR agreed to build a junction off the Clutton-Greyfield line to serve Greyfield Brickworks. The siding was later completed but it would appear not to have been greatly used since the brickworks themselves closed in about 1909. Presumably, loads of bricks were, for a short time at least, conveyed onto the North Somerset at Clutton?

The Pits at Farrington Gurney

The history of coal mining in the area east of the village of Farrington Gurney is a long and well-documented one. For example, a survey of the manors of Midsomer Norton and Farrington Gurney early in the reign of James the First (1603-1625) made no mention, at that time at least, of mines in either of these parishes. Yet, in 1615, a local partnership had set up a colliery in Midsomer Norton while, a littler earlier in 1610, further north near the Parish of Clutton, the output of two pits, then "newly entered into", was some 600 horse loads or about 70 tons a week. During the 1660s, however, we hear mention of a coal mine in Farrington Gurney itself.

In this section of the Bristol-Radstock line's collieries' history we are involved with the stories of three main collieries. These are the pits at Farrington Colliery itself; at Old Mills and at Springfield. Farrington Pit was a financial enterprise of the Mogg (later Rees-Mogg) family. The other two pits were set up by William Evans of Paulton. It was Evans who was the owner of that most famous and important Somersetshire ironworks, the foundry at Paulton. This was located just to the north of his colliery at Old Mills, of which more later, and which quite naturally supplied that, and Springfield Pit, with its foundry needs.

Farrington Colliery

Farrington Colliery appears to have been sunk shortly before 1738. The lease on the colliery was taken up, and let go, on several occasions until, on 25th October 1882, W. B. Beauchamp and Theophilius Gullick took over the lease for a 31 year period, this period beginning on 30th August 1880. With the up-and-coming Beauchamp family in the driving seat real development of the pit started to take place.

In an agreement dated 15th August 1871 the pit was to have been pulled into the Bristol & North Somerset Railway by the construction of a siding from the pit to the main line metals. Indeed, the B&NSR had agreed to put in this siding in return for concessions made when building its Bristol-Radstock section. On 11th August 1875 the contracting firm of Saunders & Ward, in an agreement with the B&NSR, the GWR and

Right: THE COLLIERY AT FARRINGTON (2)

J.E. Loaring/Dennis Rendell

FARRINGTON COLLIERY: MOTIVE POWER
A Beyer, Peacock 0-4-0 saddle tank rests between spells of shunting at Farrington Pit.

J.E. Loaring

the Earl of Warwick, undertook to install this particular siding. However, some seven years were to elapse before this was actually laid in. Indeed, some considerable works were required since the North Somerset's main line had to be slewed over so that the siding from Farrington Pit could run alongside and parallel to this main line. A junction was formed with that main route at Springfield/Old Mills where a connection was made with the exchange sidings there.

On 6th November 1882 Colonel Rich inspected the work that had been carried out. He stated that the facing points on the main passenger line at the junctions with the (Old Mills') Colliery Sidings were locked by four bolts and these, in turn, were worked by the levers that operated the Home signals. These latter were interlocked with the points, and these were worked from a raised signal cabin.

The Inspector suggested that the facing points should be controlled by four lifting bars and should be secured by four bolts

FARRINGTON COLLIERIES COMPANY,

(FARRINGTON SIDING, HALLATROW, G.W.R.)

FARRINGTON GURNEY, Nr. BRISTOL.

To________________________

For________________________

No. Date 191

Purchasers will be held responsible for demurrage on all Trucks not cleared within the time allowed, and for all Railway claims for Siding charges or otherwise.

FARRINGTON COLLIERY: WAGON LABEL

Original label: Robin Atthill

worked by separate levers. The two spare levers then existing in the locking frame could be used for this purpose. Presumably when all these conditions had been met the new works were brought into use, possibly late in November or early in December 1882. For the use of the junction at Old Mills, Farrington contributed a lump sum of £250 while it also paid a proportion of the annual costs of maintaining the junction.

At first one assumes that horses provided the motive power on the siding, since although three locomotives were believed used at Farrington, there are gaps in our knowledge as to exactly when these were actually in use. The first of these was an outside-cylindered 0-4-0ST built in 1877, by Beyer, Peacock & Co Ltd, builder's No. 1736. From the contracting firm of Meakin & Dean, a Beyer, Peacock locomotive, (builder's number unknown), was reported to be here by around 1885. This locomotive was believed sold for scrap some time after August 1904.

The second locomotive was an outside-cylindered 0-4-0ST built by W. G. Bagnall Limited, builder's No. 1432, in 1894. This locomotive came from M. W. Grazebrook Limited of Netherton in Staffordshire. It was put up for sale both in December 1921 and in July 1922, but did, in fact, consequently go for scrap.

The third of the trio was an outside-cylindered 0-4-0ST, built in 1891 by Peckett of Bristol, builder's No. 520. This engine came from G. Palmer, the contracting firm, and was on site at Farrington Colliery by November 1912. It was later sent to East Bristol Collieries Limited. However, after that its fate is unknown.

In 1905 a letter from the GWR at Bristol Divisional Headquarters to Farrington Colliery throws some interesting light on the colliery at that time. By all accounts the GWR had had a case in hand since January 1905 concerning the repair of a set of buffer stops at the Farrington Colliery private siding at Springfield/Old Mills. It appears that at the beginning of December 1904 the wooden stop blocks which, under an agreement of 8th August 1882 the colliery owners, the Radstock Coal Company, were obliged to maintain, were found by the GWR's Engineering Department to have been knocked over. The colliery manager's attention was drawn to the matter and

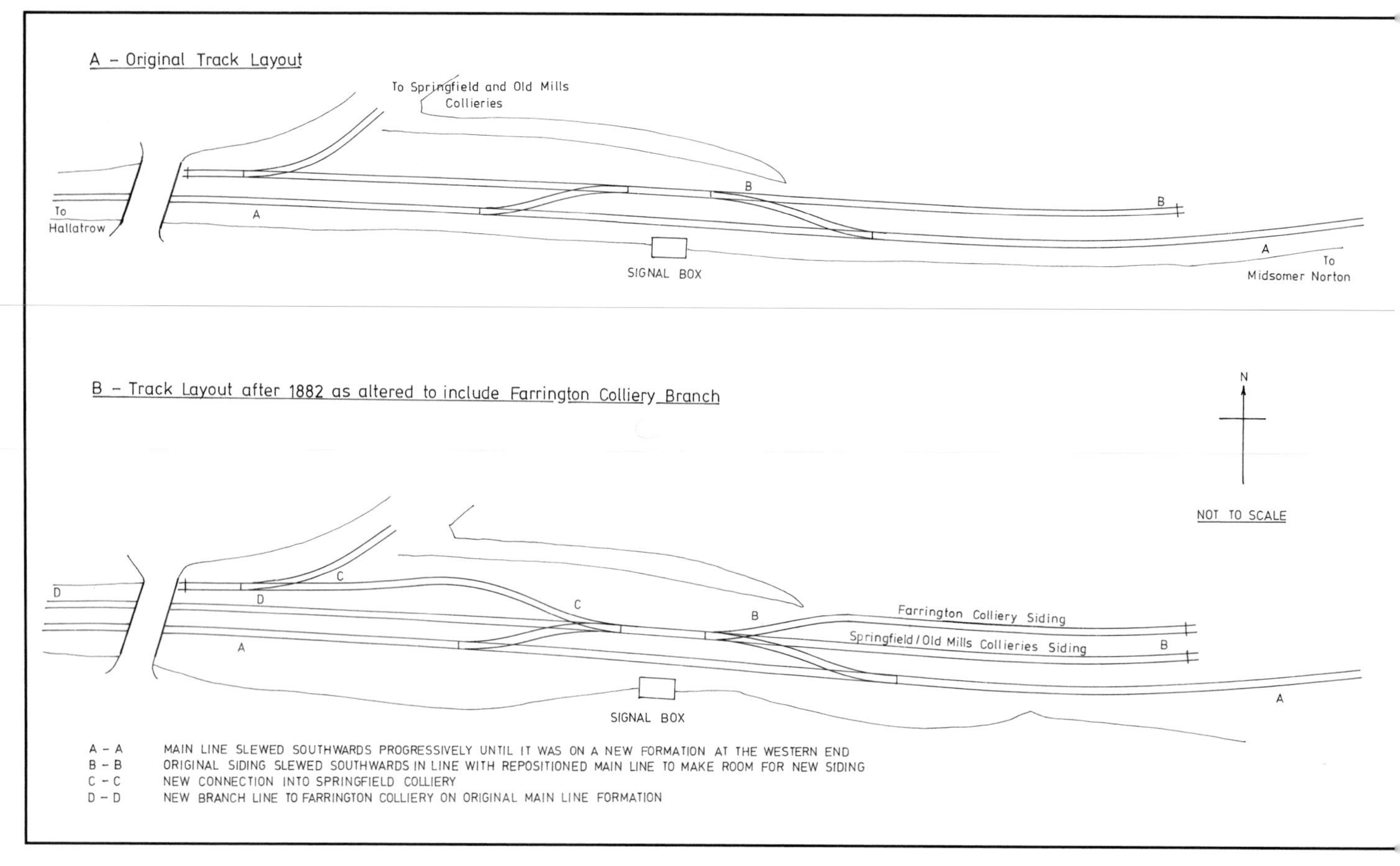

OLD MILLS COLLIERY SIDINGS *Drawings by Chris Handley*

Below: STANDING TRUCKS AND LOCO SHEDS – OLD MILLS COLLIERY (NCB)
This peaceful shot of the North Somerset's main line and loop at Old Mills shows the loco shed with its locomotive tucked away deep inside the darkness. The line running into the colliery area itself can be seen to the left of the shed.

Don Pritchard/Mike Wyatt

it was stated in reply that the damage was the result of rough shunting by one of the GWR's goods trains. Interestingly enough, the colliery company could not give exact details of the train responsible but they nevertheless felt that the GWR should put the blocks in order anyway!

The signalman at Old Mills, all the guards and all the staff working Farrington Colliery siding were interviewed about the matter but all denied knowledge of the incident. The GWR had produced evidence to show that the blocks had not been put firmly enough into the ground in the first place and so this eventual damage was not at all surprising. However, the colliery company still refused to do anything about the matter. The Divisional Engineer, Mr Lawrence, said that it would cost about £9 10s (£9.50) to put the blocks in order and the recommendation was that the colliery and the GWR should go halves on the repairs. We are left to conjecture whether or not this was what happened.

Farrington, like most other pits in silvan Somerset, was strike-bound during the confrontation of 1921. Sir Frank Beauchamp threatened closure if the men did not return underground. They did not and the pit eventually closed in October 1921. It was finally abandoned the following year.

Old Mills and Springfield Collieries

Old Mills Colliery, north of the A362 road between Welton and Farrington Gurney, was the first of this pair of pits to be sunk, work beginning around 1860. The actual sinking of

Right: OLD MILLS COLLIERY (NCB)
With a Ruston & Hornsby diesel in the background (believed to be builder's No. 200793), the photographer catches this "behind-the-scenes" view at Old Mills Colliery. The photograph was probably taken at some time during the 1950s.

John Kingman

Below: OLD MILLS COLLIERY (NCB) IN STEAM DAYS
With Old Mills Colliery buildings in the left background, Class 4500 No. 4555, now preserved and working on the Dart Valley Railway, shunts old and new style coal wagons at Old Mills' Sidings. This leisurely activity was captured on film on 20th April 1959.

P.J. Williams

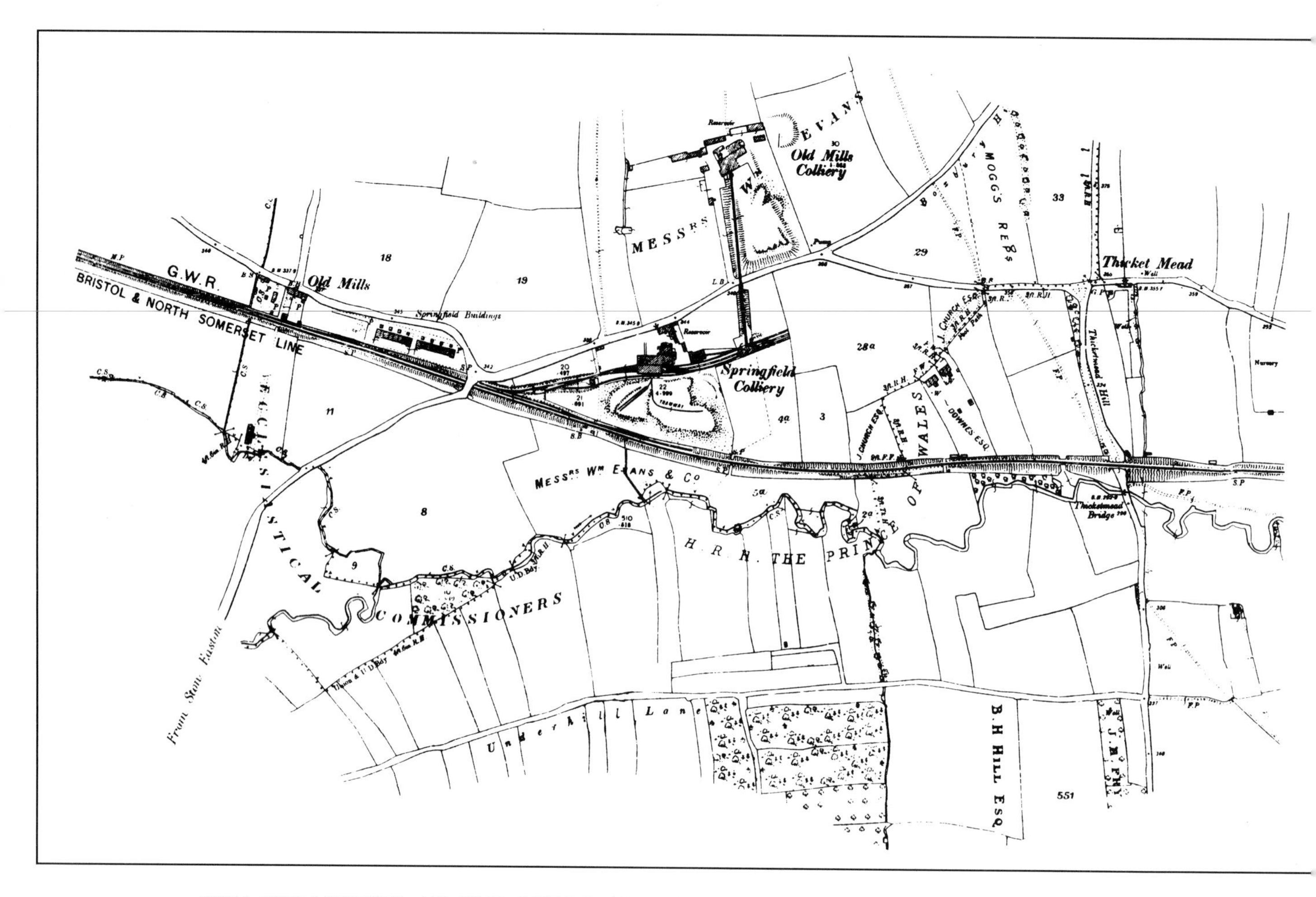

THE COLLIERIES AT OLD MILLS AND AT SPRINGFIELD *Original: A Church*

the pit probably took place in 1861, while the first recorded load of coal, twelve tons in all, left Old Mills Colliery on 3rd September 1864.

Springfield Colliery, on the other hand, is believed to have been sunk at some time after 1872, completion being carried out in 1874. On 10th June 1867 the lease for the area known as "Spring Ground" had been signed and this gave William Evans access to, and possession of, the land to start sinking operations. It also gave him an option to buy land for a railway siding adjacent to and on the north side of the B&NSR's Bristol-Radstock line. This siding was actually in position by 1875, by which time the pit itself was in operation, the private siding agreement having been reached on 5th June 1874. Indeed, on 6th April 1875 Colonel Rich inspected the sidings and connections at Springfield/Old Mills and, with the exception of

COLLIERIES AND SIGNAL CABINS
With Old Mills Colliery in the left background and Springfield Colliery in the centre middle distance, the line of the North Somerset is highlighted by the rake of wagons standing on the siding alongside that company's main line. Note the signal box to the left of the trucks.

Chris Howell

SPRINGFIELD PIT
With a somewhat doubtful chimney in the background, Springfield Pit presents its workforce to the world.
John Kingman

a few missing fishplates, found the works to be ready for traffic. The cost of the railway sidings had been £1,000. As we have seen under the previous section, an agreement of 8th August 1882 allowed Farrington Pit to link its siding into those at Springfield, the layout there remaining basically unchanged until the 1950s. The sidings were worked by horses until October 1940 when, after strengthening and improving, they became ready to receive a Ruston & Hornsby $7\frac{1}{2}$ ton diesel locomotive (builder's No. 200793).

Old Mills Colliery was connected to Springfield by a narrow gauge tramway. However, the two pits were later connected underground and, in October 1941, the Old Mills shaft was closed for coal winding, being used only for ventilation and winding supplies after this time. The combined colliery was nationalised in 1947 when it became known as the Old Mills Colliery, although the remaining installation was, in fact, *Springfield Pit* !

After 1947 use of the Springfield Washery was increased when, in 1953, coal from Pensford Pit was ferried down the Bristol & North Somerset line for washing. Bottom door hopper wagons were used for this traffic, the siding layout at Springfield being changed to accommodate these new workings and wagons. However, on the closure of Pensford, this traffic stopped in 1958 and since the bottom had fallen out of the market (!) for washed coal, the washery was closed down around 1962. At about the same time it is believed that another Ruston & Hornsby locomotive was brought to the sidings, the original being transferred away to Kilmersdon Colliery. Even with modernisation, the pit was closed on 1st April 1966, taking with it the last source of coal revenue on the North Somerset railway between Bristol and Radstock. The last colliery on this section had now gone and soon the rails would go with it.

The Pits at Welton and Clandown

Further east along the route of the B&NSR, in the Welton area, the minerals under the Somerset countryside were essentially the property of the Duchy of Cornwall. The coal was worked at three main mines: Old Welton, Welton Hill and Clandown, each pit taking in leases covering about one third of the area. We need to look closely at each of these pits since they were important feeders to the North Somerset.

Old Welton Colliery

This colliery was open by about 1783. In order to keep its workings free of water it used waterwheels for pumping and, in 1798, a new wheel was brought into use to draw coal up the shaft.

Two shafts were sunk to the Radstock series of seams and these reached a depth of 440 yards. This colliery was then tapping into the same seams as those later worked by Wellsway Pit, another colliery that ties in tightly with the North Somerset's story. From 24th May 1845 to 23rd May 1846 Old Welton raised some 13,838 tons, its target for that year being 13,850 tons.

However, during the late 1850s, through the 1860s and well into the 1870s the financial outlook was very bleak and, in 1876, when the lease came up for renewal, the then owners, John Rees-Mogg, John Moore Paget and Thomas Savage, gave up the ghost on the pit, not renewing its lease. Nevertheless the colliery remained in existence but it was not until 22nd October 1878 that a new lease was signed, this time by William Beauchamp and Thomas Gullick, and it was they who kept the pit in working order. It became the Old Welton Colliery Company and certain aspects of modernisation were carried out.

One prong of Beauchamp's modernisation programme centred around the pit's transport links with the outside world. Although the colliery was served by the Somersetshire Coal Canal's tramway, then in the ownership of the Somerset & Dorset Railway Company, it was a less than satisfactory way of getting coal from the pit to Radstock. However, the S&D could not come to an agreement with the GWR, whose North Somerset line skirted the pit, only some one hundred yards away. It would appear that Beauchamp quickly came to his own arrangements with the GWR for, in 1880, as requested by a Board of Trade Minute of the 28th May, Colonel Rich inspected permanent way work at Old Welton Colliery.

In his report dated 31st May 1880 Colonel Rich stated that he had inspected various new connections and sidings at Old Welton Colliery. The connection from the pit itself joined the

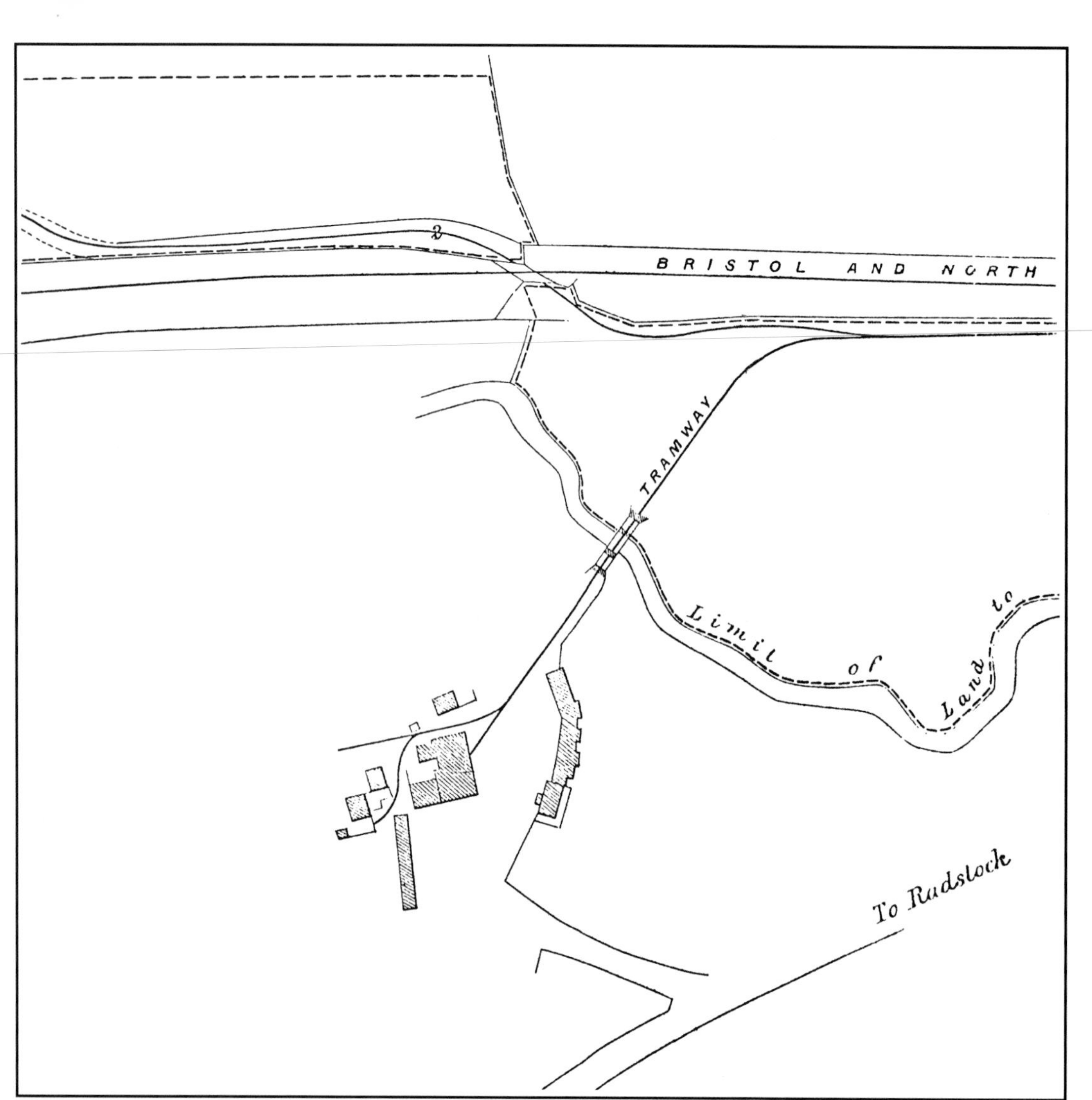

THE COLLIERY AND SCC TRAMWAY AT OLD WELTON COLLIERY c1863

Original plan: Chris Handley

main passenger line of the North Somerset about half a mile from Radstock. At this point the main Bristol-Radstock railway fell on a gradient of 1 in 128 towards Radstock but the colliery connection ran up, on a 1 in 64 grade, towards the main line. Rich noted that all loaded wagons were to be tripped from the colliery to Radstock while empty wagons were to be pushed from Radstock up to the pit. Provided this way of working be adopted he said that the various works could be

Below: WELTON HILL COLLIERY
This view of the colliery shows the pithead and the screens. The SCC tramroad from Radstock would have come in from the bottom right hand side of the photograph. The colliers look at the camera while they sit on the pit props; some of the lads look very young indeed!

John Kingman / Dennis Rendell

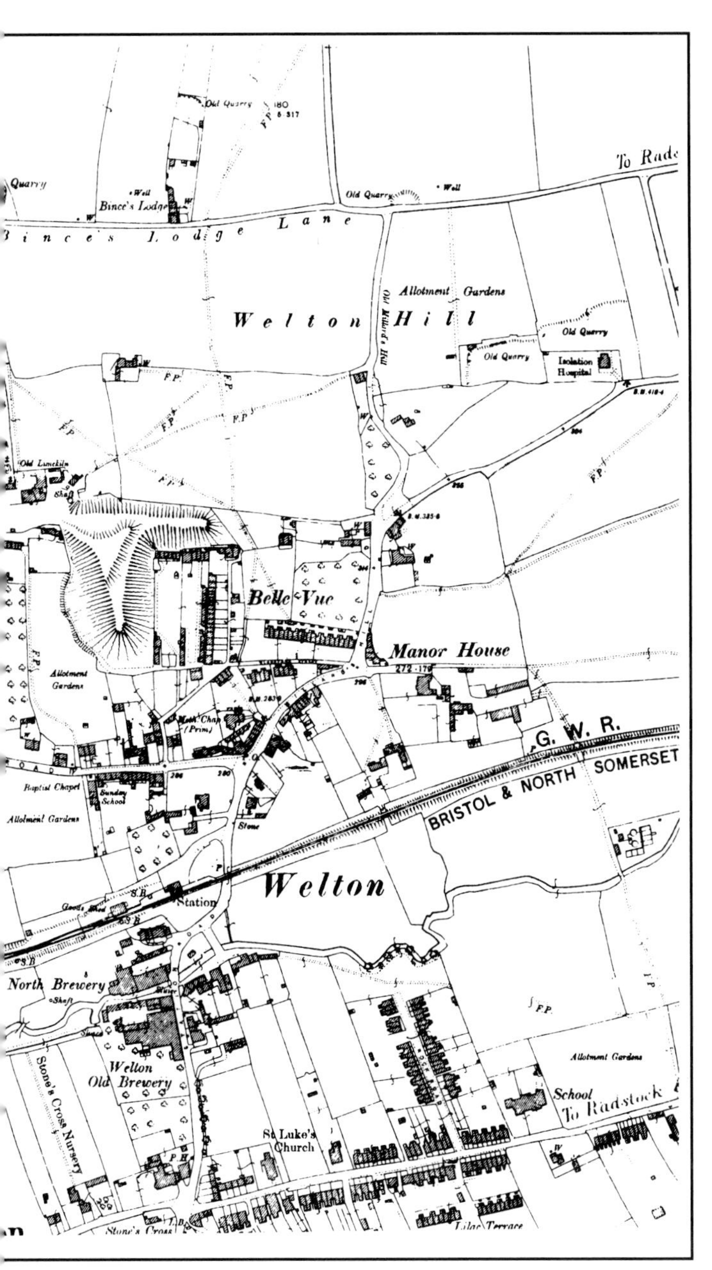

WELTON AND WELTON HILL

The North Somerset Railway can clearly be seen on this map as can the spoil tips of the old Welton Hill Colliery (situated due north of the station). The old SCC tramroad dropped southwards from the pit near the allotment gardens continuing its run east along the course of the road and footpath, directly below the words "Manor House".

Original plan: Chris Howell

brought into use. This, one assumes, is what happened soon after this inspection had taken place.

Over the 1886-88 period Beauchamp deepened the pit's northern shaft and, in order to supply bricks for this work, in 1886 he re-opened the Old Welton Brickworks. This was situated close to the colliery but, due to the poor bricks it produced, it struggled to make its way in the market place, a forerunner of the later North Somerset Brick & Tile Company's experience of which we will say more later.

All this new work on shaft, spur and sidings nearly bankrupted the business but, in spite of its financial difficulties, on 31st March 1897, the pit's lease was taken up by Mr F. J. Bird of Clandown Colliery. By May 1901 a damaged winding shaft had been put back into action but the mine never re-opened. Indeed, it is ironic that both this, and the other Welton pit, Welton Hill, were closed in 1896, the GWR losing two pits off its North Somerset supply line. On 5th May 1927 Sir Frank Beauchamp acquired Old Welton and the brickworks with the aim of increasing the coal reserves for his Norton Hill Colliery at Midsomer Norton. The Old Welton deep shaft was then brought back into use for ventilation and safety reasons.

Mr F. J. Bird's name crops up again in connection with a pre-First World War proposal to sink a new colliery at New Welton. Indeed, this new pit was twice staked out in a field called Middle Hill which was situated on the North Somerset's line. Extra land was bought up so that sidings and connections could be made with both the GWR and the S&D. Winding engines were ordered from Germany and, since the proposed new pit was on Duchy of Cornwall land, it was rumoured locally that King George V was to cut the first sod. However, the First World War broke out in August 1914 and no more was heard of this particular project. In actual fact, Welton Hill Colliery was destined to be the last pit to be sunk on the Duchy of Cornwall's Estate and it is to that colliery that we now turn.

Welton Hill Colliery

Welton Hill Colliery, situated well up the hill above the village, was certainly the last of the Duchy collieries to be sunk in the district. Sinking was delayed because the surface area required for the intended site was owned by several people and negotiations were obviously protracted. The lease was signed, nonetheless, on 8th February 1813 by Thomas Hollwey, William Coxeter James, William Kelson, John Paget and William Savage and, in accordance with the lease, work on the level began on 24th February 1813.

By January 1815, two years after sinking had begun, the first shaft, 6ft in diameter, had reached a depth of 90 yards, cutting into the Great Vein seam. To celebrate the occasion the workmen involved were given a free supper at the Greyhound Inn, Midsomer Norton. As the shaft was deepened three more seams were cut; the Little Vein and the Middle and the Sly Veins. However, when the shaft reached under Little Vein, at a depth of 200 yards, the miners came down to a fault. Water was also a problem and, at one stage, William Kelson became so alarmed at the expense and the state of the workings that one roadway was abandoned. Nonetheless, the pit started paying a freeshare royalty in March 1816, some three years after sinking had begun. In addition, two more shafts were sunk, one for pumping and one for ventilation.

In the early years of the pit, man-riding down the shaft was by hook and chain, coal raising being by hudge. A cage and wooden guides' system was successfully introduced in 1850, one of the first pits in Somerset to do so. From 24th May 1845 to 23rd May 1846, the pit produced 10,746 tons of coal.

Welton Hill, like most of the early pits in the Norton-Radstock area, was served by the SCC/S&D tramroad, a self-acting incline being used to reach the pithead. This particular piece of tramroad was the longest branch out from Radstock and, as such, the pit had laboured long under the highest tolls. Coal was lowered down the colliery inclined and, on reaching the bottom, was then horsedrawn, in sets of eight tubs each containing 27 cwts capacity, down the long trek to Radstock.

It is interesting to note that as late as the 1930s, the tramway could easily be traced from Welton to Radstock, there being stone sleeper blocks still in situ at that time. The tramrails, one yard in length, were made of a brittle cast iron, and the flat wheels of the tubs ran on the outside of the vertical flange, the gauge being 3ft 5½in. Mr Church of Welton told me that on Saturdays his grandfather had often seen people return from Radstock Market to Welton in the empty coal tubs!

To return to Welton Hill Colliery, it is clear that the SCC tramroad was severely limiting the pit and it comes, therefore, as no real surprise that, with the North Somerset Railway running along the bottom of the valley at Welton, in July 1875 the colliery applied for a siding at Welton station. Under an agreement of 31st December 1879 the colliery laid a narrow gauge line from the pit to a newly-constructed siding of the B&NSR at Welton station. Completed by June 1880, this work cost £708. The narrow gauge line was essentially a self-acting incline which ran from just below the Red Cow Inn, across the Welton-Farrington Gurney road to the new siding and screens built to the west of the station at Welton. On 11th April 1888 plans were put forward to replace the narrow gauge by standard so that through working, down the incline to the GWR, could be instituted. This proposal was never carried out, however. If this work had been executed, there would have been yet another standard gauge incline in the area.

The pit's fortunes varied during the 1870s and '80s but, by the late 1880s, the financial picture had once more become grim. By 1885 what reserves of coal remained were to be found farther away again from the shaft and capital investment would be necessary if the colliery was to survive and remain viable. The real need was to deepen the shaft so that it reached the Farrington series of seams, a project that the pit owners were not prepared to get involved in.

On 1st January 1889 William Beauchamp acquired the pit. Like his taking over of Old Welton Colliery, the reason for this particular takeover was to increase his grip on the Farrington series underlying the Duchy of Cornwall's Estate. The rundown during the 1890s was swift and, towards the end of 1896, the pit closed. After 31st March 1897 the colliery was again absorbed, this time by Mr F. J. Bird and, in spite of its declining prospects, it nevertheless acquired the impressive name of the Old Welton, Welton Hill & Clandown Amalgamated Collieries. Welton Hill, like its neighbour Old Welton, closed completely in 1897, never to re-open. An ex-Welton Hill miner, Mr Fred Maggs, told Mr Church that, by December 1897, Frank Beauchamp (his father William having died in 1894) had salvaged all that was useful at that pit and, some two years later, went on to remove the winding engine and pulley wheel for use at the new sinking then being carried on across the valley at Norton Hill Colliery.

Clandown Colliery

Clandown Colliery was never *directly* connected by standard gauge to the Bristol & North Somerset Railway but it was one of the pits from which some output found its way onto that railway. The colliery was first noted in 1793 under the title Clandown New Coal Work. The lease was signed around 1801 by John, Elizabeth and Julia Hill, William Coxeter James, Mary Langford and John Scobell. Another man was involved in this arrangement but his identity remains a mystery. Sinking began but, because of mining difficulties associated with the north/south geological fault that cuts across the manor of Radstock, it was brought to an end in November 1809. The following year, however, sinking began again and, on 24th November 1811 when the shaft was at a depth of 400 yards, coal was found. The jackpot had been struck. The pit grew quickly after this time and, in the year to September 1821, coal to the value of £12,252 was being mined.

The colliery was served by yet another branch off the Somersetshire Coal Canal's tramroad known, logically enough, as the Clan Down Railroad. This 'railroad', 5 furlongs, 1 chain in length, served other Radstock collieries at Middle Pit and Old Pit, while yet another short extension (9 chains 7 yards in this case), ran off to Smallcombe Colliery just to the east of Clandown. Just to the west of Radstock town centre, near the SCC basin, the tramways to Clandown and Welton joined each other from their respective termini.

However, once the GWR was opened from Frome to Radstock in 1854, Clandown attempted to put its coal output across to the GWR, the route being by the SCC tramway and the Waldegrave tramway to the Great Western at Radstock.

By 1862, unhappy with the high tolls incurred by this route, Clandown's owners had come up with another way of taking its coal to the rail network. They brought the coal to a siding on the SCC tramway in Radstock, from which they used a horse-drawn platform on which their coal tubs were carried from the siding to the GWR's goods yard. However, this too must have been unsatisfactory in that, by 1870, the Clandown coal was again coming down the valley to Radstock (GWR) by the SCC and Waldegrave tramways.

Nevertheless, the colliery eventually received its standard gauge connection when, on 18th September 1882, a branch off the S&D's line between Bath and Evercreech was opened and this worked traffic to and from the foot of an incline which ran up to the pithead itself. This incline was also converted to standard gauge. The S&D's Clandown extension was 44 chains in length and once opened meant, of course, the end of the coal traffic for the GWR. On 31st March 1897, F. J. Bird became the lessor of Clandown, together with the pits at Old Welton and Welton Hill, while, in May 1905 the Clandown Colliery Company became a limited liability undertaking. The following year F. J. Bird became its chairman, but along with others, he was destined to lose a good deal of money in Clandown which was now suffering with the problems of water.

In December 1924, the pit's final owner took over when Sir Frank Beauchamp bought the pit out as part of his overall strategy to buy the whole of the Duchy of Cornwall's mineral rights and their wealth. At this time the pit's coal traffic was still with the Somerset & Dorset Joint Railway. But the end was nigh, for on 24th August 1927, all the miners at the pit were given a week's notice and, on 11th November 1929, the pit was finally closed to production.

Having finally reached the Radstock area's pits by the North Somerset route let us now examine those collieries of the Earl Waldegrave that were served by the Bristol & North Somerset Railway.

The Earl Waldegrave's Radstock Collieries

> "Unquestionably the most famous Somerset colliery group in the nineteenth century was the Waldegrave family's Radstock Collieries. The family, Lords of the Manor of Radstock since the Civil War, was a relative newcomer into the coal mining business for there was at first no suggestion that coal existed at Radstock. However, either on theoretical grounds or from guesswork, the idea arose that there might, indeed, be coal there and, on 12th May 1749, James Lansdown and others took a 42 year lease to explore the area . . . In 1763, coal was found at Old Pit (as it was later known) and the sceptics were confounded."

After 1847 the various collieries under the Waldegrave banner traded under the title of the Radstock Coal Co. until, in the early 1860s, the term The Radstock Coalworks was used. In the late 1860s William Beachim, he who later went up-market and changed his name to "Beauchamp", began business under the name of the Radstock Coal Co. and this, in turn, led to Countess Waldegrave taking on a new name for her business, namely that of Frances, Countess Waldegrave, Radstock Collieries. Throughout the 1860s, '70s, '80s, '90s and into the 20th century Waldegrave coal rule was strong and steady. However, after the First World War their empire was well into decline and, in 1919, the family was forced to sell off part of its estates. The sale took place in January 1920 and Sir Frank Beauchamp, son of that wily upstart William whose company's name caused such confusion in the 1860s and '70s, was a major buyer. On 29th January 1925 Frank Beauchamp secured a licence from the ninth Earl Waldegrave to work the Radstock organisation of collieries. Profits stayed good into the 1930s under Sir Frank, the Beauchamp company's thread finally being cut with the eventual closure, in 1954, of the pit at Ludlows.

Although the Earl Waldegrave's Radstock Collieries' pits can be listed as follows: Old Pit, Smallcombe Colliery, Middle Pit, Ludlows, Wellsway and Tyning Collieries, we, as followers of the North Somerset's history are particularly interested in Wellsway, Ludlows, Middle Pit and Tyning Colliery. With the exception of Middle Pit, whose output post-1874 when the Somerset & Dorset opened was handled by that railway, all the other pits, plus Middle Pit pre-1874, had at least some, and in most cases, a substantial part of their output taken out over the GWR; either by the B&NSR or by the Wilts, Somerset & Weymouth Railway.

Wellsway Pit

As the North Somerset came swinging down the valley of the Wellow Brook from Welton, some half a mile west of Radstock, it passed the first of the Earl of Waldegrave's pits that put coal onto its tracks. This colliery was Wellsway. The lease

RADSTOCK IN THE RAIN
Although situated in a beautiful part of England, Radstock in the rain with its railways, smoking chimneys and busy coal mines makes this scene look like something out of industrial Lancashire rather than rural Somerset.

Lens of Sutton

for this particular pit was drawn up on 31st December 1828. Progress towards the production and raising of coal seems to have been slow, opening appearing to have taken place in the early 1830s, probably in 1833. Once opened, the colliery tied into the SCC's Welton Hill tramway branch. Running parallel to and then cutting across the Wellow Brook, the tramway swung almost due south towards the pit, running up an incline to the pithead itself. From its junction with the main branch to the screens themselves, the Wellsway branch was one furlong, two chains and six yards in length!

It was not until some forty years later that Wellsway was at long last connected into the Bristol & North Somerset when, on 7th January 1875, a standard gauge connection was laid in to serve the pit. Leaving the North Somerset close to Radstock, the new line ran directly to the pithead, an incline 100 yards in length being part of the new arrangements. Agreements between the North Somerset and Lady Waldegrave for the construction of this branch had been signed in both 1870 and 1871 but nothing had been done. However, an agreement between the North Somerset, the GWR, the Earl of Warwick and Saunders & Ward (contractors) of 11th August 1875 confirmed that £2,776 7s 6d (£2,776.37$\frac{1}{2}$) had been spent on the Wellsway branch (standard gauge) and that this sum included the cost of track, pointwork and signalling equipment. In addition, the agreement explained that Lady Waldegrave would have to pay the North Somerset interest at the rate of 7% per annum on the cost of building the branch, maintenance of it being the responsibility of the Bristol & North Somerset/GWR.

During the 1880s and early 1890s the North Somerset benefited from the coal put onto it by Wellsway Pit. However, during 1897 the colliery was closed for winding coal although

WELLSWAY COLLIERY: Based on a sketch of the colliery as seen from Wells Road, Radstock.

Origin unknown. Sketch via Dennis Rendell. *Drawn by C. Handley*

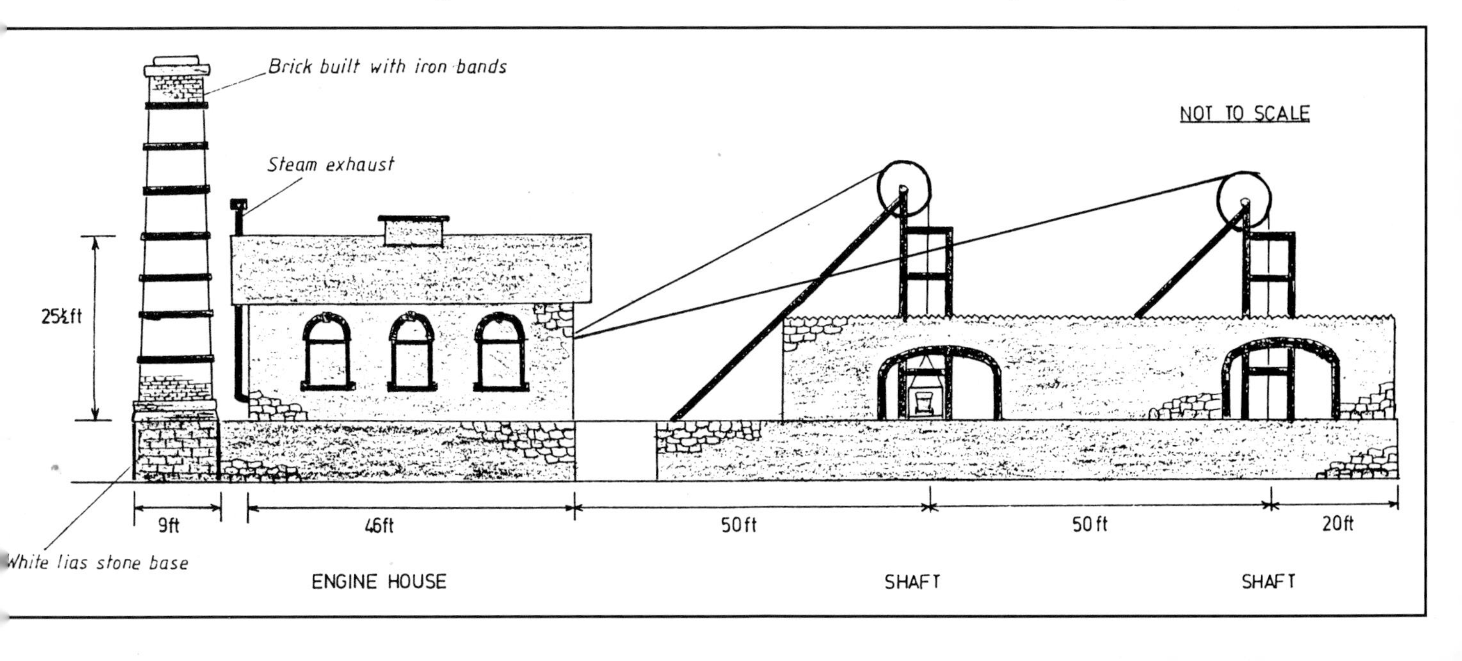

it actually remained in full production. At that time coal was being taken by a circuitous route underground, to Ludlows Pit where it was wound to the surface. On the other hand, Wellsway's shafts continued in use for winding men and materials. Once the coal was being taken to the surface at Ludlows, the standard gauge connection to Wellsway from the North Somerset, in use from 1875 to 1897, was no longer needed. However, the GWR retained Wellsway's output since Ludlows was also connected to the Great Western's well-won ways.

On 25th December 1897 (note the date and the related importance of the Victorian and capitalist work ethic!), the Radstock Collieries' manager, James McMurtrie, wrote to the GWR who were, by this time, in charge of the Bristol & North Somerset, telling them that the siding into Wellsway was no longer required. The reason he gave them was that "the coal had been exhausted at the colliery". Obviously this was not the case but can best be put down, perhaps, to "business ethics". The branch line was eventually closed in 1898 and was, at some later date, removed.

Nonetheless just because McMurtrie had said that its coal was exhausted and its connection had been removed, Wellsway was far from being finished! Indeed, it had many useful years of life stretching away in front of it. In fact, two decades of putting coal onto the GWR were to pass before the first flickerings of closures started to come to light. In January 1920 the miners were aware that closure plans were in the offing. Strikes and bad feelings were also in the air and there can be no doubt that the colliery was having a very rough time of it. C. G. Down & A. J. Warrington go on to give the following explanation:

> "The mining plans show the ridiculous methods of getting the coal away. Coal lying within a few hundred yards of Wellsway shaft had to be taken for nearly $\frac{3}{4}$ mile, with numerous interchanges, to reach the Ludlows' shaft."

Output was very low in consequence of the above, machinery was causing problems and, towards the end of August 1920, Wellsway eventually closed, some 23 years after McMurtrie had told the GWR that the pit was empty of coal!

Ludlows

Ludlows was first opened around 1784 and it was this pit that had the distinction of being the first Radstock colliery to be connected into the GWR's broad gauge line from Frome to Radstock. The private siding agreement was signed on 17th February 1853, the connection being opened the following year to handle coal and wagon repairing material. In 1857 the broad gauge branch into Ludlows was pushed on over the route and trackage of the SCC tramway to Tyning Colliery. This extension made the former 3ft $5\frac{1}{2}$in gauge SCC tramway branch from Tyning redundant but it was, nevertheless, kept and, in a remodelled form, was used, along with a similar SCC branch to Ludlows, to take spoil and dirt traffic from the two pits, up an incline, to new tipping areas in the district around Tyning. This was yet another nail in the SCC's coffin and was a further example of the way in which the Waldegraves were sending more of their own traffic out onto the GWR's seven-foot. Indeed, it is perhaps an interesting point on which to reflect that, generally speaking, most of the coal that was taken out of Radstock by the *GWR*, whether North Somerset or Wilts, Somerset & Weymouth, was bound for destinations well away from the North Somerset area.

In November 1866, Ludlows was deepened to the lower series of coal seams, while in 1894 coal winding at nearby Middle Pit was stopped, the latter colliery's coal being taken underground to be wound at Ludlows to which Middle Pit had now been joined. As we have already seen, in 1897, Wellsway Pit was connected by sinuous passages to Ludlows and Wellsway's black harvest was also brought to the surface at Ludlows, the GWR waiting to take all of this coal away from central Radstock rather than via its Wellsway branch connection.

After the struggle of the First World War, the struggle for the Waldegrave family's survival became much more intense and, by 1919, they were forced to sell a large part of their estates, an important part of which was the sale of the property's mineral rights. At the sale, held in 1920, Wellsway, Ludlows, Middle Pit and Tyning were all sold off in a package to Sir Frank Beauchamp.

On the 29th December 1925 he obtained a licence to work the Waldegrave family's Radstock Collieries' Company which, with the acquisition of Clandown Colliery in 1924, gave him

COLLIERIES AT RADSTOCK: LUDLOWS PIT
The sinking of this pit began in 1782 and the pit was completed about 1784. The last coal was dug on 19th March 1954.

Dennis Rendell

the virtual monopoly of coalfield workings in the Radstock area. It also gave him the right of access to almost all the coal *reserves* and the rights to work them, with the exception of those collieries in the Writhlington Group whose activities we have yet to look at. From all of these assets the now all-powerful Beauchamp formed Somerset Collieries Limited and among its leases were those of Wellsway, Ludlows, Middle Pit, Tyning and Clandown, as well as a number of other pits in the broader area around Radstock.

At Ludlows itself mining was extended into the Clandown area in the early 1930s with further extension towards Welton in the summer of 1936. On nationalisation the NCB soon realised that Ludlows was one of the poorer assets it had acquired within Radstock as reserves were low and methods of coal handling were old-fashioned. It came therefore as no surprise that after nationalisation the number of men working in the pit dropped until, by August 1953, only just over 200 men were still working there. Surprisingly, considering the end was so close, during the same year, much of Ludlows' Yard was resurfaced to allow local wagon shunting which, up until then had been carried out by horses, was to be handed over to a road tractor fitted with rail couplings. Less than one year later, on 19th March 1954, the last coal was dug, the last tub of coal being pushed out by Messrs O. Morgan, A. Chivers, B. Jones and B. Rowsell.

Some idea of the importance of this pit can be gauged by a letter to the local press at the time of the pit's closure. This was sent in by Mr James Hewitt who, for 40 years, had been a salesman for the Waldegrave collieries. In his letter he said that: ". . . one of four pits in Radstock that were working when, in 1895, (he) was appointed the responsible salesman for the Radstock Collieries and had to place an output of 120,000 tons per annum of house, gas and steam coal over an area from Paddington to Penzance. The other three pits, Wellsway, Tyning and Middle Pit have (all) been closed . . . and now the last of the four once owned by the Earl of Waldegrave, has sounded the "Last Post".

Mr Hewitt recalled an occasion when Viscount Chewton came of age and when the latter's father, Lord Waldegrave, gave a luncheon to the miners of the four pits mentioned above in tents at South Hill House grounds, the home of James McMurtrie, the General Manager of the pits. In proposing the toast at that function, Mr McMurtrie produced a letter dated 1870 and yellowing with age, in which the Agent of the Estate had written to the Earl of that time stating that coal had been discovered on the Somerset Estates at Radstock (presumably at Middle Pit, Radstock which was then in the process of being sunk) and asking for instructions as to the working of this pit! With Ludlows following on in 1784 the latter was clearly one of the first pits sunk and a clear moneyspinner for the North Somerset.

JAMES McMURTRIE 1839-1914
Born in 1839, James McMurtrie came down from Newcastle upon Tyne in 1862 to act as Head Bailiff for the three following collieries at Radstock: Middle Pit, Ludlows and Wellsway. He was 23 and had not been in Radstock long before the whole place came out on strike against him and there were petitions to have him removed from his job. However, his chief concern was to send £2,000 to Frances, Countess of Waldegrave, every three months to help her with her precarious financial position.

The Countess pushed McMurtrie very hard to send her the cash she so desperately needed. In turn, McMurtrie drove the workers hard, and his letters show that he was continually struggling and fighting with various groups – with coal merchants about prices, with the GWR about terms, with Stuckeys Bank about overdraft rates and, unfortunately and above all, with the miners, the hard working men who dug and raised the coal. He did all the work involved in managing what was, in those days, a large and expanding colliery business. He died in 1914. His importance to the history of Radstock cannot be over-emphasised.

Photograph: Collection of David Warnock

Caption information: Earl Waldegrave, 1970

Middle Pit

Opened about 1779 few details are known about Middle Pit's early history. As we have seen under the history of Clandown Colliery that particular pit was served by a short branch off the SCC tramroad. This "Clan Down Railroad" also served both Old Pit and Middle Pit. However, in spite of the need for better rail communications to Middle Pit it was not until 1881 that construction at last began of a short, standard gauge branch into Middle Pit off the now completed S&D line. Before that time some of Middle Pit's output went out over the GWR, but once the new standard gauge link was opened presumably most of the pit's coal went out over the S&D. The changes brought about by the new connection are well described in Chris Handley's book on *The Railways and Tramways of Radstock* when he says that the 4ft 8½in gauge railway:

"followed the route of the (SCC) tramway exactly, forming a junction with it within the siding system at the west end of the goods yard then running mixed-gauge behind the S&D's Down platform with the 3ft 2in gauge tramway down under the main road and the S&D.

Here the two lines parted company, the tramway taking its old course into Middle Pit whilst the standard gauge line took a slightly more direct route to the pit where new coal staithes were provided. The tramway into Middle Pit was retained to carry spoil and dirt, via the Ludlows' connection, up to the Tyning tipping areas whilst the extension up to Clandown Colliery continued to bring coal down. This, however, was only a temporary arrangement because during the next few months the standard gauge line was extended beyond Middle Pit right up to Clandown displacing the tramway completely over this section. This extension formed the complete S&D-owned Clandown Branch which was some 44 chains in length, and terminating at an end-on junction with the colliery incline (which was similarly converted) up to the pithead. The branch was opened in its entirety on the 18th September 1882."

In the mid-1880s plans were put into action to deepen Middle Pit and the first seam of the Farrington series was reached at a depth of 628ft below the original pit bottom. On 25th January 1886, at a total depth of 1,791ft, the sinking was ultimately completed. Beating Braysdown Colliery (of which we shall hear more later) by some 51ft, this made Middle Pit the deepest in the Somerset Coalfield, this record depth lasting until 1911 when Braysdown itself was further deepened.

In 1894 coal winding at Middle Pit was brought to a somewhat surprising end since the colliery was still in full production. Like Wellsway Pit, its output was subsequently taken underground to Ludlows where it was then handed over to the GWR. This diversion of coal to Ludlows was confirmed in a letter written on 6th March 1896 when James McMurtrie wrote to Lord Waldegrave to confirm that Middle Pit *had* been abandoned for coal winding some two years previously. However, at some later stage, the pit was re-opened only to be closed yet again in 1905 when widespread changes took place. These alterations included the building of new screens, their construction forcing other changes to be made to the railway layout on the S&D's Clandown branch.

Coal winding then continued until the days of the 1926 General Strike when, on 30th April, the pit was closed down. However, total demise was still some years away and it was not until June 1933 that Middle Pit eventually shut for good and the colliery's sidings and relatively new screens fell into disuse.

Tyning Colliery

The most easterly-positioned of the Radstock group of collieries, Tyning, perched on the northern slope of the valley of the Wellow Brook, was sunk in 1837. In that year, under leases of August and September the pit was sunk by Samuel Palmer Blacker, Jacob Collins, John Collins and Elijah Bush. At a later date, possibly in 1838, the colliery became linked, via an incline, into the SCC tramway. In 1847, some ten years after opening, the colliery passed into Waldegrave ownership.

In 1857 the broad gauge connection into Ludlows from the GWR's Frome-Radstock Branch was extended up the incline alongside the SCC tramway to serve Tyning Colliery, thus putting more coal traffic onto the GWR's freight-only line. The SCC branch up to Tyning was therefore no longer required for the purpose of coal haulage. It was re-modelled to run into the similar 3ft 5in gauge tramway branch that went into Ludlows from the SCC so that spoil and dirt traffic could be moved up the incline, into what were then new tipping areas in the Tyning district.

The pit suffered severely, and on several occasions, from water problems and, on 9th October 1876 for example, the colliery was inundated by a good deal of water from the Writhlington series of workings. Some men were drowned in the incident while a fair amount of damage was caused to the colliery itself. In July 1878 a second flood occurred, Writhlington again being held to blame. Nevertheless, in spite of its problems, the colliery continued to produce traffic for the GWR until the early years of the 20th century. By early 1905, still plagued with the problem of underground water, the colliery was coming to the end of its productive period and was working just two days a week.

At this time, the colliery was still served by both the standard gauge connection and the narrow gauge tramway. Indeed, the tramway had been stretched north-westwards into a completely new tipping area, this area dealing with the spoil produced by Ludlows and Middle Pit. However, Tyning's life was soon to be cut short and, on 11th November 1909, coal winding came to an end, although the pit continued in its role as a clearer of underground water for some years after this time. It is thought that Tyning was finally abandoned in 1922. The only activity after abandonment was the continued tipping of dirt from Middle Pit (closed 1933) and Ludlows (closed 1954), the huge coal tips being reminders even today of Tyning's location and existence.

Without doubt, the North Somerset had a good deal to be thankful for in the way of traffic over the years from the Earl Waldegrave's Radstock Collieries, especially those at Wellsway, Ludlows and Tyning.

Before we leave this group of collieries altogether it is

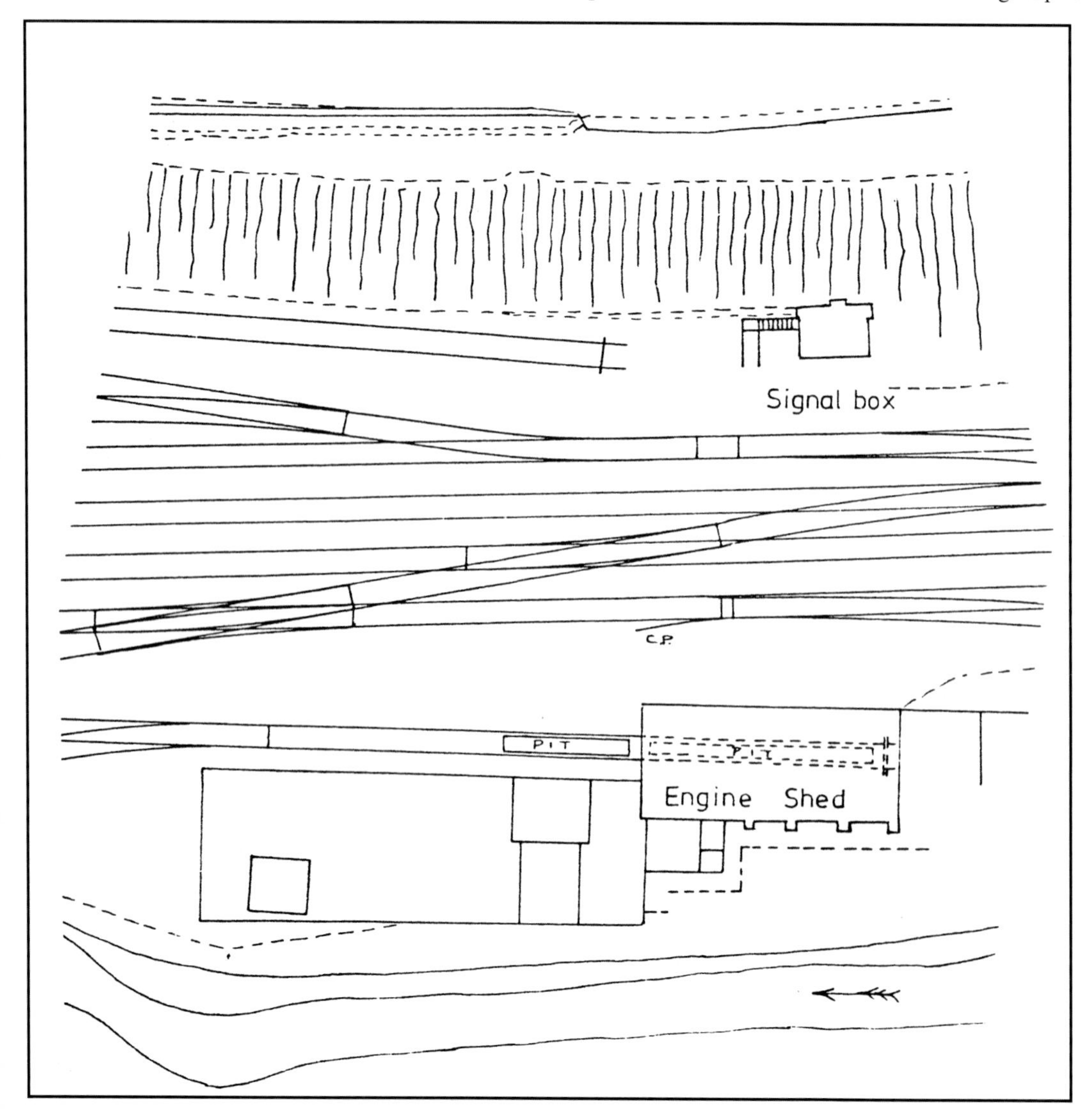

RADSTOCK (GWR): SOUTH SIGNAL BOX AND ENGINE SHED IN THE EARLY YEARS OF THE PRESENT CENTURY

Plan: Chris Handley

necessary to consider a related industry that tied in with the above-mentioned collieries. This was the gasworks at Radstock which was to be found immediately to the south of Middle Pit. Opened in the very late 1850s and extended during 1874, the works were not rail connected until 1882 when standard gauge sidings were provided off the Somerset & Dorset's Clandown Colliery branch. Upon the closure of Middle Pit in 1933, coal was brought by rail from Ludlows Colliery. The works are believed to have closed around 1950.

The Writhlington Group of Collieries

In this, our final group of collieries in the Radstock area, there were, in all, eight pits. Of these, six were involved in putting at least some of their output onto the Radstock-Mells Road section of the GWR. The pits in the group were as follows:

Kilmersdon	Linked directly to the GWR via an incline.
Lower Writhlington	Linked to the GWR via a tramway.
Upper Writhlington	Linked to the GWR via a tramway.
Braysdown	Linked to the GWR via a tramway.
Foxcote	Linked to the GWR via a tramway.
Huish	Directly linked to the GWR via an incline.
Woodborough	Not linked directly to the GWR.
Shoscombe	Not linked directly to the GWR.

All the pits in the Writhlington group stayed under essentially the same ownership right up to nationalisation in 1947 except, that is, for Braysdown which was sold to the Beauchamps in 1899. A powerful group of collieries, the remaining Writhlington collection of pits were not taken over by the Beauchamp family and remained strong competitors to it. Although the pits in the group were a mixed bag economically, the fact that Kilmersdon and Lower Writhlington were the last two remaining collieries in the Somerset Coalfield must say something about how successful their former owners had been in discovering and exploiting Somerset's coal reserves.

Kilmersdon Colliery

Running out of Radstock on the GWR towards Frome, the first Writhlington pit to be encountered was that at Kilmersdon. In November 1872 Lord Hylton of Ammerdown made a decision to offer the Writhlington coal owners a lease on all the upper series' seams of coal running under his Ammerdown Estates. In total, this was an area of some 328 acres and it was too good an offer for Writhlington to turn down, particularly considering the fact that if Writhlington had decided not to go ahead the lease was to be made available to Countess Waldegrave's Radstock Collieries!

Writhlington therefore formed the Kilmersdon Colliery Company, the lease being signed on 25th December 1873, sinking high up on Haydon Hill overlooking the WS&WR, beginning on 6th February 1874. The geology of the area, however, proved difficult and it was not until the end of 1877 that the shafts had reached their completed depth of 858ft. By April 1878 the colliery had sold its first coal and, in order to get its output away from the pithead, a standard gauge link was built from the colliery to the GWR's Wilts, Somerset & Weymouth branch between Radstock and Mells. This connection included a self-acting incline, of which more in Chapter 11, the former joining the main line at a point almost opposite the Writhlington group's colliery at Huish. The agreement for this connection and incline was duly signed on 1st September 1878.

Some twelve years later, in 1889, this railway serving the colliery underwent alteration and in its modified form the new working arrangements saw out the life of the pit in the 1970s. In the colliery's early days the traffic at the pithead itself and on the stretch of railway at the top of the incline was worked by horses. After 1896 the colliery was shunted by an, as yet unidentified, steam locomotive. On 10th September 1929 the pit's most well-known locomotive, a 23 ton Peckett 0-4-0ST (builder's No. 1788), arrived at the pit, and remained in charge through to the colliery's closure in 1973.

However, we have moved forward rather a long way in our story and we need to jump back to the 1890s for, on 6th April 1897, the Kilmersdon company was made into a limited liability business. Around the turn of the century, and certainly before the end of 1904, the shafts at the pit were deepened

KILMERSDON INCLINE AND HUISH & WRITHLINGTON SIDINGS c1905

Radstock is to the left and Mells Road is to the right. *Plan: Chris Handley*

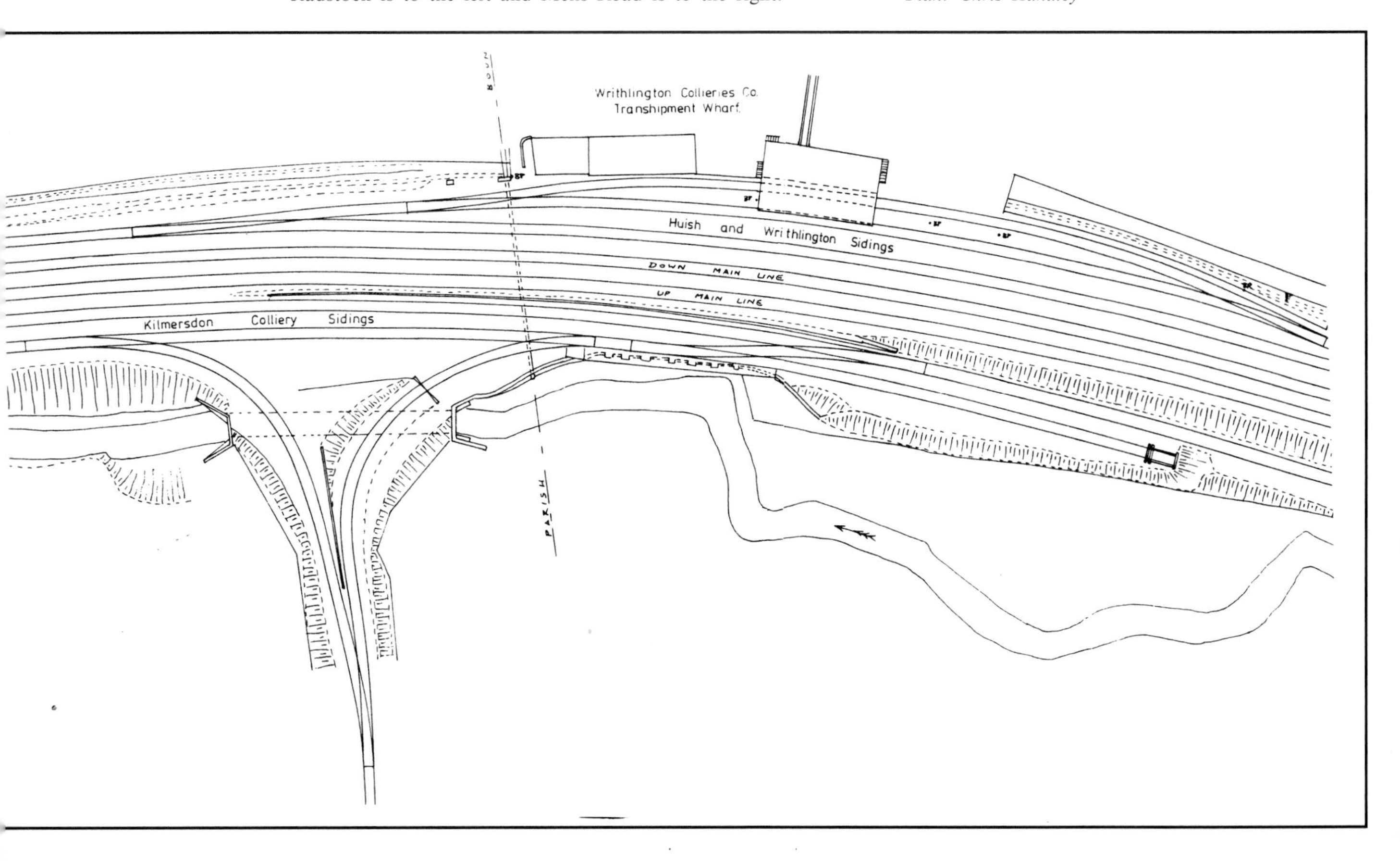

to bite into the Farrington seams of coal. The total depth of the shafts was now 1,582ft. On 6th March 1924 Writhlington signed an agreement confirming the sale to them of Kilmersdon Colliery. Water proved to be a problem in the pit for, in May 1946, flooding followed the partial collapse of the lower part of the pumping shaft. The colliery remained closed for some six months, repair work lasting into 1947 by which time the colliery had been nationalised. In due course the pit was re-opened but some two years later, flooding again proved to be a major problem. By the mid-1950s Kilmersdon had become the only pit in the Radstock area that still sent its coal away via the former GWR line, the other three active collieries in the district (Braysdown, Lower Writhlington and Norton Hill) all being served by the Somerset & Dorset's Bath-Bournemouth line.

In the late 1960s about 80 per cent of the coal being raised around Radstock was destined for two very specific markets, namely the power station at Portishead and the zinc smelting plant at Avonmouth. Due to the continuing existence of these two markets the NCB decided that both Kilmersdon and Lower Writhlington should have their lives extended to supply these users. Indeed, these two particular collieries were already linked underground and the Coal Board had decided to work them as one unit, the method of working being to bring the men up through Kilmersdon's shaft, the majority of the coal being brought to the surface at Writhlington. By 1967, the Kilmersdon railway was unique locally in that it still had its working incline. In 1968 New Rock Colliery (Chilcompton) closed and Writhlington and Kilmersdon were the only two working pits left in the county of Somerset. Together their coal

KILMERSDON COLLIERY
The last tub of Kilmersdon coal, wound a month before on 31st August 1973, still sits at the pit on 30th September 1973.

Tony Wadley

KILMERSDON COLLIERY
This view shows the tub-tipping cradle over the screens and was taken on 30th September 1973.

Tony Wadley

KILMERSDON TIP – ON THE MOVE
In the spring of 1977 special trains of spoil waste were run, on a trial basis, from the tip at Kilmersdon, the trains' loading taking place at Radstock. No. 47130 heads ten vacuum-fitted tipplers towards Frome and is seen here, east of Mells, on 23rd April 1977. No further trains of spoil were run after the trial period had ended.
Mike Miller

production still worked out at a substantial 250,000 tons of coal per year.

During the late 1960s marked changes took place in the railway network around Radstock. For Kilmersdon, however, the next key date was 1973 when the NCB announced that both Kilmersdon and Writhlington collieries were to be closed in the September of that year, their close-down being carried out together. Coal production came to a stop in September as planned although it took several weeks after that to clear remaining coal stocks. The final coal train left Writhlington Colliery on 16th November 1973 while the last remaining NCB-owned wagons at Kilmersdon were brought down the incline during early 1974. The Peckett was not sold off but was fortunately put out to the Somerset & Dorset Railway Trust on extended loan. Now with pithead and railway gone and the route of the incline landscaped, little remains of this interesting colliery and its approach incline. Incidentally, further details of this incline and its mode of operation will be found in Chapter 11.

Lower Writhlington

An important pit, Lower Writhlington Colliery was started in 1829 when two shafts were sunk in the valley bottom of the Wellow Brook near Shoscombe Pit. After 1854 Lower Writhlington Colliery was connected to the SCC's tramway but the high cost of moving coal by this was, for many years, a major problem and disadvantage. After all, the colliery had to pay the SCC to take the coal to Radstock, only to pay further tolls to the Waldegraves to transport it over their tramway, after which it could be put onto the GWR. In the 1860s various schemes were put forward to get a line built from the then developing North Somerset Railway to the pits at Writhlington, including plans to have a tunnel built under Frome Hill linking the GWR directly with the pit at Lower Writhlington. However, this line was never built and the Writhlington group were forced to think again.

In the end, the company constructed a 2ft 8½in gauge cross-country tramway running uphill and down dale, linking the collieries at Foxcote and Lower and Upper Writhlington with the GWR near Huish Colliery on the Radstock-Mells section. Once the tramway reached the GWR, and because it was high above the valley in which the railway ran, the coal tubs had to be lowered down a gravity-worked incline to a new loading dock and sidings on the Great Western Railway. These sidings, the "Writhlington and Huish Sidings", served two separate 2ft 8½in gauge lines. From the Radstock direction the first tub-line to be encountered was to be found a little beyond the Kilmersdon Colliery incline but on the north side of the valley. It terminated at the transhipment dock described above and it was this line that ran to Lower Writhlington Colliery. The other 2ft 8½in gauge tramway served by Writhlington and Huish Sidings, ran from the pithead at Huish and we shall say more about this in a later section.

The Writhlington tramline was probably opened around 1866/67 and included another long incline running up to Frome Hill where a coal depot was set up. Locomotion on the tramway was, at first, provided by horse power of the four-legged variety but after 1882 steam locomotives were used on certain stretches of the tramway. In 1886, Lower Writhlington was, at long last, connected to the nearby S&D line between Radstock and Bath, the latter having opened in 1874. A new transhipment siding was laid in almost directly opposite the colliery sidings at Braysdown.

Strange as it may seem, the Writhlington Collieries' tramway still had a good future ahead of it, although the opening of the S&D's connection was clearly yet another nail in the remnants of the SCC tramway's coffin! Indeed, it was not until 1940 that the Writhlington Collieries' group felt it was finally time to close the remaining section of their tramway which was, at that time, still in position between the steady and satisfactory pit at Lower Writhlington, the coal depot at Frome Hill and the GWR near Huish. Lower Writhlington was now clearly well-served by the S&D and, by those war years, the tramway was only being used by the one colliery (at Lower Writhlington) and by the Frome Hill coal depot.

Although various improvements were carried out through the 1950s, Lower Writhlington stayed much the same past

ALL CHANGE AT RADSTOCK
An unusual motive power combination of North British No. D6329 and "Hymek" No. D7043 come off the S&D/GW connecting line at Radstock on 9th May 1967 with a coal train for Bristol. No. D6329 had been to Evercreech to bring back rails and sleepers that had been lifted by contractors working on the S&D but had then returned light engine to Radstock. No. D7043 was on the regular coal train from Radstock to Bristol running via Mells Road, Frome and Bath.

P.J. Williams

nationalisation. As we have seen in Kilmersdon's history and lifespan, marked changes took place in the 1960s when both collieries were connected together underground and were thenceforth worked as one unit. Once the S&D closed in 1966, Lower Writhlington Pit, inaccessible by road, had to have its coal output transferred onto the former North Somerset line. In order to allow this to happen a new spur was laid in late 1965 between the S&D and the North Somerset. Ironically it was built just to the west of the notorious level crossings in Radstock town centre and was located in exactly the same place as the link proposed in the Somerset & Dorset's Bath Extension Act of 1871. At long last the two former rivals had been joined together. From 7th March 1966 the length of remaining S&D track between Lower Writhlington and Radstock, the new spur and the North Somerset became the regular route of diesel-hauled coal trains out of the Radstock area. On 16th November 1973, the final train of coal left Lower Writhlington and, with its passing the Somerset Coalfield finally disappeared from view, at last.

Upper Writhlington Colliery

First of the key Writhlington pits to be sunk, Upper Writhlington was opened in 1805. Although sunk close to the Somersetshire Coal Canal, in fact, it was not connected and it was not until the 1860s that the pit became joined to the Writhlington tramway from Lower Writhlington to the GWR near Huish. By all accounts there had been plans made to build a branch from the SCC tramway to cater for the colliery's transport needs but this railway does not seem to have been built, the pit's coal being gratefully received by the GWR, via the tramway! However, in 1898, after a somewhat quiet life, the colliery stopped winding coal and quietly died.

Memoranda re the Writhlington Collieries

In a document given to the recently-formed industrial museum at Radstock, some original and interesting information has come to light on the history of Writhlington Collieries. The document concerned was put together by the colliery company's long-standing secretary, Mr Alban Chivers. In his writings he states, among other things, that:
"In the following year (1855) I undertook the construction of the Huish Incline and Railway Sidings. In 1859, commenced the surface arrangements at the new Foxcote Colliery. Planned and superintended the buildings and erections there. Purchased a winding engine at Clutton Ham Colliery and erected the same at Foxcote Pit, and constructed Brickyard, Incline and Tramway to Lower Work."

"In 1867 I laid out and commenced the Tramway from Lower to Upper Work, the Incline to and erection of the Writhlington Depot, and in the following year carried on the same to the Great Western Railway, completing the Loading Sheds and Railway Sidings there (1868). At the same time opened out a quarry of stone and put up a Lime Kiln thus supplying the works with stone and lime on the Tramway with black carriage."

(The original document was dated 31st January 1891.)

Braysdown Colliery

Work on this particular Writhlington colliery appears to have begun about 1840 while colliery winding was certainly in progress in 1845. The coal was taken away from the pit by an incline which ran down to the SCC tramroad, this incline being built following an agreement of 23rd March 1855. Like other Writhlington collieries, Braysdown suffered from the high costs of transport incurred by the SCC tramway. It was therefore hardly surprising when, in 1875, after the arrival of the S&D in the area, new exchange sidings and screens were planned near Braysdown on the S&D's Radstock-Bath section, the connection between colliery and main line railway being filled by a new 2ft 6in gauge incline. The actual date of this work seems somewhat vague, however.

In the early 1960s the winding shaft at Braysdon was sunk to the Farrington series although this deepening proved to be a serious mistake. In 1899 the colliery had been sold to Frank B. Beauchamp and it later passed into the ownership of his Somerset Collieries Limited. Around the early 1920s it was managed jointly with Camerton Colliery. Under the NCB few changes were made but during the 1950s the pits played an important role in pumping water formerly cleared by the then recently-closed Ludlows Colliery. Braysdown eventually closed on 29th October 1959.

Foxcote Colliery

Foxcote appears to have been first mentioned in a lease of 25th March 1853 by which the Foxcote Company was permitted to lease minerals from Sir John Smyth of the Foxcote Estates. The colliery seems to have opened for business around the early part of 1859. To move the coal away from the pithead another section of the Writhlington collieries' 2ft 8½in gauge tramway was built between the pits at Foxcote and Lower Writhlington. As we have seen in our discussions about Lower Writhlington this tramway was further extended to join the GWR near Huish. However, an extension was also later made at the Foxcote Colliery end when the company built another line from the pithead some considerable way across the countryside to a landsale depot near Turners Tower, a spot on the Radstock to Trowbridge road near Ammerdown crossroads. This site proved to be very helpful in cutting costs to the local markets for coal at Trowbridge and Frome. Dates of completion for the various sections are certainly unclear but it seems very likely that the tramway was in use from Lower Writhlington all the way to the GWR by 1868, while the Foxcote-Turners Tower extension must have seen the light of day not long afterwards.

The latter section of tramway was worked by an 0-6-0ST appropriately named *Foxcote.* Built in 1890 by Hudswell, Clarke (builder's No. 369), it came new to the tramway. It was believed to have been sold for scrap around 1928/29 when it is thought that the line to Turners Tower was closed and lifted. Coal winding at Foxcote came to a halt in February 1931 and brought to an end the life of a not very successful, but nevertheless, very interesting pit.

Huish Colliery

The lease for this, the last of the Writhlington collieries that we shall be looking at, was signed on 17th July 1820 between Thomas Ams of Huish, Thomas Samuel and John Twyford Joliffe of Ammerdown and Messrs Purnell (of Woodborough House), Charles Savage, Richard Miles, Messrs Fussell, Broderip, Naish, Roach, Greenhill and John Smith of Radstock. The colliery's first coal was sold in 1824 and the colliery was rated at £720 in 1829. Coal traffic was taken out by road until 1855 when a self-acting incline of 2ft 8½in gauge was put in to link the pithead on the hill to the then recently-opened Frome-Radstock mineral only line down in the valley. Down the incline four or six tubs, each holding some eight hundredweight of coal, were lowered to screens and a transhipment dock at the two roads of Huish Collery sidings which, in turn, were accessed from the Writhlington & Huish Sidings some few chains in the Frome direction. Further development of the pit had been put forward in 1863 when it had been suggested that a new shaft should be sunk alongside the GWR's main line near Huish. However, this work was never carried out. The pit never really proved to be successful and, at the end of February 1912, it was closed as uneconomic.

Coalfield and Railway: An Overview

Looking at the overall relationship between the Somerset Coalfield and the Bristol-Radstock-Frome railway, history shows that in 1881 the southern section of the B&NSR between Radstock and Frome carried the heaviest mineral traffic, with four coal trains destined for Mells Road sidings departing from Radstock between six and half past eleven in the morning. On the other hand, goods traffic on the Radstock-Bristol section was much lighter and it was not until the GWR had taken over this part of the branch, in 1884, that traffic began to grow.

In an examination of the coalfield's production figures for the 1890s, C.G. Down & A.J. Warrington note that:

> ". . . only a third of the total coalfield output was carried by rail, even after railway construction was complete. The (Somersetshire Coal) canal would at this period have affected the figures very little, and so it must be concluded that nearly two-thirds of the coalfield output was disposed of locally by road. Secondly the GWR carried about eight times as much coal as the S&D. If we list the total number of pits connected to each system in, for example, 1899, then twelve were on the GWR and two on the S&D. The six pits at Radstock and Writhlington had connections to both systems and must have made greater use of the GWR, so the construction of the S&D benefited the coalfield little. Even after 1899 the GWR gained two new large collieries to the S&D's one, so these proportions doubtless remained similar."

Between 1901 and 1920, coal production in the Somerset Coalfield grew to almost 1¼ million tons a year. Most of this increased output was the result of the opening of the deep pits at Pensford and Dunkerton, the latter being situated in the Cam Valley. Much of this coal traffic polished the metals of the GWR's North Somerset branches. However, the depression and disputes of the 1920s started the run downhill of the coalfield. Nationalisation came at the end of 1947 while in the 1950s some pits were closed while others were modernised. In 1968 the combined output of Kilmersdon and (Lower) Writhlington was around 250,000 tons a year and it was good to see that most of this coal was still being carried out over the North Somerset branch.

Bristol-Radstock-Frome: Some Other Freight Traffic

As the railway network spread in the 19th century it created traffic for itself. This was most certainly the case for the North Somerset for, as its locomotives required coal so its tracks and stations required stone for ballast and for buildings. The limestone of the Mendips provided a ready source to meet all these needs. In return, the railways of the area provided an obvious and excellent way of carrying locally-quarried stone in bulk. For example, from 1857 the Newbury Railway south of Mells Road Goods Shed was moving limestone to the ironworks at Westbury while on the neighbouring S&D's Bath Extension, opened in 1874, stone was, for example, being put onto rail at Winsor Hill Quarry between Masbury and Shepton Mallet.

By the early years of the 20th century most of the large quarries on Mendip were linked either into the S&D or into the GWR's Bristol-Radstock-Frome line. On the North Somerset, for example, stone was being moved away by rail from such places as Hallatrow (Free's Quarry to the north of the station), Mells Road (from Vobster) and from Vallis Vale Quarries situated close to the Wilts, Somerset & Weymouth Railway between Mells Road and Frome. Between the two world wars the need for roadstone in Britain grew very quickly as did the development of new techniques of quarrying stone. On the Mendips many of the small, local quarries and groups started to merge to form larger firms, one such key amalgamation taking place in 1934 when Roads Reconstruction (1934) was put together. Nowadays, although many of the former quarries fall under the umbrella of two large publicly owned companies, ARC and English China Clays Limited, some of today's major quarries are still owned by local family groups, John Wainwright and Foster Yeoman being two good instances of this.

Most of the earlier Mendip quarries are now closed as are their connecting rail links. However, two of the major working quarries, Merehead Quarry at Cranmore, owned by Foster Yeoman and well-served by a remaining section of the former Wells-Witham branch railway and New Frome Quarry at Whatley, ARC-owned and connected by a private railway to the Radstock-Frome goods-only line, still send the stone out by the iron road, the rest of the area's stone tonnage moving out on the other kind of road! This latter traffic generates thousands of lorry movements per day, heavily increasing road congestion particularly in the areas around Frome. In addition, some quarries specialise in concrete products and this traffic once impinged upon the Radstock-Frome railway's development at the former Mells Road Station.

The B&NSR and its Associated Brickworks

Brickworks were built at several collieries along the length of the Bristol & North Somerset line with those at Greyfield, Clutton and at Tyning, Radstock coming readily to mind. One establishment that deserves a closer look is the North Somerset Brick & Tile Company at Welton. In 1925 work began on the firm's site at Lower Clewes immediately adjacent to the GWR's North Somerset station, some well-known local names appearing on the staff list including John Thatcher (Chairman) and Charles Heal, Fred Andrews and William Taylor (directors).

At first prospects seemed very good and reports of the clay at Broadway, near Clandown, were said to be excellent. In order to get the clay from the site at Broadway, an aerial ropeway was built connecting the claypit to the brickyard at Lower Clewes. Nine pylons of varying height were put up and the ropeway was about one mile in length. The skips were attached to the rope roughly every 200 yards and, apparently during use very little spillage occurred. In July 1926 the district suffered a severe electrical storm and three of the pylons were damaged by lightning. This naturally disrupted production for several weeks. At the company's station-side site, kilns, ten in number, and drying sheds were built.

The first manager at the works was a Mr John Johnson, the total workforce being some 30 men and boys with 120 tons of coal being used per month, 80 for the kilns and 40 for drying purposes. The highest output reached by the firm was 70,000 bricks per week. In the early years of the firm, work at the claypit end went well, all digging being carried out by pick and shovel. However, once a depth of 60ft had been reached, digging by hand became very awkward indeed and 24 hours a day pumping was necessary to get rid of troublesome water.

In addition to the drawback of water, landslips also caused further difficulties. The major problem was that the lime content of the finished bricks made it uphill work to get contracts and, by 1940, Welton Brickworks had closed. Most of the men employed by the firm returned to the pits. By 1941 Dawsons of Clutton had demolished the 120ft chimney that they themselves had erected when the firm had opened. The site was soon acquired by the engineering firm of Ralph Blatchford for war work.

Iron Ore and its Products

In his book on mining in Somerset in the mid-19th century, John Anstie mentions that it was hoped, with the opening of the B&NSR, that considerable deposits of iron ore known to exist at Temple Cloud would be developed. He also added that "good ironstones are known to exist in the (coal) measures of the Nettlebridge Valley" and it is in this area of North Somerset that we *can* look at some iron ore, and related, traffic that came on to the GWR's metals. For example, the output of an iron-stone mine at Nunney, opened in 1873, was sent off to the "Black Country" from Frome station.

THE STAFF OF THE NORTH SOMERSET BRICK & TILE COMPANY, WELTON
Back row (from left to right): Bonar Hamilton, Bob Snook, Arthur Johnson, Isaac Prangley and Jim Dando.
Front row (from left to right): Reg Whittock, Stanley Whittock (brothers), Jim Johnson and Reg Powell. The Johnsons were managers of the company and they had two sons, both of whom worked there.
A. Church

In the Mells area the Fussells' factories produced scythes, spades, shovels, agricultural tools for both the home and the export markets. Their business began in 1744, closing some 150 years later, in 1894. It would seem reasonable to suggest that at least some of this firm's products went out by rail, probably from Frome, most likely perhaps from the goods shed at Mells Road, and possibly even from Mells Road station itself when that finally opened in 1887. With the output of the Newbury Railway passing out through Mells, its station site and later station, this area of the Bristol-Radstock-Frome line must have been an exceptionally busy place in the 1870s and 1880s.

Also between Mells and Frome a gasworks appeared in the 1880s to provide more coal traffic for this end of the North Somerset line. Inspected in February 1887 the permanent way installations provided the gasworks with a short loop and two small sidings. The two junctions onto the main line were locked by means of an Annetts Key attached to the Train Staff, the sidings and their safety points being similarly locked. At its inspection Colonel Rich suggested that the ballast and the embankment at the Frome end should be worked upon so that if an engine or wagon ran through the safety points it would be unable to go over the embankment!

One last traffic, of incidental interest perhaps to the railway but providing some revenue for it nevertheless, was that associated with the former brewing industry on Mendip. In 1889 some 17 breweries existed in the Mendip area. By the end of the First World War there were eight. Today, essentially they are all gone. From around 1860 Coombs at Radstock and Clandown kept those districts 'wet' while there were at least four breweries at Midsomer Norton and Welton. Here Thatchers was the largest and probably the best known. In the 1880s there were some eight breweries alone in and around Frome and, indeed, Baileys, who owned the Lamb Brewery, had large maltings near the station. This firm certainly provided some traffic for the railway, even if the only merchandise it seems to have come up with was yet more coal!

FROME GASWORKS

Original plan: British Rail (Western)

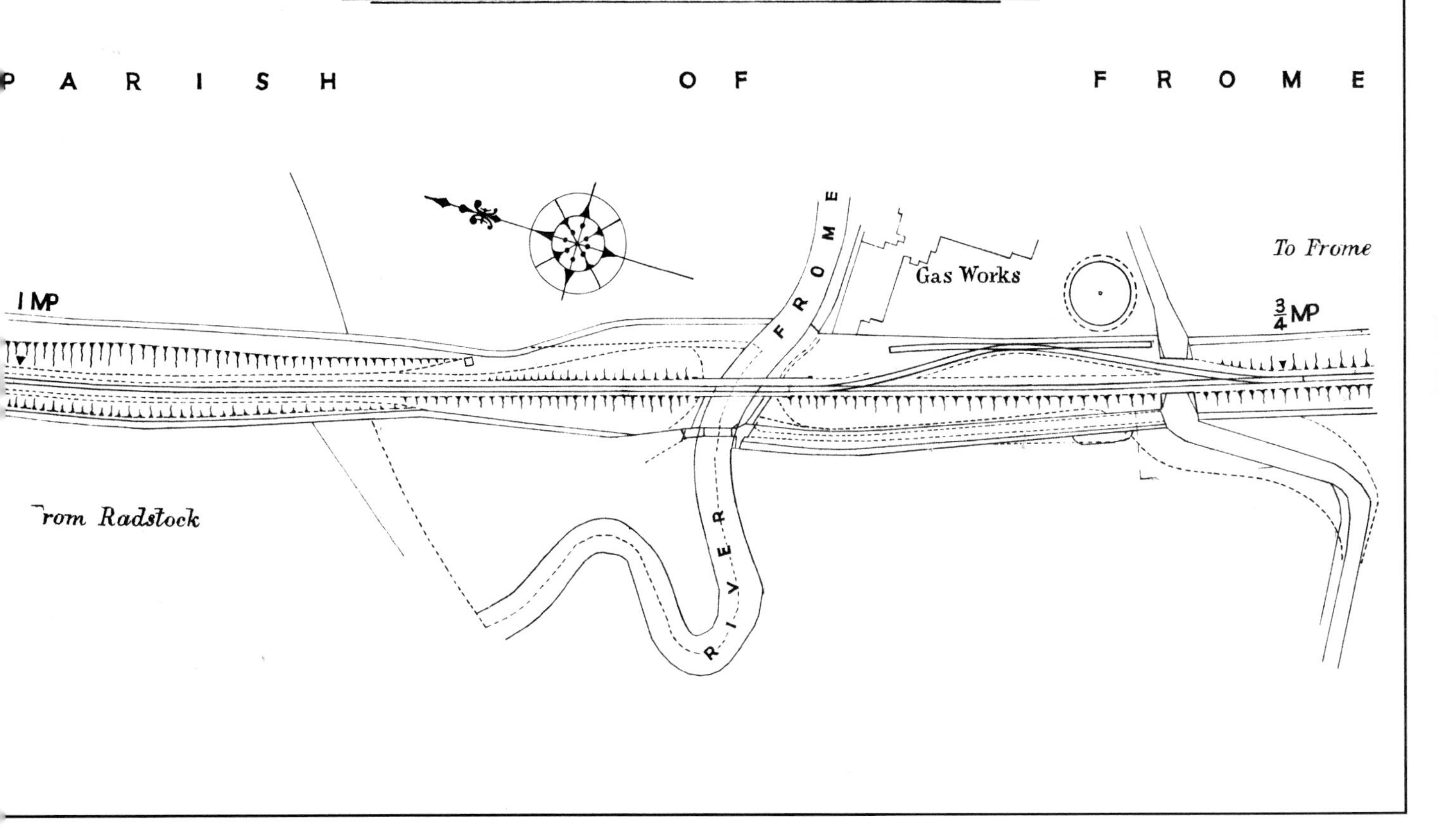

7
Hallatrow: Change for the Camerton Line

Above: HALLATROW 'TWEEN TRAINS
Hallatrow waits quietly for the arrival of the next train. Some special things worth noting include the delightfully ornate and decorated footbridge, the disc signals on that bridge and the beautifully maintained bank to the left of the picture. The station name can be seen in white stone, a popular and attractive feature of the stations at Brislington, Clutton and Hallatrow. The photograph was probably taken at some time during the 1920s. *Collection: M.J. Tozer*

During the middle years of the 19th century the idea of laying a railway to serve the collieries in the Cam Valley was not a new one. Many schemes were put forward, one of the most likely seeming to succeed being the North Somerset Railway scheme of 1860. In this, a line would have been built connecting Wells with Bristol, via Farrington Gurney, Clutton and

Below: CAM VALLEY COAL
With an empty coal train in tow, a GWR 0-6-0 saddle tank takes the lead in the beautiful Cam Valley. This photograph, probably one of the better-known of all those taken on North Somerset railways, captures something of the strange mix of rural railway and country coalfield. *Chapman & Sons*

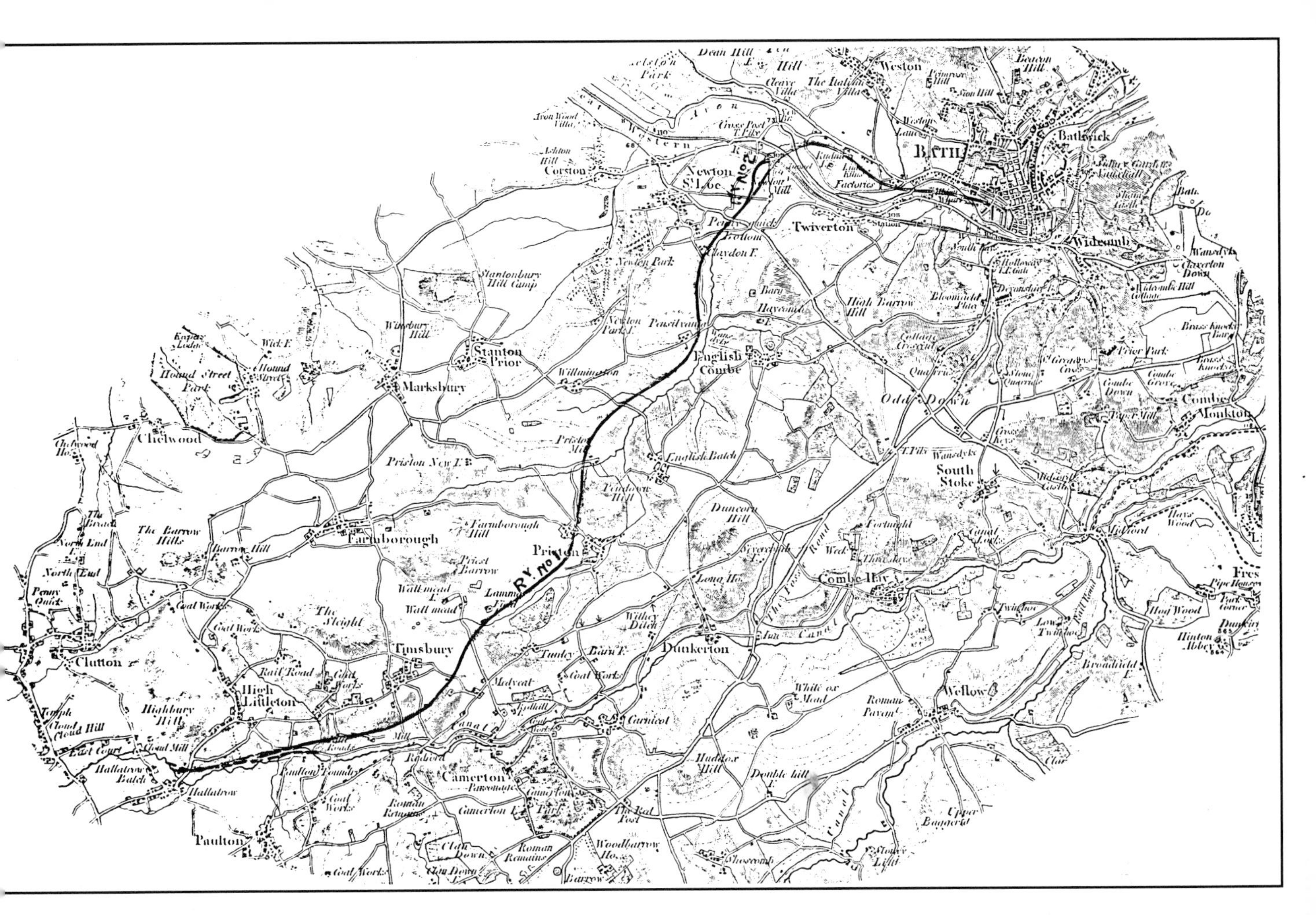

THE BRISTOL & NORTH SOMERSET RAILWAY: (BATH EXTENSION)
Plan deposited 30th November 1863 for the 1864 session.

This very clear plan shows the intended railway to Hallatrow. Note the Somersetshire Coal Canal running from near High Littleton eastwards.

Original plan: Somerset Record Office

Pensford. There would have been two branches, one to Radstock and one to Camerton. The line to Camerton would have left the main Bristol–Wells route near the village of Clutton and would have run to a terminus at Radford Mill. Unlike the railway to Radstock there would have been no triangular junction for this branch, and the line through the Cam Valley would have diverged facing towards Bristol. The branch would have been reasonably level unlike the steep climbs on the main line out of Wells and the somewhat see-saw nature of the Radstock branch. This scheme proved to be a non-starter.

Under the Somerset Coal Railway scheme of 1862 a railway was to have been built from Wincanton on the Somerset & Dorset, through the Ws of Witham Friary, Wanstrow and Whatley and on through Mells, Kilmersdon, Radstock, Midsomer Norton, Camerton, terminating at Timsbury to serve the pits in that area. This railway was also not constructed. Under the original Bristol & North Somerset Railway's Act of 1863 a railway was planned to run from the Hallatrow area to the parish of Camerton to serve the pits there. The cost of this version of the Camerton branch was put at £28,640 and hopes were high that this, and all the other railways authorised by this act, would be built. Unfortunately, the destination at Camerton was not reached by this particular act.

The following year, 1864, another plan for a Camerton branch was proposed under the B&NSR's (Bath Extension) Act. This proposal would have joined Hallatrow with Timsbury, Englishcombe, Twerton and Bath. Not built, the 1864 scheme was followed in 1865 by another such plan to link Camerton with the GWR near Bath and the then-building Midland Railway near Newton St Loe. It looked as if the 1865 scheme had a fair chance of coming to fruition in that in September of that year the area's coal owners had said that they would help towards the line's finances.

Nothing further seems to have happened, however, until 30th August 1871 when, at a B&NSR board meeting, the Company's engineer raised the question of getting parliamentary permission to build the elusive extension to Camerton. However, bearing in mind the Company's then acute financial position, the directors felt that before Camerton could be considered and constructed, the main Bristol to Radstock section had to be built first. Nevertheless, the importance of the Cam Valley scheme must have re-asserted itself for, on 31st December 1872, with help from the GWR, a bill was put forward for the following parliamentary session for reviving plans for the Camerton branch.

On 21st July 1873 the Act for the Camerton branch was passed giving a capital of £40,000 with borrowing powers for an additional £13,300. The GWR was allowed by this bill to subscribe any amount it wanted towards the North Somerset's costs of construction. This freedom proved to be very helpful to the Hallatrow-Camerton stub for, without the GWR's money, the line would not have been built at all! At a B&NSR board meeting held on 5th August 1873 Mr Clarke, the Company's engineer, was asked to prepare and submit detailed estimates for the building of the Cam Valley branch for use by the GWR. It becomes clear that it was to be much involved in the line's construction. At a 6th May meeting held in 1874 it was noted that the North Somerset Company's solicitors had received a draft agreement from the GWR allowing it to work the Camerton branch once it was actually built. At the same meeting the directors agreed to proceed at once with surveys and plans for the Camerton line and to enter into discussions with land-owners on the route. The GWR was to be asked if it could come up with cash for the line's construction and for the services of Mr Clarke, the engineer. However, no 'grass-roots' work was to be started at this stage! By early July 1874 a working agreement had been reached with the GWR.

A year later, at a board meeting held on 30th June 1875, the directors agreed to the construction of a siding at Hallatrow, while Mr Clarke was told to advertise for tenders to construct the Camerton branch. At the same time it was decided to start negotiations with the Somersetshire Coal Canal

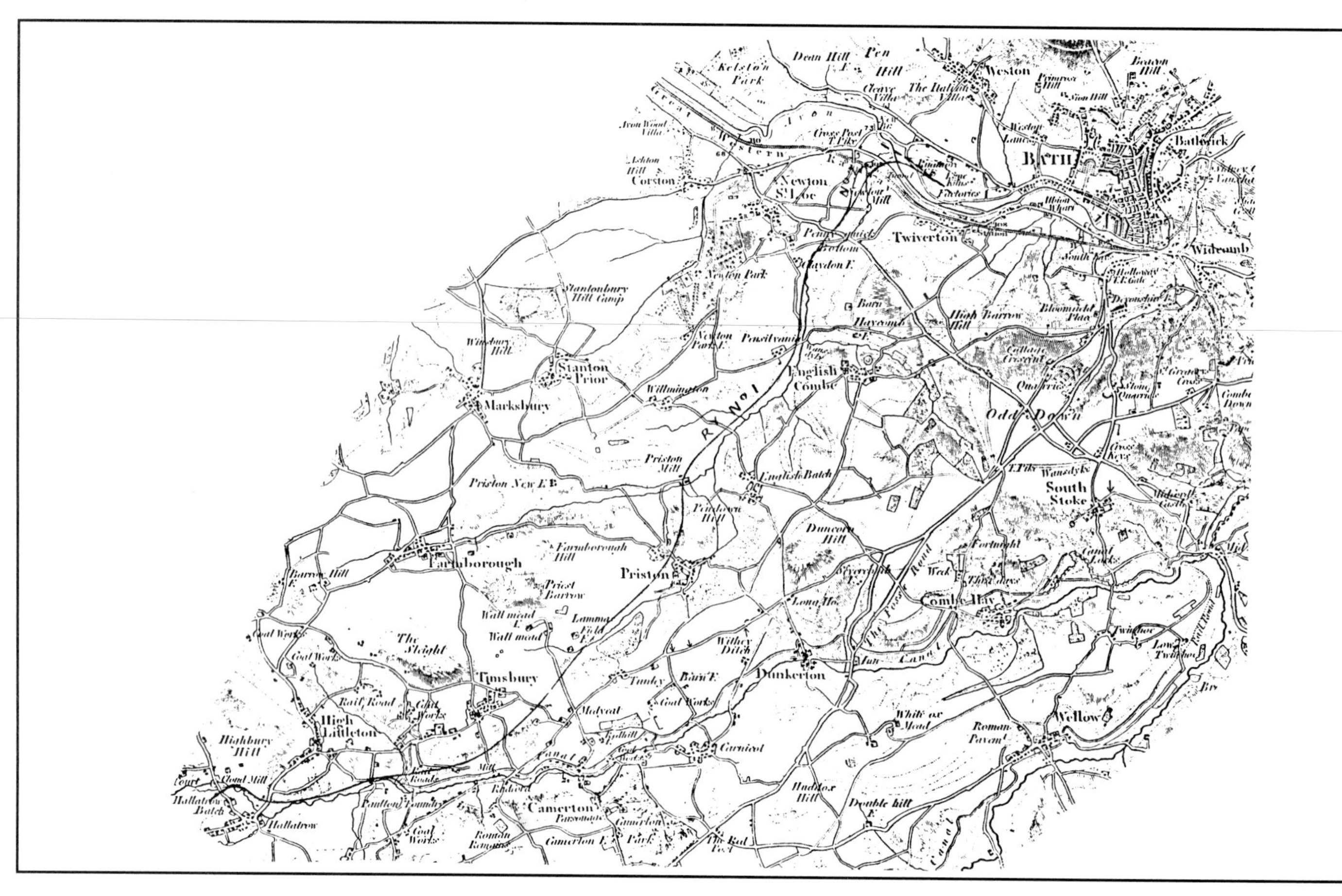

THE BRISTOL & NORTH SOMERSET RAILWAY (BRISTOL-BATH LINES)
Plan deposited 30th November 1864 for the 1865 session.

This plan shows the line running south from Bath through Englishcombe, Priston and Timsbury to Hallatrow.

Original plan: Somerset Record Office

THE JUNCTION AT HALLATROW

This plan, dated 1873, shows the planned junction of the Hallatrow-Camerton branch with the main Bristol & North Somerset line between Bristol and Radstock.

Original plan: Somerset Record Office

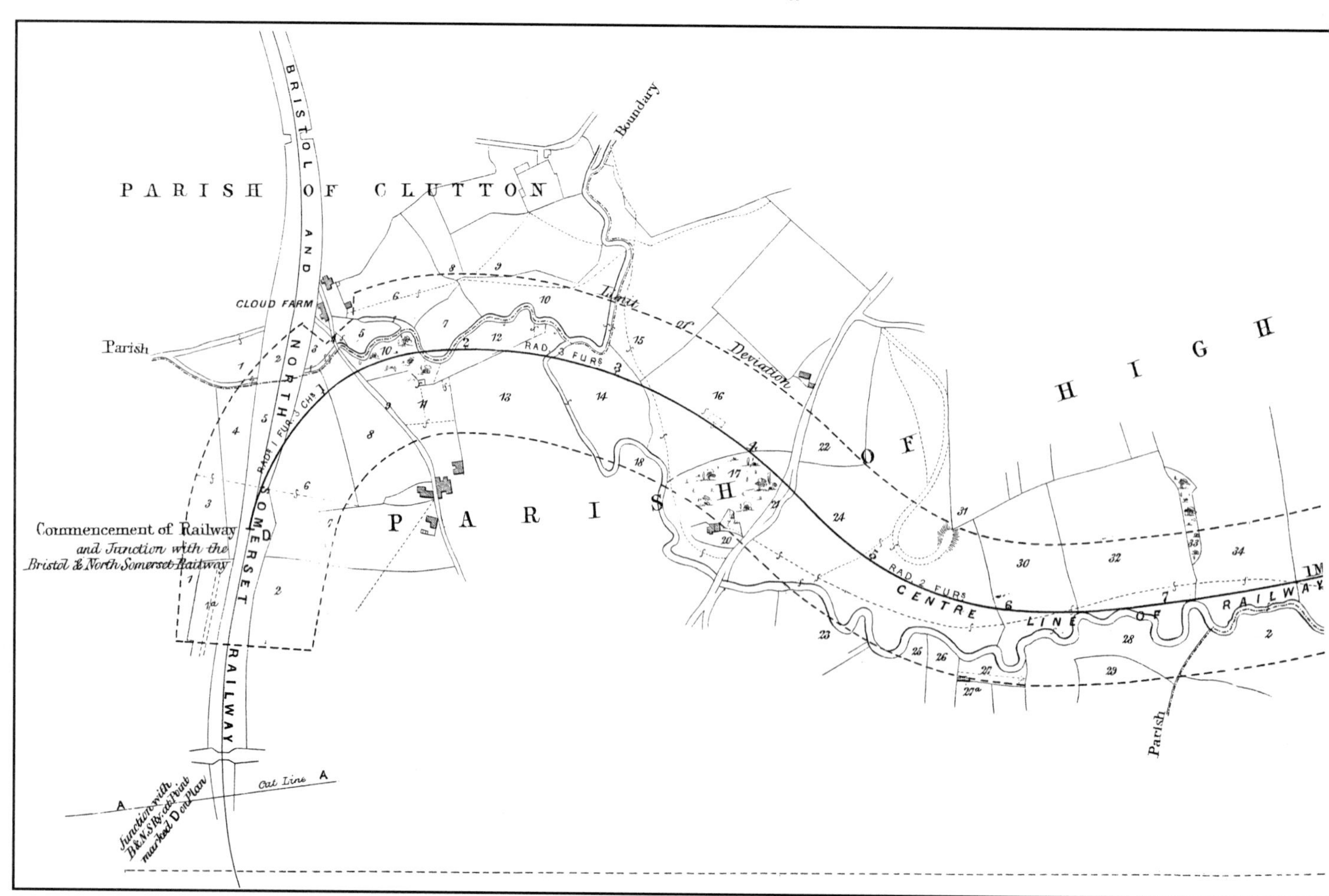

HALLATROW IN ITS PRIME
With Bristol and Frome trains crossing and with the Limpley Stoke railmotor to the extreme right of this photograph, Hallatrow nestles both into the Somerset countryside and into being busy. The struggles of its construction are all forgotten in this scene taken just after the opening of the line through to Limpley Stoke.

Chapman & Sons

to get permission to cross its canal. Work was to go ahead to give assistance(!) to the GWR and its solicitors to complete the land acquisition for the branch, the GWR bearing all the expenses incurred. In addition, the Great Western would transact the general business associated with the new branch through its own solicitors. On this occasion it looked like the North Somerset got out of some financial trouble for once!

Hallatrow, junction for the proposed branch, eventually had a station that was placed in an especially beautiful and gentle setting. Many of its former staff to whom the author has spoken have said what a pleasant position the station found itself in. One interesting aspect of the station's early history has come to light in an agreement of 11th August 1875 which stated that:

> "... during the construction of the North Somerest Railway, the GWR required as a condition of their accepting and working that railway that the North Somerset Company should provide a station at Hallatrow."

The Earl of Warwick, one of the B&NSR's strongest supporters, was at this point in time in no mood to provide funds for Hallatrow station itself. This was not at all surprising since in 1875 the B&NSR owed him over £78,000! However, the agreement also adds how necessary the construction of Hallatrow was and goes on to inform us that:

> "the said contractors (Saunders & Ward) at the request of the North Somerset Co. and of the said Earl have constructed the said Hallatrow station at a cost which has been agreed at the sum of £2,359 16s 5d (£2,359.82) ..."

An important link in the Camerton branch scheme had been forged!

At a special meeting held on 3rd September 1875 the agreement between the B&NSR and the GWR over the Camerton branch had been confirmed. On 24th October, the GWR's board of directors accepted a tender from Mr W. Monsley for the branch's construction, the job having to be completed for £19,000 and by 1st June 1880. A duplicate contract was sealed and returned by the GWR. Whether problems were encountered during the building of the stub is open to some doubt as later discussions of financial figures will suggest.

Further progress on the branch took place in 1876 when, at a special meeting held in early June, the GWR Act for the deviation of the branch at the eastern (Camerton) end was approved. The new route was to be:

> "A railway commencing in the Parish of Timsbury ... by a junction with the Camerton branch authorised to be constructed by the B&NSR Act of 1873 at or near the western side of a road called Mill Lane, which leads from Radford Mill to Timsbury ... in the Parish of Timsbury, and terminating in the Parish of Camerton at or near and on the eastern side of the Blacksmith's Shop adjoining the New Pit Colliery ... and to abandon the construction of so much of the said authorised Camerton Branch Railway as will be rendered unnecessary by the construction of the said intended railway ..."

This became the line of the Hallatrow–Camerton branch as built.

Once the plans had been finalised the project went ahead and the line was finished and subsequently inspected by the Board of Trade Inspector, Major General C.L. Hutchinson on 15th October 1880. His report read as follows:

> "Sir,
> I have the honour to report for the information of the Board of Trade, that in compliance with the instructions contained in your letter of the 8th instant, I have inspected the Camerton branch of the Bristol & North Somerset section of the Great Western Railway.
>
> The branch which joins the B&NSR line at Hallatrow station and thence runs to Camerton its present terminus, is a single line 3½miles long on the 4ft 8½in gauge. Land has been purchased and some of the overbridges constructed for a double line.
>
> The steepest gradient has an inclination of 1 in 66 and the sharpest curve a radius of 11¼ chains. The permanent way for about a mile consists of flat bottomed steel rails weighing 72lb per yard secured to each sleeper by a fang bolt or a dog spike: on the remaining 2½ miles double headed steel rails have been used weighing 82lb per yard fixed by inside keys in cast iron chairs weighing 38lb each; the rails are fished at the joints (author's comment: what a delightful expression!) Each chair is fastened to the sleepers by two iron spikes. The sleepers are creosoted and measure 8ft 11in x 10in x 5in. The ballast consists of furnace slag ashes and broken stone.
>
> There are four bridges over the line constructed with brick or masonry abutments, spanned by cast iron or

THE CAMERTON BRANCH 1873

This plan shows the Camerton branch (eastern end) as put forward under the 1873 Act.

Original plan: Somerset Record Office

THE CAMERTON BRANCH 1875/6

This related plan shows the Camerton branch (eastern end) as put forward and built under the plans and act of 1875/6.

Original plan: Somerset Record Office

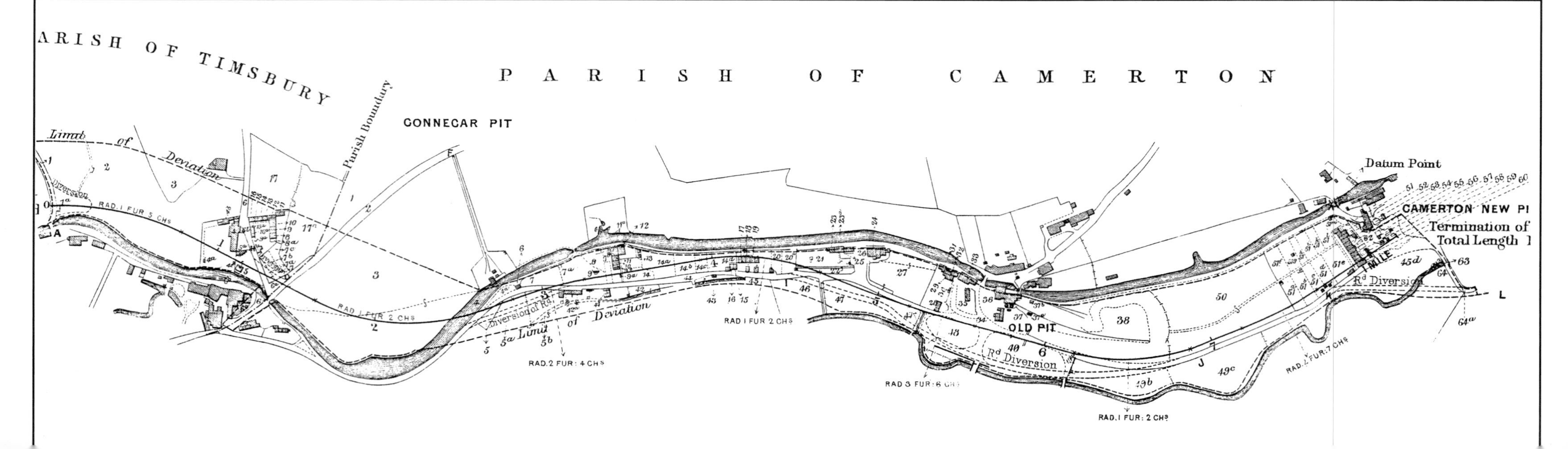

wrought iron girders with arches turned between them, largest span 30½ft. Under the line there are eleven bridges, all constructed with brick or masonry abutments, two having brick arches, and the others wrought iron type, the largest span being 26½ft. There are also five large culverts of which one (6ft span) has a timber top.

The works appear to have been all substantially constructed and to be standing well, the wood and cast iron guides have sufficient theoretical strength, and those under the line gave moderate deflections under test. There are no tunnels, and no public road level crossings. The fencing is of post and rail.

Hallatrow station has been re-modelled so as to adapt it for the reception of the branch trains, and a new station has been erected at the terminus at Camerton, there being no intermediate station; the signalling arrangements at these two stations have been properly carried out, in a raised cabin and ground frame at Hallatrow and raised cabin at Camerton.

I observed the following requirements:

(1) At Hallatrow Junction the fencing near the termination of the new platform should be removed and the platform should end in a ramp. The distant signals from Bristol and Radstock require electrical repeaters and the former should be moved further back. An additional safety point worked from the ground frame is required at the goods loop.

(2) (At Camerton station) the crossover road at the platform should be moved further back so that a train should not stand on the facing points. The 'up' home signal should be moved forward and made a starting signal. The signalman's view of the distant signal requires improving by removing the branch of a tree. Clocks are required in the station and signal cabin.

(3) Some additional fencing is required at several places as pointed out and a hand rail on the underbridge close to Camerton station.

(4) The bank close to Hallatrow station has settled during the late rains and will need careful watching and treatment.

The line is to be provided with one engine at a time under steam and the Train Staff; and an undertaking to this effect should be sent in both by the GWR and North Somerset companies.

Subject to this undertaking being duly received and the above requirements being promptly completed and an intimation of their completion sent to the Board of Trade, and to the line being re-inspected on the first convenient opportunity, the opening of the Camerton branch for passenger traffic need not be objected to.

C.S. Hutchinson
October 1880"

Finance had again become an important issue and, by a B&NSR board meeting held on 11th January 1881, the GWR confirmed, through a letter from its secretary, Mr Saunders, that £42,214 13s 8d (£42,214.67) had already been spent on constructing the branch. The GWR had therefore called for the creation and issue of the Camerton branch capital of £40,000; and for the creation of (debenture) stock for £13,300 and for the issue of sufficient of that stock to meet the balance of the £42,214.67! This the North Somerset Board agreed to do, subject to the provisos of the 1873 Act and the agreement of the 14th July 1876 mentioned earlier. These arrangements were agreed at a meeting of the GWR's Board held on 1st December 1881. In turn, these would allow the line's opening to go ahead.

Indeed, earlier in 1881, a letter from the Board of Trade to the North Somerset had stated that:

"As regards the Clutton(!) and Camerton branch of the North Somerset Railway the Board of Trade have required that the line shall be worked upon the Train Staff System . . . (and that) . . . as soon as the undertaking is given, the Board of Trade will be prepared to sanction the opening of the railway for traffic."

The requirements of this and the earlier inspection obviously having been dealt with, the line was inspected by Hutchinson yet again on 21st May 1881:

"Sir,

I have the honour to report for the information of the Board of Trade that in compliance with the instructions contained in your minute of the 9th instant I have re-inspected the Camerton branch of the Bristol & North Somerset Section of the GWR.

I find that the requirements set forth in my report of 15th October last (1880) have been complied with.

Since the date of that report a slip has occurred where the line runs near a canal. The slip seems to have been overcome for the present, but it will require most careful watching.

The chains acting as fencing across the river diversions require regulating in height some being rather too high and others too low.

Nos 2 and 3 levers at Camerton station should not be interlocked.

I enclose satisfactory undertakings with regard to the working of the traffic.

Subject to the above remarks and to these undertakings there appears to be no further objection to the Camerton branch being opened for passenger traffic.

C.S. Hutchinson
Major General R.E."

Once the GWR had agreed to the new financial arrangements of December 1881, a special meeting was held of the North Somerset's board of directors on 31st March 1882 which then allowed the company to raise the Camerton branch capital. By this time the railway had been opened for both passenger and goods traffic, the actual opening taking place on 1st March 1882. At very long last the 3½ mile long branch was in use, some 20 years after the B&NSR had first proposed its building. Perhaps the fact that this line had been built to take both freight and *passenger* traffic was a source of delay during its construction?

Once in business, the Camerton stub had an immediate impact on the Somersetshire Coal Canal along whose length the new line ran parallel. By an agreement dated 5th September 1882 connection was made into New Pit Camerton and after this time coal was moved out by rail, the SCC being the inevitable loser. Having reached Camerton in our story it would seem an opportune time to look at the Camerton collieries in a little more detail.

"Camerton itself, situate some six miles from Bath, possesses a handsome church containing some curious tombs and a churchyard which is considered to be one of the prettiest in the kingdom. Camerton Court, the seat of the Jarrett family, is an old and interesting country mansion. The adjoining parish of Dunkerton lies in a deep valley. Some little distance away is a remarkable eminence called Duncombe Hill, whereon stood a carnedd, or immense heap of stones, erected by the early Britons to commemorate a victory. Coombe Hay, on the verge of a rich "coombe" or valley, is surrounded by delightful, highly-cultivated country. Close by a Roman fosse in its original and perfect form may be seen raised very high, with a deep fosse, or ditch, on either side."
(Source: "The Camerton and Limpley Stoke Railway" by A.W. Arthurton: Railway Magazine July 1911)

The Camerton Collieries

There were two collieries at Camerton, the first of which was granted a lease on 13th November 1871. The second pit, quite understandably known as New Pit, had been sunk by 1800 and was to be found a few hundred yards to the east of Old Pit.

CAMERTON NEW PIT

There were two pits in the immediate Camerton area: Camerton Old and Camerton New. New Pit was at work as early as 1800 while Old Pit had been granted its lease some twenty years earlier in November 1781. Initially, the output of both collieries left the district by road. Later, it was transferred to the Somersetshire Coal Canal with the railway taking this job over once it was opened through to Camerton in 1882.

Old Pit closed for winding coal in about 1898 but was left open to provide an airway and an escape route for New Pit, to which it was connected underground. With the exhaustion of reserves in the Radstock Series into which New Pit tapped, the colliery wound its last coal on 14th April 1950. With its closure came the virtual demise of the Camerton-Limpley Stoke section of the former Hallatrow-Limpley Stoke, Cam Valley branch.

Bob Parsons

BRISTOL, RADSTOCK AND FROME.

The Line from Marsh Junction to Radstock is single (Pensford, Clutton and Hallatrow* are the intermediate Crossing Stations) from Radstock to Mells double, and from Mells to Frome Junction, single.

The Single portions are worked by Train Staff and Ticket and Disc Block Telegraph. The following are the particulars of the Staffs and Tickets.

SECTION.	Form of Staff and Tickets.	Colour of Ticket.
Marsh Junction and Pensford.	Square.	Red.
Pensford and Clutton.	Round.	White.
Clutton and Hallatrow.	Square.	Green.
Hallatrow and Radstock	Triangular.	Blue.
Mells and Frome Mineral Junction.	Round.	White

* Hallatrow is only available for crossing Two Goods Trains or a Goods and a Passenger Train.

For Special Instructions for working the Inclines on this Branch see Circular dated April, 1885.

Somerset Quarries Stone Siding, Frome, is worked with Annett's key, under special instructions dated February, 1894.

Gas Works Siding, Frome, is worked with Annett's key, under special instructions dated December 15th, 1886.

Market Siding, Frome, is worked under special instructions dated April, 1885.

DOWN TRAINS.—WEEK DAYS.

M.	C.	STATIONS.	1 D Goods and Coal	3	5 A Passenger.	7 D Coal.	9 D Bristol Goods & Coal.	11 D Goods.	13 A Passenger.	15 A Passenger.	17 C Trowbr'ge Engine. No. 1.	19 D Trowbr'ge Engine. No. 2.
			A.M.		A.M.	A.M.	A.M.	A.M.	A.M.	P.M.	P.M.	P.M.
—	—	Bristol (T. Meads) dep.	5 45	..	7 32	..	..	..	10 10	12 40	..	..
—	61	N. S. Junction ,,	6 0	..	7 35	..	..	..	10 13	12 43	..	..
—	—	East Depot ,,	6 25	..	—	..	8 20	9 15	—	—	..	..
—	75	Marsh Junction ,,	CS	..	CS	..	CXS	CXS	CXS	CXS	..	..
2	7	Brislington ,,	—	..	7 40	..	V	9 30	10 18	12 48	..	..
6	56	Pensford arr.	--	..	7 51	..	8X55	9X50	10 29	12X59	..	..
		Pensford dep.	6 45	..	7 52	..	9 2	10 5	10 30	1 0	..	..
9	74	Clutton arr.	6 54	..	8X0	..	9 17	10•20	10•38	1 8	..	..
		Clutton dep.	6 55	..	8 1	..	9 25	11X45	10 39	1 9	..	..
11	30	Hallatrow arr.	7 5	..	8 4	..	9X35	11 55	10 42	1 12	..	..
		Hallatrow dep.		..	8 6	..	10 0	12X20	10 44	1 14	R	..
13	34	Old Mills Siding ,,	..	..	—	..	10 25	12 50	—	—	..	..
14	39	Welton ,,	..	..	8 15	..	10 40	—	10 53	1 23	..	..
15	20	Old Welton Siding ,,	..	..	—	..	—	—	—	—	..	..
15	57	Wells Way ,,	..	..	—	RR	W	—	—	—	..	..
15	70	Radstock arr.	..	..	8 19	..	10•45	1 0	10X57	1 27	..	..
		Radstock dep.	..	..	8 22	9 30	11 20	Engine of this Train works Wells Way Sdg.	11•0	1 30	2 40	..
18	70	Mells arr.	..	..	—	9 50	11 40		—	—	CS	..
		Mells dep.	..	..	8 31	10 5	11 50		11 9	1X39	X—	3 30
—	—	Somerset Quar. Sdg ,,	..	..	—	—	12 15		—	—	—	..
23	20	Gas Works Siding ,,	..	..	—	—	12 30		—	—	—	CR
23	36	Market Siding ,,	..	..	—	—	—		—	—	—	..
23	78	Frome Mineral Junc. arr.	..	..	CS	10 30	12 35		CS	CS	3 25	3 55
24	13	Frome ,,	..	..	8 42	—	—		11 20	1 50	—	..

STATIONS.	21	23 A Passenger.	25	27	29 D Goods and Coal.	31	33 A Passenger.	35 A Passenger.	37 A Passenger.	39 D Trowbr'ge Engine. No. 2.	41 A Passenger.	SUNDAYS 43 A Passenger.	SUNDAYS 45 A Passenger.
		P.M.			P.M.		P.M.	P.M.	P.M.	P.M.	P.M.	A.M.	P.M.
Bristol (T. Meads) dep.	..	2 17	..	..	..	..	3 45	5 7	6 35	..	9 0	8 13	5 55
N. S. Junction ,,	..	2 20	..	..	..	..	3 48	5 10	6 38	..	9 3	8 16	5 58
East Depot ,,	..	—	..	..	2 25	..	—	—	—	..	—	—	—
Marsh Junction ,,	..	CS	..	..	CS	..	CS	CS	CS	..	CXS	CS	CS
Brislington ,,	..	2 25	..	..	—	..	3 53	5 15	6 43	..	9 8	8 21	6 3
Pensford arr.	..	2 37	..	..	2 55	..	4 4	5 26	6 54	..	9 19	8 32	6 14
Pensford dep.	..	2 39	..	..	3X15	..	4 5	5 27	6 55	..	9 20	8 33	6 15
Clutton arr.	..	2 49	..	..	3 30	..	4 13	5X35	7 3	..	9X28	8 41	6 23
Clutton dep.	..	2X56	..	..	3 45	..	4 14	5 38	7X4	..	9 29	8 42	6 24
Hallatrow arr.	..	2 59	..	..	3 55	..	4 17	5 41	7 7	..	9 32	8 45	6 27
Hallatrow dep.	..	3 1	..	..	4•25	..	X4•19	5 43	7 X9	..	9 34	8 47	6 29
Old Mills Siding ,,	..	—	..	..	4 50	..	—	—	—	..	—	—	—
Welton ,,	..	3 10	..	..	5 5	..	4 28	5 51	7 18	..	9 43	8 56	6 38
Old Welton Siding ,,	..	—	..	..	—	..	—	—	—	..	—	—	—
Wells Way ,,	..	—	..	..	—	..	—	—	—	..	—	—	—
Radstock arr.	..	3X14	..	..	5X10	..	4 32	5X55	7 22	..	9 47	9 0	6 42
Radstock dep.	..	Thurs. & Sats. only.	..	..	6•10	..	4 35	5•57		7 30	9 50	9 3	6 45
Mells arr.	..		..	..	6 25	..	—	—	..	7 50	—	—	—
Mells dep.	..		..	..	6 30	..	4 44	6 6	..	8X5	9 59	9 12	6 54
Somerset Quar. Sdg ,,	..		..	..	—	..	—	—	..	—	—	—	—
Gas Works Siding ,,	..		..	..	R	..	—	—	..	—	—	—	—
Market Siding ,,	..		..	..	—	..	—	—	..	—	—	—	—
Frome Mineral Junc. arr.	..		..	..	6 55	..	CXS	CS	..	8 30	CS	CS	CS
Frome ,,	..	..	..	..	—	..	4 55	6 17	..	—	10 10	9 23	7 5

P To be assisted from Hallatrow to Old Mills by Camerton Branch Engine when required and from Radstock to Mells by Trowbridge Engine, No. 1. R To be assisted from Radstock to Mells by Trowbridge Engine No. 2. S See note S, page 17. V Calls at Brislington for S T work only, and does not detach Wagons at Pensford and Clutton. W Assisted from Radstock to Mells by Trowbridge Engine No. 1. Y Via North Somerset Junction. ‡ Loco. Yard.

FROME, RADSTOCK AND BRISTOL.

UP TRAINS. WEEK DAYS.

M.C.	STATIONS.	2 D Trowbridge Engine No. 1.	4 D Goods. S	6 A Passenger.	8	10 A Passenger.	12 A Passenger.	14 A Light Engine.	16 A Passenger.	18 D Coal.
		A.M.	A.M.	A.M.		A.M.	A.M.	A.M.	A.M.	A.M.
	Frome dep.	..	..	..	..	8 10	9 5	..	10 37	..
—13	Frome Minl. Junc.	5 30	6 0	..	..	CS	CS	..	CS	Engine works Transfer Trains at Bristol, see No. 3 Section.
—57	Market Sdg. ,,	—	—	..	..	—	—	..	—	
—73	Gas W'ks Sdg. ,,	—	—	..	..	—	—	..	—	
— —	Somerset Qrs. Sdg.	—	—	..	..	—	—	..	—	
5 23	Mells arr.	5 50	6 20	..	..	8 22	9 17	..	10 49	
	Mells dep.	6 0	6 50	..	..	8 23	9 18	..	10 50	
8 23	Radstock arr.	6 15	7 5	..	..	8 31	9 26	..	10•58	
	Radstock dep.			7 42	..	8 33	9 28	..	11X0	
8 36	Wells Way ,,	..	..	—	..	—	—	..	—	
8 73	Old Welt. Sdg ,,	..	RR	—	..	—	—	RR	—	
9 54	Welton ,,	..	..	7 47	..	8 38	9 33	..	11 5	
10 59	Old Mills Sdg. ,,	..	..	—	..	—	—	10 10	..	
12 63	Hallatrow arr.	..	..	—	..	8 45	9 40	10 15	11 12	..
	Hallatrow dep.	..	..	7 55	..	8 46	9X41		11 13	11 35
14 19	Clutton arr.	..	..	7X59	..	8 50	9 45	..	11X17	11X45
	Clutton dep.	..	..	8 2	..	8 51	9 46	..	11 18	12 0
17 37	Pensford arr.	..	..	8 9	..	8 58	9X53	..	11 25	—
	Pensford dep.	..	..	8 10	..	8X59	9 54	..	11 28	CS
22 6	Brislington arr.	..	..	8 19	..	9 8	10 3	..	—	—
	Brislington dep.	..	..	8 22	..	9 11	10 6	..	—	—
23 18	Marsh Junction	..	..	CXS	..	CXS	CXS	..	CS	CXS
23 28	East Depot arr.	..	..	—	..	—	—	..	—	12 30
23 32	N. Som. Jn. arr.	..	..	8 26	..	9 15	10 10	..	11 39	..
24 13	Bristol (Tm. Ms.)	..	..	8 29	..	9 18	10 13	..	11 42	..

STATIONS.	20 D 8.5 a.m. Holt Goods & Coal.	22 D Trowbridge Engine No. 1.	24 D Trowbridge Engine No. 2.	26 A Passenger.	28 D Coal.	30 D Coal.	32 A Passenger.	34 D Goods and Coal.	36 D Bristol Goods and Coal.	38 D Trowbridge, Engine No. 2.	40 A Engine.	42 A Passenger.	44 D Coal.	SUNDAYS. 46 A Passenger.	SUNDAYS. 48 A Passenger.
	A.M.	A.M.	P.M.	P.M.	P.M.	P.M.	P.M.	P.M.	P.M.	P.M.	P.M.	P.M.	P.M.	A.M.	P.M.
Frome dep.	..	..	..	2 15	..	..	4 58	..	..	..	..	7 50	..	10 0	8 10
Frome Minl. Junc.	9 40	..	1 10	CS	..	..	CXS	..	2 30	5 10	..	CS	Thursdays and Saturdays only.	CS	CS
Market Sdg. ,,	—	..	—	—	..	..	—	..	—	—	..	—		—	—
Gas W'ks Sdg. ,,	—	..	—	—	..	..	—	..	—	5 20	..	—		—	—
Somerset Qrs. Sdg.	—	..	—	—	..	..	—	..	2 48	—	..	—		—	—
Mells arr.	10 0	..	1X30	2 27	..	..	5 10	..	3X0	5 40	..	8X2		10 12	8 22
Mells dep.	10 25	11 45	1 55	2 28	..	..	5 11	..	3 10	5 50	6 30	8 3		10 13	8 23
Radstock arr.	10•40	11 55	2 10	2 36	..	..	5•19	..	3•25	6 5	6 40	8 11		10 21	8 31
Radstock dep.	11 20			2 38	2 45	3X15	5X21	..	6X0			8 13	8 25	10 24	8 33
Wells Way ,,	—	..	..	—	—	—	—	..	—	..	..	—	—	—	—
Old Welt. Sdg ,,	—	..	..	—	—	—	—	..	—	..	..	—	—	—	—
Welton ,,	11 45	..	..	2 43	—	—	5 26	..	6 20	..	..	8 18	—	10 31	8 38
Old Mills Sdg. ,,	12 0	..	..	—	3 30	3 55	—	..	6 35	..	..	—	—	—	—
Hallatrow arr.	12X8	..	..	2 50	3X40	4X5	5 33	..	6 45	..	..	8 25	8 45	10 38	8 45
Hallatrow dep.	12 15	..	..	2 51			5 34	6 35	7X23	..	..	8 27	8 55	10 41	8 46
Clutton arr.	12 25	..	..	2X55	Thursdays and Sats. exceptd.	Thursdays and Sats. only.	5X37	6 45	7 30	..	..	8 31	9X5	10 45	8 50
Clutton dep.	12 35	..	..	2 56			5 40	7X5	7 40	..	..	8 33	9 30	10 48	8 51
Pensford arr.	12X45	..	..	3X3			5 47	7 15	7 50	..	..	8 40	—	10 55	8 58
Pensford dep.	1 0	..	..	3 4			5 50	7 25	8 0	..	..	8 42	CS	10 56	9 0
Brislington arr.	1 15	..	..	3 13			5 59	—	8 15	..	..	8 51	—	11 5	9 9
Brislington dep.	1 20	..	..	3 16			6 2	—	8 20	..	..	8 54	—	11 8	9 13
Marsh Junction	CS	..	..	CXS			CS	CS	CS	..	..	CXS	CS	CS	CS
East Depot arr.	1Y40	..	..	—		..	—	7 45	—	..	..	—	10 0	—	—
N. Som. Jn. arr.	1 30	..	..	3 20	..	..	6 7		8 30	..	..	8 58		11 12	9 17
Bristol (Tm. Ms.)		..	..	3 23	..	..	6 10	..	8 50	..	..	9 2	..	11 15	9 20

CROSSING INSTRUCTIONS.

No. 5 crosses No. 6 at Clutton.
No. 9 ,, No. 6 at Marsh Junct. No. 10 at Pensford. No. 12 at Hallatrow
No. 11 ,, No. 10 at Marsh Junct. No. 12 at Pensford. Nos. 16 & 18 at Clutton. No 20 at Hallatrow.
No. 13 crosses No. 12 at Marsh Junct. No. 16 at Radstock.
No. 15 ,, No. 18 at Marsh Junction. No. 20 at Pensford. No. 24 at Mells.
No. 17 ,, No. 36 at Mells.
No. 23 crosses No. 26 at Clutton. No. 30 at Radstock.
No. 29 ,, No. 26 at Pensford. No. 34 at Radstock.
No. 33 ,, No. 30 at Hallatrow. No. 34 at Frome Junction.
No. 35 crosses No. 34 at Clutton. No. 38 at Radstock
No. 37 ,, No. 36 at Clutton. No. 38 a Hallatrow.
No. 39 ,, No. 42 at Mells.
No. 41 ,, No. 44 at Marsh Jct. No. 46 at Clutton.

CAMERTON BRANCH.

Dist. M. C.	DOWN TRAINS. WEEK DAYS.	Mix'd A	Pass. N A	Pass. A	Goods D
		A.M.	A.M.	P.M.	P.M.
	Hallatrow .... dep.	8 15	10 50	4 30	5 50
3 34	Camerton .. .. arr.	8 28	11 0	4 40	6 0

Dist. M. C.	UP TRAINS. WEEK DAYS.	Mix'd A	Goods D	Pass. A	Goods D
		A.M.	A.M.	P.M.	P.M.
	Camerton .... dep.	9 25	11 15	5 18	6 15
3 34	Hallatrow .. .. arr.	9 38	11 25	5 28	6 25

This Branch is Single Line, and is worked by Train Staff and only one Engine in Steam at a time. No Block Telegraph on this Branch. The Shape of the Staff is Square, and the colour Red.

N To run with Brake Van only when there are no Passengers.

THE NORTH SOMERSET & CAMERTON BRANCHES; WORKING TIMETABLE 1895

Original: Public Record Office

The collieries were connected both on the surface, by tramways, and underground. There were various means of getting coal away from the pithead, road taking the load before the SCC was built. However, in October 1798, the Somersetshire Coal Canal was opened between Dunkerton and Camerton, the coal from the latter pits then being sent to Dunkerton by water and then onto Bath, the pits' main market, by road. The opening of the Hallatrow-Camerton stub improved things enormously once the $3\frac{1}{2}$ mile section was brought into use in 1882. The timing of the railway's arrival was particularly apt for the late 1800s were to be good days for Camerton coal, the maximum output being in 1903 when nearly 77,000 tons were brought to the surface in that one year alone.

We have already mentioned the tramways in use at Camerton collieries. There were two of these running away from the pithead: both are believed to have been of about 2ft 4ins gauge. One ran between Old Pit and New Pit and followed the course of the SCC. Around 1910 this particular tramway was removed and was converted into a road. The second tramway ran from the first near New Pit north-westwards up an incline to a landsale depot at Meadgate. This incline was worked by a 50hp haulage motor. On the railway side, limited siding space provided an outlet for the coal produced. Shunting in these sidings was initially carried out by horses except for a short period of time around 1926 when an 0-4-0ST from Peckett of Bristol (builder's No. 1191) was on trial there. Named *Dunkerton* (the locomotive had come from Dunkerton Colliery) the engine was obviously found wanting in some way since some months afterwards it moved on to the contracting firm of Walter, Scott & Middleton.

On nationalisation some modernisation was put in train at the sidings where a road tractor replaced the horses then being used. However, the pit was working at a loss and, after redundancies in December 1949, and again in April 1950, the colliery wound its last coal on 14th April 1950, the pit being closed officially in September 1950. The coal reserves which could be tapped had run out. So too, incidentally, had the time of the Hallatrow-Camerton-Limpley Stoke line for, once Camerton Pit closed, the line's reason for being there at that time went too. Today the key aspect of the collieries that continues to catch the eye in this beautiful part of the Cam Valley is the huge tip which still dominates the area.

However, as we have moved forward in time we have also moved too far down the line to Camerton to consider the mining developments around Timsbury that also added to the North Somerset's coal traffic. For these we need to look at the Timsbury Collieries in more detail and so it is to the pits at Upper and Lower Conygre that we now turn.

Timsbury Collieries: Upper and Lower Conygre Pits

In 1791 the first of the Timsbury Conygre (or in some old spellings of the word, Conigre) was sunk on the outskirts of Timsbury village. This 1791 sinking was of Upper Conygre Pit and was carried out by the Conygre Coal Company, although locally this firm was more generally known as the Timsbury Coal Proprietors. In the mid-1860s the name was changed to Samborne, Smith & Co after the firm's two main business partners. In 1908 Beaumont, Kennedy & Co. took over but just pre-World War One the business ran simply under the name of Kennedy & Co.

Getting coal away from Upper Conygre was almost entirely carried out by road until the pit's partner, Lower Conygre Colliery, was opened in 1858. Indeed, once the new member of the partnership had been opened a new underground connection was brought into use between the two pits and the newcomer began to take pride of place. With Lower Conygre in business, a tramway was laid in during the 1855/6 period to link the pit into the Somersetshire Coal Canal. This tramway was, however, not brought into use until 1859. The two shafts of Lower Conygre Pit were sunk to the south of the company's other colliery at Upper Conygre and from the top of the lower

THE PITHEAD AT UPPER CONYGRE COLLIERY
This delightful and somewhat ramshackle view of the pithead at Upper Conygre Colliery shows two loaded carts of coal and two somewhat well-dressed figures. Note the castellated chimney – this was built to make the view of the pit from the nearby Timsbury Manor somewhat more palatable!

Dennis Rendell

pit's western shaft, a 2ft $4\frac{1}{2}$in gauge incline ran down to serve a landsale depot, continuing on down to a wharf on the coal canal.

With the coming of the Camerton branch the SCC was becoming a less and less satisfactory way of moving coal out from the Timsbury Collieries and, since the railway closely followed the length of the canal between Hallatrow and Camerton, it was not at all surprising that in May 1894 the collieries' owners made up their minds to get a siding laid in from the GWR to serve Lower Conygre. Two proposals were put forward it seems. The first was for a wharf near Camerton station but the terms suggested by the GWR were unacceptable. The second idea, which was accepted, was for a siding to be laid in near Radford between Hallatrow and Camerton. There were problems with land acquisition, but even so, things seemed to have moved particularly slowly for it was not until September 1898 that construction of the sidings and the now-required associated incline to the colliery began. The actual private siding agreement was dated 31st July 1899.

The siding was built with facing connections with the running line in both directions while the colliery link, some half a mile in length, ran across the road between Timsbury and Radford, the crossing taking place on the level just before the new connection swung into the Camerton branch. The siding was under the control of a pair of two lever ground frames. These were released by a key on the Train Staff. From here the connection ran on up to the colliery via a cable-worked incline.

Provisional sanction for the work was given by the Board of Trade on 18th October 1899 and the work was passed fit by Board of Trade Inspector Major Pringle in his report of 15th September 1900. The self-acting, rope-worked incline was brought into use in October 1900. The narrow gauge incline stayed in use only down as far as the coal depot until February 1906 when the rails were lifted and the trackbed was turned into a dirt tip.

In retrospect, and in spite of these new transport developments, the futures of both Timsbury's pits were to prove fairly short-term. Nonetheless, during the early years of the 20th century some modernisation did take place, as did explorations for a new seam. This new seam was indeed found, but unfortunately, it proved to be badly faulted and was subsequently abandoned. The troubled year of 1911 provided disputes and a trade recession that lengthened into the following year. Lower Conygre was shut down in March 1911, re-opening in July of the same year. In January 1912 all the men and staff at both pits were sacked and the two closely-connected collieries were closed down. However, the following month it seems that virtually normal working was the rule once more!

However, it was water and difficult working, rather than management-miner warfare, that brought the final closedown of both pits. In 1914 Lower Conygre was flooded, pumping having no impact on the level of water. Eventually, following problems with the area's geology, both collieries were closed in 1916.

Reverting to our history of the Cam Valley development of the Somerset Coalfield, it was around the early years of the 20th century that several new collieries and related railway plans saw the light of day. Coal mined at Timsbury and Camerton was essentially produced for the areas of Bath, Bristol and Wiltshire. However, in the days when these pits were only served by the Hallatrow-Camerton rail link, the journey to these districts was quite a long-winded one. The coal owners wanted to get a rail link built that would run directly eastwards to serve their main markets, Bath in particular. In 1902 new coal leases were given around Dunkerton, between Camerton and Limpley Stoke, and this, in turn, forced the pace for the building of a new railway to capture this new coal.

Indeed, in May 1902, proposals had been put forward for a North Somerset Light Railway running from Greyfield Colliery at Clutton, through Timsbury, Camerton, Dunkerton and Combe Hay to Midford on the Somerset & Dorset. The line would also have had a further extension onwards from Midford to the GWR's Bathampton-Bradford-on-Avon line near Limpley Stoke. This project ran into a lot of trouble but the following year a modified scheme was put up. Running from the S&D at Midford, it would have run along the route of the former SCC to Dunkerton where it would have then swung around to the north to finish its journey at Priston, where the then Lord of the Manor (still in existence in the early years of the 20th century!), William Vaughan-Jenkins, was about to develop coal reserves underlying his estate.

This second scheme was popular in the district, so much so that the GWR who, up until this time had bathed in its somewhat usual lethargy, started to get worried. Their response

CAMERTON STATION
This view was taken just before Camerton-Limpley Stoke was opened. The connection to New Pit can be seen clearly sweeping around behind the bracket signal opposite the signal box, while the Limpley Stoke route can just be made out running under the bridge on the extreme right. *Railway Magazine*

DUNKERTON COLLIERY – LOOKING NORTH EAST
Although the Somerset Coalfield was known to be a notoriously difficult one to work, Dunkerton Colliery always had a bad name for working conditions, safety being such a low priority that dead or injured men were not an uncommon feature at its pithead. Indeed, things got so bad that during the 1908/1909 coal strike, the riots that took place at Dunkerton were some of the worst ever experienced in the coalfield.

Railway Magazine

was to propose an extension to their Hallatrow-Camerton stub through to Limpley Stoke by making use of the alignment of the old canal. Well received locally, the GWR scheme won over supporters from the North Somerset Light Railway project and the Light Railway Commissioners agreed that the GWR's line was the preferred option.

The Great Western went on to buy out the remaining assets of the SCC and, in 1904, got an Abandonment Act through Parliament so that they could build their new railway along the SCC's former canal bed. Unbeaten, however, Vaughan-Jenkins, along with three other former North Somerset Light Railway promoters put forward, in 1905, the Priston Light Railway. As its title suggests, this new line was to connect Priston with a junction at Dunkerton on the then newly-authorised Camerton-Limpley Stoke railway. The 2 mile 77 chain line was to have cost £34,736 8s 11d (£34,736.45)! In spite of the GWR's support, the line was not built and the coal from Priston Pit, of which more anon, had to go by road to a loading wharf which was constructed just on the colliery side of the Radford level crossing mentioned in our discussions of the Timsbury Collieries.

It seems logical at this point to discuss two other collieries, both already briefly mentioned, that fed a good deal of their output onto the North Somerset, although detailed histories of these two particular pits are not within the scope of this book. These two collieries were those that were once to be found at Dunkerton and Priston.

Dunkerton Colliery

C.G. Down & A.J. Warrington tell us that:

'. . . The story of Dunkerton is one of the most remarkable in the coalfield. In its short working life, only about twenty years, the pit became both the largest in Somerset and the one with the worst reputation among the men who worked there."

Plans for developing the colliery were in existence in 1898 while the contract for sinking the first shaft was signed just the other side of the new century on 11th May 1903. Massive inrushes of water seriously delayed the sinking work and it was not until 1906 that work on both shafts was actually completed.

Under an act of 15th August 1904 the building of the Camerton to Limpley Stoke section was begun and it was to be by this railway that Dunkerton Colliery was to be served. Construction of the railway was tediously slow and it was not until 4th April 1907 that coal trains were being sent away. Before this time, coal was moved away from the pithead by road. However, in the period up until 1910, it seems that transport arrangements to the developing pit were somewhat unsettled.

The sidings serving this important pit were, likewise, of equal importance and, quite naturally, were of goodly size. By an agreement, dated 27th April 1908, the GWR was responsible for providing sidings to the colliery, the private siding agreement being signed on 31st December 1908. Once constructed, these sidings were made up of two groups, one either side of Dunkerton signal box. This box, along with the line to Limpley Stoke, was brought into use on 9th May 1910. Once the sidings were completed and in use a Peckett 0-4-0ST (builder's No. 1191) was delivered to work them. This locomotive arrived on 8th August 1910, the sidings having been shunted by a stationary haulage engine prior to this. As mentioned previously, this 0-4-0ST was transferred to the Camerton Collieries in 1926. By 1915 the colliery was doing so well that the pit's No. 1 shaft was deepened to bite into the Radstock seams below the Middle Vein. Mining was also about to start in the Farrington seams and the future looked bright, especially with the demands of war. Indeed, both shafts were later used for coal winding and this was a key reason for the pit's high output levels. The Great Western Railway was doing well for itself out of Dunkerton Colliery!

However, the postwar slump set in and, in February 1920, the pit ran into money problems. Closure was put forward on a number of occasions until, on 30th May 1925, it became a reality. It seems that the pit closed on account of two main factors. First, accessible coal underground had run out while royalty problems had also pushed closure nearer. By the end of 1925 Sir Frank Beauchamp had taken charge but, on 30th August 1927, he closed the pit down yet again, this time for good. There were many later schemes to re-open Dunkerton but nothing ever came of any of them. The sidings saw little traffic after 1928 but remained in place until the 1950s when they, and the rest of the branch, were swept away.

HALLATROW AT ITS HEIGHT
With the major re-organisation of 1909 behind it, Hallatrow station shows off its recently constructed signal box to the public. With its new 'up' platform and branch through to Limpley Stoke, heavy freight in the sidings and milk traffic in churns on the platform, Hallatrow was indeed an important centre for the GWR when this photograph was taken c1910.

Alan Gregory

"The construction of the (Camerton-Limpley Stoke) railway was divided into two contracts, both of which were carried out by Messrs Pauling & Co. Ltd of Victoria Street, Westminster. One contract extended from the junction with the Camerton branch to 1 mile 45 chains, and the second from 1 mile 45 chains to the junction with the Bath and Trowbridge Railway, a total distance of 7 miles 78 chains. The original contracts expired in 1909, but owing to various unforeseen circumstances, the line was not completed and opened until the spring of 1910. The resident engineer, on behalf of the Great Western Company's new works engineer, was, during the earlier portion of the construction, Mr J.C. Blundell, and subsequently Mr H. Lott."
(Source: "The Camerton and Limpley Stoke Railway" by A.W. Arthurton – Railway Magazine July 1911)

A Great Deal of Interest . . .
"A great deal of interest was taken in the passing of the first passenger train from Camerton to Limpley Stoke this morning, and if on all the journeys the motor train will make the GWR take as much money as on that which commenced at Hallatrow junction at 7.55am, and connected with Bath and Trowbridge trains on the mainline at Limpley Stoke at 8.43, after a comfortable and punctual journey, the line will speedily be a dividend earning affair. But, of course, the novelty will wear off, and the line will depend very largely for its revenues on the mineral traffic, particularly from the Dunkerton Collieries, which will feed the line with between 200,000 and 300,000 tons of coal per annum, so Mr Egbert Spear, who was a co-passenger on the first trip this morning with a representative of The Bath Herald estimates. The line means a great deal also to the Camerton Collieries of Miss Jarrett, for although there has been a "spur" from Hallatrow . . . to Camerton Collieries the gradients have prevented more than 14 loaded trucks being made up, whereas now trains of 50 trucks can be conveyed via Limpley Stoke to all parts of the Great Western Railway Co.'s system. Nearly all mineral traffic will, we understand be dealt with in that direction, and very little is to go through Hallatrow in future . . .
. . . Thanks to the lightness of the motor trains, it was possible to open the line once it had passed Colonel Yorke, and the usual wait of two or three months for the line to be "rolled" by goods traffic was not required.

Radford and Timsbury Halt

'The little platform by the wayside without officials and minus the usual equipment of a station was thronged with cheering children who had a spice of excitement with their novelty, for the motor rail(!) overlooked the little halt and ran through! The little oversight was soon remedied and the car, being put back, was boarded by a noisy carriage load of little folk intent on celebrating the historic event at the cost of a penny and a long trudge back, by riding to Camerton. At this old established station this particular early train stays for 16 minutes, and the special reason is that on every morning of the week, save Monday, an ex-Salisbury goods passes here. With less passengers now the car was pushed on to the virgin line . . ."
(Source: Bath Chronicle 13th May 1910)

"The viaducts had had a thorough testing with large locomotives, and everything was as neat and trim as a railway need be for the beginning of business . . . In fact passengers were conscious of no oscillation whatever and the autocar, drawn by a small locomotive which can operate from either end, ran as smoothly as need be. This will, however, be supplanted, the Motor Inspector who travelled with the train informed us, by a real motor train."
(Source: Bath Chronicle 13th May 1910)

"The junction with the Salisbury line, half a mile north of Limpley Stoke station, faces in the direction of Salisbury in order to give the coal trains, which form a very large proportion of those passing over the line, a clear

RADFORD AND TIMSBURY HALT – 1910
A train from Limpley Stoke and Camerton rolls into Radford and Timsbury Halt not long after the through line from Camerton to Limpley Stoke had been opened to traffic in 1910. The locomotive, a member of the 517 class heads one of the steam rail motor cars into the spartan 150ft long wooden platform with its typical "pagoda" shelter. Judging by the number of passengers shown it looks as if "Rent-A-Crowd" has been called in for the day!

Lens of Sutton

run towards the south. The junction towards Bath, which was at first proposed, will not be made, at any rate, for the present.

Stations have been provided at Dunkerton and Monckton Coombe, with halts at Radford, Timsbury and Coombe Hay. The line . . . will deal principally with coal from the pits in the neighbourhood of Camerton, Dunkerton . . . Radford and Paulton, the passenger traffic being at the outset a comparatively minor consideration. In spite of this, however, as in other districts

DUNKERTON COLLIERY – LOOKING NORTH WEST
This photograph, although it does not actually show the Camerton & Limpley Stoke Railway (this running behind the long, low building to the middle right of the picture), it does give a good view of the colliery offices (below the chimney in the centre foreground) while the yard, in which the wooden pitprops were stored, can just be glimpsed behind these offices. The haystack on the right emphasises the way the colliery co-existed very uneasily with the rest of the beautiful Somerset countryside.

Dennis Rendell

LIMPLEY STOKE STATION IN THE EARLY YEARS OF THE 20th CENTURY

Lens of Sutton

where a new train service is provided, a healthy passenger traffic is rapidly being created. The line is served by a rail motor car, one class only, which works a shuttle service between Hallatrow and Limpley Stoke. There are five cars a day in each direction, the first leaving Hallatrow at 7.55am and the last arriving there at 8.18pm."
(Source: "The Camerton and Limpley Stoke Railway" by A.W. Arthurton – Railway Magazine July 1911)

PAULTON HALT

Original plan: British Rail (Western)

Priston Colliery (Also known as Tunley Colliery)

Priston was the last deep mine to be opened in Somerset, its sinking being masterminded by William Vaughan-Jenkins and H. Alger. The chosen site for the sinking was immediately to the west of the village, alongside the Timsbury-Tunley-Bath road. As we have already noted, Vaughan-Jenkins had also been actively involved in promoting the Priston Light Railway of 1904 but, since the scheme had not been successful, it meant that the colliery would have to rely essentially on landsale, this being a key factor in its location near a main road.

Work began on 11th March 1914 when Mrs Vaughan-Jenkins officially turned the first sod. At one o'clock in the morning of Whit Sunday, 1915, the first coal was found, the first full

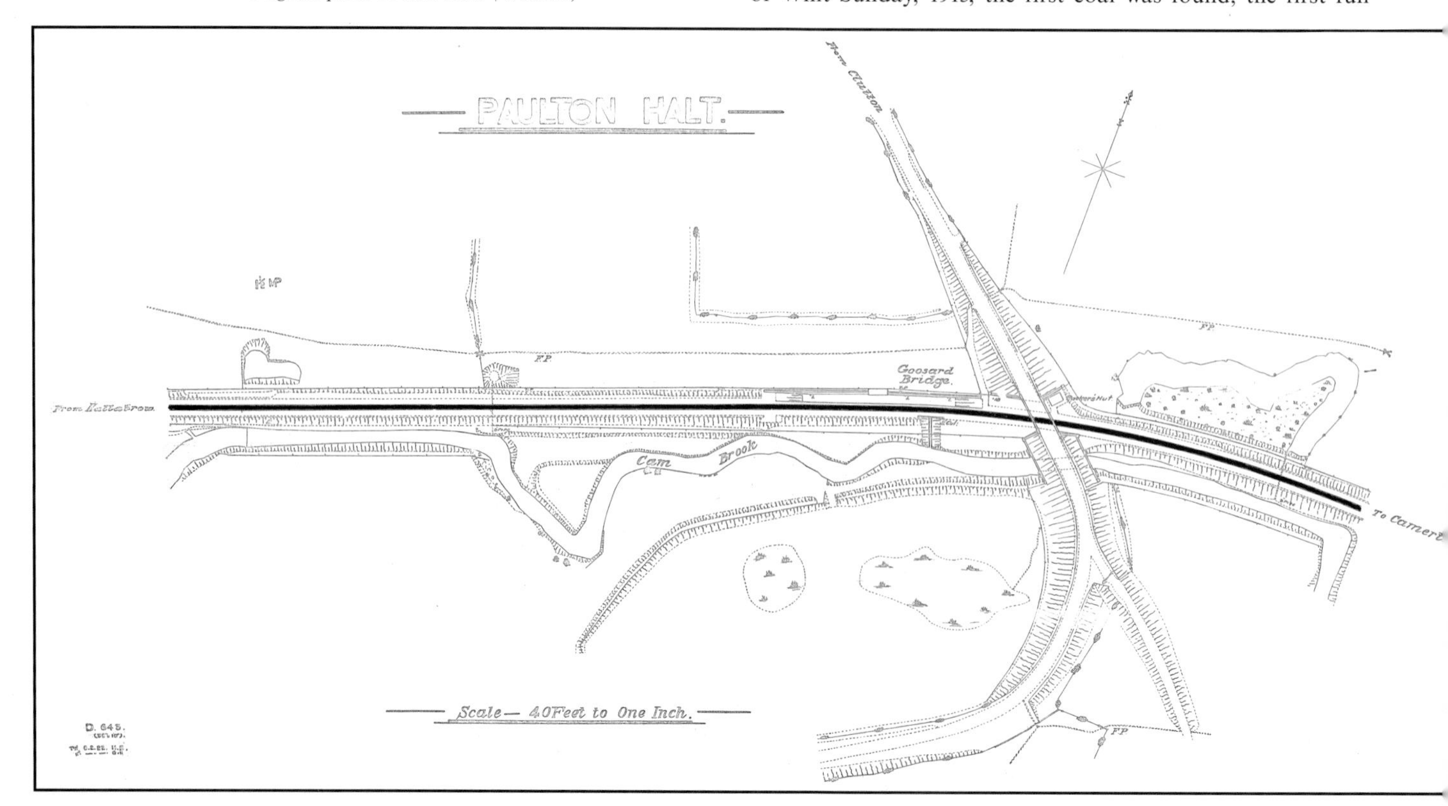

skip coming to the surface some four hours later. Coal production began about July 1915 when the first shaft had reached its fullest extent, some 750ft. Sinking of the second shaft began in 1916 and the cages began work on 1st December 1917. As can be imagined from what was said in the last paragraph, the disposal of coal from the pithead was a problem. A scheme was put forward therefore to take all of the hoped-for output of the colliery (nearly 400 tons per week) across to the GWR at Dunkerton Colliery by using an aerial ropeway. However, this was never built, the coal going by road to Radford Wharf, at the foot of the Lower Conygre Colliery incline. Here it was put onto the Hallatrow-Limpley Stoke line, the trucks being shunted into the siding by horse. Nevertheless, in spite of this initiative, it must be said that Priston was never a successful pit, mainly because its sinking was done on a very tight budget, while World War One ensured that equipment for the enterprise was both scarce and expensive.

In February 1923 the pit was sold as a going concern to Sir Frank Beauchamp. He acquired the pit for three different reasons. First, he bought the colliery in its own right; secondly, he bought it to give his Camerton Colliery good reserves of coal and thirdly, and for some strange reason, bearing in mind Priston's unsuitability for the job, he proposed winding *Dunkerton's* coal at Priston. Nonetheless, the pit at Priston survived the 1926 General Strike but, in the late 1920s, problems did start to mount. On 18th June 1930, having lost its main customer, Bath Gas Works the previous year, Priston Pit closed down for good. However, it would seem that Priston's output had helped to keep the GWR's Hallatrow-Camerton section going in the 1920s even though the passenger service on the line had finally disappeared in 1925. Once the pit at Priston fell into disuse it was only a matter of time before the Hallatrow-Camerton section would follow it into oblivion.

TWENTIETH CENTURY TRACKWORK
Although very difficult to date accurately, this marvellous photograph of a large permanent way gang is believed to have been taken during the first two decades of the 20th century, possibly around 1909/10 when the station at Hallatrow was being re-constructed. What stories these men could have told of the former Bristol & North Somerset!

Dave Fisher

CAMERTON GWR
This view of Camerton station shows it in its last days as a terminus. The photograph is taken looking towards the North Somerset's main line, although all the new development is, of course, taking place behind the camera in the direction of Limpley Stoke.

Lens of Sutton

Hallatrow: Change for Limpley Stoke

Having followed through the histories of these two pits we have moved forward rather a long way, chronologically speaking, and so it is important that we move back to Hallatrow to see what changes the extension of the Hallatrow-Camerton line through to Limpley Stoke in 1910 had had upon the junction station.

In the spring of 1909 the GWR announced that Hallatrow was to be turned into a crossing place for passenger trains, since it would seem that before this time, only two goods or one goods and a passenger train could cross there. In May 1909 the GWR applied to the Board of Trade for permission to build a new 'up' platform and to extend the then existing platform on the eastern side of the running line. In addition, more sidings were to be laid in. The new track layout required a new signal box which, when built, had 55 working and 12 spare levers.

The signal box and new works were brought into use fairly quickly but they were not inspected by the Board of Trade until 1912. When the First World War came along, Hallatrow and its new layout was well used by the heavy coal traffic that must then have been the norm.

One conspicuous source of traffic at Hallatrow from the 1880s through to the early part of the Second World War was that of stone traffic from quarries to the north of the station. It would seem that at some stage between 1882 and 1886 a new quarry was developed near Cloud Hill Farm. On 6th January 1882 the GWR's Traffic Committee gave the go-ahead for the provision of a siding to that quarry while, in May 1886, further work was undertaken at Hallatrow itself. The GWR applied to the Board of Trade for permission to carry out work to the west of the signal running line and a report of 7th July 1886, made by Colonel Rich, had the following things to say:

> "A new siding has been constructed on the west side of the single line. It has been connected with the passenger lines and sidings at the east side, and also with the single branch railway to Camerton. The signals and points have bar pointlocks and are worked from the station cabin.
>
> The pins which joined the point rods with the connecting rods to the cabin should be secured with a nut in addition to the split pin or by a strong steel cotter. Subject to these fastenings being altered I recommend that the alterations and additions at Hallatrow be approved."

On 16th July 1886 the GWR told the Board of Trade that the required changes had been carried out.

Further information about the quarry at Cloud Hill is provided in an agreement dated 19th December 1914 made between the GWR and Mr Edward Free. The private siding agreement outlines several conditions, the main ones being as follows:

(a) That the GWR would allow Free to use the sidings running north out of Hallatrow for access to and storage of stone wagons into the quarry.

(b) That the GWR sidings were to be maintained and renewed as and when necessary by the Great Western.

(c) That upon payment of the princely sum of £10, the GWR would fix gates across the sidings as they ran into the quarry area itself. Any additional costs incurred by the GWR were also to be paid by Free. Incidentally, these gates were to be maintained by the quarry company.

(d) That goods traffic was to be worked right up to the point 'A' as shown on the plan on page 113. For this service, Free would pay the GWR one penny per ton on top of the usual rate.

(e) That any quarry workers on GWR land in the vicinity of the quarry sidings were responsible to the stationmaster at Hallatrow.

Cloud Hill Quarry: Some General Background

Cloud Hill Quarry on the Warwick Estate was well-known for its pennant stone. This had a variety of uses and these included kerb and paving work, bridge building, and sea defence work. It was also used for strengthening railway embankments. There was a single running line into the quarry and this, in turn, connected with two sidings within the quarry itself. The GWR connection ran south into a run round loop which ran parallel to the North Somerset's main line to Clutton (see accompanying plan). Once trucks were in the quarry they would be moved, as required, by the men's muscle power. When loaded, trucks would be sent down to Hallatrow to be weighed since there was no rail weighbridge at the quarry site.

During the 1920s, usually at some time around 11am, the one train of the day that fed the quarry would arrive with around six to nine trucks. The train engine would pull the full wagons out and then would put the empties in. It seems that GWR four-plank open wagons were generally used to handle the traffic. Indeed, it would appear that the company had very good contacts with the GWR in that during the 1920s regular train loads of between 25 to 30 wagons supplied the GWR

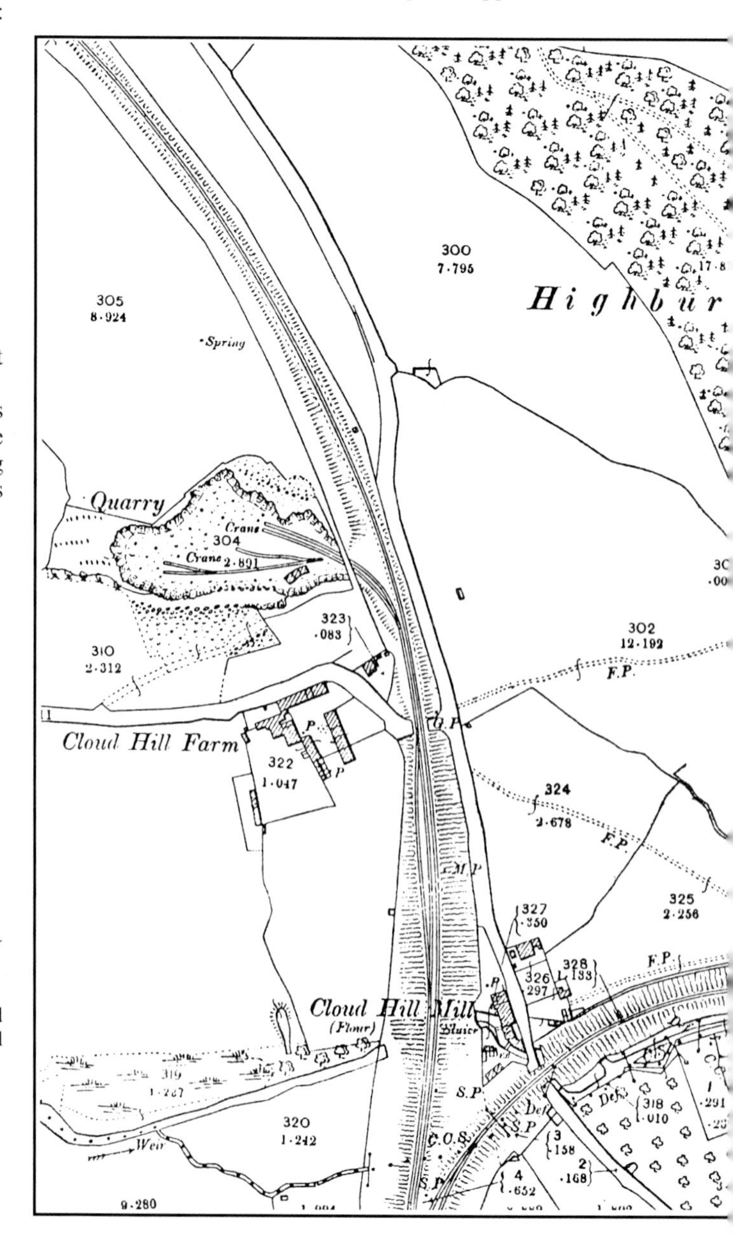

HALLATROW STATION – CLOUD HILL QUARRY

This early 20th century Ordnance Survey map shows the north end of the station limits with the long siding connection into Cloud Hill Quarry.

Original: Mike Miller

CLOUD HILL QUARRY, HALLATROW, 1914

Original plan: British Rail (Western)

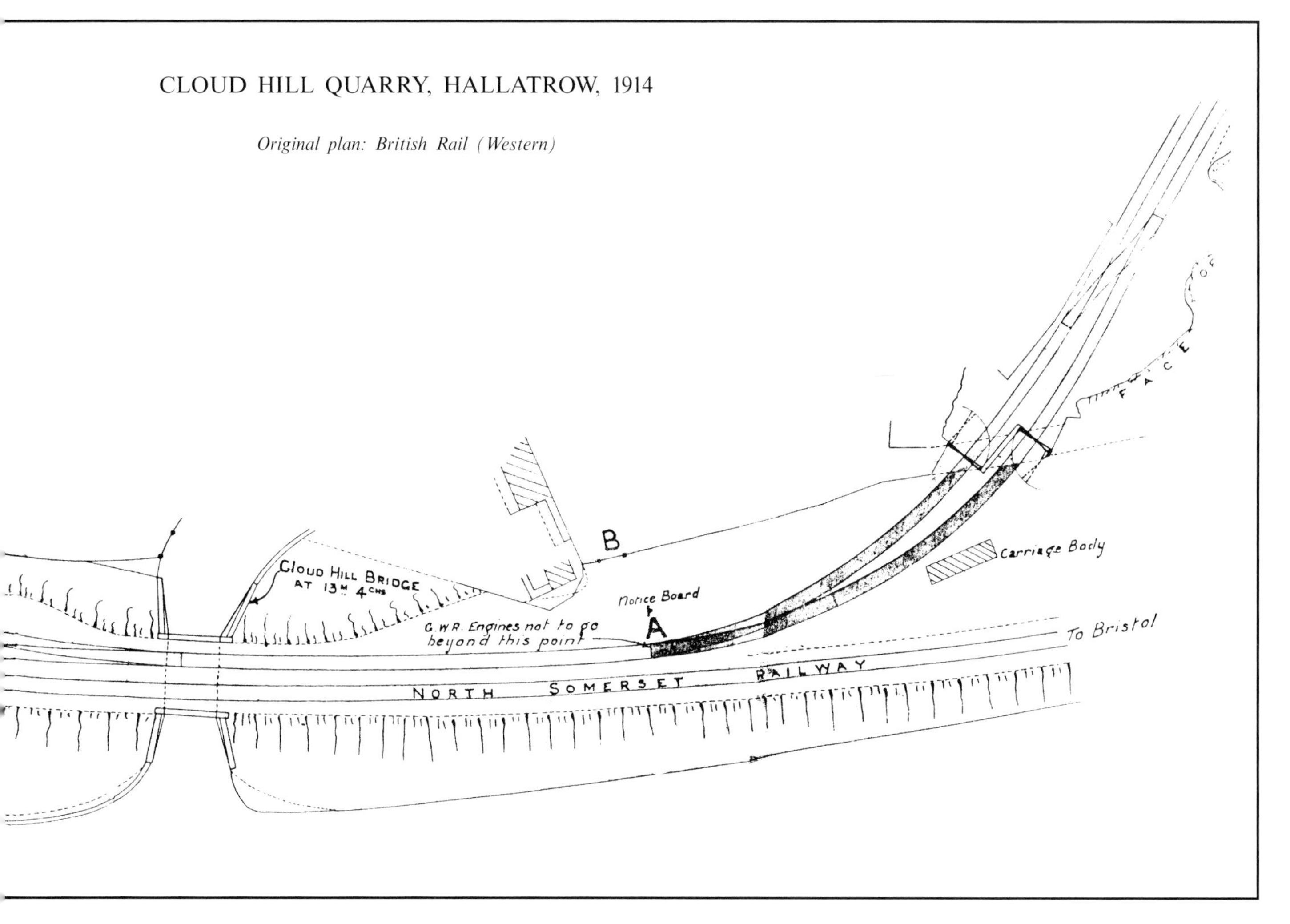

with stone from Cloud Hill for the sea wall defences at Dawlish.

The staff on site consisted of labourers, quarrymen, masons, etc. and during the late 1920s and early 1930s some ten to twelve masons were employed cutting the stone into kerb-stones or whatever. The quarry manager was Mr Free, with Mr Bob

CLOUD HILL QUARRY, HALLATROW
The human side of the quarry at Cloud Hill, Hallatrow is seen at some time during the late 1920s/early 1930s. The quarry manager, Mr. Free, stands on the extreme right. In spite of the tough life that these men undoubtedly must have had, the faces seem happy enough!

Mr & Mrs W. Perry

QUARRYING BLUE PENNANT STONE AT HALLATROW
This view clearly shows the quarry at Hallatrow and was taken looking towards the GWR's connection into Hallatrow station itself.

Gloucestershire County Library

Stock being the foreman. As the 1930s progressed, however, less stone was quarried, most of which still went out by rail. The closure of the quarry actually took place in the early years of the Second World War, probably in 1941 and, at this time, an aircraft factory producing wings and fuselages for the war effort was built within it. Indeed, further traffic for Hallatrow station was generated in that it handled nuts and bolts destined for that particular factory. Although conjectural, it is believed that the actual rail connection remained usable during the war although further information on this point would be welcomed. After the war the factory was taken over by the Ministry of Supply and further on in the chapter we will say more about this later period in the quarry's life.

Returning to Hallatrow at the time of the opening of the railway through to Limpley Stoke (1910), it is true to say that, although the line was heavily used by coal trains, the passenger traffic was never very substantial. With local bus competition this was, perhaps, hardly surprising! With the onset of World War One the passenger service was taken off on 22nd March 1915 as a wartime economy measure. The service was restored to the Cam Valley route on 9th July 1923, although Midford (GW) never returned to the railway map. The passenger service from Paulton Halt, Radford & Timsbury, Camerton, Dunkerton Colliery Halt, Dunkerton, Combe Hay and Monkton Combe was finally removed on 21st September 1925.

After the war, however, business on the main Bristol-Radstock section remained good and Hallatrow dealt with quite a heavy passenger service in spite of the fact that it was sited some distance from the surrounding villages. Apart from its regular Bristol-Frome services, Hallatrow handled a variety of specials, including football specials, particularly in the Bristol direction; Sunday specials from Frome to such South Wales resorts as Barry while excursions to the various country shows such as the ones held at Clutton and Frome were also run. All of these were invariably well patronised, often with people being packed in the guard's van as well! Special trains were regularly run to Weston-super-Mare and Weymouth, the latter often having an onward connection by ship to Cherbourg giving a very long, but adventurous day out!

On the goods side, the station dealt with a large geographical area. In the 1930s, parcels traffic on offer to surrounding

HALLATROW–CAMERTON–LIMPLEY STOKE
WORKING TIMETABLE 10th JULY 1922

Original: Peter A. Fry

HALLATROW, CAMERTON & LIMPLEY STOKE

Single Line worked by Electric Train Tablet. Intermediate Tablet Station:—Camerton, which is only available for crossing two Goods Trains or a Goods and a Passenger Train.
In no case must a Passenger Train be put into the Siding at Camerton Station for another Train to pass

Distances M	C.	UP TRAINS. STATIONS.		Station No.	Ruling Gradient 1 in.	Time Allowance for Ordinary Freight Trains. See p. 2 — P't to Point times.	Allow for stops.	Allow for start.	WEEK DAYS ONLY	2 K T'br'dge Goods	3 K Frome Goods	
						Mins.	Mins.	Mins.		P.M.	P.M.	
—	—	**Hallatrow**	dep.	1182	—	—	—	1	..	12 1	2 15	..
1	49	Paulton Halt	,,	1244	47 F	—	—	—	....	—	....	....
2	62	Timsbury Siding	,,	1194	129 F	11	1	1	..	12 23	CR	..
2	66	Radford and Timsbury Halt	,,	1195	113 F	—	—	—	....	—	—	....
3	4	Stop Board	,,	—	113 F	1	1	1	..	12P26	2P26	..
3	34	Camerton	arr.	1196	66 F	1	1	1	....	12 29	2 30	....
			dep.						..	1 30	3 0	..
4	30	Dunkerton Colliery Halt	dep.	1245	150 R	—	—	—	....	—	—	....
4	44	Dunkerton Colliery	arr.	1197	200 R	4	1	1	..	1 35	3 5	..
			dep.						....	2 0	3 25	....
6	6	Dunkerton	arr.	1198	150 F	4	1	2	..	§ Arr. 2.17	—	..
			dep.									
7	5	Combe Hay Halt	,,	1199	100 F	—	—	—	....		—	....
9	22	Midford Halt	,,	1237	100 F	—	—	—	..		—	..
10	27	Monkton Combe	,,	1200	100 F	11	1	1	..	2§27	ST	....
11	35	Limpley Stoke	arr.	552	134 R	3	1	1	....	—	3 48	..
11	72	**Freshford Exchange Sdgs.**	,,	555	242 R	[illegible]	1	—	..	2 35	4 5	..

DOWN TRAINS. STATIONS.		Ruling Gradient 1 in.	Time Allowance for Ordinary Freight Trains. See p. 2 — P't to Point times.	Allow for stops	Allow for start.	WEEK DAYS ONLY. 1 Holt Goods				
			Mins.	Mins.	Mins.	A.M.				
Freshford Exchange Sdgs	dep.	—	—	—	1	9 5	..	..	..	..
Limpley Stoke	,,	242 R	1	1	1	CS	....	....	....	....
Monkton Combe	,,	134 R	3	1	1	CR	..	..	..	..
Midford Halt	,,	100 R	—	—	—	—	....	....	....	....
Combe Hay Halt	,,	100 R	—	—	—	—	..	..	..	..
Dunkerton	arr.	—	13	1	1	—	....	....	....	....
	dep.	—				—	..	..	..	..
Dunkerton Colliery	arr.	200 F	4	1	1	9 35	....	....	....	....
	dep.					9 45	..	..	..	..
Dunkerton Colliery Halt	dep.	—	—	—	1	—	....	....	....	....
Camerton	arr.	150 F	4	1	1	9 50	..	..	..	..
	dep.					10 5	....	....	....	....
Radford and Timsbury Halt	,,	66 R	—	—	—	—	..	..	..	..
Timsbury Siding	,,	[illegible]				[illegible]	....	....	....	....
Paulton Halt	,,	129 R	3	1	1	—	..	..	..	..
Hallatrow	arr.	47 R	11	1	1	10 3[illegible]	....	....	....	....

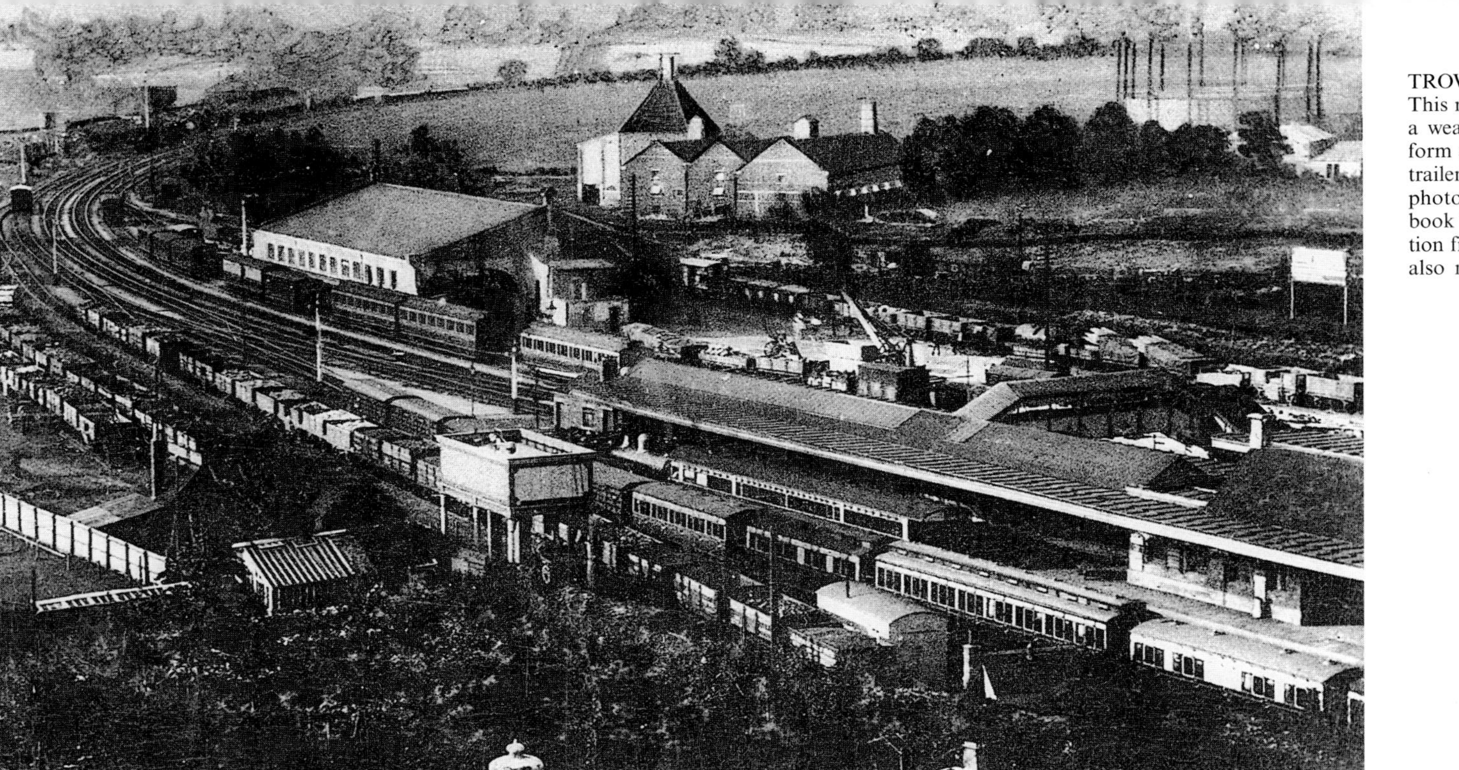

TROWBRIDGE – LOCO AND TRAILER
This marvellous view of Trowbridge station provides us with a wealth of rolling stock to look at. The train at the platform appears to be a Dean Goods hauling a steam railmotor trailer. The date is probably some time around 1906. A lovely photograph in its own right, inclusion can be justified in this book by the fact that when the Hallatrow-Limpley Stoke section first opened to passenger traffic, two midday motor trains also ran through to Trowbridge!

Lens of Sutton

CAMERTON STATION 1922

Original plan: British Rail (Western)

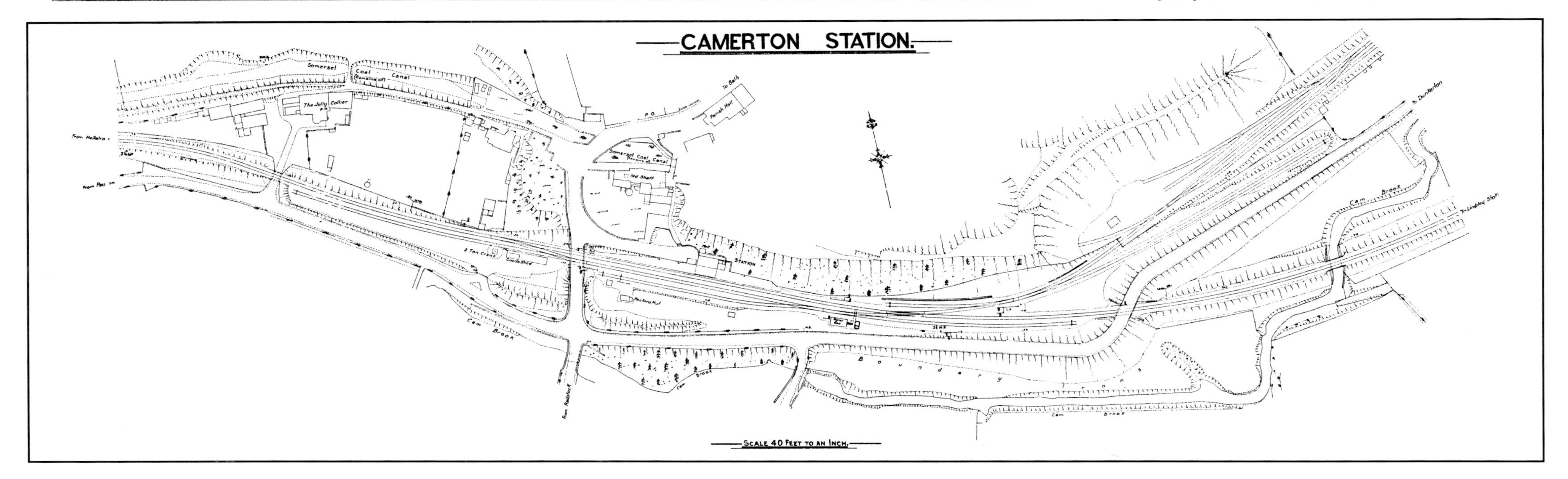

villages was handled through Hallatrow station by an agent, Mrs Cottle, and she undertook deliveries to and from Paulton. This arrangement was later replaced by the use of three GWR lorries, all stationed at Hallatrow. Two of these were three-tonners while the third was a one-tonner. In addition, a horse-drawn wagonette provided a connecting service to Paulton. This met trains on the North Somerset main line. Indeed, because of the local industries, many commercial travellers visited Paulton and they were one group of travellers who regularly made use of this service.

Mr Frank Smith was a parcels porter at Hallatrow during the period from September 1919 through to 1934. As he put it, he was given two years 'life' after 1931 when he was made redundant. Recently married and very concerned about the future he wrote to Mr Pole, the Divisional Superintendent in Bristol, who decided to prolong Mr and Mrs Smith's stay at Hallatrow by some two years. The station had a large goods office which was kept very busy. Funnily enough, the parcels office actually dealt with very little parcels traffic, although even at this time Purnells the publishers and printers at Paulton, were providing traffic for the railway. This was in the form of such items as timetables for the Southern Bus Company and invoice slips.

Strangely enough, the parcels office was actually kept busy dealing with the milk traffic of which there was a large amount before 1931. The office was especially concerned with the empty churns. These were labelled with a brass plate giving the name of the churn's home station. Most empties came in to Hallatrow via Frome. From here they were taken to the various farms for loading: Paulton, Radford, Chewton Mendip, Farrington Gurney and Ston Easton all contributing business when the traffic was at its height. There were some thirty farmers sending milk in for onward despatch and, at one time, the station generated over £300 per month in milk revenue alone.

In 1931, however, Express Dairies took over the delivery of milk by road, directly from the farms and 29 of the 30 customers were lost to road transport, the one remaining farmer living nearby in Hallatrow itself. Before the loss of the traffic the station was provided with 14 four-wheeled trolleys to handle the 17 gallon churns, each of the latter weighing some 2 cwt. Before the loss of the traffic most of the milk went out either to London (via Frome) or to Cardiff (via Bristol). All milk traffic had gone by the mid-1930s. Nonetheless, the local firm of Blannin did send its butter out by rail.

Milk Traffic Returns 1925: The North Somerset Branch

Station	Cans	Amount	Total Cans
Pensford	3,474	£332 13s 10d	3,474
Clutton	8,993	£732 17s 0d	8,993
HALLATROW	7,198	£774 19s 9d	7,198
Camerton	2,025	£260 10s 11d	2,025
Limpley Stoke	150	£16 19s 9d	150
MN & Welton	6,395	£738 11s 3d	6,395
Radstock	4,682	£441 15s 0d	4,682
Mells Road	12,641	£1,340 16s 5d	13,064+
Frome	54,231	£5,694 15s 9d	65,814++

\+ This figure includes 423 cans of Railway Clearing House traffic: Total value of all milk traffic from Mells: £1,386 3s 7d
++ This figure includes 11,583 cans of RCH traffic; Total value of all milk traffic from Frome: £7,112 15s 5d

Other goods traffic handled included quite substantial loads outwards from the former boot and shoe factories in Paulton. Free's Quarry generated stone traffic pre-World War Two, while another common sight in the 1930s, and beyond, was pigeon traffic and often the Paulton club would send away its large bird-filled cane baskets. Indeed, the pigeons were often sent by rail as far as Thurso in Scotland. Frank Smith told the author that it was a lot of work and responsibility to weigh and despatch the birds effectively!

Animal traffic of other kinds was handled at Hallatrow during the time Frank Smith worked at the station. Monday was the day for Farrington Gurney Market and a couple of individuals clearly remembered by him were two businessmen who came in by train to have dealings at the market. The men, a Mr Granick of Stoke Newington and a Mr Goldstein of Spitalfields, would buy poultry at Farrington Gurney. They would then get the produce down to Hallatrow by road carrier, taking them onwards from there to London, via the North Somerset and Bristol. Cattle traffic was often dealt with and Hallatrow would make use of its mileage porter to whitewash the large number of cattle trucks required for this traffic.

The halt at Farrington Gurney also came under the jurisdiction of Hallatrow. When the halt was opened in 1927 the

SHUNTING AND STATION STAFF AT HALLATROW
Dean Goods No. 2395 shoves trucks around at Hallatrow in the 1920s. Although the engine crew remain unidentified, the shunter can be recognised as Bert Humphries. The man on the platform, away from the engine, is Frank Smith, at this point in time parcels porter at Hallatrow, but who later went on to become one of the regular guards on the North Somerset. The parcels office itself is the wooden building to the right of Frank Smith while behind him further evidence can be seen of the line's important milk traffic.

Gerald Quartley

ROSES AND THE RAILWAY GOODS OFFICE AT HALLATROW
A splendidly rustic scene at Hallatrow just before World War Two. In this late 1930's view a Southern Railway wagon nestles alongside the brick-built goods office extension, the latter being provided in 1897.

Philip Chapman

rival bus company diverted its services to run through the hamlet of Farrington to offer competition. However, since a fair number of people lived near the halt, some use was made of it by the local community. Mr. Smith's wife, then one of Hallatrow's booking clerks, issued the first ticket at the halt on the morning of the first train along with Mrs Kingman who was, for many years, the landlady of the nearby Miner's Arms

THE HALLATROW STAFF IN THE THIRTIES
Back row (from left to right) Mr Kingsbury, Jack Smewin (son of the then Pensford stationmaster), Harry Payne, Walt Thatcher, Anon, Wilf Edwards, Bill Oatley.

Front row (from left to right) Philip Chapman, Bob Edwards, Rowley Best (stationmaster), Mr Griffin, Mr Jarvis.

Philip Chapman

Above: HALLATROW STATION LOOKING SOUTH (1)
The view towards the station buildings and the signal cabin in the late 1930s. *Philip Chapman*

BRISTOL–RADSTOCK–FROME WORKING TIMETABLE JUNE/SEPT 1890

Original: Public Record Office

Bristol, Radstock, and Frome.

For Service between Bristol and Weymouth, *vid* Trowbridge, see pages 54 and 55.

WEEK DAYS.								SUNDAYS.		
Class between Bristol and Frome.		1,2,P. AM.	AM.	PM.	PM.	PM.	1,2,P. PM.	1,2,P. AM.	PM.	
BRISTOL (Temple Meads)	dep.	7 32	10 20	12 28	4 20	6 30	8 20	8 17	5 58	......
Brislington	"	7 39	—	12 36	4 28	6 38	8 30	8 24	6 3	—
Pensford	"	7 52	10 37	12 48	4 40	6 50	8 42	8 35	6 15	......
Clutton	"	8 1	10 46	12 57	4 49	6 59	8 52	8 44	6 25	—
Hallatrow	"	8 5	10 50	1 1	4 53	7 3	8 56	8 48	6 29	......
Camerton	dep.	—	—	—	—	—	—	—	—	—
	arr.	8 20	11*10	......	5* 10	......	......	......	......	......
Welton (for Midsomer N.)	dep.	8 13	10 58	1 9	5 2	7 11	9 4	8 56	6 37	—
RADSTOCK	"	8 20	11 6	1 16	5 9	7 15	9 10	9 3	6 44	......
Mells	"	8 29	11 14	1 25	5 17		9 18	9 11	6 53	—
FROME	arr.	8 40	11 25	1 37	5 28	......	9 30	9 22	7 5	--
Frome (for Chippenham)	dep.	9 7	11 54	2 1	5 34	—	—	12 56	7 10	—
Westbury	arr.	9 17	—	2 12	5 44	......	......	1 6	7 20	......
Trowbridge	"	9 27	12 9	2 26	5 54	—	—	1 19	7 34	—
Chippenham	"	9 57	12 30	3 3	6 18	......	......	1 50	—	......
Frome (for Weymouth)	dep.	—	11 38	1 51	6 8	—	9 40	9 41	7 59	—
Yeovil (Pen Mill)	arr.	......	12 39	2 39	7 3	......	10 27	10 32	9 10	......
Dorchester	"	—	1 38	3 21	7 57	—	11 17	11 22	10 6	—
WEYMOUTH	"	......	1 55	3 36	8 15	......	11 32	11 40	10 25	......

WEEK DAYS.								SUNDAYS.		
Class between Frome and Bristol.		AM.	1,2,P. AM.	AM.	AM.	PM.	1,2,P. PM.	1,2,P. AM.	PM.	
WEYMOUTH	dep.	......	7 0	8 25	11 50	2 45	5 5	......	5 0	......
Dorchester	"	—	7 20	8 44	12 12	3 6	5 26	—	5 15	—
Yeovil (Pen Mill)	"	......	8 10	9 36	12 59	4 0	6 26	......	6 5	......
Frome	arr.	—	9 7	10 39	2 1	4 55	7 32	—	7 10	—
Chippenham	dep.	......	6 32	......	1 4	2 40	5 15	......	7 0	......
Trowbridge	"	—	7 8	—	1 28	3 19	5 42	9 17	7 32	—
Westbury	"	......	7 24	......	1 38	3 38	5 53	9 27	7 45	......
Frome	arr.	—	7 39	—	1 51	3 57	6 8	9 41	7 59	—
FROME (for Bristol)	dep.	......	9 15	10 42	2 10	4 58	7 50	10 0	8 10	......
Mells	"	—	9 29	10 55	2 25	5 12	8 5	10 15	8 25	—
RADSTOCK	"	7 25	9 39	11 5	2 35	5 23	8 15	10 25	8 35	......
Welton (for Midsomer N.)	"	7 30	9 44	11 10	2 40	5 28	8 20	10 30	8 40	—
Camerton	dep.	—	9 35	—	—	5*25	—	—	—	—
	arr.	8*20	11 10	......	......	......	......	......	......	......
Hallatrow	dep.	7 38	9 52	11 18	2 48	5 38	8 28	10 40	8 50	......
Clutton	"	7 43	9 56	11 22	2 53	5 43	8 33	10 45	8 55	—
Pensford	"	7 51	10 4	11 31	3 1	5 51	8 43	10 55	9 5	......
Brislington	"	8 3	10 16	......	3 13	6 3	8 55	11 8	9 17	—
BRISTOL (T. Meads)	arr.	8 10	10 23	11 45	3 20	6 10	9 2	11 15	9 25	......

* Parliamentary as between Hallatrow and Camerton.

BRISTOL–RADSTOCK–FROME PUBLIC TIMETABLE 5th OCTOBER 1942

Original: Public Record Office

BRISTOL, RADSTOCK AND FROME. 47

		Week Days.							Suns.	
		a.m.	a.m.	a.m.	p.m.	p.m.	p.m.	p.m.	a.m.	p.m.
Bristol (Temple Meads)	dep.	6X50	...	10 20	1S 30	5 20	6 30	9 40	9 40	4 50
Brislington	"	6X57	.	10 27	1S 37	5 27	6 37	9 47	9 47	4 57
Whitchurch Halt	"	7X 5	...	10 34	1S 44	5 34	6 44	9 54	9 54	5 4
Pensford	"	7X12	.	10 41	1S 52	5 41	6 51	10 1	10 1	5 11
Clutton	"	7X24	...	10 50	2S 0	5 50	7 0	10 10	10 10	5 20
Hallatrow	"	7X29	.	10 54	2S 5	5 54	7 5	10 13	10 14	5 24
Farrington Gurney	"	7X34	...	10 58	2S 10	5 58	7 10	10 17	10 18	5 28
Midsomer Norton & Welton	"	7X39	.	11 2	2S 14	6 2	7 14	10 21	10 22	5 32
Radstock *	"	7X44	9X35	11 7	2S 18	6 7	7 19	10 25	10 26	5 36
Mells Road	"	7X54	9X44	11 15	2S 26	6 17	7 27	10 33	10 34	5 44
Frome	arr.	8X 6	9X55	11 25	2S 36	6 27	7 37	10 43	10 44	5 54

		Week Days.							Suns.	
		a.m.	a.m.	a.m.	p.m.	p.m.	p.m.	p.m.	noon	p.m.
Frome	dep.	7 37	8X55	10 47	1 35	3S 30	6X 0	9 18	12 0	9 0
Mells Road	"	7 49	9X 9	10 59	1 47	3S 42	6X14	9 30	12 12	9 12
Radstock *	"	7 56	9X15	11 6	1 54	3S 49	6X20	9 37	12 19	9 21
Midsomer N'ton & W'ton	"	8 0	—	11 10	1 58	3S 53	6X25	9 41	12 23	9 25
Farrington Gurney	"	8 4	...	11 14	2 2	3S 57	6X31	9 45	12 27	9 29
Hallatrow	"	8 8	.	11 18	2 6	4S 1	6X35	9 49	12 31	9 33
Clutton	"	8 12	...	11 22	2 10	4S 5	6X40	9 53	12 35	9 37
Pensford	"	8 20	.	11 30	2 20	4S 13	6X52	10 2	12 43	9 45
Whitchurch Halt	"	8 27	...	...	2 27	4S 20	7X 0	10 9	12 50	9 52
Brislington	"	8 31	.	W	2 32	4S 25	7X 5	10 14	12 55	9 57
Bristol (T'ple Meads)	arr.	8 38	...	11 45	2 40	4S 32	7X12	10 21	1 6	10 6

S—Saturdays only.
V—Runs Friday and Saturdays nights only.
W—On Saturdays only calls at Brislington at 11.38 a.m. to set down passengers. X—Third class only (limited accommodation).

③—Third class only.
¶—One mile to Southern Railway Station.
*—Adjoins Somerset and Dorset Railway Station.
‡—Paignton arr. 7.58 p.m. §—Paignton arr. 10.10 p.m.

HALLATROW STATION LOOKING SOUTH (2)
This time showing the loops and sidings to the north of the station in the late 1930s.

Philip Chapman

public house and agent for the railway in that locality.

Hallatrow station had a prize possession in the form of a railway push-bike which was only used by certain privileged members of staff! The stationmaster would use it to cycle out into the district to placate irate customers and to deal with complaints generally, while the parcels porter would use it to deliver accounts to the surrounding farmers. In addition, the station's wagon examiner would use it to cycle to Camerton to examine wagons standing in the colliery sidings there. Although no permanent wagon repairs were carried out at Hallatrow, running or spot repairs were often made at the station.

On the station side of the roadbridge, at the south end of the 'down' platform, there was a water tank, installed during the major reconstruction of 1909/10, which was fed by water from the nearby River Cam. The tank supplied the station's water columns but in the summer months it would also serve as an unofficial place for staff to bathe! Various railwaymen have said that Hallatrow was a very pleasant place to work. As parcels porter, Frank Smith did his own graphics on posters advertising the railway company's services and, indeed, so successful was he at this that when he left Hallatrow in 1934 he was offered the chance to do professional graphic design work with the local press!

The delightful grassy bank and garden on the Bristol side platform was a well-known feature of the station. Mr Williams, the stationmaster in 1919, was responsible for the development of the long flower bed which was a centrepiece of that 'up' platform. The station was a winner in the "Best Station" award on a couple of occasions, competition being fierce locally with Clutton just up the line. Frank Smith had the idea of putting the name "Hallatrow" into stone chippings, the letters tapering down in size from the large "H". This garden and station name was destroyed under government orders at the outbreak of the Second World War so as not to aid the Germans. Presumably this form of destruction took place at other stations on the line that had this feature, that is, Clutton and possibly Brislington.

Hallatrow in Later Days

During the 1930s Mr Rowley Best was stationmaster at Hallatrow. Around 1938/39 Mr Best, who went on to do relief work, was replaced by Mr Gait. He stayed for some 16 years, his place being taken over by Mr Toy c1955. He remained there until the passenger service was removed in 1959. However, he continued to live in the station house after that time.

Incidentally, before coming to Hallatrow, Mr Gait had been relief stationmaster at Wanstrow. He then moved onto Wrington doing relief work around the area before finally becoming stationmaster at Hallatrow. During his time on the railway, Mr Gait worked at no less than 103 stations in the GWR's Bristol Division.

In 1947, Mr Gerald Dagger went to Hallatrow station, as a porter, a job his brother had held before Gerald's arrival. Later, Gerald went on to become a lorry driver based there. By the 1950s passenger traffic was well on the decline although the goods side was still busy. There were a good number of parcels deliveries particularly at Christmas while, with the continual growth of Purnells, two small and one large parcels lorries were all kept busy. Indeed, by this time Hallatrow dealt with a substantial amount of traffic for Purnells, many small parcels going out to the Woolworth chain of stores. Any urgent parcels or small packages were sent away by passenger train, larger consignments being handled through the goods depot.

As mentioned above, Christmas was usually a very hectic time. Almost all the parcels, sometimes up to 2,000 per day in number, went out by passenger train. Because of the workload, extra staff would have to be called in from Bristol. At other times of the year Gerald's normal week as a parcels lorry driver would look much like this:

Monday
am: Hallatrow/Farrington Gurney/High Littleton
pm: Timsbury/Tunley/Camerton and Dunkerton
Tuesday am/pm: Chewton Mendip/Ston Easton areas
Wednesday: Spare day
Thursday: Timsbury/Tunley/Camerton and Dunkerton
Friday: Chewton Mendip/Ston Easton

GAS PIPES AND GOODS SHED AT HALLATROW
In the 1935-1939 period a very large contract was put through for the installation of gas pipes in the area around Hallatrow. With a Thornycroft tractor and trailer prominent in this view, another cargo of pipes awaits distribution in the goods yard at Hallatrow station.

Philip Chapman

CARNIVAL, COMMUNITY AND THE GWR
With a heavily disguised Thornycroft wagon acting as the basis for a tableau, staff from stations on the North Somerset branch raise funds for Paulton Hospital on the occasion of one of the carnivals held annually in Midsomer Norton.

Philip Chapman

HALLATROW STAFF IN THE FIFTIES
Back row (left to right) Reg Edwards, John Stokes, Harold Box, Bert Durbin, Bert Tovey, Bill Oatley, Tom Owen, Bill Bolt, George Denning.
Centre row (left to right) Reg Dance, Harold Grist, Dulcie Stock, Dorothy Bishop, Joan Routley (now Gregory).
Front row (left to right) Mr and Mrs Gait (on his retirement as stationmaster at Hallatrow).

Alan and Joan Gregory

In addition, outward parcels would be picked up from Purnells most afternoons and, in fact, this traffic stayed with the railway until the removal of the North Somerset passenger service in 1959.

Another important source of traffic both during and after World War Two was provided by the Ministry of Food's Buffer Depot, a series of large single-storeyed sheds to the south-west of Hallatrow station and within sight of it. Naturally busy during the war, the sheds were still well in use in 1947 when consignments of corned beef and sugar were brought in by rail, the use of these sheds continuing into the mid-1950s at least. The corned beef came in heavy wooden boxes which were carried in open wagons and it was these boxes which proved very difficult for railway staff to handle. Sugar from the West Indies was also a frequent visitor to the platforms of Hallatrow on its way to the Buffer Depot.

The Depot was well used by American servicemen during the war and the station yard at Hallatrow was frequently full of jeeps and GI's. Stores held in the depot were often unloaded by detainees from the nearby Shepton Mallet jail. Not unnaturally, these detainees were kept under armed guard! The aeroplane components factory in the quarry at Cloud Hill produced all kinds of items during the war. These would go out in box vans from Hallatrow although it is not known whether these went out over the former rail link to the quarry itself. Post war, Purnells produced railway publications such as working timetables and rules and regulations and these were also shipped out by train.

On the goods side, in January 1947, a zonal scheme was instigated with a view to speeding up the collection and delivery of goods in the West of England. The aim of the scheme was to save delay by reducing the number of small stations that had a role as goods agencies. In the North Somerset area this meant that the traffic of some 35 stations was handled by five, these being Bristol, Bath, Hallatrow, Wells and Weston-super-Mare. Similarly the stations in the West Wiltshire area at Trowbridge, Melksham, Frome, Warminster and Castle Cary became concentration points for traffic which had previously been worked through 18 stations.

Calf traffic started from Hallatrow around 1950, this being handled on behalf of dealers at Hinton Blewett and Bishop Sutton. In the late 1950s horseboxes were used, the calves being sent out loose in the box. The consignments were bound for various destinations and these included Scotland, East Anglia, Abergavenny, Chepstow and Hereford. Passengers must surely have been surprised when their Bristol-bound trains were shunted into the former Camerton bay to pick up the odd horsebox! This traffic 'tailed-off' by 1959. Horses were also sent out during the 1950s period by a local horse breeder, Rodney Carpenter of Cloud Hill Farm, who would occasionally send out his stock through Hallatrow. Meanwhile, the pigeon traffic was still heavy in the spring and summer months with most of the business going north.

Mrs Joan Gregory worked in the goods office at Hallatrow during the 1953-58 period. She tells of the still heavy traffic from Purnells which by this time included books for Littlewoods, Marks & Spencer, Menzies, W.H. Smith's and Woolworth. Initially, she says that the books were taken out by train but, later on in the 1950s, the traffic went out by road although the revenue was still actually booked to Hallatrow. This particular traffic was very heavy right up until 1959. During her time there Joan says that the goods office was rebuilt and extended to help handle all the goods traffic then on offer, the goods office staff working in a camping coach while the extension was being built. One unusual category of freight dealt with were the containers of glass which were bound for the nearby firm of Franco-British Glass. These particular consignments originated from the Continent and were thoroughly packed in straw, the railway staff at Hallatrow having to burn the latter!

Above: FROME GRAMMAR AT HALLATROW
In November 1961 Frome Grammar School's Railway Circle organised a brake van trip over the North Somerset. This well-posed shot shows the entire group (less photographer, of course!) at Hallatrow station. Inspector Henry Skinner of Westbury obviously has things well in hand here!

John Keeping

Below: OFF THE RAILS AT HALLATROW!
Class 6100 No. 6148 simmers and settles gently into the sand drag at the south end of Hallatrow station on 15th August 1963. Intense concentration is obviously being given to the first wagon of the freight train which remains firmly on the rails, while the engine, well and truly stuck in the sand, seems to merit no attention at all!

P.J. Williams

BEHIND THE SCENES AT HALLATROW
This perspective of the station approach road looks towards Temple Cloud. Generally speaking, passenger traffic towards Frome was much quieter than that towards Bristol which was always respectably heavy. In the days post World War One until the removal of the passenger service in 1925, the Camerton branch was always quiet from Hallatrow, any travellers tending to be visitors from Bristol.
Author's collection

A B&NSR SPECIAL
Having lost its regular passenger service some three years earlier, Hallatrow welcomes a somewhat unusual passenger carrier for this branch at least! This three-car dmu ran on 15th September 1962 and is seen here leaving the loop at the south end of the station. *Ivo Peters*

Chapter 9 will provide us with fuller details of the loss of the line's passenger traffic, suffice it to say at this point that at Hallatrow the total parcels revenue alone for 1958 amounted to some £28,000 which included £7,000 for live calf traffic. The balance of £21,000 was almost wholly derived from Purnell's forwardings, although as we have seen much of this traffic actually left the area by road! It would seem that with freight, parcel, livestock and passenger traffic the branch through Hallatrow was, *as a whole,* very profitable. Indeed, Post Office traffic from Purnells added another £76,000 to Hallatrow's revenue in 1958! Nonetheless, in November 1959 the station lost its passenger and parcels' services. The livestock traffic was transferred to Binegar station on the S&D where it stayed until that railway closed in 1966. Robin Atthill states:

> "One of the banking turns from Radstock (S&D) involved 'doing the Binegar calf' that is, attaching the vans to the rear of an 'up' afternoon train to Bath and beyond."

For Hallatrow the loss of all this traffic seemed a sad end to what had once been a very fine and busy junction station on the former Bristol & North Somerset Railway.

Of all things however, the branch is probably best remembered for its record in films. In 1935 *The Ghost Train* was filmed (along with other locations) at Camerton, Dunkerton and Mells Road. In 1937, the Edgar Wallace thriller *Kate Plus Ten* was shot at Dunkerton Colliery sidings while, in 1953, *The Titfield Thunderbolt* was put onto film at Camerton, Dunkerton and Monkton Combe.

NORTHBOUND MEETS SOUTHBOUND AT HALLATROW
Class 5101 2-6-2T No. 4103 waits with the southbound 2.40pm goods from Bristol, whilst 6100 class No. 6148 runs in with the 5.00pm northbound coal train from Radstock. This 26th March 1964 picture shows that even with the passenger trains gone, Hallatrow station was still worth a visit!

Ivo Peters

8
World War One and Beyond

MIDSOMER NORTON & WELTON STATION
A party of schoolchildren on their way to Windsor for a day out found themselves having an extra "trip" on a station trolley at Midsomer Norton & Welton station in 1933. The children were all pupils from Midsomer Norton School. The porter, Ernest Goulding, has kindly contributed both information and the photograph, and who knows, some of these children may now be readers of this book!

Ernest Goulding

As the North Somerset Railway entered the 20th century new works running into and along its length became the order of the day. One early example of this was a 1903 proposal which involved the building of a railway from Pensford to Blagdon, the latter being the then existing terminus of a short branch from Congresbury on the GWR's Cheddar Valley line between Wells and Yatton. This short branch, the Wrington Vale Light Railway, opened on 4th December 1901 and served small villages at Wrington, Langford, Burrington and Blagdon. However, in 1903, pressure was brought to bear on the GWR by Sir Edward Strachey to take up a scheme to build a railway from Blagdon to the North Somerset at Pensford in order to rail connect the Chew Valley.

At that time the GWR was favourable to the project but it was not prepared to make any initial moves. The company felt that if the inhabitants of the Chew Valley wanted a railway then it was up to them to do something about it! It was to this end, therefore, that a meeting was called in the first week of January 1905 at the Grand Hotel, Bristol to consider the advisability of applying for a Light Railway Order for the new scheme. Sir Edward Strachey was chairman at the meeting and, naturally enough, he was a staunch supporter of the line.

At this 1905 meeting Mr William Foxlee, a member of the Institute of Civil Engineers, said that the proposed railway, some 10¼ miles in length, would begin at a junction with the existing Wrington Vale Light Railway at Blagdon, and would have proceeded along the southern side of the Bristol Waterworks reservoir. Passing Ubley, and a little to the north of Compton Martin, it would have crossed the main road from the Harptrees near the Blue Bowl Inn. Turning in a north-easterly direction, it would have then followed the main road to Sutton Wick for a distance of about a mile. Having passed Stratford Bridge, it would have swung to the north, crossing the valley of the River Chew, and following along the western side of that stream to Chew Stoke. On leaving there the line would have continued up the valley to Chew Magna, where it would have crossed the main street at the southern end of the village.

After running parallel to the Chelwood Road it would have passed a little to the north of Bromley Colliery (see Chapter 6), thence turning north-east and forming a junction with the North Somerset branch at the southern end of Pensford Viaduct. It was proposed to provide stations or stopping places for Blagdon, Ubley and near the Blue Bowl Inn to serve Compton Martin and East and West Harptree. There would also have been halts at Sutton Wick, Chew Stoke, Chew Magna and Stanton Drew. The line was to have been constructed under the 1896 Light Railway Act. Its supporters believed that it would be a valuable feeder to the GWR and they hoped that it would develop regular commuter traffic into Bristol.

Incidentally, an alternative and more direct route had also been examined. This would have left the line described above at Stratford Bridge and, running to the east of Bishop Sutton, it would then have taken up the line of the route as first intended. If that route had been adopted a saving of some 1½ miles would have been made in the distance between Blagdon and Pensford and the cost of construction would have fallen by around £18,000 to £20,000. However, the main snag with this was that neither Chew Stoke nor Chew Magna would have been served by the new railway!

STATION STAFF AT CONGRESBURY
This pastoral shot shows the station staff at Congresbury on the GWR's Cheddar Valley line, probably in the years just before World War One. Junction for the short branch to Blagdon, hopes were high at Congresbury in Edwardian days that the branch could be extended through to Pensford on the North Somerset.

Gerald Quartley

Traffic prospects for the new extension were said to be good. The possible passenger traffic looked healthy while the line was planned to tap some likely lead seams in the Ubley area. In addition, and rather over-optimistically it would seem, Bromley Colliery promised to put at least 1,000 tons of coal a week onto the B&PLR! Agricultural traffic from Ubley, Compton Martin, the Harptrees and the Chew Valley all appeared a reasonable bet, particularly bearing in mind that the local farmers had just tried to use motor vehicles for their milk traffic. This initiative had been a failure and milk transport had reverted to horse haulage.

At its close, the promoters' meeting was undecided on two crucial points. It had not agreed the route that the new railway should take nor had it decided where the money to finance the project was to come from! Nevertheless, at an inquiry at the Pelican Hotel, Chew Magna the following year, the Light Railway Commissioners granted a Light Railway Order for the Blagdon & Pensford. However, in spite of local enthusiasm the line was never built and Pensford never became a junction, although it would have been fascinating to have seen the result of the changes if it had!

Although the Blagdon & Pensford project never came into being, the years up until World War One saw a goodly number of other changes taking place on the North Somerset branch as the GWR consolidated the route's role as a substantial cross-country railway. On 18th August 1906 additional siding accommodation was provided at Brislington while, two years later, on 14th April 1908 the two dead end loops then in use at the station were converted into loops. An additional ground frame was then provided at the north end of the station to control the new connection into the main line. On 25th April 1908 the extended platform was brought into use at the station while a new approach road was provided to the goods yard on the 'down' side.

In lieu of a/c previously opened with W. Thatcher.

(2113) GREAT WESTERN RAILWAY.

C.A. 57/65 / 131201

AUDIT OFFICE,

Paddington, 13. Dec 1901

Dear Sir,

Please to open a Monthly Ledger Account in your Station books with Messrs Thatchers Breweries Ltd of Welton Old Brewery, Midsomer Norton for charges on Merchandise conveyed to or from your Station; the account must be promptly and regularly forwarded to this Office to be rendered, and the amount of same is to be collected by you within SEVEN DAYS after delivery, of which you will be duly advised.

Be so good as to fill up the attached receipt, and return it to this Office by an early Train.

Yours truly,
J. FRYERS,
per

Welton Station.
Near Radstock

In lieu of a/c with Thatchers Breweries L

(2,000—K 10—12 09) Copyable (2118)

GREAT WESTERN RAILWAY.

C.A. 80/215

AUDIT OFFICE,

Paddington, 12th Decr 1911

Dear Sir,

Please to open a Monthly Ledger Account in your Station books with Welton Breweries Ld of Midsomer Norton nr Bath for charges on Merchandise; the account must be promptly and regularly rendered by you, and the amount of same is to be collected within SEVEN DAYS after delivery.

Be so good as to fill up the attached receipt, and return it to this office by an early Train.

In the event of any change in the constitution of the Firm or of any change of address, please advise me.

Yours truly,
D. W. B. PRICE,
per

Midsomer Norton Station.

AT ALL STATIONS ONE PENNY.

"HOLIDAY HAUNTS," 1907.

With List of HOTELS, BOARDING HOUSES, SEASIDE, FARMHOUSE, and COUNTRY LODGINGS.

GREAT WESTERN RAILWAY.

NORTH-EAST SOMERSET FARMERS' CLUB SHOW

AT

SALTFORD.

On WEDNESDAY, AUGUST 28th,

CHEAP TICKETS

will be issued to

SALTFORD

FROM	AT		Return Fares.		
			1st Cl.	2nd Cl.	3rd Cl.
	A.M.	P.M.	s. d.	s. d.	s. d.
Hallatrow	10 38	1 2	3 9	2 6	1 11
Clutton	10 43	1 7	3 6	2 3	1 9
Pensford	10 53	1 15	2 10	1 10	1 5
Brislington	11 3	1 24	1 11	1 3	1 0

Passengers may return by any train on day of issue only.

Children under Twelve Years of age, Half-Price. No Luggage allowed.

The Tickets are not transferable. Should an Excursion or Cheap Ticket be used for any other Station than those named upon it, or by any other Train than those specified above it will be rendered void, and therefore the fare paid will be liable to forfeiture, and the full Ordinary Fare will become chargeable.

For information respecting Pleasure Party and Excursion arrangements, and Special Trips on the Great Western Railway, application should be made to Mr. C. Kislingbury, Divisional Superintendent, Temple Meads Station, Bristol; or at any of the Stations.

Paddington, Aug., 1907. JAMES C. INGLIS, General Manager.

(Bristol – 500 R. 8vo, 2 sides.) Arrowsmith, Printer, Quay Street, Bristol. (B 692)

AT ALL STATIONS ONE PENNY.

"HOLIDAY HAUNTS," 1907.

With List of HOTELS, BOARDING HOUSES, SEASIDE, FARMHOUSE, and COUNTRY LODGINGS.

GREAT WESTERN RAILWAY

A Day at the Seaside!

On SATURDAY, August 17th,

A Day-Trip Excursion

WILL RUN TO

WEYMOUTH

LEAVING	AT	RETURN FARES, THIRD CLASS.
	A.M.	s. d.
RADSTOCK	7 35	3 9
MELLS ROAD	7 45	3 3

The Return Train will leave Weymouth at 8.20 p.m. the same day.

Children under Twelve years of age, half-price.

NO LUGGAGE ALLOWED.

The Tickets are not transferable. Should an Excursion or Cheap Ticket be used for any other Station than those named upon it, or by any other Train than those specified above, it will be rendered void, and therefore the fare paid will be liable to forfeiture, and the full Ordinary Fare will become chargeable.

For information respecting Pleasure Party Arrangements, and Excursions and Special Trips on the Great Western Railway, application should be made to Mr. C. Kislingbury, Divisional Superintendent, Temple Meads Station, Bristol; or at any of the Stations.

Paddington, Aug., 1907. JAMES C. INGLIS, General Manager.

(Bristol—1000 R. 8vo, 2 sides.) Arrowsmith, Printer, Quay Street, Bristol. (B 673)

SONS OF THE SOIL AT SALTFORD, 1907 *Original: M Wyatt* A DAY OUT TO WEYMOUTH, 1907 *Original: M Wyatt*

THE PROPOSED ROUTE OF THE BLAGDON & PENSFORD LIGHT RAILWAY – 1905

Original plan: Somerset Record Office

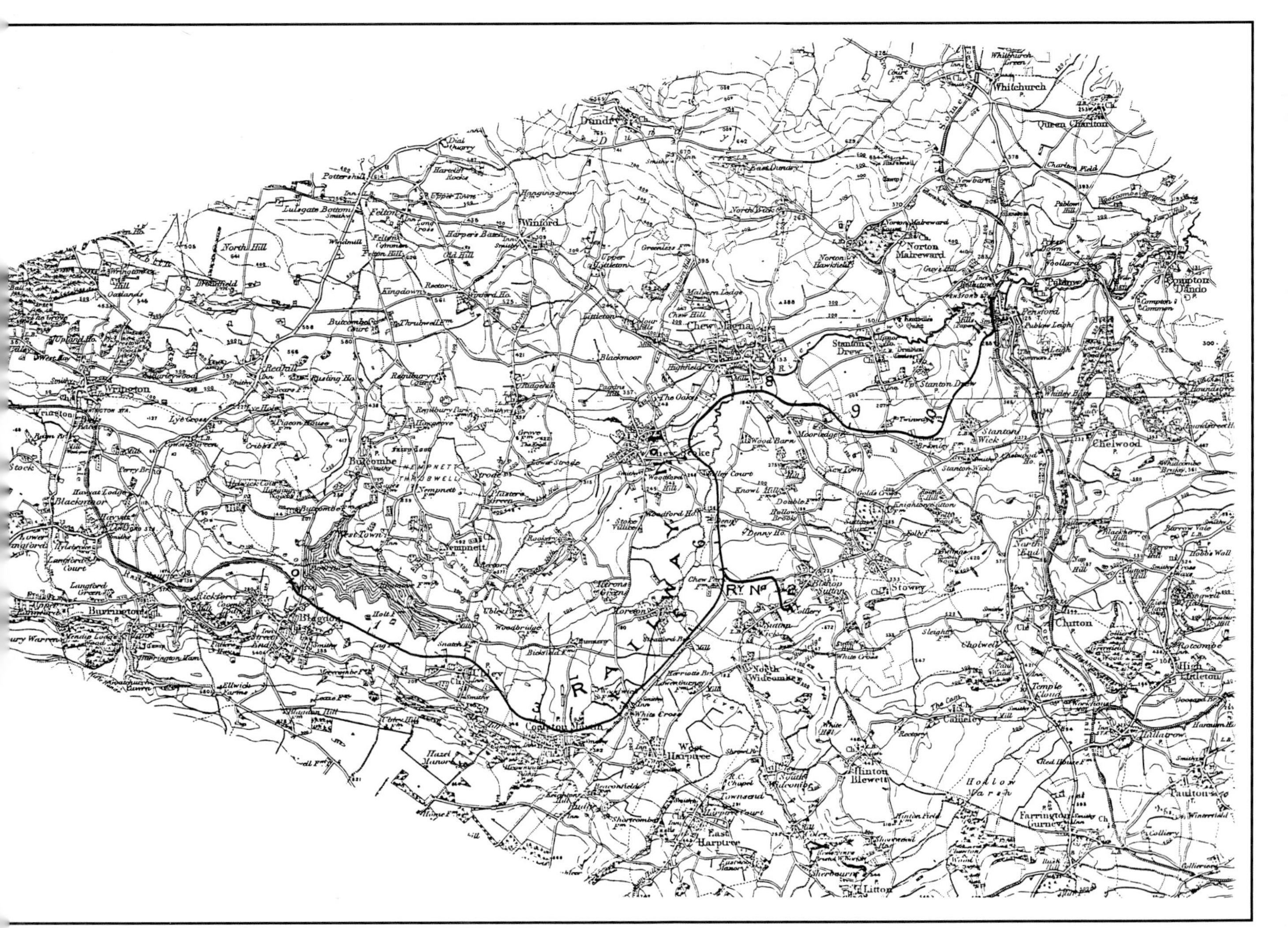

Blagdon and Pensford Light Railway.

Estimate of Expense.

SUMMARY.

	Length.				Cost.		
	M.	F.	C.		£	s.	d.
Railway No. 1	11	3	5		74,800	7	3
Railway No. 2	0	7	3·3		2,587	17	1
Total length	12	2	8·3	Total cost	£77,388	4	4

Dated this 31st day of May, 1905.

WILLIAM T. FOXLEE,
Engineer.

On 4th July 1908 Board of Trade Inspector Yorke produced the following report:

'Sir, I have the honour to report for the information of the Board of Trade, that in compliance with the instructions contained in your Minute of the 1st instant, I have inspected the new siding connection and extension of platform at Brislington, on the GWR.

The line is single, and is worked upon the Electric Train Staff system."

During World War One a fair number of changes took place in the Bristol area around St Philip's Marsh, Dr Day's Sidings and Marsh Junction. Although these changes affected the North Somerset only indirectly, these additional works were of some significance to the branch, being at its northern end. On 30th July 1915 £568 was spent on providing accommodation at St Philip's Marsh, the War Ministry bearing the cost of this work. In the same year, on 22nd March, the Camerton-Limpley Stoke line was closed for passenger traffic in order to release staff for other war work.

On 16th March 1917 plans were made to spend £8,144 on new carriage sidings at Marsh Junction with a further £1,365 to be spent at Dr Day's, both sets of sidings to be built to store ecs then being used by trains serving the huge Munitions Depot under construction at that time at Henbury on the Avonmouth-Filton line (see the author's companion title *Lines to Avonmouth* OPC for further information). However, on 8th June 1917, with the entry of the USA into the war, the Henbury project was abandoned. In turn, this led to a severe reduction in the number and scope of several associated railway projects in the Bristol and Severnside areas. Sidings being laid in for ecs storage at St Philip's Marsh were expected to be abandoned as were the above-mentioned sidings at Marsh Junction and Dr Day's, this work being in direct consequence of the abandonment of the Henbury scheme. Nonetheless, all was not lost for, in October 1917 the go-ahead was given to spend £210 on the lighting of sidings at Marsh Junction while, at the same location, the work of providing stabling accommodation for workmens' trains, on the intensive passenger service to the very busy Avonmouth area, was regarded as being of such importance that it should be completed at an estimated cost of £700. In addition, the tracks at Dr Day's Sidings were also taken over for general railway purposes.

Around the same period, but at the other end of the line, new siding connections at Frome were also under scrutiny on 4th May 1916 when Colonel P.G. Von Donop, an Inspecting Officer with the Board of Trade, presented the following report:

Below: AN INTERESTING MIGHT-HAVE-BEEN
Locomotive No. 1384 makes a fine sight at the head of the Wrington Vale train. It is an interesting thought that if the Blagdon & Pensford Light Railway scheme of 1905/6 had gone ahead and the Wrington Vale Light Railway had been linked with the North Somerset, this locomotive and its three coach rake would have been regular visitors to the Bristol & North Somerset's station at Pensford.

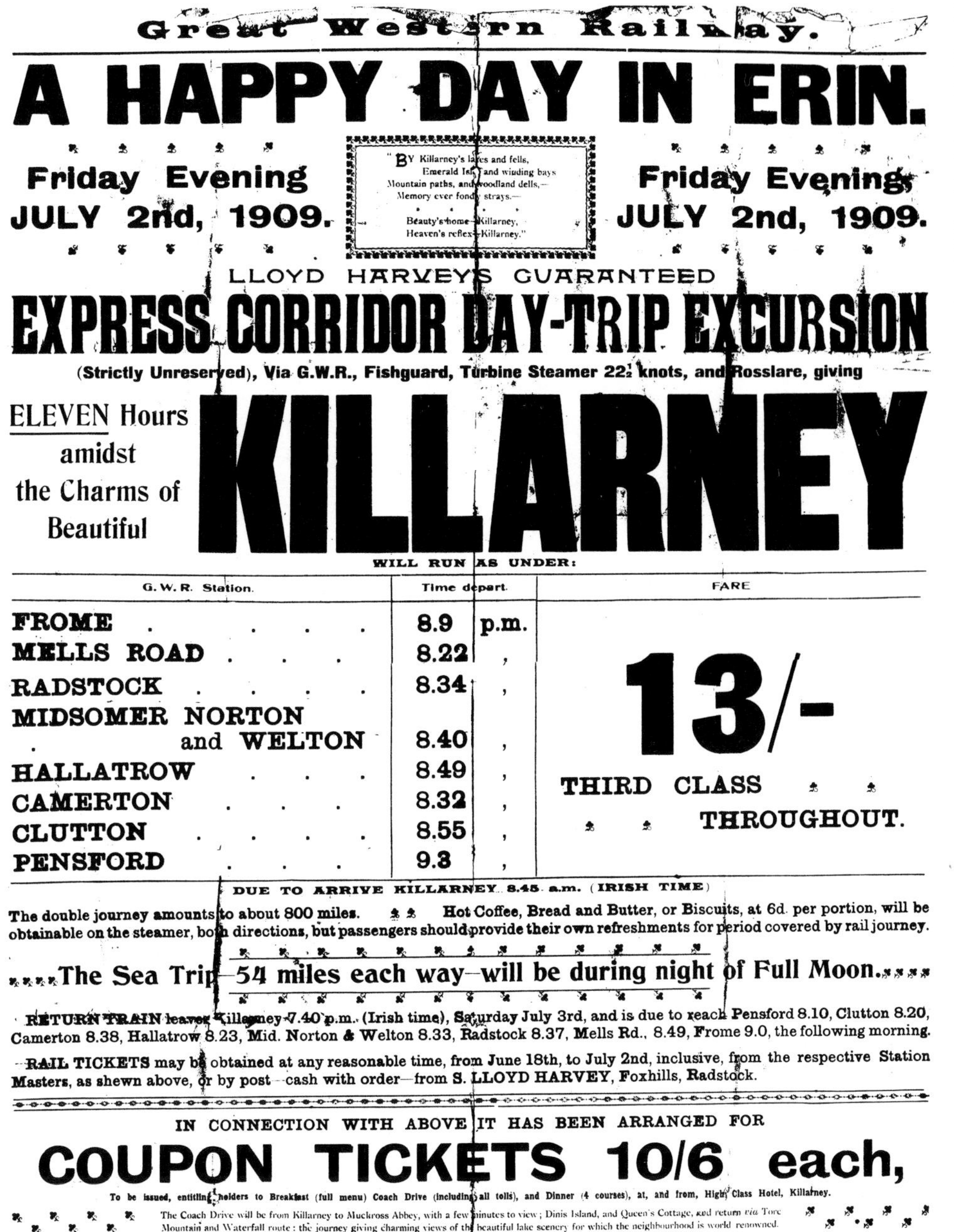

A HAPPY DAY IN ERIN
Mr S. Lloyd Harvey, the organiser of the above excursion, was a native of Weston-super-Mare who, at the age of 17, joined the GWR. He spent some 18 years with the company, eventually becoming stationmaster at Welton station. In later life he left the GWR to join the Radstock Coal & Wagon Company where he remained until his retirement at the age of 70.

The GWR Magazine of August 1909 reported that the special corridor train, with more than 300 passengers on board, left Frome at 8.09pm on Friday 2nd July 1909. Its travellers reached Killarney at 8.45am the next morning, spot on the scheduled time. The excursionists spent eleven hours in Killarney and reached their home stations only three minutes after the advertised time. By train and steamer they had covered over 800 miles in 36 hours – strong souls indeed!

Original poster: Chris Smith

Caption information: Dennis Chedgy

'Sir, I have the honour to report for the Board of Trade, that in compliance with the instructions contained in your Minute of 29th February (1916) I have inspected the new works at Frome, on the GWR.

At the Radstock Branch Junction, near Frome, a new trailing connection has been added on the 'up' line, leading from sidings. The points and signals are worked from the Frome West signal box – an existing signal box, containing a frame of 18 working and 2 spare levers.

The interlocking is correct and the arrangements are satisfactory, so I can recommend the Board of Trade to sanction the new works being brought into use."

Once the war was over, the line reverted to a more normal pattern of working and our narrative now continues by examining the everyday life and traffic of stations along the route during the 1920s and 1930s and it is to the first of these, Clutton, that we now turn.

When the First World War broke out on 1st August 1914 it happened on a day that all of Clutton had been looking forward to, namely the day of its famous Flower Show. Special trains had been booked to run from both Bristol and Frome, while plans had been made for the Somerset Yeomanry to put on a display. At the last minute, however, they were called up for duty and for them, the village and for Western Europe generally things would never be the same again. The period after the war also brought its own problems, one of which was that petrol was in generally short supply. It was therefore not unusual to find steam wagons being used to carry goods. Burning the best steam coal from South Wales, they did some ten miles to the hundredweight! In the Clutton area this particular coal came in via the North Somerset and cost some 15s (75p) per ton, surely a real case of "taking coals to Newcastle"!

In conversation with Mrs Weaver from Clutton she told me about her father, Mr Albert Gibbs, who was one of the regular signalmen at Clutton from around 1917 to 20th May 1940. Formerly at Pill on the GWR's Bristol-Portishead branch, he had moved to the busy wartime station at Clutton partially because of his strong local railway connections. For example, one of his uncles, Mr Reg Cooke, was a guard based at Frome while another uncle, Mr Bill Poole, was a ganger on the North Somerset (see photographs on pages 58, 133 and 144). Bill was well-respectedlocally as a highly capable railwayman: he was also well-known for supplying the men in his permanent way gang with cider!

While at Clutton, Mr Gibbs worked with fellow signalman, Mr Ticknell, with Mr Cecil Greenslade also working there as signal porter, later moving on to Hallatrow where he became one of that station's signalmen. He eventually went on to the post of stationmaster at the very small station at Wanstrow on the East Somerset Railway near Witham. Clutton's stationmasters in the order it is believed they were there were as follows: Mr Gosling, Mr Williams, Mr Attwood, Mr Rust and Mr Nailor. With the exception of Mr Nailor, of whom more in the next chapter, all of the others were at Clutton during the same time as Mr Gibbs.

A well-known railway family in the Clutton area was the Edwards' family. There were three brothers in the family during the 1920s and 1930s, all of whom were known to Mr Gibbs. The three brothers Luther ('Lou'), Wilfrid and Reginald were all bred into a railway background, their father having been a porter at Clutton, probably in the period before the First World War. Lou was both porter and signalporter at Clutton while Reginald also worked here during the time of Mr Gibbs' stay, later moving on to Pensford. Wilf is known to have worked at Hallatrow as lad porter in the late 1930s although his progress has been very much more difficult to follow. The Edwards were yet another instance of the way in which the North Somerset was very much a family railway and a full community in itself.

During the 1926 General Strike most of the local railwaymen came out although Mr Gibbs himself stayed in work. He was offered police protection but during the actual period of the Strike he only went down to the box once a day. During the 1930s Clutton won the 'Best Station in the South West Award' mainly due to the hard work of Mr Joseph Attwood who was stationmaster at the time. He maintained an absolutely beautiful station garden, this being taken over by Mr Gibbs when Mr Attwood moved on. One key feature of the floral and decorative arrangements was that the station's name was outlined in stone chippings in the grassy banks that surrounded the station. Like the displays at Brislington and Hallatrow, it became a well-known 'trade-mark' for Clutton station.

On the passenger side at this time, one regular traffic carried by the trains from Clutton to Bristol and return was the boys of Bristol Grammar School and the girls of Colston Girls School. It must be mentioned, however, that it was felt advisable to keep them apart in separate compartments! Office workers used the North Somerset to get into Bristol while the trains were, of course, very well used for the heavy milk traffic put

BRISLINGTON STATION 1908
With the ground frame at the north end of the station prominent in the foreground, a Bristol-Frome train approaches Brislington station in 1908. It is headed by 'Metro' class 2-4-0T No. 632 and 'Buffalo' class 0-6-0ST No. 1819.
M.B. Warburton

BRISTOL (TEMPLE MEADS)
This peaceful photograph shows Bristol Temple Meads, looking west, before the station was rebuilt in the early 1930s.
Lens of Sutton

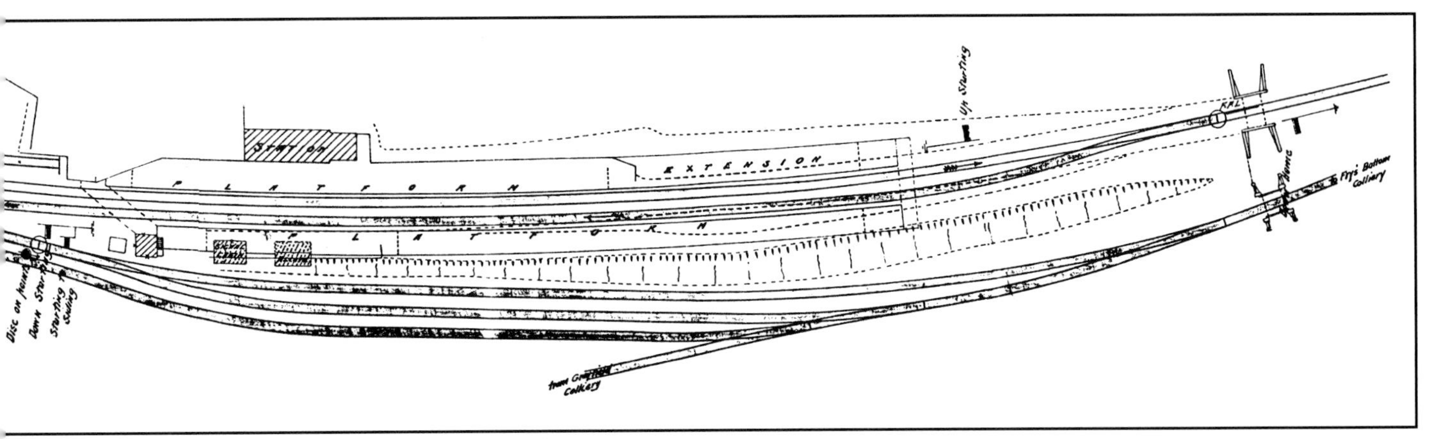

CLUTTON STATION SHOWING THE CHANGES MADE IN 1890

Original plan: Public Record Office

CLUTTON STATION STAFF IN THE 1920s
With further evidence of milk traffic in clear view, Clutton's station staff pose proudly for the camera. Mr Gibbs, one of the station's signalmen is on the extreme left, while the stationmaster, Mr Williams, is the person third from the left. In the background can be seen the station's parcels office.

Mrs Weaver

through the station. Indeed, the station yard would be full of carts bringing milk churns in from the neighbouring farms during all of the 1920s and into the early 1930s. Sadly, this traffic was lost to road about 1935/36.

As we mentioned earlier, on Clutton Flower Show days special trains would be run. These would be very well-loaded, people standing in additional Siphon G milk vans. The station handled excursion traffic to places such as Weston-super-Mare, Weymouth and Barry Island while, each year, towards the end of the spring, special trains would be run in connection with the pilgrimages at Glastonbury. Incidentally, one excursion that was frequently mentioned in the Clutton area was one run in 1911 when, on 15th July of that year, a returning miners' excursion was rammed at Clutton by its own pilot engine. The latter had returned from Pensford where it had picked up a guard who had been accidentally left there. No serious damage was done but the event seems to have become part of local folklore.

Between the wars, Clutton, like Hallatrow to the south, also dealt with pigeon traffic while, during the same period, cattle, coal and bricks were all being handled through Clutton yard. Mr Ernest A. Rivers, trading as the Burchill Brick Company, had his own private siding, this being opened on 5th July 1927. The agreement for this was signed on 27th June of the same year. Another private siding agreement was signed for Clutton on 24th November 1927 when the Bristol & Clutton Wagon Company Limited continued the tradition of wagon repairing at the station, the local collieries having long provided the business. This repair work was later taken up by an outstation of Marcroft's of Radstock whose history is outlined in Chapter 11.

The yard at Clutton also played host to a small railway workshop which was based here. The district's P.W. Inspector and gang were located at Clutton while the two stone masons who worked out of Hallatrow, George and Bill Comer, along with their mate, Mr Stephens, were also regular visitors to the site. The wagon examiner based at Hallatrow would often visit Clutton on an if-and-when-required basis. All this activity was, nonetheless, fairly shortlived for, by the 1930s, all the collieries and brickworks had closed down although the tracks that

Left: CLUTTON SIGNAL BOX
This close-up view of the signal box at Clutton shows Mr Gibbs up in the box itself. Miss Brookman and Stationmaster Gosling appear in the group standing in front of the signal cabin. Vegetation seems to be flourishing inside the building!

Mrs Weaver

Below: CLUTTON STATION LOOKING NORTH TOWARDS BRISTOL

Lens of Sutton

Bottom: CLUTTON STATION LOOKING SOUTH TOWARDS RADSTOCK

Lens of Sutton

The two lower photographs on the facing page illustrate the importance of milk traffic to the North Somerset branch in the early 20th century. Just to give one set of sample figures, the 1911 "Milk Traffic Statement" given below shows the value of this traffic to the line's revenue

	Number of churns	Amount
Brislington	–	–
Pensford	11,919	£471 8s 0d
Clutton	**18,701**	**£935 0s 0d**
Hallatrow	34,423	£1,942 9s 1d
MN & Welton	12,498	£744 5s 4d
Radstock	7,814	£492 2s 7d
Mells Road	32,539	£2,028 0s 4d
Frome	68,541	£4,719 0s 6d

Public Record Office/Dick Kelham

CLUTTON P.W. GANG c1933 (1)
This photograph, taken at Hallatrow station, shows the Clutton permanent way gang.
From left to right: Back row Bill Poole (ganger), Jimmy Gatehouse (and dog!), George Tiley, Tom Bourton, Dan Perry (the gang's second man).
Front row Tom Owen and Jack Brain

Ken Tiley

CLUTTON P.W. GANG c1933 (2)
Another nostalgic view taken at Hallatrow showing the P.W. gang from Clutton.
From left to right: Bill Poole, Tom Bourton, Jimmy Gatehouse, Jack Brain, Tom Owen, Dan Perry, George Tiley.

Ken Tiley

once served them remained in place for quite some time after and it was not until 1936/37, for example, that the line to Grey field was believed to have been lifted.

Hallatrow Station

The station at Hallatrow was closely examined in the last chapter but the following are some additional and general details about this junction station that seem worth adding in at this point. During the late 1930s two permanent stationmasters were in post at Hallatrow. These were Mr Rowley Best who was later succeeded by Mr Jack Gait. However, when not on duty the stationmaster's job was covered by a Bristol Relief Stationmaster, a role often played by Mr Reginald Palmer. Still on the staff side, one common occurrence for many of the railwaymen at Hallatrow, and for other men on the North Somerset for that matter, was their carrying out ticket collection duties at local holiday resort stations such as Severn Beach and Portishead over Bank Holidays. As one railwayman put it to me, this was always a useful way of earning a 'few extra bob'.

Around this time Hallatrow was the scene of an accident when a regular driver, then stationed at Radstock (GW) shed, a Mr Benny Flower, was injured while walking over the barrow crossing at that station, in front of his own freight train. Apparently, the fireman moved the locomotive forward unaware of Mr Flower's position, seriously injuring him. By all accounts, Mr Flower had quite a local reputation on the railway. He usually worked freight trains over the Radstock-Hallatrow section in addition to his regular banking duties from Radstock to Mells Road. Indeed, his day-to-day freight working over the North Somerset was known in the district as 'Benny's Goods'. However, the high point was that once a year he would drive an 'up' passenger train from Frome to Bristol. A railwayman who was part of the railway scene indeed!

GWR TICKET OFFICE FARRINGTON GURNEY
The Miners' Arms pub was about forty yards from Farrington Gurney Halt on the North Somerset line. The halt itself never had a booking office, tickets being issued at the Miners' Arms. Here, a tiny room, with a window facing towards the halt was converted into a booking office, complete with ticket issuing case, dating press, train and fares' books, and a supply of handbills and posters.

The booking office was just behind the public bar but there was no direct entrance from there. Tickets could be bought up until 7.00pm on weekdays but the office was not open on Sundays unless any specials were running and they called at the halt.

Collection A.H. Parsons

RAILWAY TICKETS TO BRISTOL AND GEORGES' BRISTOL BEERS; THE TICKET OFFICE AT THE MINERS' ARMS, FARRINGTON GURNEY

This broad view of the Miners' Arms at Farrington Gurney shows the GWR ticket office in relation to the rest of the pub. It seems rather a nice place to get your ticket, your travel and your pint of best bitter!

Incidentally, it was in a field near here that two coal drifts were begun late in 1921 by men who had lost their jobs on the closure of Farrington Colliery in 1921. These drifts were known as Farrington or Ruett Slant. It was a very small set-up and was worked on a shoestring basis. Dangers from the flooded workings of the former colliery at Farrington led to the closure of these workings in 1923.

John Kingman

SHUNTING AT HALLATROW

GWR 2-6-0 No. 4347 rests awhile between shunting moves while the crew face the photographer. From left to right are Len Kingsbury, Bill Oatley and an unidentified guard from Bristol. The photograph was taken in the late 1930s. *Philip Chapman*

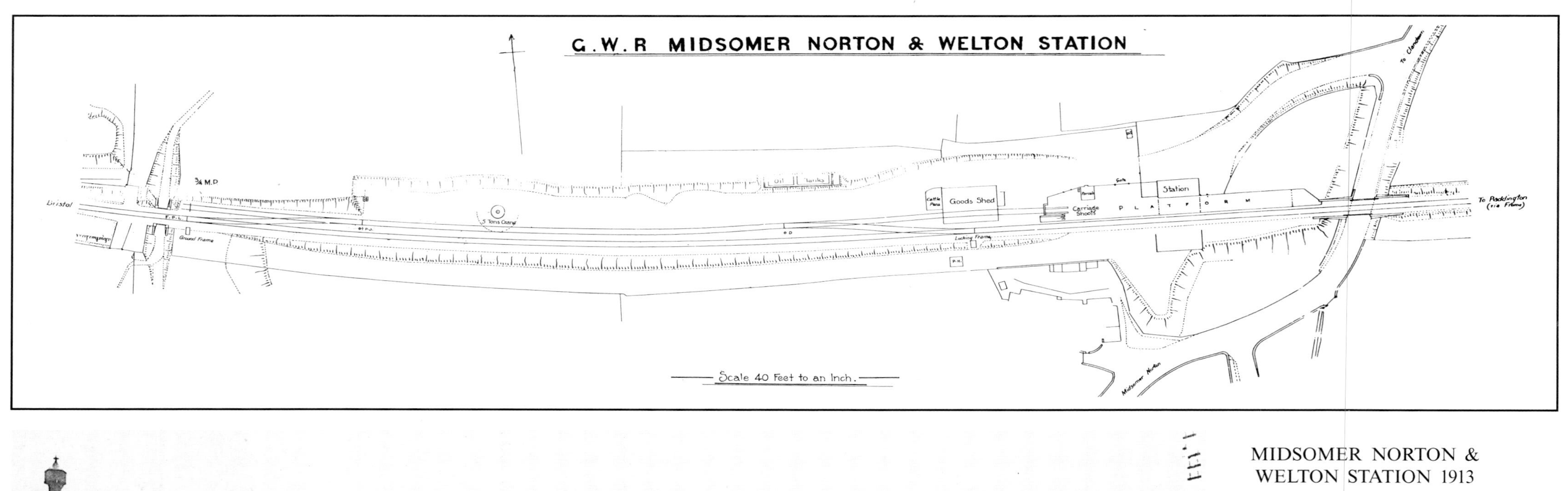

MIDSOMER NORTON & WELTON STATION 1913

Original plan: British Rail (Western)

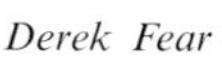

RADSTOCK (GW) STATION
In the early autumn of 1922 Radstock (GW) station advertises its various excursions to the public; for example, for 1s 3d (6p) you could sample the delights of Frome Show by train. On the wall of the main station building a host of advertisements encourages travellers to buy a real variety of wares!

Derek Fear

The Cloud Hill Colliery Project
A Scheme that Never got Underground!

In April 1923, after some preliminary explorations had been made in 1918, a plan was put forward to lease 200 acres of coal south of Clutton for a proposed Cloud Hill Colliery near Hallatrow (GWR). For the project a pair of drifts was to have been put down to the Rudge seam of coal, a capital sum of some £17,000 having to be raised in order to lease the land. From the two drifts a tramway would have been laid across the fields to Cloud Hill Quarry, the latter as we know, being served off existing sidings at Hallatrow station. However, in spite of the fact that a large amount of surplus plant from other collieries, including those at Burchells and Greyfield of Clutton, was put aside for the venture, the project never got established.

On the freight side there was very little coal traffic handled at Hallatrow, strange bearing in mind how much coal rumbled and clattered over the station's tracks and crossings. Some coal that was dealt with by the station was that sent out from the firm of Dunkerton Coal Factors. Since all of that firm's wagons were labelled "Empty to Hallatrow" it was not unnatural that during the late 1930s a daily telephone call was made by Mr Brock of the company to discover the latest number of private owner wagons held on the company's behalf at Hallatrow. Another traffic worth mentioning during this pre-Second World War period was that of gas pipes. These came in by rail for distribution and fitting in the area around Hallatrow, then being supplied for the first time with piped gas from the Bristol area.

The printing firm of Purnells produced heavy traffic throughout the 1930s. By the latter end of the decade business was very brisk and, by an agreement with the GWR, the company stipulated that the Great Western would collect the firm's business up until midnight. On some nights loadings would be so heavy that the 7.30pm ex-Radstock freight would be given a clear run through to Bristol so that it could have more time for loading at Hallatrow. On some occasions, driver, fireman and guard would all have to help with the loading! Once this freight had left, any further traffic due for despatch that evening would have to go to Bristol by road. In addition, Purnells would often produce paperbacks for Penguin Books, these being destined for Harmondsworth in Middlesex. This particular source of revenue was dealt with at Paddington Special Siding from which the books were road hauled to Harmondsworth, where arrival would be before 9.00am the following day. Some days around 70 to 80 tons would be handled through Hallatrow.

Midsomer Norton & Welton Station

Mr Ernest Goulding joined the station staff at Midsomer Norton & Welton station in 1924 as a goods porter, taking over the job from Mr Ernest Davey, the latter moving on to a post at Radstock (GW) station. Mr Goulding was appointed on a three month trial basis, but he actually stayed there for twelve years. From Welton, as the station was still known locally, he moved to stations at Pilning, Yeovil and Filton, returning to the North Somerset line in 1938 when he started work at Hallatrow as a lorry driver. In those days he received £2 15s (£2.75) a week but the poor money was obviously no deterrent to his being in railway work for he remained at Hallatrow until 1963!

During his time as goods porter at Welton one aspect of his work he clearly remembers was that since there was no work for him as a goods porter on Bank Holidays he was often sent over to Brislington, the last station on the North Somerset before Bristol, and to Clifton Bridge (Bristol-Portishead branch) in order to collect tickets, Bristol (Temple Meads) being an 'open station' in those days. Portishead was another regular location for his extra ticket collecting activities.

At Welton traffic on the goods side was really quite busy between the two wars. The North Somerset Brick & Tile Company had its sidings just to the Bristol side of the station, the private siding agreement for this being signed on 23rd August 1926. This siding could hold eight wagons and ran alongside a loading bank and storage area. It had a wheelstop at the station end to prevent wagons running into the goods loop at Welton station. According to the Bristol Division's Annual Report for 1926 the North Somerset Brick & Tile Company's siding had been completed but was not, as yet, opened.

Although these brickworks were rail connected, it would appear that very little *brick* traffic actually went out by rail. Most was locally delivered by road steam wagon. Nonetheless, a small percentage of the brick business was sent out via the GWR connection. However, one job that the railway was apparently called upon to do was that of bringing in and taking away the new and old ropes that were employed by the aerial ropeway linking claypit to brickyard.

SIGNAL CABIN/PARCELS OFFICE AT MIDSOMER NORTON & WELTON
This very good view of Midsomer Norton & Welton station in the 1930s shows what was once a signal cabin on the platform. However, at the time this photograph was taken it was serving as the parcels office. This station was opened under the simple title "Welton"; it was renamed "Welton & Midsomer Norton" on 2nd May 1898, its name changing yet again on 1st May 1904 when it became "Midsomer Norton & Welton".

Philip Chapman

MEN AND THEIR LORRIES AT WELTON STATION
The lorries are Thornycrofts: the men are, from left to right C. Bishop, F. Blatchford, A. Chapman (stationmaster), H. Grist, E. Goulding, Mr Denning and M.V. Oakhill. The photograph was taken in 1931.

Philip Chapman/Ernest Goulding

HANDLING THE MILK AT WELTON
Ernest Goulding handles milk churns at Welton. An expert with the churns, he could keep three on the move at any one time!

Philip Chapman

During the 1930s Midsomer Norton & Welton station was an agency for two competing cement companies. The two firms involved, Aberthaw and Blue Circle, provided rival outlets for builders, farmers, etc in the district. The cement was stored in two grounded box vans and, in those days, this traffic was very good business indeed. In addition, the station handled a variety of other traffics and these included parcels which went out every day from the Standard Cheque works in Welton. Some milk was still taken out, while the firm of Prattens, well-known in the area for the manufacture of wooden chalets, poultryhouses and greenhouses, sent out some of its products

Above: RETIREMENT AT WELTON
This photograph shows the retirement ceremony of Mr Chapman (Senior) as stationmaster at Midsomer Norton & Welton. Taken at the station itself on 2nd April 1949 it shows the gifts received by Mr Chapman: a radio, a table lamp and a wallet with cash donations. Mr & Mrs Chapman are seen in the centre of the photograph with Cliff Bishop to their right (behind the radio) while Frank Blatchford stands to Mr Chapman's immediate left. *Philip Chapman*

Below: A LOAD OF BULL AT MIDSOMER NORTON & WELTON

Original Document: Bob Parsons

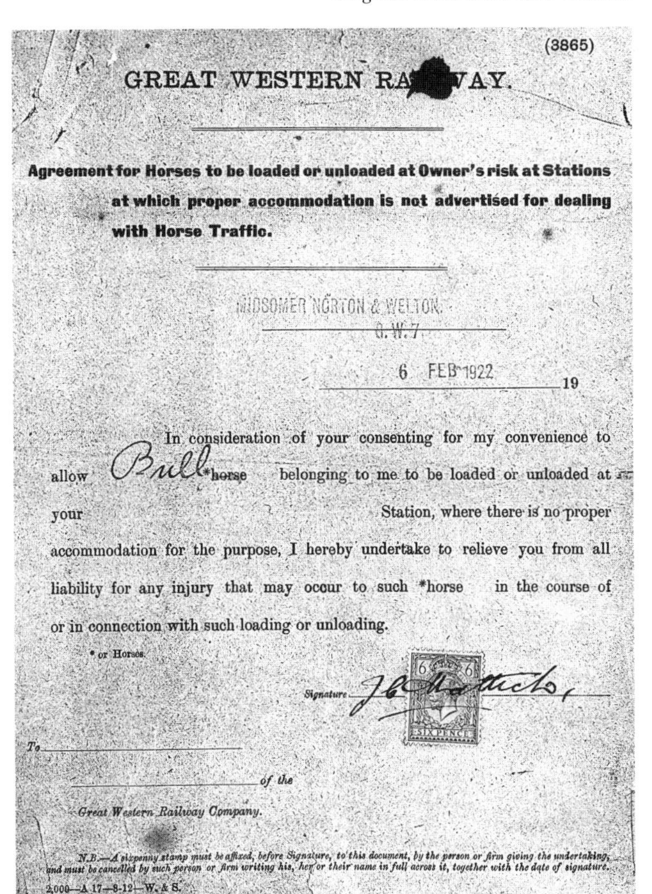

(3865)

GREAT WESTERN RAILWAY.

Agreement for Horses to be loaded or unloaded at Owner's risk at Stations at which proper accommodation is not advertised for dealing with Horse Traffic.

MIDSOMER NORTON & WELTON.
G.W.R.

6 FEB 1922 19

In consideration of your consenting for my convenience to allow Bull *horse belonging to me to be loaded or unloaded at your Station, where there is no proper accommodation for the purpose, I hereby undertake to relieve you from all liability for any injury that may occur to such *horse in the course of or in connection with such loading or unloading.

* or Horses.

Signature J. G. Mattocks

To ____________________
____________________ of the
Great Western Railway Company.

N.B.—A sixpenny stamp must be affixed, before Signature, to this document, by the person or firm giving the undertaking, and must be cancelled by such person or firm writing his, her or their name in full across it, together with the date of signature.

2,000—A 17—8-12—W. & S.

Great Western Railway.

On SATURDAY, OCTOBER 2nd

A HALF-DAY EXPRESS EXCURSION will run to

LONDON

Leaving	At	Return Fares, Third Class.
	p.m.	
Whitchurch Halt	12 22	6/-
Pensford	12 33	
Clutton	12 43	
Hallatrow	12 48	
Midsomer Norton & Welton	12 56	
Radstock	1 3	5/6
Mells Road	1 13	
Frome	1 35	
Paddington .. .. arr.	3 40	

The Return Train will leave Paddington Station at 12.20 a.m. (early Sunday morning).

TAKE YOUR TICKET IN ADVANCE.

Children under three years of age, FREE; three and under twelve, HALF-PRICE. NO LUGGAGE ALLOWED.

FELIX J. C. POLE, General Manager.

PADDINGTON STATION, Sept., 1926.

Bristol, 3,000 Burleigh Ltd., Printers, Bristol. B7/1091

Above: A HALF-DAY EXPRESS EXCURSION TO LONDON FROM WHITCHURCH HALT
This must have been quite an occasion for it seems likely that the excursion would have come from the Bristol direction, there being no run-round facilities at the halt itself. It would have passed through Brislington and started its journey to the metropolis from one of the smallest passenger stops on the line. It is possible that this train may have been a theatre special.

The halt opened for traffic on 1st January 1925.

Original handbill: M. Wyatt

through the station, glass coming in from the firm of Pilkington to meet Prattens' needs.

Timber that had come in through the Port of Bristol at Avonmouth was railed to Welton station where it was distributed locally by horse drawn wagons. Malt from George's Brewery in Bristol also followed the same route down the North Somerset, this being used for cattle feed purposes around Midsomer Norton and Welton. The nearby firm of Frank Shearn, millers and corn factors, also provided the GWR with animal feeding stuffs at Welton. Before the 1939-1945 conflict the Welton Bag Company also did business with the GWR but, after the war, this account and that of Ralph Blatchford, whose company carried on a good deal of war work, were both transferred to Frome in May 1952. Perhaps even then the storm clouds could be seen gathering for the branch. All in all, however, it was very true to say that in the 1930s, at least, Midsomer Norton & Welton was a small but busy station that really served the community of which it was a real part.

Radstock (GW): The Station and its Surrounding Area

As the 20th century came in on the Somerset Coalfield, the time of peak production was being reached. During the first decade of the new century 1¼ million tons of coal per annum was raised, the GWR line moving about 425,000 tons of this total, 50,000 tons going out by the Somerset & Dorset with the rest of the output being moved away by road or being sold locally. With the growing years of the century the smaller pits were being closed down with the emphasis of production being based on the larger and more profitable pits. Around Radstock the wealth and strength of the Beauchamp family continued to grow while that of the Waldegraves waned. It was now left to the Writhlington Collieries group to put up reasonable competition to the strengthening Beauchamps.

After the First World War the local railways and collieries, hammered and misused during the long years of hostilities, took time to get back on to their feet. This required money and energy and, with the post-war recession setting in, the pits around Radstock and their associated railways were about to begin the long and tortuous slide into decline that eventually led to the disappearance of all the collieries and virtually all of the railways in the North Somerset area in the early 1970s.

Mells Road Station

As we have already seen in Chapter 7, Hallatrow was the scene of a major reconstruction in 1909/10 when it was upgraded in its role as crossing place and when it had extra siding space added in preparation for the opening, in 1910, of the Camerton-Limpley Stoke railway. However, in the same year as the work was going on at Hallatrow, considerable alterations were taking place at another junction station further down the line towards Frome, namely that at Mells Road. During 1909 both platforms were extended here by an additional 90ft, their full length now becoming 288ft. On the 'up' side a new milk platform, waiting room and lock-up were also provided. New track arrangements were brought into use when a new connection was installed from the down main to the goods shed, the lengthening of the Bristol-bound platform entailing the removal of a crossover. The plans for this work were signed on 10th August 1909 so presumably the works were completed later that year.

Around this time changes were also made to the signalling arrangements at Mells. Plans were revealed for one signal box to replace the two then in use. The new box was sited on the Frome side of the station adjacent to the Frome-bound track, some five miles and two chains from Frome. Its estimated costs were £928 on the civil engineering side, and £830 on the signal engineer's account. Both old boxes, North and South, closed on 13th March 1910, the new box taking over on the same day. Post 1910, the signal box, facing south as it did, was home to many a crop of geraniums. The 37 levers in the box shone while, throughout the years, the box was kept in excellent condition internally with a beautifully polished floor and shining range as one has come to expect from rural railwaymen.

Mr Keen had been a signalman at Mells Road for a number of years, having joined the GWR in the Worcester area in March 1914. Around 1916 he moved to Bristol where he worked in signal boxes at Shirehampton, Henbury, Hallen Junction and Pilning (Low Level). He clearly remembers the Irish navvies working on the important munitions factory at Henbury on the Avonmouth and Filton line that was mentioned earlier in the chapter. From Bristol he moved to the thriving station at Mells Road where, with coal from the collieries at Mells and Newbury, and the stone traffic from Vobster Quarry he reckoned that towards the end of World War One the station's turnover was some £60,000 per annum (for further details of the collieries and quarries in this area, see Chapter 11).

Mr Keen remembers that some of the coal from the nearby Newbury Pit went out by rail to the paper mills at Wookey near Wells, while milk traffic from the station was very substantial, the churns coming in from farms in the Norton St Philip and Faulkland areas. One other traffic handled during the First World War was that of timber for, close to the station, a government sawmills was established. This was worked by POWs and provided a considerable number of loads for the railway.

Further traffic came to the railway when, in 1924, plans were made to install a new siding for the firm of Beauchamp Brothers, trading under the name of the Mells Quarry Company, at Mells Road station. The new siding actually ran off part of the Newbury Railway but its position meant that part of the station's existing goods road into the goods shed had to be kept clear for shunting to take place to this new siding of Beauchamp's. Therefore the GWR insisted that a new mileage siding be constructed and it was this which helped to account for the following costs: civil engineer £1,500, signal engineer £10! This new work was agreed by the GWR's Traffic Committee on 18th December 1924. The private siding agreement was signed on 14th October 1925 with the siding opening to roadstone traffic on 23rd November 1926.

Another private siding was planned and installed at Mells Road over the 1926/27 period when the firm of S.G. Gilson & Sons requested a siding to be built for their roadstone traffic. This was generated at the company's Cooks Wood Quarry and was to be brought to Mells Road station by road. On 25th November 1926 the GWR's Traffic Committee approved an estimated expenditure of £435 for the construction of a private siding with its own loading bank at Mells Road. Designed to hold nine wagons, the siding's estimated cost on the civil engineering side was £305, with £130 to be spent by the signalling engineer giving the £435 total mentioned. The loading bank was 20ft x 40ft x 6ft 6in high. The private siding agreement was signed on 23rd September 1927. One interesting aspect of that agreement was that Gilson's were themselves responsible for carrying out all the earthworks in connection with the new siding, in addition to building the loading bank previously mentioned. Once in use, the siding and bank handled stone and chippings, the loads from the quarry to Mells Road being carried by steam wagons from Holcombe. These loads were later transported by former "Bristol" buses which had been converted to lorries.

In 1931 both the North Somerset and the Camerton branch were used for the production, by Gainsborough Pictures, of the film *The Ghost Train.* Although most of the filming was carried out on the Hallatrow-Limpley Stoke line, some action also took place on the double track section between Radstock and Mells Road.

Non-Stop on the North Somerset!

During the period of the 1932 summer timetable (18th July-11th September) there was a Saturdays Only through Boat Express from Birmingham to Weymouth. Nominally this ran non-stop over the North Somerset branch up until 29th August. Although the train did not call at any of the stations on the branch, staffs were, of course, exchanged at slow speed at passing loops. The

MEANDERING INTO MELLS ROAD
With the double track section from Radstock in the background, pannier tank No. 9628 meanders into Mells Road on a dull June day with the 10.17am from Bristol to Frome.

Hugh Ballantyne

THE SOMERSET STANDARD – FRIDAY 14th MARCH 1902

FROME TO BRISTOL.
(Via Radstock.)

		A.M	A.M	A.M.	P.M	P.M	P.M	A.M.	P.M.
FROME	dep	8 5	9 55	11 45	3 15	5 47	8 45	10 0	8 15
Mells Road	,,	8 18	10 8	12 0	3 28	6 0	9 1	10 15	8 31
Radstock ..	,,	8 28	1018	12 12	3 38	6 13	9 13	10 25	8 41
Welton	,,	8 34	1023	12 18	3 43	6 20	9 19	10 31	8 47
Camerton	,,	..	1010	..	..	6 10	..	..	..
Hallatrow ..	,,	8 44	1032	12 28	3 51	6 30	9 28	10 41	8 54
Clutton	,,	8 51	1037	12 34	3 56	6 38	9 33	10 48	9 4
Pensford ..	,,	8 59	1047	12 45	4 8	6 50	9 44	10 56	9 14
Brislington.	,,	9 8	1057	12 55	4 17	7 0	9 54	11 5	9 23
Bristol......	arr	9 18	1110	1 7	4 28	7 12	10 5	11 15	9 34

A train also leaves Radstock at 7.35 a.m. and reaches Bristol at 8.22.

BRISTOL TO FROME.
(Via Radstock.)

		A.M	A. M.	P. M.	P.M	P.M	P.M	A.M.	P.M
Bristol......	dep	7 25	10 25	1220	3 30	5 0	9 5	8 13	5 55
Brislington.	,,	7 33	10 33	1230	3 38	5 9	9 13	8 21	6 3
Pensford ..	,,	7 45	10 45	1244	3 50	5 21	9 25	8 33	6 15
Clutton	,,	7 54	10 55	1254	3 59	5 31	9 35	8 42	6 24
Hallatrow..	,,	7 59	11 0	1 0	4 4	5 38	9 41	8 47	6 29
Camerton	arr	8 23	11 17	..	4 25	5*55	..	..	..
Welton	dep	8 8	11 9	1 10	4 13	5 47	9 51	8 56	6 38
Radstock ..	,,	8 12	11 13	1 15	4 17	5 51	9 55	9 0	6 42
Mells Road	,,	8 24	11 27	1 29	4 29	6 4	10 7	9 12	6 54
FROME....	arr	8 35	11 40	1 40	4 40	6 15	1020	9 28	7 5

* Thursdays only.

A train leaves Bristol for Radstock (Thursdays and Saturdays only) at 2.5 p.m., arriving at 2.52. A train leaves Bristol for Radstock at 6.30 p.m., arriving at 7.20

FROME TO BRISTOL.
(Via Bath.)

		A.M	A.M	A.M	P.M	P.M	P.M	P.M	P.M	P.M
FROME ...	dep	6 50	8 45	10 5	12 3	5 43	7 8	8 36	1254	7 20
Westbury ..	,,	7 15	8 58	1022	1215	6 3	7 31	8 49	1 6	7 35
Trowbridge	,,	7 28	9 10	1033	1230	6 13	8 1	9 0	1 30	7 49
Bradford ..	,,	7 39	9 20	1044	1241	6 24	..	9 12	1 41	8 0
Freshford ..	,,	7 45	9 26	1051	1247	6 30	..	9 18	1 47	8 6
Lmply. Stoke	,,	7 49	9 30	1056	1251	6 34	..	9 23	1 51	8 10
Bathampton	,,	7 58	..	11 5	1 0	6 43	..	9 32	2 0	8 19
Bath........	arr	8 3	9 41	1110	1 5	6 48	8 30	9 37	2 5	8 24
Bristol......	,,	8 38	1013	1135	1 29	7 10	8 55	10 0	2 30	9 2

Trains leave Trowbridge at 8.0, 11.1, and 11.30 a.m., 2.26, 3.55, and 6.31 p.m. for Bristol, arriving at 9.2 and 11.47 a.m., 12.33, 3.30, 4.48, and 7.25 p.m.

Trains leave Frome at 10.29 a.m., 1.55 and 3.11 p.m. for Bristol, arriving at 11.47 a.m., 3.30 and 4.48 p.m.

On Sundays a train leaves Westbury at 9.18 a.m., arriving at Bristol at 10.40 a.m.

BRISTOL TO FROME.
(Via Bath).

		A.M	A. M	A.M	P.M	P.M	P.M	P.M	A.M	P.M
Bristol ...	dep	6 5	8 12	10 5	1 15	2 15	5 0	6 43	8 10	6 25
Bath........	,,	6 23	8 36	1026	1 32	2 45	5 17	7 15	8 40	6 55
Bathampton	,,	6 34	8 46	1036	..	2 54	5 27	7 26	8 50	7 5
Lmply. Stoke	,,	6 43	8 55	1045	1 49	3 3	5 36	7 36	8 59	7 14
Freshford ..	,,	6 47	8 59	1049	1 54	3 8	5 40	7 41	9 3	7 18
Bradford ..	,,	6 53	9 6	1055	2 2	3 15	5 46	7 50	9 10	7 25
Trowbridge	arr	7 2	9 14	11 3	2 10	3 23	5 54	8 0	9 18	7 33
Westbury ..	,,	7 18	9 26	1115	2 25	3 43	6 5	8 13	9 30	7 44
FROME	,,	7 34	9 45	1154	3 0	4 0	6 34	8 25	9 42	8 0

11.32 (Weds. only).

Trains also leave Bristol for Trowbridge at 3.55, 6.0, 8.40 and 11 p.m. on week-days, and 3.45 p.m. on Sundays.

Trains also leave Bristol for Frome at 3.55 and 6.0 p.m., arriving at Frome at 5.19 and 7.37 p.m.; also on Saturdays at 11.0 p.m., arriving at Frome at 12.15 midnight.

FROME TO WELLS.

		A.M	A.M	P.M	P.M	P.M	P.M	A.M	P.M
FROME..........	dep	7 37	9 55	1222	3 5	6 37	9 3	9 44	..
Witham Friary	arr	7 49	10 7	1234	3 16	6 49	9 15	9 56	..
Ditto..........	dep	8 5	1020	1244	3 30	7 0	9 25	..	4 30
Wanstrow	,,	8 15	1030	1254	3 40	7 10	..	..	..
Cranmore	,,	8 27	1042	1 4	3 50	7 20	9 40	..	4 38
Shepton Mallet.	,,	8 42	1113	1 13	4 3	7 30	9 51	..	4 48
Wells	arr	8 54	1125	1 25	4 15	7 43	10 3	..	5 0

WELLS TO FROME.

		A.M	A.M	A.M	P.M	P.M	P.M	P.M	P.M
Wells..........	dep	7 5	8 30	11 0	2 5	4 37	7 5	..	3 5
Shepton Mallet	,,	7 20	8 55	1119	2 20	4 53	7 37	..	3 25
Cranmore	,,	7 30	9 7	1129	2 31	5 3	7 55	..	3 38
Wanstrow	,,	7 37	9 16	1136	2 39	5 13	..	..	3 47
Witham Friary	arr	7 43	9 22	1142	2 45	5 19	8 10	..	3 55
Ditto..........	dep	7 47	9 39	1149	2 58	5 29	8 20	..	4 30
FROME..........	arr	7 56	9 48	12 0	3 7	5 38	8 32	..	4 45

WELLS TO YATTON.

		A.M	A.M	A.M	A.M	P.M	P.M	P.M	P.M
Wells............	dep.	7 20	9 3	9 50	1140	2 15	4 55	8 15	5 5
Wookey	,,	7 24	..	9 54	1144	2 19	4 59	8 19	5 9
Lodge Hill........	,,	7 31	9 12	10 1	1151	2 26	5 6	8 28	5 16
Draycott	,,	7 36	9 17	10 6	1156	2 31	5 11	8 34	5 22
Cheddar	,,	7 42	9 24	1014	12 4	2 39	5 21	8 45	5 31
Axbridge	,,	7 48	9 32	1022	1213	2 48	5 30	8 56	5 41
Winscombe	,,	7 54	9 38	1030	1220	2 56	5 38	9 4	5 48
Sandford & Banwell	,,	7 58	9 41	1036	1225	3 2	5 44	9 10	5 53
Congresbury	,,	8 4	*	1042	1231	3 8	5 50	9 16	5 59
Yatton	arr.	8 10	9 52	1050	1237	3 15	5 56	9 23	6 5

* Calls Thursdays, also sets down from Axbridge or beyond.

A train leaves Wells at 7.55 a.m., calling at all intermediate stations, and arrives at Yatton at 9.9.

YATTON TO WELLS.

		A.M	A.M	A.M	P.M	P.M	P.M	P.M	P.M
Yatton	dep.	8 10	9 55	1150	2 15	3 35	5 57	9 40	2 0
Congresbury	,,	8 15	10 2	1154	2 21	3 40	6 1	9 44	2 4
Sandford & Banwell	,,	8 21	10 8	12 1	2 29	3 47	6 8	9 50	2 11
Winscombe	,,	8 26	1013	12 6	2 35	3 52	6 13	9 55	2 16
Axbridge	dep.	8 33	1020	1213	2 42	4 0	6 20	10 1	2 24
Cheddar	,,	8 39	1027	1221	2 52	4 7	6 27	10 7	2 31
Draycott	,,	8 44	1032	1226	2 57	4 12	6 32	1012	2 36
Lodge Hill ..	,,	8 49	1038	1232	3 3	4 18	6 38	1018	2 42
Wookey ..	,,	8 55	1044	1238	3 9	4 24	6 44	1024	2 48
Wells........	arr.	9 1	1050	1245	3 15	4 30	6 50	1030	2 55

A train leaves Yatton at 6.45 p.m., calling at all stations, and arrives at Wells at 7.40.

FROME TO YEOVIL & TAUNTON.

		A.M	A.M	A.M	P.M	P.M	P.M	P.M	
FROME..........	dep.	..	7 37	9 55	1222	3 5	..	6 37	..
Yeovil (Pen Mill)	,,	..	8 55	1125	1 45	4 17	..	7 45	..
Ditto (Town) ..	,,	6 25	9 0	1135	1 50	4 24	..	7 55	..
Montacute	,,	6 36	9 11	1146	2 4	4 35	..	8 8	..
Martock	,,	6 43	9 18	1153	2 12	4 43	..	8 16	..
Langport	,,	6 54	9 29	12 4	2 24	4 55	..	8 28	..
Athelney	,,	7 2	9 37	1212	2 33	5 4	..	8 37	..
Durston..........	arr.	7 10	9 45	1220	2 42	5 12	..	8 45	..
Taunton	,,	7 35	1013	1247	3 5	5 25	..	9 5	..

TAUNTON TO YEOVIL & FROME.

		A.M	A.M	P.M	P.M	P.M	P.M	P.M	
Taunton	dep.	7 5	9 43	1225	2 25	..	5 58	8 40	..
Durston	,,	7 35	1010	1246	2 48	..	6 18	9 0	..
Athelney	,,	7 40	1015	1252	2 53	..	6 24	9 7	..
Langport	,,	7 52	1027	1 4	3 5	..	6 36	9 18	..
Martock	,,	8 4	1038	1 16	3 17	..	6 48	9 29	..
Montacute	,,	8 9	1043	1 21	3 22	..	6 53	9 34	..
Yeovil (Town)	arr.	8 23	1057	1 35	3 37	..	7 5	9 53	..
Ditto (Pen Mill)	,,	8 25	11 1	1 40	3 40	..	7 11	9 56	..
FROME	,,	9 48	12 0	3 7	5 38	..	8 32	..	..

train had an "A" headcode and, in the Bristol area, it called at Stapleton Road (11.45/11.50). It passed Marsh Junction at 11.55 and 30 seconds (!) arriving at Frome Mineral Junction for staff changing at 12.56 (passing time). Arrival at Frome was at 12.58, departure being at 1.01.

The train went on to Yeovil where it called and then ran non-stop to Weymouth where arrival was at 2.10pm.

Passenger traffic was quite brisk from the station with cheap tickets to Frome Market on Wednesdays while on Saturday evenings cheap tickets were available for a night out in Bristol. With the Hylton family living close by on the estate at Ammerdown, Mells Road would be kept busy handling milk and fresh vegetables from that estate when they were on their way up "to town". The same was true when the Horner family from nearby Mells Manor were in the metropolis, their estate's produce also going out through Mells Road.

During both world wars the stately home at Longleat near Warminster was used for medical and caring purposes. In World War One it was employed as a hospital for convalescing English soldiers, while during World War Two it was used by the Americans in the same role. Certainly during the latter conflict hospital trains came to Mells Road station. From there, casualties were taken onto Longleat by a fleet of ambulances, arrival at Longleat usually being around the early evening. Whether similar arrangements took place during the First World War is conjectural but possible.

In the early 1930s, possibly around 1934, a halt was requested at Kilmersdon by the local community. One was never built, the reason given by the GWR hinging upon the awkwardness of the site proposed, located as it would have been on the difficult gradient between Radstock and Mells Road.

Generally speaking, the station at Mells Road dealt with a wide variety of goods traffic. Being in a very rural area it was not surprising that farm equipment came in via the station. Flour also went through Mells Road on its way to the CWS store at Coleford which had its own bakery. Like many other country stations newspapers were a daily traffic in the form of cattle feed was also common. Surprisingly, considering the large production of coal within the neighbourhood, anthracite dust was brought in from South Wales for working withthe lime from Mells. In addition, lime itself went out by rail to glove factories in the Yeovil area. Broom and rake handles and other such similar implements from the firm of Ashmans at Leigh-on-Mendip could be seen being dealt with by the staff at the station. Post World War Two, South Wales was a destination for small amounts of timber despatched from Mells Road.

Stone Traffic from Mells Road Station: 1926/27

	1926	1927
Mells Road	50,297 tons/£16,543	71,099 tons/£24,877
Frome	29,453 tons/£6,986	27,002 tons/£6,831

Source: Bristol Division Annual Report 1927

Incidentally, also in 1927, the North Somerset Line was passed for use by the GWR's Group 'D' Locomotives. The employment of more powerful engines pulling increased loads was estimated to give a saving of nearly £3,000 per annum.

Frome: The Station and its Surrounding Area

At the Frome end of the line a process of continuing change and improvement went on during the 1920s. For example, in 1921, additional passenger and goods accommodation was provided at Frome station and this work involved extending some of the sidings and one of the platforms. On the goods side a private siding agreement was signed on 28th February 1921 providing a private siding for the firm of Edward Cockey & Son. Edward Cockey, whose family had been braziers in the town since 1685, had premises, in 1808, in Frome's Upper Market Place but later in its history the company moved over to ironfounding and, with this change, to a new site in Palmer Street.

However, it was not until 1831 that the firm started to become really successful for it was after that date that gas lighting was introduced into the town. In that year Mr Penny lit his shop in Bath Street with gas for the first time, and, after that, Edward Cockey's main manufactures became items such as gas holders and standards, although the business also made steam engines, boilers and iron roofs among other products. The firm continued in work until 31st March 1960 when it ceased trading altogether. Presumably the private siding became completely disused soon after this time?

The New Avoiding Lines at Westbury and Frome Stations

In the 1930s two new sections of the GWR's main line to the West Country were completed at Westbury (Wilts) and Frome. The new sections by-passed the two stations serving the towns, the point behind their construction being the avoidance of fairly severe speed limits at the stations themselves. The total cost of the work was around £220,000 and the work was carried out by Logan & Hemingway of Doncaster.

Since we are particularly interested in the Frome area and its North Somerset connection, it is worth adding that the new Frome avoiding line was served, at its London end, by a junction at Clink Road while, at the Taunton end, new connections and signal box were installed at Blatchbridge Junction.

The Frome cut-off was opened on 2nd January 1933.

THE NEW AVOIDING LINES AT WESTBURY AND FROME STATIONS

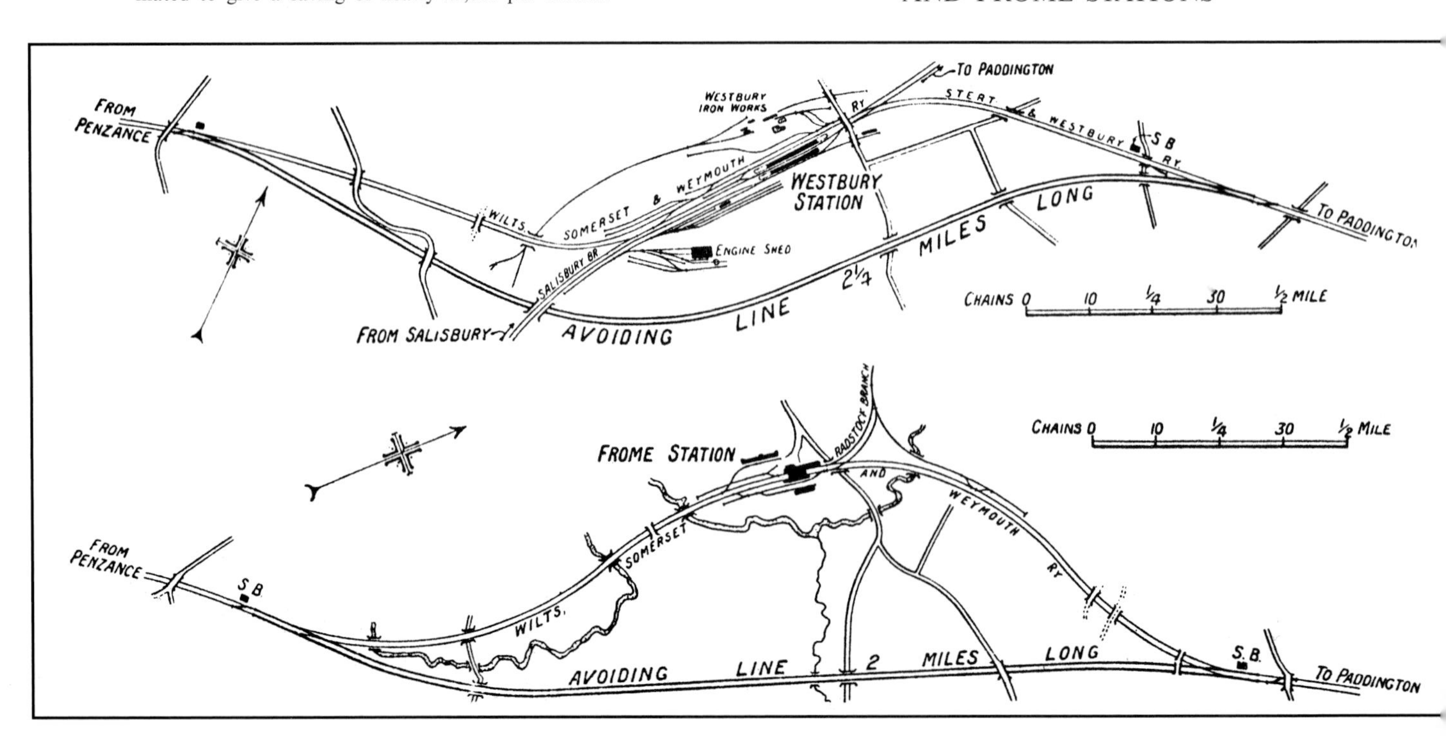

9
World War Two and Beyond

STATION STAFF SMILE AT RADSTOCK (WEST)
This nostalgic photograph shows the station staff at Radstock during the last years of the line's passenger services.
It shows, from left to right: Tom Tamblyn (porter/signalman), Fred Scott (booking clerk at Radstock West), Stationmaster Dennis Cridland, Gordon Bennett (booking clerk at Radstock North S&D), Bert Dark (porter at Radstock West).
P.J. Williams

During World War Two the B&NSR itself seems to have suffered very little real, structural damage. Nevertheless, events at the Bristol end of the line and in the Bath area caused considerable disruption to services on the branch. On 25th June 1940 about 15 bombs were dropped in the vicinity of Bristol (Temple Meads). No-one was hurt and only slight damage was done to buildings. The reason for there being no injuries was that several of the bombs failed to explode. Nonetheless, six passenger coaches were severely damaged while an ambulance train was also hit. On 24th November 1940, during an intensive air raid, Temple Meads received three direct hits. Several platforms and their adjacent running lines were blocked, the station's overall roof being damaged as well. A considerable amount of roof glass was broken. Bombs were dropped at many places, temporarily blocking the running lines at Bedminster, Lawrence Hill and Bristol, East Depot.

On 2nd December 1940 two platforms at Temple Meads were damaged by high explosive bombs. Fire caused by incendiaries damaged the overall roof in several places while the Ladies' Waiting Room also received some damage. On 6th December a train was hit whilst leaving No. 6 platform, the driver being killed and the fireman seriously injured. Fifteen passengers were killed and 23 were seriously injured. Another train of empty coaches was set on fire, three being totally destroyed. Debris struck the rear coach of yet another train and several of its passengers were injured. Incendiary bombs yet again damaged the station's fine roof, the telegraph office and luggage lift also sustaining hits. In addition, a quantity of parcels and letters were destroyed.

In April 1942, the North Somerset branch was very severely affected by the results of bomb damage on neighbouring GWR tracks when, in air raids on the Georgian city of Bath carried out on 25th and 26th of that month, the Great Western's main Bristol-Paddington line was hit in nine places between Twerton Tunnel and Bath station. On 26th April, at the Bath end of the tunnel, 100ft of the 30ft high retaining wall was demolished, leaving the 'up' main line unsupported for roughly the same distance. The 'down' main line was also seriously undermined.

However, the GWR's Chief Engineer, along with Sir Robert McAlpine & Sons Limited, rapidly carried out repairs at Twerton, so much so in fact, that by slewing the Down Main over, at 10.30am on 28th April, single line working was restored. Below the Up Main, piles were driven into the 100ft gap and these carried the line while permanent repairs were completed. Traffic was fully restored to both tracks by 15th May. While this important restoration work was being carried out some trains were diverted over North Somerset metals, an important event in that railway's history. While the damage at Twerton was being repaired, one of the trains regularly diverted was the 1.20am goods from Bristol to Weymouth, Bristol men working this to Westbury. Workings, via Radstock, were handled by a variety of motive power, including 'Manors', 'Bulldogs' and locomotives of the ROD 2-8-0, the 2600 and 4300 classes. The line was so busy that all Radstock Link men were taken off other jobs to keep the trains running. Indeed, although it was exceptionally well-used during this period, the North Somerset seems to have been able to cope remarkably effectively with the additional traffic. During wartime the

Above: DAN PERRY'S RETIREMENT
This photograph, taken at Clutton station just after the Second World War, shows Dan Perry's retirement ceremony. On the left, Stationmaster Russ hands "Danno", as he was known, his retirement gift. The group features, from left to right: George Bailey, Albert Selway (standing), George Tiley, Jack Brain, Bill Poole (ganger at Clutton) and Cath Heywood (signalwoman). *Ken Tiley*

Below: BARRY ISLAND BOUND
On a beautiful summer's day, 2-6-0 No. 6358 heads a Barry Island excursion through the warm, crop-laden fields near Chelwood Bridge. Judging by the width of the railway land as seen here between the two boundary fences, it is quite clear that the small, local company had great expansion plans in mind when it first acquired the land for its Bristol to Radstock section.

The locomotive and its coaches slip quietly by on 19th July 1959, the last summer of regular passenger working. *P.J. Williams*

"TICKETS PLEASE!"
A selection from the Bristol-Radstock (West)-Frome branch.

Original tickets: M. Wyatt

Photography: W. Harbor

branch was used to handle troop trains from Bristol to Westbury and southwards to the English Channel ports. These ran throughout the night, although as various railwaymen have said they believe that the B&NSR was only used in a limited way for diversions due to the fearsome nature of some of the gradients along its route.

Having mentioned earlier the air raids that were inflicted on the two cities of Bristol and Bath it is a logical place to mention that when these were taking place on Bristol, trains were often held at Pensford, Clutton and Hallatrow stations. One Bristol driver told the author that some very pleasant hours had been spent at the Station Hotel at Hallatrow waiting for the "all-clear" to be given!

One never-to-be-built project emanating from the 1942 air raids on Bath was that of a joint station to replace the LMSR and GWR stations in the city. Although not a popular idea when first suggested by Bath planners in 1943, by 1947 the GWR, at least, were seriously considering the proposals! The scheme put forward was for a new joint GW/LMS station to be built on the GWR's main line between Oldfield Park station and the skew bridge over the River Avon, just to the west of the present Bath Spa station. A new connection would have been built from the former Midland line between Bath and Bristol, just west of Twerton Tunnel at Saltford (GW), so that LMS trains could run straight into the new joint station from the western end. Once through this station, a new line would then have been constructed, heading eastwards, under the Widcombe area of Bath. Coming out of the tunnel at Monkton Combe a triangular junction would have linked the new chord with the Bathampton-Bradford-on-Avon railway, the other two arms of the junction combining to swing parallel with the former Limpley Stoke-Hallatrow branch as far as Midford. Here connections were to have been made with both the Somerset & Dorset and the former Camerton branch. The new railway would have been double track through the tunnel, the former S&D tunnels at Devonshire and Combe Down being abandoned under the plan. A new marshalling yard was to have been built at Twerton.

HALLATROW WITH PASTORAL PANNIER
Pannier tank No. 4647 heads south from Hallatrow with a "B" set in the early evening of 6th July 1959.

R.C. Riley

BRISTOL, RADSTOCK AND FROME.

DOWN TRAINS. WEEK DAYS.

Mile Post Mileage M.	C.	Distance from Bristol (T.M.) M.	C.	STATIONS.		Ruling Gradient 1 in.	Time Allowance for Ordinary Freight Trains. See page 2. Point-to-Point Times.	Allow for Stop.	Allow for Start.
							Mins.	Mins.	Mins.
24	8	—	--	BRISTOL (T.M.)	dep.				
—	—	—	—	East Depot	,,		—	—	1
23	19	—	78	Marsh Junction	,,		4	—	—
22	1	2	7	Brislington	,,	62 R.	5	1	1
19	73	4	15	Whitchurch Halt	,,	60 R.	—	—	—
19	7	5	0	Stop Board	,,	60 R.	14	1	1
17	31	6	57	Pensford	arr. / dep.	66 F.	6	2	1
16	52	7	36	Pensford and Bromley Siding	arr. / dep.	60 R.	3	1	2
14	13	9	75	Clutton	arr. / dep.	60 R.	12	2	1
13	51	10	37	Stop Board	,,	71 F.	2	1	1
12	57	11	31	Hallatrow	arr. / dep.	58 F.	4	1	2
11	52	12	36	Stop Board	,,	65 R.	4	1	1
11	39	12	49	Farrington Gurney	,,	73 F.	—	—	—
10	50	13	37	Old Mills Siding	arr. / dep.	73 F.	4	1	1
9	47	14	41	Midsomer Norton and Welton	arr / dep.	177 F.	4	1	1
8	16	15	72	RADSTOCK	arr. / dep.	128 F.	4	1	2
5	18	18	70	Mells Road	arr. / dep.	69 R.	15	1	1
3	74	20	14	Stop Board	,,	204 F.	3	1	1
2	8	21	79	Somerset Quar. Siding	,,	48 F.	7	2	2
—	63	23	24	Gas Works Siding	,,	51 F.	4	1	1
—	47	23	41	Market Siding	,,	276 R.	—	—	—
—	—	23	73	Frome Mineral Junction	arr.	76 R.	3	1	—
—	—	24	16	FROME	arr. / dep.	76 R.	5	1	—

STATIONS.		B	K	K	K	B	K	B	K	K	B	K	B	K		K		
		Bruton Diesel.	Stone	Frght and Coal. SO	Frght and Coal. SX	Wells Diesel. WSO Radstock to Frome.	Frght	Witham Pass.	Stone	Frght SO	Pass.	Frght. SX	Pass.	Frght SX		Westbury Frght SX		
		a.m.	a.m.	a.m.	a.m.	a.m.	a.m.	a.m.	p.m.	a.m.	p.m.	p.m.	p.m.	p.m.		p.m.		
BRISTOL (T.M.)	dep.	6 50	....	....	....	....	....	10 17	....	....	1 32	....	2 55	....	....	....	....	....
East Depot	,,	..	..	8 32	8 32			..			..	2 5	..					
Marsh Junction	,,	CS		CS	CS			CS			CS	CS	CS					
Brislington	,,	6 58		8 53	8 55			10 25			1 39	—	3 2					
Whitchurch Halt	,,	7 6		—	—			10 32			1 46	—	3 9					
Stop Board	,,	—		9P12	9P14			—			—	2P33	—					
Pensford	arr.	7 12		9 21	9 23			10 38			1 52	—	3 15					
	dep.	7X13		9 33	9 35			10 39			1X55	CS	3 16					
Pensford and Bromley Siding	arr.	—		—	9 40			CS			CS	—	CS					
	dep.	—		—	10 6			—			—	—	—					
Clutton	arr.	7 24		9 41	10 16			10 47			2 3	2 57	3 24					
	dep.	7 25		9 51				10 48			2 4	3 7	3 25	12 50				
Stop Board	,,	—		9P57				—			—	3P14	—	12P57				
Hallatrow	arr.	7 28		10 3				10 51			2 7	3•20	3 28	1 3				
	dep.	7 29		10 23				10 52			2 8	3 45	3 29	2X25				
Stop Board	,,	—		10P32				—			—	3P55	—	2P35				
Farrington Gurney	,,	7 34		—				10 56			2 12	—	3 33	—				
Old Mills Siding	arr.	—		—				—			—	—	—	2 41				
	dep.	—		—				—			—	—	—	3 0				
Midsomer Norton and Welton	arr	7 37		10 42				10 59			2 15	—	3 36	—				
	dep.	7 38		10 52			9 55	11 0			2 16	—	3 37	—				
RADSTOCK	arr.	7 41		10 57			10 1	11X 3			2 19	4 9	3 40	3 10				
	dep.	7 42				9 40		11 5		11 45	2 20		3 41	4 0				
Mells Road	arr.	7 50				9 48		11 12		12 3	2 27		3 48	4 18				
	dep.	7 51				9 49		11 13		12 35	2 28		3 49	4 20		5 10		
Stop Board	,,	—				—		—		12P45	—		—	4P28		5P18		
Somerset Quar. Siding	,,	—	8 40			—		—	12 10	—	—		—	—		•—		
Gas Works Siding	,,	—	—			—		—	—	—	—		—	—		—		
Market Siding	,,	—	—			—		—	—	—	—		—	—		—		
Frome Mineral Junction	arr.	—	8 50			—		—	12 15	1 1	—		—	4 44		5 34		
FROME	arr.	8 2				10 0		11 24			2 38		4 0					
	dep.	8N10				10 10		11 46										

N—Saturdays and School Holidays excepted between Frome and Bruton.

BRISTOL, RADSTOCK AND FROME.

DOWN TRAINS. STATIONS.		WEEK DAYS. B			B	B	B			SUNDAYS. B		B	
		Wells Pass.			Pass.	Pass.	Pass.			Pass.		Pass.	
		p.m.			p.m.	p.m.	p.m.			a.m.		p.m.	
BRISTOL (T.M.)	dep.	5 20	....	....	6 15	8 12	9 48	....	....	9 40	....	4 50	....
East Depot	,,	..			..	..	..			..		..	
Marsh Junction	,,	CS			CS	CS	CS			CS		CS	
Brislington	,,	5 27			6 22	8 20	9 55			9 47		4 57	
Whitchurch Halt	,,	5 34			6 29	8 27	10 2			9 54		5 4	
Stop Board	,,	—			—	—	—			—		—	
Pensford	arr.	5 40			6X35	8 33	10X 8			10 0		5 10	
	dep.	5 41			6 36	8 34	10 10			10 1		5 11	
Pensford and Bromley Siding	arr.	—			—	—	—			—		—	
	dep.	—			—	—	—			—		—	
Clutton	arr.	5 49			6 44	8 42	10 18			10 9		5 19	
	dep.	5 50			6X48	8 43	10 19			10 10		5 20	
Stop Board	,,	—			—	—	—			—		—	
Hallatrow	arr.	5 53			6 51	8 46	10 22			10 13		5 23	
	dep.	5 54			6 52	8 47	10 23			10 14		5 24	
Stop Board	,,	—			—	—	—			—		—	
Farrington Gurney	,,	5 58			6 56	8 51	10 27			10 18		5 28	
Old Mills Siding	arr.	—			—	—	—			—		—	
	dep.	—			—	—	—			—		—	
Midsomer Norton and Welton	arr.	6 1			6 59	8 54	10 30			10 21		5 31	
	dep.	6 2			7 0	8 55	10 31			10 22		5 32	
RADSTOCK	arr.	6 5			7 3	8 58	10 34			10 25		5 35	
	dep.	6 7			7 4	9 0	10 35			10 26		5 36	
Mells Road	arr.	6 14			7 11	9 7	10 42			10 33		5 43	
	dep.	6X20			7 12	9 8	10 43			10 34		5 44	
Stop Board	,,	—			—	—	—			—		—	
Somerset Quarries Siding	,,	—			—	—	—			—		—	
Gas Works Siding	,,	—			—	—	—			—		—	
Market Siding	,,	—			—	—	—			—		—	
Frome Mineral Junction	arr.	—			—	—	—			—		—	
FROME	arr.	6 31	....	....	7 22	9 19	10 53	....	....	10 44	....	5 54	....
	dep.	6 35											

Single Line, Marsh Junction to Radstock Station worked by Electric Train Token Marsh Junction to Pensford, and Electric Train Staff Pensford to Radstock, the Staff Stations and crossing places being Marsh Junction, Pensford, Pensford and Bromley Siding‡, Clutton, Hallatrow, and Radstock Station.

Electric Train Token worked between Clutton and Pensford when Pensford and Bromley Siding is out of circuit.

‡Pensford and Bromley Siding is only available for shunting a light Engine, or Freight Train (at Old Mills short Freight Train only can be shunted), for a train to pass in the same or opposite direction.

Double Line, Radstock Station to Mells Road South End.

Single Line, Mells Road South End to Frome worked by Electric Train Token, Mells Road and Frome South Box being the Token Stations.

SERVICE TIMETABLE BR (WR)
May 31 to September 26
inclusive 1948

Left: IN-BETWEEN TIMES AT MONKTON COMBE
1400 class 0-4-2T No. 1456 rests between shots at Monkton Combe during the filming of *The Titfield Thunderbolt* in the summer of 1952. For the film, Monkton Combe station was renamed "Titfield", part of a small, rural railway fighting for its very existence against the onslaught of the motor car.

This photograph seems an admirable epitaph to the passing of a more leisurely "branch-line" way of life.

Lens of Sutton/R.R. Bowler

Following Nationalisation the scheme was put "on the shelf" but it was not until 1958, when the Western Region took over the Somerset & Dorset's northern half that the plan was finally and formally abandoned! However, to return to the days of war, we find that in April 1944 a Sherman tank being carried on a tank transporter became jammed under the bridge at Thicket Mead, near Welton. Mr Amos Church, who was waiting at Welton station for the 8.30am train to Frome, said that the railway staff, fearing that the bridge was unsafe, decided to get a motor coach to take the waiting passengers into Radstock. This duly came and very quickly whisked all concerned down to Radstock (GW) station. Here passengers caught the 8.50am to Frome, where they made the London connection. Buses were used for some three or four days after the incident while the damage was put right, the buses again ferrying passengers as far as Radstock (Great Western).

Particularly busy during the Second World War, the line handled large amounts of coal from the collieries at Pensford, Bromley, Old Mills and from those in the Radstock area. In addition, the shadow factory in the former quarry and the government's buffer depot, both near Hallatrow, generated heavy traffic. There was also a good deal of wartime traffic to and from Blatchford's at Welton station. During the 1939-45 period the various wagon works and out-stations along the line were very active and this included the one at Clutton. Freight workings south from Bristol would put crippled wagons into the works on their way towards Radstock. Once repaired, these wagons would be tripped to Pensford & Bromley Collieries' sidings from where they would be taken back to East Depot.

As we saw in the history of its construction, one problem that the Bristol & North Somerset Railway had always suffered from was that of landslips. On 28th December 1946 another landslip, this time of the colliery tip at Pensford, dislocated railway working over the branch. It seems that a bout of wet weather had caused part of the tip to fall away, forcing the track out of alignment. On Monday 30th December the tip was still moving even though railwaymen had been hard at work the entire weekend trying to clear the line and making sure that there would be no further slides.

FROME, RADSTOCK, AND BRISTOL.

UP TRAINS. — WEEK DAYS.

Mile Post Distance from Frome M.	C.	STATIONS.		Ruling Gradient 1 in.	Time Allowance for Ordinary Freight Trains. See page 2. Point-to-Point Times	Allow for Stop	Allow for Start.	B	K	B	K	B	K	B	K	K	K	K	B	B	K		A	B	
								Pass.	Frght. and Empties.	Pass.	E'ties	Diesel. W80	Frght SX	Pass.	Frght SO	Frght SX	E'ties	Frght. SX	Pass.	Pass.	Kingsland Road Frght and Coal. SX		Pass.	Diesel	
M.	C.				Mins.	Mins.	Mins.	a.m.	a.m.	a.m.	a.m.	a.m.	a.m.	a.m.	a.m.	a.m.	a.m.	p.m.	p.m.	p.m.	p.m.		p.m.	p.m.	
—	—	FROME	arr.	—	—	—	1	..	..	..	..		..	..	..	..	..	..	..	..	..	..	..	..	..
			dep.		—	—	—	6 27	....	7 37	....	*8 55*	....	10 47	....	....	....	....	1 10	4 5	....	....	5 55	6 6	....
—	21	Frome Mineral Jct.	,,	76 F.	—	—	1	—	7 0	—	8 15	—	..	—	..	..	11 50	12 45	—	—	..	..	—	—	..
—	53	Market Siding	,,	76 F.	—	—	—	—	—	—	—	—	....	—	..	....	—	—	—	—	....	....	—	—	....
—	70	Gas Works Siding	,,	276 F.	4	1	1	—	—	—	—	—	..	—	..	..	—	—	—	—	..	..	—	—	..
2	15	Somerset Quar. Sdg.	,,	51 R.	3	2	2	—	—	—	8 25	—	....	—	....	....	11 55	—	—	—	..	..	—	—	..
5	26	Mells Road	arr.	48 R.	11	1	1	6 38	7 20	7 48		*9 8*	..	10 58	..	..		1 5	1 21	4 16	....	....	CS	6 19	....
			dep.					6 39	8 0	7 49	..	*9 9*	....	10 59	....	....	..	1●40	1 22	4 17	..	..	—	6 20	..
5	27	Stop Board	,,	69 F.	1	1	1	—	8P6	—	....	—	..	—	..	..	....	1P45	—	—	....	....	—	—	....
8	24	RADSTOCK	arr.	69 F.	8	1	1	6 45	8 16	7 55	..	*9 15*	....	11 5	....	..	..	1 55	1 28	4 23	..	..	6 11	6 26	..
			dep.					6 46	9 10	7 56	....		..	11X 6	*11 20*	11 25	....		1 30	4 24	5 0	....	6 12	6 27	....
9	55	Midsomer Norton and Welton	arr.	128 R.	3	1	1	6 49	9 15	7 59	..	..	....	11 9	—	11 30	..	..	1 33	4 27	—	..	—	6 31	..
			dep.					6 50		8 0	....	....	..	11 10	CR	11 40	....	....	1 34	4 28	—	....	—	6 32	....
10	59	Old Mills Siding	arr.	177 R.	4	1	1	—	..	—	..	..	....	—	—	11 46	..	..	—	—	—	..	—	—	..
			dep.					—	....	—	....	....	..	—	—	12 0	....	....	—	—	—	....	—	—	....
—	—	Farrington Gurney	,,	73 R.	—	—	—	6 54	..	8 4	..	..	....	11 14	—	—	..	..	1 38	4 32	—	..	—	6 38	..
11	62	Stop Board	,,	73 R.	4	1	1	—	....	—	....	....	..	—	*11P36*	12P9	....	....	—	—	5P16	....	—	—	....
12	65	Hallatrow	arr.	65 F.	4	1	1	6 57	..	8 7	..	..	....	11 17	*11 42*	12 15	..	..	1 41	4 35	5 22	..	—	6 41	..
			dep.					6X59	....	8 8	....	....	..	11 18	*11 53*	12 30	....	....	1X42	4 36	5 32	....	CS	6 42	....
14	21	Clutton	arr.	58 R.	6	1	2	7 2	..	8 11	..	..	....	11 21	—	12 38	..	..	1 45	4 39	5 40	..	—	6 46	..
			dep.					7 3	....	8 12	....	....	11 0	11X22	CR		....	....	1 46	4 40	7X 0	....	CS	6X49	....
14	57	Stop Board	,,	71 R.	3	1	1	—	..	—	..	..	11P9	—	*12P11*	..	..	..	—	—	7P6	..	—	—	..
16	60	Pensford and Bromley Siding	arr.	—	—	—	—	—	....	—	....	....	11 18	—	*12 20*	....	....	....	CS	—	—	....	—	—	....
			dep.	60 F.	6	2	1	—	..	—	..	..	12●0	CX S	*12 43*	..	..	..	—	—	—	..	—	—	..
17	39	Pensford	arr.	60 F.	2	1	2	7 10	....	8 19	....	....	12 4	11 29	*12 47*	....	....	....	1 53	4 47	—	....	6 32	6 56	....
			dep.					7X14	..	8 20	..	..	12 25	11 30	*12 55*	..	..	..	1X54	4 48	C7 17S	..	6X37	6 59	..
19	20	Stop Board	,,	66 R.	8	1	1	—	....	—	....	....	12P39	—	*1P9*	....	....	....	—	—	7P29	....	—	—	....
20	1	Whitchurch Halt	,,	60 F.	—	—	—	7 21	..	8 27	..	..	—	—	—	..	..	..	2 1	4 55	—	..	—	7 8	..
22	9	Brislington	arr.	60 F.	8	1	1	7 25	....	8 31	....	....	12 49	N	*1 19*	....	....	....	2 5	4 59	7 39	....	—	7 13	....
			dep.					7 26	..	8 32	..	..	1 5	—	*1P22*	..	..	..	2 6	5 0	7P41	..	—	7 15	..
23	18	Marsh Junction	dep.	62 F.	3	1	1	CS	....	CS	....	....	1*16	CS	CS	....	....	....	CS	CS	C7*50S	....	CS	CS	....
23	63	East Depot	arr.	—	4	1	—	..	..	..	..	..	1 22	..	*1 38*	..	..	..	..	..	..	..	..	..	..
23	34	North Somerset Jct.	arr.	—	—	—	—	—	....	—	....	....		—	....	....	....	....	—	—	7V55	....	—	—	....
24	16	BRISTOL (T.M.)	,,	—	—	—	—	7 32	..	8 38	..	..	..	11 45	..	..	..	..	2 12	5 6		..	6 52	7 24	..

N—Calls at Brislington on Saturdays. V—Kingsland Road.

FROME, RADSTOCK AND BRISTOL.

UP TRAINS.		WEEK DAYS. B								SUNDAYS.	B					B
STATIONS.		Pass.									Pass.					Pass.
		p.m.									noon					p.m.
FROME	arr.	..	..	..	..	..	..	..	..	..	..	..	..	..	..	..
	dep.	9 25	....	....	....	....	....	....	....	....	12 0	....	....	....	....	9 35
Frome Mineral Junction	,,	—	..	..	..	..	..	..	..	..	—	..	..	..	..	—
Market Siding	,,	—	....	....	....	....	....	....	....	....	—	....	....	....	....	—
Gas Works Siding	,,	—	..	..	..	..	..	..	..	..	—	..	..	..	..	—
Somerset Quarries Siding	,,	—	....	....	....	....	....	....	....	....	—	....	....	....	....	—
Mells Road	arr.	9 36	..	..	..	..	..	..	..	..	12 11	..	..	..	..	9 46
	dep.	9 37	....	....	....	....	....	....	....	....	12 12	....	....	....	....	9 47
Stop Board	,,	—	..	..	..	..	..	..	..	..	—	..	..	..	..	—
RADSTOCK	arr.	9 43	....	....	....	....	....	....	....	....	12 18	....	....	....	....	9 53
	dep.	9 44	..	..	..	..	..	..	..	..	12 19	..	..	..	..	9 55
Midsomer Norton and Welton	arr.	—	....	....	....	....	....	....	....	....	12 22	....	....	....	....	9 58
	dep.	9 48	..	..	..	..	..	..	..	..	12 23	..	..	..	..	9 59
Old Mills Siding	arr.	—	....	....	....	....	....	....	....	....	—	....	....	....	....	—
	dep.	—	..	..	..	..	..	..	..	..	—	..	..	..	..	—
Farrington Gurney	,,	9 52	....	....	....	....	....	....	....	....	12 27	....	....	....	....	10 3
Stop Board	,,	—	..	..	..	..	..	..	..	..	—	..	..	..	..	—
Hallatrow	arr.	9 55	....	....	....	....	....	....	....	....	12 30	....	....	....	....	10 6
	dep.	9 56	..	..	..	..	..	..	..	..	12 31	..	..	..	..	10 7
Clutton	arr.	9 59	....	....	....	....	....	....	....	....	12 34	....	....	....	....	10 10
	dep.	10 0	..	..	..	..	..	..	..	..	12 35	..	..	..	..	10 11
Stop Board	,,	—	....	....	....	....	....	....	....	....	—	....	....	....	....	—
Pensford and Bromley Sdg.	arr.	—	..	..	..	..	..	..	..	..	—	..	..	..	..	—
	dep.	—	....	....	....	....	....	....	....	....	—	....	....	....	....	—
Pensford	arr.	10X 7	..	..	..	..	..	..	..	..	12 42	..	..	..	..	10 18
	dep.	10 9	....	....	....	....	....	....	....	....	12 43	....	....	....	....	10 19
Stop Board	,,	—	..	..	..	..	..	..	..	..	—	..	..	..	..	—
Whitchurch Halt	dep.	10 16	....	....	....	....	....	....	....	....	12 50	....	....	....	....	10 26
Brislington	arr.	—	..	..	..	..	..	..	..	..	12 54	..	..	..	..	10 30
	dep.	10 21	....	....	....	....	....	....	....	....	12 55	....	....	....	....	10 31
Marsh Junction	dep.	CS	..	..	..	..	..	..	..	..	CS	..	..	..	..	CS
East Depot	arr.	....	....	....	....	....	....	....	....	....	....	....	....	....	....	....
North Somerset Junction	,,	—	..	..	..	..	..	..	..	..	—	..	..	..	..	—
BRISTOL (T.M.)	,,	10 28	....	....	....	....	....	....	....	....	1 4	....	....	....	....	10 38

V—Kingsland Road.

In order to by-pass the blockage, rail passengers were taken by road between Bristol (Temple Meads) and Clutton. They were picked up by substitute coaches near Brislington station, at Whitchurch Halt and at Pensford station. From Clutton, trains took them southwards towards Frome. It seems that by the end of January 1947 all was working normally again, just in time for one of the worst winters on record.

One well-known, and very knowledgeable, local railwayman is Mr Ken Evans. He worked at Radstock (GW) from 1946, when he joined the GWR as a relief lorry driver. In May 1947 he went on to become a signalman in the Radstock area, working locally until 1973 when, with the final closure of the Somerset Coalfield and its associated rail traffic, he moved to a TOPS job at Westbury for two years. He told the author that in the late 1940s and through most of the 1950s the station and the goods yard at Radstock were very busy with heavy passenger and excursion traffic. In addition, bullion traffic for the banks at Radstock also came in by passenger train. The passenger service was particularly well patronised during the extremely bad winter of 1947 when local buses could not venture out onto the treacherous Mendip roads. There was also a wide variety of freight and this included coal, tar, stone, general freight and repaired freight wagons from the nearby wagon works at Marcroft. At that time, the business out of Marcroft was heavy enough to justify its own Carriage & Wagon Inspector while the company's outstations at Mells Road and Clutton were still busy with running repairs.

The post war days of austerity still saw a substantial station staff at Radstock (West). This included a stationmaster, two passenger porters, one signalporter, one clerk, one junior clerk, one goods agent, one chief goods porter, one Carriage

Above: KEN EVANS ON DUTY AT "THE GATES"
Ken Evans takes a break from his signalling activities at Radstock North signal box to have his photo taken for posterity.

Collection: Ken Evans

Below: WORKING FOR THE GWR
This photograph shows a copy of the certificate obtained by Ken Evans, allowing him to work signal boxes in the Radstock area. It was issued in the last year of the GWR's reign.

Original document: Ken Evans

Photography: W. Harbor

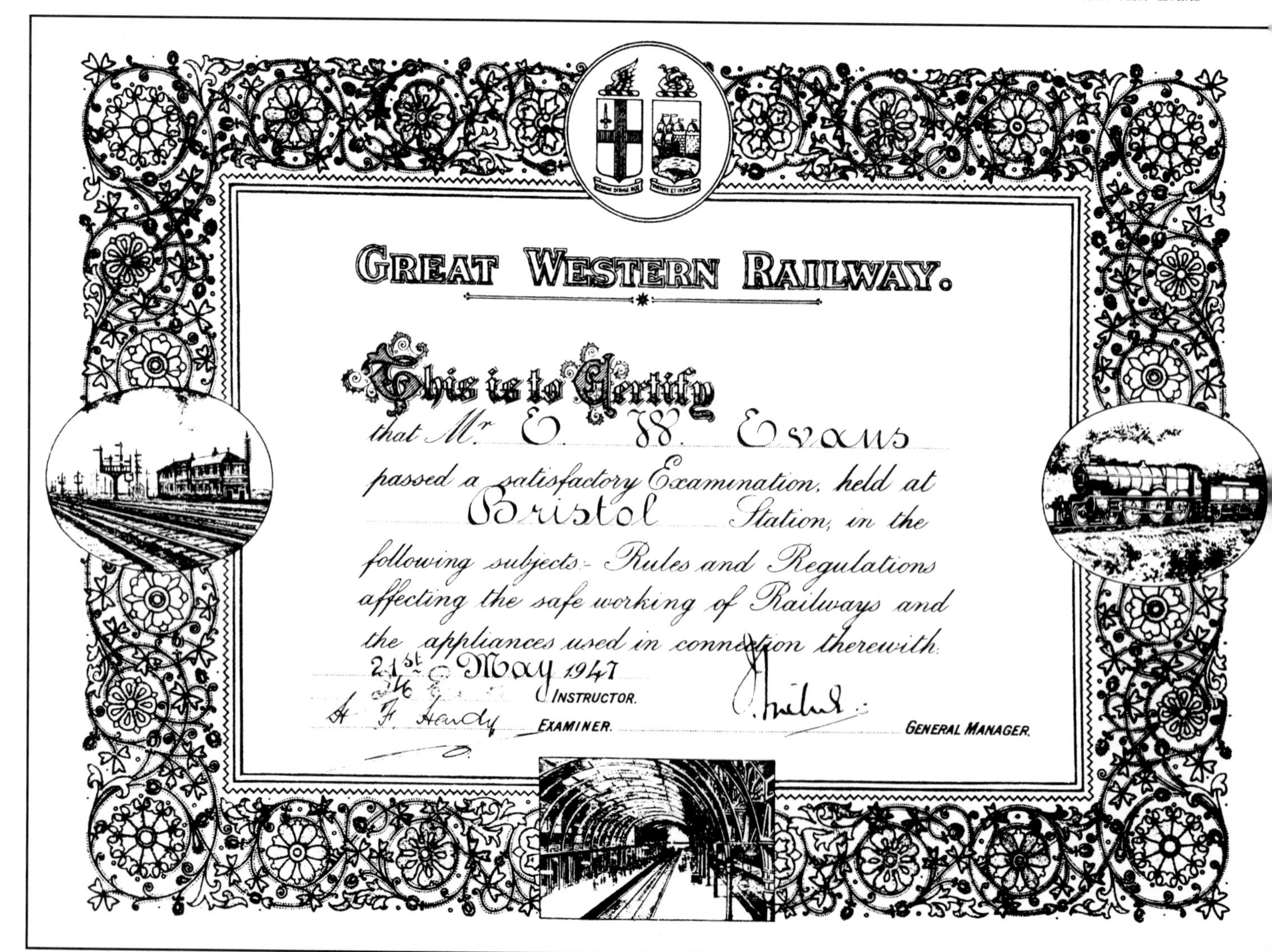

GREAT WESTERN RAILWAY.

This is to Certify that Mr E. W. Evans passed a satisfactory Examination, held at Bristol Station, in the following subjects:- Rules and Regulations affecting the safe working of Railways and the appliances used in connection therewith.

21st May 1947

INSTRUCTOR.

A. F. Hardy EXAMINER.

GENERAL MANAGER.

& Wagon Inspector (based at Marcroft's Wagon Works), a lamp boy and a ganger with his gang of six men. Local parcels deliveries were made by driver Bert Dark and his horse and cart! In the 1950s, on the signalling side, the two signal boxes then in use had, as their regular signalmen, Mr Evans and Mr Jefferies at Radstock North (the "Gates") while at Radstock South (the "Yard") Mr Frank Carter and Mr Henry Hawkins were the regular men.

After the war, and up until the removal of the passenger service in 1959, one very important working on the North Somerset was the line's famous "Boat Train" which provided Frome, Radstock and Pensford with a quick, early evening service across North Somerset to Bristol. Running "A" headlamps, this train connected with the Channel Islands-Paddington boat train at Frome and was due into Bristol at 6.52pm. If the train was running late for any reason, Frome station staff would wire ahead to Bristol to make sure that passengers needing to make connections for the North would still get their trains. The locomotive off the 5.55pm would later work the 8.12pm back to Frome, a pannier tank or 45/55XX normally handling these workings. This fast service was followed by an all-stations "stopper", the 6.06pm from Frome and this was often handled by a GWR diesel railcar.

From 1937 to the early years of the Second World War, Mr E. White was employed on the signalling side at Pensford station. After one year working there as signal porter, he was made up to signalman until, some three years later, he moved to Clifton Bridge station on the Bristol-Portishead line. Whilst at Pensford, Ernest's fellow signalman was Mr Stan Way, while Stationmaster Smewing was in charge. In addition to his signalling duties, the signal porter at Pensford had to do all the station work including checking the weighbridge tallies. Mr White said that Sundays were often terribly long in that, although there were pairs of trains crossing throughout the day, there were also some very long boring periods in between.

Pre-war at Pensford, the passenger business was still in pretty fair shape. Indeed, the 8.20am into Bristol, for example, was always packed with office workers and schoolchildren. On the freight side, coal empties came out from Bristol early in the morning and were past Pensford at 5.30am. Often this train would load to some 28/30 wagons and would be headed by a 45/55XX 2-6-2T, a 2200 0-6-0 or by a 4300 2-6-0 locomotive. The return working from Radstock would be through in the afternoon with around 25 on, the wagons being of the ten or twelve ton variety. Around 12.30pm a late morning freight would leave Pensford & Bromley Collieries' sidings for Bristol.

As far as the North Somerset was concerned, there were various things to note about the Pensford area during the Second World War. For example, when severe air raids took place in Bristol during the early years of the war, the last train from Frome into that city terminated at Pensford. From here it returned to Frome. In addition, at the time of the very worst raids, people would come out on the trains in the evening to stay overnight in the areas around Pensford, Clutton and Hallatrow, going back to Bristol in the morning to find who-knows-what after the bombs had done their terrifying work. Pensford station itself, however, did remain generally unscathed by war damage although, on one memorable occasion, a bomb crater some four coaches long was made at the back of the signal box!

After the war, Mr Fry became signalman at Pensford station from June 1953 to the end of 1955 and he recalls life at the station during the mid-1950s. At that time Mr Maul was his fellow signalman while Mr H.J. (Harry) Wyatt was porter and it was he who took over from Mr Fry when he left. The stationmaster at that time was Mr Bob Collins. The signalmens' turns in those days were from 6.45am to 2.45pm and from

FARRINGTON GURNEY TWILIGHT
With the 6.26pm passenger off Radstock, BR Standard Class 3 2-6-2T No. 82002 and its two coach train wait at Farrington Gurney Halt before heading north towards Bristol, on the evening of 24th June 1958.

Farrington Gurney was opened on 11th July 1927, the opening being celebrated by the running of a special excursion to Weston-super-Mare. The cost of the return fare was just 2s (10p). It was, therefore, not surprising that over 300 adults and 140 children took advantage of this offer.

P.J. Williams

2.45pm to 10.55pm, with the finish time being 11.15pm on Wednesdays and Saturdays only. After 6pm the signalman on duty would also collect the tickets as well as carry out his other tasks. The box was opened for 15 Sundays in the summer, the shifts being 10.15am to 1.10pm and 5.pm to 10pm.

Along the line, Pensford & Bromley Collieries' signal box was switched in for the mornings-only basically and, in January 1952 for example, this meant that the signalman's turn was 7.45am to 3.45pm, the box actually being switched out at 2.10pm. The signalman would then walk over to Pensford station to make out the invoices for coal traffic handled from Pensford & Bromley Collieries that day.

In the 1950s, the passenger traffic into Bristol was still pretty brisk, the first pair of passenger trains of the day crossing at Pensford. Another pair would cross around lunchtime while a third pair crossed early in the evening. As with most cross-country lines there were delightful stories to recall, such as the one where guards on southbound freights from East Depot would give the signalman at Pensford their orders for apples. These orders would then be taken to a farm below the nearby viaduct, the apples being delivered to the station around lunchtime, just in time for the guards' return on the northbound working! Incidentally, the Bristol-bound afternoon freight would also call at Brislington station to shunt both coal and scrap traffic there.

On the freight side at Pensford, the siding was still much in use with the goods shed handling potatoes for pig food, while potatoes for human consumption were also handled in season. A local gas purification firm used the goods yard, its products being exported to Hong Kong, their journey starting out in covered vans from Pensford station. During the spring and summer months Friday evenings were particularly busy times for the station, for it was then that the North Somerset Combine, a local pigeon-racing group, would make use of British Railways to convey their precious cargoes, the pigeons being conveyed in General Utility Vans. The birds were generally ringed in the station's goods store.

Pensford station closed to passenger traffic on 2nd November 1959 and to goods traffic on 15th June 1964. On the latter date, the signal box was closed and signalman H.J. Wyatt was made redundant. He retired on 27th June 1964. Leading porter J. Brimble, who was then still working at the station, was transferred to Radstock. The boxes at Clutton and Hallatrow were closed at the same time as the one at Pensford and, with all these closures, the signalling section stretched from Marsh Junction to Radstock. In December 1965 the signal box and goods shed were demolished. Today, the station site has become the location for a new housing estate.

In 1949 Mr G.W. Nailor took over the stationmaster's job at Clutton station from Mr Rust. He remained there until June 1956 and, in conversation with him, we get a full and vivid picture of the life of the station at that time. On the passenger side local traffic was holding up well while, during the summer months, specials continued to work along the branch to such well-established destinations as Weymouth. In addition, there was still the odd excursion to the South Wales resorts and these were often very well filled, as were the pantomime trains which ran into Bristol around Christmastime. Pigeon specials

JAMES ROBERTSON & SONS – THEIR FACTORY AT BRISLINGTON, 1952

Robertson's factory at Brislington was opened in 1915. At first, the firm used the railway a good deal for the transport of its products but the traffic was never believed to have been put onto rail at Brislington station itself. It was always collected by lorry and taken straight to Temple Meads for onward distribution.

Once road transport started to compete forcefully with rail the traffic went over completely to road. It would seem, therefore, that in spite of its closeness to the North Somerset the factory of James Robertson & Sons never made significant use of the railway! After the line closed to freight, Robertson's acquired some railway land at Brislington station on a short-term lease.

However, times have really changed now and the factory has been completely demolished. A new superstore has been built on the site and on part of the North Somerset's route southwards.

James Robertson & Sons/Aerofilms

Above: MIDSOMER NORTON & WELTON STATION (1)
This view shows a lull in traffic at Midsomer Norton & Welton station. Milk traffic is well in evidence on the right.
M.B. Warburton/P. Rutherford

Below: MIDSOMER NORTON & WELTON STATION (2)
Pannier tank No. 9615 and its two coach "B" set pause amidst the flower beds at Midsomer Norton & Welton station with the 4.05pm train from Frome to Bristol on 12th September 1959.
Hugh Ballantyne

continued to be a regular feature of the line during the summer period while the level of inwards parcels for the Harptrees, Chew Magna, Bishop Sutton and Timsbury remained healthy.

Occasionally, passenger trains to Weymouth were diverted over the branch instead of running via Westbury. These workings were sometimes doubleheaded with 0-6-0 and 2-6-2 tanks, the workings continuing through until at least 1956 when Mr Nailor left Clutton for Witham station. In those days, this latter station included responsibility for the halt and station respectively at Wanstrow and Cranmore on the East Somerset branch. The writing was clearly on the wall for Clutton in that when Mr Nailor left, another stationmaster was not appointed.

In 1949 other station staff included porters Tom Owen and Anthony Church, with signalmen Luther Edwards and Harry Dando. When the latter died, Anthony Church became signalman in his place, with his job, in turn, being taken up by Mr Leslie Stowe. At this time, the Clutton ganger-in-charge was Mr E.J. Brain but, when he was promoted to work in Bristol, "Gunner" Lockyer took over his job. In those days, Clutton really was a railway village!

On the goods side the wagon repair depot at Clutton continued to flourish, the work now being carried out under the auspices of Marcroft's Wagon Works. For the work of repairing and restoring the wooden bodies then in general use on railway wagons, the station received timber inwards. However, work on wagon wheels, axles, etc. took place at the firm's Radstock works. Repairs at the Clutton outstation were handled by Mr Farnham Bailey and his capable group of around a dozen workers. With a fair number of trucks being repaired in the yard, storage space was required for those awaiting attention. This was provided by the former colliery line to Fry's Bottom, 60 to 70 wagons often being stabled here. This long stretch of overgrown track, somewhat switchback in nature, would really make locomotives "cough" as they put trucks away!

During George Nailor's time at Clutton thousands of cast-iron pipes were handled by the station. Arriving at Clutton on bogie bolster wagons, the pipes were being laid in from Clutton to Bishop Sutton by Bristol Waterworks. A seven days a week job, this pipe contract was very good business for Clutton station while it lasted. Occasionally, the station handled sugar beet traffic, while blue-stained potatoes also came in, these being used for animal feeding purposes within the local area. In addition, coal traffic for the Clutton firm of Bromilows provided loads for around four wagons a week on average.

Further to the south at Welton station, very little outwards traffic was handled. Nonetheless, a variety of traffic came in and this included explosives delivered by rail from Penrhyndeudraeth in North Wales for the local firm of Caswells. Caswells also received about a dozen wagons of cement a week through Welton, the railways delivering it directly to the firm's customers from the station. Explosives for the colliery at Norton Hill came from Stevenson in Scotland, via the Somerset & Dorset.

Blatchford's private siding at Welton was served by British Railways' bogie bolster wagons which brought steel into the firm, the company also receiving ex-army tanks which came to them for cutting up. Lighter traffic in the form of maize and cereals also passed in through the station. Every winter *one* wagonload of salt was delivered to Welton for use on local roads. This was certainly not heavy traffic but, at least it was regular! During the 1950s, while Mr Derek Fear was clerk, Mr May was stationmaster at Welton. The station also had an early and late goods porter. The parcels van driver was Frank Blatchford while Les Stowe was the driver of the station's goods van. Parcels work was concentrated at Radstock (West) although there can be no doubt that this traffic was affected by the 1955 ASLEF strike when a serious loss of local parcels traffic took place, including that of the Standard Cheque company's account.

Mr Derek Fear also recalls his experiences as a junior clerk at Radstock (West) station in the 1950s. He was in a post there from 31st December 1956 until the passenger service was taken off in November 1959, when he moved across to Midsomer Norton (South) on the Somerset & Dorset. Mr Newbury was then stationmaster at Radstock (West). Mr Fred Scott was the station's clerk while Bert Dark was porter. Interestingly enough, there was still rivalry between old railwaymen working on the GWR and S&D at Radstock. By this time the staff at the spotless South signal box were Mr Bert Hawkins and his son, Alan.

The passenger service was still being handled by 45/55XXs and a variety of pannier tanks, although the 6.06pm "stopper" from Frome was often in the hands of a single GWR railcar, the three-car formation being a much rarer visitor to the district. Twice or three times a year Sunday excursions were still run to South Wales destinations such as Barry Island and Porthcawl, these being headed by a 2-6-0, or a pair of tank engines, either 2-6-2s or 0-6-0s. Weymouth specials were often "diverted" over the North Somerset and these six and seven coach trains were usually hauled by a 2-6-0 of the 43/53/63XX type. In the late days of the passenger service, particularly in the 1958/59 period, Standard Class 3, 82XXX 2-6-2 tanks, although heavy on coal, were also in evidence on passenger trains.

In the early 1950s, some of the ROD class 2-8-0 locomotives of Great Central Railway design were regular runners on the freight trains on the branch. The locomotives most used were Nos 3017 and 3032, although 3014 was another member of the class often seen. However, by 1956, the RODs had gone and so the freight traffic was dealt with by 41XX series 2-6-2Ts from Bristol (East Depot), locomotive No. 4131 being an especial favourite, and by pannier tanks which worked in from the Frome direction. Occasionally, 22XXs, 32XXs, 84XXs and very rarely 61XXs were also seen polishing the tracks around Radstock (West), while the weedkilling train would bring an Ivatt 2-6-0 to the district. Still on the freight side, there were three shunters and a goods foreman at Radstock (West) and this gives some idea of how busy the station was even into the line's later days of decline.

One point of interest about freight workings on the North Somerset branch was that, generally speaking, Radstock, with its small loco shed, was the end of the journey for locomen from the Bristol district. In the other direction, Frome men would work goods trains through Mells Road to Radstock. It is fascinating to see how these workings reflected, until late on in the line's history, the railway's initial pattern of construction, namely, its being built in two sections, Frome-Radstock and Bristol-Radstock. Because of this fact Bristol and Frome-based goods enginemen were, in a strange kind of way, remote from one another. On the other hand, Bristol (Bath Road) passenger drivers (No. 4 Link) worked along the whole length of the line. Indeed, their turns took them and their colleagues from the sheds at Frome, Westbury and Yatton over the neighbouring East Somerset Railway as well.

Further east from Radstock, Mells Road was an interesting and busy place to be, post war, with stone still being handled by the private Newbury Railway which served the quarry at Vobster. Some half a dozen wagons would be pushed out onto the GWR by the quarry's own engine, the stone being taken out, via Frome and Westbury, to London where it was used as ballast by London Transport. The station pilot at Frome would also work the neighbouring Somerset Quarry Sidings as part of its day's duties. Here private owner locomotives belonging to the quarry firm of ARC, would push the full wagons of stone out into the exchange sidings for the branch locomotives to Frome. (For more information on these workings, please see Chapter 11.)

During the research for this book, one local railwayman had told the author that the North Somerset had been "an easy line" from which to remove the passenger services. It is therefore quite surprising that when the "crunch" came to their removal, the railway authorities made very heavy going of the whole process. It fell to the South Western Transport Users Consultative Committee, the SWTUCC, to consider the railways' proposal to withdraw the passenger service between Bristol, Radstock (West) and Frome. At the same time, the Western Region's proposals also sought, what became controversial permission, to remove parcels facilities from Brislington, Pensford, Clutton, Hallatrow, Midsomer Norton & Welton and Radstock (West) stations. The railway would remain open for freight traffic.

Not surprisingly, many groups and bodies objected to the

RADSTOCK (WEST) IN THE 1950s
This evocative 1958 shot shows a Bristol-bound train running gently across the GW level crossing at Radstock behind BR Standard Class 3 2-6-2T No. 82043.

Taken in the last days of the North Somerset's passenger service, this photograph highlights such gems as the Vauxhall Velox car waiting at the gates while the poster on the station wall leads one to consider the delights, not of scrumpy, but of Irish Guinness! *Terry Paget*

THE NORTH SOMERSET RAILTOUR, 28th April 1957 (1)
Two 2-6-2 tank locomotives, Nos 41202 and 41203, work the RCTS special over the Bristol Harbour line between Bathurst Basin and Ashton Swing Bridge. The two bicycles provide a rather good contrast in methods of transport! *R.J. Leonard*

line's closure to passengers. These groups included trades' councils at Radstock and Frome, various parish and urban district councils served by the line, including Somerset County Council, while a 100 signature petition from the Clutton area showed just how strong public opinion was against the removal of the service. Interestingly and strangely enough, the city council in Bristol had no objection to the proposals!

In defence of its case, the Western Region had provided some alternative rail facilities, one of these being a replacement service, via Westbury, for the former 5.55 pm "Boat Train" from Frome to Bristol, via Radstock. The railway authorities said that they had also considered the introduction of diesel multiple units on the North Somerset but had found that this would have cost at least £42,500. This, they insisted, was an unacceptable figure bearing in mind the loss already incurred by the passenger service which, once they had "amended" their figures, BR claimed was £18,542 a year.

Supporters of the line reiterated the fact that even British

TESTING THE BRISTOL COMMERCIAL VEHICLES' RAILBUS CHASSIS (1)
This view shows the BCV railbus chassis on test at the southern end of Brislington station. This, and the following photograph, were taken on 19th April 1958. *M.B. Warburton*

TESTING THE BRISTOL COMMERCIAL VEHICLES' RAILBUS CHASSIS (2)
With its test temporarily halted, the BCV railbus chassis rests awhile at Brislington station while it comes under some intense scrutiny. This was one of two railbuses supplied to BR in 1958 (Nos SC79958 and SC79959), with bodywork by Eastern Counties Coachworks Ltd of Lowestoft and powered by a 6-cylinder Gardner engine. They survived until 1968. *M.B. Warburton*

THE NORTH SOMERSET RAILTOUR (2)
The second outing of GWR 4-4-0 *City of Truro* after its 1950's restoration at Swindon Works provided, perhaps, the finest sight ever seen on the Bristol & North Somerset branch. This lovely engine is seen here coming across Pensford Viaduct piloting (although in actuality the inside locomotive is the pilot!) 2-6-2T No. 5528 on the RCTS special "The North Somerset Railtour", returning to Paddington on 28th April 1957.
Hugh Ballantyne

THE NORTH SOMERSET RAILTOUR (3)
An absolutely spotless No. 3440 *City of Truro* approaches Frome on the same railtour as above. It is so good to know that this beautiful locomotive is still in fine order.
Peter A. Fry

Railways' own figures for 1958 showed revenue of £173,000 and £137,000 for freight and coal traffic respectively. Indeed, one particular councillor reported that the parcels traffic alone for Hallatrow station had been worth some £28,000 in 1958 while, in the same period, some £76,000 worth of GPO traffic had been generated. Even today, it must be said that these figures impress! In addition, the North Somerset's use as a diversionary route was mentioned as was its usefulness in the wild, winter months on Mendip. Comments were also made about the unhelpfulness of the emergency timetable then in operation on the branch.

The railway authorities had claimed that for an extra £373 in cartage costs they could retain some £28,000 worth of parcels revenue then being handled by Hallatrow station for the firm of Purnells at Paulton. The SWTUCC questioned as to how this was to be done. The Western Region responded by saying that large quantities of the traffic would be put onto the S&D and that no long haulage was involved. It seems clear that a clever manoeuvre had been made by railway officialdom here.

The feelings of dissatisfaction on the part of the objectors with the way things had been handled was also expressed by the chairman of the SWTUCC, Mr Mark Whitwill, when he said that he was not convinced that every attempt had been made to keep the passenger service going. He reckoned that dmus should have been tried on the line, although he did have doubts about the units' ability to carry the volume of parcels then on offer. The WR agreed with him on this point and added that the multiple units would also experience difficulties with "automatic signalling arrangements at both the Bristol and Frome ends"!

In their final set of recommendations, the SWTUCC put forward the following points. First, and not altogether unexpectedly, the North Somerset should lose its passenger and parcels services. Secondly, that the major cause for the line's decline was the enormous growth in road transport, although the inconvenience of many of the stations along the route had not helped the railways' case. Thirdly, the committee viewed with disfavour:

> ". . . the defeatist attitude adopted by the (British Transport) Commission in dealing with branch line problems and, whilst we are informed that difficulties are being experienced with automatic signalling arrangements in respect of lightweight railbuses over the main lines at the Bristol and Frome ends of the journey, it was unanimously considered that a period of experimental dieselisation should have been tried on this Branch before submission of the proposal."

In addition:

> "The members (of the SWTUCC) are also strongly of the opinion that the principle of divorcing revenue for parcels, livestock and GPO conveyed by passenger train at the appropriate rates from purely passenger revenue is not in accord with the 1952 agreement."

It also made a farce of the railways' own statement of costs!

In June 1959, the matter was highlighted yet again at a meeting of the Central Transport Consultative Committee held in Glasgow when that body drew attention to the Western Region's very poorly framed and evidenced withdrawal proposal for the Bristol, Radstock (West) and Frome service. Nevertheless, in spite of all the economic, social and administrative arguments and mistakes, the removal of the North Somerset's passenger services was sanctioned, the agreed date being given as 2nd November 1959.

On the evening of Saturday, 31st October 1959 the last passenger train passed over the Bristol-Radstock (West)-Frome branch. It left Frome punctually at 9.25pm. Throughout the Saturday the trains on the branch had been pretty busy. Indeed, on the Saturday afternoon, 160 members and friends of the Bristol & District RCTS joined the 2.35pm from Temple Meads for the run across to Frome. The service was formed with three corridor coaches and a two-coach "B" set headed by 2-6-2T No. 5532 of Frome shed.

The group's return was made on the 5.55pm "Boat Express", again with the same engine and stock. Not only was this the last boat train on the North Somerset but it was also the last occasion that through Weymouth-Paddington coaches were being run. From this time on, passengers from the Channel Islands to Bristol and beyond would have to make their own way from Weymouth Quay to Weymouth Town station. Here they would have to catch the 4.15pm train as far as Westbury,

COAL OFF THE COALFIELD
In June 1959, 2-6-2T No. 4102 shuffles a coal train of uniformly-shaped wooden-bodied wagons through Brislington. The locomotive is in green livery.

M.B. Warburton

BLAST AND CHIMNEY BARK AT BRISLINGTON
A rather grimy "B" set is taken away from Brislington station by a 4500 class 2-6-2T. This autumnal scene was captured on film on 5th October 1954.
M.B. Warburton

changing there for Bristol and travelling via Trowbridge and Bath.

Still headed by No. 5532 and its same five coaches, the very last train from Bristol to Frome (via Radstock) left Temple Meads at 7.45pm. Apart from the RCTS group relatively few passengers were making the trip in this direction. Noticeably, Clutton gave this train a good send-off with some 60 detonators laid on its tracks. At Frome, the final passenger train to Bristol pulled out spot on time at 9.25pm hauled by 2-6-2T No. 41203 and piloted by pannier tank No. 9612. In true GWR fashion, the pannier was attached inside the train engine. The train's drivers were Mr R. Tonkin and Mr C. Webb, while firemen Mr E. Rogers and Mr K. Shearn kept the fires strong. The guard was Mr H.C. Barnes.

The 9.25's five coaches were packed and there was a large crowd at Frome station to see it off. It pulled out to shouting, singing and cheering; to the explosion of detonators and the throwing of fireworks. It was a particularly nostalgic occasion for Mr George Coleman, one of the Frome signalmen, for it was the last train that he signalled out before officially retiring at 10.00pm that evening. He had worked for just over 50 years as a signalman with the GWR and BR. He had served first at Bristol, then in South Wales and, finally, for 25 years at Frome.

At Mells, the pannier came off the train, leaving No. 41203 to finish the sad journey to Bristol. There were small clusters of people at most stations but again it was left to Clutton to provide the noisiest departure. It was reckoned that over 100 detonators were let off at this once busy colliery and railway village. With its arrival in Bristol late that Saturday evening, the 9.25pm from Frome, via Radstock, marked the disappearance of yet another West Country railway's passenger service.

The 1960s and Station Closures on the Bristol-Radstock (West)-Frome Line

Brislington Station
The station at Brislington was closed to passengers on 2nd November 1959. It remained open to goods traffic, essentially coal and scrap, until 7th October 1963 when it closed entirely.

Whitchurch Halt
This halt closed to all traffic on 2nd November 1959.

Pensford Station
The station here lost its passenger service on 2nd November 1959, goods traffic lasting until 15th June 1964 when Pensford closed altogether.

Hallatrow Station
The passenger service here was removed on 2nd November 1959. However, freight survived at this once busy junction until 15th June 1964.

Farrington Gurney Halt
This halt closed in its entirety on 2nd November 1959.

Midsomer Norton & Welton Station
Once the passenger service had been removed in 1959 the station remained in use for freight until 15th June 1964.

Radstock West
Busy with freight after November 1959, especially coal and wagon repairs, the station itself was eventually closed on 29th November 1965, the coal depot having closed some six months earlier on 17th May. The neighbouring collieries at Kilmersdon and, after 1966, Writhlington, continued to be served by the former Bristol & North Somerset Railway until the closure of the two pits in the 1970s.

Mells Road
Once passengers were no longer on the scene at Mells, the station remained in use for stone and tar traffic. Its final closure took place on 15th June 1964.

STONE TRUCKS OFF THE ROAD AT FROME (1)
This photograph shows the result of a partial breakaway of a train that was heading up Frome Mineral Loop on 8th July 1959.

John Keeping

STONE TRUCKS OFF THE ROAD AT FROME (2)
A GWR Mogul No. 6309 comes to the rescue of the trucks shown in the above derailment. In spite of the mess the train service between Bristol, Radstock (GW) and Frome continued to run. This photograph was taken on 17th July 1959.

John Keeping

10
Days of Decline, Closure and Growth Again

CLIMBING TO CHELWOOD BRIDGE
"Hymek" No. D7039 climbs towards Chelwood Bridge between Pensford and Clutton with the 11.30am Portishead to Radstock coal empties on 28th May 1968. In the author's view this is one of the most striking and attractive pictures in the entire book – an absolute gem for the railway modeller!

Ivo Peters

Once the Radstock and Bristol line had lost its passenger service, the west curve at Frome, which ran from the North Somerset branch into the station itself, was removed. This took place some four years after the last passenger train had steamed out in 1959. In 1970 major track and signalling changes took place in the Frome area, one of the most significant being the singling of the line through the station from Frome (North) signal box to the southern junction of the Frome avoiding line at Blatchbridge. The removal of the 'down' line naturally meant that only the 'up' line and platform remained in use. At the same time, most of the station's goods sidings and the lines into the nearby engine shed were taken out of use. Frome (South) signal box was closed, leaving only the box at Frome North in working condition. As we shall see, there would be further major changes in the mid-1980s when multiple aspect signalling controlled from Westbury Power Box was brought into use, but we shall say more about those developments later in our story.

In the bitter January of the very bad winter of 1963, a 2-6-0 of the 63XX type, under the control of driver Mr Ronald Ayres, ventured along the North Somerset branch to Mells Road, to free a breakdown train which had become stuck there in deep snow. The one coach train carried some forty permanent way staff to dig the trapped train out. However, by the time the would-be rescuers had reached Radstock, the breakdown train had been freed from the snow, and so no further assistance was required! In the depths of winter and before the introduction of diesels on North Somerset freight, generally speaking, locomen preferred the comfort provided by former GWR tank locomotives. For example, conditions were often so chill on the former ROD 2-8-0s that when these engines worked the branch tender first from East Depot, drivers would often rig up additional sheets across the back of the cab to protect them from the vicious cold of Mendip!

On 28th April 1964 the D7XXX ("Hymek") class diesel-hydraulic locomotive was first tested on the Bristol-Radstock line. The locomotive chosen went down on the 8.20am East Depot-Radstock coal empties, testing all the various station and colliery sidings on its way to Radstock. It returned on the 12.00 noon working from Radstock to East Depot with three empty Vanfits and 21 loaded 16 ton mineral wagons. The locomotive had no trouble handling this load and soon after this the "Hymeks" became regular, reliable and generally trouble-free workhorses over the North Somerset.

On 6th March 1966 the new link between the S&D and the Great Western line at Radstock was installed. The S&D track itself was severed, slewed as required and then tied into the new single line connection. From the morning of the 6th the level crossing-gate gear was disconnected in the centre of Radstock, all traffic on the days of 5th and 6th March being hand-signalled through Radstock. Although the branch was freight-only in the 1960s, it is important to realise that it was still carrying large quantities of coal. For example, in 1967 13,000 wagons of coal were being worked in circuit between Radstock and Portishead, via Pensford.

THE FROME GRAMMAR SCHOOL SPECIAL SHUNTS MIDSOMER NORTON & WELTON STATION
With the guards van remaining on the main running road, the rest of the train is shunted into the loop at Midsomer Norton & Welton station. The smell of smoke and steam is strong in this November 1967 picture of the once-familiar, pick-up goods. *John Keeping*

PASSENGERS NO MORE AT HALLATROW
The sign says "Passengers are requested to cross the line by the bridge" but by the time this photograph was taken passengers were a very rare sight indeed at Hallatrow station. Here, on 31st March 1964, a goods-only Hallatrow sees 6100 class 2-6-2T No. 6148 hauling a coal train from Old Mills Colliery north towards Bristol. *Ivo Peters*

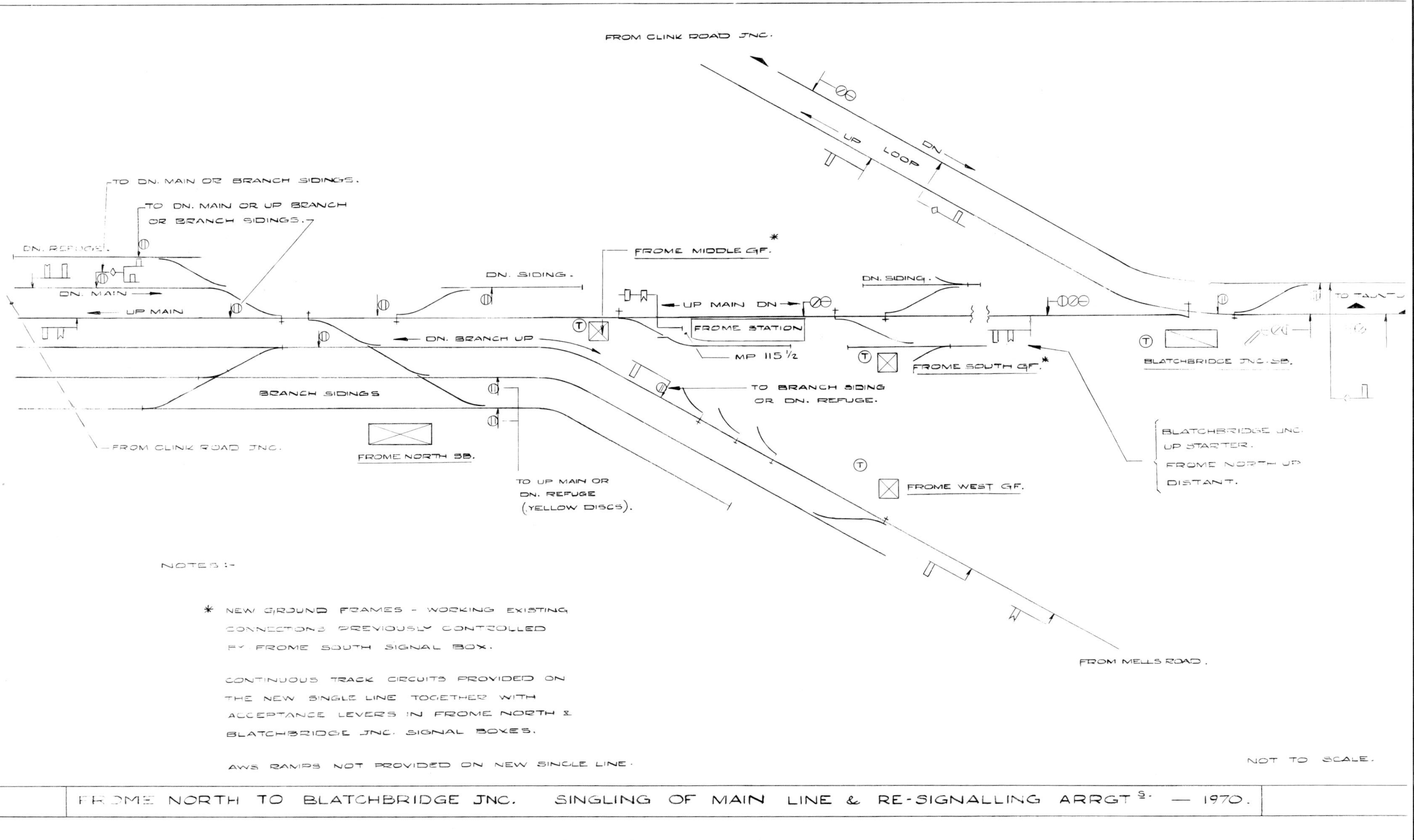

FROME NORTH RESIGNALLING 1970

Original plan: British Rail (Western). Redrawn by John Durnford

ENGINEER'S INSPECTION ON THE NORTH SOMERSET
With an unidentified member of the "Hymek" class of diesels doing the work, an engineer's special winds its way uphill towards Clutton on 22nd March 1968. Bearing in mind the fact that the line had lost its passenger services some nine years before, the permanent way looks in pretty tidy condition as the engineers do their work. *P.J. Williams*

COAL THROUGH CLUTTON
With a really good head of steam blowing against a windy, spring sky, pannier tank No. 7782 climbs past Clutton's fixed distant and heads the 5.00pm train from Radstock towards Bristol on 23rd April 1964. *Ivo Peters*

However, it was not only goods trains using the line, for on Saturday, 6th April 1968 an RCTS railtour on a Paddington - Swindon - Melksham - Frome - Radstock (GW) - Bristol - Portishead - St Philip's Marsh - Filton Junction - Paddington itinerary visited the North Somerset. On 29th June, yet another railtour visited the branch. Originally planned for September 1968, "The North Somerset Farewell Railtour" had been brought forward to 29th June for, with closure imminent, this was the last date on which through running was to be possible over the North Somerset. Although this railtour ran to a more locally-based itinerary, it was no less interesting for that. It started at Bristol (Temple Meads) and visited Avonmouth, Severn Beach, Pilning, Yate, Bath (Green Park), St Philip's Marsh and Portishead before traversing the Bristol & North Somerset itself to Radstock and Writhlington Colliery. The train then returned to Bristol via Frome, Chippenham and Bath.

On 15th August 1966 the Radstock-Mells Road section was closed to all traffic but fortunately, as future events will show, the track was allowed to remain in place. BR had already taken the decision to close the Bristol-Radstock section of the North Somerset and to re-route all goods traffic through Mells Road and Frome, the closure date for these arrangements having been set for 30th June 1968. However, before closure could take place, a certain amount of S&T work was necessary in order to re-connect Radstock with Frome. In the event, this work was not complete by the time closure had been planned and so the latter was put back two weeks.

On the evening of 10th July exceptionally bad weather in the shape of a torrential thunderstorm struck the North Somerset area only four days before the revised closure date. Although this bad weather did cause washouts on both the Bristol and Frome sides of Radstock, with the 9.00pm freight from that town just getting through before the route was severed, it would appear that this was not really the cause of closure, although various sources have given it as so. However, as a result of the atrocious weather Radstock was totally cut off from the rest of the BR system for several days. No attempt was made to repair the Bristol-Radstock line and, once various other repairs had been completed, all goods traffic from Radstock went out via Frome. One interesting snippet of information in all this is that figures from BR suggest that the cost of repairs to the very serious slip that occurred at Pensford would have been in the region of some £40,000. After the Bristol-Radstock section had been severed, a token instrument was installed at Mells and trains into Radstock were then worked on a "one engine in steam" basis.

Incidentally, in late April 1968 the bridge at Thicketmead came in for yet another battering when a lorry carrying a container ran into it, a crane being needed to put the container back on the lorry. The bridge suffered as well in that it was moved some three inches out of position. Interestingly, the local newspapers revealed the following facts about the railway's future:

> "The line is only used for freight and is to be closed within the next few months. Trains, therefore, have been allowed to continue using the bridge, though under a 5mph speed restriction."

Quite clearly the railways had already planned the line's total

COASTING DOWN TO CHELWOOD
The rain clouds and the autumn draw in on this view taken on 26th September 1963. 6100 class 2-6-2T No. 6148 coasts down the grade towards Chelwood Bridge and Pensford with the 5.00pm coal train from Radstock.

Ivo Peters

THE LINK IS MADE AT LAST (1)
0-6-0 diesel-electric shunter No. D3185 puts a rake of coal wagons across the new connecting link at Radstock. The wagons are heading towards the photographer, onto the North Somerset branch which runs from left to right in the foreground of the picture. *Hugh Ballantyne*

THE LINK IS MADE AT LAST (2)
With the new connecting line between the Bristol & North Somerset Railway and the S&D prominent in the foreground No. 33049 propels stock owned by The Somerset & Dorset Railway Museum Trust across that connecting line. The stock was being moved from the Trust's former museum site at Radstock, via the North Somerset, to the West Somerset Railway. The photograph was taken on 16th October 1975. *Mike Miller*

'WESTERNS' ON THE PORTISHEAD COAL
'Western' class locomotive No. D1040 *Western Queen* approaches Mells Road station with a string of coal empties from the power station at Portishead on 25th April 1969. *Ivo Peters*

"HYMEKS" ON THE RADSTOCK TRIP
After shunting some oil tanks onto the former quarry siding, "Hymek" No. D7064 leaves Mells Road for Radstock. With coal sacks and coal trucks in abundance, the wagons rumble past the photographer on 15th April 1970. *G.F. Gillham*

WHATLEY QUARRY TRAFFIC IN STEAM DAYS
Pannier tank No. 4673 runs out from Frome with a load of empty wagons bound for the quarry at Whatley. This short, steam-hauled pick-up freight makes a strong contrast with today's diesel-hauled air-braked stone trains.
Ivo Peters

KILMERSDON COAL TRAFFIC IN DIESEL DAYS
On 15th April 1970 "Hymek" No. D7064 passes Somerset Quarry Siding (and the branch to Whatley Quarry) with a Radstock-Portishead coal train.
G.F. Gillham

closure. The bad weather of June 1968 was just a convenient and helpful excuse!

On the former Somerset & Dorset line at this time, demolition had only reached as far as Midsomer Norton, at which point the lifting contract was terminated. The final 'demolition train' ran on 12th July 1968 when Radstock's resident Class 08 diesel shunter, with no other work to do in the isolated Radstock Yard, ran up to Midsomer Norton to fetch the last of the wagons that had been loaded by the contractors. The final section of the S&D from Midsomer Norton over the B&NSR and back to the (in)famous level crossing gates at Radstock was finally dismantled. It is thought that this event took place in the spring of 1969.

In August 1969 the former station at Midsomer Norton & Welton, so often the scene of happy memories for local people in the district, was demolished. Indeed, some locals were so concerned about this that when they saw flames shooting from the former booking office and waiting room at the station, they called in the emergency services and, very soon, firemen from Paulton and Radstock arrived on the scene. Strange as it may seem, however, the firemen allowed the flames to continue for the fire was part of the demolition work then being carried out on the site by Bristol contractors, S.J. Wring Limited. With the timbers still burning, giant bulldozers quickly reduced the building to a heap of rubble and yet another reminder of the line had disappeared for ever. In the following May, the old station overbridge at Clutton, so long a feature of the village, was also removed. Unlike its construction, the line's destruction and removal from the face of the earth seemed to be taking place at great speed.

Even though passenger trains had disappeared from the North Somerset in 1959, substantial loads of coal from Radstock were still handled during the 1960s and up until 1973 when the last coal train ran. Steam locomotives remained in charge until the mid-1960s when the diesels took over. Around 1967, the turntable at Radstock (West) was removed, diesels being in sole charge, these new motive power units having no need of this particular piece of equipment. At that time, coal to the power station at Portishead was being carried in BR Standard 16 ton wagons, although during the early 1970s, coal was taken on a merry-go-round (mgr) basis to Didcot Power Station. These trains were formed of modern HAA stock, loadings being 34 wagons for a 'Western' class diesel-hydraulic and 36 for a Brush Class 47. Locomotives from the 'Warship' class were also used but these proved to be poor hauliers, being restricted to some 30, 16 ton wagons. Their use on the branch was fairly restricted because of this, unlike that of the "Hymeks" which were very regular visitors to the Radstock area until their eventual demise.

In order to shunt and trip work the coal traffic, an 08 class diesel shunter was stationed at Radstock. At any one time, this would take five mgr wagons across the new chord line. When first used on these duties, the locomotive was changed once a week, but eventually one was more permanently stationed there, the changeover then occurring every six weeks, with the 08 going back to Westbury depot during Saturday afternoon. The shunter resided in the old S&D loco shed and was filled with fuel from a BP road tanker, the locomotive being parked at a convenient place for this to happen. The diesel would handle some four trains of coal a day, although Saturdays could be better for business, when up to six could be dealt with.

What could have been a frightening disaster took place on 7th January 1971 when 24 coal wagons ran out of control through the middle of Radstock, crashing into the North Somerset's level crossing gates in the centre of the town. Fortunately, no-one was injured although a very serious situation could have occurred had the accident taken place later in the day when the roads in the area would have been busier. It seems that a 32 wagon train had been brought in from Westbury and that eight wagons had been taken out of the train for repair at Marcroft's. When the shunter, Mr Stan Tote, arrived to move the remaining wagons they had gone! The next thing he knew was that the local newsagent Mr Malcolm Moon, had arrived on the scene to say that the wagons had crashed into the crossing gates!

The last coal from Writhlington Colliery left Radstock on 16th November 1973. The pit had ceased mining operations at the end of September, but since that time work had been going on at the colliery stacking coal on the surface. Shortly before midday on the 16th the last wagonload left the colliery. Ken Evans informed the author that it had been a very sad day for him. It really was "the end of an era . . . Our relationship with the NCB had always been good". Many motorists in the area, however, must have breathed a sigh of relief, for while the coal trains had been working over the new 1966 spur the delays to road traffic had continued to occur. Nowadays, the new road layout at the spot continues to hinder motorists in their travels!

Motorists were delayed yet again, this time by an unusual load, when on 16th October 1975 a Class 33 diesel-electric, No 33049, was diagrammed to take the Somerset & Dorset Trust's locomotive, 2-8-0 No. 53808, and other stock from the S&D loco shed to the North Somerset and then down to Washford on the West Somerset Railway. Some two years later more unusual workings ran in the form of trains of spoil waste from Kilmersdon tip. These ran, on a trial basis, during the spring of 1977. It seems, however, that the exercise was not a success for no further spoil trains were run after the trial period.

The early 1970s heralded good news on the freight side for a short portion of the northern section of the North Somerset. In 1913 a paperboard mill had been opened at St Anne's in Brislington. This mill was supplied with woodpulp via the City Docks in Bristol and, from here, it was taken by boat through The Feeder to the mill's site where it was off-loaded into large storage sheds. Although this process did involve transhipping the woodpulp from ocean-going ships into lighters for the latter part of their journey, right up until the 1960s this practice was regarded as the most efficient and economical way of doing things. However, with the closure of the City Docks about to take place, the mill's owners decided that it needed to find a new storage site, adjacent to a quay, to which woodpulp could be discharged directly. The mill's requirements could then be met direct from store.

The company decided that Portishead Dock was the ideal location for such a storage site and so an area of nearly five acres was leased to the St Anne's Board Mill Company to be used for their new woodpulp terminal. From here the woodpulp was loaded directly into specially-built rail wagons to form block trains to Marsh Ponds. This latter site on the North Somerset had formerly been the location for a set of carriage sidings, added during the First World War, and was conveniently close to the board mill at St Anne's. Beginning in 1971, the traffic finished in 1977. To get some idea of how much woodpulp was moved from Portishead to Marsh Ponds, suffice it to say that in one year alone the traffic amounted to some 55,000 tons. At the start of the trade there was a fleet of 52 wagons to handle the bales of woodpulp, this number increasing to 57 by the end of the contract.

In November 1986 a scheme for a privately funded light rail network for Bristol costing £385 million was unveiled by Bristol's former MEP, Richard Cottrell. His company, Advanced Transport for Avon Limited (ATA), had been set up to promote the scheme, which itself was a development of another proposal previously advanced by Mr Cottrell in late 1979. This earlier plan foundered when local authorities in the area absolutely refused to fund it. Without any doubt, the 1986 project is the hardest and most concrete proposition to date.

ATA's plan is to construct a privately-financed, rail-based passenger transit system to serve the developing County of Avon and to relieve increasingly bad traffic congestion within Bristol and Bath. If, and once, full parliamentary permission is given to the *total* project, the system would be built to link Bristol's city centre with Portishead, Bath, Weston-super-Mare, Yate/Sodbury and other growing areas within the county. Over 100 miles of track, much of it already in existence, would be used. Indeed, according to initial plans at least, part of the former North Somerset's alignment could possibly be incorporated into the new rapid transit.

ATA have met local BR management to discuss the matter and they, along with senior British Rail management in the South West, have indicated an acceptance that the service is definitely needed. However, they are somewhat sceptical about

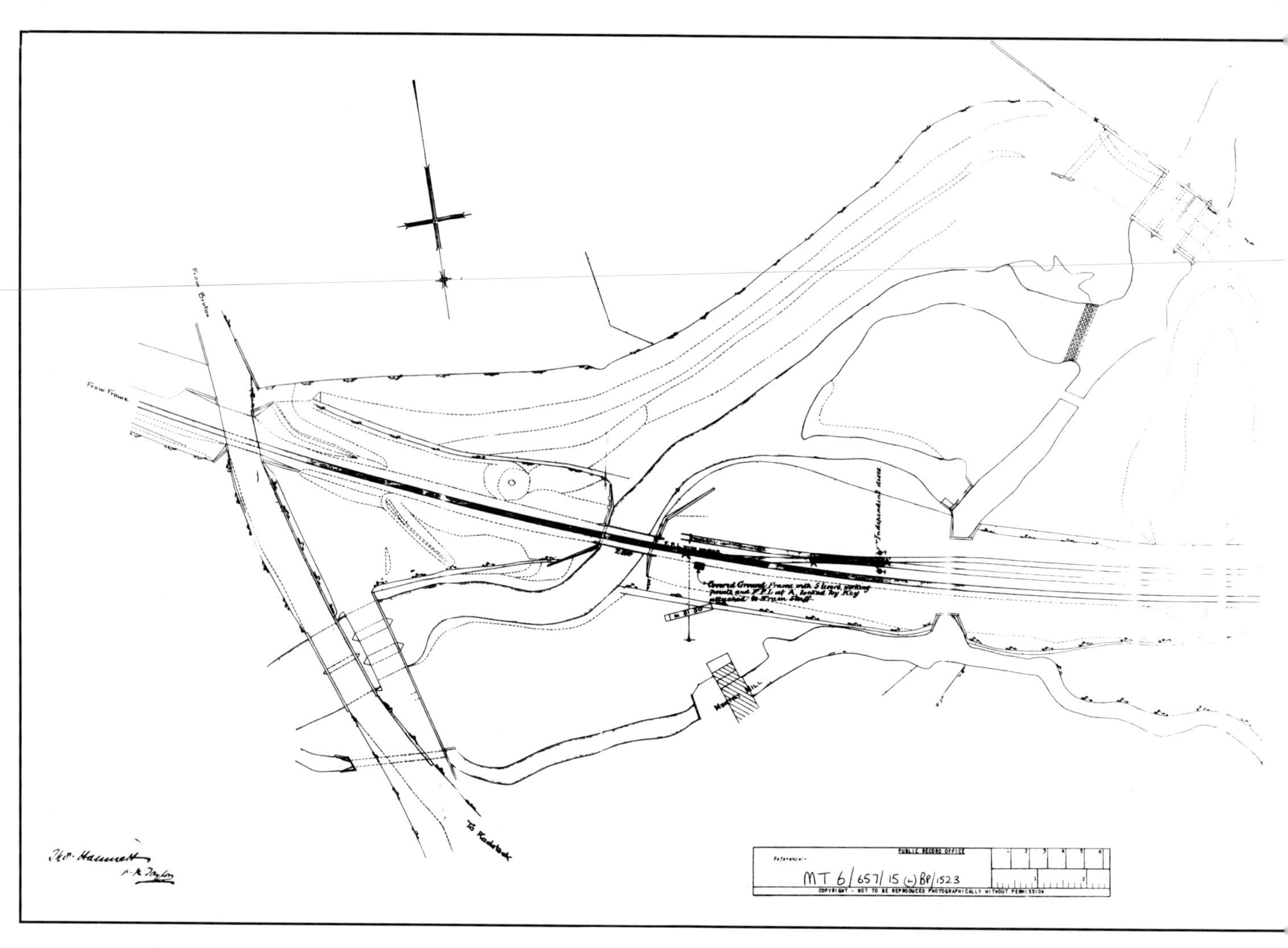

SOMERSET STONE QUARRIES' SIDINGS 1893/4

Original plan: Public Record Office

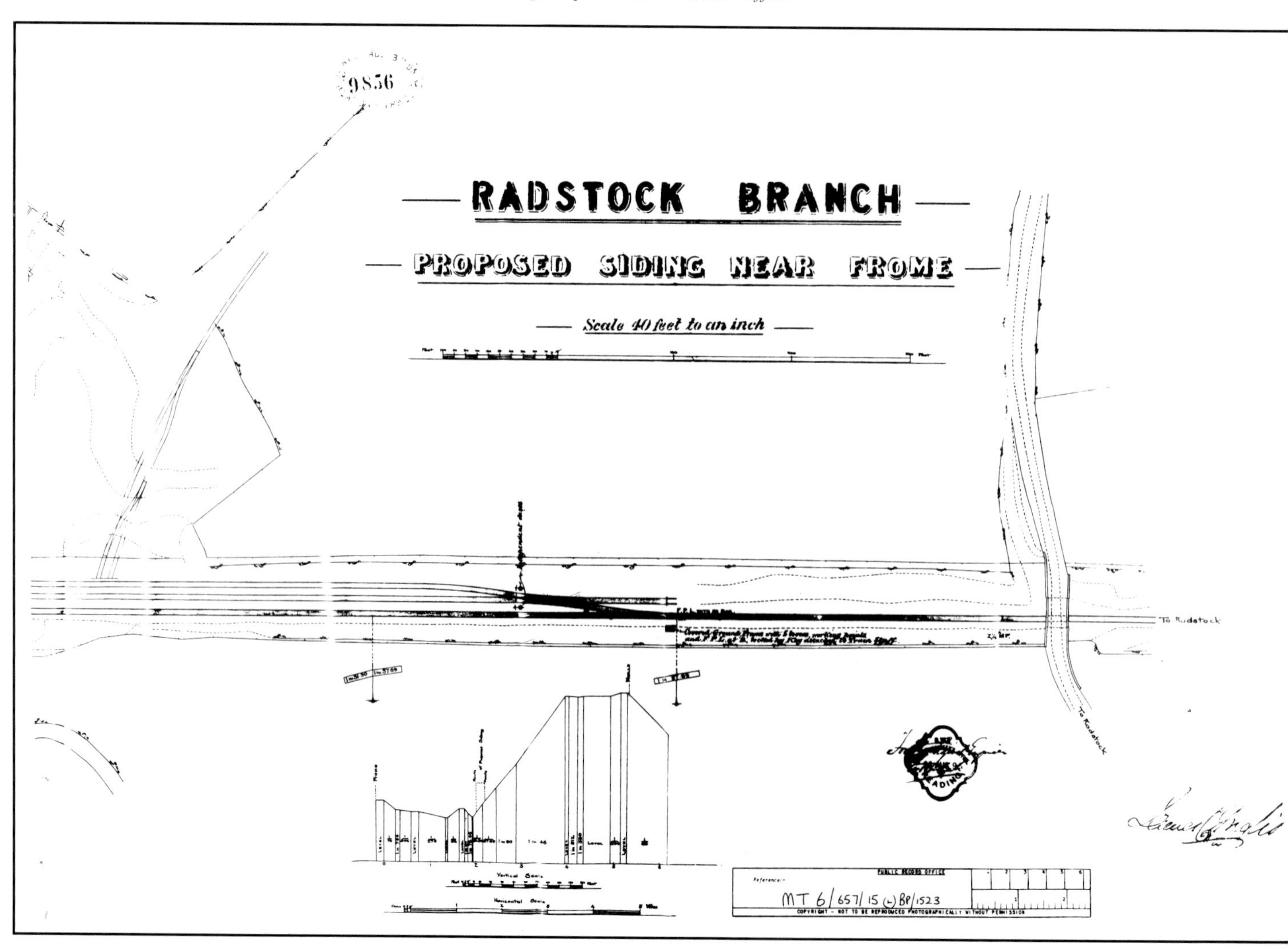

the ATA's ability to raise the cash needed. They have also indicated that there could be no question of ATA using British Rail's main line trackage on the routes from Bristol to Bath and Weston-super-Mare. A spokesman for Avon County Council said that the scheme would be of "considerable benefit" so long as it was completed in one unbroken programme. In common with other interested parties, the county fears what could happen if the system was started and not finished. It is also concerned about the impact of extended construction work in the city's centre. Because of these factors it would seem that the question of funding the system will have to be fully settled before work can start.

Who knows, it may be that at least some parts of the Bristol & North Somerset Railway's alignment could be carrying light rapid transit trains into the 21st century!

One regular, real and long-standing source of traffic for the Radstock-Mells Road-Frome stretch of railway has been stone. Much of this was from the quarry at Vobster near Mells, the quarry being linked to the GWR by the privately-owned Newbury Railway which ran south for two miles from Mells Road station. Opened as a broad gauge line in 1857, the Newbury Railway was first worked by horses. Maintenance costs of the railway were shared by its users and, later in the line's history, each had its own locomotives. This remarkable railway lasted into the 1960s and a more detailed history of it can be found in the next chapter.

At the present time, steadily growing quantities of stone traffic for the remaining single track Hapsford Junction-Frome section are being generated by the quarry at Whatley. Worked by ARC, this quarry is linked to the former Wilts, Somerset & Weymouth's Radstock branch by its own private railway. Whatley is 4 miles 15 chains from Frome North Junction and generates such significant traffic for Railfreight's Construction Sub-Sector that its development warrants looking at in more detail.

It would appear that today's major workings at Whatley had their very small beginnings in the 1890s when an agreement of 26th October 1893 was entered into between the GWR and James Dovell Armstrong, of Vallis Farm, Frome, and Jonathon Drew Knight of Innox Hill House, Frome. These two men traded under the name of the Somerset Stone Quarry Company and it was they who wanted to get their stone out of the district by rail. The above-mentioned 1893 agreement had been entered into:

". . . in respect of certain Junctions, Sidings and Works which have been constructed for the convenience of the traffic from the works of the tenants known as the Somerset Stone Quarries, Murtry, Frome . . ."

In the following year, on 13th February 1894, another agreement was signed by which the GWR laid in two running loops from the Radstock-Frome line (see accompanying plan) along with the associated point and signalling work, the estimated cost of which was £79. The company agreed to pay the GWR the rate of 6d ($2\frac{1}{2}$p) over and above the then current rates for every truck worked over the new connections onto the GWR. In addition, a minimum sum of 2s 6d ($12\frac{1}{2}$p) had to be paid for each trip working made!

On 8th May 1894, an Inspecting Officer from the Board of Trade produced the following report on the new works:

"Sir,

I have the honour to report for the information of the Board of Trade, that in compliance with your Minute of the 17th ult. I have inspected the new loop and siding connections for the Somersetshire Stone Quarries on the Radstock Branch of the GWR near Frome.

The connections are worked from two 5-lever frames locked by the Train Staff with which this single line is worked. I can recommend that the use of the new connections may be sanctioned."

In an article in the June 1898 edition of "The Quarry" journal there is an extensive article on the Vallis Vale limestone quarries which gives a good picture of the workings at that time.

The article states:

". . . that there is some singularly picturesque countryside in and around the Mendip Hills, in Somersetshire, especially so in the case of the romantic vale where these quarries are situated. They are about a mile to the west of Frome and, unlike many works, do not detract from the beauty around, but afford a pleasant break in the steep wooded slopes. The Vallis stream flows through the vale to join the River Frome, about half a mile below the works.

The neighbourhood has a classic interest to geologists as being the scene of the labours of some of our most distinguished geologists, from the time of the Father of Geology – William Smith – to the more recent investigations of Charles Moore, Sanders, Greenwell, McMurtrie and others.

The quarries have been worked for the last four years by a company, of which Mr J.D. Armstrong is manager, and under whose vigorous management an extensive trade has been secured in Somerset and the neighbouring counties. The works give employment to about 40 men.

There are four faces working at present. The stone is easily quarried, and can be produced remarkably clean. The chief difficulty in working is due to the stone dipping inwards, which necessitates driving ahead, and then working the stone outwards. But this difficulty only presents itself on the west side of the valley. The overburden, consisting of Inferior Oolite and a somewhat loose conglomerate, about 5 to 8 feet thick, is easily removed.

The stone is blasted with gelignite (from Nobel's of Glasgow) or gunpowder (from Curtiss & Harvey), according to circumstances. The greater part of the stone being used for road metal, there is not the necessity for producing large blocks. The present yield of the quarries is about 100 tons per day, about 90 per cent of which is broken for road metalling, and the remainder is burnt in two ordinary kilns, producing lime for agriculture, water softening and sewage purposes.

The limestone is conveyed from the working faces in narrow gauge wagons, technically known as "tubs". The tubs are drawn about half-a-mile by horses to the foot of a short incline at Hapsford Mill, where the horses are detached, and return to the quarries with the empty tubs standing alongside. A wire rope is attached to the full tubs, which are wound up to a higher level, ready for removal to the automatic tips. The full tub, on arrival at the tips is turned over, and the contents emptied into a hopper communicating with the stone breakers.

The stone breaking plant consists of two Baxter's knapping motion machines, one 20 inch by 12 inch, and another 18 inch by 9 inch, producing stone up to 3 inch cube. The power to work the stone breakers and winding drum is taken from an old breast-wheel, of nine horsepower and a ten horsepower turbine, by Gilkes & Co. of Kendal. A 10 horsepower portable steam engine (built by Brown & May of Devizes) is used when the quantity of water in the river is insufficient for power purposes. The stone, after passing through the screens, falls direct into the (stone) company's own trucks, or those of the Great Western Railway Company.

The (stone) company have a private branch line, about a quarter of a mile long, connecting the works with the Radstock Branch of the GWR."

The tramways mentioned were laid to a gauge of 2ft 3in the tubs being hauled initially by horse, as indicated in the above extract. However, in 1907, steam motive power was brought into use on the tramway when an outside cylindered 0-4-0ST named *Midge*, built by the firm of Kerr Stuart (builder's No. 1017) came to work for the Somerset Quarry Company. This locomotive must have been a success for, in 1910, a similar engine, named *Wren* (builder's No. 1188) was also purchased, new, from the same manufacturer. In the 1930s, this narrow gauge system and its stock were taken over by the then newly-formed firm of Roads Reconstruction (1934) Limited, although exact details of the fate of SQC's locomotives and rolling stock still remain shrouded in mystery.

Once taken over, the Somerset Quarry Company Limited had its quarries and tramway incorporated into the New Frome Quarry Company's system, this firm itself having been one of the merger partners forming Roads Reconstruction (1934) Limited. The quarry workings were then served by a 2ft gauge tramway. In 1940 a stone processing plant was installed at Hapsford, while a new quarry was opened up at Whatley itself. A line, some two and a half miles long, linked the quarry at Whatley with Hapsford Plant. Running along the valley bottom, this railway closely followed the twisting Mells River. However, this narrow gauge link was severely restricting and so the whole system from Hapsford to the quarry faces was converted to standard gauge during 1943, the former tramway being lifted in 1945.

In addition to the standard gauge locomotives used at Hapsford since the wartime conversion, three new engines arrived there during 1947 and 1948 (for full details of these and of other industrial and contractors' locomotives used in this area, see Appendix II). Four-wheeled, vertical-boilered, chain-driven machines (builder's Nos 9374, 9386 and 9387) and built by the firm of Sentinel of Shrewsbury, they were painted in a rather pleasant shade of mid-green. They sported the circular "RR" motif.

In the mid-1950s, the primary crushing plant was transferred from the site at Hapsford to the quarry at Whatley. However, various processing facilities still remained at Hapsford Plant, as did the firm's lorry servicing depot. The line's locomotive sheds, of which there were two, were also to be found there. A small, single track locomotive shed was situated opposite the work's office. The other shed was situated on the Whatley side of the Hapsford Plant site. With the gradual drifting of facilities from the Hapsford to the quarry end of the private railway, it was inevitable that a stone processing plant would be built at Whatley. This was in use by 1965.

In the early 1960s diesel-hydraulic locomotives started to arrive on the railway, the first being delivered in 1963. Used until the mid-1980s, although painted in ARC yellow rather than their original dark green livery, they were delivered new, but with two of them being complete rebuilds from Sentinel geared steam locomotives. The company purchased four in total (numbered 1, 2 and 3, the fourth remaining unnumbered) from the firm of Thomas Hill (Rotherham) Limited (builder's numbers 133C, 136C, 152V and 200V). These locomotives have proved useful and long-lasting, locomotive No. 1 being fitted with a new engine in 1983.

During the 1960s, with new traction arriving on the quarry

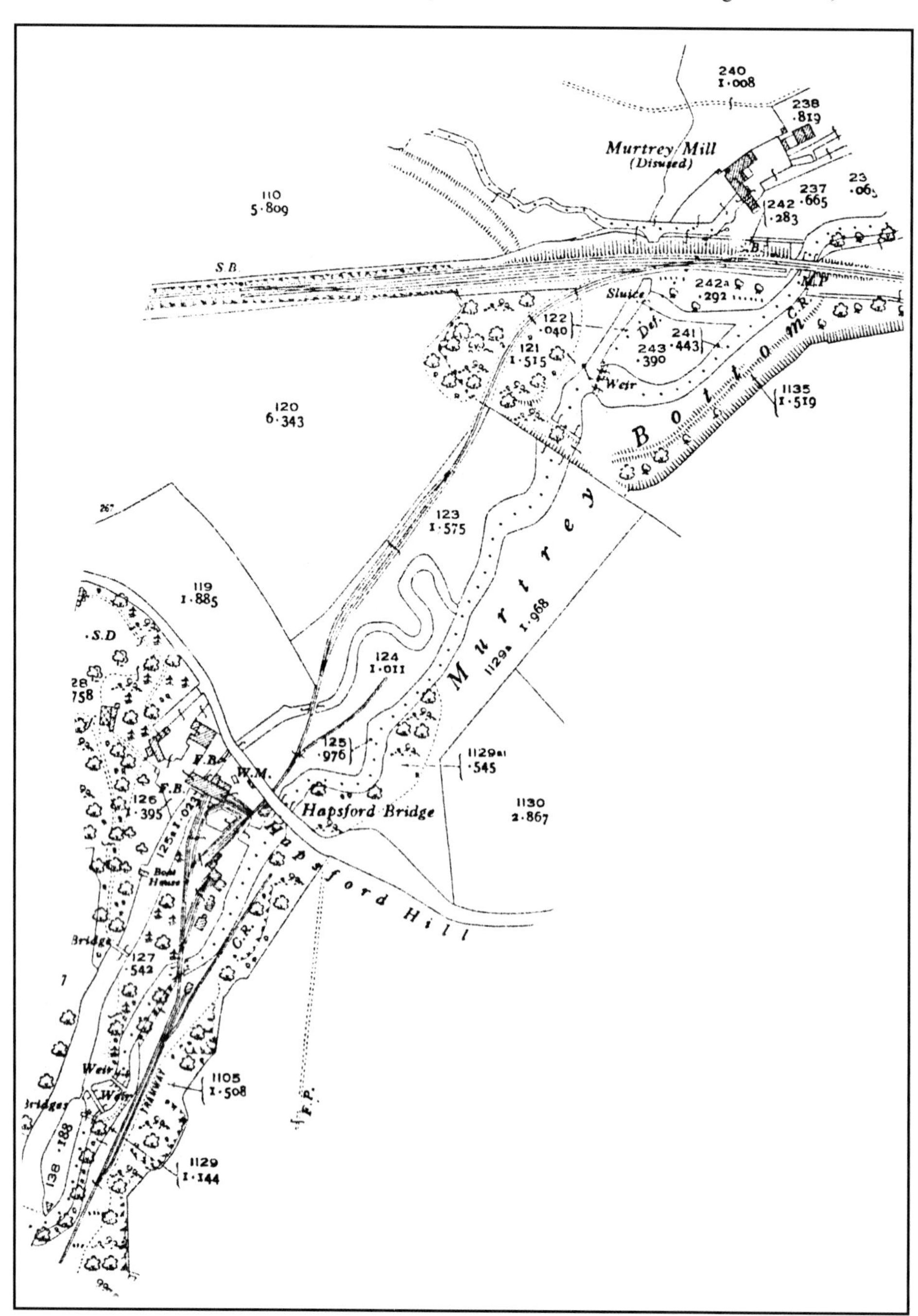

THE AREA AROUND HAPSFORD 1930

Original map: Ordnance Survey

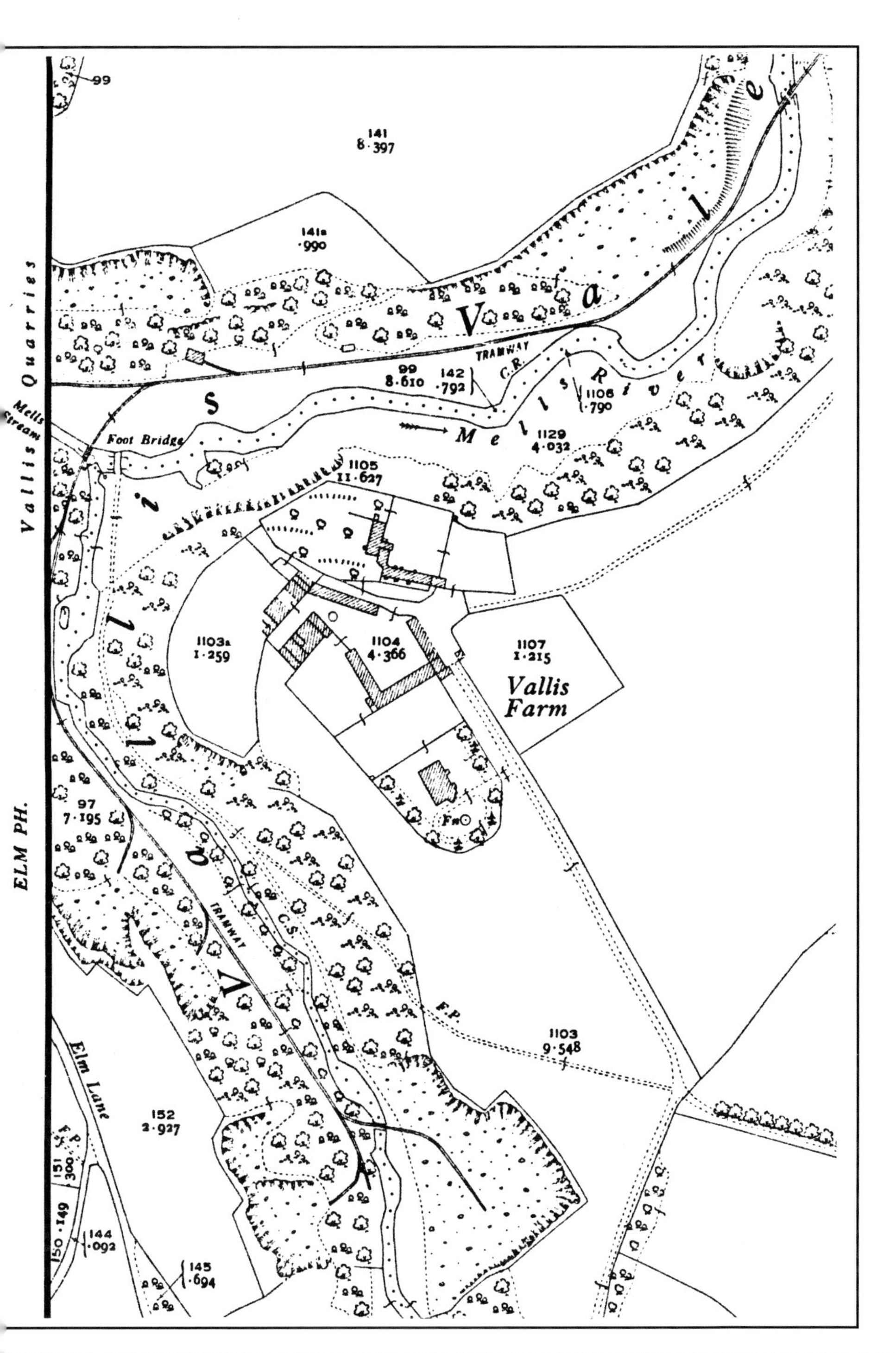

THE QUARRIES AROUND VALLIS 1930

Original map: Ordnance Survey

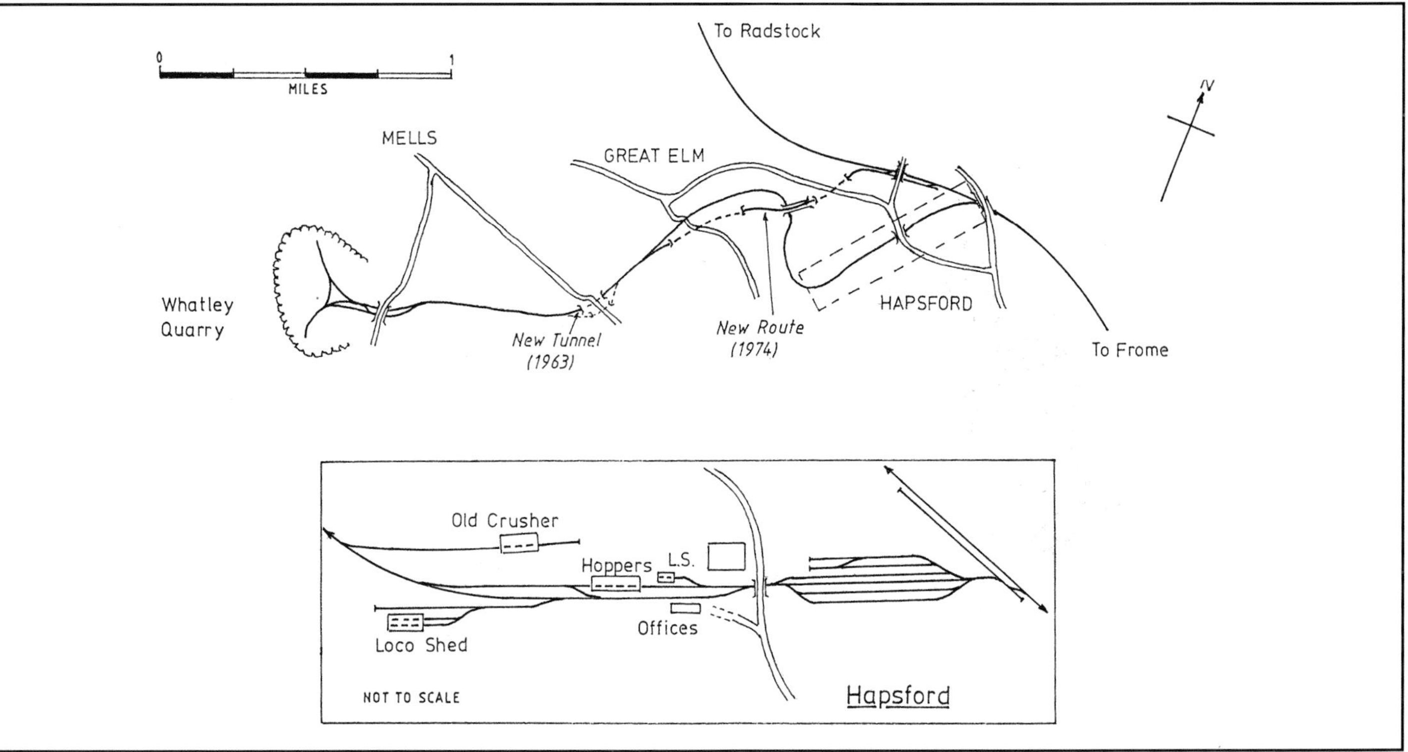

NEW FROME QUARRIES

Original plan: IRS
Redrawn: Chris Handley

company's railway, improvements also started to take place on the permanent way side. Traffic was on the increase and, in 1963, a new tunnel, alongside and replacing an already existing bore at Murder Combe, was excavated under the road leading to Mells. This allowed larger wagons to travel down the branch. Relaying and general upgrading of the right-of-way between Hapsford Depot and the quarry at Whatley continued apace, along with the provision of a large group of sidings between Hapsford Depot and the run round loops on the main Frome-Radstock section. All this work took place before the end of 1965.

In 1967 further improvements were carried out to the track between Hapsford and the quarry itself. Nonetheless, in spite of all the work that had been put in to improve the Whatley Quarry-Hapsford section, main line locomotives were still unable to run through from British Railways' metals to the site of the quarry itself: all that they could do was run as far as the exchange sidings at Hapsford.

However, in the early 1970s all of this was to change and, in 1973, a start was made on a new, 1,100 yard long deviation line. The new route left the Frome-Radstock main just to the north of the original exchange sidings. It entailed the construction of two new tunnels (one at Bedlam(!) and one at Great Elm) and a substantial overbridge at Great Elm where the

HAPSFORD YARD – CONTRAST IN MOTIVE POWER
Steam locomotive No. 1 (Sentinel 9374 of 1947) and a well-travelled and somewhat worn-looking member of the "Hymek" type sit alongside one another at Hapsford Yard. This photograph gives some idea of just how busy the yard could be and shows a good variety of BR wagon stock.

Ivo Peters

ALL CHANGE AT THE EXCHANGE
Following construction of the new alignment of the Whatley Quarry line at its junction end, Hapsford Yard was made redundant. This scene, dated October 1974, shows dismantling work well in hand at the former exchange roads.

Geoff Carter

much straighter new route was carried above the former, more sinuous route from the quarry. The new railway avoided the road level crossing at Great Elm Lake and construction was well started by October 1973. The whole enterprise opened for traffic on 9th September 1974. With the new alignment in use, the track from the junction of the old and new lines near Great Elm level crossing, through Hapsford Depot to the former exchange sidings with British Railways at Hapsford Yard, was taken out of use. It was then lifted, this work occurring late in 1974.

As part of the rebuilding of the Whatley Quarry line, the loop at Somerset Quarry Siding was lengthened considerably. With these changes in place, North ground frame was to be found at 2 miles 38 chains from Frome whilst Somerset Stone Quarries' South ground frame was located at 1 mile 78 chains. Around January 1974 the former North ground frame and the old loop arrangements were taken out of use. In the autumn of the same year, and with the opening of the new alignment, the new loop was brought into operation. It was, however, severely damaged in a derailment that occurred on Friday, 5th November 1976 when the last vehicle of a 41-wagon train, loaded and on its way to Theale came off the road. The

OBSTRUCTION ON THE QUARRY LINE!
All traffic came to a halt on the Whatley Quarry branch when this tree fell across the main running line near the quarry itself on 14th March 1975.

Mike Miller

SOMERSET QUARRY NORTH GROUND FRAME
This view shows the north end of Hapsford Loop looking towards Mells Road (right hand track) and Whatley Quarry (left hand, descending track). The view was taken from the brake van of a returning Radstock trip freight and shows that the points have already been re-set for the Whatley Quarry line. The loop at Hapsford was in use for roughly two years, this photograph being taken on 21st March 1975.

Mike Miller

accompanying photograph clearly shows the amount of damage caused!

Once the upgraded line was in operation, BR locomotives could work trains as far as the exchange sidings at the quarry itself. On the new alignment, a variety of diesel types were to be seen. These included 'Westerns', Class 33s (often in pairs), 45s, 46s, 47s and, in today's Railfreight era, Class 56s. From the exchange sidings ARC's own diesels would take empty wagons into the quarry area, bringing out full trains in return. Under these new arrangements, the Thomas Hill/Rolls-Royce diesels were restricted essentially to the exchange sidings and to the quarry area. In addition, a new locomotive shed was built near these exchange sidings.

As the mid-1980s rolled by, further major developments took place at Whatley. An indication of this new work was given in October 1986 when "Modern Railways" magazine reported that:

> "The Department of Transport has awarded the biggest-ever grant under Section 8 of the 1974 Railways Act to (the) Amey Roadstone Corporation. The grant, totalling £3.7 million, will be invested in its Whatley Quarry . . . and will secure rail transport of the quarry's stone, thereby avoiding a number of lorry movements in environmentally-sensitive areas."

In fact, over three years, total investment actually topped the £25 million mark. Under this new wave of modernisation, the road bridge over the entrance to the quarry, once large enough to take only a single track, was swept away, allowing a much more substantial bridge to be built. This has permitted two well-laid tracks to have a clear, straight run into the quarry itself. In the exchange sidings three new roads have been installed, one for reception (the middle road), one for running round a train (on the left as a train approaches Whatley Quarry from the Frome end) and a departure road (on the right). Under a British Rail working notice for the period of Saturday 7th February to Friday 13th February 1987, these new facilities were shown to be in working order. In these sidings, exchange with the ARC shunter normally takes place although, under this latest redevelopment, BR locomotives can also be given access to the quarry should this be necessary.

As part of this recent work, more trees have been cleared, the river at Whatley has been diverted yet again, and track has been further realigned and relaid. Continuously welded rail and strong manganese crossings are now the order of the day. Within the quarry, the shot rock is transported to a primary crusher by dumptrucks which carry some 85 tonnes of stone. "Modern Railways" for January 1988 reported that:

> ". . . Centrepiece of the new project is a British-built Hazemag primary impact crusher, where boulders up to three tonnes in weight are reduced to pieces no larger than a human hand by the 43 tonne impact motor. The machine is capable of a throughput of 2,500 tonnes per hour, the whole crushing and screening process being controlled by a single operator through a computerised central console.
>
> Empty wagons arriving at Whatley pass over a Dactron weighbridge for tare weighing, and a microprocessor-controlled system calculates and calls up the exact net weight of material for each wagon. A travelling rail loader supplied by Butterley Engineering is capable of loading any of four sidings, each with capacity for a 2,000 tonne train. With the potential use of trains up to 4,000 tonnes capacity, each equivalent to 200 heavy goods vehicles, the redevelopment will save a further 13 million lorry miles a year by the early 1990s."

Trains are shunted under the new travelling rail loader by a 750hp 'Steelman' 6-wheel diesel-hydraulic shunter built by Thomas Hill Limited and named *Pride of Whatley* (builder's No. 325V). One of the smaller Thomas Hill/Rolls-Royce diesel shunters (builder's No. 200V) also works at Whatley as required (but the other three are now stored out of use). These locomotives and the ARC wagon fleet are all maintained in a new wagon repair shop at Whatley Bottom.

On 29th October 1987, the redevelopment project at Whatley was officially opened by HRH The Princess Royal. The enlarged rail layout now enables most trains to be run to the quarry directly, thus eliminating the need to marshal trains at Westbury prior to working to their destinations. However, trains are still tripped to Westbury soon after loading to clear the sidings at Whatley even if this results in a long layover in Westbury yard. On BR metals the Class 56s generally used on these workings nowadays are being repainted in two tone grey with Railfreight Construction Sub-Sector symbols. The first to be dealt with was No. 56001, which was specially prepared so that it could be named *Whatley* by HRH The Princess Royal at the redevelopment's official opening in October 1987. The Westbury White Horse has been adopted as Westbury loco depot's symbol and this is being displayed on all locomotives dedicated to Mendip stone traffic. The introduction of the new Class 60 locomotives is likely to be the next exciting motive power event on these Mendip stone workings and it will be fascinating to see how they cope with these increasingly-heavy stone trains, although ARC have now placed an order for their own General Motors locomotives, similar to Foster Yeoman's Class 59s.

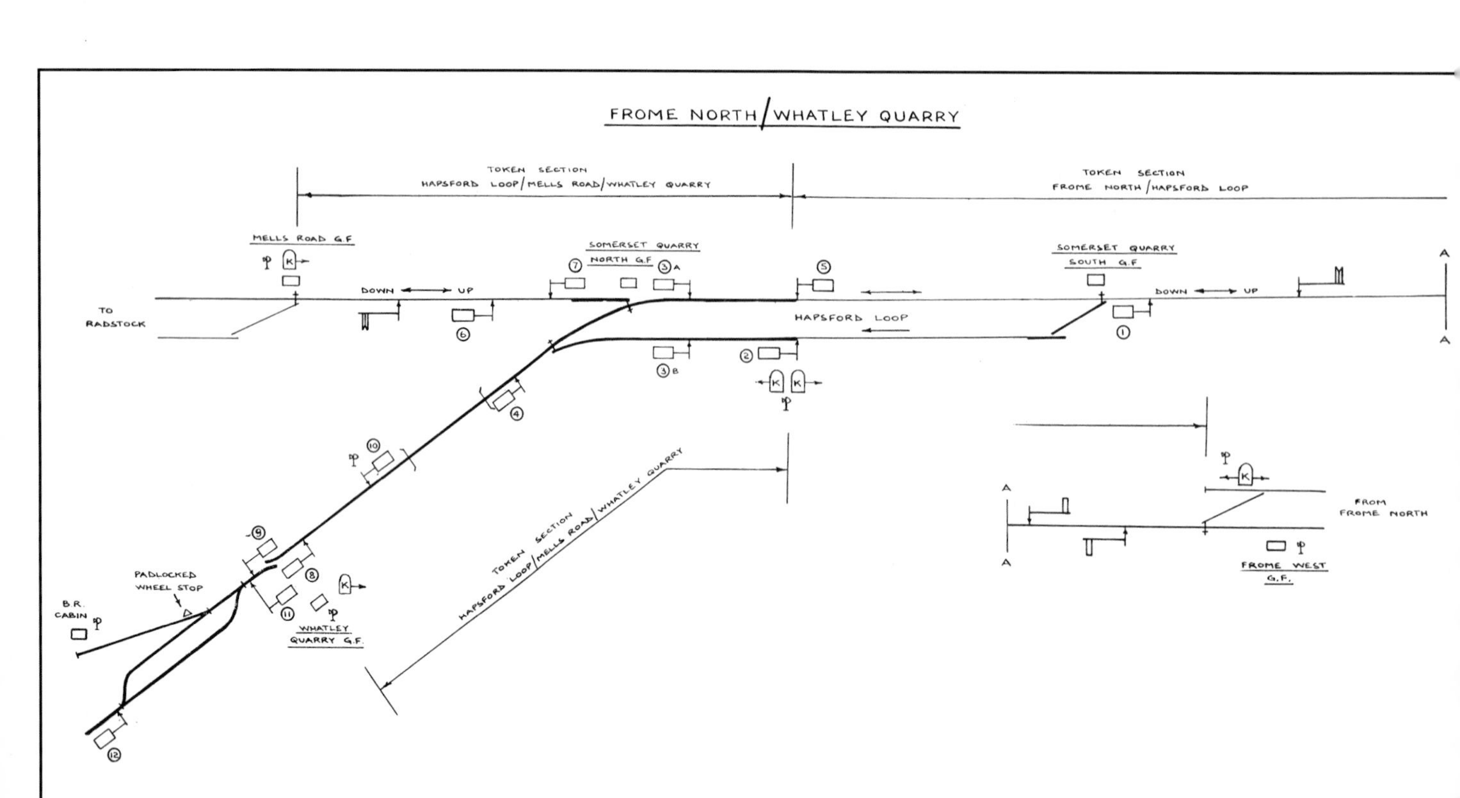

Turning to the company's wagon requirements, 1987 saw the last of the 27 ton MSV mineral wagons, so long a common sight on the Mendip stone traffic workings. Increasingly unreliable, they offered no comparison with the modern privately owned, high capacity wagons then coming into service. In December 1988 ARC's wagon fleet was made up of 312 PGA's, 17 PXA type and 50 PTA type; PGA, PXA and PTA being the TOPS codes for particular classes of wagons. The PGAs are the mainstay of the firm's wagon fleet and are 51 tonne, two-axle hopper wagons. Of the PGAs, roughly half work from Whatley whilst the other half works out of ARC's Tytherington Quarry in North Avon. Tarmac also operate 36 PGAs for the Hothfield and Hayes and Harlington workings (see accompanying diagram of workings). There is a strong likelihood that ARC will acquire some new high capacity hopper wagons in the near future. In the tradition of the old private owner wagons of the past, ARC wagons are distinctive with their clean ochre paintwork and large ARC legend.

The wagon fleets for both Whatley and neighbouring Merehead quarries are leased from CAIB (UK) Limited, ex-Procor, Tiger Rail or Tiphook Rail. Maintenance is usually carried out by the wagon owner at facilities provided at and by the quarry. This minimises the time that wagons are out of service. Wherever possible, routine maintenance is carried out during seasonal lulls in traffic, while heavy repair work is occasionally carried out at the Procor workshops at Horbury or, until its recent closure by CAIB (UK) Limited, at Marcroft's at Radstock.

The Mendip stone rail operations, to Whatley and Merehead, are managed from the Railfreight Construction Sub-Sector office at Westbury. Central to the whole rail operation is the BR TOPS system, terminals for which are provided at both Whatley and Merehead via British Telecom telex. Stone is delivered to the depots indicated on the accompanying table and it is worth noting that, as well as its own depots, ARC trains also supply Tarmac and Redland terminals as well. The quarry has a potential capacity of some 10 million tons of stone per annum and, if the recent past is anything to go by, it would seem that further expansion will keep the rails of the former WS&WR's Radstock branch well-polished right into the 21st century!

SERVICES INTO WHATLEY QUARRY – DECEMBER 1988

ARC Southern Whatley Quarry Inward-Bound Services

WTT	Time	Train Details		Locomotive Class	Normal Load
6A07	0211	West Drayton-Whatley	(0540)MX	56	36PGA
6A66	0535	Westbury-Whatley	(0603)MO	56	36PGA
6A19	0650	Westbury-Whatley (Tarmac)	(0728)MSO	56	21PGA & 9 PHA
6A43	0804	Appleford-Whatley	(1035)SX		18PTA
6A43	0700	Oxford (Banbury Road)-Whatley	(1035)SX		18PTA
6V60	0952	Fareham-Whatley	(1223)SO	56	18PTA
6200	1030	Fareham-Whatley	(1305)QFO	56	18PTA
6200	1100	Fareham-Whatley	(1345)QFSX	56	18PTA
6V98 } or	0900	Hothfield-Whatley	(1422)SX	56	36PGA
6V95 }	0952	Bat & Ball (Redland)-Whatley	(1422)SX	56	36PGA
6V95 } or	0900	Hothfield-Whatley	(1435)SO	56	36PGA
6V95 }	0952	Bat & Ball (Redland)-Whatley	(1435)SO	56	36PGA
6V59	0955	Ardingly-Whatley	(1545)FX	56	36PGA
6A48	1415	West Drayton-Whatley	(1750)SX	56	36PGA
6V38	1210	Tolworth-Whatley	(1729)TO	47	24PGA
6V84	1400	Salfords-Whatley	(1841)SO	47	26PGA
6A81	1524	Theale (ARC)-Whatley	(1844)SX	56**	24PTA
6V84	1400	Allington-Whatley	(1928)QThFO	56	36PGA
6A25	1712	Hayes (Tarmac)-Whatley (Westbury arr 2005)	FO	56	21PGA & 9PHA
6V28	1100	Barking-Acton	TTh(FO)Q	56	25PTA
6V90	1146	Chislehurst-Acton-Whatley	(2037)MF		11PTA
6V18	1541	Mile End-Whatley	(2100)WO	37+ 37**	18PHA
6V85	1850	Fareham-Whatley	(2303)SX	56	18PTA
6V73	1625	Woking (Redland)-Whatley	MTThO	56	18PXA or 12PTA +pl6PHA

*All services subject to weekly traffic requirements.
**Last Theale-Whatley can be 37 + 37 ThFO. ***Mile End working can be 31 + 31.
Note Trains from Whatley work around diagrams with other operations at Stoke Gifford and Mile End. This sometimes results in an imbalance of services to certain locations.

SERVICES OUT OF WHATLEY QUARRY – DECEMBER 1988

Outward-Bound Services

WTT	Time	Train Details		Locomotive Class	Normal Load
6L66	0050	Westbury-Barking	MO	56	25PTA
6L66	0013	Whatley-Acton-Barking	TuWTh(FOQ)	56	25PTA
6O90		-Chislehurst	M-F	56	11PTA
7A15	0100	Whatley-Oxford (Banbury Road) or Appleford	SX	56	18PTA
6O38	0058	Westbury-Tolworth	TO	47	24PGA
6O55	0235	Westbury-Salfords	SO	47	26PGA
6Z86	0310	Whatley-Ashford (Sevington)	SO	56	32PGA
7O59	0350	Whatley-Fareham	SO	56	18PTA
6O80	0630	Whatley-Allington	MFO	56	36PGA
6L50	0640	Whatley-Mile End empties on to Marks Tey)	SO	37+37	18PHA
6O89	0645	Whatley-Woking (Redland)	MTThO	56	18PXA or 12PTA & 6PHA
6M24	0725	Whatley-Wolverton	SO	56	37PGA
6A17	0745	Whatley-Theale	SX	56**	24PTA
6A26	0800	Whatley-West Drayton	SO	56	43PGA
6A26	0803	Whatley-West Drayton	SX	56	43PGA
6O53	0855	Whatley-Hothfield (Tarmac)	Tho	56	12PHA
6Z81	0915	Whatley-Allington	MWTho(Q)	56	36PGA
6A26	1100	Whatley-Hayes (Tarmac)	M & SO	56	21PGA & 9PHA
7O83	1209	Whatley-Fareham	SX	56	18PTA
6A77	1605	Whatley-Westbury	SO	56	
6O40	1925	Whatley-Ardingly	SX	56	36PGA
6A03	1950	Whatley-West Drayton	SX	56	43PGA
6O37	2135	Whatley-Hothfield	Sunday O	56	36PGA
6O37	2107 } or	Whatley-Hothfield (Tarmac)	SX	56	36PGA
6O95	2107 }	Whatley-Bat & Ball (Redland)	SX	56	36PGA
6A19	2335	Whatley-Westbury	FO	56	

*All services subject to weekly traffic requirements.
**6A17 0745 Whatley-Theale can be 37 + 37 ThFO.

(Source "Rail Enthusiast" – December 1988)

Pre-1988, trains from Whatley would share the same tracks as the former trip freights to Marcroft's Wagon Works at Radstock. These latter workings would usually run once, possibly twice a week. Nowadays, the points at Hapsford Ground Frame normally lie for the Whatley direction and, before the resignalling work carried out under the Frome area of the Westbury powerbox scheme came into use on 8th October 1984, the guard of a train running down to Radstock would change them by pulling levers. In those days, the procedure was to ring the signal box at Frome North to get the token instrument for the Radstock line released. The guard could then get a key token out of the machine, set the road for Radstock, move the train into the Radstock section, and reset the road for Whatley before going down to Radstock itself.

Adrian Vaughan, in his comprehensive book entitled *The*

MEETING AT MURDER COMBE
Stone trains working between Whatley Quarry and the screens at Hapsford were made up of four rakes each of eight Hudson skips. Two small diesel locomotives ran a shuttle service and these met at the passing loop at Murder Combe. In this photograph No. 2 (Hill 136C) has just left this loop and is about to enter the very restricted tunnel under the Egford-Mells road. Today this tunnel is bricked-up but the entrance can still be seen alongside the newer bore which is currently in use. Note the "telegraph pole" made from narrow gauge rail that can be seen just behind the first wagon. The picture was taken in the early 1960s.

Geoff Carter

THE WHATLEY QUARRY BRANCH
On 25th September 1977, a Sunday, a tunnel inspection takes place at Murder Combe. No. 47147 is in charge of this somewhat unusual working.

Mike Miller

WHATLEY QUARRY – THE LOADING PLANT
Three of ARC's Thomas Hill 4-wheel diesel-hydraulic locomotives wait alongside the loading plant at Whatley Quarry on 14th March 1975.

Mike Miller

THE WHATLEY QUARRY BRANCH – 33s IN TANDEM
On 10th August 1982 Class 33s Nos 33062 and 33028 head a rake of air-braked 51 tonne hoppers across the new bridge at Bedlam with a full load of stone from the quarry.

Mike Miller

THE WHATLEY QUARRY BRANCH – 'WESTERN' IN THE WOODS
On 15th June 1976, 'Western' class No. D1001 *Western Pathfinder* wanders quietly through the woods at Bedlam on its way to the quarry.

Mike Miller

THE WHATLEY QUARRY BRANCH
'Western' No. D1001 runs light engine through Murder Combe on its way to Whatley Quarry. This picture, taken on 16th May 1976, exemplifies the beautiful setting of this tranquil but well-used branch.

Mike Miller

HAPSFORD LOOP
Ooops . . . this view shows the damaged line at Hapsford Loop following the derailment of a freight train on Friday, 5th November 1976.

Mike Miller

THE WHATLEY QUARRY BRANCH
A "Neptune" Track Recording Trolley slips through sylvan Murder Combe on Saturday, 11th October 1980. Note the train identification number, 7Z06.

Mike Miller

WEAVER'S LOOP MELLS ROAD
On 25th August 1982, Class 47 No. 47262 heads the return Radstock trip. It is seen here passing Weaver's Loop at Mells Road.

Mike Miller

West of England Resignalling (Ian Allan), described modern working over the Whatley Quarry Junction-Radstock section in the following way:

> "Since the introduction of the Westbury Panel the guard obtains a release from the signalman at Westbury for a token, and having removed the 60 year-old device from the instrument he is in sole possession of authority over the single track branch and can therefore be permitted to operate the mini-panel. This is within an 18-in square box fixed to a post. He unlocks the door and again asks the Panelman for a release; having got one he can press down the relevant button to motor the points for the Radstock direction. The train passes onto the branch, the guard resets the points for the quarry line and having checked with the panel that all is in order, goes off with the token to join his train."

Looking in greater detail at the Whatley Quarry Junction-Radstock section in its later days, one important industry that needs to be mentioned at Mells Road station was a tar distilling company by the name of Berry-Wiggins. This company had a plant at the junction of the Mells Road-Vobster Quarry line. This provided traffic which, in turn, partly compensated for the loss of the line's earlier coal traffic. The tar traffic continued into the 1960s when, in 1964, Berry-Wiggins ceased production. Then all that was left of this once thriving goods centre was the weekly train of wagons for repair at Marcroft Wagon Works. These trains were generally worked by Class 31s and 47s. The site at Mells Road is still used, however, for the storage and cutting up of redundant sleepers. These are despatched by road by the firm of Weaver Plant Limited, of Temple Cloud.

Since 1963 the firm of Weaver's, plant and transport contractors and dealers in railway materials have worked on sections of the North Somerset line and at the stations at Radstock, Mells Road and Frome. However, most of their operations have taken place since around 1974. Initially based in the rail triangle at Frome, the firm rented part of this site for a period of around seven years, the location being used to store up to 50,000 sleepers. These came in by rail from a wide variety of depots including Radyr, Evesham, Millerhill

THE LINERCRANE LIES OVER AT RADSTOCK
In the spring of 1985, the Linercrane, a combined transfer and container movement vehicle, rail-mounted, self-propelled, powered by a 190hp Rolls-Royce engine, and built by the firm of Ralph Blatchford at Midsomer Norton, lies over between trials in the former station at Radstock (West).

Mike Miller

in Scotland and Woking, Surrey. However, when the stone firm of Tarmac wanted the use of this site, Weaver's vacated it and moved to Mells Road. Weaver's were also involved in the lifting of the Bristol & North Somerset Railway between Bristol and Radstock. This operation was carried out by British Rail and a Welsh company called Woodfield Limited. This latter firm, now no longer in business, put the sleepers through the hands of Weaver Plant who sold them on behalf of the Welsh company. In addition, in May 1983, when various redundant sidings were lifted in the goods yard at Radstock, it was Weaver Plant who carried out the contract.

Mentioning Radstock provides an opportunity to say that by February 1980 the general arrangement of trackwork in Radstock West Yard was that the former 'up' main line terminated just to the east of the level crossing in the middle of Radstock. The 'down' sidings were still largely intact as were the 'up' sidings. The metals into the former colliery at Ludlows still ran as far as the boundary fence but beyond that they had disappeared. The engine shed and the turntable road were still in place but the water column had been removed. Although not easy to locate, the site of the former signal box at Radstock South was still discernible.

Marcroft Wagon Repair Works were still very active with a number of modern private owner wagons either under repair or waiting repair or collection in the yard outside. Some wagons were being stored on the Kilmersdon Colliery exchange siding which, at this date, still ran its full distance past the foot of the former colliery incline. However, the rails on the incline itself had been lifted. On the Radstock-Mells Road section the Down Main had been terminated some yards beyond the site of Kilmersdon Colliery incline and adjacent to the former Writhlington Colliery screens of which there was little to see by this late date.

Around the late 1970s and early 1980s the possible demolition of the Brunellian station at Frome aroused a great deal of local and national controversy. In 1978 British Rail applied for permission to demolish the station buildings, the intention being to replace them with a very basic single storey timber building. Fortunately, this application was turned down and, in October 1979, renovation work started at the station which, at that time, had been described as a "disgrace to the town". The £46,000 facelift, which was to include the provision of new waiting rooms, offices and platform buildings, also planned for the restoration of the original Brunel train shed. Once under way, however, the restoration programme revealed structural faults in the buildings and experts estimated that the final repair bill could reach more than £160,000! Eventually, however, money was forthcoming for the renovation and the rotting timbers, peeling paint and emergency roof supports of the autumn of 1981 gave way, in the spring of the following year, to a station which had been beautifully renovated and completely transformed.

Around Frome station itself, there are various and varied sources of freight traffic still being handled by the railways. For example, in 1984 another substantial trainload flow of aggregate traffic from Mendip became established and this, like ARC's business out of Whatley Quarry, used the rump of the former Bristol-Radstock (West)-Frome line. On 10th September 1982 a new stone train service began from an equally new stone depot which had been established in the former triangle of lines at Frome. With locomotive No 56056 in charge, the stone was taken out in 36 trucks, each handling 37½ tons, which were privately owned by the Tarmac Company. The stone had been brought into Frome North by a fleet of some 25 lorries from a new quarry jointly established at Westdow by Tarmac Roadstone and Redland Aggregates. Taking around three hours to get loaded, the stone was put to rail by Volvo 4600 loading shovels. The train had 1,350 tons of aggregate on board and was bound for Tarmac's Asphalt Plant at Hayes in Middlesex. It left Frome North Yard at 12.30pm, Westbury at 1.35pm arriving at Hayes at 3.30pm.

In the first week of operation two trains a week were being handled by the depot and this was the average for the first month of operation. During November 1982 the weekly average number of trains increased to three per week, their loads being used to construct the then growing M25 motorway at Denham Interchange. The average dropped again to around two a week during December, this continuing into early 1983. In the summer of that year the average dropped to around one a week. The costings of the Hayes workings were very interesting in that by road, throughout from the quarry to Hayes, the cost to the company was £7.50 per ton. By rail the

NORTH SOMERSET RAILTOURS (1)
Class 33 No. 33109 and 4TC set No. 417 form "The Quarryman" railtour. It is seen here climbing the 1 in 48 bank between Hapsford and Mells Road on its way to Radstock. This particular special ran on Sunday, 16th September 1974. *Mike Miller*

NORTH SOMERSET RAILTOURS (2)
This delightful scene, full of foliage and railfans, shows a three-car dmu (unit No. B820) heading a Great Western Society railtour from Cardiff. It is seen here, at Batch Farm, between Radstock and Mells Road. This railtour continued its journey on to Meeth and Meldon, deep in the heart of the West Country. This special ran on 11th October 1980. *Mike Miller*

cost was £4 per ton plus £1 road transport costs into Frome, plus 50p per ton loading costs, a saving of two pounds over the road-throughout price.

However, it was intended that the arrangements at Frome were to be temporary. As a more permanent way of working, the company had hoped to put its stone onto British Rail via a cross-country conveyor from the quarry at Westdow to a possible private siding on the East Somerset line in the area around Leighton. This proposal was not to be, however, and the arrangements at Frome North continue, the entrance/exit to the sidings there being under the direct control of the signalling panel at Westbury.

On 4th July 1983 another first was notched up for Tarmac when one of its stone trains left Frome North for the quaintly-named Bat & Ball station, near Sevenoaks in Kent, where Tarmac and Redland have a joint depot. This service employed a smaller set of wagons than that used by the Hayes train, the rakes running to around 24/26 wagons, some 975 tons in all. In the Frome area, these workings were handled over Tuesdays and Wednesdays in the following way. The "Bat & Ball" was usually loaded by lunchtime on the Tuesday and then was tripped to Westbury where it was held until 1.00am the following day. It left for its destination at that time, running via the Berks & Hants line to Reading.

Also at Frome is the Mobil depot which is situated in the station yard. This depot handles bituminous materials for use in road making. Nowadays, the materials are brought in by rail from the firm's Coryton Refinery in Essex where standard gauge tracks connect that depot into British Rail's London, Tilbury & Southend system. The loads travel across from Essex, taking some two days in all. Each wagon carries between 26 and 32 tons of material and each train is made up of between 24 and 36 wagons. Quite often the trains are trip worked from Westbury, Class 47s being common on this duty, the train engine shunting the wagons into the depot since the latter has no device within the perimeter fence for moving trucks around. A "considerable traffic" is handled each year, the loads being taken away from the depot by road tanker. In 1987 Mobil was using BR's Speedlink service from London to Severn Tunnel Junction to carry its goods westwards and this, in a typical working, was bringing up to ten wagons overnight from Coryton.

In the recent past, Frome station has also seen trains of bitumen traffic from Ellesmere Port in Cheshire. Once in the West Country these trains were split at Westbury, one portion going to Cranmore on the East Somerset, the other terminating at Frome. The journey from the North was often in the care of two Class 25 locomotives, while the journey out to Cranmore itself was handled by one of the pair. Nowadays, however, the installation at Cranmore is no longer in use. A traffic of a different kind seen at Frome station during the 1980s has been that of modern furniture which has been handled for the firm of Benchairs.

It is at Frome that our journey along the Bristol-Radstock (West)-Frome railway itself must come to an end. Although the Bristol & North Somerset Railway has all but disappeared from the face of the earth, the former freight-only Wilts, Somerset & Weymouth's branch from Frome to Radstock partially remains in use. Although coal does not move through Frome West any more and wagons are no longer repaired at Radstock West, stone does rumble its way eastwards and it does so in enormous quantities. It is with that reassuring thought that we move to the next and last chapter where we shall look in much more detail at the inclined planes and the railway wagons that once served the North Somerset Coalfield. At the same time we will be throwing more light on the areas around Mells and Vobster where loads of coal and stone once thumped their way over the well-worn metals of the Newbury Railway.

THE RADSTOCK-FROME BRANCH IN THE 1980s (1)
This pair of pictures shows two staple traffics on the Whatley Quarry/Radstock/Frome sections of freight-only trackage during the early and mid-1980s.

Class 56 No. 56056, well-employed on today's stone trains, joins the main Berks & Hants line with a substantial train of limestone in tow. This traffic has been the saviour of this section of the WS&WR. This and the following photograph were taken on 15th April 1983 at Clink Lane Junction, Frome.

R. Hateley

THE RADSTOCK-FROME BRANCH IN THE 1980s (2)
At the same location and on the same date, Class 47 No. 47327 runs past on a lengthy train of repaired wagons from Marcroft's Wagon Works.

R. Hateley

11
Inclined Planes, Wagon Works and Industrial Lines

PASTORAL SCENES NEAR PENSFORD
Ex-GWR 2-6-2T No. 4131, a regular on the North Somerset, heads towards Bristol with an ex-Radstock coal train. It is seen here between Pensford and Whitchurch on 10th June 1964.
Tony Wadley

The Colliery Inclines at Pensford, Huish and Kilmersdon Collieries

Pensford Colliery Incline

The colliery at Pensford was one of a number of pits in the Somerset Coalfield where there was a marked difference in height between the pithead itself and the railway sidings serving that pit. In Pensford's case, the colliery was to be found some 100 feet above the Bristol & North Somerset branch. The colliery's rope haulage incline fed sidings to the west of that branch and it is to this incline that we now turn our attention.

An agreement for an incline was signed on 9th September 1910 but as the original plans would have made working difficult, they were changed on 15th March 1911, and the new proposals made the incline somewhat longer and rather less steep. The way of working the incline was also changed with a haulage engine taking on the job from the previous idea of having a self-acting incline. Opened by 1912, the incline saw some small use in the January of that year but it was not until 1917 that both it and the colliery were in full use.

The North Somerset's sidings serving the colliery were laid out as shown in the accompanying diagram. The method of actually working the incline was well described by Colin G. Maggs in his article on the "Railways at Pensford Colliery" where he states:

"A short rake of empty wagons was allowed to run by gravity across the foot of the incline by means of a diamond crossing, momentum causing them to run into another siding. From there, they were run singly to the foot of the incline, where the coupling chain was hooked on to the steel cable taken from a wagon just descended. A hawser was looped round the leading axle and hooked to the cable as a safety precaution in the event of the coupling chain breaking. When all was ready, a ring was given on the bell signal in operation between the winding house and the hut at the foot of the incline. On arrival at the head of the incline empty wagons were run back by gravity into the pithead sidings while still attached to the cable. Loaded wagons were hauled singly from the pithead sidings to the head of the incline and lowered to its foot where they were unhooked and allowed to gravitate to the lower sidings. The incline was capable of despatching up to eight loaded wagons an hour, though the normal daily traffic was about 30 10-ton wagons."

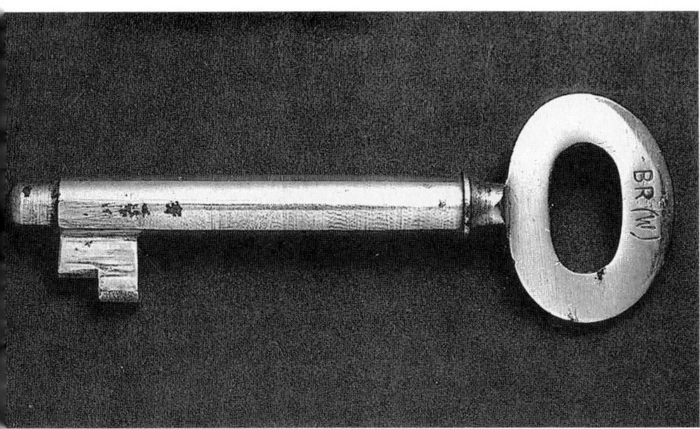

Left: PENSFORD SIGNAL BOX – THE KEY TO THE DOOR!
This illustration shows the key to the signal box that once existed at Pensford station. This particular box, the last to work the loop and signals at the station, was closed on 14th June 1964.

Original key: H. Wyatt

Above: PENSFORD & BROMLEY COLLIERIES' SIDINGS
This photograph, taken from the bottom of the incline leading up to Pensford Pit, looks towards the station itself at Pensford. It shows the main line from Bristol to Radstock swinging in from left to right, while it also shows the connection from the collieries' sidings into the main running track. The signals show a rather interesting, if somewhat conflicting, state of affairs in this scene which was taken on 2nd October 1954.

M.B. Warburton

PENSFORD COLLIERY INCLINE
With the Bristol-Radstock line just visible on the far right, a wagon comes down the incline serving Pensford Colliery. The peace of the operation was captured on 8th September 1953.

Colin G. Maggs

PENSFORD COLLIERY INCLINE (1)
With a wagon descending, the photographer points his camera up the incline at Pensford. With weed-strewn track and wooden-bodied wagon this picture captures an entirely different era on the railways. *Colin G. Maggs*

PENSFORD COLLIERY INCLINE (2)
With the wagon now safely in the sidings at the bottom of the incline, the shunter uncouples the rope that was responsible for the wagon's safe descent. *Colin G. Maggs*

PENSFORD & BROMLEY COLLIERIES SIDINGS SIGNAL BOX
This view gives a general scene showing the box and sidings at Pensford & Bromley Collieries Sidings Signal Box, with BR Standard Class 3 2-6-2T No. 82042 coming through fast with the 4.50pm (Sundays Only) Bristol to Frome passenger. This photograph was taken on 13th September 1959, the last day of Sunday working.

Hugh Ballantyne

COLLIERY FEEDERS TO THE NORTH SOMERSET LINE (SOUTHERN SECTION)

Huish Colliery Incline

In our description of the history of Huish Colliery (Chapter 6) we noted that the first coal was raised and sold in the spring of 1824. However, it was not until 1855, by which time the GWR's broad gauge line had reached Radstock from Frome, that the coal from this colliery actually went out by rail. Before this the pit's output was taken out by road.

The self-acting incline which took the coal from the pithead, the latter being well above the valley floor, was of 2ft $8\frac{1}{2}$in gauge. Four or six tubs, each holding 8cwt of coal, were let down the incline to the GWR. The plan on page 188 shows the bottom of the incline feeding into the screens which were themselves served by sidings off the Radstock-Mells Road section. It would be especially fascinating to see some photographs of this particular incline assuming, of course, that any were taken and that they are still in existence! The colliery was closed in 1912.

Kilmersdon Colliery Incline

The lease for Kilmersdon Colliery was signed on 25th December 1873, with the shafts reaching completion late in 1877. The first coal was sold in 1878, by which time the colliery incline

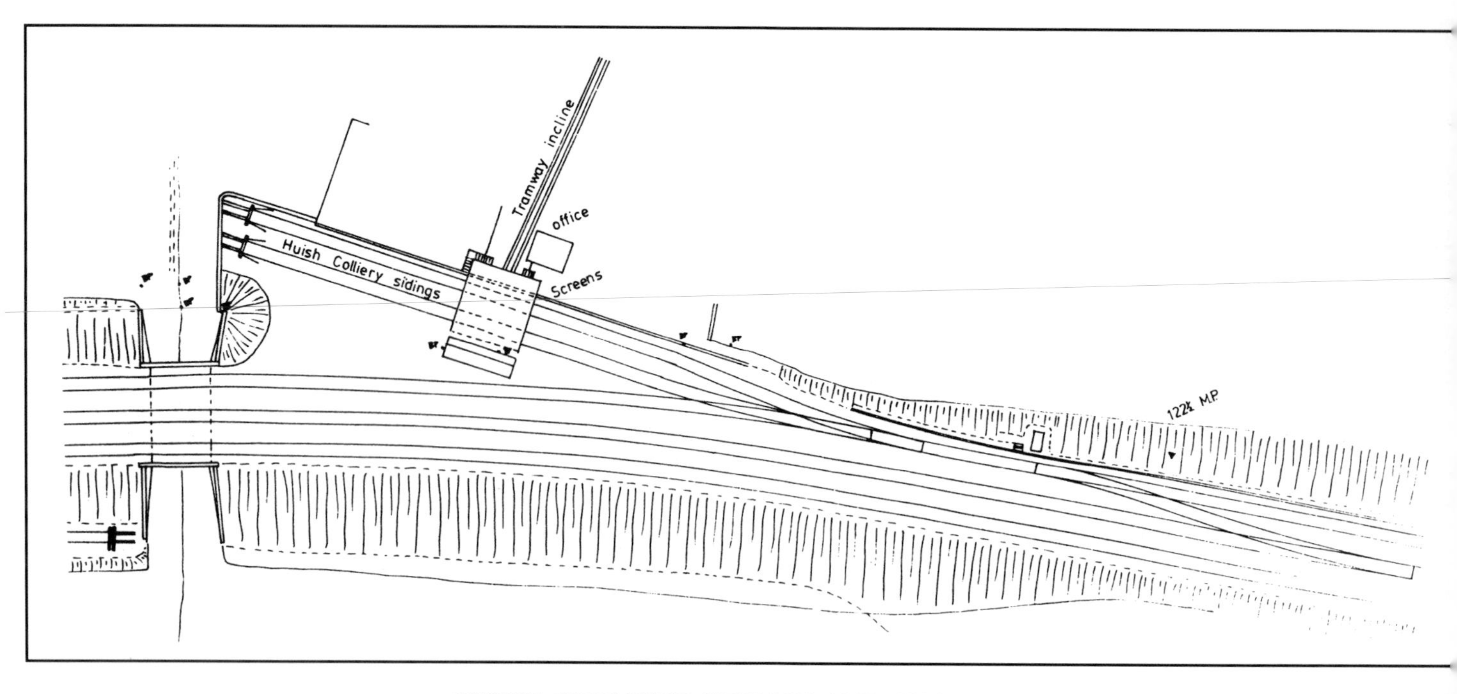

HUISH COLLIERY SIDINGS AND INCLINE

Original plan: Chris Handley

may well have been in action since the agreement for it had been reached and signed on 1st September 1877.

The 1877 agreement was made between the GWR and the Kilmersdon Colliery Company, W.B. Naish and W. Busfield, both directors of the company signing on behalf of the then-growing colliery. It would appear from the agreement and the plans that went with it that the work to be done by the GWR essentially involved the installation of two sidings on the western side of the Radstock-Mells Road section with a connection to the pit running off the westernmost siding. In turn, this connection led to the bottom of the colliery incline. The new sidings then linked into the GWR through an existing siding in that company's goods yard near the Radstock Wagon Company's premises, this latter company being found on the site of what later became Marcroft's Wagon Works. The estimated cost of the work was £1,401 12s 6d (£1,401.57½), £500 of which was paid on the date of the agreement, the balance following as the work progressed. The whole amount had to be paid before the sidings were brought into use. It would appear that the GWR would only be responsible for the installation of trackwork to and at the base of the incline – presumably the latter was installed by another contractor?

In addition, the colliery company also consented to pay any extra costs incurred by the installation of signalling. On top of all this it had to pay other costs that might be generated to the GWR by Board of Trade requirements. The maintenance of the sidings and associated new works was the responsibility of the GWR with the exception of a short stretch of track at the base of the incline which was to be looked after by the

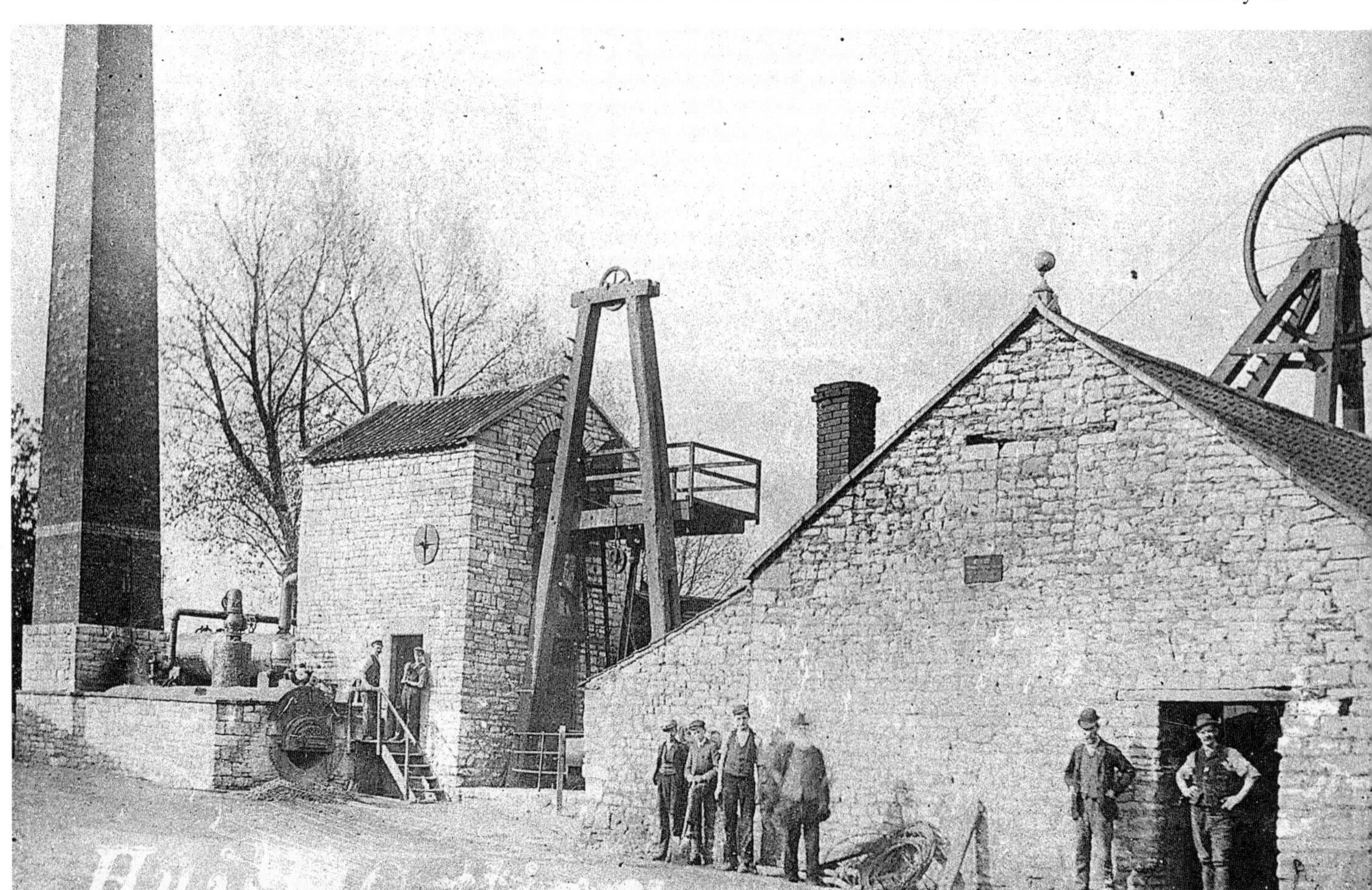

COLLIERIES AT RADSTOCK: HUISH PIT
Probably taken about 1870 this photograph shows the pit at Huish. Although not a particularly successful pit, its life nonetheless stretched into the 20th century, eventually closing in February 1912, when it was declared uneconomic.

Dennis Rendell

SUBSIDENCE AT KILMERSDON (1)
With the Frome-Radstock branch to the extreme right of this photograph, gangers alongside this main line survey the results of subsidence at the bottom of Kilmersdon Incline. Constructed in 1889, the connecting chord that has subsided in this view has upon it, a marvellous variety of private owner wagons from local pits and firms. By all accounts, the rather large dip in the track was caused by a culvert becoming blocked, this, in turn, causing flooding which consequently led to the subsidence shown here. *P.J. Williams*

SUBSIDENCE AT KILMERSDON (2)
This second scene of the subsidence problems encountered at Kilmersdon is taken looking up the incline. This view illustrates very clearly just how much of a drop has occurred at track level. Of interest in this photograph are the different types of track in the foreground while the small cluster of onlookers in the background reveals the human touch! Note too one or two examples of trucks with dumb buffers. The date of the incident is probably at some time during the early years of the present century. *P.J. Williams*

colliery company, but to the satisfaction of the GWR's Permanent Way Engineer.

As part of the agreement the colliery company was to pay £5 annual rent to the GWR for the right of way required by the new sidings, the first payment being made on 1st January 1878. Incidentally, if the GWR required further sidings to be laid in to work traffic to and from Kilmersdon, the colliery company would have to construct and maintain these additional sidings on their own land and at their own expense. One final point to remember is that under this particular agreement the GWR's connection to the incline itself was from the Frome end only.

However, it would seem that with the increasingly successful development of the pit, better rail access was needed and, under an agreement of 1st August 1889, this was provided. Under this agreement the colliery company lengthened the approach sidings at the bottom of the incline, at the same time, adding in a third spur from these sidings to the bottom of the incline. In this way a triangular junction was created at the base of the incline. The work was funded by the Kilmersdon Colliery Company but was checked by the GWR's Civil Engineer. The maintenance of the new works was to be carried out by the GWR, the colliery company again paying the bill! In addition, the company also had to pay an extra 5s (25p) rent on top of the £5 agreed in the 1877 document.

An interesting clause in the 1889 agreement gave the GWR's Civil Engineer the right to tip colliery spoil at the base of the incline so that the two sidings that lay parallel to the Radstock-Mells main line could be extended. These sidings were kept for "consigned" and "unconsigned" wagons and under this agreement they were to be lengthened as and when it was felt necessary. It was in this form and layout that these sidings and connections were to remain until the incline's closure in the 1970s. Yet another agreement, this time dated 15th June 1905, clarified the maintenance obligations of the railway and colliery companies. In 1925 one more agreement worthy of note was signed when, on 15th May of that year, the liquidator to the Kilmersdon Colliery Company agreed that the 1877 and 1889 agreements would stand under the pit's new owners, the Writhlington Collieries Company.

Having filled in some historical background to the incline, a full description of the way that it was worked might now prove helpful. For the following information I am greatly indebted to an article by C.J. Peacock who finely detailed the operation of the colliery and incline in October 1965.

At that time the main shaft was 1,740ft deep and down this

KILMERSDON COLLIERY EXCHANGE SIDINGS 1877

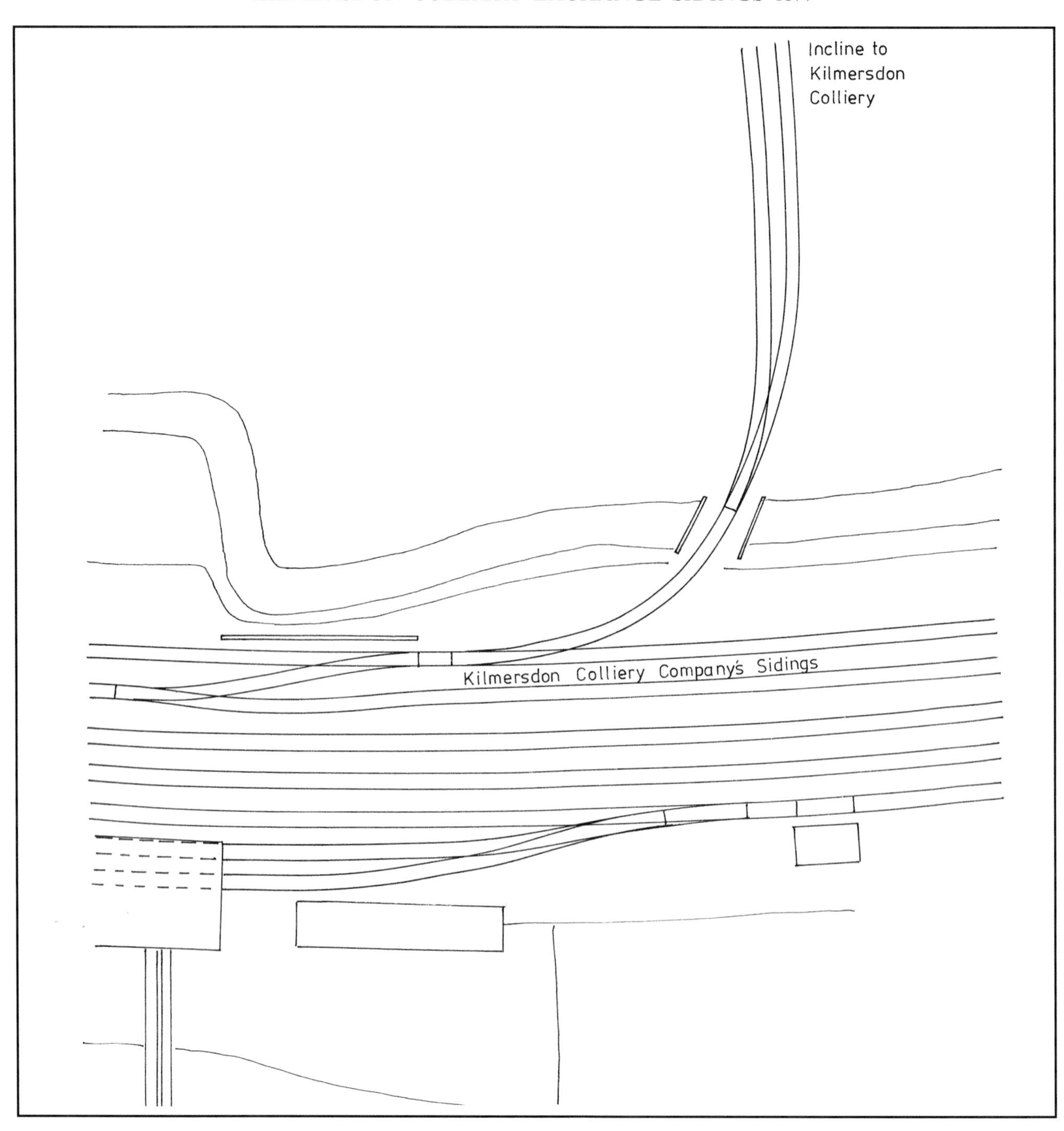

a cage could descend in just over one minute. The winding drums were powered by a GEC 650hp electric motor and one cage could bring up either 18 miners on two levels, or three tubs on three. Output at that period in the colliery's history was some 800 tons per day. This coal was brought to the surface in the above-mentioned steel tubs, each with a capacity of 19cwt and each running on 2ft 8¼in gauge track. At the pithead the tubs were taken to a building in which they were emptied by two rotary tippers onto the screens below. Once they had been tipped the tubs were returned down an elevated track to the pithead.

In the mid-1960s each day roughly 100 tons of coal left the pit by road, with some 700 tons of lower grade coal going out by rail, via the incline, to be used by the power station at Portishead. (For further reference to the workings at Portishead see the author's related book *Reflections on the Portishead Branch*, OPC 1983.) With an average wagon load of 14 tons, the average number of wagons disappearing down the incline to British Rail was around 50 wagons a day.

Looking at the ways in which the two grades of coal were handled, the household coal was screened into NCB internal user wagons. These were wagons owned by the NCB for use inside the colliery boundary, and had been purchased from the pre-Nationalisation railway companies or from local colliery owners. The internal user wagons at Kilmersdon were allowed to run, by gravity, from under the screening house into the colliery yard where the coal was bagged and sent out by road. The lower grade coal was loaded direct into BR wagons for its trip to Portishead. These latter wagons were taken, two or three at a time, by the 23 ton Peckett-built tank locomotive, to the top of the incline for their journey onto main line metals.

From the colliery yard to the head of the incline the track along which the BR wagons ran was pretty well level, if not immaculately laid! Once out through the colliery yard the line crossed the Radstock-Kilmersdon road on Haydon Hill by an ungated level crosing. All trains had to stop here. Along the route the rails were chaired to the sleepers but there was little or no stone ballast.

The incline itself dropped down to the valley floor some 100ft below at an average grade of roughly 1 in 6½. There was a slight easing of the gradient over the top third of the incline while, where it began and finished at the top and the bottom, very sharp changes in gradient took place. The trackwork, of flat bottom rail spiked direct to every second sleeper and welded to flat steel plates, the latter themselves bolted to the other sleeper, was not stone ballasted on the incline. At intervals,

KILMERSDON COLLIERY EXCHANGE SIDINGS REVISED LAYOUT 1889

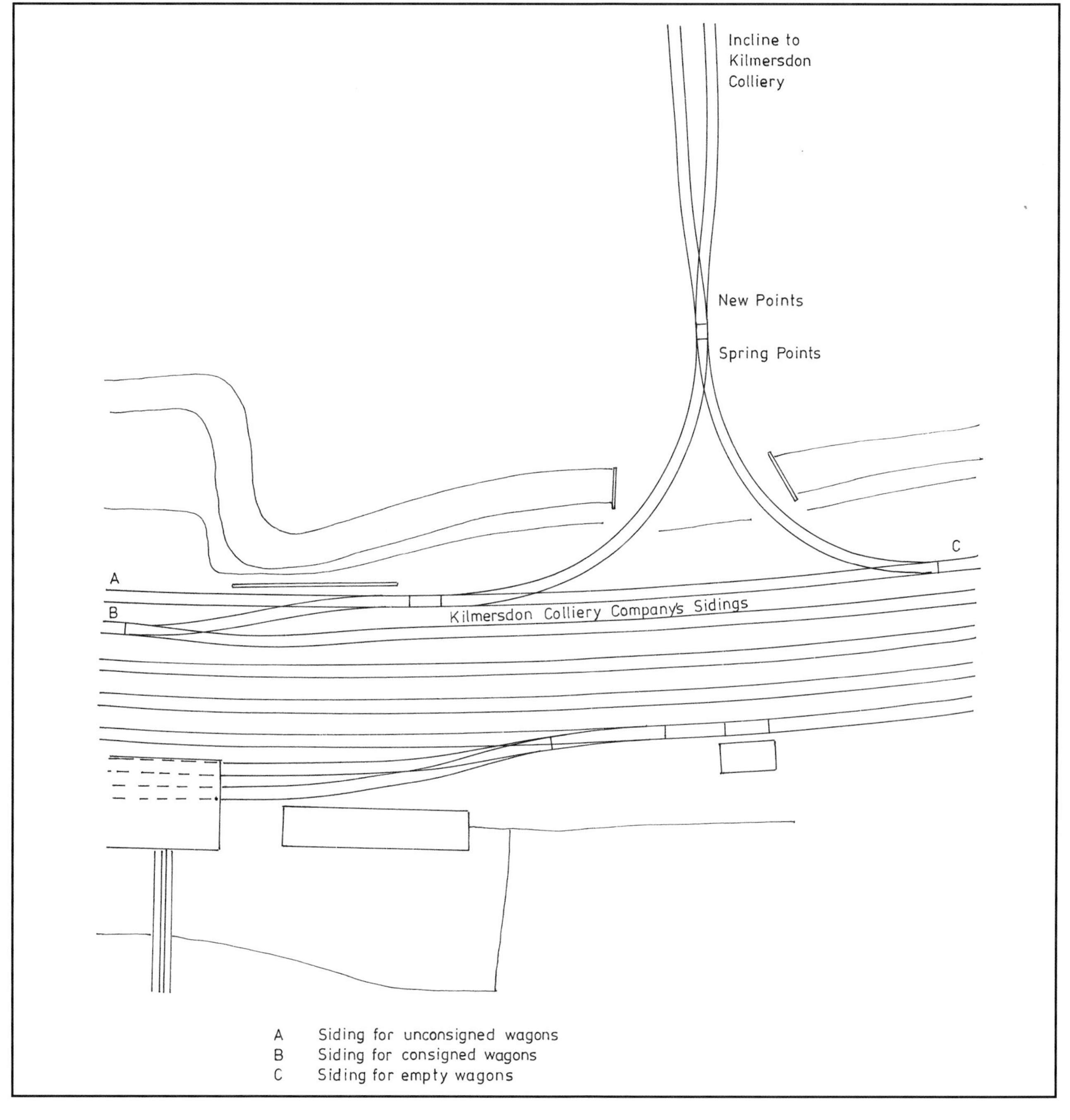

Above: KILMERSDON COLLIERY
GWR and S&DJR rail chairs sit side by side on NCB track at Kilmersdon Colliery on 30th September 1973.

Tony Wadley

Left: KILMERSDON COLLIERY
The pithead at Kilmersdon stands out clearly against the sky on 30th September 1973.

Tony Wadley

KILMERSDON COLLIERY
A DIAGRAMMATIC VIEW – 1965

Original (with thanks): C. J. Peacock

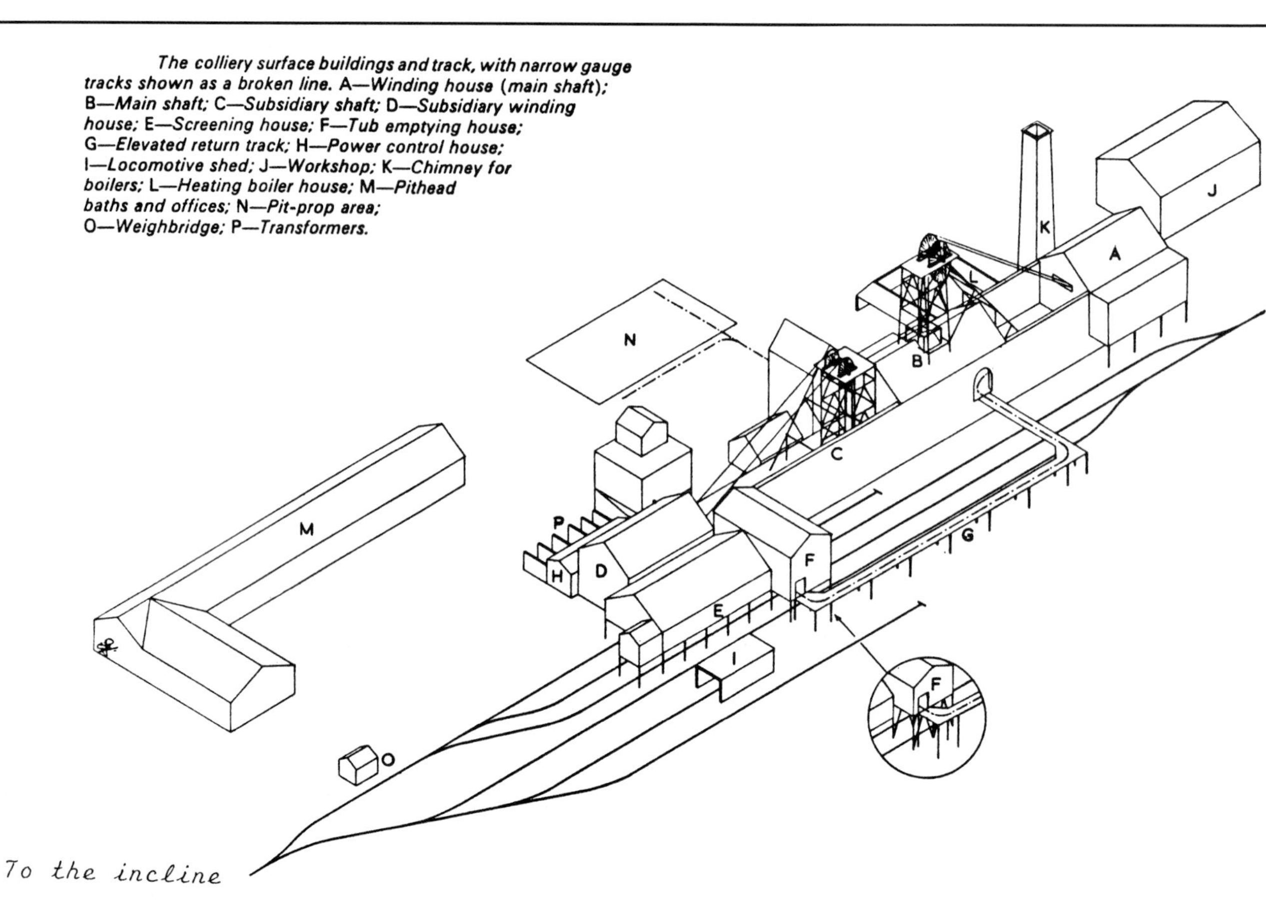

KILMERSDON INCLINE
On the way down – a loaded wagon starts to descend the incline on 18th August 1966. *Tony Wadley*

KILMERSDON INCLINE
On the way up and down – a loaded wagon descends while an empty starts the journey up. The Somerset countryside is at its best in the summer of 1961. *P.J. Williams*

Above: CHAOS ON KILMERSDON INCLINE
Ruston & Hornsby 4-wheeled diesel No. 200793 makes something of a mess of the trackwork at Kilmersdon Colliery Incline. In spite of appearances, very little real damage was actually done!
H. Loader/Dennis Rendell

The Mishap on Kilmersdon Colliery Incline

When one of the regular engines at Norton Hill Colliery was away for repairs, the Kilmersdon Peckett would act as a stand-in. In turn, the above locomotive was used as the Peckett's replacement. Unfortunately, the substitute was poorly provided with brakes while its four wheels and 7 ton weight did little for good adhesion. Indeed, in the mishap shown in the photograph three trucks of coal being shunted at the top of the incline had simply pulled the engine through the stop-blocks at the top and onto the incline itself! Somewhat unbelievably, the engine was undamaged by the crash, although it did lose its radiator cap in the process. Not unsurprisingly, the Peckett's return was strongly welcomed.

Below: KILMERSDON INCLINE
An empty wagon arrives at the top of the incline. The engine driver, Herb Loader, is standing on the right while his son Nelson is seen working the brake levers.
Tony Wadley

HUNSLET IN A HEAP AT KILMERSDON

This sad view shows Hunslet 0-4-0T, builder's No. 1684, at Kilmersdon. Built in 1931 this locomotive came from Norton Hill Colliery in 1966 when that pit closed. In October 1971 it was moved to the Somerset Railway Museum situated at the former Bleadon & Uphill railway station between Weston-super-Mare and Taunton. In 1986 the locomotive was moved to the Peak Railway's Buxton Steam Centre, Derbyshire, and in 1990 to the Swanage Railway, Dorset.

Author's collection/John Kingman

KILMERSDON COLLIERY

Driver Herb Loader is seen here on the footplate of Peckett No. 1788. This reflective shot shows a man obviously happy in his work.

Tony Wadley

lengths of rail or baulks of wood were fitted between the running rails to maintain the gauge while, in some places, other lengths of rail were fixed on the outside of the running rails to the stone banks.

At the top of the incline the winding house was a stone-built structure with a corrugated iron roof. Inside it there were two 9ft 6in diameter drums on a common shaft, one for the up cable and one for the down. Between them was a brake drum upon which the brake linings would come to bear. Right at the top of the incline there were two sets of levers, one for applying the brakes to the cable drums and one to operate the catch-points halfway down the incline. On the upper part of the incline the cables ran over rollers set between the rails. There were stopgates or blocks at the head of the incline to prevent wagons running down over, although, as the photograph on page 194 shows, accidents did occur!

The method of working the incline was as follows. The Peckett would bring two or three wagons to the top of the incline where they would be stabled onto the northern track, that is, the left hand road looking down the incline. They were sent down one at a time and as the full wagon went down it, in turn, pulled up an empty. As the empties arrived at the top, the locomotive collected them, thence taking them along the short stretch of railway to the colliery itself. This operation was repeated until the pit's daily output had been cleared. The shunter on the locomotive acted as the brakesman and it was he who controlled the speed of the wagons on the incline through the use of the brake levers. He also coupled the wagons to, and uncoupled them from, the cable while another man at the bottom of the incline coupled and uncoupled wagons at that end. As a safety measure, the end of each cable had two attachments; first there were links to go over the coupling hook on the wagon, while there was also a hook to pick up the wagon links themselves.

For over thirty years, until the colliery incline closed in 1974 in fact, the Peckett at Kilmersdon had, as its regular driver, Mr Herbert "Herb" Loader. It was indeed a sad day for him when the incline closed and the locomotive was no longer required. Indeed, on closure, the Peckett was still in excellent condition thanks to the skill and care lavished upon it by Mr Loader and it was given by the NCB, on indefinite loan, to the Somerset & Dorset Railway Trust. Initially the locomotive was retained at Radstock but was later moved to the West Somerset Railway once the former site had been closed. As for the Kilmersdon Colliery incline this was believed to have been used for the last time on Sunday, 9th June 1974 when seven trucks, some the property of the S&D Trust, were lowered to the sidings alongside the BR line. Members of the Trust helped the Loaders, Herbert and his son, Nelson, to get the wagons down the incline. At the bottom, the trucks were uncoupled by the then vice-chairman of Norton-Radstock Council, Cecil Jones, himself a former employee of Kilmersdon Colliery. Another delightful piece of Victorian engineering fell into disuse. Today, it is hard to realise that an incline was ever there!

Marcroft's Wagon Works, Radstock

Private Owners Wagons: Some Background Information

By Act of Parliament, the early UK railways were "common carriers". Stated simply, this implied that they had to transport, on demand, almost any form of freight traffic then on offer. This "common carrier" requirement meant that anything from meat to machinery, coal to bananas, tar to tomatoes, cattle to packing cases all had to be catered for. As can be imagined, these various traffics called for many different kinds of freight wagons.

By the early 1860s, when the Bristol & North Somerset Railway was in its infancy, the national railway system had developed to the stage where private companies such as collieries, coal traders, gas and electricity undertakings, fishing companies, mills, factories and the like all found they had a new and reliable way of moving their goods. It was therefore a natural step for these companies to begin to buy their own wagons, these being built in a wide selection of styles and colours. At first, these freight wagons carried the owner's name, the type of goods carried, and the destination painted on the sides of the wagons. Soon, however, the advertising potential was realised and they began to carry advertising slogans and company liveries, the latter becoming quite complicated as time went on.

In addition, companies found that there were other benefits to be had by owning their own wagons. They could be held at coal yards and factory sidings without incurring the

MARCROFT, RADSTOCK – STONE WAGONS UNDER REPAIR
Maintaining a long tradition of repairing stone carrying wagons and standing among a variety of BR's own permanent way wagons, some modern 51 tonne, two-axle wagons from the Mendip quarrying firm of Foster Yeoman await attention at Marcroft.

Marcroft, Radstock

demurrage charges which had to be paid by industrial firms to the various railway companies for letting them use their rolling stock. Nevertheless, the railways still extracted a "Shunting and Siding Rent" charge. This was later covered by a Commuted Scheme, owners/operators contributing to this scheme either having plates or stencils with the logo "C" affixed to their wagons.

Before the railway companies amalgamated into four main companies, the GWR, the LNER, the LMSR and the SR, a large proportion of the UK's coal traffic was handled by the railways in wagons which were, for the most part at least, of 8, 10 or 12 tons capacity. This state of affairs continued right up to the time when wagon fleets were pooled in September 1939. Numerous efforts were made by the railway companies to get rid of the wagons which were of the lower carrying capacities but these attempts were resisted by the owners who,

PRIVATE OWNER WAGON E. BAILY & SON, FROME (1)
Built to take coal to the maltsters of Frome, this black bodywork with white lettering wagon was built by the Gloucester Railway Carriage & Wagon Company in March 1893. (Note mis-spelling of word "Maltsters".) *Gloucester RCW. Co.*

PRIVATE OWNER WAGON E. BAILY & SON, FROME (2)
In the same livery and built by the same company as the wagon shown above, this later example of the wagon builder's art was constructed for use in January 1903. *Gloucester RCW Co.*

RADSTOCK COAL CO. IN THE 1800s
Eddie Dowding was generous enough to contribute the accompanying photograph which shows the Radstock Coal Company's wagon works in the late 1800s. This wagon works was taken over by Marcroft in the early years of the present century.

The workmen are, from left to right:

Back row Bill Nuth, Albert Ashman, Bill Ashman and Dave Nuth.

Front row F. Moon, S. Biggs, Walter Dowding, Bill Nuth (Senior). The young lad was John Seymour.

Mr Walter Dowding (Eddie's father) was born in 1873 and was employed by Sir Frank Beauchamp, the local colliery owner, as a clerk in the office of the Radstock Coal Company Wagon Works. While Mr Dowding (Senior) was working for Beauchamp he became acquainted with the well-known entrepreneur, Mr Samuel Lloyd Harvey, whose name we have encountered elsewhere in this book.

Other items worthy of note in the photograph are the wagons with dumb buffers (these are obviously being converted to self-contained spring buffers), and the office and wagon works themselves looming large in the background. Incidentally, while Mr Dowding (Junior) was working at Marcroft, these sheds were extended by the currently-existing steel structures.

E. Dowding

as customers of the railways, were able to exert their strong influence.

With the standardisation of design at the 1923 Grouping the 12 ton wagons with a timber body, one door at each side and one end door, became the accepted vehicle for coal traffic. By World War Two the majority of 12 ton wagons were still of the timber type but all-steel construction was being favoured for larger wagons. The GWR in particular actively tried to make the 20 tonner popular, especially for coal shipments. Nevertheless, the 20 tonner did not become generally accepted as the greater part of the domestic coal handled was for delivery to small merchants and to these the larger wagons were unwelcome since the sidings and handling facilities of many large coal users, and of some collieries as well, were not built to take such large vehicles.

In these conditions, the 12 tonner remained standard. This meant that the railways had to indulge in a good deal of shunting and, on the outward journey from a colliery, a train of say fifty wagons could quite possibly include loads of 30/40 different consignees based on 20/30 different stations. When the wagons were empty each had to be returned to the colliery, as indicated by the owner, so that a considerable amount of shunting was needed, much as had been the case on the way out!

Once the Second World War came along the private owner wagon fleet was pooled so that detailed and precise shunting of empties was no longer necessary. If, at a given time, twenty wagons were cleared empty from one yard, they could all be sent away without any further marshalling to the same colliery. They could easily have been transferred to a neighbouring gasworks to load coke or to a local goods yard for scrap metal. Without any doubt, the pool proved very useful in reducing shunting and empty mileage to a minimum. Certain private owner wagons were not included in the common pool. Special traffic wagons not part of the common arrangements included those carrying tarred roadstone, tar and petrol tanks, covered salt wagons plus various other unusual vehicles.

One interesting by-product of wartime economy was that private owner wagons, like those of the railway companies, were repainted in a much simpler style. Before the war most owners favoured scarlet, grey or black for their wagons, with white block lettering which, on red and light grey vehicles, were usually shaded with black. On black and dark grey wagons the lettering was more often than not unshaded, although red shading was occasionally seen. The majority of the Welsh colliery companies preferred black wagons with bold, white, unshaded lettering. Usually reduced to the name of the company, or perhaps its initials, this style, when cleanly done, was possible one of the most effective. The same style, on red, grey and black wagons, was popular with the larger colliery companies elsewhere and also with the larger businesses and merchants.

Many thousands of private owner wagons were still in use on the railways until the Nationalisation of the coal industry took place in 1947 and of the railway network in 1948. After Nationalisation a few private wagons were allowed to remain in traffic for carrying tar, oil, cement and lime while, more recently British Rail have relaxed the rules to allow the transporting of minerals other than coal, and of some other commodities, in private owner wagons, the latter often in their own colourful liveries. Our story really does seem to have come full circle!

The Somerset Coalfield and the Mendip Quarries

Some Private Owners' Liveries c1930

Name of Company	Body Colour	Lettering Colour
CAMERTON COLLIERY	Black	White
DUNKERTON COAL FACTORS	Lead	White, shaded black
RADSTOCK COAL COMPANY	Black	White
LUDLOWS PIT	Black	White
NORTON HILL COLLIERY	Black	White
BRAYSDOWN	Black	White
WRITHLINGTON COLLIERY	Bauxite	White
FOXCOTE COLLIERY	Bauxite	White
KILMERSDON COLLIERY	Bauxite	White
MELLS ROAD TAR WORKS	Black	White
S.C. GILSON & SONS (Mells Road)	Red	White

(This company is believed to have had no more than two or three wagons under its ownership.)

Name of Company	Body Colour	Lettering Colour
ROAD RECONSTRUCTION (1934) LIMITED	Grey	White
MELLS COLLIERY	Lead	White, shaded black
MELLS STONE QUARRY (BILBAO)	Red	White
NEWBURY COLLIERY	Lead	White

A Short History of Marcroft's Wagon Works

(Grateful acknowledgements to Mr Wilf White for his help with this section.)

According to a plan attached to the 1877 GWR/Kilmersdon Colliery agreement a "Radstock Wagon Works" existed, in the late 1870s, on the site that later became occupied by Marcroft's Wagon Works, the subject of our story in this section. It is believed that these early works were used not only as wagon repair shops but were also employed in the repair and maintenance of colliery locomotives. In addition, pit wagons and other ironwork needed in the collieries were manufactured here as well.

The firm of E. Marcroft & Co. was founded in the Radstock area by Mr Ernest Marcroft. With its head offices in Swansea, the company had previously been seen working on railway sidings in Radstock and the surrounding districts. Records at Somerset Collieries Limited state that Ernest Marcroft bought the freehold to the then-existing wagon works on the GWR on 8th June 1920, so presumably the site was only leased before that time. It would seem very likely that the ground was originally leased from the Waldegraves and was included among that family's assets when Sir Frank Beauchamp bought up all the Waldegrave mineral rights in 1919, the selling off of the freehold to the firm of Marcroft being one way of realising some of the unwanted assets.

In 1924 Marcroft became a public company with Ernest Marcroft, as chairman and managing director. Two of his brothers were also in the business with him. When Ernest Marcroft died in 1947, his nephew, Mr Robert Marcroft, succeeded him but, in 1973, the company was the subject of a reverse takeover and ownership passed to the York Trust Limited and, later again, became part of Maurice James' Industries, an industrial group based in the Midlands.

Although the early premises at Radstock were limited as to the number of wagons which could be accommodated (less than half a dozen, in fact), the firm had a foundry where axleboxes, buffer castings and various other cast-iron components were made. There were also facilities for re-tyring wheels but at some later date these fell into disuse. In 1929, a large wagon shop was added to the resources then on offer. This was capable of handling 20 wagons on four sets of tracks. The shop contained what was, at that time, a real luxury, namely, two overhead cranes covering the whole of the working area. The cranes proved of considerable use in that it meant that one end of a wagon then in current usage could be easily lifted without the manhandling of heavy jacks that had previously been the case. Heavy frame timbers, buffer springs, etc. could also be lifted into position with a lot less manual effort.

In earlier years, it seems that the buildings were used for other activities than those of wagon repair work for, at one time, they were reputed to have had their own cock-fighting enthusiasts. In addition, one section of one of the workshop walls had been plastered and decorated. This was pointed out to Mr Wilf White, who had joined the business in 1931, as being part of an organ room where Mr George Hamblin, the secretary to the works' previous owners and an accomplished organist, used to play an organ which had been kept there. In a field adjoining the works the Radstock Town Quoits Club had its quoits beds but these were later moved to the back of the Waldegrave Hotel after first being moved to the Tyning Inn.

When Mr White started work at Radstock, the wagon frames and bodies were of all-wood construction. Mainly of 8 and 10 ton carrying capacity, they had grease lubricated axleboxes and brass bearings. A large proportion of these wagons were either of the "converted" or "reconstructed" types, these terms indicating that the wagons were originally of the dead-buffered variety. These wagons had all been modernised, essentially by the addition of spring buffers and continuous drawgear. Many of these wagons had wheels with cast iron bosses. There were also "New Specification" wagons which were of more modern construction and had been built to the first specification of the Railway Clearing House (RCH). All the wagons repaired by the works in the 1920s and '30s carried either coal or stone.

In the 1930s working conditions were not at all attractive. For example, practically all the woodworking activities along with the blacksmithing were, of necessity, carried out by hand. Such machinery as there was – one lathe for turning wheel tyres and one for turning axle journals; several bolt threading machines, a sawbench drilling machine, a punch and shearing machine, and fans (the latter providing air blast to the blacksmiths' forges) – were all driven by a single-cylinder steam engine, the boiler of which also provided steam for the steam hammer in the blacksmiths' shop. On top of all this, the steam powered a small dynamo which provided a fluctuating supply of electric light! The light for working underneath the wagons during hours of darkness was provided by oil lamps of the "teapot" variety, namely, those where the wick protruded from the spout. When lit, these lamps were smoky and smelly, but even worse, they gave a poor light.

The bulk of the work undertaken by Marcroft was on a contract basis. Such contracts were taken out with wagon owners for a period of years for which an annual rate was agreed. For this, the repairer did all the work necessary in repairing, maintaining, repainting and relettering the wagons. The latter activity was usually carried out twice during a seven year contract. These contracts were obtained in the face of very severe competition.

At Marcroft, in common with other wagon repairers of the time, there were a variety of trades represented and employed in the works. These included wagon repairers who dealt with the carpentry and with other work on the frames and the bodies. There were lifters who lifted the wagons off their wheels so that these could be inspected, serviced or changed, painters who cleaned down and repainted the wagons and letterers who relettered the wagons in the liveries of their particular owners.

MARCROFT, RADSTOCK
This picture shows the blacksmiths' shop which is busily engaged in the manufacture and reconditioning of various items of wagon ironwork, including springs.
Marcroft, Radstock

MARCROFT, RADSTOCK
The fitting shop, where wheel tyres and axle journals were machined, is shown here. In the foreground a stack of steel bars were being cut to length before being made into brake pushrods.
Marcroft, Radstock

There were also blacksmiths who made and reconditioned all the ironwork while springsmiths reconditioned the side and buffer springs. In addition, there was a wheelturner whose job it was to reprofile worn wheel tyres on the wheel lathe and a fitter who, amongst many other duties, turned journals and refitted bearings damaged when axleboxes ran hot as they very often did at that time. Wagons for repair were shunted into the works by the Great Western Railway's locomotives. However, to get them to the actual spot in the workshops where they were needed for repair a gang of men would be called together and they would push the wagons to the required spot!

Away from South Wales, Radstock was the first works that the company acquired but, as the business expanded, other locations were needed and, eventually, there were six main sites. These were at Radstock, Coalville (near Leicester), Cardiff, Port Talbot, Danygraig and Burry Port. In addition, a large number of outstations were spread around the country as well. The Radstock works, for example, supplied materials and back-up services to outstation depots which had been established at the various collieries and quarries in the locality where wagons were based. There were also outstation depots at the more important railway junctions and marshalling yards, their job being to carry out general maintenance and running repairs.

Marcroft had outstations at various places on the Bristol & North Somerset Railway and on the section from Radstock to Frome. One of these was at Mells Road and this dealt with wagons from Mells Colliery, Mells Stone Quarries (Bilboa), Newbury Colliery and Vobster (see the next section of this chapter for more information on these locations). The trustees of the Earl Waldegrave, the Radstock Coal Company, the Somerset Collieries and Writhlington Collieries' wagons and Pensford & Bromley Collieries' wagons all provided work for Marcroft. Although not directly connected to the B&NSR, Bristol (Kingsland Road) also provided business for the company.

Further afield were the outstations at Camerton, Cranmore and Sandford (the latter two being on the East Somerset and Cheddar Valley branches respectively); Tytherington Quarry on the Thornbury branch just north of Bristol, Westerleigh sidings near Yate, Bath (Green Park), Norton Hill Colliery and Newton Abbot in Devon. In later years further outstations were established at Swindon, Salisbury, Lydney, Old Oak Common and Brent Junction, the last two being in the London area. A repair service was also provided in the Templecombe and Yeovil localities on the former LSWR's lines.

Back in North Somerset, a wagon repairing facility existed for many years at Clutton. This was in the form of a small works established by the Earl of Warwick for the repair of wagons used in his collieries. The works later became the Bristol & Clutton Wagon Company, the private siding agreement for which was dated 24th November 1927. During a good number of years this company was run by a Mr Ernest Rivers. When the works closed, Marcroft operated a wagon repair service here on an outstation basis.

Marcroft had its own fleet of some 5,000 wagons which were let out to customers on hire or lease. In the depths of the depression of the 1930s, business was so difficult that one customer on Mendip hired wagons on a day-to-day basis so precarious were the daily demands for his products! Given below are some of Marcroft's many local customers prior to World War Two:

Binegar, C. Dailey & Co. Ltd
Bridgwater, Sully & Co.
Bristol, Coal Agencies
Bristol, Alfred J. Smith
Dunkerton, Dunkerton Coal Factors
Frome, Roads Reconstruction (1934) Ltd
Glastonbury, John Snow & Co.
Mells, Mells Colliery
Mells, Mells Stone Quarries (Bilbao)
Moorewood, Moorewood Colliery Co.
Newton Abbot, Stoneycombe Lime & Stone Co.
Pensford, Pensford & Bromley Collieries Ltd
Radstock, Somerset Collieries Ltd
Radstock, Writhlington Collieries Co.
Stratton on the Fosse, New Rock Colliery
Wells, Underwood Quarry
Weymouth, G. Bryer Ash
Wickwar, Gloucestershire, Wickwar Quarries.

One Man's View . . .

(Thanks are due to both Mr and the late Mrs Dowding for their help and hospitality.)

On 3rd February 1908, Mr Edmund ("Eddie") Dowding was born in the now-demolished cottages owned by and situated to the rear of the firm of Marcroft. Coincidentally, he was taken on by the very same company around 1924/25, being employed there for nearly twenty years. He finally left the firm in 1943.

In conversation with the author, Eddie Dowding said that while at Marcroft he worked as a carpenter, repairing and building the many wooden-bodied wagons then in traffic. During his stay with the company some 50 people were on the payroll, Mr Henry Ludlam being in charge of the workforce for part of that time.

Within the carpentry shop, Eddie worked with Jim Curtis, Albert Lear, Alfred Marchment, Godfrey Miles, Harry Shellard and, later to become foreman, Mr Stan Smith. Maurice Ladd was also a carpenter at Marcroft. He was one of a group of three or four men almost permanently engaged on outstation work.

Incidentally, the GWR's engine shed at Radstock, later to become part of the wagon works itself, was under the control of Mr Tom Griffin during Mr Dowding's early few years at Marcroft.

In the blacksmith's shop, Eddie remembers Jock Mounty and Ernest Fear. Another colleague, Jack Sherborn, was a wheel lathe turner while Harold Ludlam was in charge of the fitting shop. In the 1920s Joe Nash worked as a signwriter while Douglas Britten was later engaged in this work. The Churchill brothers from Peasedown St John both worked at Marcroft, one being a lifter, the other working as a carpenter.

Eddie remembers how the wagon building and repairing business was hard and slogging sledgehammer work, with such activities as removing bolts that were well corroded into the wagon, especially those that had seen heavy service in areas near the sea. He went on to say that in the Radstock area people always saw the men at the neighbouring collieries and quarries as having a tough time of things but he made the point that wagon building was also a part of this same harsh, outdoor and heavily manual league. Strangely enough, however, the industry's arduous conditions were frequently overlooked. Nevertheless, in spite of these difficult ways of working, the men at Marcroft had a strong sense of humour and, once in the job, tended to stay in it. Nonetheless, one occasion when their absence was noted was during the time of the General Strike of 1926 when the workforce came out for nine days.

A booklet entitled *"Marcroft: Works & Depots"* published around 1932 gives the following information. It says that Marcroft Wagons Limited were the owners of:

The Margam Wagon Works & Forge, Port Talbot.
The Cardiff & Newport Wagon Works, Cardiff.
The Radstock Wagon & Wheel Works, Radstock.
The Coalville Wagon Works, Coalville.

At this time, the head office was at Swansea but it also had works and branch offices at Cardiff, Port Talbot, Radstock and Coalville. In addition, it had outstation depots at Burry Port, Swansea, Bristol (Kingsland Road), Gloucester, Lydney, Old Oak Common, Brent, Swindon, Newport, Rogerstone, Neath (Low Level station), Newton Abbot, Bath, Gowerton, Gurnos, Westerleigh, Yate, Binegar, Cranmore, Teign Valley (Bovey Tracey), Pantyffynnon, Salisbury, Abercrave, Birmingham and Leicester (South Wigston).

The telephone number for the Radstock Works was 3!

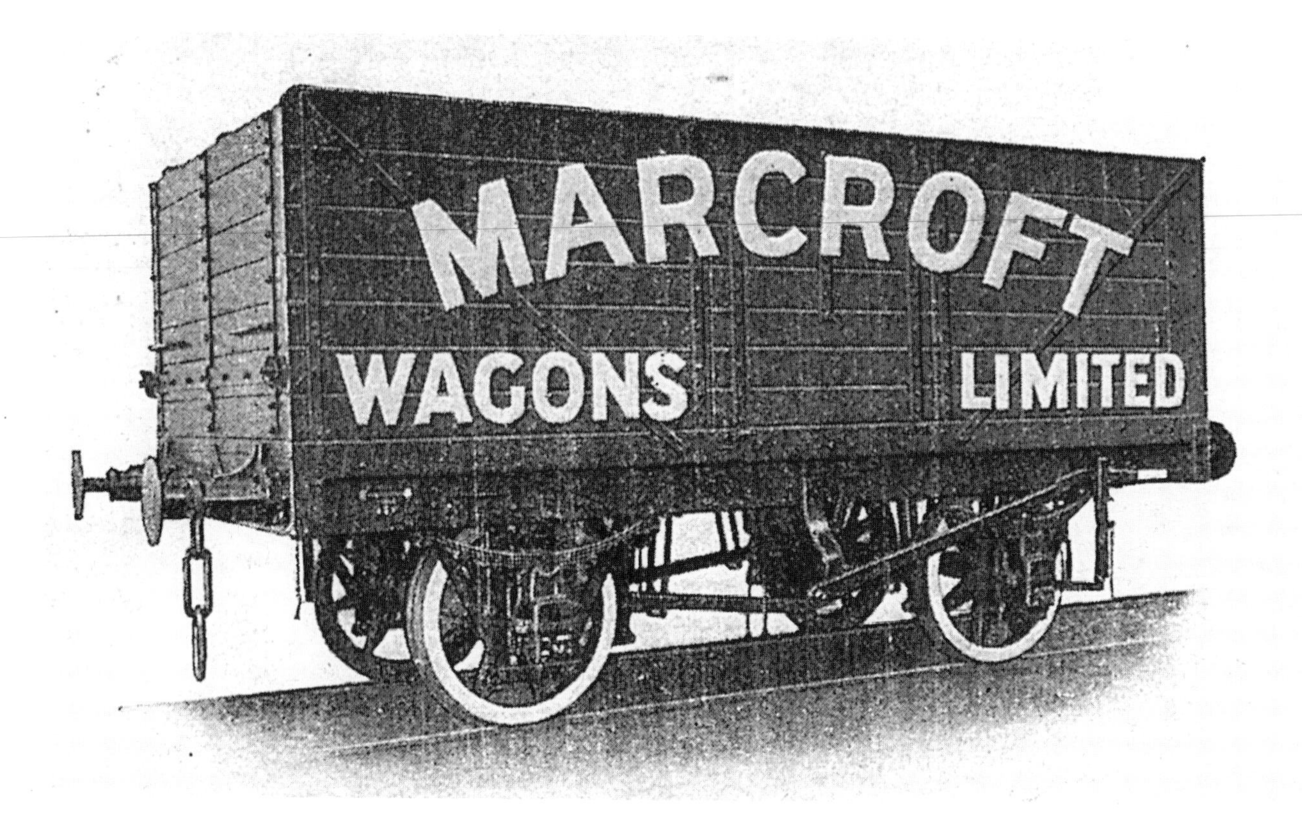

MARCROFT WAGONS LIMITED: AN EXAMPLE OF THEIR WORK

Author's collection

Wagons in Wartime

To appreciate how the pattern of the wagon repair business was altered by the outbreak of the Second World War, it needs to be realised that all over the country there were a great many wagon firms involved in the repair of a large number of privately owned wagons. These firms were all working on the same basis and were in fierce competition with one another. In addition, the four main railway companies (the GWR, LMSR, LNER and the Southern) also had fleets of their own wagons. However, upon declaration of war on the 3rd September 1939 practically all railway wagons were requisitioned by the Ministry of Supply, the Ministry taking over complete responsibility for the necessary repair and maintenance of these wagons. One of the immediate benefits to arise from this takeover was the elimination of much empty haulage. Thus, if a Writhlington Collieries' wagon ran loaded from Radstock to Barnstaple instead of returning empty, it could be loaded with something else at Barnstaple and sent on to another destination. It can readily be seen from this that local wagons quickly disappeared, their place being taken up by wagons from other parts of the county.

Wagon repairing was given a high priority during the war and most of the personnel in the industry were given "Reserved Occupation" status, this exempting them from military service. At Marcroft there was a continual demand for repaired wagons and many, many long hours of overtime were worked during the difficult years of the war. The pressures of the conflict made it necessary to improve facilities and, in 1939, the wagon repair shop in existence when the works were acquired, was rebuilt. In 1940 this was followed by the addition of a woodworking shop with up-to-date machinery. Of necessity for the new equipment, the works were connected to the main power supply and all existing machines were then motorised. A modern lighting system was also installed. Two other wartime activities in which Marcroft became involved were the building of some new 12 ton wood framed wagons for the Ministry of Supply while the repair of petrol and oil tankers was carried out for the Petroleum Board.

The final demise of the pre-war privately owned wagon fleets came with the Nationalisation of the railways in 1947 when all the wagons still remaining from those pooled on 3rd September 1939 were taken over. Marcroft continued to repair these wagons but their original names and numbers were dispensed with, new numbers being allocated, these being given a "P" prefix. Steel frames and all steel ex-railway companies' wagons which had previously been repaired exclusively by railway company workshops were allowed into privately-owned repair shops. For Marcroft, this meant the need to install air compressors, riveting tools and electric welding equipment. Some of these steel wagons were also fitted with vacuum brakes. These had to be periodically overhauled and again new equipment in the form of vacuum exhausters had to be installed, men having to be trained in the new ways.

The earlier relationship with the Petroleum Board continued in the shape of further work from Shell-Mex and BP and a large number of petrol and oil tankers were dealt with. The volume of work on steel wagons increased when BR's fleet of 16 ton all steel mineral wagons began to fall due for repair and another workshop was added in 1951. This was equipped with an overhead crane and additional roof height. From now on steel frame and all steel wagons began to dominate the scene as the all wood wagons were phased out. A descaling and repainting programme was introduced for the 16 ton wagons and, eventually this work, which involved spray painting, was carried out in the former GWR engine shed which had been rented by Marcroft for many years.

The scope of the work undertaken for British Railways continued to widen with repairs being carried out on covered goods vans, permanent way wagons, 21 ton hopper wagons and 'Walrus' wagons which were then used in connection with the stone traffic on Mendip. However the scene, as regards outstations, was changing drastically. Several had already been lost through the closure of local pits such as those at Camerton and Pensford, while others had disappeared through a reorganisation scheme. This had been introduced in an attempt to reduce the number of repairing firms at any one geographical point to just one. In addition, another blow was struck in 1957 when the allocation of work to Cranmore on the East Somerset was withdrawn by British Railways on the grounds of economy.

About this same time Marcroft secured a contract with the Port of Bristol Authority (PBA) to recondition and repaint a fleet of wagons which they had purchased from BR for internal use on the Authority's rail network at their docks. A

MARCROFT, RADSTOCK
A broad view of the sawmill and woodworking shop is given here. In the left foreground Mr Harold Green is seen machining a headstock on the mortising and boring machine. *Marcroft, Radstock*

MARCROFT, RADSTOCK
A major overhaul, here being carried out by Mr George Latchem and Mr Wilf Young, is seen in progress in this photograph. Only two of the main frames' members remained when this picture was taken. All remaining parts of the wagon would be renewed before the work was completed. *Marcroft, Radstock*

special, temporary workshop was built for this work and the contract occupied a gang of 7-8 men for several years. Around this time, another contract was also secured, this one being with Shell-Mex & BP Limited, to service their tank car fleet at their Avonmouth installation, then rail connected.

In 1961 a major expansion of the Radstock works was achieved through the addition of another workshop. It was equipped with a 10 ton, overhead electric crane on a gantry some thirty feet above rail level. This facility considerably widened the range of work which could be handled. One example of its usefulness occurred when it off-loaded a number of wagons which had been extensively damaged in a mishap near Frome. The damage was so severe that they had to be lifted onto low-loading bogie wagons and sent to Marcroft for repair. Without this off-loading facility these twisted vehicles would have been sent elsewhere and a substantial order would have been lost.

When the wagon fleets were nationalised there were some 1.25 million wagons in use. However, since that time there has been a continual reduction in the size of the fleet which has been brought about by a constantly changing economic and commercial climate. The withdrawal of large numbers of wagons has been accomplished by setting tight limits on the amount of money which can be spent on repairs. If the estimated cost of repairing the wagon exceeds the limit set, the wagon is scrapped and sold for breaking up. As a result of this latter procedure, and with a constantly dwindling wagon fleet, it was obvious that, long term, the future was not very bright for wagon repairers and many of them considered it prudent to look around for other, alternative business. It was reasoned that if possible this should use equipment such as electric welding which was already installed. The first effort in this diversification by Marcroft was the manufacture of some simple agricultural equipment which, for several years at least, proved quite successful. To further this policy of diversification, in 1965, the blacksmiths' shop was turned over to general engineering and, with the closure of Norton Hill Colliery and the loss of the outstation depot there in 1966, two of the men were transferred to the engineering shop for re-training and subsequently made very efficient machinists.

In 1966, following the closure of the Somerset & Dorset, the coal from Writhlington Colliery was transferred to the North Somerset via the already-mentioned link west of the two former stations at Radstock. This coal, together with that from Kilmersdon, was sent mainly to Portishead via Bristol. Marcroft's works were also fed with wagons from the Bristol end. However, as we have seen, in 1968 the Bristol-Radstock section of line was closed and coal traffic was re-routed via the single and re-opened line between Mells Road and Frome. This re-opening was to be a very significant event for the future of Marcroft's base at Radstock.

A Working Day At Marcroft's Wagon Works – Winter 1963

by C. J. Peacock

In October 1965 a visitor to Marcroft's Wagon Works described the site and its activities in the following way. At the time of his visit he said that among the wagons under repair there were tank wagons belonging to Shell, Shell/BP and National. In addition, there, were BR 16 ton mineral, 13 ton 5-plank open and 13 ton 'Hybar' wagons; there were ballast wagons of the 'Walrus', 'Herring', 'Dogfish' and 'Grampus' varieties while a 20 ton steel hopper with wooden extension planks, a 20 ton coke wagon, an ex-private owner 21 ton steel mineral wagon and an ex-GWR 13 ton 6-plank wagon all added to the diversity.

Work actually being carried out included the renewing of brake shoes, buffers, wheel springs and brake gear, replacing of body panels and doors on steel wagons and the renewing of floors and side planks on wooden

MARCROFT, RADSTOCK – WORK IN PROGRESS

Marcroft, Radstock

MARCROFT, RADSTOCK – SHUNTING THE YARD

Marcroft, Radstock

wagons. Some wagons were over pits or on trestles with wheels, axleboxes and springs removed. Others were jacked up at one end and had just one pair of wheels removed. In the machine shop were centre lathes, shapers, slotters, guillotines, welding and riveting equipment, pillar drills and a wheel turning lathe. Spares to be seen dotted about the place included springs, "V" hangers, buffers and buffer guides, axleboxes, brake shoe castings, couplings and wheels. Painting was being carried out in the former GWR engine shed, while an adjacent grounded van body was being used as a paint store. Within the works themselves, movement of wagons was being carried out by a small shunting tractor.

With the end of the Somerset Coalfield in 1973 Marcroft became the only company at Radstock that still required rail-connected facilities. At the same time BR decided that they still needed repair facilities at Radstock and, after a survey of the line from Hapsford Loop to Radstock, decided that the freight service over this stretch of track should continue. It would seem most unlikely that Marcroft would have remained rail-connected if this had involved BR keeping in use the 15 odd miles of track from Bristol to Pensford including, as it did, the viaduct at Pensford and the level crossing at Radstock.

In the light of continuing reductions in BR's wagon fleet and their policy that in future they would only *haul* freight trains, the provision of wagons in that train being left to the customer, steps were taken to secure business from companies already operating privately-owned fleets. This move met with a large measure of success and saw the arrival at Radstock of yet more varieties of rail freight vehicles.

In the late 1960s and early '70s, a new generation of freight wagons was being introduced onto British Rail's tracks, their main strength over their predecessors being their ability to carry much larger loads at higher speeds. As an example, a bogie tank wagon with a gross laden weight of 100 tons could carry over 200,000 gallons of petroleum spirit while a two axle wagon with a gross laden weight of 45 tons could carry between 8 and 9,000 gallons of heavy fuel oil. Many of these wagons were fitted with a more advanced type of vacuum braking system incorporating an automatic empty load changeover device. They also had a more sophisticated type of suspension. Variations on the 1 in 20 tyre profile were introduced to meet new working conditions out on the railway.

Soon, vacuum brakes were superseded by air brakes and a 51 ton GLW two-axle vehicle appeared in neighbouring Mendip quarries. This type of wagon was equipped with disc brakes and could carry 37½ tons of stone at 60 mph – a very far cry from the 8 and 10 ton capacity all wood and grease axlebox wagons of the 1920s and '30s! A large number of these wagons were repaired at Radstock and a representative of one local quarry owner stated that but for the repair facility at Radstock their business on Mendip would probably have never become established! As well as the business in stone traffic wagons, Marcroft had for many years been repairing BR's permanent way wagons. However, with the upgrading of the Western Region's Bristol Parkway-Swindon-London main line for IC125 trains in the 1970s Marcroft was kept particularly busy repairing fleets of permanent way wagons which were then being much used on the upgrading work.

In 1975 an important contact was established with a London-based company, Storage & Transport Systems (STS), who owned a fleet of tank wagons carrying a wide variety of chemicals. A number of different types of these vehicles were sent to Radstock and, as a result, facilities were installed for shot-blasting and spray painting. The former GWR engine shed was again brought into use for this purpose. In turn, this brought work from other customers. A cement manufacturer sent in a fleet of wagons used for the transport of gypsum, these wagons being similar in design to the coal-carrying

REPAIRED WAGONS FROM RADSTOCK (1)
Class 47 No. 47068 winds its way and its train of repaired wagons past Batch Farm, west of Mells Road, on 4th December 1975.
Mike Miller

REPAIRED WAGONS FROM RADSTOCK (2)
Class 47 No. 47055 crosses the rolling countryside of Mells Down with a marvellous assortment of repaired wagons from Marcroft's Wagon Works at Radstock. The photograph was taken on 22nd April 1980.
Mike Miller

FROME GRAMMAR SCHOOL RAILWAY CLUB'S RAILTOUR NOVEMBER 1961
In its trip along the North Somerset the brake van special called at Marcroft's Wagon Works where a Portland Cement van on the firm's traverser was the centre of attraction.

John Keeping

mgr wagons. These had to be completely overhauled, shot-blasted and repainted.

Work was also undertaken on the modification of the 51 ton GLW wagons used by the Mendip quarry firms of ARC and Foster Yeoman. This involved having equipment to rotate them to the upside-down position so that work could be carried out on their underframes. A loss of work occurred, however, in 1978 when British Rail decided that it no longer needed a repair facility at Radstock and withdrew its allocation of business. The wheel had turned full circle and the situation that had existed prior to the outbreak of the 1939/45 war, namely that all the work needed to keep the company going had to be got from the owners of private fleets, now applied again. This situation had been foreseen at the Radstock works and so enough business was available to keep the company operating.

In 1980 STS acquired the company, one objective of this takeover being to have the firm's own repair facility for its own fleet. In fact, STS was the UK subsidiary of the Belgian group, N.V. CAIB S.A., Europe's largest rail transport services group. CAIB owned some 28,000 wagons, five major repair shops and two wagon building works. Their operational field spread throughout Western Europe. In the United Kingdom STS owned a fleet of nearly 600 wagons of all types, some of which were soon seen at the Radstock works bearing their red STS sign. STS's business in the UK over the last 30 years or so has been in the hiring of specialised wagons, mainly to the chemical, petroleum and fertilizer industries. In 1986, however, another re-organisation took place when a new company CAIB UK was formed. The then four existing companies: Storage & Transport System Limited (STS), Marcroft Engineering Limited, Railcall Limited and Traffic Services Limited were combined, each one trading as separate divisions of the new company.

Back on the ground in North Somerset, Monday 29th February 1988 saw Bath Fire Service carrying out a firefighting exercise in the former goods yard at Radstock (GW). This entailed the use of Chemical Sub-Sector Class 47 No. 47053 which arrived at Radstock from Westbury at 09.30 hauling one coal hopper and two tank wagons. In addition, Marcroft Engineering had also given the Fire Service permission to make use of a line of private owner tank wagons in their exercise. Stabled at Radstock for some considerable time, these were due to be converted into static tanks by the company.

The exercise itself was completed by 10.30 but, unfortunately for BR, the day's incidents were not over, for while the locomotive was propelling its train back over a double slip in the yard it became rerailed. This was due to the very poor condition of the track which spread under the weight of the locomotive, thus derailing one of its bogies. It was not re-railed until 15.00 that afternoon by crews who had come out by road from Westbury depot!

More bad news was to follow in the spring of 1988 when it was announced that Marcroft's Radstock Works were going to be closed at the end of June. This would involve the loss of three clerical and 22 engineering jobs. It was therefore a sad occasion when, on the morning of 29th June 1988, what was probably the last "official" freight train to serve Radstock arrived at Marcroft Engineering from Westbury. Headed by Railfreight Class 47 No. 47370 the train was made up of an open wagon and a brake van carrying a number of camera-clicking BR officials. Around 10.45 the train was greeted by a goodly number of local children and residents.

The open wagon was left at the repair works for the loading of items from the works for transfer to other parts of the parent company. At some stage in July this wagon formed the last train to serve the works but the running of this was carried out without fuss and notice. Meanwhile, back on the 29th the 47/3 went on to gather some 16 wagons to take back to Westbury. As these had been in store at Radstock for quite some time, trouble was experienced with some of the wagons' brakes. The locomotive and its train were due to return at 11.00 but it was not until 12.32 that the train actually left for its return to Westbury. The intention had been to have the brake van next to the locomotive but because of the brake trouble it had to be placed at the rear of the train.

Mr R. C. Bunyar, who kindly supplied the above information stated that he had earlier requested a charter dmu for a last run down to Radstock but that BR had told him that this request could not be granted due to the poor condition of the permanent way. Ironically enough, some two weeks before the clearance train described above had run, the Civil Engineer's Department two-car 'Sprinter' Track Recording Train had run right down into the former GWR yard at Radstock!

However, all may not be lost for the Radstock-Mells Road-Whatley Quarry Junction section for plans are afoot that could rejuvenate this line's damp and decaying trackage. Although a sad event in itself, the closure of the wagon repair shops at

SEG RAILTOUR AT RADSTOCK – JULY 1981
With Marcroft's in the background, a three-car dmu set No. L416 arrives at Radstock with a railtour on 25th July 1981. *Mike Miller*

FIREFIGHTING AT RADSTOCK
With No. 47053 in the background, a lone Bath fireman is seen in action against a line of tank wagons in the former GWR yard at Radstock on 29th February 1988. *R. C. Bunyar*

CLEARING UP AT THE WORKS (1)
With a heavy train of wagons in tow, Class 47 No. 47370 waits at the foot of Mells Bank before returning to Westbury on 29th June 1988.
R. C. Bunyar

CLEARING UP AT THE WORKS (2)
With a shunting tractor providing the motive power, two open wagons containing wagon wheels are propelled out of the shops and towards the train waiting to take them along the remaining section of the former Wilts, Somerset & Weymouth Railway. *R. C. Bunyar*

Marcroft has opened up the possibility of the Frome-Radstock section being reinstated as a steam-operated tourist railway. With growth taking place, both in the local and tourist population of North Somerset, the market possibilities would seem to be very hopeful indeed, and the Somerset & Avon Railway Co. Ltd was formed in early 1989.

It is estimated that £200,000 would be needed to bring the line up to passenger carrying standards. Along with this service it is planned that a museum, industrial heritage centre and children's activity centre could be built at Radstock. At Frome, a new station will be built and that at Mells Road reopened.

Dennis Haines of Frome, one of the main proponents of the scheme, said that:

> "(It) . . . will bring enormous benefits to the area and will restore an important part of Radstock. The railway and heritage centre together will form an easily identifiable attraction and a viable commercial activity."

He reckons that the route could attract some 48,000 passengers a year. Funding for the venture would come from a share issue and through long-term leases from Avon and Somerset County Councils. The Somerset and Avon Railway Association has been set up to support the project. Who knows, if this project succeeds, Mells Bank could once more reverberate to the blasting exhaust of hard-working steam locomotives and Kilmersdon see the opening of a station – at last!

MEDITATIONS AT MARCROFT
Class 47 No. 47185 simmers in the early spring sun at Marcroft's while working the Saturday morning trip from Westbury on 2nd March 1974.

Grenville R. Hounsell

Coal Mining and Quarrying in the Mells Area

Apart from weaving, coal mining was the oldest industry in the area around Mells and, in the reign of Charles II, the hamlet of Mells is specifically mentioned as one of the places in ". . . the forest of Mendippe where coalpits are . . ." Indeed it was fortunate that the unemployment caused by the decline of the weaving industry was, to some extent at least, ameliorated by the growth in the coal industry and in the arrival in Mells of the firm of Fussells (see Chapter 6). Actually, in relation to the mining of coal, Collington in 1791 says:

> "There are several coalworks in the parish, in some of which is a stratum of clay, equal to the Stourbridge in the manufacture of crucibles; lead, manganese, pipe clay and fuller's earth. In a hill called Vobster Tor, from the hamlet of Vobster, is a vein of ash-coloured marble streaked with red. (In 1798 there was calamine) . . . At the time a large quantity was raised in Mells, remarkably pure and of excellent quality."

However, our story directs us back to the mining of coal, iron ore and limestone and the ways in which they were

brought together in the areas around Mells and Westbury to cater for the growing demand for iron during the mid and late Victorian period.

Along the Line of the Newbury Railway

Pre 1887 the Newbury Railway made connection with the GWR's Radstock-Frome line at Mells good shed and, after that time, with Mells Road station itself, the latter being opened in that year. Naturally enough, there were exchange sidings at Mells Road and these handled the coal, coke and limestone generated by the collieries and quarries along the route of the Newbury Railway and its associated tramways.

Heading southwards from the GWR and running in a

WESTBURY STATION & WESTBURY IRONWORKS
This view of Westbury station, probably taken in the early years of the 20th century, clearly shows the Westbury Ironworks on the extreme left. The photograph was taken looking towards London.
Lens of Sutton

THE NEWBURY RAILWAY 1882

Original plan: Ordnance Survey

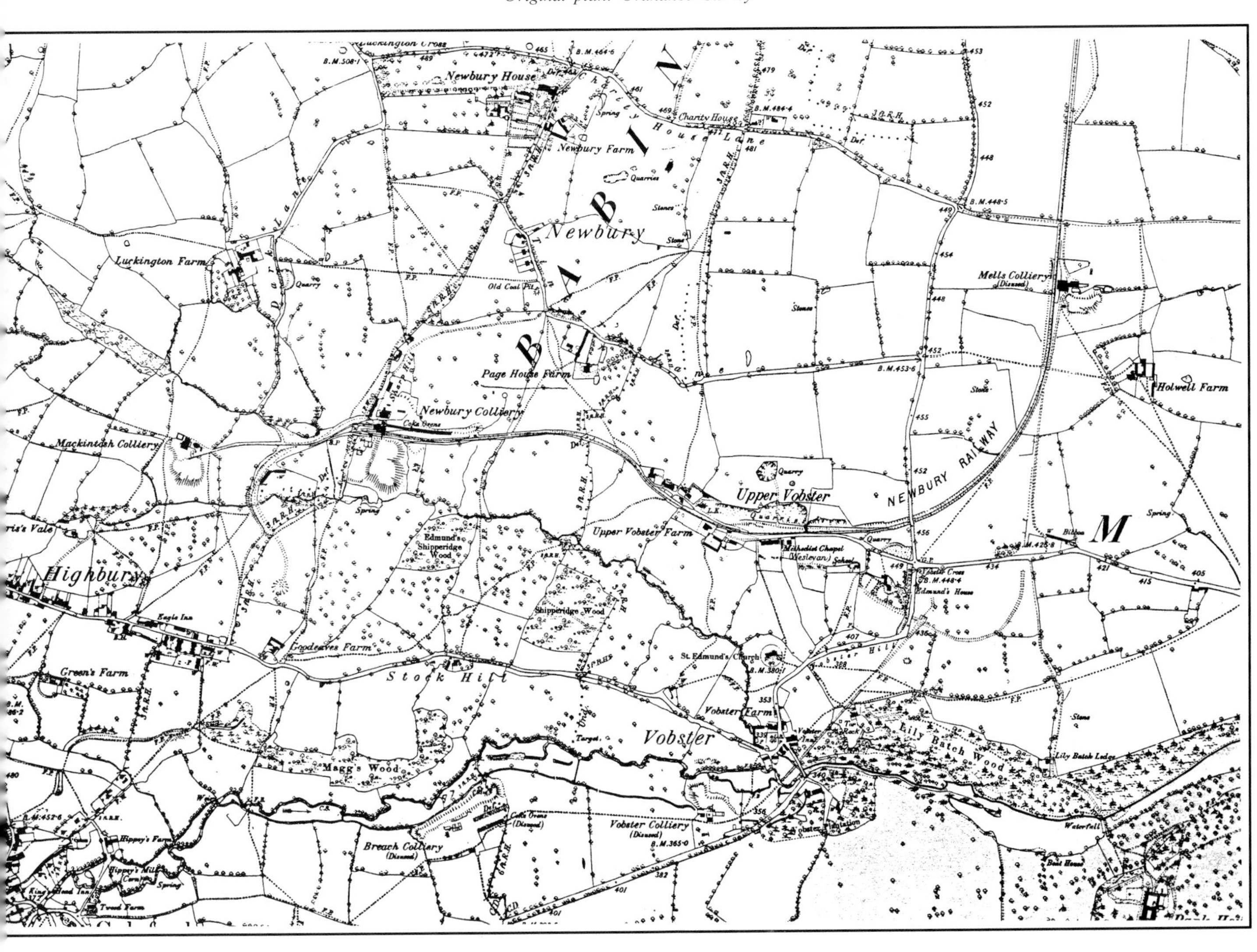

straight line through the Somerset countryside, the Newbury Railway cut across and through the route of the once partially constructed, but never completed, Dorset & Somerset Canal. Three quarters of a mile out, and around the year of 1863, sidings were built to serve Mells Colliery which was situated on the eastern side of the line here (see plan on page 215). These sidings were removed in the 1880s after the colliery's first closure. During 1909 they were laid in for a second time when the colliery re-opened for business. During World War Two they were removed for the final time after the pit had been abandoned once more.

Once past Mells Colliery, the Newbury Railway swung around to the west, passing Vobster Cross and serving Vobster Quarry, the latter being served by a long siding on the Newbury line's northern side some mile and a quarter from Mells Road. Passing to the south of the quarry the "Newbury" then continued westwards for another quarter of a mile, terminating at Newbury Colliery itself, a distance of two miles from the GWR. Here capacious coke ovens had been built on the northern side of the line. In 1891 these were served simply by a solitary siding but, by 1904, a loading bank had been built. At Newbury three lines ran under the colliery screens, two being used for loading coal, the third running right through the screens to serve a loco shed which was situated on the Mackintosh side of the pithead at Newbury.

There were plans to extend the standard gauge line of the Newbury Railway (it was broad gauge from its opening c1857 to 1874) from Newbury Colliery on through to Mackintosh Colliery but, although this work was started in 1918, the extension was never completed, Mackintosh closing in 1919. In the event the two pits were linked by a narrow gauge tubline, a portion of which was made up of a three-rail incline. The tramway was worked by a hauling engine located at the Mackintosh end although shunting was carried out by horses at Newbury. This latter colliery closed in 1927. Today parts of the Newbury Railway can still be seen between Vobster and the former junction at Mells Road.

Looking at the Newbury Railway's connections in the Mells and Vobster areas there were two sidings that are worth exploring in a little more detail. One of these ran in a south-easterly direction to serve to serve Mells, or as it was otherwise known, Bilboa Quarry, the route of this line diverging from the Newbury Railway south of the site of Mells Colliery. The second siding ran off the NR in a south-westerly direction, possibly close to the line of the footpath shown in the Ordnance Survey map (1882) running from the NR to Vobster Cross. There is some doubt, however, as to whether or not this siding actually made *direct* interchange with the then-running Vobster tramway which connected Vobster Breach and Vobster Collieries with the area around Vobster Cross. Certainly a landsale depot was in use at some stage at Vobster Cross. In addition, it would seem reasonable to assume that Vobster Collieries' good coking coal would be in demand at Westbury Ironworks. Nevertheless, whether or not the tramway and the Newbury Railway had direct interchange remains an open question at this time.

Before bringing this section to a close a few further details of the Vobster tramway may prove helpful (again see map on page 211). Starting near Vobster Cross the tramway ran towards the south-west for about a quarter of a mile passing close by the Vobster Inn. It then turned west through the yard of Vobster Colliery, continuing westwards yet again before reaching its terminus at Vobster Breach Colliery. Here, generous siding provision served three banks of coke ovens, with another siding linking in directly to the pit-head. It seems likely that much of the coal went straight from pithead to coke oven

THE COLLIERIES AT MACKINTOSH AND NEWBURY

Mackintosh and Newbury Collieries as shown by the second edition of the Ordnance Survey (1904).

Original: Tim Venton

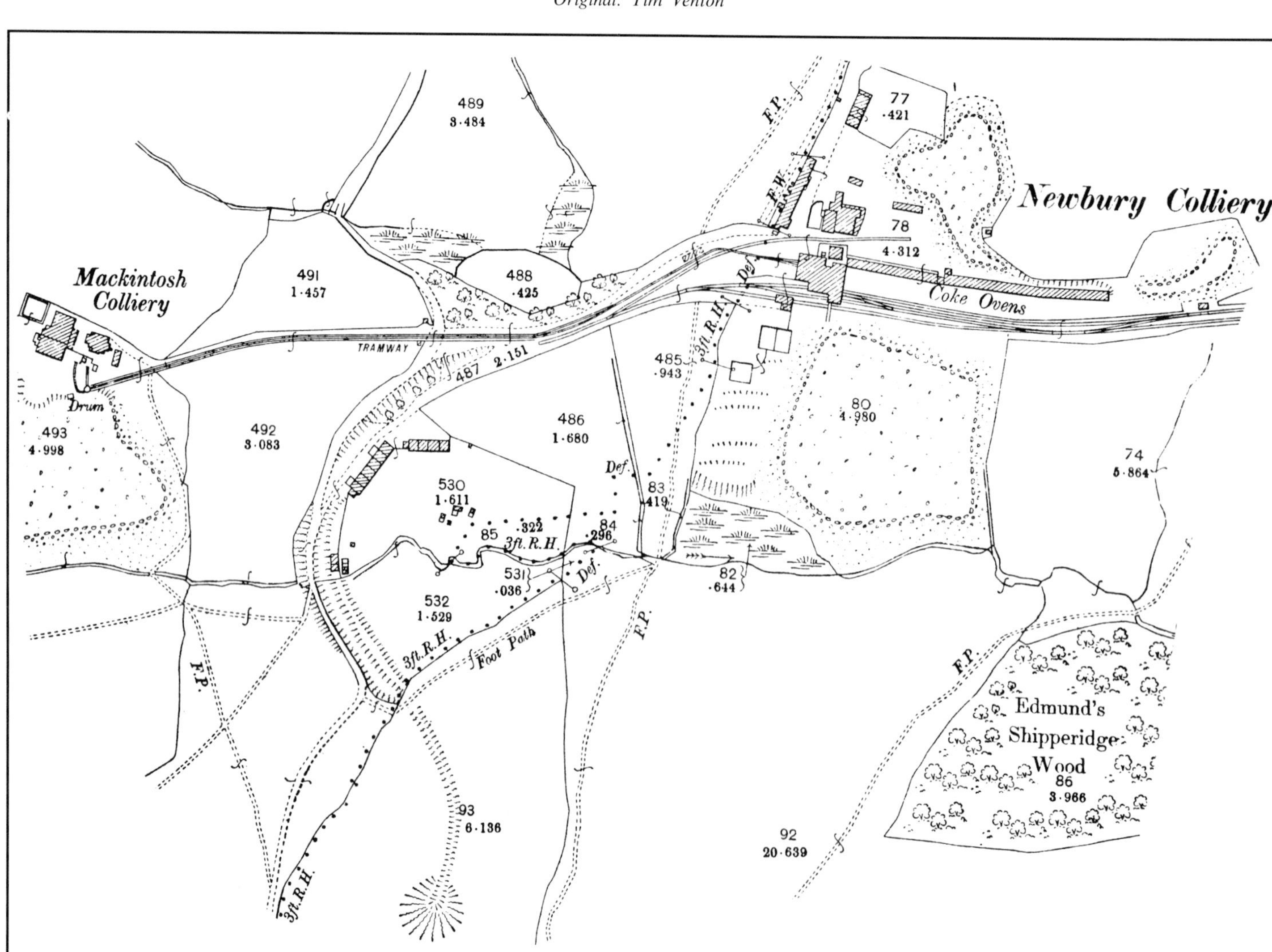

NEWBURY COLLIERY (1)
This photograph shows Newbury Colliery about 1918. On the left can be seen the tubline connecting Newbury with Mackintosh Colliery. It was planned to convert this into a standard gauge connection but this never came about. The view is looking east towards Mells.

Robin Atthill

and then, perhaps, on to Westbury Ironworks? Along with the pits on its route, the Vobster tramway was believed to have closed around 1878.

The Newbury Railway and the Collieries at Mells, Newbury and Mackintosh

On 24th July 1857 the Westbury Iron Company was formed in order to work and to smelt deposits of ironstone found at Westbury in Wiltshire. About 1855 iron ore had been discovered at various sites near the GWR's station at Westbury by G.C. Greenwell, a name we will recognise in connection with his work at the Earl Waldegrave's Radstock Collieries and it was he, along with another local coal owner, W. B. Naish, and ten others, all of whom had local coal and iron interests, that went on to form the Westbury Iron Company.

In 1857 the company began to build blast furnaces near Westbury station close to the iron deposits. Naturally enough, coal and limestone were also essential ingredients for the workings of these furnaces and, some ten convenient miles away, were the Mendips, source of both commodities. As we know, in 1854, Radstock was linked by the Wilts, Somerset & Weymouth's broad gauge railway from Frome (and Westbury) and

NEWBURY COLLIERY (2)
Another fascinating photograph of the colliery, this time showing the extensive coal ovens that were in use at this pit. As always, everything stops for the photographer! With one of John Wainwright's private owner wagons in view, this scene was probably taken during the time of Wainwright's ownership of the pit, that is at some time between 1905 and 1912.

Robin Atthill

NEWBURY COLLIERY (3)
This view at Newbury was taken from the pit's chimney looking towards Mackintosh Colliery. Note the way the narrow gauge crosses the standard gauge in the foreground! It would seem that the date is probably some time in the early 1920s, the narrow gauge connection to Mackintosh having been cut short. The loco shed was on the extreme left hand road. Newbury Colliery closed for good in 1927, although the section of line through to Vobster Quarry continued in use until 1965.

Robin Atthill

this was an obvious rail corridor over which to carry the coal required. However, the Westbury Iron Co.'s interests lay in the Newbury Colliery, a small, somewhat antiquated pit some two miles to the west of the WS&WR's line. And so, on 31st August 1858, the Westbury company took a lease from the colliery's owner, Mr John Moore Paget, and, in turn, laid a single, broad gauge railway between the pithead and the GWR at what later became the site of Mells Road station. This branch was built without a formal agreement with the GWR so the exact dates of its building are unknown, although it does seem most likely that the railway was in use from about 1858.

The line was generally known as the "Newbury Railway" although the GWR referred to it as the "Vobster Branch". The earliest reference to the railway is reckoned to be August 1863 when limestone was being excavated in the Newbury Railway's cutting at Vobster Cross. Two years later, in 1865, truckloads of stone were winding down the branch and onto the GWR to run across to the ironworks at Westbury. It seems likely that pretty soon after the opening of the Newbury Railway a narrow gauge tramway was laid in from Vobster Breach Colliery, via the Colliery at Vobster itself, up an incline towards the Newbury Railway where there may have been transhipment facilities and/or a landsale depot. Vobster coal was certainly of good coking quality and would have surely been welcomed at Westbury Ironworks.

As was mentioned in the introduction to this section, the area around Vobster had a long and respectable history in the mining of coal, the main pit in the district, pre 1857, being Vobster Colliery, which was also known as "Vobster Coal Works". Nevertheless, with the opening of the new railway and the active support of the Westbury Iron Company, new pits were opened or extended in the area served by the branch. In 1861, a new colliery was sunk to the west of Vobster Colliery. This pit was Vobster Breach while, about 1863, Mackintosh Colliery was sunk to the west of Newbury Colliery. Some four years later Mackintosh Pit opened in 1867. The deep, 1,620ft shaft of Mackintosh was sunk in order to bite into the deeper seams which Newbury Pit was unable to cut into from its own 720ft deep shaft. Once coal was at the pithead at Mackintosh it was sent, by a narrow gauge tubline, to Newbury Colliery where it was then put onto the Newbury Railway. Due to a trade recession Mackintosh Colliery closed on 30th March 1895, re-opening some five years later. It eventually closed for good on 5th December 1919 after an accident in which the winding rope broke.

Mells Colliery was sunk about 1863, being in production a year later. Its coal was easily and conveniently transferred to the Newbury Railway which ran alongside the pit in a north/south direction. This colliery was originally owned by Messrs Naish and Steeds but, in later years, the two pits at Vobster (Vobster itself and Vobster Breach) and the colliery at Mells were all worked by the Vobster & Mells Coal Company. Mells Colliery was believed closed in 1876 while the Vobster Pits closed at some stage after the summer of the same year. Down & Warrington suggest that the final date of closure was 30th September 1878. It was most certainly disused by 1882. One reason for these various closures was likely to have been a decline in the workload at Westbury Iron Works.

To get some idea of the tonnage then being handled by the Newbury Railway it is useful to remember that during the years 1869 to 1874 Mells Colliery raised some 106,000 tons of coal with the Vobster Pits lifting some 28,000 tons of coal and 59,000 tons of coke over the same period. The Newbury Railway and the Vobster tramway must have groaned under the load! It seems likely that in broad gauge days (pre 1874) that this traffic was worked along the entire length of the railway to the GWR by horses, although one school of thought has suggested that the line was *built* using horses but that, once opened, it was actually worked by broad gauge locomotives from the GWR. These would have run through to the various users' sidings where wagons would then have been shunted by horse. Some further discussion of the line's locomotive history can be found in Appendix II.

The 1870s were important years for the Newbury Railway. In 1874 the proposed Nettlebridge Valley Railway was to have run from the GWR at Mells Road to connect with the Somerset & Dorset Railway near Binegar. This particular scheme

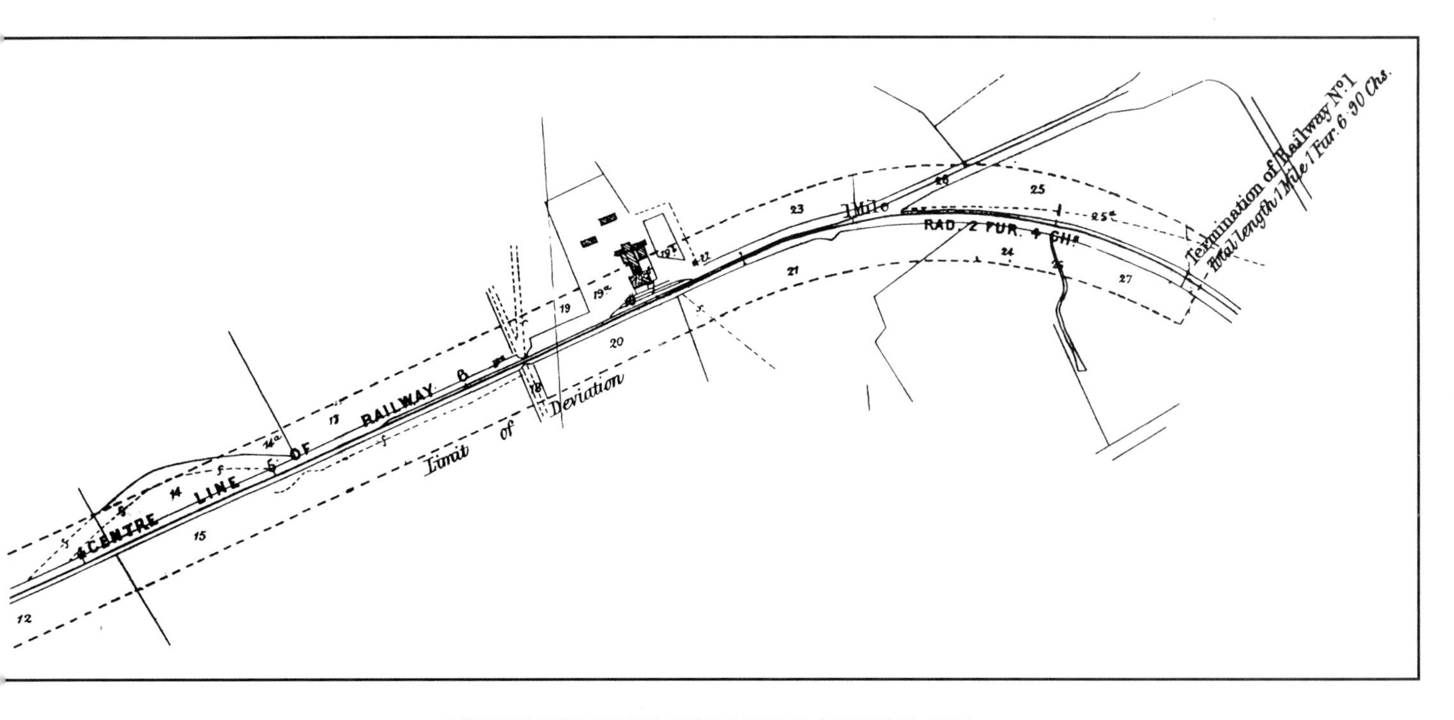

NETTLEBRIDGE VALLEY RAILWAY 1874

This plan of the proposed NVR is interesting in that it shows the stretch of the Newbury Railway near its junction with the Radstock-Frome section at Mells Good Shed. The colliery in the centre of the plan is Mells Colliery, which closed in 1876. A stretch of the abandoned Dorset & Somerset Canal can also be seen, to the left. The line on the right swings round to Newbury and Mackintosh Collieries.

Original plan: Lord Oxford

MELLS COLLIERY 1920
This view of Mells Colliery was taken looking towards the east and shows, quite clearly, the line of the Newbury Railway which runs across the picture in front of the screens. Mells Road station is to the left. This view also shows a fascinating collection of private owner wagons.

John Cornwell

envisaged following the route of the Newbury Railway to Vobster Cross, then running through the Nettlebridge Valley itself, immediately to the north of Vobster Breach Colliery as shown on the plan on page 216. However, like so many schemes discussed in this book the NVR was never built. The Westbury Iron Co. had sunk Moorewood Colliery (near Chilcompton) in the hope that the NVR would be built and partially because of this got itself into severe financial trouble. Through the 1870s, with the closures of Mells and the Vobster Pits, things started to go badly wrong for the company. In addition, the situation was made worse by the decline of ironmaking at its Westbury furnaces. In 1878 only two of these were at work, while by 1881 only one furnace was still in production. Because of this, Newbury Colliery became more and more of a liability in that its coal was essentially suited to foundry work and was not particularly good for the domestic market.

In 1897 the colliery's lease came up for renewal. At this time the Westbury Iron Co. leased and worked the Newbury

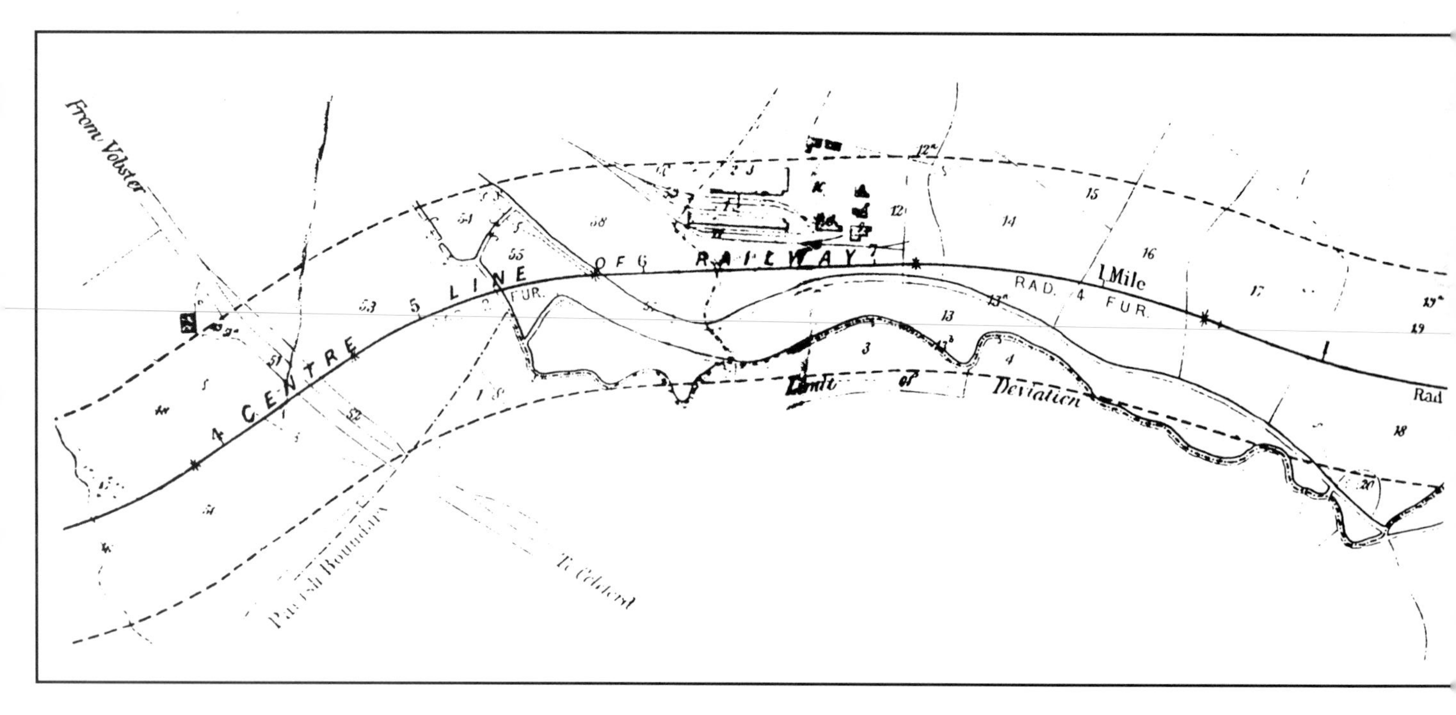

NETTLEBRIDGE VALLEY RAILWAY 1874

In the 1874 scheme, the NVR was intended to swing very close to the colliery at Vobster Breach. This colliery is seen here. The line veering away to the left of the pit itself ran to Vobster Colliery.

Original plan: Lord Oxford

Railway, the colliery at Newbury and the now growing-in-importance quarry at Vobster. In spite of the company's financial problems and apparent lack of enthusiasm for the railway and the quarry, Westbury Iron took on the new lease without any hesitation. Signed on 19th October 1898, it was for a 25 year term, that period beginning from 1st July 1898. It was about the turn of the century, however, that the Westbury Iron Co. appears to have got itself into real financial problems. These were likely caused by a slump in business and so, in June 1901, the company decided to re-organise itself. It also said that if this re-organisation failed it would have to sell off Newbury Colliery. In spite of all the difficulties, the company's re-constitution was successfully carried out with the *New* Westbury Iron Company Limited being incorporated on 6th June 1903. This new company took over only the ironworks at Westbury; the Newbury Railway, the Newbury Colliery and the Quarry at Vobster staying in the hands of the former Westbury Iron Company which had just entered into voluntary liquidation.

Various offers came forward for the old company but the best and, as it turned out, the most successful came from the local quarrying family of John Wainwright & Co. Limited. This company offered £300 per year for the lease of Vobster Quarry, £50 per year for the use of the Newbury Railway and 4d (1½p) per ton on stone for the asphalt plant situated on the Newbury Railway near Mells Road station. Although Wainwright's was firmly established in the quarrying business on Mendip at this time John Wainwright wanted to have a quarry that linked into the GWR, and of course Vobster did this. It was also clear that the asphalt plant at Mells Road would make a useful addition to Wainwright's large tar business. His offer was therefore accepted by the Westbury Iron Company's liquidator and, by 1905, Vobster Quarry, Newbury Colliery and Railway had all moved into Wainwright's hands. The former Westbury Iron Co. was now completely wound up, this unhappy event taking place on 27th November 1907.

In 1909 work was taken in hand to get Mells Colliery re-opened. A new lease was taken out by the Mells Collieries Limited on 22nd September 1909, coal winding probably taking place in 1911 or 1912. It would seem to be the case that it was around this time that the Mells Sidings' Committee was created, this committee being made up from the representatives from each of the Newbury Railway's users. It was formed so that there could be liaison between groups using the line, as well as for accounting purposes. However, its key function was to actually *run* the Newbury Railway.

According to Down & Warrington, it would seem likely that when the committee came into being, each locomotive owner on the Newbury Railway would put his locomotives into a common-user pool. When things were running normally on the railway this would mean no change from the situation that had existed before the committee had been formed, namely that each locomotive would work its own owners' area of work (for example, the "Mells Loco" or the "Newbury Colliery Loco"). However, if things ran out-of-course and someone's locomotive failed, the Committee's Traffic Manager could pool the rest of the locomotive stock to cover the gap. It is important to remember that the Committee itself never owned any locomotives, it simply used those on loan from companies served by the Newbury Railway.

Post World War One Newbury Colliery had a difficult time of it even though it was producing some 40-50,000 tons of coal a year. In August 1927 the colliery succumbed and was closed, even though there were some 15 million tons of coal within reach. However, to get at this coal the shaft would have had to have been deepened and the colliery at Mackintosh re-opened and, for this, the money was simply not available.

The business of Mells Collieries Limited was also struggling at this time. In August 1930 the company went into receivership. In this case, however, the colliery's landlords, the Horner Trustees, kept the pit at Mells going until 15th January 1934 when Mells Coal Industry Limited took the whole operation over. From 5th August 1937 New Mells Colliery Company Limited became the pit's new owner until the mine's final closure took place on 30th October 1943.

At this stage it might be useful to add in a couple more points about the Newbury Railway itself. On 27th May 1938 a new siding agreement was signed with the GWR while another agreement of the same date was undertaken between the firm of Roads Reconstruction (1934) Limited, of which more later, and the New Mells Colliery Company Limited in relation to the joint use of the GWR siding connection between the Newbury Railway and the Great Western at Mells Road station. In addition, the new agreement stated that the payment of the line's maintenance was to be in proportion to the tonnage carried by the Newbury Railway on behalf of the various firms using it.

Notwithstanding the line's early problems, the Newbury Railway continued to be used until the mid-1960s, the actual date of disuse being around 1965/6. Road transport was used after that time to move stone from Vobster Quarry, then still in production. At the Mells Road end of the railway a siding

MELLS ROAD STATION STAFF
This photograph shows the station staff at Mells Road station in 1946. The members of staff are as follows, from left to right:
Back row Mr Wilson, Mr Keen, Jim Trimby, Ted Dunford.
Front row Harold Withers, Anon, Mr Sharman's daughter, Mr Sharman (stationmaster) and Charlie Jacobs.

Collection: Mr Keen

linking the now, once-more goods-only line from Radstock to Frome was retained to run into the bitumen terminal situated there. This terminal was an important railhead for bitumen supplies from various quarries across Mendip. This siding also served the ARC concrete pipe works which, although it is still in use today, is no longer rail connected. The sidings to the bitumen works were disused by 1978, while the connection linking these sidings into British Rail was also severed at some time during the 1970s. In addition, the Newbury Railway which had survived remarkably well up until this time (with the exception of some lifting at Vobster Quarry) was in the process of being removed during the summer of 1973. It had gone completely by 1978.

Vobster and Bilboa Quarries

As we have already said, the Newbury Railway was constructed in the late 1850s to provide transport for the coal supplying the ironworks which had been built by the Westbury Iron Co. During the laying down of the Newbury Railway an area of limestone, the "flux" used in the making of iron, was uncovered at Vobster Cross and on which the Westbury Iron Co. took a lease, opening a quarry to the north of the Newbury Railway in this area. A limekiln was also built and indeed, it is believed that a limekiln continued to work at Vobster into the 1900s, but in the later period this was to be found to the *west* of the quarry rather than to the north-west of Vobster crossroads as the earlier one had been.

On reflection, it seems true to say that the only industry that really prospered along the route of the Newbury Railway was the quarry at Vobster. The quarry's initial development was simply an extension, or "bulge" northwards from the Newbury Railway itself, the excavations spreading away from the railway until, in the 1880s, the limestone ran out when the latter banged up against a ridge of shales. "Upper Vobster" or "Old Vobster", as it was then known, had to develop in a new direction and, as the O.S. map of 1904 shows, this was towards the north where another large mass of limestone was encountered. A tunnel was driven between the old and new workings, these later being connected by a 2ft gauge railway.

The importance of Vobster Quarry to the Newbury Railway was enormous and turn-of-the-century figures give some idea of the scope of its significance. For 1900, 1901 and 1902 Vobster's rail traffic had totalled 35,593; 38,757 and 37,572 tons of stone respectively. In 1903, the lease for this valuable quarry property came up for renewal. In the advertisement concerning the lease, prospective lessees were told that the quarry lease would cover some 17 acres and that the future tenant would have the right to use the Newbury Railway, paying maintenance in proportion to the tonnage carried on his/her behalf. All the plant at the quarry, along with the asphalt works at Mells Road station, were to be included in the deal. This latter works seems to have been first mentioned in 1902 when it was operated by the Asphaltic Limestone Concrete Company Limited. It seems reasonable to assume that some of the limestone from Vobster Quarry would have been sent to the plant at Mells Road for coating with tar for use on the growing network of roads which were then seeing the beginnings of motor transport.

Various tenders for the quarry were received but that of John Wainwright's clinched the deal. Wainwright's firm had been incorporated on 19th March 1902 when it had had an authorised capital of £23,000. With the Newbury Railway and Colliery and Vobster Quarry off its hands the Westbury Iron Co. was wound up in 1907 as we saw in the earlier section. In 1934 John Wainwright's, along with three other groupings of quarries, was itself taken over by the firm of Roads Reconstruction Limited. On 17th February 1934 this expanded company was incorporated in the city of Bristol, its authorised capital standing at £675,000. Strangely enough, in December 1960, the firm reverted to its original title of Roads Reconstruction Limited while, on 1st November 1967, the whole of the ordinary and preference share capital of that company was taken up by the Amalgamated Roadstone Corporation (ARC). ARC was the immediate parent company but the overall holding company was then, and is now, Consolidated Gold Fields Limited. Since 1st January 1973 the initials ARC have stood for the Amey Roadstone Corporation, itself a product of

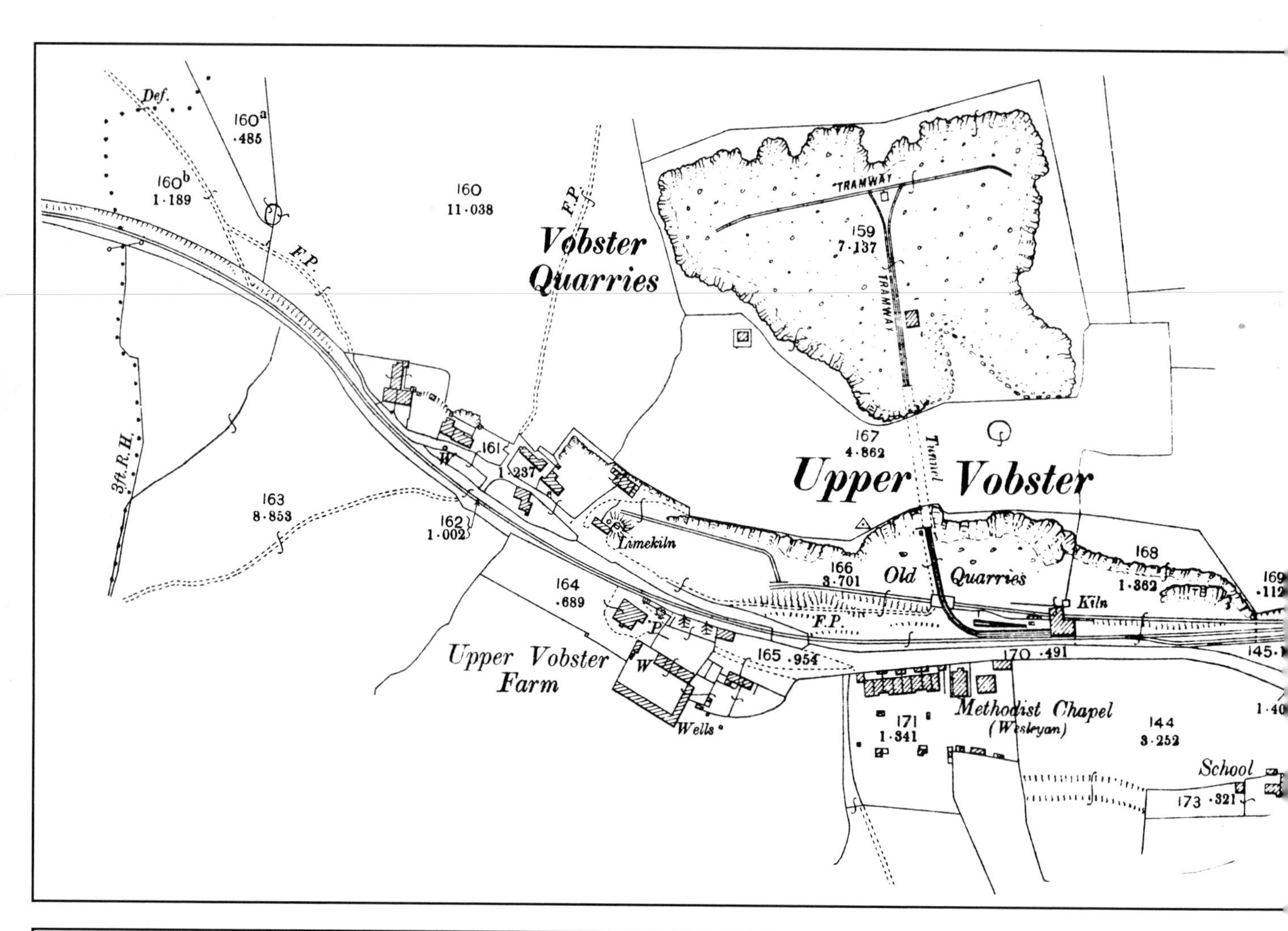

VOBSTER QUARRIES

The quarry faces at Vobster showing the Newbury Railway and the associated tramways serving those quarries (1904).

Original: Tim Venton

FROME, RADSTOCK AND BRISTOL.

UP TRAINS. — WEEK DAYS.

Distances From Frome M.	C.	STATIONS.		Station No.	Ruling Gradient 1 in	Time Allow. for Ordinary Freight Trains—See page 2: Point to Point T (ins.)	Allow for Stop. (Mins.)	Allow for Start. (Mins.)	1B Passenger. A.M.	2K Goods.	3K Coal Empties. A.M.	4K Goods. U A.M.	5K Coal. A.M.	6B Passenger. A.M.	7K Goods. NOON.	8K Goods and Coal. A.M.	9K Goods. A.M.	10K 10.55 a.m. Westby Goods. P.M.	11B Passenger. P.M.	12K Holt Coal Empties. P.M.	13K Goods. P.M.	14 Passenger. P.M.	15B Passenger. P.M.	16	17 Goods and Coal. P.M.	18K Goods and Coal. P.M.	19K Coal. P.M.
—	—	Frome	arr.	585		—	—	1	..	..	..	..	..	..	..	..	..	..	..	..	..	..	..	..	..	..	..
			dep.	—		—	—	—	7 25	....	....	8V50	Suspended.	10 35	....	....	....	....	1240	....	3 5	3 25	4 50	....	Suspended.	....	....
—	21	Frome Minl. Junc.		582	76 F	—	—	1	CS	..	8 30	—		CS	..	..	11 48	12 20	—	2 45	CS	CS	CS	..		..	..
—	53	Market Sdg.	,,	1193	76 F	—	—	—	—	....	—	—		—	....	....	—	....	—	—	—	—	—	....		....	....
—	70	Gas W'ks Sdg.	,,	1192	276 F	4	1	1	—	..	—	—		—	..	..	CR	..	—	2 55	—	—	—	..		..	..
2	15	Somerset Qrs. Sdg.		1191	51 R	3	2	2	—	....	—	9 0		—	Suspended.	....	—	....	—	—	—	—	—	....		SX	....
5	23	Mells Rd.	arr.	1190	48 R	11	1	1	7 37	..	8 50			10 47		..	12 8	12 40	12 52	3 10	3 25	3 37	5 2	..		..	RR
			dep.						7 40	....	9 30			10 49		8 40	12 18	1 10	12 54		3 45	3 38	5 3	....	Sats. only.	....	6 5
5	25	Stop Board	,,	—	L	1	1	1	—	..	9P35		..	—		8P48	12P23	1P15	—	..	3P 50	—	—	..	....	..	6P15
8	22	Radstock	arr.	1187	69 F	8	1	1	7 47	....	9 45	V Mineral Loop.	MSX	10 55		8 50	12X33	1 25	1 1	....	4 0	3 45	5X10	....	....	....	6 20
			dep.						7X52	..			..	10 5		11X25	1e25		1X2	..		3 47	5 12	..	..	5 0	
9	53	M. Nort. & Welton	arr.	1184	128 R	3	1	1	7 56	....	....		....	10 59		11 30	—	....	1 6	....	....	3 51	5 16	....	....	—	TSO
			dep.						7 59	..	..		..	11 1	..	11 45	—	..	1 7	..	..	3 32	5 18	..	..	—	..
10	57	Old Mills Sg.	arr.	1183	177 R	4	1	1	—	....	....		....	—	....	11 49	1 34	....	—	....	....	—	—	....	....	5e8	....
			dep.						CS	..	..		RR	CS	..	12 10	—	..	—	..	..	—	CS	..	4 30	5X50	..
11	66	Stop Board	,,	—	73 R	4	1	1	—	....	....		....	—	....	12P18	1P40	....	—	....	....	—	—	....	4P38	5P58	....
12	61	Hallatrow	arr.	1182	65 F	4	1	1	8 5	..	..		..	11X8	..	12X28	1X45	..	1 14	..	..	3 58	5 25	..	4 43	6 3	..
			dep.						8 9	10 28	....	....	10 28	11 12	MSX	1 0	2 15	....	1 16	....	....	4X0	5 27	....	6X5	6X5	....
14	20	Clutton	arr.	1181	58 R	6	1	2	8X13	10e36	..	..	10X36	11 16	....	1e8		..	1 20	..	..	4 4	5X31	..	6 12	6 12	..
			dep.						8 16	11X25	....	....	11 18	11X18	..	1X48	....	....	1 23	....	..	4X6	5 36	....	6 25	6 25	....
14	63	Stop Board	,,	—	71 R	3	1	1	—	11P30	..	..	11P25	—	....	1P55	..	..	—	..	....	—	—	..	6P30	6P30	..
16	60	Pensford & Bromley Sid	arr.	—	—	—	—	—	—	11e37	....	....	11 30	—	..	2X0	....	....	—	....	..	CS	—	....	6 35	6 35	....
			dep.	1241	60 F	6	2	1	—	12 0	..	..		—	1 0	2 25	..	..	—	..	....	—	—	..	7X10	7X10	..
17	36	Pensford	arr.	1180	60 F	2	1	2	8 23	—	....	....	Does not run when No. 2 is running.	11 25	1eX5	2X31	....	....	1 30	....	..	4 13	5 44	....	7 15	7 15	....
			dep.						8 26	CS	..	..		11 28	1 46	3 15	..	..	1X37	..	....	4 15	5 46	..	7 45	7 45	..
19	26	Stop Board	,,	—	66 R	8	1	1	—	12P15	....	....		—	1P50	3P28	....	....	—	....	..	—	—	....	7P58	7P58	....
22	7	Brislington	arr.	1179	60 F	8	1	1	8 35	—	..	..		11 37	2P 0	3P36	..	..	1 46	..	....	4 24	5 56	..	—	—	..
			dep.						8 39	12P25	....	....		11 40	—	3 55	....	....	1 50	....	..	4 27	6 1	....	8P8	8P8	....
23	16	Marsh Junction		1069	62 F	3	1	1	CS	CS	..	..		CS	CS	CS	..	..	—	..	....	CS	CS	..	CS	CS	..
23	61	East Depot	arr.	1067	500 R	4	1	1	....	12 35	....	....		..	2 10	4 5	....	....	—	....	..	—	..	....	8 18	8 18	....
23	32	N. Som. Jun.	arr.	1073	—	—	—	—	—		..	..		—			..	..	—	..	....	—	—	..			..
24	14	Bristol (Tm. Ms.)		1079	—	—	—	—	8 47		....	....		11 50	....	....	....	....	2 0	....	....	4 35	6 12	....	....	....	....

U Worked by Frome Engine, Shunter and Porter.

Frome Shunting Engine.—Must assist Goods Trains as required from Frome to Mells Road.

FROME, RADSTOCK AND BRISTOL.

STATIONS.		UP TRAINS—WEEK DAYS. 20B Pass. P.M.	21K Goods. P.M.	22K Goods. P.M.	23B Portishead Pass. P.M.	24	25K Goods and Coal. P.M.	26	SUNDAYS. 1B Pass. NOON.	2	3B Pass. P.M.	4
Frome	arr.	..	..	..	8 0	..	..	..	..	..	..	..
	dep.	6 20		....	8 5	....	Suspended Tuesdays to Saturdays.	....	12 0	....	6 45	...
Frome Mineral Junction	,,	CS	TSO	..	CS	..		..	CS	..	CS	..
Market Siding	,,	—		....	—	....		....	—	....	—	...
Gas Works Siding	,,	—		RR	—	..		..	—	..	—	..
Somerset Quarries Siding	,,	—		....	—	....		....	—	....	—	...
Mells Road	arr.	6 32	....	..	8 17	..		..	12 12	..	6 56	..
	dep.	6 34	..	7 30	8 18	....		....	12 19	....	7 0	...
Stop Board	,,	—	....	7P33	—	..		..	—	..	—	..
Radstock	arr.	6X41	..	7 43	8 23	....	....	....	12 26	....	7 7	..
	dep.	6 43	7 35		8 27	..	8 35	..	12 28	..	7 10	..
Midsomer Norton and Welton.	arr.	6 47	—	....	8 31	....	8 40	....	12 32	....	7 14	...
	dep.	6 48	—	..	8 33	..	8 55	..	12 35	..	7 17	..
Old Mills Siding	arr.	—	7 45	....	—	....	—	....	—	....	—	...
	dep.	CS	7 52	..	—	..	—	..	—	..	—	..
Stop Board	,,	—	8P0	....	—	....	9P7	....	—	....	—	...
Hallatrow	arr.	6X55	8 5	..	8 40	..	9 12	..	12 42	..	7 24	..
	dep.	6 57	8 25	....	8 43	....	9 35	....	12 48	....	7 29	...
Clutton	arr.	7 1	8 33	..	8 47	..	9 43	..	12 52	..	7 33	..
	dep.	7 3	9 5	....	8 49	....	10X3	....	12 58	....	7 37	...
Stop Board	,,	—	9P12	..	—	..	10P10	..	—	..	—	..
Pensford & Bromley Siding	arr.	—	—	....	—	....	—	....	—	....	—	...
	dep.	—	—	..	—	..	—	..	—	..	—	..
Pensford	arr.	7 10	9 22	....	8 56	....	10 18	....	1 5	....	7 44	...
	dep.	7 11	9X55	..	8 57	..	10 20	..	1 6	..	7 47	..
Stop Board	,,	--	10P8	....	—	....	10P43	....	—	....	—	...
Brislington	arr.	7 20	—	..	9 6	..	—	..	1 15	..	7 56	..
	dep.	7 23	10P18	....	9 10	....	10P53	....	1 17	....	8 2	...
Marsh Junction	,,	—	—	..	CS	..	CS	..	CS	..	CS	..
East Depot	arr.	—	10 25	....	..	....		....	..	....	..	...
North Somerset Junction	,,	—		..	—	..	11V 0	..	—	..	—	..
Bristol (Temple Meads)	,,	7 32	....	....	9 18	....		....	1 23	....	8 10	...

Working of Engines—Bristol, Radstock, Frome and Camerton.

1.—5.30 a.m. East Depôt to Mells Road 8.40 a.m. Mells Road to East Depôt.

2.—6.12 a.m. East Depot to Hallatrow. 10.28 a.m. Hallatrow to Bristol. 4.0 p.m. East Depot to Mells Road. 8.28 p.m. Mells Road to East Depot.

3.—8.40 a.m. East Depôt to Radstock, assist 4.45 p.m. Radstock to Mells Road if required. 8.35 p.m. Radstock to Bristol.

4.—1.25 p.m. East Depôt to Radstock, 5.0 p.m. Radstock to Bristol (SX) 4.30 p.m. ex Old Mills (SO).

5.—TSO 2.12 p.m. Passenger Train Temple Meads to Radstock, 3.30 p.m. Special Radstock or Mells Road to Castle Cary or beyond, 5.10 or 7.0 p.m. R.R. (TSO) Radstock to Mells Road and back, 7.35 p.m. Radstock to Bristol (TSO). When the 3.30 p.m. Special runs, the engine and men ordinarily working the 8.35 p.m. ex Radstock to work the 7.35 p.m. Radstock to Bristol and the 2.12 p.m. engine, guard, and van if the Special they work terminates at a convenient local point, to return to Radstock, to work a Special Radstock to Bristol (calling at the same places as the 8.35 p.m. Radstock to Bristol, which will not run), provided that such train can clear off the North Somerset Line not later than 12.45 a.m. If the Special will be too late to work via Radstock, working to be arranged according to circumstances.

6.—8.30 a.m. Frome to Radstock, 1.0 p.m. Radstock to Frome.

7.—11.48 a.m. Frome to Freshford and Frome.

8.—(Trowbridge Engine) 12.25 p.m. Holt Junction to Mells Road, 6.48 p.m. Mells Road to Patney, etc.

9.—3.5 p.m. Frome to Radstock, RR trips to Mells Road if required, 8.20 p.m. Radstock to Frome.

10.—10.55 a.m. Westbury to Radstock, 4.45 p.m. Radstock to Westbury.

V Kingsland Road.

BRISTOL-RADSTOCK-FROME SERVICE TIMETABLE 10th JULY 1922

Original: Peter A Fry

MIXED FREIGHT AT MELLS ROAD
BR(W) Class 35 "Hymek" diesel-hydraulic No. D7064 arrives at Mells Road with the daily 09.40 Frome-Radstock freight on 15th April 1970. The signal box on the left had been closed on 15th August 1966.

G. F. Gillham

BRISTOL, RADSTOCK AND FROME.

DOWN TRAINS.—WEEK DAYS.

Distance from Bristol P.M. M	C.	STATIONS.		Ruling Gradient 1 in	Time Allow. for Ordinary Freight Trains See page 2: Point to Point Times.	Allow for Stop.	Allow for Start.	1 K Goods and Coal.	2 K Goods and Coal.	3 B Passenger.	4 K Stone.	5 K Coal Empties.	6 K Goods.	7 B Passenger.	8 K Coal Empties.	9 B Passenger.	10 K Coal.
					Mins.	Mins.	Mns.	A.M.	A.M.	A.M.	P.M.	A.M.	A.M.	A.M.	A.M.	P.M.	P.M.
—	—	Bristol (Tmpl.Mds)	dep.							7 0				10 32		1 12	
—	—	East Depot	"		..	..	1	5 30	6 12				8 40		11 35		
—	78	Marsh Junction	"		4	...	...	CS	CS	CS		MSX	CS	CS	CS	CS	
2	7	Brislington	"	62 R	5	1	1	—	—	7 8			8 55	10 40	—	1 20	
5	0	Stop Board	"	60 R	14	1	1	5P58	6P37	—		RR	9P11	—	12 P 0	—	
6	58	Pensford	arr. / dep.	66 F	6	2	1	6 6 / 6 15	CS / —	7 19 / 7 20			9 20 / 9 30	10 51 / 10 53	CS / —	1 31 / 1X33	
7	34	Pensford and Bromley Siding	arr. / dep.	60 R	3	1	2	CS	6 48 / 7e29	— / —		9 40	9 34 / 10 0	CS / —	12 15	CS / —	
9	74	Clutton	arr. / dep.	60 R	12	2	1	6ST33 / 6L 43	7 45 / 8X15	7 28 / 7 30		— / CS	10e15 / 11X18	11 0 / 11 2		1X40 / 1 42	
11	37	Stop Board	"	71 F	2	1	1	6P48	8P20	—		9P57	11P23	—		—	
11	33	Hallatrow	arr. / dep.	58 F	4	1	2	6ST54 / 7 5	8 26	7 33 / 7 36		10 2	11 28 / 12X25	11 5 / 11X10	MSX	1X45 / 1 47	
12	36	Stop Board	"	65 E	4	1	1	7P13		—		Suspended.	12P32	—	Suspended.	—	
13	37	Old Mills Siding	arr. / dep.	7[illegible]	4	1	1	CS		— / —			12 37 / 12 50	CS / —		CS / —	
14	11	Midsomer Norton & Welton	arr. / dep.	177 F	4	1	1	7 28 / 7 30		7 44 / 7 46			— / —	11 18 / 11 19		1 55 / 1 56	
15	72	Radstock	arr. / dep.	128 F	4	1	2	7X35 / 8 5		7X50 / 7 52			1 X 0	11X23 / 11 26		2 0 / 2 2	1 0
18	71	Mells Road	arr. / dep.	69 R	15	1	1	8 25		8 0 / 8 X 3				11 34 / 11 37		2 10 / 2 12	1 20 / 3 15
20	14	Stop Board	"	204 F	3	1	1			—				—		—	3P20
21	79	Somerset Quar. Sdg	"	48 F	7	2	2			—	9 15			—		—	—
23	24	Gas Works Siding	"	51 F	4	1	1			—	—			—		—	—
23	41	Market Siding	"	276 R	..	..	...			—	—			—		—	—
23	73	Frome Mineral Junc.	arr.	76 R	3	1	...			CS	9 25			CS		CS	—
24	14	Frome	arr. / dep.	76 R	5	1	...			8 14 / 8 27				11 48		2 28 / 3 5	3 35

STATIONS.		11 K Goods and Coal.	12 K Goods.	13 B Passenger.	14 B Passenger.	15 K Westbury Goods.	16 Coal.	17 K Goods.	18 B Passenger.	19 K Pattney & C. Coal.
		P.M.	P.M.	P.M.	P.M.	P.M.	P.M.	P.M.	P.M.	P.M.
Bristol (Tmpl.Mds)	dep.	V		2 15	2 52				5 5	
East Depot	"	1 25	1 55	TSO				4 0		
Marsh Junction	"	CS	CS	CS	—			CS	CS	
Brislington	"	—	—	2 24	—			—	5 13	
Stop Board	"	1P48	2P16	—	—			4P26	—	
Pensford	arr. / dep.	1 55 / 2 5	2 23 / 2X35	2X35 / 2 37	3 8 / 3X10		TSO	4 34 / 4 45	5 24 / 5 26	
Pensford and Bromley Siding	arr. / dep.	C X S / —	2 39 / 2X50	— / —	— / —			— / —	— / —	
Clutton	arr. / dep.	2 20 / 2 50	3 2 / 3 45	2 45 / 2 50	3 17 / 3 19			5e12 / 5X40	5X34 / 5 36	
Stop Board	"	2P55	3P58	—	—		RR	5P45	—	
Hallatrow	arr. / dep.	3 0 / 3 10	3X57 / 4 20	2 53 / 2 55	3 22 / 3 24			5 51 / 6 X 5	5 39 / 5 42	
Stop Board	"	3P17	4P28	—	—			6P12	—	
Old Mills Siding	arr. / dep.	3 22 / 3 55	4 35 / 5 0	CS / —	— / —			6 18 / 6 30	CS / —	
Midsomer Norton & Welton	arr. / dep.	4 2 / 4 12	— / —	3 2 / 3 4	3 32 / 3 34			— / —	5 48 / 5 51	
Radstock	arr. / dep.	4 17 / To be kept clear of 2.15 p.m. TSO Terminates at Old Mills on Saturdays.	5X10	3 8	3 38 / 3 40	4 43	5 10	6X40 / 7e25	5 55 / 5 57	
Mells Road	arr. / dep.		TSX		3 48 / 3 50	CR	5 28	7 45 / 8X28	6 5 / 6 8	6 48
Stop Board	"		Suspended.		—	5P10		8P35	—	6P57
Somerset Quar. Sdg	"				—	—		—	—	—
Gas Works Siding	"				—	—		8P50	—	—
Market Siding	"				—	—		—	—	—
Frome Mineral Junc.	arr.				—	5 26		9 5	CS	7 13
Frome	arr. / dep.				4 2				6 20 / 6 40	

V Suspended Tuesdays to Saturdays.

Radstock and Mells Road, RR Trip. In addition to the trips shewn in the Tables, a trip from Radstock to Mells Road and back will be run daily, worked by Train Engine available at most convenient time.

BRISTOL, RADSTOCK AND FROME.

STATIONS.		Down Trains.—Week Days. 20 K Goods.	21 B Passenger.	22	23 K Coal.	24 K Coal.	25 B Passenger.	26	Sundays. 1 B Passenger.	2	3 B Passenger.	4
		P.M.	P.M.		P.M.	P.M.	P.M.		A.M.		P.M.	
Bristol (Temple Meads)	dep.		6 20				9 35		9 25		4 50	
East Depot	"						—					
Marsh Junction	"		CS				CS		CS		CS	
Brislington	"		6 28				9 42		9 33		4 58	
Stop Board	"		—				—		—		—	
Pensford	arr. / dep.		6 39 / 6 40				9X51 / 9 52		9 44 / 9 46		5 9 / 5 17	
Pensford & Bromley Sdg.	arr. / dep.		— / —				— / —		— / —		— / —	
Clutton	arr. / dep.		6 48 / 6 50				10 X 0 / 10 1		9 54 / 9 58		5 25 / 5 32	
Stop Board	"		—				—		—		—	
Hallatrow	arr. / dep.		6 53 / 6X59				10 4 / 10 5		10 1 / 10 8		5 35 / 5 37	
Stop Board	"		—				—		—		—	
Old Mills Siding	arr. / dep.		CS / —			RR	— / —		— / —		— / —	
Midsomer Norton & Welton	arr. / dep.		7 7 / 7 8				10 13 / 10 14		10 16 / 10 23		5 45 / 5 48	
Radstock	arr. / dep.	RR / 7 0	7 12 / 7 15		8 20		10 18 / 10 20		10 27 / 10 30		5 52 / 5 54	
Mells Road	arr. / dep.	7 20	7 23 / 7 24		8 38 / 9 20	9 53	Y / —		10 38 / 10 44		6 2 / 6 3	
Stop Board	"		—		9P25	9P57	—		—		—	
Somerset Quarries Siding	"		—			—	—		—		—	
Gas Works Siding	"		—		9 45	—	—		—		—	
Market Siding	"		—			—	—		—		—	
Frome Mineral Junction	arr.		CS		CS	CS	CS		CS		CS	
Frome	arr. / dep.		7 35		9 58	10 18	10 41		10 53		6 14	

Single Line, Marsh Junction to Radstock Station worked by Electric Train Staff, the Staff Stations and crossing places being Marsh Junc., Pensford, Pensford and Bromley Siding‡, Clutton, Hallatrow, Old Mills‡, and Radstock Station.

Electric Train Tablet worked between Clutton and Pensford when Pensford and Bromley Colliery is out of circuit.

‡Pensford and Bromley Siding and Old Mills are only available for shunting a light Engine, or Goods Train (at Old Mills short Goods Train only can be shunted), for a Train to pass in the same or opposite direction.

Double Line, Radstock Station to Mells Road South End.

Single Line, Mells Road South End to Frome Mineral Junction, worked by Electric Train Staff, Mells Road and Frome West Box being the Staff Stations.

Y calls at Mells Road to set down only. Running time Mells Road to Frome, when not required to call, 17 minutes.

Special Trains to clear North Somerset Line of Surplus Coal Traffic.

Radstock must advise Control Office, Bristol, when specials are required to any point on North Somerset Line to clear traffic, and arrangements will be made accordingly.

FROME-RADSTOCK-BRISTOL
SERVICE TIMETABLE
10th JULY 1922

Original: Peter A Fry

MORE FROM MARCROFT
Class 31 No. 31293 heads a fine mix of repaired wagons past Conduit Belt on Mells Down on 1st July 1976.

Mike Miller

Amalgamated Roadstone and the Amey Group Limited.

One more feature of quarrying in the Mells area that we need to consider in our narrative is that of Bilboa Quarry. Bilboa's name is connected to a family whose name we have already encountered in this book. The family name was that of William Beachim, or William Beachim Beauchamp as he became known in 1876. As we have seen in Chapter 6 it was his sons who were intimately connected with Somerset's coalmining industry in the late 19th century. It was, however, a somewhat remote branch of the family made up of Dudley, Gilbert, Ralph and Ross Beauchamp who formed a partnership which was known as the Mells Quarry Company. Under this title they re-opened the Bilboa Quarry which was situated close to Vobster Cross.

In 1911, the quarry had been described as "long disused" but a 1922 report had the quarry "recently re-opened". One puzzling aspect of the quarry's story is that under an agreement with the GWR dated 14th October 1925 a standard gauge railway was laid from the GWR near Jericho Bridge (what an evocative name!) down to the quarry at Bilboa. The metals ran north/south, their route taking them almost parallel to the tracks of the Newbury Railway. In the quarries themselves, for there were, in fact, two of these working under the term "Bilboa Quarry", narrow gauge lines were used to move stone from the faces to the processing plants.

Although the Bilboa concern prospered in the very early years of the 1930s, it would seem that by 1933 the losses were such that the quarry had to close. The firm of Roads Reconstruction (1934) Limited then went on to buy the quarry and its associated railway from the GWR. An all-in price of £80,000 was paid for these two groups of questionable assets! Once the new company was in charge it closed the Bilboa Railway and a new siding was built linking the quarry faces into the Newbury Railway south of the site of Mells Colliery and near to Vobster Cross. It seems more than likely that this new connection saw very little use since it is not at all certain that the quarry was ever re-opened. Part of the short-lived Bilboa Railway was lifted in 1937 with the majority of it going just pre-World War Two in 1939. The actual junction with the GWR's Mells Road-Frome section was not removed, however, until the autumn of 1940.

DOWN THE MAIN FROM MELLS ROAD
Pannier tank No. 4636 bowls down Mells Bank with a local in the 1950s. By this time Mells Road station had lost pretty well all of its former glory.

Peter A. Fry

Appendix I

The Bristol & North Somerset Branch – A Survey of Locomotive Power

UNUSUAL POWER ON THE BRANCH
On 6th April 1968 a four-car dmu crosses the viaduct at Pensford. The unit was rostered on an RCTS special from London, similar to the run made some eleven years before in the care of 4-4-0 *City of Truro* except that this time the journey was made in a bone-shaking, non-corridor suburban dmu! The uncomfortable stock was not the fault of the RCTS but was the result of poor organisation by the Western Region at the London end. Unlike most of the engines seen in this locomotive montage, this is an example of *unusual* motive power on the North Somerset branch.
Hugh Ballantyne

FROME STATION (1)
This view has something of interest for those readers who like GWR locomotives, signals and trackwork. The engine on the right is one of the 517 class 0-4-2Ts built in batches at Wolverhampton between 1868 and 1885. There is rather a nice array of signals on the left while the ground signal in the centre of the picture between the two running lines is of an early pattern, which revolved through 90 degrees. The one on the end of the left hand platform is of a later design having a miniature signal arm.
The track is also worth a second glance in that it is a later survivor of the Brunellian baulked road.
Lens of Sutton

FROME STATION (2)
The locomotive seen in this picture is one of the large 'Metro' class 2-4-0 tanks built at Swindon. It has an S4 boiler and carries two jacks, one on either side of the running plate. Again the track, ground signal, milk churns and gas lamp are all items that deserve closer inspection.
R. Atthill/A. Church

A 'RIVER' IN BRISTOL
'River' class locomotive No. 73 *Isis* stands at Bristol Temple Meads c1906. The seven engines in this class were rebuilt from 2-2-2s over the 1895-7 period while No. 73 itself was reconstructed in October 1895. It was withdrawn from service in 1918. It is quite possible that this class of locomotive worked over Bristol-Frome metals in the late 1890s/early 1900s.
Brian Armen

Above: 517 CLASS ON FROME SHED

Chass 517 No. 558 rests easily on Frome Shed c1921. This 0-4-2T was one of Lot G (Nos 553-564) built in 1869. This particular class of engine was built progressively over the years from 1869 to 1885 for use on branch lines such as the North Somerset.

Brian Armen

Left: HEAT, BUT LITTLE WORK, AT CAMERTON STATION

A 2721 class 0-6-0 saddle tank and crew shunt quietly at Camerton station sometime around 1905/06.

Collection: Gerald Quartley

Left: A 'BUFFALO', A BACKING SIGNAL AND HALLATROW STATION BEFORE THE 1909/10 RECONSTRUCTION

An unidentified member of the 1076 'Buffalo' class 0-6-0 saddle tanks rests at Hallatrow station around 1908. The engine has a three segment saddle tank and carries the old form of lamp bracket. The signal in the foreground is interesting in that it carries a backing signal as well as the usual arm.

Lens of Sutton

Left: RADSTOCK (GW) STATION
This delightful and tranquil view shows Radstock (GW) station in the early years of the present century. Prominent in the picture is the original wooden North signal box in front of which is passing a small 'Metro' tank in immaculate condition. These locomotives were built in batches between 1869 and 1892. The train's leading vehicle is a six-wheeled 'Siphon' while the second vehicle appears to be an example of a six-wheeled brake. With late Victorian/early Edwardian fashions highlighted on the platform, this photograph truly captures the rural railway peace pre-World War One.

W. White

Left, below: RESTING AT RADSTOCK (GW)
With an impressive line up of staff, including the stationmaster who turned out especially for the occasion, a saddle tank and a pannier tank sit quietly in the yard while the photographer goes about his work. The saddle tank is one of the outside frame 1076 class introduced in 1870 and built in batches until 1881. The class numbered 266 engines in all. The member shown here is in later condition with short chimney and three-course saddle tank.

The pannier tank is one of the 2721 class introduced in 1897, and which covered 80 engines in all, these being built in four lots until 1901. Although originally built as saddle tanks, pannier tanks were progressively fitted from 1909. The number of this locomotive appears to be 2795 which was built in 1901, rebuilt with pannier tanks in 1911 and withdrawn in 1949. The elegant yard lamp is also a real scene stealer in this view which was taken c1920.

Gerald Quartley

Below: AN ROD SHUNTS THE COAL
With a mixed freight in tow, ROD 2-8-0 No. 3032 sits on the through line at Brislington station on 17th March 1955. This engine and its companion, No. 3017, regularly worked the North Somerset, although No. 3014 was also seen on the route occasionally. After the decline of the RODs in the mid-1950s 2-6-2T No. 4131 became well-known on these coal trains.

M. B. Warburton

Above: PRAIRIE AND PANNIER FOR PORTHCAWL!

Much-travelled locomotive No. 4555 and pannier tank No. 4647 are seen here in charge of an excursion to Porthcawl. The place is Brislington station and the date is 20th July 1958. Even one year before the removal of the line's passenger services, it is interesting to note that the permanent way work is exemplary!

M. B. Warburton

Left: AN ROD ROLLS HOME

One of the ROD 2-8-0 locomotives pulls upgrade out of Pensford station with a freight for Bristol. This locomotive, No. 3032, was stationed at St Philip's Marsh engine shed as were most of the goods engines that ran over the Radstock branch from Bristol. Generally working tender-first out of East Depot they would, as one railwayman at the "Marsh" put it, ". . . quite happily plod over the contours of Somerset with only 80lb of steam on the clock"! This particular ROD plods homewards on 2nd November 1954.

M. B. Warburton

Left: SHOVING THE STONE AT HAPSFORD

Pannier tank No. 4647, another well-known engine on the Bristol-Radstock (West)-Frome route, is seen here shoving trucks into the sidings at Hapsford Loop. An average pannier working an ordinary, everyday duty providing a scene that seemed to be changeless but which was destined to disappear in a remarkably short time.

Peter A. Fry

Above: KILMERSDON COLLIERY
Naked to the world, Peckett 0-4-0 saddle tank No. 1788 stands stripped down for boiler inspection on 28th July 1970. *Tony Wadley*

Below left: A 57XX FILLS UP AT FROME
Introduced in 1933, this 5700 class pannier tank No. 3735 nears the end of its working life. Photographed during the period of declining and disappearing steam, this sad and shabby locomotive was seen taking water at Frome station in the early 1960s. The former Radstock bay runs in from the left although, by the time this picture was taken, the passenger service over the North Somerset had been removed.
Collection: Gerald Quartley

Below right: A LIGHT LOAD MOVES SOUTH
With a solitary brake van in tow, Class 6100 2-6-2T No. 6148 heads south towards Radstock with the 2.05pm from Bristol (East Depot). Locomotive and van are seen here between Pensford and Clutton. The Prairie tank was built at Swindon in 1933 and was scrapped some 31 years later in 1964. *Ivo Peters*

A HEAVY LOAD MOVES NORTH
With a tidy rake of BR 16 ton steel mineral wagons behind, "Hymek" No. D7039 moves down towards Chelwood Bridge with the 2.30pm Radstock to Portishead coal train. In the 1960s the "Hymeks" were a common, and to the author at least(!), a welcome sight on the old North Somerset.
Ivo Peters

33s TO THE FORE AT FROME
Class 33 No. 33026 passes the site of Frome Market Siding on 19th June 1978. Made up of 'Sealion' and 'Whale' wagons, the train itself carries ballast for the Southern Region. Stone and train began their journey at ARC's quarry at Whatley.
Mike Miller

FROME NORTH – JUNCTION FOR THE RADSTOCK LINE
On 13th May 1981 Brush Class 47 No. 47122 is seen at Frome North signal box in charge of a Whatley Quarry to Westbury stone working. Signalman Quartley takes the token. The original signal box here was known as Frome Mineral Junction and it was inspected, after its construction, by Captain Tyler of the Board of Trade in September 1875. He described the box as "a good signal cabin".

It controlled the points and signals between the GWR's Westbury-Castle Cary line and Frome Mineral Sidings, the latter being found in the triangle formed by the Radstock-Westbury and Frome lines. Tyler did actually have "occasion to recommend that levers Nos 14 and 15 in the locking frame should lead lever No. 16 as well as that the necessary figures should be painted on the various levers"; otherwise he found everything to his satisfaction. *Mike Miller*

RADSTOCK – "THE GATES"
With the gates held aloft, Class 33 No. 33049 runs over the GWR level crossing in the centre of Radstock. The locomotive was involved in the removal of stock from the Somerset & Dorset Trust's site at Radstock to the West Somerset Railway. These workings were photographed on 16th October 1975. *Mike Miller*

Appendix II.

Industrial Locomotives

This appendix gives details of industrial locomotives that have worked on industrial lines or have been found in locations linked either directly to or connected indirectly with the Bristol & North Somerset Railway and the areas it served.
(All locomotives were outside cylindered, unless stated otherwise.)

Bromley Collieries (until 1909), later Pensford & Bromley Collieries Limited

2ft gauge
Bromley No. 1 was an 0-4-0T built by Avonside in 1911, builder's No. 1593. It was bought new and, after a very short life at the pit, was sold around 1913 to the Old Delabole Slate Company, Cornwall.

Construction of Blagdon Reservoir for Bristol Waterworks Company: Meakin & Dean

Standard gauge
For the construction of Blagdon Reservoir an inside cylindered 0-6-0ST Manning Wardle was used. This locomotive was built in 1861, its builder's number being 21. It had come from a contract in Birkenhead, and, once the Somerset contract was completed, went on to the Hundred of Manhood & Selsey Tramway, Sussex in 1907. On that railway the locomotive was given the number 2 and the name *Sidlesham*.

A second locomotive was an 0-4-0ST from the firm of Beyer, Peacock & Company. Its builder's number was 1736, the locomotive being built 1877. It is possible that it came here new. It went to Farrington Collieries Company, possibly by 1885.

Earl of Warwick's Somerset Collieries: Fry's Bottom, Greyfield and Clutton Collieries

Standard gauge
The locomotives that were believed to have worked at these collieries were as follows:
Frances, an 0-4-0ST built in 1885 by R. & W. Hawthorn, builder's No. 2040. It was delivered new to Clutton and was scrapped on site around 1895.
Daisy, an 0-4-0ST built in 1894 by the Bristol firm of Peckett. Its builder's number was 581. Around 1911 it went to Clutton Colliery from Greyfield Colliery and around 1922 it went to Wynnstay Collieries Limited, Denbighshire (now Clwyd).
Emlyn, an 0-4-0ST, builder unknown, which came to Clutton on hire from C. D. Phillips, Newport, Monmouthshire (now Gwent) by c1900. Around 1910, it returned off hire to C. D. Phillips. Nothing else is known about this particular locomotive.

Hallatrow: (J. Perry & Co.)
After the construction of the Bristol & North Someret Railway had finished in 1873, two unidentified 0-6-0 saddle tanks went up for sale at Hallatrow on completion of Perry's contract. No further information is known about these.

Somerset Collieries Limited: Camerton & Dunkerton Collieries –

Camerton Colliery

Standard gauge
Camerton Colliery (see Chapter 7) used horses to move its wagons except for a brief period when a locomotive was here on trials. To 4ft 8½in gauge, the locomotive, named *Dunkerton*, came from the nearby colliery of the same name around 1926. An 0-4-0ST built by Peckett, builder's No. 1191, this locomotive was built in 1910. The trials would appear to have been unsuccessful, the engine moving on in the same year to the contractors, Walter, Scott & Middleton.

Dunkerton Colliery

Standard gauge
This colliery was serviced by the 0-4-0ST mentioned above. *Dunkerton* came new to Dunkerton Colliery in 1910 and was in use there until 1926 when it went for trials at Camerton, and then on to Walter, Scott and Middleton, contractors as mentioned above.

Pauling & Elliot (Contractors for the construction of the Camerton-Limpley Stoke Branch for the GWR 1908/1910)

In 1907, six locomotives were involved in the construction of the above railway, details of two standard gauge locomotives used on the Dunkerton-Limpley Stoke section having survived.

Both of the locomotives concerned were inside cylindered 0-6-0STs built by Manning Wardle & Co. The first of these, Pauling's No. 26, was named *Tyersall* and this had been built in 1888, builder's No. 1068. The locomotive had come to the Somerset area after having worked on the contract for the GW/GC joint railway between Northolt Junction and High Wycombe. After the Dunkerton-Limpley Stoke work was finished it moved back to the London area at Greenford, later moving to J. Lyons & Company Limited of Greenford in 1919.

The second locomotive, *Northolt*, builder's No. 1555, (Pauling's No. 56), was built in 1902 and also came from the GW/GC contract. Once the Cam Valley work was completed this engine was sold in June 1913, to the Freshwater, Yarmouth & Newport Railway on the Isle of Wight.

A. P. Gardner (Tunley near Camerton)

Standard gauge
In November 1970, a 4-wheeled vertical boilered geared tank locomotive, built by Sentinel, builder's No. 7492, was brought to the above site. It had come from Grove Scrap Iron & Steel Merchants Limited, Fishponds, in Bristol. It had previously been in the possession of J. S. Fry & Sons Limited and the move to the Tunley site was with the intention of preserving the locomotive. However, the engine, built in 1928, went on to R. Finbow of Bacton, Suffolk in 1971.

Farrington Collieries Company, Farrington Colliery (Also traded under the title "Radstock Coal Company" and "Radstock Coal & Wagon Company")

At least three locomotives are known to have been used at the small colliery at Farrington. The first of these was an 0-4-0ST built in 1877, by Beyer, Peacock & Co Ltd, builder's No. 1736. From the contracting firm of Meakin & Dean, a Beyer, Peacock locomotive, builder's number unknown, was known to be here by around 1885. This locomotive was believed sold for scrap some time after August 1904.

The second locomotive was an 0-4-0ST built by W. G. Bagnall Limited, builder's No. 1432, in 1894. This locomotive came from M. W. Grazebrook Limited of Netherton in Staffordshire. It was put up for sale both in December 1921 and in July 1922 but did, in fact, consequently go for scrap.

The third of the trio was an 0-4-0, built in 1891 by Peckett of Bristol, builder's No. 520. This engine came from G. Palmer, the contracting firm, and was on site at Farrington Colliery by November 1912. It was later sent to East Bristol Collieries Limited. After that its fate is unknown.

E. J. King & Sons Limited, Scrap Merchants, Farrington Gurney

2ft gauge
A 4-wheeled diesel mechanical locomotive was moved to the above site for scrap. This locomotive, built by R. A. Lister & Company (builder's No. 8023) in 1936 with a JAP petrol engine, it had come from J. S. Fry & Sons Limited of Somerdale, Keynsham in 1972 where it had been used to haul *standard* gauge wagons, on a parallel track. It was sent to M.E. Engineering of Cricklewood, in London in August 1974, where it was restored for re-sale for further industrial use.

Old Mills & Springfield Collieries (Old Mills Colliery Company and William Evans until 1931)

Standard gauge
In 1940, a new 4-wheeled diesel mechanical locomotive built by Ruston & Hornsby Limited, builder's No. 200793, came to the site. On nationalisation on 1st January 1947, it became the property of Division 7, Area 8 of the new National Coal Board.

Some industrial Locations in the Radstock area

The Somersetshire Coal Canal

The company of Proprietors of the Somersetshire Coal Canal navigation built a seven mile long tramway from the collieries at Radstock to its main canal at Midford. This used the course of an unsuccessful canal. Opened in 1815, the tramway used horses to haul the coal tubs. In 1825, a steam locomotive was built by William Ashman of Clandown Colliery, Radstock. This was put to work on the tramway in August 1827. It is thought that this locomotive was relegated to being a stationary hauling engine after it frequently broke the rails of the tramway. It was later sold for scrap. The tramway stayed in use with horse traction until it was sold in 1871, its route then being used for the Bath Extension of the Somerset & Dorset Railway.

Writhlington Collieries Company Limited

The group was made up of five major collieries, three of which used locomotives:

Foxcote Colliery

2ft 8in gauge
The locomotive used on the Foxcote Colliery line (see Chapter 6) was named *Foxcote* and was an 0-6-0ST built by Hudswell, Clarke & Co. Ltd. Its builder's number was 369 and it was built in 1890. It went new to the narrow gauge Foxcote line, being sold for scrap at some unkown date.

Kilmersdon Colliery

Standard gauge
At least four steam locomotives are known to have worked the standard gauge sidings from the colliery's pithead to the top of the cable worked incline to the Radstock (West)-Frome line.

The first of these was an 0-4-0ST built by Hudswell, Clarke and named *Kilmersdon*. Its builder's number was 464 and it came new to the colliery when it was built in 1896. It was, at some unknown date, possibly in the late 1920s/early 1930s, sold for scrap.

The second, and best known locomotive at this colliery, a Peckett 0-4-0ST, builder's No. 1788, came to Kilmersdon new in 1929. In 1973, on the closure of the colliery, it went on permanent loan to the S&D Railway Museum Trust. It now resides on the West Somerset Railway.

The third locomotive, an 0-6-0ST named *Albert* came on loan around 1936 from "the Docks at Bristol". Details about this engine are very scant indeed, except to say that after a very short visit, it returned off loan sometime in 1937.

The fourth steam locomotive here was Hunslet 1684, built in 1931, an 0-4-0 side tank which was transferred from Norton Hill Colliery in March 1966. It is now preserved on the Swanage Railway, Dorset.

In addition, two Ruston & Hornsby 4-wheeled diesels were here during the period of NCB control at the pit. No. 200793, built in 1940, came to Kilmersdon from Old Mills Colliery before 1961 and returned again at some time during 1964.

It passed on to Southern Counties Preservation at Droxford in Hampshire in July 1967 and was believed to have been cut up sometime after 1972. This 48bhp locomotive can be seen in the photograph on page 194.

The other Ruston & Hornsby locomotive used at Kilmersdon was No. 242869, built in 1946. This came from Old Mills in 1968, later going on to Merthyr Vale Colliery in South Wales. This was a larger locomotive of 80hp.

Lower Writhlington Colliery

2ft 8½in gauge
Three locomotives were used at this pit. The first was named *Enterprise* and was an inside cylindered, 0-4-0ST built in 1882 by the firm of Hunslet. Its builder's number was 279 and it was delivered new. It was believed to have been sold for scrap to William Evans at Writhlington Foundry at a site adjacent to the colliery around 1940, as were the other two locomotives used by this particular pit.

The second locomotive was named *Writhlington* and was an 0-6-0ST built by Hudswell, Clarke & Company. Constructed in 1900, builder's No. 546, it was delivered new to the pit.

The final locomotive was an 0-4-0ST built by Peckett. Builder's number 1546, this locomotive arrived new at Writhlington in 1920.

(The other two pits in the group, without locomotives, were Upper Writhlington and Huish.)

The Somerset & Dorset Railway Trust (Somerset & Dorset Railway Circle until 1974)

Standard gauge
During the 1970-1975 period various preserved locomotives and items of rolling stock were kept at the former S&DJR loco shed. They were infrequently run over the BR line as far as Writhlington Colliery but during the mid-1970s the stock was moved, essentially to the West and East Somerset Railways. A list of the standard gauge items moved and their destinations is given below:
No. 53808 2-8-0 ex-S&DJR: West Somerset Railway, Washford.
Bagnall 2668 0-6-0ST *Cranford No. 2*: Steamtown Museum, Carnforth.
Fox, Walker 242 0-6-0ST No.3: Bristol Suburban Railway, Bitton.
Avonside 1764 0-6-0ST S3 *Portbury*: West Somerset Railway, Washford.
Peckett 1940 0-6-0ST S9 *Henbury*: West Somerset Railway, Washford.
Hawthorn, Leslie 3437 0-6-0ST *Isabel*: West Somerset Railway.
Barclay 1398 0-4-0ST *Lord Fisher*: East Somerset Railway, Cranmore.

Ruston & Hornsby 210479 4wDM: West Somerset Railway, Washford.
No. 47493 0-6-0T ex-LMSR: East Somerset Railway, Cranmore.
Barclay 1719 0-4-0ST *Glenfield*: East Somerset Railway, Cranmore.
Peckett 1788 0-4-0ST: West Somerset Railway, Washford.*
Bagnall 2473 0-4-0 Fireless No. 1: West Somerset Railway, Washford.
Peckett 1636 0-6-0ST *Fonmon*: Bristol Suburban Railway, Bitton.
Wickham 6967 4-wheeled rail trolley: West Somerset Railway, Washford.
* This is the locomotive that formerly worked at Kilmersdon Colliery.
(Note, some of these locomotives have been moved again subsequently, to different locations.)

Some Industrial Locations in the Mells/Mells Road Areas

(For further information about this general area see Chapter 11)

New Mells Colliery Company Limited, Mells Colliery

(This had been Mells Collieries Limited until 23rd August 1930: Horner Trustees from that time until 15th January 1934 and Mells Coal Industry Limited from then until 5th January 1937. This colliery was served by sidings off the Newbury Railway which ran from Mells Road station. This latter railway, initially broad, then standard gauge, served other industrial locations along its length and was, at one time, operated by the Mells Siding Committee).

Standard gauge
Two locomotives are listed under the above company, the first of which was believed to be an outside cylindered 0-4-0ST built by Hunslet. It is possible that it came from Newbury Collieries Limited around August 1927, going for scrap at some undetermined date.

The second locomotive was No. 820, an 0-6-0T built by Chapman & Furneaux Limited, builder's No. 1161. The engine was built in 1898 and came from the GWR in March 1931. It went to the firm of Cohen in London for scrap in February 1945.

Newbury Collieries Limited (Newbury Colliery)

This company had become Llwydcoed Collieries Limited by April 1912 and Newbury Collieries by 1917. The colliery at Newbury was to be found at the end of the Newbury Railway. From here, a narrow gauge connection linked it with Mackintosh Colliery. By 1910, a locomotive was shedded here, presumably this was purchased from John Wainwright by Llwydcoed Collieries Limited. Mackintosh Colliery closed in August 1927 and it is possible that the locomotive was sold either to Mendip Mountain Quarries Limited or to Mells Collieries Limited by or around this date.

Mells Quarry Company: Bilboa Quarry, Mells

Standard gauge
Mells Quarry Company had its own locomotive. This was believed to have been an 0-4-0. At an unknown date, it was sold for scrap.

Vobster Quarry

Standard gauge connections to the quarry.
2ft gauge connections within the quarry.
This quarry was served by the Newbury Railway. It was operated by the Vobster Quarry Company as a part of Roads Reconstruction (1934) Limited. A narrow gauge (2ft) line was worked within the quarry itself but this was replaced by conveyors and dumpers around 1949. Some two years later the narrow gauge track was lifted. In 1965 standard gauge rail traffic ceased and the quarry was closed around one year later.

2ft gauge
Six locomotives are known to have worked the narrow gauge network within the quarry. No. 190 "D8", was an 0-4-0 diesel mechanical locomotive built in 1931 by Motorenfabrik Deutz A. G. of Cologne in Germany. Its builder's number was 9898 and it came to the quarry from Grovesend Quarry, Gloucestershire around 1948. It was scrapped around 1954.

No. 548 was a 4-wheeled diesel mechanical locomotive built by Ruston & Hornsby as were all the following engines used at Vobster. No. 548, builder's No. 164329, was built in 1931 and at some unspecified date came from Emborough, another Mendip quarry. After Vobster, the locomotive moved to the firm of Pugsley at Stoke Gifford, near Bristol.

No. 549 "D3", builder's No. 164331, was also built in 1931 and it too came to Vobster from Emborough. This locomotive was sold for scrap in 1953.

No. 675, builder's No. 182145, was built in 1936 and, in 1939, it came from the Borough of Slough. Around 1953, it went to Devizes Brick & Tile Company Limited.

No. 701 "D6", builder's No. 198313, was constructed in 1940 and came, at some stage, from New Frome Quarry. It went to Emborough Quarry in 1951.

The only details known of the last diesel locomotive was that it carried as identity "Locofax Comessa, Strasbourg 6295". This was scrapped around 1955.

No. 820 AT MELLS COLLIERY
Chapman & Furneaux 1161 of 1898, acquired from the GWR in 1931.

F. Jones

NIDD
Kerr, Stuart 3112 of 1918 which worked at both Vobster and New Frome Quarries.
F. Jones

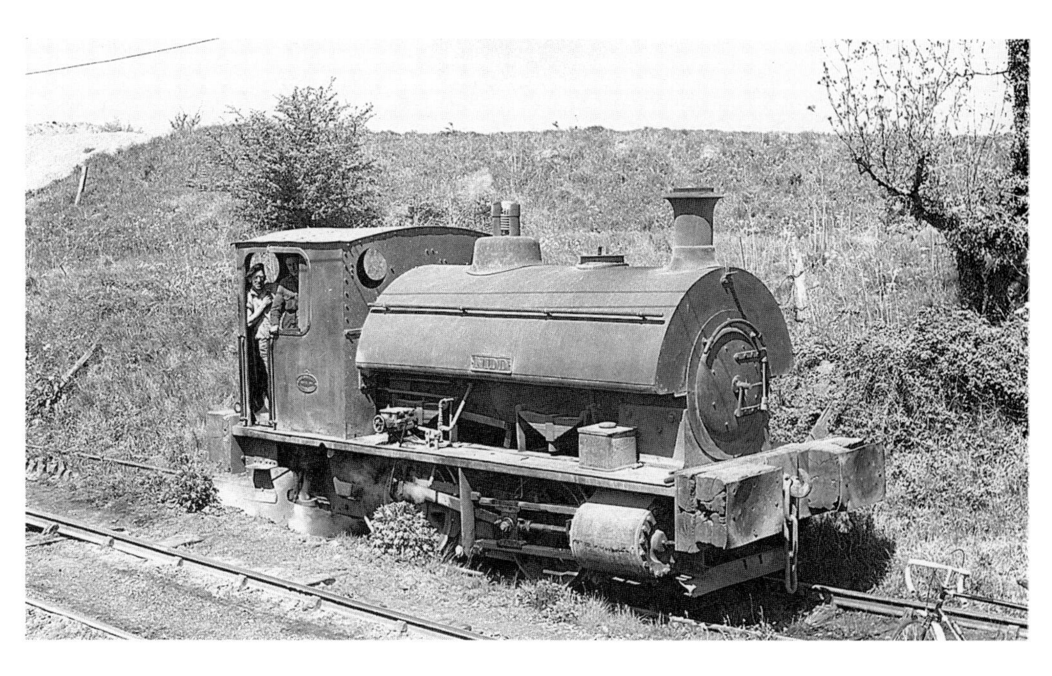

Standard gauge
There were 13 known standard gauge locomotives used at Vobster, one of which was an outside cylindered 0-6-0ST which had possibly come from the firm of John Wainwright and which, at some later date, was sold for scrap.

No. 292 *Nidd* was an 0-4-0ST, built in 1918 by Kerr, Stuart builder's No.3112. It came from Conygar Quarry near Clevedon, later going to New Frome Quarry. It returned to Vobster around 1949, finally being scrapped around 1955.

No. 385, formerly No. 33 *Mildred*, was an 0-6-0ST, and came from the Avonside Engine Company. Its builder's number was 1763. Built in 1917, it was at Vobster by June 1920 having come from Inland Waterways & Docks at Purfleet in Essex. It was scrapped in February 1959.

No. 386, an 0-6-0ST, was built in 1874 by Hudswell, Clarke & Rodgers, builder's No. 153. It probably came from John Wainwright & Company Limited around 1918, going for scrap at some later, unknown date.

No. 1700 was an 0-4-0 vertical boilered side tank built by Sentinel around 1927, builder's No. 6219. No more details have, as yet, come to light about this engine.

Another locomotive was a rebuild from an 0-4-0 petrol driven locomotive, with mechanical transmission, built by Manning, Wardle in 1918, builder's No. 1954. It came to Vobster from Cranmore Depot around 1927 and at some later date went on to Sandford Quarry at Banwell, on the Yatton-Wells railway line.

Vobster also saw the use of two 4-wheeled, vertical boilered Sentinel geared steam locomotives: *Sentinel* and No. 1. No. 752, Sentinel, builder's number 9398, was built in 1950 and had come from the firm of Sentinel around May 1953. In January 1965, it was sent to Thomas Hill, of Kilnhurst, West Yorkshire.

No. 784, No.1 was built in 1947, builder's No. 9374, and came to Vobster from New Frome Quarry around 1963. It returned there in August 1965.

The remaining five locomotives were all 4-wheeled, battery-powered electric locomotives built by the English Electric Company Limited. The builder's numbers were 712 to 716 inclusive and they were all built in 1927. They all came to Vobster new, their dates of scrapping being unknown.

Somerset Quarry Company Limited, Vallis Vale, Near Frome

2ft 3in gauge
This company had two 0-4-0STs; *Midge* and *Wren* built by Kerr, Stuart. *Midge* was built in 1907, builder's No. 1017, while *Wren* was built in 1910, builder's No. 1188. Both came to Vallis Vale new. At some later, uncertain date they went for scrapping.

ARC (Southern) Limited, New Frome Quarry/Whatley Quarry

(This company had formerly been Roads Reconstruction (1934) Limited. For a detailed history of this, and associated companies, see Chapter 11.)

2ft gauge
Four locomotives are known to have worked at New Frome Quarry, the first of these, No. 41, being an 0-4-2ST built by Kerr, Stuart. Constructed in 1918, builder's No 3065, it came to the quarry via a number of firms. Around 1920, it came from the Air Ministry, at Eastleigh in Hampshire (through the Sussex Trading Company Limited) arriving at Cranmore Depot by April 1924. It eventually left Tytherington Quarry, Gloucestershire some time after July 1933. The locomotive moved back to Cranmore Depot from New Frome around 1948.

An 0-4-0T locomotive, built by Avonside, came from Pugsley around November 1941. Built in 1933, builder's No. 2072, it had formerly been No. 84, *Aukland*. After its time at New Frome, the engine went on to Cranmore Depot.

The other two narrow gauge locomotives were both 4-wheeled, diesel mechanicals. Both of them were built by Ruston & Hornsby in 1940. Their builders' numbers were 198313 and 200507 respectively. However, they did differ as to where they went after New Frome. No. 198313 went to Vobster Quarry while 200507 was acquired by Emborough Quarry.

Standard gauge
Fourteen standard gauge locomotives have been recorded at New Frome and these are as follows. *Medway* was an 0-4-0ST built in 1903 by Andrew Barclay. Its builder's number was 969 and it came to New Frome around 1943 from APCM's Burnham Works, Kent via the dealer, Cohen. It was dismantled in 1956, its frame and tank being retained as a water carrier until scrapped in November 1974.

No. 154 was a 4-wheeled vertical boilered tank geared steam locomotive built by Sentinel in 1925, builder's No. 6090. It came from Cranmore Depot around September 1944 and was scrapped some five years later in April 1949.

No. 292 *Nidd* was an 0-4-0ST, built in 1918 by Kerr, Stuart builder's No. 3112. It came from Vobster Quarry, returning there around 1949.

The next locomotive to note is No. 758 an 0-4-0ST built by Vulcan Foundry in 1876. Builder's No. 798, this locomotive came from Sandford Quarry circa 1946, being scrapped around August 1949.

A batch of three locomotives are our next concern. All were 4-wheeled vertical boilered tank geared steam locomotives built by Sentinel. Nos 784 (1), 789 (2) and 794 (3) had the following builder's numbers, 9374, 9386 and 9387. No. 1 was built in 1947, the other two being constructed the following year. All came to New Frome Quarry new. Eventually, No. 1 went to Vobster Quarry in 1963; No. 2 was scrapped on site by Bidwell of Clandown, near Radstock, in June 1967, while No. 3 went to Welsh Mill Children's Adventure Playground, Frome in November 1971 where it remains to this day.

No. 153 was an 0-4-0 diesel mechanical built by John Fowler

Left: WHATLEY QUARRY RAILWAY – 1948
The crew of this then brand new Sentinel (not yet carrying a running number) take a rest in the loop at Murder Combe on a very hot May afternoon. They are all waiting to pass a train coming from the quarry. The railway had not long been regauged to standard when this picture was taken on 18th May 1948.

Hugh Ballantyne

Above: WHATLEY QUARRY RAILWAY – 1952
This photograph shows a good view of Murder Combe loop in the bleak depths of deep winter. No. 2 Sentinel 9386 of 1948 enters the loop with its train on 30th December 1952.

Hugh Ballantyne

Left: WHATLEY QUARRY – 1948
Sentinel locomotive 6090, built 1925, is seen at the crushing plant on the former Roads Reconstruction line on 18th May 1948.

Hugh Ballantyne

Right: ROADS RECONSTRUCTION (1934) LTD – 1948
This locomotive is believed to be No. 758, Vulcan 798 and built in 1876. It was photographed standing out of use near the then new standard gauge shed at Vallis Vale on 18th May 1948. It was eventually scrapped in August 1949.

Hugh Ballantyne

Below: WHATLEY QUARRY – 1948
One of the then new Sentinel locomotives waits patiently at the quarry face while loading takes place into a train of tippler wagons. The photograph recaptures the scene on 18th May 1948.

Hugh Ballantyne

Right: WHATLEY QUARRY – 1952
Similar to the above photograph, except in this case 0-4-0ST *Medway* (Barclay 959 of 1903) is now employed on shunting duties. The action was recorded on 30th December 1952.

Hugh Ballantyne

Below: WHATLEY QUARRY – 1975
This general view of Whatley Quarry was taken on 14th March 1975 with one of the Thomas Hill 4-wheel diesel-hydraulics at work.

Mike Miller

Above: LITTLE HAPPENING AT HAPSFORD
Prior to 1960 the "exchange yard" at Hapsford was little more than a run-round loop set in a leafy, North Somerset glade just off a loop on the main Frome-Radstock line. However, during the early 1960s a nine track marshalling yard was installed by Darlington Sidings. Rolls-Royce engined Thomas Hill diesels Nos 1 and 2 (133C and 136C) take a midday break in the yard, having just worked a full train of stone down from Whatley, the 'Dogfish' wagons in the background having formed that train. Incidentally, this breed of locomotive was almost invariably worked cab-to-cab by ARC in contrast to BR's current practice, for example, with its Class 20 locomotives.

Geoff Carter

Left: THE WHATLEY QUARRY RAILWAY
One of ARC's Thomas Hills carries out a permanent way duty in Murder Combe on Sunday 27th April 1980.

Mike Miller

WHATLEY QUARRY – 1988
Pride of Whatley, Thos Hill V325, a 750hp 'Steelman Royale' 6-wheel diesel, passes beneath the loading gantry with a rake of empties on the evening of 30th June 1988.
Peter Nicholson

& Co. in 1932, builder's No. 19645. The engine came from Cranmore Depot at some unspecified date, eventually going on to Sandford Quarry.

No. 1262 was yet another 4-wheeled, vertical boiler tank locomotive built by Sentinel, builder's No. 9391. This engine was built in 1949, coming from Sandford Quarry in September 1964, going to Thomas Hill at Kilnhurst in January 1965.

In recent years all motive power has come from the Thomas Hill stable. The first, No. 2162, later No. 1 was builder's No. 133C which was a 4-wheel diesel-hydraulic rebuilt from a Sentinel 4-wheel geared steam locomotive in 1963. The following year saw the arrival of No. 2166, later No. 2, builder's No. 136C, a similar rebuild to No. 1. No. 2317, Thomas Hill No. 149C however, although a rebuild from a Sentinel geared steam locomotive frame and wheels, was an un-powered brake tender for use with the diesel locomotives. This was delivered in 1965 but was scrapped in 1969 after being damaged in a collision.

No. 3 was also built in 1965, builder's No. 152V and is now in store. The last of this series was built in 1968 and is builder's No. 200V and still sees regular use. Nos 1 and 2 have been purchased for the Somerset and Avon Railway project, and were moved to Mells Road on 23rd June 1990.

From June 1987 a 350hp 0-6-0 diesel-hydraulic, Thomas Hill No. 261V was received on hire from the builders until Spring 1988. In the meantime, a new locomotive was acquired, Thomas Hill No. V325 a 750hp 'Steelman Royale' 6-wheel diesel-hydraulic with a Caterpillar diesel engine, in common with dumper trucks etc. used in the quarry. This locomotive was formally named *Pride of Whatley* in September 1987 by David Mitchell, then Secretary of State for Transport when he visited the quarry to open the new loading facilities.

Westbury Iron Company Limited: After February 1922 John Wainwright & Company Limited, Newbury Railway, Mells.

Standard gauge
A number of locomotives were believed to have been used by this firm, the first of which was an 0-6-0ST. This had been built in 1874, builder's No. 153, by the company of Hudswell,Clarke & Rodgers of Leeds. It was bought new for use on the Newbury Railway, once that had been regauged (to standard from broad) in the summer of 1874. It went to Mendip Mountain Quarries around 1918.

It also seems likely that two two other locomotives were purchased around the 1908/10 period from the company of John Aird & Sons who were, around this time (1902/1908) working on the building of the Royal Edward Dock and other works at Avonmouth near Bristol. One of these locomotives is presumed scrapped after a collision, the other was possibly sent to Llwydcoed Collieries Limited, Newbury Colliery by April 1912.

Another locomotive known to have worked for Wainwright's was an inside cylindered 0-6-0ST built by Manning, Wardle in 1898, builder's No. 1426. Around 1912, this had come from Stockport Corporation where it had been used on the construction of the Kinder Reservoir at Hayfield in Derbyshire. It was later sold or scrapped.

This company also saw the use of No. 33 *Mildred*, an 0-6-0ST built by Avonside in 1917, builder's No. 1763. This locomotive had come from Inland Waterways & Docks, of Purfleet in Essex by June 1920. On 1st January 1934 it went to Roads Reconstruction Limited (also see under Vobster Quarry).

Logan & Hemingway: Construction of the Frome Avoiding Line (Clink Road Junction/Blatchbridge Junction) for the GWR 1931/34

Standard gauge
Three locomotives were used on this contract, all of which were inside cylindered 0-6-0STs built by Manning, Wardle. The first of these, No. 3, was built in 1918, builder's No. 1966. By January 1931, it had come from a contract at Barnt Green in Worcestershire. After the Frome contract was completed, the locomotive went to the Midland Ironstone Company of Scunthorpe.

The second 0-6-0ST, No. 5, came from the same Barnt Green contract, arriving in the Frome area by March 1931. This was built in 1912 and had builder's number 1793. It was sold for scrap sometime after July 1934.

The third engine, No. 8, was built in 1888, builder's No. 1079. This was rebuilt by Manning Wardle in 1908. It came from the Hattersley Tunnel Contract at Mottram, Cheshire and was on the Frome contract by March 1932. It was sold for scrap sometime after July 1934.

Appendix III

Signalling Matters: An Introduction

At various stages in the history of the Bristol & North Somerset Railway, the following signal boxes and ground frames were in existence on the railway and its WS&WR/GWR extension to Mells Road and Frome.

North Somerset Junction
Marsh Junction
Bristol MAS Panel Box
Contractors Siding
Brislington Station (Box/Ground Frames)
Pensford Station
Pensford & Bromley Collieries Sidings
Clutton Station
Hallatrow Station
Camerton Station (Camerton/Limpley Stoke branch)
Old Mills (Box/Ground Frames)
Welton Station (Box/Ground Frames)

Radstock (North)
(South)
(No. 3)
Mells (North)
(South)
Mells Road (Box/Ground Frame)
Ground Frames at: Somerset Quarry Siding
Frome Gasworks Siding
Frome Market Siding
Frome West (Box/Ground Frame)
Frome North
Boxes at Frome Middle and Frome South
Westbury MAS Panel Box

At its opening in 1873, the Bristol & North Somerset Railway between Bristol and Radstock, was equipped with McKenzie & Holland Type 1 signal boxes.

Below: NORTH SOMERSET JUNCTION SIGNAL BOX *Mr E. White*

North Somerset Junction

The two boxes at this site were located at a point where the Bristol & North Somerset Railway left the main Bristol/Paddington line to the east of Bristol (Temple Meads) station.

The first box here was in place by 1873. It was closed on 22nd March 1886 as part of the quadrupling works then being undertaken in the Bristol area in connection with the opening of the Severn Tunnel.

The second box at this location was of Type 23 and opened on 22rd March 1886. This box was of timber, the frame being 5¼in centres between levers. Neither the first nor the second of the two boxes were fitted with a block switch.

In June 1909 further modifications took place when the box's frame was changed to an horizontal tappet 3 bar type with 4in centres, having 92 levers. On 6th September 1945, the locking was converted to 5 bar vertical tappet. This box was closed on 20th July 1970 as part of work undertaken for the Bristol MAS scheme. The actual junction was singled over the period from 23rd November 1974 to 9th December 1974.

Marsh Junction

When the B&NSR was first opened it made a double junction in a south-easterly direction with the Paddington line at North Somerset Junction. It then swung southwards in a gentle curve towards Brislington to become single track south of the junction itself. After 10th April 1892, the North Somerset travelled south in a tighter curve making a triangular junction with a similar curve from Bristol (East Depot). Once these two arms had come together two further arms diverged, one feeding the North Somerset towards the east, and the other feeding the Bristol (Avoiding Line) through St Philip's Marsh towards the west. It was on a site in the actual divergence of the two routes that the boxes at Marsh Junction were to be found. From Marsh Junction itself, the double tracks of the North Somerset continued towards the Avon Viaduct becoming single before crossing the river itself. It was at Marsh Junction during 1917 that the carriage sidings at Marsh Pond were brought into use.

The first box at Marsh Junction was in use by 1890. Around 1908 it was given a new horizontal tappet frame of 35 levers,

these being at $5\frac{1}{4}$in centres. In 1917, to deal with the enlarged layout brought about by the addition of the nearby carriage sidings, it received a third frame. This was of the vertical tappet type and had 46 levers at 4in centres.

On 2nd March 1959 the original box was replaced by a brick box of the Western Region's Type 17 design with flat roof. This housed an 87 lever vertical tappet 5 bar frame, with 4in centres. This box remained in use until 20th July 1970 when its functions were taken over by Bristol panel box. The frame was removed and part of it installed at Frome North Signal Box (see later entry).

Bristol MAS Panel Box

As part of the Western Region's resignalling programe, the Bristol area came under a new signalling panel which was brought into use in stages in the early 1970s. This panel took over what was left of the former B&NSR to Radstock.

Contractors Siding

This temporary box was in use by 1890, doubtless in connection with the construction of the Bristol Avoiding Line. It is presumed to have closed when the new lines were opened.

Brislington Station: Box and Ground Frames

A signal box once existed at Brislington station and was shown to be in place in 1891 when a British Rail plan indicates a cabin at the Pensford end of the single platform. At that time, the signal cabin controlled six signals, and two points, having one spare lever as well. At some time after 1891 and before 1908 the box was replaced by a ground frame at the southern end. On 14th April 1908 a new connection and ground frame was brought into use at the northern end of the station. Both ground frames and all sidings and connections were taken out of use on 14th June 1964. It does not appear that Brislington was a staff station at any time in the railway's history.

Pensford Station: Signal Boxes

The date of the opening of the first box at Pensford is almost certain to have been 1873 since a crossing loop was known

Below: PENSFORD SIGNAL BOX – AN INTERIOR SHOT
Collection H. Wyatt

Below: PENSFORD SIGNAL BOX

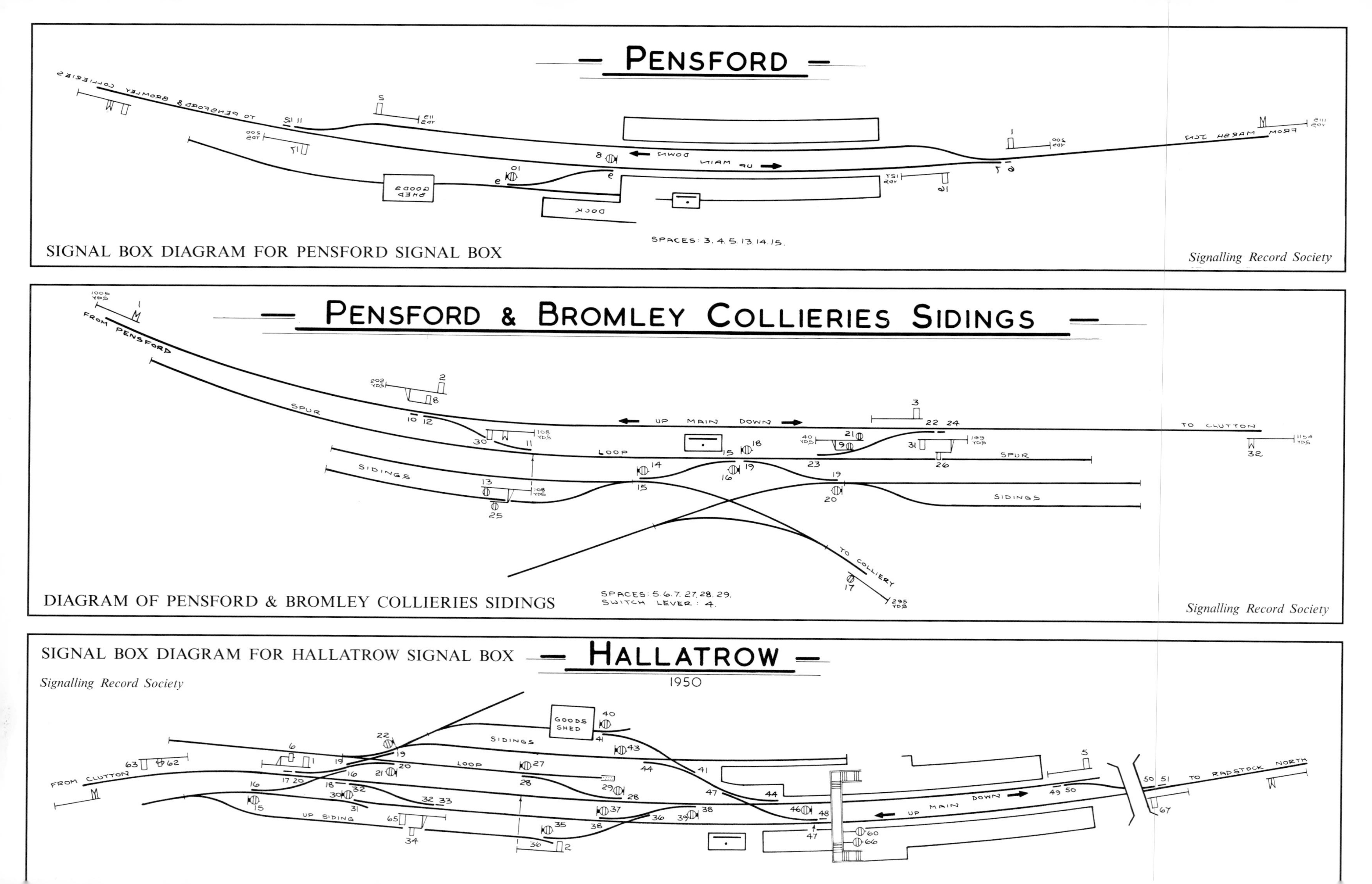

PENSFORD
TO PENSFORD & BROMLEY COLLIERIES
FROM MARSH JCT
DOWN MAIN
UP MAIN
GOODS SHED
DOCK
SPACES: 3. 4. 5. 13. 14. 15.
SIGNAL BOX DIAGRAM FOR PENSFORD SIGNAL BOX
Signalling Record Society
PENSFORD & BROMLEY COLLIERIES SIDINGS
FROM PENSFORD
SPUR
UP MAIN DOWN
TO CLUTTON
LOOP
SIDINGS
SPUR
SIDINGS
TO COLLIERY
SPACES: 5. 6. 7. 27. 28. 29.
SWITCH LEVER: 4.
DIAGRAM OF PENSFORD & BROMLEY COLLIERIES SIDINGS
Signalling Record Society
SIGNAL BOX DIAGRAM FOR HALLATROW SIGNAL BOX
HALLATROW
1950
Signalling Record Society
FROM CLUTTON
GOODS SHED
SIDINGS
LOOP
UP SIDING
UP MAIN DOWN
TO RADSTOCK NORTH

to have been in existence by 1877. A cabin shown on a plan of 1883 had ten levers in all, three of them being spares. However, the plan also shows that a new signal box was about to be built on the 'up' platform on the site of the later, second box. New signals were also being installed, all of which were to be operated by the new box. These signals were the Down Starting, the Up Starting and Down Home, the latter two being situated on the same post, and the Up Home giving three new posts in all. The coal stage was also under construction at this time in the goods yard.

When the second box did come into use, it was of Type 7A and was 21ft x12ft x 8ft in size. Initially, it had 15 levers in the frame but modifications carried out in September 1916 gave it a stud frame with 5¼in centres and 17 levers. The box did not have a block switch. It was closed on 14th June 1964.

Pensford & Bromley Collieries Sidings Box

There was only ever one box at this location and this was brought into use on 27th August 1911 and was of Type 27C. It was 25ft x 9ft 6in x 8ft in size and had a vertical tappet 3 bar locking frame with 4in centres and 32 levers. The box was equipped with a block switch and was believed to have closed on 22nd March 1960. Incidentally, this box could be switched-out for "long-section" working.

Clutton Signal Box

The signal box at Clutton was opened in September 1890 when the new loop and second platform were brought into use at the station (see Chapter 8). Before that time, signalling arrangements for the connections from the collieries at Fry's Bottom and Greyfield into the main running line of the Bristol & North Somerset Railway remain conjectural, although the existence of a ground frame seems most likely. The box was of Type 5 and it had a double twist locking frame with 29 levers at 5¼in centres. The box was not equipped with a block switch. It closed on 14th June 1964. In this book, the box is well illustrated due to the kindness of Mrs Weaver, of Clutton, who generously allowed her photographs to be used.

Hallatrow Station:
Ground Frame and Signal Boxes

When the station at Hallatrow was first opened there was no signal box, access to the small goods yard being by a ground frame. When the Camerton branch opened in 1882 (see Chapter 7) a brick signal box was built by McKenzie & Holland. This cost £680 15s (£680.75) and measured 20ft x 10ft 6in. It had a locking frame containing 24 working and 6 spare levers. It closed on 16th September 1909 when the reconstruction of the station led to the need for a new and larger signal box.

Of Type 7D, this box was 38ft x 12ft x 9ft in size and had a horizontal tappet 3 bar locking frame with 55 working and 12 spare levers. The levers were at 4in centres. At the north end of the station a ground frame was installed to work the quarry siding connection beyond the loop, its two levers being locked by a key on the Electric Train Staff. The box had no block switch. It was closed on 14th June 1964.

Camerton Station:
Signal Boxes/Ground Frames

Two signal boxes existed at Camerton. It is believed that the first of these was brought into use in 1882 when the Camerton branch was opened to traffic. This box was located by the road bridge at the Hallatrow end of the station. Although it is known that the box was provided by McKenzie & Holland, further information about the actual signalling arrangements around this time are very scanty indeed. We do know that the box was reduced to G.F. status by 1898, although it may have been upgraded again in 1908.

Adjacent to the connection into Camerton Colliery siding, the second box was brought into use when the layout was relaid and resignalled for the extension of the line through from Camerton to Limpley Stoke. The opening of the box took place on 3rd May 1910. It was of Type 7D, being 25ft x 12ft x 9ft in size. It had 35 levers in the frame, 25 working and 10 spare. The box was not equipped with a block switch and was closed on 23rd February 1938, when two new ground frames were provided to replace it. Presumably these remained in use until 1951 when the line closed completely.

(Further details of the Hallatrow-Limpley Stoke line and its signalling can be found in *The Camerton Branch* by Colin G. Maggs & Gerry Beale, and I gladly acknowledge that particular source in providing information for the sections on Hallatrow & Camerton.)

Old Mills: Signal Box and Ground Frames

The history of the signalling arrangements at Old Mills is both unclear and complex. The box here was known to be in place by 1882. It controlled the connections into three collieries namely those at Farrington, Springfield and Old Mills (see Chapter 6). It seems likely that the connections to the latter two pits were worked by ground frame prior to the box being brought into use. Around 1931 it was reduced to ground frame status. It is believed to have closed on 26th April 1953 when an open ground frame was provided. Eventually three ground frames were in use here.

The private siding agreement for Old Mills was terminated on 15th February 1967, the sidings remaining being taken out of use on 23rd April of the same year.

Midsomer Norton & Welton Station:
Signal Box and Ground Frames

Although it appears likely that a signal box existed here in the railway's very early days, an informed guess would suggest that the box was reduced to ground frame status very early on. In later times, it became the station's parcels office. Replaced by two ground frames, North and South, these controlled entry into the small goods yard and siding. On 31st December 1968 the siding at Midsomer Norton & Welton was taken out of use as were the ground frames, the private siding agreement with the adjacent firm of Blatchford having been terminated on 6th July 1968.

Radstock (Great Western):
Signal Boxes and Ground Frames

There was certainly a box at the level crossing over the main Bath-Wells road when the line opened since one was mentioned in the Inspecting Officer's Report taken at the time. This box was called "Radstock No. 1". It was built by the firm of McKenzie & Holland as were all the boxes on the North Somerset at its opening. It seems likely that this original box was rebuilt around 1908.

After the changes had taken place, the box had a brick base some 8ft high, some 6ft of which had been part of the earlier box. The latter building was 18ft x 12ft in size. It had a double twist locking frame with 5¼in centres. There were 24 levers in the frame, the time of the installation of this frame being 1896. The box did not have a block switch. It was renamed North and then Radstock West, the latter change of title probably occurring in 1951 when the nearby S&D boxes were renamed, the adjacent S&D box becoming Radstock North "B". Clearly, this could have led to some confusion!

Radstock West was reduced to ground frame status on 14th July 1968 and was finally closed on 17th January 1973. On 6th March 1968, a ground frame had been brought into use to control the new connection to the ex-S&D line.

By this time, the Bristol Group of the Great Western Society were interested in buying the box and, after protracted negotiations, BR offered them the box, and one level crossing

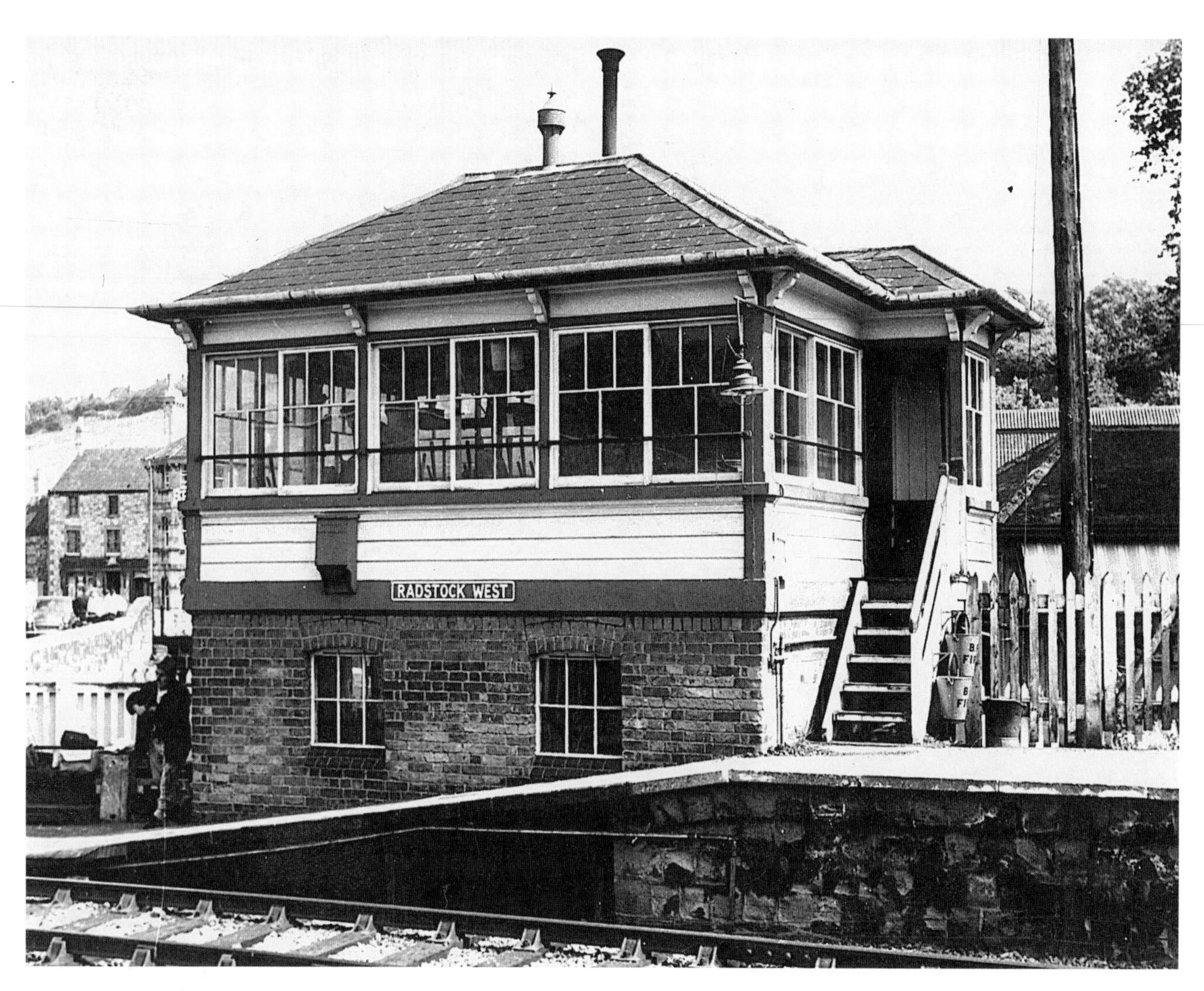

RADSTOCK WEST SIGNAL BOX *Collection Ken Evans*

FROME WEST GROUND FRAME

Original drawings: Tim Venton

Above: RADSTOCK WEST – AN INTERIOR SHOT

Collection Ken Evans

Above: RADSTOCK WEST – THE TRACK DIAGRAM

Collection Ken Evans

Right: RADSTOCK NORTH SIGNAL BOX

Mrs G. Shearn

Below: RADSTOCK NORTH SIGNAL BOX

Chris Howell

RADSTOCK SOUTH SIGNAL BOX

Collection: Ken Evans

RADSTOCK SOUTH – THE TRACK DIAGRAM

Collection: Ken Evans

gate with post, for £53 at the end of September 1975. A week later the box belonged to the Society! After the removal, by road, of the box's top half and lever frame from Radstock, it has now been fully restored and is in working condition at Didcot.

Incidentally, there was a Siemen's Mercury Treadle at the "Five Arches" bridge to the west of Radstock to warn the signalman at Radstock North (West) Signal Box of an approaching train. This treadle worked a bell provided on the outside front of the box after about 1930, but it must have been located somewhere else prior to this as it had been previously mentioned in the 1920 Sectional Appendix as well.

Since there was a "Radstock No. 1" when the line originally opened, and there was also a "Radstock No. 2" it is clear that this latter became the later Radstock South Signal Box ("The Yard"). A Type 2 box, it had a stud frame. Signalling Record Society information confirms the installation date for this frame as being 1911. This frame had 21 levers at $5\frac{1}{4}$in centres. The box did have a block switch and it closed on 15th August 1966.

A No. 3 Signal Box existed in this area circa 1890. This box could have been located at the site of the later ground frame at Huish & Writhlington Siding since this was a very important location in the 1880s with a number of tramways converging on it (see Chapter 6). The ground frame here was later locked from the box at Radstock South, the frame being some

500 yards in advance of the box from the Frome direction. It was controlled by an Annett's Key from the South Signal Box, where the key formed part of the locking arrangement.

Mells Road: Signal Boxes and Ground Frames

In the early years of the 20th century, the layout at Mells Road was kept busy handling coal and stone traffic, etc. All this traffic was worked by two signal boxes, Mells North Signal Box (with 30 levers in the frame), and Mells South Signal Box.

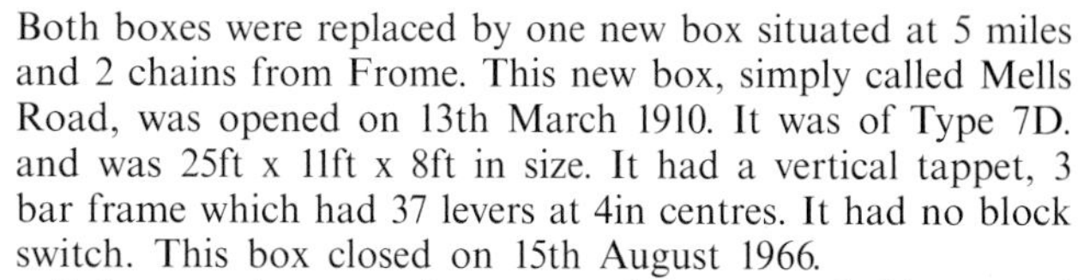

Both boxes were replaced by one new box situated at 5 miles and 2 chains from Frome. This new box, simply called Mells Road, was opened on 13th March 1910. It was of Type 7D. and was 25ft x 11ft x 8ft in size. It had a vertical tappet, 3 bar frame which had 37 levers at 4in centres. It had no block switch. This box closed on 15th August 1966.

Subsequently, a two lever ground frame, probably opened when the Radstock-Mells section reopened in 1968, was provided at the South end of the layout to control access to the remaining sidings. This was unlocked by the key token from the Frome North-Mells Road section. In May 1982, a short run-round loop was brought into use at Mells Road.

WHATLEY GROUND FRAME
Photograph taken on 14th March 1975.

Mike Miller

SOMERSET STONE QUARRIES GROUND FRAME
This photograph shows the damage incurred following the derailment here on 5th November 1976.

Mike Miller

Somerset Quarry Siding: Ground Frames

The two ground frames at Somerset Quarry Siding North (2 miles 15 chains from Frome) and South (2m 1c) were brought into use in May 1894. Both lever frame had five levers. Few changes seemed to have taken place and the track and point-work arrangements appear to have remained essentially as they had been when the two double-ended sidings had been opened, although by the 1960s the inner of these had been lifted. Around September 1943 it would appear that the sidings here were out of use for a time, although it is not certain as to when the lines were brought back into operation again.

Even more major changes took place in the 1970s when, with the marked growth of stone traffic from the now greatly modified and improved Whatley Quarry line (see Chapter 10), the loop at Somerset Quarry Siding was considerably lengthened, becoming known as Hapsford Loop. With the new works in place, the original Somerset Quarry Siding North Ground Frame was replaced by a Hapsford North G.F., situated at 2 miles 38 chains from Frome whilst Hapsford (Somerset Stone Quarries' Siding) South G.F. was located at 1m 78c.

Around January 1974 the former North G.F. and the old loop arrangements had been taken out of use, while the new layout was brought into operation in the autumn of the same year. The loop was severely damaged in a derailment that occurred on Friday, 5th November 1976 and was taken out of use after that together with the South G.F. At the time of writing (1989), the whole of the line from Frome North to Whatley Quarry (including the junction for Radstock) comes under the control of the Westbury Panel Box (see later section), the Whatley Quarry route having now become the "Main" and the line to Radstock, the "branch".

Frome Gasworks' Siding Ground Frame

This gasworks was served by a short loop off the main North Somerset running line between Frome West Junction Signal Box and the Somerset Quarry Siding. Situated between the viaducts at Leonards Mill and Gas House, the siding was inspected, and then presumably opened, in February 1887. It was controlled by a ground frame which remained in use until it, and its associated connections and loop, were all removed on 8th February 1948. Further information about this siding can be found in Chapter 6.

Frome Market Siding

This siding was to be found between Willow Vale Viaduct and North Row Viaduct between the junction at Frome West and Frome Gasworks' Siding. Inspected and opened in September 1875 (see Chapter 5 for further details), Frome Market Siding was originally provided with a signal cabin and locking frame. The box was never a block post and it was later replaced by ground frames. In later years, two ground frames, North and South, were to be found at 50 and 42 chains respectively from Frome. The siding was taken out of use on 30th October 1968.

Frome West Signal Box

Frome West Junction was to be found where the original branch to Radstock from Frome North Junction Signal Box (originally Frome Mineral Junction) met the later curve from the Radstock branch into Frome station itself. This latter curve, which joined the main line to Weymouth over Radstock Branch Junction at the approach to Frome station, was added when the passenger service from Bristol (via Radstock) was instituted in 1874.

Believed opened in 1874, Frome West Junction was a Type 2 box. On 24th September 1933 the box was reduced in status to a ground frame with five levers, the other levers being removed. This ground frame was eventually taken out of use on 13th December 1975, being replaced by a new frame. Incidentally, it was in close vicinity to these ground frames that the private siding of the firm of E. Cockey & Sons was to be found, the agreement for which was terminated in early 1964.

Frome North Signal Box

Frome North Signal Box, or Frome Mineral Junction as it was known by 1895, was opened in 1875. Of Type 2, it was a small box with a hip roof and an external staircase. The top of the box was a three quarter wooden structure, prefabricated at Reading. This top was married to a cheap brick base built in

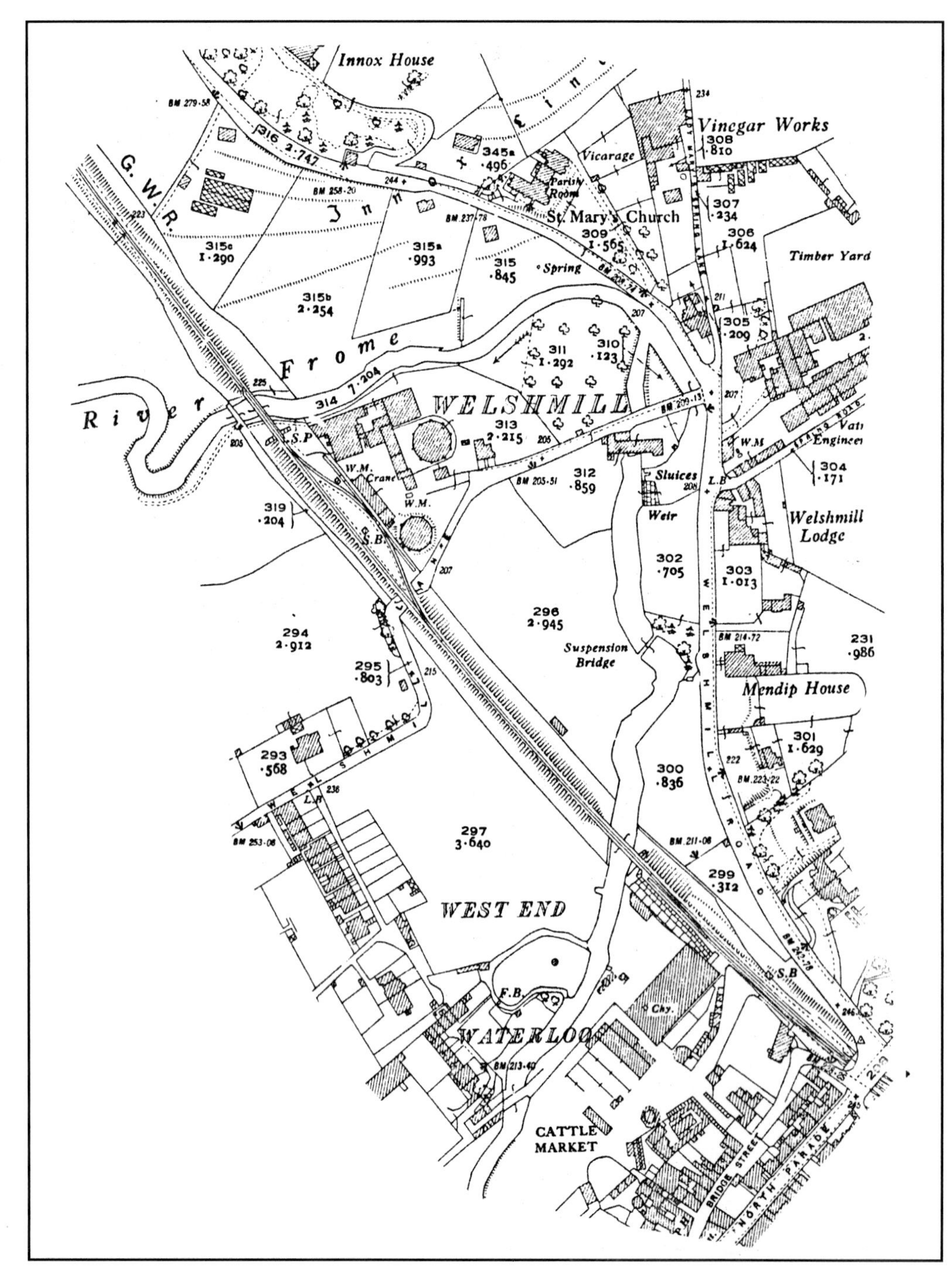

FROME GASWORKS SIDING & FROME MARKET SIDING 1930

THE SITE OF FROME MARKET SIDING
This view shows concrete troughing for MAS cables being unloaded at the site of the former siding at Frome Market. No. 47095 propels the train towards Radstock on 6th December 1981.

Mike Miller

Flemish bond. It was almost certainly built by a local contractor.

Over the years several alterations and additions took place. A porch was added, the vertical planking beneath the windows removed and the space bricked up.

The box had had three locking frames. Of the frames, the one that was possibly second in the sequence had 29 levers. The last frame in use at the box was built new for Marsh Junction Signal Box in Bristol. It was moved to Frome when that box closed. When in use at Frome it had 34 levers. This move took place in 1970 when there were major changes in the layout through Frome.

The box closed on 6th October 1984, the wooden superstructure being moved for restoration to the Great Western Society at Didcot where it has now been restored and is back in working use along with its former Somerset neighbour, Radstock North.

JERICHO BRIDGE, MELLS ROAD
Having obtained the token, the Radstock "trip" is ready to resume its journey back to Frome North and Westbury. The locomotive is No. 46013, unusual power for the Radstock branch. The date is 21st March 1975.

Mike Miller

FROME NORTH SIGNAL BOX
This photograph was taken on 2nd March 1973. *G. F. Gillham*

FROME SOUTH SIGNAL BOX
This photograph was taken on 26th March 1970. The train, formed of two three-car diesel units, is the 11.23 Westbury-Weymouth. *G. F. Gillham*

FROME WEST GROUND FRAME
Photographed in September 1975. *Tim Venton*

Frome Middle and South Signal Boxes

The boxes at both Frome Middle and Frome South were in use c1874. Frome Middle, a Type 2 box, had 23 levers. Both boxes were closed on 17th September 1933.

The closure of these took place as part of a rolling programme by the GWR to reduce signal boxes, particularly those situated at each end of stations. A new box, again called Frome South, was built near to the site of the old Middle box and this opened on 17th September 1933. This one box replaced three, if Frome West becoming a ground frame is included.

Frome South was of Type 9, one of, if not the last, Type 9 to be built, its internal dimensions being 36ft 3in x 11ft x 6ft 6in. The box had a 73 lever vertical tappet 3 bar locking frame with 4in centres. The box had a block switch. Under a major rationalisation plan for the Frome area, it closed on 19th August 1970.

Westbury MAS Panel Box

As part of the resignalling plans for the West Country, the Western Region has extended Multiple Aspect Signalling (MAS) down its West of England main line through Westbury, Taunton, Exeter and beyond. From Monday 8th October 1984, the area around Frome, including the single lines from Frome to Whatley Quarry and Radstock, were brought under the control of the new panel box at Westbury. From that date, the "No Signalman Token" system on the Frome North-Whatley Quarry-Mells Road section and the "One Train Working" system on the Mells Road-Radstock section were withdrawn.

The section between Frome North and Whatley Quarry is now worked by the Track Circuit Block System controlled from Westbury Panel. The section between Hapsford and Radstock is worked by the "One Train Working" system. The Train Staff is currently kept in an instrument provided at Hapsford and is released from Westbury Panel. With the opening of this stage of the MAS scheme, the former token instrument at Mells Road was recovered. Under existing arrangements, a key is attached to the Train Staff and this is used to release the padlock provided on the point clips by which each end of the loop at Mells Road is secured.

The former Hapsford (North) Ground Frame was recovered and the points converted to power operation, worked locally upon release from Westbury. In addition, AWS was provided on the Frome North-Whatley Quarry section.

As a final comment, it is worth saying that it is rather unusual to find track circuit block and colour light signalling on purely mineral lines. In this respect, the Whatley Quarry branch, with its frequent freight train service, is somewhat special, perhaps? It is certainly an indication of how valuable the stone traffic is to the Western Region's revenue account!

Block Working on the Branch: Some Observations

The Annual Return to the Board of Trade for 31st December 1873 shows North Somerset Junction to Radstock as being worked by Absolute Block in addition to the use of Train Staff. Indeed, Colonel Rich's Report at the opening of the line to passenger traffic in 1873 states that all the points and signals on the North Somerset were worked from boxes and were interlocked. At the time of Rich's inspection, the arrangements for working the branch on the Block Telegraph system were nearly completed (see Chapter 5 for more information). Between 1895 and 1898 E. T. Staff was added on the single sections while block switches were added at Radstock South and Mells North around 1895.

Block Sections and/or Shape and Form of Staff and Tickets: 1877

At this time the line from Bristol to Radstock was single, Pensford being the intermediate crossing place, while the section from Radstock to Mells was double with Mells to Frome Junction, single. The following are details of the Staffs and Tickets:

Section	**Form of Staff and Ticket/Colour**
Bristol & Pensford	Square/Red
Pensford & Radstock	Triangular/Blue
Mells & Frome Jcn	Round/White

1884

Bristol & Pensford	Square/Red	Plus Disc Block Telegraph
Pensford & Hallatrow	Round/White	
Hallatrow & Radstock	Triangular/Blue	
Mells & Frome	Round/White	
Hallatrow/Camerton	Square/Red	(Staff Only)

Non-Block Posts existed at Old Mills, Old Welton Colliery, Wells Way and Market Siding

1890

N. Som. Jcn & Contractors Siding	Round/Blue
Contractors Siding & Pensford	Square/Red
Pensford & Clutton	Round/White
Clutton & Hallatrow	Square/Green
To Camerton as 1884	(No Block)
Hallatrow & Radstock	Triangular/Blue
Mells & Frome	Round/White

1895

The line from Marsh Junction to Radstock was single with intermediate crossing places at Pensford, Clutton and Hallatrow. There was double track between Radstock and Mells with Mells to Frome Junction being single. The single portion was worked by Train Staff and Ticket and Disc Block Telegraph. The following are the details of the Staffs and Tickets:

Marsh Junction & Pensford	Square/Red
Pensford & Clutton	Round/White
Clutton & Hallatrow	Square/Green
Hallatrow & Radstock	Triangular/Blue
Mells & Frome Mineral Jcn	Round/White

Hallatrow was only available for crossing two goods trains or a goods and a passenger train.

Somerset Quarries Stone Siding, Frome, was worked with

Annett's Key, under special instructions dated February 1894.

Gas Works Siding, Frome was worked with Annett's Key, under special instructions dated 15th December 1886.

Market Siding, Frome was worked under special instructions dated April 1885.

By around 1898 Old Mills was fitted with a switch.

1913

By 1913 the sections were the same as those given above except that Pensford & Bromley Siding Signal Box had now been brought into use. When this box was switched out, a long section of E.T. tablet applied between Pensford and Clutton boxes. This was later converted to Token. On closure of Old Mills, the long section, or by now the only remaining one between Hallatrow and Radstock North, was also altered to Token Working.

1922

The Service Timetable for 1922 gives the following information. The single line from Marsh Junction to Radstock station was worked by Electric Train Staff, the Staff Stations and crossing places being at Marsh Junction, Pensford, Pensford & Bromley Siding, Clutton, Hallatrow, Old Mills and Radstock station. Electric Train Tablet working applied between Clutton and Pensford when Pensford & Bromley was out of circuit. Pensford & Bromley Siding and Old Mills were only available for shunting a light engine, or a goods train (at Old Mills only short goods trains could be shunted!) or for trains to pass in the same or opposite direction.

The single line from Mells Road South End to Frome Mineral Junction was worked by Electric Train Staff, Mells Road and Frome West Box being Staff Stations.

1948

In 1948 the Block Sections were as follows:

Marsh Junction & Pensford	
Pensford & Pensford & Bromley Colliery Siding	(short section)
Pensford & Bromley Colliery & Clutton	(short section)
Pensford & Clutton	(long section)
Clutton & Hallatrow	
Hallatrow & Radstock North	
Radstock North & Radstock South	(double line section)
Radstock South & Mells Road	(double line section)

Mells Road and Frome South

It may be of interest to mention that Marsh Junction and Pensford & Bromley were the only signal boxes between Bristol and Radstock that had picking up and setting down posts.

Following the reopening of the Radstock-Mells Road section in 1968, the signalling situation in this area gets rather complicated! By 1969/70 "no signalman" Electric Token (NSKT) ("D" configuration) was in use between Frome North and Mells Road, with intermediate instruments provided at Somerset Quarry Siding and Frome West Ground Frame but, by 1975, Frome West Ground Frame was equipped with an Annett's Key instrument, released from Frome North. The Mells Road-Radstock section was "One Train Working" (OTW) with a wooden Train Staff.

Following the opening of the Hapsford Loop, the situation became

Frome North-Hapsford	NSKT ("D" configuration).
Hapsford Whatley-Mells Road	A "combined" section using one set of NSKT.
Mells Road-Radstock	OTW with wooden Train Staff.

At a later date, presumably after the removal of Hapsford Loop, the arrangement was:

Frome North-Whatley-Mells Road: a combined section using NSKT.

Mells Road-Radstock: OTW with wooden Train Staff.

The OTW Staff was kept at Frome North, and given to the guard of a 'down ' train. He then gave it to the driver on arrival at Mells, after putting the NSKT in the instrument there. The procedure was reversed on the return journey.

BRITISH RAILWAYS SECTIONAL APPENDIX 1960

NORTH SOMERSET BRANCH.

MARSH JUNCTION TO FROME.

OCCUPATION OF LINE BETWEEN BRISTOL (MARSH JUNCTION) AND RADSTOCK WEST SIGNAL BOX BY THE ENGINEERING DEPARTMENT.

The Motor Trolley System of maintenance operates from 22m. 76ch. near Marsh Junction to 8m. 23ch. near Radstock West Signal Box.

The home stations of the engineering gangs responsible for the Section of Line are Pensford and Clutton.

The Pensford gang maintain the line between 22m. 76ch. and 14m. 20ch., and the Clutton gang maintain the line between 14m. 20ch. and 8m. 23ch.

The Instructions for the Motor Trolley System of Maintenance on Single Lines worked by Electric Token apply.

Places where Telephones and Occupation Key Boxes are fixed, giving the mileage and number of hut.

Section—Marsh Junction to Pensford (One Key).

Gang No. 126 .. .. 22m. 76ch. to 17m. 30ch.

Marsh Junction Signal Box.	M.	CH.
Box No. 1	22	10
Box No. 2	21	11
Box No. 3	20	16
Box No. 4	19	32
Box No. 5	18	26

Pensford Signal Box.

The Telephones communicate with the Signalman at Pensford.

Section—Pensford to Clutton (One Key).

Gang. No. 126 .. .. .. 17m. 30ch. to 14m. 20ch.

Pensford Signal Box.

Pensford & Bromley Old Signal Box (In box outside).	M.	CH.
Box No. 6	15	65
Box No. 7	14	78

Clutton Signal Box.

The Telephones communicate with the Signalman at Clutton.

Section—Clutton to Hallatrow (One Key).

Gang No. 125 .. .. .. 14m. 20ch. to 12m. 58ch.

Clutton Signal Box.	M.	CH.
Box No. 8	13	34

Hallatrow Signal Box.

The Telephones communicate with the Signalman at Clutton.

193

Section—Hallatrow to Radstock (One Key).

Gang No. 125 .. .. .. 12m. 58ch. to 8m. 23ch.

Hallatrow Signal Box.	M.	CH.
Box No. 9	11	54
Box No. 10	10	50
Box No. 11	9	66
Box No. 12	9	2

Radstock West Signal Box.

The Telephones communicate with the Signalman at Radstock West.

For the section Clutton—Pensford a control instrument with three Slides, (1) Control (2) Occupation Key, Clutton—Pensford & Bromley (3) Occupation Key, Pensford & Bromley—Pensford, is provided at Clutton. The instrument should be operated in the same manner as described in the Standard Instructions, with the addition that it will be necessary for the Signalman at Clutton to ask the Ganger to press the plunger provided in connection with Occupation Key Box to enable the Signalman to withdraw the Occupation Slide applicable, i.e., 2 or 3.

It is possible to have occupation of the Clutton—Pensford & Bromley and Pensford & Bromley—Pensford Sections simultaneously, but both occupation Keys must be restored before the token working can be resumed.

The Signal Box at Pensford & Bromley is now closed.

BRISLINGTON.

Ground Frames are fixed on Up Side of Line at Brislington (one at each end of the Station) for working the points leading to and from the Sidings.

The Frames are locked by key on the Token, and the Station Master or Porter will be responsible for working same.

The points at the Bristol end of the Sidings may only be used by trains coming from the direction of Radstock.

See separate instructions in regard to propelling Freight trains between East Depot and Brislington on page 122.

CLUTTON.

No vehicle, unless fitted with a hand brake, must be allowed to stand on either Loop Line.

British Railways engines must not, under any circumstances, go beyond the Stop Board fixed on the Bristol side of the Under-bridge in the Fry's Bottom Line.

When it is necessary for Shunting purposes to foul or shunt on to the Fry's Bottom Line, such operations must not be carried out unless a competent man of the Clutton Station Staff is present, and he is held responsible for seeing that the Siding Points and crossings are left absolutely clear after the work has been completed.

HALLATROW.

BELL COMMUNICATION.

A bell is provided in the Signal Box operated from a push fixed on the Down Home Signal, to facilitate shunting operations.

OLD MILLS SIDINGS.

These Sidings must only be used as a Crossing place for engines or short Freight trains. Before dispatching a Freight train to be shunted here, it must be ascertained that there is sufficient Siding room to accommodate same.

Freight trains calling at these Sidings to do work come to a stand on a gradient falling towards Midsomer Norton & Welton. The Guard in charge of any such train must, before allowing the engine to be detached, see that his van brake is tightly applied and that the wagon nearest the brake van of an Up train and the leading vehicle of a Down train is spragged so as to prevent the possibility of the train or any portion of it moving.

An Intermediate Token Instrument is installed in a wooden hut situated on the Upside of the Line between Old Mills East and Middle Ground Frames for the receipt and issue of Tokens for the Hallatrow—Radstock West section in accordance with the Standard Instructions. Telephone communication with Hallatrow and Radstock West Station Signal Boxes is provided outside the wooden hut.

Three Ground Frames, Old Mills West, Middle and East operate the connections and Facing Point Locks at the Sidings, and are released by the Electric Token.

When an engine or train is ready to leave the Sidings the man in charge, after having withdrawn the Token, must operate the points for the train to be drawn on to the Single Line, after which the points must be reversed and the Ground Frame locked, and the train can then proceed to Radstock West Home Signal or Hallatrow Home Signal, as the case may be, the Driver carrying the Token in the ordinary way. When handing the Token to the Driver the man in charge must verbally instruct him that the Section is only clear to the Home Signal at Radstock West or Hallatrow.

194

When the man in charge requires to draw the Token for the purpose of running an engine with or without vehicles over the Main Line between the two connections, he must telephone to Hallatrow Box and advise the Signalman there what is required. When the shunt has been made and the Main Line is again clear and the man in charge has replaced the Token in the instrument he must advise the Signalman at Hallatrow and Radstock West.

The Guards of trains calling at the Siding will be in charge of the working there and must record the numbers of the wagons put off and taken on at the Sidings and send particulars to the Station Master at Hallatrow.

Action to be taken by Colliery Staff in event of a mishap in the Sidings fouling the Running Line.

In the event of a derailment occurring during shunting operations in the Old Mills Sidings or any other mishap, which fouls the main line, the Colliery staff must take immediate action to protect the obstruction and prevent any train which may be approaching on the Main Line from running into the obstruction, by placing three detonators 10 yards apart on the rails on each side of the obstruction and exhibiting a danger hand signal at least ¾ mile from the obstruction or as far as possible from the obstruction should a train be observed approaching.

The Colliery staff must also take immediate action to advise the Signalmen at Hallatrow and Radstock of the mishap by means of the telephone provided in the Box located outside the wooden hut, located between Old Mills East and Middle Ground Frames and act on any instructions given by the Signalmen. The Signalmen must upon receipt of the advice from the Colliery Staff take such emergency action as is necessary and advise all concerned in regard to the clearing of the obstruction and running of trains.

MIDSOMER NORTON & WELTON.

Freight trains calling at these Sidings to do work come to a stand on a gradient falling towards Radstock. The Guard in charge of any such train must, before allowing the engine to be detached, see that his van brake is tightly applied and that the wagon nearest the brake van of an Up train and the leading vehicle of a Down train is spragged so as to prevent the possibility of the train or any portion of it moving.

RALPH BLATCHFORD & CO. SIDING.

This siding is on a gradient of 1 in 40 falling towards Midsomer Norton & Welton Station.

Special care must be taken when shunting operations into these sidings have been completed, to see that wagons are secured with brakes and the two wheel stops are padlocked across the rail.

The keys of the padlocks must be kept in the Station Master's possession and he must see that these instructions are strictly carried out.

RADSTOCK WEST.

PROPELLING FREIGHT TRAINS BETWEEN RADSTOCK WEST AND MIDSOMER NORTON & WELTON.

When necessary during daylight and in clear weather not more than 12 wagons may be propelled with brake van leading, in which the Guard must ride, keep a good look-out and be prepared to Signal to the Driver as required, from Radstock West to Midsomer Norton & Welton. On arrival ad Midsomer Norton the brake van must be detached and the whole of the shunting performed at the North Ground Frame, if practicable. When necessary, however, the shunting may be performed at the South Ground Frame. The speed of the train when being propelled must not exceed 10 miles per hour at any point and not more than 4 miles per hour when running through Facing Points and Crossings.

LEVEL CROSSING GATES.

With a view to minimising the delay to road vehicles at the Level Crossing at Radstock, the following regulations must be carried out in connection with the working of Fixed Signals and Level Crossing Gates:

1. The normal position of the Gates is across the Railway.

2. The Gates must be kept across the Line until the electric treadle bell rings for Down trains, and until the Fixed Signals are whistled for by Up Freight trains.

3. In the event of trains crossing at Radstock West Station, the Gates must be placed across the Line if necessary when either train has come to a stand, if the margin as laid down in Clause 2 can be adopted for Up or Down train as the case may be.

4. Shunting operations must cease to allow the Gates to be worked if vehicles require to cross.

COAL TRAFFIC FROM KILMERSDON SIDINGS.

When absolutely necessary for wagons of coal to be gravitated from these Sidings into the Yard the work must be performed with the greatest care. If an engine is upon the Sidings at the time it must be sent into the Station Yard clear of the road into which the wagons are intended to be placed

before the latter are allowed to move forward. When the engine is clear the Engineman must give a "Crow" on the whistle and the man at the Sidings (who must be a competent Shunter) in charge of the wagons must then release only a sufficient number of brakes to admit of the wagons moving steadily towards the Yard.

The Shunter in charge must walk by the side of the wagons and he will be held responsible for having the wagons under such complete control at all times that they may be brought to a stand at any point required when moving towards or reaching the Yard.

This working is prohibited after sunset and during fog or falling snow.

TRAFFIC FROM NORTH SOMERSET LINE.

Traffic from Pensford, Clutton, Hallatrow, Old Mills and Radstock for South Wales, Bristol, and adjacent stations below Keynsham (inclusive), also to the Cheddar Valley (except Wells), must work **via BRISTOL.**

Traffic from Old Mills, Radstock and Mells Road for Taunton and West thereof, Melksham, Holt Junction, Devizes Line, Trowbridge, Bradford-on-Avon, Salisbury and Weymouth Lines, must work **via FROME.**

MELLS ROAD.

As the Radstock end of this Station is on the summit of a steep gradient falling 1 in 69 towards Radstock, it is important that special care should be exercised in carrying out shunting operations.

No such operations must be carried out on the Down Line unless an engine is always leading towards Radstock, or the points leading from the Down Line are set for the Goods Shed Sidings.

Great care must be exercised in shunting into and out of the Goods Shed road at Mells Road Station.

All wagons shunted from the Down Main Line to the Goods Shed Siding must remain coupled to the engine or train until they have been propelled on to the Siding Line and under no circumstances must wagons be loose shunted from the Down Main Line to the Goods Shed Siding.

The Station Master is held responsible for seeing that not less than two hand scotches and a brake stick are always available at the Radstock end of the platform for use whenever required, and he is also held responsible for satisfying himself that every member of the Staff is fully conversant with the requirements and these instructions.

The crossing of long coaching stock and other vehicles over 60 feet in length from Up to Down Lines and vice versa through the Crossover Junction at 5m. 12chs. is prohibited. Such movement should be carried out over the junction to the Up and Down Lines at 4m. 71chs.

COMMUNICATION BETWEEN SIGNAL BOX AND SIDINGS.

Bell communication is provided between the Sidings and Mells Road Signal Box.

MELLS QUARRY COMPANY'S SIDINGS—MELLS ROAD.

The above Private Sidings have a connection with the Up Refuge Siding at Mells Road (4m. 67ch.).

There are two Sidings each holding 12 wagons—one for the reception of empties and the other for loaded wagons for despatch; and a connection from the Private Sidings to the Quarries.

The connection from the Refuge Siding to the Private Sidings is on a falling gradient of 1 in 100.

Wagons placed in the Sidings must remain coupled to the engine until they have been propelled inside the gate, and in no case must wagons be loosely shunted to the Sidings.

When the Sidings are not in use the gate must be padlocked across the Line and the lever working the points of the connection with the Refuge Siding chained and padlocked. The keys of both padlocks must be kept in the Signal Box.

SIDINGS BETWEEN MELLS ROAD AND FROME.

NEW FROME QUARRY COMPANY'S SIDINGS, ABOUT TWO MILES FROM FROME STATION.

1. These Sidings are on the Up Side, and the Main Line at this point is on a gradient of 1 in 51, falling towards Frome. There are two sidings, the one adjacent and running parallel to the Main Line having a connection with the Main Line at each end. The other siding runs to the Quarry. Each of the Main Line connections is worked from a Ground Frame, the latter being released by the key on the Electric Token for the Mells Road—Frome South Section. There are no Signals in connection with the Sidings. The Guard in charge of a train calling at the Sidings is responsible for working the points, and when the work is finished he must, after locking the Points and Ground Frames, hand the Token to the Driver. A Shunter or competent Porter must accompany the train to assist the Guard. No train must call at the Sidings during darkness.

2. The Siding adjacent and parallel to the Main Line must always be kept absolutely clear for a train calling at the Sidings, which must in all cases be shunted into it, and not allowed (or any part of a train) to stand on the Main Line without the engine being attached.

3. Before the engine is detached for shunting purposes, the Guard in charge must satisfy himself that a sufficient number of brakes is applied to prevent the wagons moving.

4. Loaded wagons must be attached through the Junction at the Frome end; and Western Region engines are authorised to run over the Quarry Siding for this purpose, as far as the Warning Board.

5. The Frome Goods Agent will allocate a Porter to record the numbers of all empty and loaded wagons to and from the Quarry Sidings, prior to the scheduled trips leaving and upon arrival back at Frome North respectively. Should there be any variation in the times of the scheduled trips, or should it be necessary to run any special trips to the Quarry Sidings, the Station Master must inform the Goods Agent who will endeavour to cover the numbertaking, but in the event of this not being possible, the Station Master must arrange for staff to cover the emergency and record the numbers of the vehicles and pass the details to the Goods Agent.

Should it be necessary for empty vehicles to be substituted at Frome North for vehicles which have already been recorded by the Goods Agents Staff, the Station Master must advise the Goods Agent accordingly giving the necessary details.

6. The Frome Station Master is responsible for working the traffic to and from the sidings and orders for rolling stock from the Quarry Company are dealt with by the Goods Agent to whom also the consignment notes for outwards traffic are sent direct by the Firm.

WORKING OF MARKET SIDING (FROME).

This Siding is on the Up Line side, and has Up and Down connections with the Main Line.

There are no Signals in connection with the Siding.

The Points are worked from a Ground Frame, and are secured by Annett's Key, attached to the Token for working the Frome and Mells Road Section.

As a rule this Siding will be worked by Special Engines from the Frome end, and in such cases wagons may be worked to and from the Siding without a Brake Van and propelled in either direction. A competent man must, however, ride in the leading vehicle when propelled, and the rear vehicle when drawn, and he must keep a sharp-look out and be prepared to give any necessary hand signal to the Driver. Trips to be worked as arranged by the Frome Station Master.

The speed of Trains working to and from this Siding and Frome Station must not exceed 10 miles per hour, and whilst running the men in charge must keep a sharp look-out.

Through Trains may call at the Siding as arranged from time to time in accordance with the Working Time Table.

NEW FROME QUARRY COMPANY AND MARKET SIDINGS.

Traffic to and from these Sidings will usually be worked by Pilot trips as arranged by the Frome Station Master.

FROME WEST GROUND FRAME.

The Ground Frame at Frome West controls the connections to Frome Mineral Loop Lines and Sidings on the Up side.

An Intermediate Electric Token Instrument is fixed in the Ground Frame Cabin for the receipt and issue of Tokens for the Frome—Mells Road Section in accordance with the Standard Instructions. Telephone communication is provided with Frome South Signal Box.

During time trains or engines are locked in the Sidings or have passed clear of the single line on to the Mineral Loops trains may be passed over the Single Line between Frome and Mells Road in the ordinary way.

When an engine or train is ready to leave the Sidings or Mineral Loops the man in charge must after having withdrawn the Token, operate the points for the train to be drawn on to the Single Line, after which the points must be reversed and the Ground Frame locked. The train can then proceed to Frome South or Mells Road as the case may be, the Driver carrying the Token in the ordinary way. When handing the Token to the Driver the man in charge must verbally instruct him that the section is only clear to the Home Signal at Frome South or Mells Road.

When the man in charge requires to draw a Token for the purpose of shunting the Sidings on the Main Line he must telephone to Frome South Signal Box and advise the Signalman there what is required. When the shunt has been made and the Main Line is again clear the man in charge at the Ground Frame must replace the Token in the instrument and advise the Signalman at Frome South.

Trains or engines requiring to do work at the Sidings must be accompanied by a Guard or Shunter.

Trains from the direction of Mells Road to Frome North via the Mineral Loops must be brought to a stand immediately before reaching the facing points worked from Frome West Ground Frame. A shunter will be in attendance at the Ground Frame for each train proceeding via the Mineral Loops and he will obtain the Token from the driver, operate the Ground Frame and, when the points are correctly set, authorise the driver by hand signal to proceed. Until the shunter's hand signal is received the train must not pass over the facing points.

The guard must remain in his brake-van whilst the train is being drawn from the Main Line on to the Mineral Loop. If necessary an engine must be provided to assist the train on the Up gradient to Frome North.

Before a train is allowed to draw on to the Mineral Loop the Shunter must communicate by telephone with Frome North and obtain permission for this to be done.

Trains off the Mineral Loops must be met at the Ground Frame by a Shunter who will obtain the Token from the instrument and operate the Ground Frame, afterwards handing the Token to the Driver.

Before a train or engine is allowed to proceed from Frome North Signal Box to Frome West Ground Frame over the Mineral Loop Lines, the Signalman at Frome North must satisfy himself that no conflicting movement is being made in the reverse direction at the West Ground Frame.

A key of the Ground Frame will be kept at Frome South Signal Box and another at Frome North Signal Box. When the shunter has fininished work at the Ground Frame it must be locked and the key returned to the Signal Box from which it was taken.

TURNING OF ENGINES—FROME.

Engines must not be turned at Frome by means of the triangle unless absolutely necessary, and in such circumstances the above instructions under Frome West Ground Frame must be strictly observed.

Select Bibliography

Atthill, R.	*Mendip: A New Study* 1976 David & Charles
Clew, K. R.	*The Somersetshire Coal Canal and Railways* 1970 David & Charles
Cooke, R. A.	*Track Layout Diagrams of the GWR and BR (WR) (Section 21)*
Down, C. G. & Warrington, A. J.	*The Newbury Railway* Industrial Railway Society
Down, C. G. & Warrington, A. J.	*The History of the Somerset Coalfield* 1974 David & Charles
Handley, C.	*The Railways & Tramways of Radstock* 1979 Somerset & Dorset Railway Museum Trust
Harris, P.J.	*Bristol's "Railway Mania"* 1987 Bristol Branch of the Historical Association The University, Bristol
Hateley, R.	*Industrial Locomotives of South Western England* Industrial Railway Society
Maggs, C. G.	*The Bath To Weymouth Line* 1982 Oakwood Press
Maggs, C. G. & Beale, G.	*The Camerton Branch* 1985 Wild Swan Publications
McDermot, E. T. & Clinker, C. R.	*History of the Great Western Railway* Ian Allan
McGarvie, M.	*The Book of Frome* 1984 Barracuda Press
Vincent, M.	*Reflections on the Portishead Branch* 1983 Oxford Publishing Company
Warnock, D.	*The Bristol & North Somerset Railway 1863-1884* 1978 Temple Cloud Publications
Warnock, D. W. & Parsons, R. G.	*The Bristol & North Somerset Since 1884* Avon-Anglia

Some additional key references:

Atthill, R.	*The Somerset & Dorset Railway* (New Ed) 1985 David & Charles
Booker, F.	*The GWR: A New History* 1985 David & Charles
Fellows, R. B.	*Rival Routes to Bristol* Parts 1/2 "Railway World" Nov/Dec 1960

Chapter 3

Harris, P. J.	*Projected Railways in Bristol 1862-1864* (Unpublished paper)
Lord, J. & Southam, J.	*The Floating Harbour* 1983 The Redcliffe Press
Maggs, C. G.	*The East Somerset Railway: 1858-1972* 1977 Avon-Anglia

Chapter 4

This chapter has drawn particularly heavily on the following three sources of information
The Bristol & North Somerset Railway Minute Books at the Public Record Office, Kew.

Warnock, D. W.	*The Bristol & North Somerset Railway 1863-1884* 1978 Temple Cloud Publications
Warnock, D. W. & Parsons, R. G.	*The Bristol & North Somerset Railway Since 1884* Avon-Anglia

Chapter 7

I am most grateful to the staff at the Somerset Record Office, Taunton for their help in the provision of a wide variety of maps for this chapter.

Chapter 8

I would particularly like to thank Dick Kelham for his work at the Public Record Office at Kew which has enriched this, and other chapters throughout the book, with interesting snippets of information on stone and milk traffic etc.

Chapter 10

McNicol, S.	*Rails around Frome* 1984 Railmac Publications
Vaughan, A.	*The West of England Resignalling* 1987 Ian Allan

Chapter 11

Everard, S.	*Private Owners' Wagons* The Railway Magazine September/October 1942
Maggs, C. G.	*Railways at Pensford Colliery* "British Railway Journal" No. 7 Spring 1985
Peacock, C. J.	*Marcroft Wagon Repair Works* "Model Railway Constructor" June 1968
Peacock, C. J.	*Kilmersdon Colliery & Incline* "Model Railway Constructor" Sept 1967

Appendix II

I offer my grateful thanks to Roger Hateley, the Industrial Railway Society, Peter Nicholson and Derek Stoyel for their help with this section.

Appendix III

I would like to thank Chris Handley, Reg Instone, John Morris, Chris Osment, Alan Price and Kevin Weston for their significant and most helpful contributions to this section. In addition, the support and work of the Signalling Record Society has been very much appreciated.

Signalling Study Group *The Signal Box* 1986 OPC

Index

MELLS ROAD 1990
The first locomotive for the Somerset & Avon Railway is craned off its road transport at Mells Road on 23rd June 1990. This is No.1 (Thos Hill 133C of 1963) purchased from ARC, Whatley Quarry, together with sister No. 2 (Thos Hill 136C), which arrived on site later the same day.

Peter Nicholson